Twentieth
Century
Literary
Theory

INTERSECTIONS: PHILOSOPHY AND CRITICAL THEORY

A SUNY Series edited by Rodolphe Gasché
and Mark C. Taylor

Twentieth Century Literary Theory

An

Introductory

Anthology

edited by

Vassilis Lambropoulos
David Neal Miller

STATE UNIVERSITY OF NEW YORK PRESS

Published by
State University of New York Press, Albany

Printed in the United States of America

For information, address State University of New York
Press, State University Plaza, Albany, N.Y. 12246

Library of Congress Cataloging in Publication Data

Twentieth century literary theory.

   (Suny series in intersection. Philosophy and
literary theory)
   Includes index.
   1. Literature—Philosophy.   I. Lambropoulos,
Vassilis, 1953-   II. Miller, David Neal.
III. Series.
PN45.T94   1986   801′ .95′0904   86-5837
ISBN 0-88706-265-2
ISBN 0-88706-266-0 (pbk.)

10   9   8   7   6   5   4   3   2   1

Contents

Five: Conventions

Six: Style

Seven: Narrative

Eight: Interpretation

Nine: Reception

Ten: Evaluation

Introduction

When we started putting together this anthology, we realized with much satisfaction that recent developments in the humanities and the social sciences have called into question attempts to define theory (or any other concept) on the basis of attributes rather than of use: as long as people these days are arguing about "theory," graduating in "theory," and publishing on "theory," we at least can live with or without those quotation marks and leave static definitions to the lexicographers. For our own purposes in this volume, we take theory to mean what gets taught, published, reviewed, and read as theory—and the currently acceptable public uses of the term. In this sense, *Twentieth-Century Literary Theory: An Introductory Anthology* is itself a contribution to the process and project of definition.

Because we want to avoid endorsing the false distinction between theory and practice, we must add here one qualification; that we also take theory to signify the self-reflexivity of the specialist: the questions he or she raises about the enterprise—its assumptions, methods, and procedures. In this case, the specialist is the professional reader of literature, scholar or critic, as well as its educated practitioner—the informed author. This shared reflexivity is directed to their respective practices, the reading and writing of literature. This anthology, then, is meant to introduce the student and every other interested person to the problematics of twentieth-century literary criticism—the self-reflexive (and often self-inflicted) anguish of the literary scholar or writer over the nature of his or her subject, the scope of his or her investigation, and the validity of his or her methods.

The urgent need for a book of this kind became apparent to us while we were preparing together a course with the same title: we discovered, much to our surprise, that the last similar effort remains David Lodge's excellent (and unduly neglected in the United States) *Twentieth-Century Literary Criticism: A Reader* (London: Longman, 1972). That anthology served its purposes very well at the time of its publication, but today its age shows at least in three respects: first, because it stops at the threshold of structuralism, since its last selection dates back to 1966; second, because it concentrated more on criticism than on theory; and third, because the compilation does not include figures and texts which have only recently acquired a significant prominence. What we felt we needed was a new reader that would respond to contemporary course and class requirements; one that would focus exclusively on theoretical questions and include writers representing more national languages and literatures; and one that would present older as well as very recent pieces which reflect the state and the orientation of this art in the 1980s—the age when theory not only invaded academia but became part of pop culture too.

Although the spectacular spread of interest in theory made it easier for us to shun a clear-cut definition of the popular term, a series of difficult choices had to be made at every stage of the compilation process. This introduction intends to give all the necessary explanations about our decisions and allow, perhaps even help, the reader to make his own whenever he finds himself in disagreement. Of course, the main difficulty was found in exercising our judgement with a self-reflexive awareness worthy of our subject and its commentators: since we were to collect some of the most interesting instances of the self-criticisms of literary criticism, our practice would have to draw guidance from those very questions which had inspired the texts selected. The best help in this impossible task came from our own educational experience, the course that we had the opportunity to co-teach and build in our University.

Out of our teaching practice and the consistently fascinating exchange of ideas with our undergraduates and graduates grew the plan of this book and all its strategic choices: it was constructed for and out of the results of an experiment in meta-theoretical communication that worked. Obviously, this local success does not guarantee that our collection will be of ideal or uniform use to all instructors and students; but we happen to believe that its wealth is open and adaptable enough to serve a variety of propaedeutic needs and satisfy a wide spectrum of tastes and inclinations. With this due acknowledgment to the institutional origins of the book made, we can proceed now to account for our editorial decisions.

First, let it be simply stated that the anthology covers only the twentieth century because there was no literary theory before (if by literary theory one means a considered body of knowledge rather than isolated texts of theoretical import). In fact, we feel that our choice was directly dictated by the historical constitution of our subject. An anthology of criticism, of course, could extend back and include far more names and trends (although it might have to stop at the twilight of Neo-Classicism and the decline of interest in rhetoric which allowed what was first conceived as criticism by the Romantics to emerge). But theoretical questions about the very possibility of the critical enterprise had generally been avoided, and this is the fundamental epistemological difference that we chose to respect and implicitly emphasize. The first self-reflexive moment which heralded the appearance of literary theory coincided with the first truly self-reflexive moment of literature itself, the rebellions of Modernism, and developments in the former followed in close correspondence the evolution of the latter. Clearly, it is only in this century that literary theory emerged as a legitimate subject of knowledge in itself, influenced literary studies in general, and participated in many productive dialogues with other disciplines inside and outside the humanities; and it is only in the cultural and intellectual context of the modern era that its emergence can be properly understood. As it has been often publicly admitted, ours is the Age of Theory—of a theory which is perhaps about the nineteenth century, the Age of Criticism.

After demarcating the time limits of the anthology, the next and most important question we dealt with was that of the arrangement of the material—what was called earlier the plan of the book and its strategic choices. Those choices had to be strategic for many reasons: because we did not want, as editors, to take a pretentious stance of innocence or disinterested distance, as if our involvement and mediation in the field were unbiased; because we intended to propose a particular plan for discussion and research; because we conceived our collection as a reflection of and response to current epistemic attitudes and epistemological concerns; finally, because we were trying to crystallize in a textbook form an arrangement that had worked effectively in class.

Different possibilities were considered. The random (say, alphabetical) arrangement was rejected from the beginning for reasons mentioned above: to avoid the temptation of a scholarly aloofness that prizes disinterested objectivity as a valid approach. Being part of the present (academic) community of theorists, we felt that the risk of displeasing everybody involved in proposing a particular guide to the subject was preferable to the dangers inherent in the philological fallacy of editing-as-presenting. Here, we present by pre-setting. The view may be panoramic but the sensitive reader should remember that there is only one particular cultural point which validates it—that of the early 1980s; as such, the view is just another point of view, another version of the world of theory, whose best chance is to make sense here and now.

The second possibility examined was that of chronological ordering. But the first list we made showed us that this kind of arrangement presupposes a greater degree of sequential discourse than historical cultural experience confirms; it also adheres to the traditional model of linear history, according to which events follow each other in an evolutionary order that can be reasonably accounted for in terms of cause and effect. We thought that a plan of this kind would neutralize silences, inconsistencies, discontinuities, and marginal developments, and would impose the perspective or organicist historicism which has suppressed difference in the name of allegedly higher values or historical necessity.

The same danger we suspected lurking behind another alternative, that of organizing the material according to critical "schools" and literary "movements." Again, these units would have to be arranged chronologically and examined separately, as if each one constituted an autonomous body of knowledge—a tactic that would create artificial divisions by emphasizing unity and coherence. Also, every school does not address itself to every major issue; and when it does, it does so on its own presuppositions and terms. What is more, important figures (like Abrams, Burke, and Frye) cannot be easily identified with particular schools. In the final analysis, our anthology was certainly not intended to be a companion to a History of Twentieth-Century Theory of Literature and to supplement its successive chapters with original sources. It was another sense and awareness of history that we would like to exhibit and propose—one of its presentness rather than of its continuity.

Finally, we opted for the most challenging choice: the arrangement of material according to main topics. Of course, time and circumstances will tell if the challenge will work, as we hoped, both ways—for the editors and the readers. At this stage, we can only state our belief that the ten heading we chose represent adequately the prevailing concerns of literary theory these days. They are not meant to be permanent: if we were to revise this edition after a reasonable (say, five) number of years, some parts of it might change; they are not meant to be all-inclusive: we tried to identify and respond to the ideological character of the historical moment, admitting that its epistemological preoccupations unavoidedly limit the horizon of current inquiry and affect its orientation; nor are they means to be absolute: quite a few of the texts might conceivably be moved to different sections of the book and operate under a different light. In other words, we did not anthologize the classics of the century but rather selected those texts which make most sense for theory in the 1980s, trying at the same time to suggest a variety of perspectives available to the hermeneutic imagination.

This is consciously meant to be a functional reader, offering a series of carefully planned working suggestions for study. The ten topics reflect contemporary theoretical interests and attempt to orient the student's attention toward today's fundamental questions about the practices of criticism. Since supplementary bibliographical, biographical, and historical information is readily available in other sources, we felt free to omit it altogether and let the texts speak for themselves. Here, the student is encouraged to think about issues, compare existing approaches, and explore further possibilities. Our list of topics remains open to discussion and revision, while their arrangement, although itself an imposition of projected homogeneity, could always change in different educational environments, if specific requirements or needs dictate some adjustment. But the point to be stressed is that the study of the book should be the actualization of the study plan incorporated in it, a plan which guides the reader from the formation to the uses of theory and from the constitution to the interpretation of literature.

The anthology opens with discussion of Theory that address themselves to the nature of its origins, subjects, politics, and limitations. Then the basic questions of Literature as writing, art, action, and institution are raised. The possible roles played by its craftsman, the Author, are examined: is he a creator, a literary hero himself, or an irrecoverable (and therefore irrelevant) source or a cultural fiction? Whatever the role and privileges of the author, literature is necessarily read against a Tradition, a relevant context whose dialectics have been attributed to its own inner dynamics, to institutional changes, cultural influences, or historical circumstances. Furthermore, this context includes not only individual works but also various Conventions—rules and norms which affect writing methods and reading practices, techniques of composition and reception. The application of compositional techniques and the resulting concrete formation of stock or original devices in a particular work is commonly perceived as Style. But where does it inhere: in the work itself or in its relationships with other, extratextual factors? A similar question is asked next about the nature of the Narrative: is fictiveness immanent to literature, verbal discourse, the human psyche, or historical experience? and which are its elementary units?

At this point, the very question of Interpretation is posed: what do we do when we interpret, and how can this activity be distinguished (if at all) from reading, explicating, analyzing, and understanding? This question in turn leads to the one about the roles of the reader and the extent of his participation in the event of Reception. Finally, since his involvement will produce an experience and result in an Evaluation, the appropriate criteria are discussed along with their epistemological assumptions and political implications. Essentially, the volume opens with the question: *what does theory do?*, devotes eight chapters to discussing *how?*, and closes with another question, *why?*. After the last text, perhaps it would be interesting to attempt to return to the very first one, though this might entail rereading the whole book in a rather different way.

We turn now to our decision to include only one text from each critic, scholar, or author. This is an anthology of texts and a presentation of issues, not a survey of writers or critical movements. We tried to make a place for as many critics as possible without establishing a canon of great names or articles. The texts chosen from each writer's work are not always their "best" or most famous, but rather the ones that fitted our plan best in terms of relevance, strength, and concisiveness. On the other hand, the absence of certain well-known names (like those of V. Shklovski, F. R. Leavis, and . . .) from our list is in most cases due to the fact that, despite their impact, those critics did not work directly on theory but included their influential theoretical statements in pieces of criticism where they could not be legitimately isolated for our own purposes. The exclusion of criticism from our collection (to the degree that it was possible) serves not only the concentration of a very significant twentieth-century intellectual phenomenon—literary theory itself—but also the tactical distraction of interest from a literary canon which has dominated the field for at least one hundred years now.

This anthology thus attempts to resist two kinds of canonization which have overtaken literary studies in general—that of "great" critics and schools of criticism, and that of "major" national literatures. For reasons of theoretical soundness, we did not want to include arguments that depend heavily on their applications; and for reasons of political vigilance we did not want to privilege applications which deal with the "masterpieces" of western tradition and the Great Masters of the English-centered and -modeled canon. Moreover, we chose to respect the radical insularity of the margins of contemporary theoretical discourse—feminist criticism, for example.

We would like this selection of texts to be available to students of all national languages and literatures and all scholars, irrespective of what their writers studied or propagated. Only inquiries beyond the boundaries of British Romanticism, French Symbolism, and American Modernism will enable us to ascertain the validity of any theoretical statements by transgressing the decorum of scholarship imposed by the discourses of critical nationalism. In this respect, it is not an accident (or an unpromising sign) that recent discussions of cultural imperialism, feminism, and popular culture have drawn valuable attention to the wider politics of interpretation and the violent power of institutional knowledge. They have also shown convincingly that western social, political, moral, literary, or any other theory depends by its very constitution on the premises of a certain dominant tradition (which has been called phallocratic, logocentric, metaphysical, capitalist, Protestant, etc.) and that, therefore, any theory deals necessarily with questions pertaining to the operations of its sustaining tradition only. It was in realization of these cultural (and hence epistemological) limitations that we decided to go against the grain of the established notions of what literature and criticism are and include texts that seem to bear no apparent relation to literary theory (like those by Derrida, Wittgenstein and others). Thus, we felt, we respond to challenges from other fields that literary theory itself has already eagerly taken up.

We also invite our readers to examine assumptions about language, writing, art, and reality informing the very concept of literature, and ask themselves how recent developments in other disciplines can help us improve or revise our approaches to texts. The deliberate inclusion of ideas from the theories of history, philosophy, and the human sciences is an expression of our belief that literary studies (or the texts they cherish) cannot survive in self-satisfied isolation any longer but need to participate in the open debates that these days center around the question of scientific theory and its philosophies.

For each one of the ten sections in this book, we have selected three texts as required reading and we have suggested five others as recommended. We would like to have published all eighty texts here, but that would have resulted in a bulky and uneconomical volume. Thus we give only bibliographical references for the supplementary material, and our encouragement that these texts be consulted. In our own course, taught under a quarterly system, we discuss (rather than lecture on) the main texts but we urge students to read on their own the rest too, and on this condition we feel free to make occasional references to them in class. Despite its demands, the method has worked very well: the course has proven to be an intensive one but the range of questions posed in the thirty texts, as well as their intellectual breadth, is such that continuous attention, exploration, and participation are almost automatically required and, in our experience, have not been refused.

Since the anthology focuses on issues rather than schools, works, or critics, the number of texts in each section is one that allows for enough familiarity and diversity; this allows a sufficient number of alternative treatments of the same topic to be presented. In the third chapter, for example, we have chosen texts which in turn suggest that the examination of the artist's literary biography is a valid subject for literary studies, ostracize intentionality from the proper concerns of close reading as irrelevant, and reject as a cultural construct all notions of the creator. The aim of such a selection is obviously to alert the reader to the multiple dimensions of the problem by exposing him to different, opposing, or even incommensurable positions. As has been affirmed, it is not answers or solutions that we intended to provide but rather questions and issues that we hoped to raise. We felt, however, that in this respect information about the schools of thought represented by these interpretations or their exponents, although potentially helpful, was not of primary importance and could also distract attention from problems of immediate relevance; those interested may chose to research those matters elsewhere. Although certain schools were given their fair say under certain topics (like structuralism in the section on Narrative or phenomenology in that on Reception), no special emphasis was added to that share.

The recommended texts supplement the required readings in various ways: they expand viewpoints, they examine alternative aspects, or they even counter positions advanced in the main list (as, for example, in the cases of Valéry and Lukács). But again we refrained from pointing out all these internal correspondences, preferring to let the reader himself engage the texts in possible correlations, if he wishes to explore the dialectics of our selection. In fact, the additional texts give ample ground for home work, including a return to the required ones for different kinds of cross-reading. Eventually, the interpretive freedom the reader will feel competent to exercise can be one of the better measures of the volume's success.

The last major editorial decision we were faced with was the order of texts, which, like the order of things, reflects the state of a discourse and its respective domain of knowledge. Our final arrangement is neither chronological nor hierarchical but the one we thought was (and found out in practice to be) the most educational—the one that introduces (and intrigues) the reader into the problematics of the topic. Usually, the first text in each chapter is the most conservative of the three (without this meaning that we consider it to be a truly conservative one): it maps a territory with some clarity, certainty, and safety along rather conventional lines that normally are not expected to surprise the student. The other two progressively blur those demarcations, with the last one often arguing that they are altogether impossible to draw, at least not without questioning some fundamental assumptions about the character of the topic itself. Ideally, at the end of every chapter one should go back and review it as a unit in order to grasp the range of questions asked or not asked by those writers.

With a single exception, texts are printed in full. In most cases we chose to print them as they originally appeared and in all cases we found uniformity an insufficient reason for any editorial intervention. This principle was followed even in matters of transliteration and orthography. Whether a text is an essay, an article, a paper, or part of a book is indicated by the bibliographical reference provided at is end. Different available translations were compared for imaginative adherence to the original or, in the case of the Slavic languages, meaningful lucidity. All the titles belong to the authors. Since we did not want to create a historical anthology nor, on the other hand, encourage an ahistorical (or what some might consider "purely philosophical") approach to our selection, we added as an Appendix a list of all eighty texts included or mentioned in strict chronological order to show the linear path of time that modern theoretical debates have followed—from the 1920s, when a literary work was generally expected to be and not mean anything in particular, to the present day and the return of axiology to prominence.

In closing, we would like to repeat that this anthology is not meant for posterity but for specific and productive contemporary uses. It is by these uses that its value should be judged. We present a guide to the problematics of twentieth-century literary theory fully aware of the fact that even this seemingly impersonal work entails taking sides. We tried to leave much room for the reader's and the instructor's initiative and to suggest an approach which integrates a coherent series of working ideas. As an implicit evaluation, this selection directs interest and inquiry to issues and arguments, rather than artworks or personalities. Compiling this volume has been a thoroughly fascinating experience which owes more than we want to express to more than we can mention at this closing point. We are grateful to our colleagues for their support, to our students for their understanding, to our educators for their guidance, and to our friends for their devotion—in reverse order. We are also grateful to each other for sharing the same office and what still strikes the other party as in incomprehensibly affectionate tolerance.

February 1984

Acknowledgments

M. H. Abrams, "Orientation of Critical Theories," is reprinted from *The Mirror and the Lamp: Romantic Theory and the Critical Tradition*, with permission of the Oxford University Press.

Jurij Tynjanov and Roman Jakobson, "Problems in the Study of Literature and Language," is reprinted from *Russian Poetics: Formalist and Structuralist Views*, edited by Ladislav Matejka and Krystyna Pomorska, with permission of the Massachusetts Institute of Technology Press.

Jacques Derrida, "Structure, Sign, and Play in the Human Sciences," is reprinted from *The Structuralist Controversy: The Languages of Criticism and the Sciences of Man* with permission of the Johns Hopkins University Press.

Yvor Winters, "Preliminary Problems," is reprinted from *In Defense of Reason* with permission of the Ohio University Press.

René Wellek, "The Mode of Existence of the Literary Work," is reprinted from the *Southern Review* (Spring, 1942) with permission of the Louisiana State University Press.

Kenneth Burke, "Symbolic Action" is reprinted from *The Philosophy of Literary Form* with permission of the University of California Press.

W. K. Wimsatt, Jr., and Monroe C. Beardsley, "The Intentional Fallacy" is reprinted from *The Verbal Icon: Studies in the Meaning of Poetry* with permission of the University of Kentucky Press.

Boris Tomashevsky, "Literature and Biography," is reprinted from *Russian Poetics: Formalist and Structuralist Views*, edited by Ladislav Matejka and Krystyna Pomorska, with permission of the Massachusetts Institute of Technology Press.

Michel Foucault, "What Is an Author?" is reprinted from *Language, Counter-Memory, Practice: Selected Essays and Interviews by Michel Foucault*, (trans. by Donald F. Bouchard and Sherry Simon, and edited by Donald F. Bouchard, Copyright © 1977 by Cornell University) with permission of Cornell University Press and the Bulletin de la Societé Francaise de Philosophie.

T.S. Eliot, "Tradition and the Individual Talent," is reprinted from *Selected Essays* with permission of Faber and Faber Ltd., London.

Jurij Tynjanov, "On Literary Evolution" is reprinted from *Poetics: Formalist and Structuralist Views*, edited by Ladislav Matejka and Krystyna Pomorska, with permission of the Massachusetts Institute of Technology Press.

Harold Bloom, "The Dialectics of Poetic Tradition" is reprinted from *A Map of Misreading* (Copyright © 1975 by Oxford University Press, Inc.,) with permission of Oxford University Press.

Ludvig Wittgenstein, Sections 156-67, 197-203, reprinted from *Philosophical Investigations* with permission of Basil Blackwell publishers.

Raymond Williams, "Conventions," is reprinted from *Marxism and Literature* (Copywright © 1977 by Oxford University Press) with permission of Oxford University Press.

Tzvetan Todorov, "Literary Genres," is reprinted from *The Fantastic: A Structural Approach to a Literary Genre* with permission of Case Western University Press and Editions du Seuil.

Leo Spitzer, "Linguistics and Literary History," is reprinted from *Linguistics and Literary History: Essays in Stylistics* (Copyright © 1948, renewed 1976, by Princeton University Press) is reprinted with permission of Princeton University Press.

Cleanth Brooks, "The Heresy of Paraphrase" is reprinted from *The Well Wrought Urn* by permission of Harcourt Brace Jovanovich, Inc.

Nelson Goodman, "The Status of Style," is reprinted from *Critical Inquiry*, Vol. 1, no. 4 (June 1975) by permission of the author and the University of Chicago Press.

Wayne Booth, "Distance and Point of View" is reprinted from *Essays in Criticism* (edited by Stephen Wall) with the permission of the editor and author.

Mixail Baxtin, "Discourse Typology in Prose," tr. by Richard Balthazar and I. R. Titunik in *Readings in Russian Poetics: Formalist and Structuralist Views* (edited by Ladislav Matejka and Krystyna Pomorska) is reprinted with permission of Michigan Slavic Publications.

A.J. Greimas "Elements of a Narrative Grammar," is reprinted from *Diacritics 7* (March 1977) by permission of the Johns Hopkins University Press.

Paul Ricoeur, "What Is a Text? Explanation and Uniderstanding" is reprinted from *Hermeneutics and the Human Sciences,* edited by John B. Thompson, with permission of the Cambridge University Press.

Stanley Fish, "Demonstration vs. Persuasion: Two Models of Critical Activity" is reprinted from *Is There a Text in This Class?* by Stanley Fish (Copyright © 1980 by the President and Fellows of Harvard College) with permission of the Harvard University Press.

Julia Kristeva, "Psychoanalysis and the Polis," is reprinted from *Critical Inquiry* vol. 9, no. 1 (Sept. 1982) by permission of the author and the University of Chicago Press.

Wolfgang Iser, "The Reading Process: A Phenomenological Approach," is reprinted from *New Literary History,* 3 (1972) with permission of the Johns Hopkins University Press.

Walter J. Ong, "The Writer's Audience is Always a Fiction," is reprinted from *PMLA* 90 (1975) with permission of the Modern Language Association of America.

Umberto Eco, "Introduction," is reprinted from *The Role of the Reader* with permission of the Indiana University Press.

Benedetto Croce, "Taste and the Reproduction of Art," is reprinted from *Aesthetic as Science of Expression and General Linguistic,* edited by Douglas Ainslie, with permission of MacMillan Company.

Monroe c. Beardsley, "Reasons and Judgments," is reprinted from *The Possibility of Criticism* with permission of the Wayne State University Press.

Barbara Herrnstein-Smith, "Contingencies of Value," is reprinted from *Critical Inquiry,* vol. 10, no. 1 (Sept. 1983) with permission of the author and the University of Chicago Press.

One
theory

M. H. Abrams

Orientation of Critical Theories

> BOSWELL. 'Then, Sir, what is poetry?'
> JOHNSON. 'Why, Sir, it is much easier to say what it
> is not. We all *know* what light is; but it is not easy
> to *tell* what it is.'
>
> It is the mark of an educated man to look for
> precision in each class of things just so far as the
> nature of the subject admits.
>
> —ARISTOTLE, *Nicomachean Ethics*

To pose and answer aesthetic questions in terms of the relation of art to
the artist, rather than to external nature, or to the audience, or to the internal requirements of the work itself, was the characteristic tendency of
modern criticism up to a few decades ago, and it continues to be the propensity of a great many—perhaps the majority—of critics today. This
point of view is very young measured against the twenty-five-hundred-
year history of the Western theory of art, for its emergence as a comprehensive approach to art, shared by a large number of critics, dates back not
much more than a century and a half. The intention of this book is to
chronicle the evolution and (in the early nineteenth century) the triumph,
in its diverse forms, of this radical shift to the artist in the alignment of
aesthetic thinking, and to describe the principal alternate theories
against which this approach had to compete. In particular, I shall be concerned with the momentous consequences of these new bearings in criticism for the identification, the analysis, the evaluation, and the writing
of poetry.

The field of aesthetics presents an especially difficult problem to the
historian. Recent theorists of art have been quick to profess that much, if
not all, that has been said by their predecessors is wavering, chaotic,
phantasmal. 'What has gone by the name of the philosophy of art' seemed
to Santayana 'sheer verbiage.' D. W. Prall, who himself wrote two excellent books on the subject, commented that traditional aesthetics 'is in
fact only a pseudo-science or pseudo-philosophy.'

3

Its subject-matter is such wavering and deceptive stuff as dreams
are made of; its method is neither logical nor scientific, nor quite
whole-heartedly and empirically matter of fact ... without
application in practice to test it and without an orthodox
terminology to make it into an honest superstition or a
thoroughgoing, soul satisfying cult. It is neither useful to creative
artists nor a help to amateurs in appreciation.[1]

And I. A. Richards, in his *Principles of Literary Criticism*, labeled his
first chapter 'The Chaos of Critical Theories,' and justified the pejorative
attribute by quoting, as 'the apices of critical theory,' more than a score of
isolated and violently discrepant utterances about art, from Aristotle to
the present time.[2] With the optimism of his youth, Richards himself
went on to attempt a solid grounding of literary evaluation in the science
of psychology.

It is true that the course of aesthetic theory displays its full measure
of the rhetoric and logomachy which seem an inseparable part of man's
discourse about all things that really matter. But a good deal of our im-
patience with the diversity and seeming chaos in philosophies of art is
rooted in a demand from criticism for something it cannot do, at the cost
of overlooking many of its genuine powers. We still need to face up to the
full consequences of the realization that criticism is not a physical, nor
even a psychological, science. By setting out from and terminating in an
appeal to the facts, any good aesthetic theory is, indeed, empirical in
method. Its aim, however, is not to establish correlations between facts
which will enable us to predict the future by reference to the past, but to
establish principles enabling us to justify, order, and clarify our interpretation and appraisal of the aesthetic facts themselves. And as we shall see,
these facts turn out to have the curious and scientifically reprehensible
property of being conspicuously altered by the nature of the very principles which appeal to them for their support. Because many critical statements of fact are thus partially relative to the perspective of the theory
within which they occur, they are not 'true,' in the strict scientific sense
that they approach the ideal of being verifiable by any intelligent human
being, no matter what his point of view. Any hope, therefore, for the kind
of basic agreement in criticism that we have learned to expect in the exact
sciences is doomed to disappointment.

A good critical theory, nevertheless, has its own kind of validity. The
criterion is not the scientific verifiability of its single propositions, but
the scope, precision, and coherence of the insights that it yields into the
properties of single works of art and the adequacy with which it accounts
for diverse kinds of art. Such a criterion will, of course, justify not one, but
a number of valid theories, all in their several ways self-consistent, appli-

cable, and relatively adequate to the range of aesthetic phenomena; but this diversity is not to be deplored. One lesson we gain from a survey of the history of criticism, in fact, is the great debt we owe to the variety of the criticism of the past. Contrary to Prall's pessimistic appraisal, these theories have not been futile, but as working conceptions of the matter, end, and ordonnance of art, have been greatly effective in shaping the activities of creative artists. Even an aesthetic philosophy so abstract and seemingly academic as that of Kant can be shown to have modified the work of poets. In modern times, new departures in literature almost invariably have been accompanied by novel critical pronouncements, whose very inadequacies sometimes help to form the characteristic qualities of the correlated literary achievements, so that if our critics had not disagreed so violently, our artistic inheritance would doubtless have been less rich and various. Also, the very fact that any well-grounded critical theory in some degree alters the aesthetic perceptions it purports to discover is a source of its value to the amateur of art, for it may open his senses to aspects of a work which other theories, with a different focus and different categories of discrimination, have on principle overlooked, underestimated, or obscured.

The diversity of aesthetic theories, however, makes the task of the historian a very difficult one. It is not only that answers to such questions as 'What is art?' or 'What is poetry?' disagree. The fact is that many theories of art cannot readily be compared at all, because they lack a common ground on which to meet and clash. They seem incommensurable because stated in diverse terms, or in identical terms with diverse signification, or because they are an integral part of larger systems of thought which differ in assumptions and procedure. As a result it is hard to find where they agree, where disagree, or even, what the points at issue are.

Our first need, then, is to find a frame of reference simple enough to be readily manageable, yet flexible enough so that, without undue violence to any one set of statements about art, it will translate as many sets as possible onto a single plane of discourse. Most writers bold enough to undertake the history of aesthetic theory have achieved this end by silently translating the basic terms of all theories into their own favorite philosophical vocabulary, but this procedure unduly distorts its subject matter, and merely multiplies the complications to be unraveled. The more promising method is to adopt an analytic scheme which avoids imposing its own philosophy, by utilizing those key distinctions which are already common to the largest possible number of the theories to be compared, and then to apply the scheme warily, in constant readiness to introduce such further distinctions as seem to be needed for the purpose in hand.

Some Co-ordinates of Art Criticism

Four elements in the total situation of a work of art are discriminated and
made salient, by one or another synonym, in almost all theories which
aim to be comprehensive. First, there is the *work*, the artistic product itself. And since this is a human product, an artifact, the second common
element is the artificer, the *artist*. Third, the work is taken to have a subject which, directly or deviously, is derived from existing things—to be
about, or signify, or reflect something which either is, or bears some relation to, an objective state of affairs. This third element, whether held to
consist of people and actions, ideas and feelings, material things and
events, or super-sensible essences, has frequently been denoted by that
word-of-all-work, 'nature'; but let us use the more neutral and comprehensive term, *universe*, instead. For the final element we have the *audience:* the listeners, spectators, or readers to whom the work is addressed,
or to whose attention, at any rate, it becomes available.

On this framework of artist, work, universe, and audience I wish to
spread out various theories for comparison. To emphasize the artificiality
of the device, and at the same time make it easier to visualize the analyses, let us arrange the four co-ordinates in a convenient pattern. A triangle will do, with the work of art, the thing to be explained, in the center.

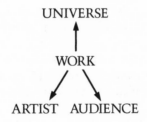

Although any reasonably adequate theory takes some account of all four
elements, almost all theories, as we shall see, exhibit a discernible orientation toward one only. That is, a critic tends to derive from one of these
terms his principal categories for defining, classifying, and analyzing a
work of art, as well as the major criteria by which he judges its value. Application of this analytic scheme, therefore, will sort attempts to explain
the nature and worth of a work of art into four broad classes. Three will
explain the work of art principally by relating it to another thing: the universe, the audience, or the artist. The fourth will explain the work by considering it in isolation, as an autonomous whole, whose significance and
value are determined without any reference beyond itself.

To find the major orientation of a critical theory, however, is only the
beginning of an adequate analysis. For one thing, these four co-ordinates

are not constants, but variables; they differ in significance according to the theory in which they occur. Take what I have called the *universe* as an example. In any one theory, the aspects of nature which an artist is said to imitate, or is exhorted to imitate, may be either particulars or types, and they may be only the beautiful or the moral aspects of the world, or else any aspect without discrimination. It may be maintained that the artist's world is that of imaginative intuition, or of common sense, or of natural science; and this world may be held to include, or not to include, gods, witches, chimeras, and Platonic Ideas. Consequently, theories which agree in assigning to the represented universe the primary control over a legitimate work of art may vary from recommending the most uncompromising realism to the most remote idealism. Each of our other terms, as we shall see, also varies, both in meaning and functioning, according to the critical theory in which it occurs, the method of reasoning which the theorist characteristically uses, and the explicit or implicit 'world-view' of which these theories are an integral part.

It would be possible, of course, to devise more complex methods of analysis which, even in a preliminary classification, would make more subtle distinctions.[3] By multiplying differentiae, however, we sharpen our capacity to discriminate at the expense both of easy manageability and the ability to make broad initial generalizations. For our historical purpose, the scheme I have proposed has this important virtue, that it will enable us to bring out the one essential attribute which most early nineteenth-century theories had in common: the persistent recourse to the poet to explain the nature and criteria of poetry. Historians have recently been instructed to speak only of 'romanticisms,' in the plural, but from our point of vantage there turns out to be one distinctively romantic criticism, although this remains a unity amid variety.

Mimetic Theories

The mimetic orientation—the explanation of art as essentially an imitation of aspects of the universe—was probably the most primitive aesthetic theory, but mimesis is no simple concept by the time it makes its first recorded appearance in the dialogues of Plato. The arts of painting, poetry, music, dancing, and sculpture, Socrates says, are all imitations.[4] 'Imitation' is a relational term, signifying two items and some correspondence between them. But although in many later mimetic theories everything is comprehended in two categories, the imitable and the imitation, the philosopher in the Platonic dialogues characteristically operates with three categories. The first category is that of the eternal and unchanging Ideas; the second, reflecting this, is the world of sense, natural or artifi-

cial; and the third category, in turn reflecting the second, comprises such
things as shadows, images in water and mirrors, and the fine arts.

Around this three-stage regress—complicated still further by various supplementary distinctions, as well as by his exploitation of the poly-
semism of his key terms—Plato weaves his dazzling dialectic.[5] But from
the shifting arguments emerges a recurrent pattern, exemplified in the famous passage in the tenth book of the *Republic.* In discussing the nature
of art, Socrates makes the point that there are three beds: the Idea which
'is the essence of the bed' and is made by God, the bed made by the car-
penter, and the bed found in a painting. How shall we describe the painter
of this third bed?

> I think, he said, that we may fairly designate him as the
> imitator of that which the others make.
> Good, I said; then you call him who is third in the descent from
> nature an imitator?
> Certainly, he said.
> And the tragic poet is an imitator, and therefore, like all other
> imitators, he is thrice removed from the king and from the truth?
> That appears to be so.[6]

From the initial position that art imitates the world of appearance
and not of Essence, it follows that works of art have a lowly status in the
order of existing things. Furthermore, since the realm of Ideas is the ultimate locus not only of reality but of value, the determination that art is
at second remove from the truth automatically establishes its equal re-
moteness from the beautiful and good. Despite the elaborate dialectic—
or more accurately, by means of it—Plato's remains a philosophy of a single standard; for all things, including art, are ultimately judged by the one
criterion of their relation to the same Ideas. On these grounds, the poet is
inescapably the competitor of the artisan, the lawmaker, and the moralist; indeed, any one of these can be regarded as himself the truer poet, successfully achieving that imitation of the Ideas which the traditional poet
attempts under conditions dooming him to failure. Thus the lawmaker is
able to reply to the poets seeking admission to his city, 'Best of strangers—

> we also according to our ability are tragic poets, and our tragedy is
> the best and noblest; for our whole state is an imitation of the best
> and noblest life, which we affirm to be indeed the very truth of
> tragedy. You are poets and we are poets . . . rivals and antagonists in
> the noblest of dramas . . . [7]

And the poor opinion of ordinary poetry to which we are committed on
the basis of its mimetic character, is merely confirmed when Plato points
out that its effects on its auditors are bad because it represents appear-

ance rather than truth, and nourishes their feelings rather than their reason; or by demonstrating that the poet in composing (as Socrates jockeys poor obtuse Ion into admitting) cannot depend on his art and knowledge, but must wait upon the divine afflatus and the loss of his right mind.[8]

The Socratic dialogues, then, contain no aesthetics proper, for neither the structure of Plato's cosmos nor the pattern of his dialectic permits us to consider poetry as poetry—as a special kind of product having its own criteria and reason for being. In the dialogues there is only one direction possible, and one issue, that is, the perfecting of the social state and the state of man; so that the question of art can never be separated from questions of truth, justice, and virtue. 'For great is the issue at stake,' Socrates says in concluding his discussion of poetry in the *Republic*, 'greater than appears, whether a man is to be good or bad.'[9]

Aristotle in the *Poetics* also defines poetry as imitation. 'Epic poetry and Tragedy, as also Comedy, Dithyrambic poetry, and most flute-playing and lyre-playing, are all, viewed as a whole, modes of imitation'; and 'the objects the imitator represents are actions ... '[10] But the difference between the way the term 'imitation' functions in Aristotle and in Plato distinguishes radically their consideration of art. In the *Poetics*, as in the Platonic dialogues, the term implies that a work of art is constructed according to prior models in the nature of things, but since Aristotle has shorn away the other world of criterion-Ideas, there is no longer anything invidious in that fact. Imitation is also made a term specific to the arts, distinguishing these from everything else in the universe, and thereby freeing them from rivalry with other human activities. Furthermore, in his analysis of the fine arts, Aristotle at once introduces supplementary distinctions according to the objects imitated, the medium of imitation, and the manner—dramatic, narrative, or mixed, for example—in which the imitation is accomplished. By successive exploitation of these distinctions in object, means, and manner, he is able first to distinguish poetry from other kinds of art, and then to differentiate the various poetic genres, such as epic and drama, tragedy and comedy. When he focuses on the genre of tragedy, the same analytic instrument is applied to the discrimination of the parts constituting the individual whole: plot, character, thought, and so on. Aristotle's criticism, therefore, is not only criticism of art as art, independent of statesmanship, being, and morality, but also of poetry as poetry, and of each kind of poem by the criteria appropriate to its particular nature. As a result of this procedure, Aristotle bequeathed an arsenal of instruments for technical analysis of poetic forms and their elements which have proved indispensable to critics ever since, however diverse the uses to which these instruments have been put.

A salient quality of the *Poetics* is the way it considers a work of art in various of its external relations, affording each its due function as one of the 'causes' of the work. This procedure results in a scope and flexibility that makes the treatise resist a ready classification into any one kind of orientation. Tragedy cannot be fully defined, for example, nor can the total determinants of its construction be understood, without taking into account its proper effect on the audience: the achievement of the specifically 'tragic pleasure,' which is 'that of pity and fear.'[11] It is apparent, however, that the mimetic concept—the reference of a work to the subject matter which it imitates—is primary in Aristotle's critical system, even if it is *primus inter pares*. Their character as an imitation of human actions is what defines the arts in general, and the kind of action imitated serves as one important differentia of an artistic species. The historical genesis of art is traced to the natural human instinct for imitating, and to the natural tendency to find pleasure in seeing imitations. Even the unity essential to any work of art is mimetically grounded, since 'one imitation is always of one thing,' and in poetry 'the story, as an imitation of action, must represent one action, a complete whole ... '[12] And the 'form' of a work, the presiding principle determining the choice and order and internal adjustments of all the parts, is derived from the form of the object that is imitated. It is the fable or plot 'that is the end and purpose of tragedy,' its 'life and soul, so to speak,' and this because

> tragedy is essentially an imitation not of persons but of action and life ... We maintain that Tragedy is primarily an imitation of action, and that it is mainly for the sake of the action that it imitates the personal agents.[13]

If we refer again to our analytic diagram, one other general aspect of the *Poetics* presses on our attention, particularly when we have the distinctive orientation of romantic criticism in mind. While Aristotle makes a distribution (though an unequal one) among the objects imitated, the necessary emotional effects on an audience, and the internal demands of the product itself, as determinants of this or that aspect of a poem, he does not assign a determinative function to the poet himself. The poet is the indispensable efficient cause, the agent who, by his skill, extracts the form from natural things and imposes it upon an artificial medium; but his personal faculties, feelings, or desires are not called on to explain the subject matter or form of a poem. In the *Poetics*, the poet is invoked only to explain the historical divergence of comic from serious forms, and to be advised of certain aids toward the construction of plot and the choice of diction.[14] In Plato, the poet is considered from the point of view of politics, not of art. When the poets make a personal appearance all the major ones are dismissed, with extravagant courtesy, from the ideal Republic; upon later application, a somewhat greater number are admitted to the second-best state of the *Laws*, but with a radically diminished repertory.[15]

'Imitation' continued to be a prominent item in the critical vocabulary for a long time after Aristotle—all the way through the eighteenth century, in fact. The systematic importance given to the term differed greatly from critic to critic; those objects in the universe that art imitates, or should imitate, were variously conceived as either actual or in some sense ideal; and from the first, there was a tendency to replace Aristotle's 'action' as the principal object of imitation with such elements as human character, or thought, or even inanimate things. But particularly after the recovery of the *Poetics* and the great burst of aesthetic theory in sixteenth-century Italy, whenever a critic was moved to get down to fundamentals and frame a comprehensive definition of art, the predicate usually included the word 'imitation,' or else one of those parallel terms which, whatever differences they might imply, all faced in the same direction: 'reflection,' 'representation,' 'counterfeiting,' 'feigning,' 'copy,' or 'image.'

Through most of the eighteenth century, the tenet that art is an imitation seemed almost too obvious to need iteration or proof. As Richard Hurd said in his 'Discourse on Poetical Imitation,' published in 1751, 'All *Poetry*, to speak with Aristotle and the Greek critics (if for so plain a point authorities be thought wanting) is, properly, *imitation*. It is, indeed, the noblest and most extensive of the mimetic arts; having all creation for its object, and ranging the entire circuit of universal being.'[16] Even the reputedly radical proponents of 'original genius' in the second half of the century commonly found that a work of genius was no less an imitation for being an original. *'Imitations,'* Young wrote in his *Conjectures on Original Composition,* 'are of two kinds: one of nature, one of authors. The first we call *Originals* ... ' The original genius in fact turns out to be a kind of scientific investigator: 'The wide field of nature lies open before it, where it may range unconfined, make what discoveries it can ... as far as visible nature extends ... '[17] Later the Reverend J. Moir, an extremist in his demand for originality in poetry, conceived genius to lie in the ability to discover 'a thousand new variations, distinctions, and resemblances' in the 'familiar phenomena of nature,' and declared that original genius always gives 'the identical impression it receives.'[18] In this identification of the poet's task as novelty of discovery and particularity of description we have moved a long way from Aristotle's conception of mimesis, except in this respect, that criticism still looks to one or another aspect of the given world for the essential source and subject matter of poetry.

Instead of heaping up quotations, it will be better to cite a few eighteenth-century discussions of imitation that are of special interest. My first example is the French critic, Charles Batteux, whose *Les Beaux Arts réduits à un même principe* (1747) found some favor in England and had immense influence in Germany, as well as in his native country. The rules of art, Batteux thought, which are now so numerous, must surely be reducible to a single principle. 'Let us,' he cries, 'imitate the true physicists, who assemble experiments and then on these found a system which reduces them to a principle.'

That Batteux proposes for his procedure 'to begin with a clear and distinct idea'—a principle 'simple enough to be grasped instantly, and extensive enough to absorb all the little detailed rules'—is sufficient clue that he will follow in method not Newton, the physicist, but rather Euclid and Descartes. In pursuance of his clear and distinct idea, he burrowed industriously through the standard French critics until, he says ingenuously, 'it occurred to me to open Aristotle, whose *Poetics* I had heard praised.' Then came the revelation; all details fell neatly into place. The source of illumination?—none other than 'the principle of imitation which the Greek philosopher established for the fine arts.'[19] This imitation, however, is not of crude everyday reality, but of 'la belle nature'; that is, 'le vrai-semblable,' formed by assembling traits taken from individual things to compose a model possessing 'all the perfections it is able to receive.'[20] From this principle Batteux goes on, lengthily and with great show of rigor, to extract one by one the rules of taste—both the general rules for poetry and painting and the detailed rules for the special genres. For

> the majority of known rules refer back to imitation, and form a sort
> of chain, by which the mind seizes at the same instant
> consequences and principle, as a whole perfectly joined, in which all
> the parts are mutually sustained.[21]

Next to this classic instance of a priori and deductive aesthetics I shall set a German document, Lessing's *Laokoon*, published in 1776. Lessing undertook to undo the confusion in theory and practice between poetry and the graphic and plastic arts which, he believed, resulted from an uninquisitive acceptance of Simonides' maxim that 'painting is dumb poetry and poetry a speaking painting.' His own procedure, he promises, will be continually to test abstract theory against 'the individual instance.' Repeatedly he derides German critics for their reliance on deduction. 'We Germans have no lack of systematic books. We are the most expert of any nation in the world at deducing, from a few given verbal explanations, and in the most beautiful order, anything whatever that we wish.' 'How many things would prove incontestable in theory, had not genius succeeded in proving the contrary in fact!'[22] Lessing's intention, then, is to establish aesthetic principles by an inductive logic which is deliberately opposed to the procedure of Batteux. Nevertheless, like Batteux, Lessing concludes that poetry, no less than painting, is imitation. The diversity between these arts follows from their difference in medium, which imposes necessary differences in the objects each is competent to imitate. But although poetry consists of a sequence of articulate sounds in time rather than of forms and colors fixed in space, and although, instead of being limited, like painting, to a static but pregnant moment, its special power is the reproduction of progressive action, Lessing reiterates for it the standard formula: 'Nachahmung' is still for the poet the attribute 'which constitutes the essence of his art.'[23]

As the century drew on, various English critics began to scrutinize the concept of imitation very closely, and they ended by finding (Aristotle to the contrary) that differences in medium between the arts were such as to disqualify all but a limited number from being classed as mimetic, in any strict sense. The trend may be indicated by a few examples. In 1744 James Harris still maintained, in 'A Discourse on Music, Painting, and Poetry,' that imitation was common to all three arts. 'They agree, by being all mimetic or imitative. They differ, as they imitate by different media . . . '[24] In 1762 Kames declared that 'of all the fine arts, painting only and sculpture are in their nature imitative'; music, like architecture, 'is productive of originals, and copies not from nature'; while language copies from nature only in those instances in which it 'is imitative of sound or motion.'[25] And by 1789, in two closely reasoned dissertations prefixed to his translation of the *Poetics*, Thomas Twining confirmed this distinction between arts whose media are 'iconic' (in the later terminology of the Chicago semiotician, Charles Morris), in that they resemble what they denote, and those which are significant only by convention. Only works in which the resemblance between copy and object is both 'immediate' and 'obvious,' Twining says, can be described as imitative in a strict sense. Dramatic poetry, therefore, in which we mimic speech by speech, is the only kind of poetry which is properly imitation; music must be struck from the list of imitative arts; and he concludes by saying that painting, sculpture, and the arts of design in general are 'the only arts that are *obviously* and *essentially* imitative.'[26]

The concept that art is imitation, then, played an important part in neoclassic aesthetics; but closer inspection shows that it did not, in most theories, play the dominant part. Art, it was commonly said, is an imitation—but an imitation which is only instrumental toward producing effects upon an audience. In fact, the near-unanimity with which post-Renaissance critics lauded and echoed Aristotle's *Poetics* is deceptive. The focus of interest had shifted, and, on our diagram, this later criticism is primarily oriented, not from work to universe, but from work to audience. The nature and consequences of this change of direction is clearly indicated by the first classic of English criticism, written sometime in the early 1580's, Sir Philip Sidney's *The Apologie for Poetry*.

Pragmatic Theories

> Poesy therefore [said Sidney] is an arte of imitation, for so Aristotle
> termeth it in the word *Mimesis,* that is to say, a representing,
> counterfetting, or figuring foorth—to speake metaphorically, a
> speaking picture: with this end, to teach and delight.[27]

In spite of the appeal to Aristotle, this is not an Aristotelian formulation. To Sidney, poetry, by definition, has a purpose—to achieve certain
effects in an audience. It imitates only as a means to the proximate end of
pleasing, and pleases, it turns out, only as a means to the ultimate end of
teaching; for 'right poets' are those who 'imitate both to delight and teach,
and delight to move men to take that goodnes in hande, which without
delight they would flye as from a stranger ... '[28] As a result, throughout
this essay the needs of the audience become the fertile grounds for critical
distinctions and standards. In order 'to teach and delight,' poets imitate
not 'what is, hath been, or shall be,' but only 'what may be, and should be,'
so that the very objects of imitation become such as to guarantee the
moral purpose. The poet is distinguished from, and elevated above, the
moral philosopher and the historian by his capacity to move his auditors
more forcefully to virtue, since he couples 'the general notion' of the philosopher with 'the particular example' of the historian; while by disguis-
ing his doctrine in a tale, he entices even 'harde harted evill men,' unaware, into the love of goodness, 'as if they tooke a medicine of Cherries.'
The genres of poetry are discussed and ranked from the point of view of
the moral and social effect each is suited to achieve: the epic poem thus
demonstrates itself to be the king of poetry because it 'most inflameth
the mind with desire to be worthy,' and even the lowly love lyric is conceived as an instrument for persuading a mistress of the genuineness of
her lover's passion.[29] A history of criticism could be written solely on the
basis of successive interpretations of salient passages from Aristotle's *Poetics.* In this instance, with no sense of strain, Sidney follows his Italian
guides (who in turn had read Aristotle through the spectacles of Horace,
Cicero, and the Church fathers) in bending one after another of the key
statements of the *Poetics* to fit his own theoretical frame.[30]

For convenience we may name criticism that, like Sidney's, is ordered toward the audience, a 'pragmatic theory,' since it looks at the work
of art chiefly as a means to an end, an instrument for getting something
done, and tends to judge its value according to its success in achieving that
aim. There is, of course, the greatest variance in emphasis and detail, but
the central tendency of the pragmatic critic is to conceive a poem as something made in order to effect requisite responses in its readers; to consider
the author from the point of view of the powers and training he must have
in order to achieve this end; to ground the classification and anatomy of

poems in large part on the special effects each kind and component is most competent to achieve; and to derive the norms of the poetic art and canons of critical appraisal from the needs and legitimate demands of the audience to whom the poetry is addressed.

The perspective, much of the basic vocabulary, and many of the characteristic topics of pragmatic criticism originated in the classical theory of rhetoric. For rhetoric had been universally regarded as an instrument for achieving persuasion in an audience, and most theorists agreed with Cicero that in order to persuade, the orator must conciliate, inform, and move the minds of his auditors.[31] The great classical exemplar of the application of the rhetorical point of view to poetry was, of course, the *Ars Poetica* of Horace. As Richard McKeon points out, 'Horace's criticism is directed in the main to instruct the poet how to keep his audience in their seats until the end, how to induce cheers and applause, how to please a Roman audience, and by the same token, how to please all audiences and win immortality.'[32]

In what became for later critics the focal passage of the *Ars Poetica*, Horace advised that 'the poet's aim is either to profit or to please, or to blend in one the delightful and the useful.' The context shows that Horace held pleasure to be the chief purpose of poetry, for he recommends the profitable merely as a means to give pleasure to the elders, who, in contrast to the young aristocrats, 'rail at what contains no serviceable lesson.'[33] But *prodesse* and *delectare*, to teach and to please, together with another term introduced from rhetoric, *movere*, to move, served for centuries to collect under three heads the sum of aesthetic effects on the reader. The balance between these terms altered in the course of time. To the overwhelming majority of Renaissance critics, as to Sir Philip Sidney, the moral effect was the terminal aim, to which delight and emotion were auxiliary. From the time of the critical essays of Dryden through the eighteenth century, pleasure tended to become the ultimate end, although poetry without profit was often held to be trivial, and the optimistic moralist believed with James Beattie that if poetry instructs, it only pleases the more effectually.[34]

Looking upon a poem as a 'making,' a contrivance for affecting an audience, the typical pragmatic critic is engrossed with formulating the methods—the 'skill, or Crafte of making' as Ben Jonson called it—for achieving the effects desired. These methods, traditionally comprehended under the term *poesis*, or 'art' (in phrases such as 'the art of poetry'), are formulated as precepts and rules whose warrant consists either in their being derived from the qualities of works whose success and long survival have proved their adaptation to human nature, or else in their being grounded directly on the psychological laws governing the responses of men in general. The rules, therefore, are inherent in the qualities of each excellent work of art, and when excerpted and codified these rules serve equally to guide the artist in making and the critics in judging any future product. 'Dryden,' said Dr. Johnson, 'may be properly considered as the father of English criticism, as the writer who first taught us to determine upon principles the merit of composition.'[35] Dryden's method of establishing those principles was to point out that poetry, like painting, has an end, which is to please; that imitation of nature is the general means for attaining this end; and that rules serve to specify the means for accomplishing this end in detail:

> Having thus shewn that imitation pleases, and why it pleases in both these arts, it follows, that some rules of imitation are necessary to obtain the end; for without rules there can be no art, any more than there can be a house without a door to conduct you into it.[36]

Emphasis on the rules and maxims of an art is native to all criticism that grounds itself in the demands of an audience, and it survives today in the magazines and manuals devoted to teaching fledgling authors 'how to write stories that sell.' But rulebooks based on the lowest common denominator of the modern buying public are only gross caricatures of the complex and subtly rationalized neo-classic ideals of literary craftsmanship. Through the early part of the eighteenth century, the poet could rely confidently on the trained taste and expert connoisseurship of a limited circle of readers, whether these were Horace's Roman contemporaries under Emperor Augustus, or Vida's at the papal court of Leo X, or Sidney's fellow-courtiers under Elizabeth, or the London audience of Dryden and Pope; while, in theory, the voices even of the best contemporary judges were subordinated to the voice of the ages. Some neo-classic critics were also certain that the rules of art, though empirically derived, were ultimately validated by conforming to that objective structure of norms whose existence guaranteed the rational order and harmony of the universe. In a strict sense, as John Dennis made explicit what was often implied, Nature 'is nothing but that Rule and Order, and Harmony, which we find in the visible Creation'; so 'Poetry, which is an imitation of Nature,' must demonstrate the same properties. The renowned masters among the ancients wrote not

> to please a tumultuous transitory Assembly, or a Handful of Men, who were call'd their Countrymen; They wrote to their Fellow-Citizens of the Universe, to all Countries, and to all Ages ... They were clearly convinc'd, that nothing could transmit their Immortal Works to Posterity, but something like that harmonious Order which maintains the Universe ...[37]

Although they disagreed concerning specific rules, and although many English critics repudiated such formal French requisites as the unity of time and place, and the purity of comedy and tragedy, all but a few eccentrics among eighteenth-century critics believed in the validity of some set of universal rules. At about mid-century, it became popular to demonstrate and expound all the major rules for poetry, or even for art in general, in a single inclusive critical system. The pattern of the pragmatic reasoning usually employed may conveniently be studied in such a compendious treatment as James Beattie's *Essay on Poetry and Music as they affect the Mind* (1762), or more succinctly still, in Richard Hurd's 'Dissertation of the Idea of Universal Poetry' (1766). Universal poetry, no matter what the genre, Hurd says, is an art whose end is the maximum possible pleasure. 'When we speak of poetry, as an *art*, we mean *such a way or method of treating a subject, as is found most pleasing and delightful to us.'* And this idea 'if kept steadily in view, will unfold to us all the mysteries of the poetic art. There needs but to evolve the philosopher's idea, and to apply it, as occasion serves.' From this major premise Hurd evolves three properties, essential to all poetry if it is to effect the greatest possible delight: figurative language, 'fiction' (that is to say, a departure from what is actual, or empirically possible), and versification. The mode and degree in which these three universal qualities are to be combined in any one species of poetry, however, will depend on its peculiar end, because each poetic kind must exploit that special pleasure which it is generically adapted to achieve. 'For the art of every *kind* of poetry is only this general art so modified as the *nature* of each, that is, its more immediate and subordinate end, may respectively require.'

> For the name of poem will belong to every composition, whose primary end is to *please*, provided it be so constructed as to afford *all* the pleasure, which its kind or *sort* will permit.[38]

On the basis of isolated passages from his *Letters on Chivalry and Romance,* Hurd is commonly treated as a 'pre-romantic' critic. But in the summation of his poetic creed in the 'Idea of Universal Poetry,' the rigidly deductive logic which Hurd employs to 'unfold' the rules of poetry from a primitive definition, permitting 'the reason of the thing' to override the evidence of the actual practice of poets, brings him as close as anyone in England to the geometric method of Charles Batteux, though without that critic's Cartesian apparatus. The difference is that Batteux evolves his rules from the definition of poetry as the imitation of *la belle nature,* and Hurd, from its definition as the art of treating a subject so as to afford the reader a maximum pleasure; and this involves his assuming that he possesses an empirical knowledge of the psychology of the reader. For if the end of poetry is to gratify the mind of the reader, Hurd says, knowledge of the laws of mind is necessary to establish its rules, which are 'but so many MEANS, which experience finds most conducive to that end.'[39] Since Batteux and Hurd, however, are both intent on rationalizing what is mainly a common body of poetic lore, it need not surprise us that, though they set out from different points of the compass, their paths often coincide.[40]

But to appreciate the power and illumination of which a refined and flexible pragmatic criticism is capable, we must turn from these abstract systematizers of current methods and maxims to such a practical critic as Samuel Johnson. Johnson's literary criticism assumes approximately the frame of critical reference I have described, but Johnson, who distrusts rigid and abstract theorizing, applies the method with a constant appeal to specific literary examples, deference to the opinions of other readers, but ultimately, reliance on his own expert responses to the text. As a result Johnson's comments on poets and poems have persistently afforded a jumping-off point for later critics whose frame of reference and particular judgments differ radically from his own. For an instance of Johnson's procedure which is especially interesting because it shows how the notion of the imitation of nature is co-ordinated with the judgment of poetry in terms of its end and effects, consider that monument of neo-classic criticism, Johnson's *Preface to Shakespeare*.

Johnson undertakes in his *Preface* to establish Shakespeare's rank among poets, and to do so, he is led to rate Shakespeare's native abilities against the general level of taste and achievement in the Elizabethan age, and to measure these abilities in turn 'by their proportion to the general and collective ability of man.'[41] Since the powers and excellence of an author, however, can only be inferred from the nature and excellence of the works he achieves, Johnson addresses himself to a general examination of Shakespeare's dramas. In this systematic appraisal of the works themselves, we find that mimesis retains for Johnson a measure of authority as criterion. Repeatedly Johnson maintains that 'this therefore is the praise of *Shakespeare*, that his drama is the mirrour of life,' and of inanimate nature as well: 'He was an exact surveyor of the inanimate world ... *Shakespeare*, whether life or nature be his subject, shews plainly, that he has seen with his own eyes ... '[42] But, Johnson also claims, 'The end of writing is to instruct; the end of poetry is to instruct by pleasing.'[43] It is to this function of poetry, and to the demonstrated effect of a poem upon its audience, that Johnson awards priority as aesthetic criterion. If a poem fails to please, whatever its character otherwise, it is, as a work of art, nothing; though Johnson insists, with a strenuous moralism that must already have seemed old-fashioned to contemporary readers, it must please without violating the standards of truth and virtue. Accordingly,

Johnson discriminates those elements in Shakespeare's plays which were introduced to appeal to the local and passing tastes of the rather barbarous audience of his own time ('He knew,' said Johnson, 'how he should most please'),[44] from those elements which are proportioned to the tastes of the common readers of all time. And since in works 'appealing wholly to observation and experience, no other test can be applied than length of duration and continuance of esteem,' Shakespeare's long survival as a poet 'read without any other reason than the desire for pleasure' is the best evidence for his artistic excellence. The reason for this survival Johnson explains on the subsidiary principle that 'nothing can please many, and please long, but just representations of general nature.' Shakespeare exhibits the eternal 'species' of human character, moved by 'those general passions and principles by which all minds are agitated.'[45] Thus Shakespeare's excellence in holding up the mirror to general nature turns out, in the long run, to be justified by the superior criterion of the appeal this achievement holds for the enduring tastes of the general literary public.

A number of Johnson's individual observations and judgments exhibit a play of the argument between the two principles of the nature of the world the poet must reflect, and the nature and legitimate requirements of the poet's audience. For the most part the two principles co-operate toward a single conclusion. For example, both the empirical nature of the universe and of the universal reader demonstrate the fallacy of those who censure Shakespeare for mixing his comic and tragic scenes. Shakespeare's plays, Johnson says, exhibit 'the real state of sublunary nature, which partakes of good and evil, joy and sorrow, mingled with endless variety.' In addition, 'the mingled drama may convey all the instruction of tragedy or comedy' by approaching nearer 'to the appearance of life'; while the objection that the change of scene 'wants at last the power to move' is a specious reasoning 'received as true even by those who in daily experience feel it to be false.'[46] But when the actual state of sublunary affairs conflicts with the poet's obligation to his audience, the latter is the court of final appeal. It is Shakespeare's defect, says Johnson,

> that he seems to write without any moral purpose ... He makes no just distribution of good or evil, nor is always careful to shew in the virtuous a disapprobation of the wicked ... It is always a writer's duty to make the world better, and justice is a virtue independant on time or place.[47]

The pragmatic orientation, ordering the aim of the artist and the character of the work to the nature, the needs, and the springs of pleasure in the audience, characterized by far the greatest part of criticism from the time of Horace through the eighteenth century. Measured either by its duration or the number of its adherents, therefore, the pragmatic view,

broadly conceived, has been the principal aesthetic attitude of the Western world. But inherent in this system were the elements of its dissolu-
tion. Ancient rhetoric had bequeathed to criticism not only its stress on
affecting the audience but also (since its main concern was with educat-
ing the orator) its detailed attention to the powers and activities of the
speaker himself—his 'nature,' or innate powers and genius, as distinguished from his culture and art, and also the process of invention, disposition, and expression involved in his discourse.[48] In the course of time,
and particularly after the psychological contributions of Hobbes and
Locke in the seventeenth century, increasing attention was given to the
mental constitution of the poet, the quality and degree of his 'genius,' and
the play of his faculties in the act of composition. Through most of the
eighteenth century, the poet's invention and imagination were made thoroughly dependent for their materials—their ideas and 'images'—on the
external universe and the literary models the poet had to imitate; while
the persistent stress laid on his need for judgment and art—the mental
surrogates, in effect, of the requirements of a cultivated audience—held
the poet strictly responsible to the audience for whose pleasure he exerted
his creative ability. Gradually, however, the stress was shifted more and
more to the poet's natural genius, creative imagination, and emotional
spontaneity, at the expense of the opposing attributes of judgment, learning, and artful restraints. As a result the audience gradually receded into
the background, giving place to the poet himself, and his own mental
powers and emotional needs, as the predominant cause and even the end
and test of art. By this time other developments, which we shall have occasion to talk about later, were also helping to shift the focus of critical
interest from audience to artist and thus to introduce a new orientation
into the theory of art.

Expressive Theories

'Poetry,' Wordsworth announced in his Preface to the *Lyrical Ballads* of
1800, 'is the spontaneous overflow of powerful feelings.' He thought well
enough of this formulation to use it twice in the same essay, and on this,
as the ground-idea, he founded his theory of the proper subjects, language,
effects, and value of poetry. Almost all the major critics of the English romantic generation phrased definitions or key statements showing a parallel alignment from work to poet. Poetry is the overflow, utterance, or
projection of the thought and feelings of the poet; or else (in the chief variant formulation) poetry is defined in terms of the imaginative process
which modifies and synthesizes the images, thoughts, and feelings of the
poet. This way of thinking, in which the artist himself becomes the ma-

jor element generating both the artistic product and the criteria by which it is to be judged, I shall call the expressive theory of art.

Setting the date at which this point of view became predominant in critical theory, like marking the point at which orange becomes yellow in the color spectrum, must be a somewhat arbitrary procedure. As we shall see, an approach to the expressive orientation, though isolated in history and partial in scope, is to be found as early as Longinus' discussion of the sublime style as having its main sources in the thought and emotions of the speaker; and it recurs in a variant form in Bacon's brief analysis of poetry as pertaining to the imagination and 'accommodating the shows of things to the desires of the mind.' Even Wordsworth's theory, it will appear, is much more embedded in a traditional matrix of interests and emphases, and is, therefore, less radical than are the theories of his followers of the 1830's. The year 1800 is a good round number, however, and Wordsworth's Preface a convenient document, by which to signalize the displacement of the mimetic and pragmatic by the expressive view of art in English criticism.

In general terms, the central tendency of the expressive theory may be summarized in this way: A work of art is essentially the internal made external, resulting from a creative process operating under the impulse of feeling, and embodying the combined product of the poet's perceptions, thoughts, and feelings. The primary source and subject matter of a poem, therefore, are the attributes and actions of the poet's own mind; or if aspects of the external world, then these only as they are converted from fact to poetry by the feelings and operations of the poet's mind. ('Thus the Poetry ... ' Wordsworth wrote, 'proceeds whence it ought to do, from the soul of Man, communicating its creative energies to the images of the external world.')[49] The paramount cause of poetry is not, as in Aristotle, a formal cause, determined primarily by the human actions and qualities imitated; nor, as in neo-classic criticism, a final cause, the effect intended upon the audience; but instead an efficient cause—the impulse within the poet of feelings and desires seeking expression, or the compulsion of the 'creative' imagination which, like God the creator, has its internal source of motion. The propensity is to grade the arts by the extent to which their media are amenable to the undistorted expression of the feelings or mental powers of the artist, and to classify the species of an art, and evaluate their instances, by the qualities or states of mind of which they are a sign. Of the elements constituting a poem, the element of diction, especially figures of speech, becomes primary; and the burning question is, whether these are the natural utterance of emotion and imagination or the deliberate aping of poetic conventions. The first test any poem must pass is no longer, 'Is it true to nature?' or 'Is it appropriate to the requirements either of the best judges or the generality of mankind?'

but a criterion looking in a different direction; namely, 'Is it sincere? Is it genuine? Does it match the intention, the feeling, and the actual state of mind of the poet while composing?' The work ceases then to be regarded as primarily a reflection of nature, actual or improved; the mirror held up to nature becomes transparent and yields the reader insights into the mind and heart of the poet himself. The exploitation of literature as an index to personality first manifests itself in the early nineteenth century; it is the inevitable consequence of the expressive point of view.

The sources, details, and historical results of this reorientation of criticism, in its various forms, will be a principal concern of the rest of this book. Now, while we have some of the earlier facts fresh in mind, let me indicate what happened to salient elements of traditional criticism in the essays 'What Is Poetry?' and 'The Two Kinds of Poetry,' written by John Stuart Mill in 1833. Mill relied in large part on Wordsworth's Preface to the *Lyrical Ballads,* but in the intervening thirty years the expressive theory had emerged from the network of qualifications in which Wordsworth had carefully placed it, and had worked out its own destiny unhindered. Mill's logic in answering the question, 'What Is Poetry?' is not *more geometrico,* like that of Batteux, nor stiffly formal, like Richard Hurd's; nonetheless, his theory turns out to be just as tightly dependent upon a central principle as theirs. For whatever Mill's empirical pretensions, his initial assumption about the essential nature of poetry remains continuously though silently effective in selecting, interpreting, and ordering the facts to be explained.

The primitive proposition of Mill's theory is: Poetry is 'the expression or uttering forth of feeling.'[50] Exploration of the data of aesthetics from this starting point leads, among other things, to the following drastic alterations in the great commonplaces of the critical tradition:

(1) *The poetic kinds.* Mill reinterprets and inverts the neo-classic ranking of the poetic kinds. As the purest expression of feeling, lyric poetry is 'more eminently and peculiarly poetry than any other ... ' Other forms are all alloyed by non-poetic elements, whether descriptive, didactic, or narrative, which serve merely as convenient occasions for the poetic utterances of feeling either by the poet or by one of his invented characters. To Aristotle, tragedy had been the highest form of poetry, and the plot, representing the action being imitated, had been its 'soul'; while most neo-classic critics had agreed that, whether judged by greatness of subject matter or of effect, epic and tragedy are the king and queen of poetic forms. It serves as an index to the revolution in critical norms to notice that to Mill, plot becomes a kind of necessary evil. An epic poem 'in so far as it is epic (i.e. narrative) ... is not poetry at all,' but only a suitable frame for the greatest diversity of genuinely poetic passages; while the interest in plot and story 'merely as a story' characterizes rude stages of so-

ciety, children, and the 'shallowest and emptiest' of civilized adults.[51] Similarly with the other arts; in music, painting, sculpture, and architecture Mill distinguishes between that which is 'simple imitation or description' and that which 'expresses human feeling' and is, therefore, poetry.[52]

(2) *Spontaneity as criterion.* Mill accepts the venerable assumption that a man's emotional susceptibility is innate, but his knowledge and skill—his art—are acquired. On this basis, he distinguishes poets into two classes: poets who are born and poets who are made, or those who are poets 'by nature,' and those who are poets 'by culture.' Natural poetry is identifiable because it 'is Feeling itself, employing Thought only as the medium of its utterance'; on the other hand, the poetry of 'a cultivated but not naturally poetic mind,' is written with 'a distinct aim,' and in it the thought remains the conspicuous object, however surrounded by 'a halo of feeling.' Natural poetry, it turns out, is 'poetry in a far higher sense, than any other; since ... that which constitutes poetry, human feeling, enters far more largely into this than into the poetry of culture.' Among the moderns, Shelley represents the poet born and Wordsworth the poet made; and with unconscious irony Mill turns Wordsworth's own criterion, 'the spontaneous overflow of feeling,' against its sponsor. Wordsworth's poetry 'has little even of the appearance of spontaneousness: the well is never so full that it overflows.'[53]

(3) *The external world.* In so far as a literary product simply imitates objects, it is not poetry at all. As a result, reference of poetry to the external universe disappears from Mill's theory, except to the extent that sensible objects may serve as a stimulus or 'occasion for the generation of poetry,' and then, 'the poetry is not in the object itself,' but 'in the state of mind' in which it is contemplated. When a poet describes a lion he 'is describing the lion professedly, but the state of excitement of the spectator really,' and the poetry must be true not to the object, but to 'the human emotion.'[54] Thus severed from the external world, the objects signified by a poem tend to be regarded as no more than a projected equivalent—an extended and articulated symbol—for the poet's inner state of mind. Poetry, said Mill, in a phrasing which anticipates T. E. Hulme and lays the theoretical groundwork for the practice of symbolists from Baudelaire through T. S. Eliot, embodies 'itself in symbols, which are the nearest possible representations of the feeling in the exact shape in which it exists in the poet's mind.'[55] Tennyson, Mill wrote in a review of that poet's early poems, excels in 'scene-painting, in the higher sense of the term'; and this is

> not the mere power of producing that rather vapid species of composition usually termed descriptive poetry ... but the power of *creating* scenery, in keeping with some state of human feeling; so

fitted to it as to be the embodied symbol of it, and to summon up the state of feeling itself, with a force not to be surpassed by anything but reality.[56]

And as an indication of the degree to which the innovations of the romantics persist as the commonplaces of modern critics—even of those who purport to found their theory on anti-romantic principles—notice how striking is the parallel between the passage above and a famous comment by T. S. Eliot:

> The only way of expressing emotion in the form of art is by finding an 'objective correlative'; in other words, a set of objects, a situation, a chain of events which shall be the formula of that *particular* emotion; such that when the external facts, which must terminate in sensory experience, are given, the emotion is immediately evoked.[57]

(4) *The audience.* No less drastic is the fate of the audience. According to Mill, 'Poetry is feeling, confessing itself to itself in moments of solitude ... ' The poet's audience is reduced to a single member, consisting of the poet himself. 'All poetry,' as Mill puts it, 'is of the nature of soliloquy.' The purpose of producing effects upon other men, which for centuries had been the defining character of the art of poetry, now serves precisely the opposite function: it disqualifies a poem by proving it to be rhetoric instead. When the poet's

> act of utterance is not itself the end, but a means to an end—viz. by the feelings he himself expresses, to work upon the feelings, or upon the belief, or the will, of another,—when the expression of his emotions ... is tinged also by that purpose, by that desire of making an impression upon another mind, then it ceases to be poetry, and becomes eloquence.[58]
>
> There is, in fact, something singularly fatal to the audience in the romantic point of view. Or, in terms of historical causes, it might be conjectured that the disappearance of a homogeneous and discriminating reading public fostered a criticism which on principle diminished the importance of the audience as a determinant of poetry and poetic value. Wordsworth still insisted that 'Poets do not write for Poets alone, but for Men,' and that each of his poems 'has a worthy purpose'; even though it turns out that the pleasure and profit of the audience is an automatic consequence of the poet's *spontaneous* overflow of feeling, provided that the appropriate associations between thoughts and feelings have been established by the poet in advance.[59] Keats, however, affirmed roundly that 'I never wrote one single line of Poetry with the least Shadow of public thought.'[60] 'A poet is a nightingale,' according to Shelley, 'who sits in darkness and sings to cheer its own solitude

with sweet sounds; his auditors are as men entranced by the melody of an unseen musician ... '[61] For Carlyle, the poet utterly replaces the audience as the generator of aesthetic norms.

> On the whole, Genius has privileges of its own; it selects an orbit for itself; and be this never so eccentric, if it is indeed a celestial orbit, we mere star-gazers must at last compose ourselves; must cease to cavil at it, and begin to observe it, and calculate its laws.[62]

The evolution is complete, from the mimetic poet, assigned the minimal role of holding a mirror up to nature, through the pragmatic poet who, whatever his natural gifts, is ultimately measured by his capacity to satisfy the public taste, to Carlyle's Poet as Hero, the chosen one who, because he is 'a Force of Nature,' writes as he must, and through the degree of homage he evokes, serves as the measure of his *reader's* piety and taste.[63]

Objective Theories

All types of theory described so far, in their practical applications, get down to dealing with the work of art itself, in its parts and their mutual relations, whether the premises on which these elements are discriminated and evaluated relate them primarily to the spectator, the artist, or the world without. But there is also a fourth procedure, the 'objective orientation,' which on principle regards the work of art in isolation from all these external points of reference, analyzes it as a self-sufficient entity constituted by its parts in their internal relations, and sets out to judge it solely by criteria intrinsic to its own mode of being.

This point of view has been comparatively rare in literary criticism. The one early attempt at the analysis of an art form which is both objective and comprehensive occurs in the central portion of Aristotle's *Poetics.* I have chosen to discuss Aristotle's theory of art under the heading of mimetic theories, because it sets out from, and makes frequent reference back to the concept of imitation. Such is the flexibility of Aristotle's procedure, however, that after he has isolated the species 'tragedy,' and established its relation to the universe as an imitation of a certain kind of action, and to the audience through its observed effect of purging pity and fear, his method becomes centripetal, and assimilates these external elements into attributes of the work proper. In this second consideration of tragedy as an object in itself, the actions and agents that are imitated reenter the discussion as the plot, character, and thought which, together with diction, melody, and spectacle, make up the six elements of a tragedy; and even pity and fear are reconsidered as that pleasurable quality proper to tragedy, to be distinguished from the pleasures characteristic of comedy and other forms.[64] The tragic work itself can now be analyzed formally as a self-determining whole made up of parts, all organized around the controlling part, the tragic plot—itself a unity in which the component incidents are integrated by the internal relations of 'necessity or probability.'

As an all-inclusive approach to poetry, the objective orientation was just beginning to emerge in the late eighteenth and early nineteenth century. We shall see later on that some critics were undertaking to explore the concept of the poem as a heterocosm, a world of its own, independent of the world into which we are born, whose end is not to instruct or please but simply to exist. Certain critics, particularly in Germany, were expanding upon Kant's formula that a work of art exhibits *Zweckmässigkeit ohne Zweck* (purposiveness without purpose), together with his concept that the contemplation of beauty is disinterested and without regard to utility, while neglecting Kant's characteristic reference of an aesthetic product to the mental faculties of its creator and receptor. The aim to consider a poem, as Poe expressed it, as a 'poem *per se* ... written solely for the poem's sake,'[65] in isolation from external causes and ulterior ends, came to constitute one element of the diverse doctrines usually huddled together by historians under the heading 'Art for Art's Sake.' And with differing emphases and adequacy, and in a great variety of theoretical contexts, the objective approach to poetry has become one of the most prominent elements in the innovative criticism of the last two or three decades. T. S. Eliot's dictum of 1928, that 'when we are considering poetry we must consider it primarily as poetry and not another thing' is widely approved, however far Eliot's own criticism sometimes departs from this ideal; and it is often joined with MacLeish's verse aphorism, 'A poem should not mean But be.' The subtle and incisive criticism of criticism by the Chicago Neo-Aristotelians and their advocacy of an instrument adapted to dealing with poetry as such have been largely effective toward a similar end. In his 'ontological criticism,' John Crowe Ransom has been calling for recognition of 'the autonomy of the work itself as existing for its own sake';[66] campaigns have been organized against 'the personal heresy,' 'the intentional fallacy,' and 'the affective fallacy'; the widely influential handbook, *The Theory of Literature*, written by René Wellek and Austin Warren, proposes that criticism deal with a poem *qua* poem, independently of 'extrinsic' factors; and similar views are being expressed, with increasing frequency, not only in our literary but in our scholarly journals. In America, at least, some form of the objective point of view has already gone far to displace its rivals as the reigning mode of literary criticism.

According to our scheme of analysis, then, there have been four major orientations, each one of which has seemed to various acute minds adequate for a satisfactory criticism of art in general. And by and large the historic progression, from the beginning through the early nineteenth century, has been from the mimetic theory of Plato and (in a qualified fashion) Aristotle, through the pragmatic theory, lasting from the conflation of rhetoric with poetic in the Hellenistic and Roman era almost through the eighteenth century, to the expressive theory of English (and somewhat earlier, German) romantic criticism.

Of course romantic criticism, like that of any period, was not uniform in its outlook. As late as 1831 Macaulay (whose thinking usually followed traditional patterns) still insists, as an eternal rule 'founded in reason and in the nature of things,' that 'poetry is, as was said more than two thousand years ago, imitation,' and differentiates between the arts on the basis of their diverse media and objects of imitation. Then, in an essay packed with eighteenth-century catch-lines, he ungratefully employs the mimetic principle to justify his elevation of Scott, Wordsworth, and Coleridge over the eighteenth-century poets because they imitate nature more accurately, and attacks the neo-classic rules of correctness on the ground that they 'tend to make ... imitations less perfect than they otherwise would be ... '[67] The mode of criticism which subjects art and the artist to the audience also continued to flourish, usually in a vulgarized form, among influential journalists such as Francis Jeffrey, who deliberately set themselves to voice the literary standards of the middle class and to preserve unsullied what Jeffrey called 'the purity of the female character.'[68]

But these are not the innovative critical writings which contributed to the predominant temper of what Shelley, in his 'Defence of Poetry,' called 'the spirit of the age'; and the radical difference between the characteristic points of view of neo-classic and romantic criticism remains unmistakable. Take such representative productions of the 1760's and '70's as Johnson's *Preface to Shakespeare,* Kames's *Elements of Criticism,* Richard Hurd's 'On the Idea of Universal Poetry,' *The Art of Poetry on a New Plan* (of dubious authorship), Beattie's *Essays on Poetry and Music,* and the first eight *Discourses* of Sir Joshua Reynolds. Place these next to the major inquiries into poetry and art of the romantic generation: Wordsworth's Prefaces and collateral essays, Coleridge's *Biographia Literaria* and Shakespearean lectures, Hazlitt's 'On Poetry in General' and other essays, even Shelley's Platonistic 'Defence of Poetry'; then add to this group such later documents as Carlyle's 'Characteristics' and early literary reviews, J. S. Mill's two essays on poetry, John Keble's *Lectures on Poetry,* and Leigh Hunt's 'What Is Poetry?'. Whatever the continuity of certain terms and topics between individual members of the two eras, and however important the methodological and doctrinal differences which divide the members within a single group, one decisive change marks off the criticism in the Age of Wordsworth from that in the Age of Johnson. The poet has moved into the center of the critical system and taken over many of the prerogatives which had once been exercised by his readers, the nature of the world in which he found himself, and the inherited precepts and examples of his poetic art.

NOTES

1. Foreword to *Philosophies of Beauty*, ed. E. F. Carritt (Oxford, 1931), p. ix.
2. (5th ed.; London, 1934), pp. 6–7. Richards' later change of emphasis is indicated by his recent statement that ' "Semantics" which began by finding nonsense everywhere may well end up as a technique for widening understanding' (*Modern Language Notes*, LX, 1945, p. 350).
3. For a subtle and elaborate analysis of diverse critical theories, see Richard McKeon, 'Philosophic Bases of Art and Criticism,' *Critics and Criticism, Ancient and Modern*, ed. R. S. Crane (The University of Chicago Press, Chicago, 1952).
4. *Republic* (trans. Jowett) x. 596–7; *Laws* ii. 667–8, vii. 814–16.
5. See Richard McKeon, 'Literary Criticism and the Concept of Imitation in Antiquity,' *Critics and Criticism*, ed. Crane, pp. 147–9. The article exhibits those multiple shifts in Plato's use of the term 'imitation' which have trapped many later commentators as successfully as they once did the rash spirits who engaged Socrates in controversy.
6. *Republic* x. 597.
7. *Laws* vii. 817.
8. *Republic* x. 603–5; *Ion* 535–6; cf. *Apology* 22.
9. *Republic* x. 608.
10. *Poetics* (trans. Ingram Bywater) 1. 1447ª, 1448ª. On imitation in Aristotle's criticism see McKeon, 'The Concept of Imitation,' op. cit. pp. 160–68.
11. *Poetics* 6. 1449ᵇ, 14. 1453ᵇ.
12. Ibid. 8. 1451ª.
13. Ibid. 6. 1450ª–1450ᵇ.
14. Ibid. 4. 1448ᵇ, 17. 1455ª–1455ᵇ.
15. *Republic* iii. 398, x. 606–8; *Laws* vii. 817.
16. *The Works of Richard Hurd* (London, 1811), 11, 111–12.
17. Edward Young, *Conjectures on Original Composition*, ed. Edith Morley (Manchester, 1918), pp. 6, 18. See also William Duff, *Essay on Original Genius* (London, 1767), p. 192n. John Ogilvie reconciles creative genius and original invention with 'the great principle of *poetic imitation*' (*Philosophical and Critical Observations on the Nature, Characters, and Various Species of Composition*, London, 1774, 1, 105–7). Joseph Warton, familiar proponent of a 'boundless imagination,' enthusiasm, and 'the romantic, the

wonderful, and the wild,' still agrees with Richard Hurd that poetry is 'an art, whose essence is imitation,' and whose objects are 'material or animate, extraneous or internal' (*Essay on the Writings and Genius of Pope*, London, 1756, 1, 89–90). Cf. Robert Wood, *Essay on the Original Genius and Writings of Homer* (1769), London, 1824, pp. 6–7, 178.

18. 'Originality,' *Gleanings* (London, 1785), 1, 107, 109.

19. Charles Batteux, *Les Beaux Arts réduits à un même principe* (Paris, 1747), pp. i-viii.

20. Ibid. pp. 9–27.

21. Ibid. p. xiii. For the important place of imitation in earlier French neo-classic theories, see René Bray, *La Formation de la doctrine classique en France* (Lausanne, 1931), pp. 140ff.

22. Lessing, *Laokoon*, ed. W. G. Howard (New York, 1910), pp. 23–5, 42.

23. Ibid. pp. 99–102, 64.

24. *Three Treatises*, in *The Works of James Harris* (London, 1803), 1, 58. Cf. Adam Smith, 'Of the Nature of that Imitation which Takes Place in What Are Called the Imitative Arts,' *Essays Philosophical and Literary* (London, n.d.), pp. 405ff.

25. Henry Home, Lord Kames, *Elements of Criticism* (Boston, 1796), 11, 1 (chap. xviii).

26. Thomas Twining, ed., *Aristotle's Treatise on Poetry* (London, 1789), pp. 4, 21-2, 60–61.

27. Sir Philip Sidney, 'An Apology for Poetry,' *Elizabethan Critical Essays*, ed. G. Gregory Smith (London, 1904), 1, 158.

28. Ibid. 1, 159.

29. Ibid. 1, 159, 161–4, 171–80, 201.

30. See, e.g., his use of Aristotle's statement that poetry is more philosophical than history (1, 167–8), and that painful things can be made pleasant by imitations (p. 171); and his wrenching of Aristotle's central term, *praxis*—the actions which are imitated by poetry—to signify the moral action which a poem moves the spectator to practise (p. 171).

31. Cicero, *De oratore* 11. xxviii.

32. 'The Concept of Imitation,' op. cit. p. 173.

33. Horace, *Ars Poetica*, trans. E. H. Blakeney, in *Literary Criticism, Plato to Dryden*, ed. Allan H. Gilbert (New York, 1940), p. 139.

34. *Essays on Poetry and Music* (3d ed.; London, 1779), p. 10.

35. 'Dryden,' *Lives of the English Poets*, ed. Birkbeck Hill (Oxford, 1905), 1, 410.

36. 'Parallel of Poetry and Painting' (1695), *Essays*, ed. W. P. Ker (Oxford, 1926), 11, 138. See Hoyt Trowbridge, 'The Place of Rules in Dryden's Criticism,' *Modern Philology*, XLIV (1946), 84ff.

37. *The Advancement and Reformation of Modern Poetry* (1701), in *The Critical Works of John Dennis*, ed. E. N. Hooker (Baltimore, 1939), 1, 202–3. For Dennis' derivation of specific rules from the end of art, which is 'to delight and reform the mind,' see *The Grounds of Criticism in Poetry* (1704), ibid. pp. 336ff.

38. 'Dissertation on the Idea of Universal Poetry,' *Works*, 11, 3–4, 25–6, 7. For a parallel argument see Alexander Gerard, *An Essay on Taste* (London, 1759), p. 40.

39. 'Idea of Universal Poetry,' *Works*, 11, 3–4. On the rationale underlying the
     body of Hurd's criticism, see the article by Hoyt Trowbridge, 'Bishop Hurd:
     A Reinterpretation,' *PMLA*, LVIII (1943), 450ff.

40. E.g., Batteux 'deduces' from the idea that poetry is the imitation, not of un-
     adorned reality, but of *la belle nature*, that its end can only be 'to please, to
     move, to touch, in a word, pleasure' (*Les Beaux Arts*, pp. 81, 151). Conversely,
     Hurd infers from the fact that the end of poetry is pleasure that the poet's
     duty is 'to illustrate and adorn' reality, and to delineate it 'in the most taking
     forms' ('Idea of Universal Poetry,' *Works*, 11, 8). For purposes of a specialized
     investigation into the evidences for plagiarism among poets, Hurd himself,
     in another essay, shifts his ground, and like Batteux, sets out from a defini-
     tion of poetry as an imitation, specifically, of 'the fairest forms of things'
     ('Discourse on Poetic Imitation,' *Works*, 11, 111).

41. *Johnson on Shakespeare*, ed. Walter Raleigh (Oxford, 1908), pp. 10, 30–31.

42. Ibid. pp. 14, 39. Cf. pp. 11, 31, 33, 37, etc.

43. Ibid. p. 16.

44. Ibid. pp. 31–3, 41.

45. Ibid. pp. 9–12.

46. Ibid. pp. 15–17. See also Johnson's defense of Shakespeare for violating the
     decorum of character-types, by the appeal to 'nature' as against 'accident';
     and for breaking the unities of time and place, by the appeal both to the ac-
     tual experience of dramatic auditors, and to the principle that 'the greatest
     graces of a play, are to copy nature and instruct life' (ibid. pp. 14–15, 25–30).
     Cf. *Rambler* No. 156.

47. Ibid. pp. 20–21. The logic appears even more clearly in Johnson's early paper
     on 'works of fiction,' in *Rambler* No. 4, 1750 (*The Works of Samuel Johnson*,
     ed. Arthur Murphy, London, 1824, IV, 23): 'It is justly considered as the great-
     est excellency of art, to imitate nature; but it is necessary to distinguish
     those parts of nature which are most proper for imitation,' etc. For a detailed
     analysis of Johnson's critical methods, see W. R. Keast, 'The Theoretical
     Foundations of Johnson's Criticism,' *Critics and Criticism*, ed. R. S. Crane,
     pp. 389–407.

48. See the masterly précis of the complex movements within English neo-clas-
     sic criticism by R. S. Crane, 'English Neoclassical Criticism,' *Critics and
     Criticism*, pp. 372–88.

49. *Letters of William and Dorothy Wordsworth: The Middle Years*, ed. E. de
     Selincourt (Oxford, 1937), 11, 705; 18 Jan. 1816.

50. *Early Essays by John Stuart Mill*, ed. J. W. M. Gibbs (London, 1897), p. 208.

51. Ibid. pp. 228, 205–6, 213, 203–4.

52. Ibid. pp. 211–17.

53. Ibid. pp. 222–31.

54. Ibid. pp. 206–7.

55. Ibid. pp. 208–9. Cf. Hulme, 'If it is sincere in the accurate sense... the whole
     of the analogy is necessary to get out the exact curve of the feeling or thing
     you want to express...' ('Romanticism and Classicism,' *Speculations*, Lon-
     don, 1936, p. 138).

56. Review, written in 1835, of Tennyson's *Poems Chiefly Lyrical* (1830) and *Poems* (1833), in *Early Essays*, p. 242.
57. 'Hamlet,' *Selected Essays 1917–32* (London, 1932), p. 145.
58. *Early Essays*, pp. 208–9. Cf. John Keble, *Lectures on Poetry* (1832–41), trans. E. K. Francis (Oxford, 1912), 1, 48–9: 'Cicero is always the orator' because 'he always has in mind the theatre, the benches, the audience'; whereas Plato is 'more poetical than Homer himself' because 'he writes to please himself, not to win over others.'
59. Preface to the *Lyrical Ballads, Wordsworth's Literary Criticism*, ed. N. C. Smith (London, 1905), pp. 30, 15–16.
60. *Letters*, ed. Maurice Buxton Forman (3d ed.; New York, 1948), p. 131 (to Reynolds, 9 Apr. 1818).
61. 'Defence of Poetry,' *Shelley's Literary and Philosophical Criticism*, ed. John Shawcross (London, 1909), p. 129.
62. 'Jean Paul Friedrich Richter' (1827), *Works*, ed. H. D. Traill (London, 1905), XXVI, 20.
63. See *Heroes, Hero-Worship, and the Heroic in History*, in *Works*, v, esp. pp. 80–85, 108–12. Cf. Jones Very's indignant denial of the inference that because the general ear takes delight in Shakespeare, 'his motive was to please ... We degrade those whom the world has pronounced poets, when we assume any other cause of their song than the divine and original action of the soul in humble obedience to the Holy Spirit upon whom they call' ['Shakespeare' (1838), *Poems and Essays*, Boston and New York, 1886, pp. 45–6].
64. 'Not every kind of pleasure should be required of a tragedy, but only its own proper pleasure. The tragic pleasure is that of pity and fear ... ' (*Poetics* 14. 1453^b).
65. 'The Poetic Principle,' *Representative Selections*, ed. Margaret Alterton and Hardin Craig (New York, 1935), pp. 382–3.
66. See John Crowe Ransom, *The World's Body* (New York, 1938), esp. pp. 327ff., and 'Criticism as Pure Speculation,' *The Intent of the Critic*, ed. Donald Stauffer (Princeton, 1941).
67. 'Moore's *Life of Lord Byron*,' in *Critical and Historical Essays* (Everyman's Library; London, 1907), 11, 622–8.
68. *Edinburgh Review*, VIII (1806), 459–60. On Jeffrey's use of an elaborate associationist aesthetics in order to justify the demand that an author or artist have as his aim 'to give as much [pleasure] and to as many persons as possible,' and that he 'fashion his productions according to the rules of taste which may be deduced' from an investigation of the most widespread public preferences, see his *Contributions to the Edinburgh Review* (London, 1844), 1, 76–8, 128; 111, 53–4. For contemporary justifications, on sociological and moral grounds, for instituting a petticoat government over the republic of letters, see, e.g., John Bowring's review of Tennyson's *Poems*, in *Westminster Review*, XIV (1831), 223; *Lockhart's Literary Criticism*, ed. M. C. Hildyard (Oxford, 1931), p. 66; Christopher North (John Wilson), *Works*, ed. Ferrier (Edinburgh and London, 1857), IX, 194–5, 228.

Jurij Tynjanov
Roman Jakobson

Problems in the Study of Literature and Language*

1. The immediate problems facing Russian literary and linguistic science demand a precision of the theoretical platform. They require a firm dissociation from the increasing tendency to paste together mechanically the new methodology and the old discarded methods; they necessitate a determined refusal of the contraband offer of naive psychologism and other methodological hand-me-downs in the guise of new terminology.

Furthermore, academic eclecticism, scholastic "formalism"—which replaces analysis by terminology and the classification of phenomena—and the repeated attempts to shift literary and linguistic studies from a systematic science to episodic and anecdotal genres should be rejected.

2. The history of literature (art), being simultaneous with other historical series, is characterized, as is each of these series, by an involved complex of specific structural laws. Without an elucidation of these laws, it is impossible to establish in a scientific manner the correlation between the literary series and other historical series.

3. The evolution of literature cannot be understood until the evolutionary problem ceases to be obscured by questions of episodic, nonsystemic origin, whether literary (for example, so-called "literary influences") or extraliterary. The literary and extraliterary material used in literature may be introduced into the orbit of scientific investigation only when it is considered from a functional point of view.

4. The sharp opposition of synchronic (static) and diachronic cross sections has recently become a fruitful working hypothesis, both for linguistics and for the history of literature; this opposition reveals the na-

*"Problemy izučenija literatury i jazyka," *Novyj Lef.* 12 (1928), pp. 36–37. Translated by Herbert Eagle.

ture of language (literature) as a system at each individual moment of its existence. At the present time, the achievements of the synchronic concept force us to reconsider the principles of diachrony as well. The idea of the mechanical agglomeration of material, having been replaced by the concept of system or structure in the realm of synchronic study, underwent a corresponding replacement in the realm of diachronic study as well. The history of a system is in turn a system. Pure synchronism now proves to be an illusion: every synchronic system has its past and its future as inseparable structural elements of the system: (a) archaism as a fact of style; the linguistic and literary background recognized as the rejected old-fashioned style; (b) the tendency in language and literature recognized as innovation in the system.

The opposition between synchrony and diachrony was an opposition between the concept of system and the concept of evolution; thus it loses its importance in principle as soon as we recognize that every system necessarily exists as an evolution, whereas, on the other hand, evolution is inescapably of a systemic nature.

5. The concept of a synchronic literary system does not coincide with the naively envisaged concept of a chronological epoch, since the former embraces not only works of art which are close to each other in time but also works which are drawn into the orbit of the system from foreign literatures or previous epochs. An indifferent cataloguing of coexisting phenomena is not sufficient; what is important is their hierarchical significance for the given epoch.

6. The assertion of two differing concepts—*la langue* and *la parole*—and the analysis of the relationship between them (the Geneva school) has been exceedingly fruitful for linguistic science. The principles involved in relating these two categories (i.e., the existing norm and the individual utterances) as applied to literature must now be elaborated. In this latter case, the individual utterance cannot be considered without reference to the existing complex of norms. (The investigator, in isolating the former from the latter, inescapably deforms the system of artistic values under consideration, thus losing the possibility of establishing its immanent laws.)

7. An analysis of the structural laws of language and literature and their evolution inevitably leads to the establishment of a limited series of actually existing structural types (types of structural evolution).

8. A disclosure of the immanent laws of the history of literature (language) allows us to determine the character of each specific change in literary (linguistic) systems. However, these laws do not allow us to explain the tempo of evolution or the chosen path of evolution when several, theoretically possible, evolutionary paths are given. This is owing to the fact that the immanent laws of literary (linguistic) evolution form an indeter-

minate equation; although they admit only a limited number of possible solutions, they do not necessarily specify a unique solution. The question of a specific choice of path, or at least of the dominant, can be solved only by means of an analysis of the correlation between the literary series and other historical series. This correlation (a system of systems) has its own structural laws, which must be submitted to investigation. It would be methodologically fatal to consider the correlation of systems without taking into account the immanent laws of each system.

Jacques Derrida

Structure, Sign, and Play in the Discourse of the Human Sciences[1]

Perhaps something has occurred in the history of the concept of structure that could be called an "event," if this loaded word did not entail a meaning which it is precisely the function of structural—or structuralist—thought to reduce or to suspect. But let me use the term "event" anyway, employing it with caution and as if in quotation marks. In this sense, this event will have the exterior form of a *rupture* and a *redoubling*.

It would be easy enough to show that the concept of structure and even the word "structure" itself are as old as the *epistèmè*—that is to say, as old as western science and western philosophy—and that their roots thrust deep into the soil of ordinary language, into whose deepest recesses the *epistèmè* plunges to gather them together once more, making them part of itself in a metaphorical displacement. Nevertheless, up until the event which I wish to mark out and define, structure—or rather the structurality of structure—although it has always been involved, has always been neutralized or reduced, and this by a process of giving it a center or referring it to a point of presence, a fixed origin. The function of this center was not only to orient, balance, and organize the structure—one cannot in fact conceive of an unorganized structure—but above all to make sure that the organizing principle of the structure would limit what we might call the *freeplay* of the structure. No doubt that by orienting and organizing the coherence of the system, the center of a structure permits the freeplay of its elements inside the total form. And even today the notion of a structure lacking any center represents the unthinkable itself.

Nevertheless, the center also closes off the freeplay it opens up and makes possible. *Qua* center, it is the point at which the substitution of contents, elements, or terms is no longer possible. At the center, the permutation or the transformation of elements (which may of course be structures enclosed within a structure) is forbidden. At least this permutation has always remained *inderdicted*[2] (I use this word deliberately).

35

Thus it has always been thought that the center, which is by definition unique, constituted that very thing within a structure which governs the structure, while escaping structurality. This is why classical thought concerning structure could say that the center is, paradoxically, *within* the structure and *outside* it. The center is at the center of the totality, and yet, since the center does not belong to the totality (is not part of the totality), the totality *has its center elsewhere*. The center is not the center. The concept of centered structure—although it represents coherence itself, the condition of the *epistème* as philosophy or science—is contradictorily coherent. And, as always, coherence in contradiction expresses the force of a desire. The concept of centered structure is in fact the concept of a freeplay based on a fundamental ground, a freeplay which is constituted upon a fundamental immobility and a reassuring certitude, which is itself beyond the reach of the freeplay. With this certitude anxiety can be mastered, for anxiety is invariably the result of a certain mode of being implicated in the game, of being caught by the game, of being as it were from the very beginning at stake in the game.[3] From the basis of what we therefore call the center (and which, because it can be either inside or outside, is as readily called the origin as the end, as readily *archè* as *telos*), the repetitions, the substitutions, the transformations, and the permutations are always *taken* from a history of meaning [*sens*]—that is, a history, period—whose origin may always be revealed or whose end may always be anticipated in the form of presence. This is why one could perhaps say that the movement of any archeology, like that of any eschatology, is an accomplice of this reduction of the structurality of structure and always attempts to conceive of structure from the basis of a full presence which is out of play.

If this is so, the whole history of the concept of structure, before the rupture I spoke of, must be thought of as a series of substitutions of center for center, as a linked chain of determinations of the center. Successively, and in a regulated fashion, the center receives different forms or names. The history of metaphysics, like the history of the West, is the history of these metaphors and metonymies. Its matrix—if you will pardon me for demonstrating so little and for being so elliptical in order to bring me more quickly to my principal theme—is the determination of being as *presence* in all the senses of this word. It would be possible to show that all the names related to fundamentals, to principles, or to the center have always designated the constant of a presence—*eidos, archè, telos, energeia, ousia* (essence, existence, substance, subject) *aletheia,* transcendentality, consciousness, or conscience, God, man, and so forth.

The event I called a rupture, the disruption I alluded to at the beginning of this paper, would presumably have come about when the structurality of structure had to begin to be thought, that is to say, repeated, and this is why I said that this disruption was repetition in all of the senses of this word. From then on it became necessary to think the law which governed, as it were, the desire for the center in the constitution of structure and the process of signification prescribing its displacements and its substitutions for this law of the central presence—but a central presence which was never itself, which has always already been transported outside itself in its surrogate. The surrogate does not substitute itself for anything which has somehow pre-existed it. From then on it was probably necessary to begin to think that there was no center, that the center could not be thought in the form of a being-present, that the center had no natural locus, that it was not a fixed locus but a function, a sort of non-locus in which an infinite number of sign-substitutions came into play. This moment was that in which language invaded the universal problematic; that in which, in the absence of a center or origin, everything became discourse—provided we can agree on this word—that is to say, when everything became a system where the central signified, the original or transcendental signified, is never absolutely present outside a system of differences. The absence of the transcendental signified extends the domain and the interplay of signification *ad infinitum.*

Where and how does this decentering, this notion of the structurality of structure, occur? It would be somewhat naïve to refer to an event, a doctrine, or an author in order to designate this occurrence. It is no doubt part of the totality of an era, our own, but still it has already begun to proclaim itself and begun to *work*. Nevertheless, if I wished to give some sort of indication by choosing one or two "names," and by recalling those authors in whose discourses this occurrence has most nearly maintained its most radical formulation, I would probably cite the Nietzschean critique of metaphysics, the critique of the concepts of being and truth, for which were substituted the concepts of play, interpretation, and sign (sign without truth present); the Freudian critique or self-presence, that is, the critique of consciousness, of the subject, of self-identity and of self-proximity or self-possession; and, more radically, the Heideggerean destruction of metaphysics, of onto-theology, of the determination of being as presence. But all these destructive discourses and all their analogues are trapped in a sort of circle. This circle is unique. It describes the form of the relationship between the history of metaphysics and the destruction of the history of metaphysics. *There is no sense* in doing without the concepts of metaphysics in order to attack metaphysics. We have no language—no syntax and no lexicon—which is alien to this history; we cannot utter a single destructive proposition which has not already slipped into the form, the logic, and the implicit postulations of precisely what it seeks to contest. To pick out one example from many: the metaphysics of presence is attacked with the help of the concept of the *sign.* But from the

moment anyone wishes this to show, as I suggested a moment ago, that
there is no transcendental or privileged signified and that the domain or
the interplay of signification has, henceforth, no limit, he ought to extend
his refusal to the concept and to the word sign itself—which is precisely
what cannot be done. For the signification "sign" has always been comprehended and determined, in its sense, as sign-of, signifier referring to a
signified, signifier different from its signified. If one erases the radical difference between signifier and signified, it is the word signifier itself
which ought to be abandoned as a metaphysical concept. When Lévi-
Strauss says in the preface to *The Raw and the Cooked*[4] that he has
"sought to transcend the opposition between the sensible and the intelligible by placing [himself] from the very beginning at the level of signs,"
the necessity, the force, and the legitimacy of his act cannot make us forget that the concept of the sign cannot in itself surpass or bypass this opposition between the sensible and the intelligible. The concept of the sign
is determined by this opposition: through and throughout the totality of
its history and by its system. But we cannot do without the concept of the
sign, we cannot give up this metaphysical complicity without also giving
up the critique we are directing against this complicity, without the risk
of erasing difference [altogether] in the self-identity of a signified reducing
into itself its signifier, or, what amounts to the same thing, simply expel-
ling it outside itself. For there are two heterogenous ways of erasing the
difference between the signifier and the signified: one, the classic way,
consists in reducing or deriving the signifier, that is to say, ultimately in
submitting the sign to thought; the other, the one we are using here
against the first one, consists in putting into question the system in
which the preceding reduction functioned: first and foremost, the opposition between the sensible and the intelligible. The *paradox* is that the
metaphysical reduction of the sign needed the opposition it was reducing.
The opposition is part of the system, along with the reduction. And what
I am saying here about the sign can be extended to all the concepts and all
the sentences of metaphysics, in particular to the discourse on "structure." But there are many ways of being caught in this circle. They are all
more or less naïve, more or less empirical, more or less systematic, more
or less close to the formulation or even to the formalization of this circle.
It is these differences which explain the multiplicity of destructive discourses and the disagreement between those who make them. It was
within concepts inherited from metaphysics that Nietzsche, Freud, and
Heidegger worked, for example. Since these concepts are not elements or
atoms and since they are taken from a syntax and a system, every particular borrowing drags along with it the whole of metaphysics. This is what
allows these destroyers to destroy each other reciprocally—for example,
Heidegger considering Nietzsche, with as much lucidity and rigor as bad

faith and misconstruction, as the last metaphysician, the last "Platonist." One could do the same for Heidegger himself, for Freud, or for a number of others. And today no exercise is more widespread.

What is the relevance of this formal schéma when we turn to what are called the "human sciences"? One of them perhaps occupies a privileged place—ethnology. One can in fact assume that ethnology could have been born as a science only at the moment when a de-centering had come about: at the moment when European culture—and, in consequence, the history of metaphysics and of its concepts—had been *dislocated*, driven from its locus, and forced to stop considering itself as the culture of reference. This moment is not first and foremost a moment of philosophical or scientific discourse, it is also a moment which is political, economic, technical, and so forth. One can say in total assurance that there is nothing fortuitous about the fact that the critique of ethnocentrism—the very condition of ethnology—should be systematically and historically contemporaneous with the destruction of the history of metaphysics. Both belong to a single and same era.

Ethnology—like any science—comes about within the element of discourse. And it is primarily a European science employing traditional concepts, however much it may struggle against them. Consequently, whether he wants to or not—and this does not depend on a decision on his part—the ethnologist accepts into his discourse the premises of ethnocentrism at the very moment when he is employed in denouncing them. This necessity is irreducible; it is not a historical contingency. We ought to consider very carefully all its implications. But if nobody can escape this necessity, and if no one is therefore responsible for giving in to it, however little, this does not mean that all the ways of giving in to it are of an equal pertinence. The quality and the fecundity of a discourse are perhaps measured by the critical rigor with which this relationship to the history of metaphysics and to inherited concepts is thought. Here it is a question of a critical relationship to the language of the human sciences and a question of a critical responsibility of the discourse. It is a question of putting expressly and systematically the problem of the status of a discourse which borrows from a heritage the resources necessary for the deconstruction of that heritage itself. A problem of *economy* and *strategy.*

If I now go on to employ an examination of the texts of Lévi-Strauss as an example, it is not only because of the privilege accorded to ethnology among the human sciences, nor yet because the thought of Lévi-Strauss weighs heavily on the contemporary theoretical situation. It is above all because a certain choice has made itself evident in the work of Lévi-Strauss and because a certain doctrine has been elaborated there, and precisely in a *more or less explicit manner*, in relation to this critique of language and to this critical language in the human sciences.

In order to follow this movement in the text of Lévi-Strauss, let me choose as one guiding thread among others the opposition between nature and culture. In spite of all its rejuvenations and its disguises, this opposition is congenital to philosophy. It is even older than Plato. It is at least as old as the Sophists. Since the statement of the opposition—*physis/nomos, physis/technè*—it has been passed on to us by a whole historical chain which opposes "nature" to the law, to education, to art, to technics—and also to liberty, to the arbitrary, to history, to society, to the mind, and so on. From the beginnings of his quest and from his first book, *The Elementary Structures of Kinship*,[5] Lévi-Strauss has felt at one and the same time the necessity of utilizing this opposition and the impossibility of making it acceptable. In the *Elementary Structures*, he begins from this axiom or definition: that belongs to nature which is *universal* and spontaneous, not depending on any particular culture or on any determinate norm. That belongs to culture, on the other hand, which depends on a system of *norms* regulating society and is therefore capable of *varying* from one social structure to another. These two definitions are of the traditional type. But, in the very first pages of the *Elementary Structures*, Lévi-Strauss, who has begun to give these concepts an acceptable standing, encounters what he calls a *scandal*, that is to say, something which no longer tolerates the nature/culture opposition he has accepted and which seems to require *at one and the same time* the predicates of nature and those of culture. This scandal is the *incest-prohibition*. The incest-prohibition is universal; in this sense one could call it natural. But it is also a prohibition, a system of norms and interdicts; in this sense one could call it cultural.

> Let us assume therefore that everything universal in man derives from the order of nature and is characterized by spontaneity, that everything which is subject to a norm belongs to culture and presents the attributes of the relative and the particular. We then find ourselves confronted by a fact, or rather an ensemble of facts, which, in the light of the preceding definitions, is not far from appearing as a scandal: the prohibition of incest presents without the least equivocation, and indissolubly linked together, the two characteristics in which we recognized the contradictory attributes of two exclusive orders. The prohibition of incest constitutes a rule, but a rule, alone of all the social rules, which possesses at the same time a universal character (p. 9).

Obviously there is no scandal except in the *interior* of a system of concepts sanctioning the difference between nature and culture. In beginning his work with the *factum* of the incest-prohibition, Lévi-Strauss thus puts himself in a position entailing that this difference, which has always been assumed to be self-evident, becomes obliterated or disputed.

For, from the moment that the incest-prohibition can no longer be conceived within the nature/culture opposition, it can no longer be said that it is a scandalous fact, a nucleus of opacity within a network of transparent significations. The incest-prohibition is no longer a scandal one meets with or comes up against in the domain of traditional concepts; it is something which escapes these concepts and certainly precedes them— probably as the condition of their possibility. It could perhaps be said that the whole of philosophical conceptualization, systematically relating itself to the nature/culture opposition, is designed to leave in the domain of the unthinkable the very thing that makes this conceptualization possible: the origin of the prohibition of incest.

I have dealt too cursorily with this example, only one among so many others, but the example nevertheless reveals that language bears within itself the necessity of its own critique. This critique may be undertaken along two tracks, in two "manners." Once the limit of nature/culture opposition makes itself felt, one might want to question systematically and rigorously the history of these concepts. This is a first action. Such a systematic and historic questioning would be neither a philological nor a philosophical action in the classic sense of these words. Concerning oneself with the founding concepts of the whole history of philosophy, deconstituting them, is not to undertake the task of the philologist or of the classic historian of philosophy. In spite of appearances, it is probably the most daring way of making the beginnings of a step outside of philosophy. The step "outside philosophy" is much more difficult to conceive than is generally imagined by those who think they made it long ago with cavalier ease, and who are in general swallowed up in metaphysics by the whole body of the discourse that they claim to have disengaged from it.

In order to avoid the possibly sterilizing effect of the first way, the other choice—which I feel corresponds more nearly to the way chosen by Lévi-Strauss—consists in conserving in the field of empirical discovery all these old concepts, while at the same time exposing here and there their limits, treating them as tools which can still be of use. No longer is any truth-value attributed to them; there is a readiness to abandon them if necessary if other instruments should appear more useful. In the meantime, their relative efficacy is exploited, and they are employed to destroy the old machinery to which they belong and of which they themselves are pieces. Thus it is that the language of the human sciences criticizes *itself*. Lévi-Strauss thinks that in this way he can separate *method* from *truth*, the instruments of the method and the objective significations aimed at by it. One could almost say that this is the primary affirmation of Lévi-Strauss; in any event, the first words of the *Elementary Structures* are: "One begins to understand that the distinction between state of nature and state of society (we would be more apt to say today: state of nature

and state of culture), while lacking any acceptable historical signification, presents a value which fully justifies its use by modern sociology: its
value as a methodological instrument."

Lévi-Strauss will always remain faithful to this double intention: to
preserve as an instrument that whose truth-value he criticizes.

On the one hand, he will continue in effect to contest the value of the
nature/culture opposition. More than thirteen years after the *Elementary Structures, The Savage Mind*[6] faithfully echoes the text I have just
quoted: "The opposition between nature and culture which I have previously insisted on seems today to offer a value which is above all methodological." And this methodological value is not affected by its "ontological" non-value (as could be said, if this notion were not suspect here): "It
would not be enough to have absorbed particular humanities into a general humanity; this first enterprise prepares the way for others ... which
belong to the natural and exact sciences: to reintegrate culture into nature, and finally, to reintegrate life into the totality of its physiochemical
conditions" (p. 327).

On the other hand, still in *The Savage Mind*, he presents as what he
calls *bricolage*[7] what might be called the discourse of this method. The
bricoleur, says Lévi-Strauss, is someone who uses "the means at hand,"
that is, the instruments he finds at his disposition around him, those
which are already there, which had not been especially conceived with an
eye to the operation for which they are to be used and to which one tries
by trial and error to adapt them, not hesitating to change them whenever
it appears necessary, or to try several of them at once, even if their form
and their origin are heterogenous—and so forth. There is therefore a critique of language in the form of *bricolage*, and it has even been possible
to say that *bricolage* is the critical language itself. I am thinking in particular of the article by G. Genette, "Structuralisme et Critique littéraire," published in homage to Lévi-Strauss in a special issue of *L'Arc*
(no. 26, 1965), where it is stated that the analysis of *bricolage* could "be
applied almost word for word" to criticism, and especially to "literary
criticism."[8]

If one calls *bricolage* the necessity of borrowing one's concepts from
the text of a heritage which is more or less coherent or ruined, it must be
said that every discourse is *bricoleur*. The engineer, whom Lévi-Strauss
opposes to the *bricoleur*, should be the one to construct the totality of his
language, syntax, and lexicon. In this sense the engineer is a myth. A subject who would supposedly be the absolute origin of his own discourse
and would supposedly construct it "out of nothing," "out of whole cloth,"
would be the creator of the *verbe*, the *verbe* itself. The notion of the engineer who had supposedly broken with all forms of *bricolage* is therefore
a theological idea; and since Lévi-Strauss tells us elsewhere that *bricolage* is mythopoetic, the odds are that the engineer is a myth produced by

the *bricoleur.* From the moment that we cease to believe in such an engineer and in a discourse breaking with the received historical discourse, as soon as it is admitted that every finite discourse is bound by a certain *bricolage,* and that the engineer and the scientist are also species of *bricoleurs* then the very idea of *bricolage* is menaced and the difference in which it took on its meaning decomposes.

This brings out the second thread which might guide us in what is being unraveled here.

Lévi-Strauss describes *bricolage* not only as an intellectual activity but also as a mythopoetical activity. One reads in *The Savage Mind,* "Like *bricolage* on the technical level, mythical reflection can attain brilliant and unforeseen results on the intellectual level. Reciprocally, the mythopoetical character of *bricolage* has often been noted" (p. 26).

But the remarkable endeavor of Lévi-Strauss is not simply to put forward, notably in the most recent of his investigations, a structural science or knowledge of myths and of mythological activity. His endeavor also appears—I would say almost from the first—in the status which he accords to his own discourse on myths, to what he calls his "mythologicals." It is here that his discourse on the myth reflects on itself and criticizes itself. And this moment, this critical period, is evidently of concern to all the languages which share the field of the human sciences. What does Lévi-Strauss say of his "mythologicals"? It is here that we rediscover the mythopoetical virtue (power) of *bricolage.* In effect, what appears most fascinating in this critical search for a new status of the discourse is the stated abandonment of all reference to a *center,* to a *subject,* to a privileged *reference,* to an origin, or to an absolute *archè.* The theme of this decentering could be followed throughout the "Overture" to his last book, *The Raw and the Cooked.* I shall simply remark on a few key points.

1) From the very start, Lévi-Strauss recognizes that the Bororo myth which he employs in the book as the "reference-myth" does not merit this name and this treatment. The name is specious and the use of the myth improper. This myth deserves no more than any other its referential privilege:

> In fact the Bororo myth which will from now on be designated by
> the name *reference-myth* is, as I shall try to show, nothing other
> than a more or less forced transformation of other myths
> originating either in the same society or in societies more or less far
> removed. It would therefore have been legitimate to choose as my
> point of departure any representative of the group whatsoever. From
> this point of view, the interest of the reference-myth does not
> depend on its typical character, but rather on its irregular position
> in the midst of a group (p. 10).

2) There is no unity or absolute source of the myth. The focus or the source of the myth are always shadows and virtualities which are elusive, unactualizable, and nonexistent in the first place. Everything begins with the structure, the configuration, the relationship. The discourse on this acentric structure, the myth, that is, cannot itself have an absolute subject or an absolute center. In order not to short change the form and the movement of the myth, that violence which consists in centering a language which is describing an acentric structure must be avoided. In this context, therefore it is necessary to forego scientific or philosophical discourse, to renounce the *epistèmè* which absolutely requires, which is the absolute requirement that we go back to the source, to the center, to the founding basis, to the principle, and so on. In opposition to *epistèmic* discourse, structural discourse on myths—*mythological* discourse—must itself be *mythomorphic*. It must have the form of that of which it speaks. This is what Lévi-Strauss says in *The Raw and the Cooked*, from which I would now like to quote a long and remarkable passage:

> In effect the study of myths poses a methodological problem by the fact that it cannot conform to the Cartesian principle of dividing the difficulty into as many parts as are necessary to resolve it. There exists no veritable end or term to mythical analysis, no secret unity which could be grasped at the end of the work of decomposition. The themes duplicate themselves to infinity. When we think we have disentangled them from each other and can hold them separate, it is only to realize that they are joining together again, in response to the attraction of unforeseen affinities. In consequence, the unity of the myth is only tendential and projective; it never reflects a state or a moment of the myth. An imaginary phenomenon implied by the endeavor to interpret, its role is to give a synthetic form to the myth and to impede its dissolution into the confusion of contraries. It could therefore be said that the science or knowledge of myths is an *anaclastic*, taking this ancient term in the widest sense authorized by its etymology, a science which admits into its definition the study of the reflected rays along with that of the broken ones. But, unlike philosophical reflection, which claims to go all the way back to its source, the reflections in question here concern rays without any other than a virtual focus. ... In wanting to imitate the spontaneous movement of mythical thought, my enterprise, itself too brief and too long, has had to yield to its demands and respect its rhythm. Thus is this book, on myths itself and in its own way, a myth.

This statement is repeated a little farther on (p. 20): "Since myths themselves rest on second-order codes (the first-order codes being those in which language consists), this book thus offers the rough draft of a third-order code, destined to insure the reciprocal possibility of translation of several myths. This is why it would not be wrong to consider it a myth: the myth of mythology, as it were." It is by this absence of any real and fixed center of the mythical or mythological discourse that the musical model chosen by Lévi-Strauss for the composition of his book is apparently justified. The absence of a center is here the absence of a subject and the absence of an author: "The myth and the musical work thus appear as orchestra conductors whose listeners are the silent performers. If it be asked where the real focus of the work is to be found, it must be replied that its determination is impossible. Music and mythology bring man face to face with virtual objects whose shadow alone is actual. . . . Myths have no authors" (p. 25).

Thus it is at this point that ethnographic *bricolage* deliberately assumes its mythopoetic function. But by the same token, this function makes the philosophical or epistemological requirement of a center appear as mythological, that is to say, as a historical illusion.

Nevertheless, even if one yields to the necessity of what Lévi-Strauss has done, one cannot ignore its risks. If the mythological is mythomorphic, are all discourses on myths equivalent? Shall we have to abandon any epistemological requirement which permits us to distinguish between several qualities of discourse on the myth? A classic question, but inevitable. We cannot reply—and I do not believe Lévi-Strauss replies to it—as long as the problem of the relationships between the philosopheme or the theorem, on the one hand, and the mytheme or the mythopoem(e), on the other, has not been expressly posed. This is no small problem. For lack of expressly posing this problem, we condemn ourselves to transforming the claimed transgression of philosophy into an unperceived fault in the interior of the philosophical field. Empiricism would be the genus of which these faults would always be the species. Trans-philosophical concepts would be transformed into philosophical naïvetés. One could give many examples to demonstrate this risk: the concepts of sign, history, truth, and so forth. What I want to emphasize is simply that the passage beyond philosophy does not consist in turning the page of philosophy (which usually comes down to philosophizing badly), but in continuing to read philosophers *in a certain way*. The risk I am speaking of is always assumed by Lévi-Strauss and it is the very price of his endeavor. I have said that empiricism is the matrix of all the faults menacing a discourse which continues, as with Lévi-Strauss in particular, to elect to be scientific. If we wanted to pose the problem of empiricism and *bricolage* in depth, we would probably end up very quickly with a number of propositions absolutely contradictory in relation to the status of discourse in structural ethnography. On the one hand, structuralism justly claims to be the critique of empiricism. But at the same time there is not a single book or study by Lévi-Strauss which does not offer itself as an empirical essay which can always be completed or invalidated by new information. The structural schemata are always proposed as hypotheses resulting from a finite quantity of information and which are subjected to the proof of experience. Numerous texts could be used to demonstrate this double postulation. Let us turn once again to the "Overture" of *The Raw and the Cooked,* where it seems clear that if this postulation is double, it is because it is a question here of a language on language:

> Critics who might take me to task for not having begun by making an exhaustive inventory of South American myths before analyzing them would be making a serious mistake about the nature and the role of these documents. The totality of the myths of a people is of the order of the discourse. Provided that this people does not become physically or morally extinct, this totality is never closed. Such a criticism would therefore be equivalent to reproaching a linguist with writing the grammar of a language without having recorded the totality of the words which have been uttered since that language came into existence and without knowing the verbal exchanges which will take place as long as the language continues to exist. Experience proves that an absurdly small number of sentences . . . allows the linguist to elaborate a grammar of the language he is studying. And even a partial grammar or an outline of a grammar represents valuable acquisitions in the case of unknown languages. Syntax does not wait until it has been possible to enumerate a theoretically unlimited series of events before becoming manifest, because syntax consists in the body of rules which presides over the generation of these events. And it is precisely a syntax of South American mythology that I wanted to outline. Should new texts appear to enrich the mythical discourse, then this will provide an opportunity to check or modify the way in which certain grammatical laws have been formulated, an opportunity to discard certain of them and an opportunity to discover new ones. But in no instance can the requirement of a total mythical discourse be raised as an objection. For we have just seen that such a requirement has no meaning (pp. 15–16).

Totalization is therefore defined at one time as *useless,* at another time as *impossible.* This is no doubt the result of the fact that there are two ways of conceiving the limit of totalization. And I assert once again that these two determinations coexist implicitly in the discourses of Lévi-Strauss. Totalization can be judged impossible in the classical style: one then refers to the empirical endeavor of a subject or of a finite discourse in a vain and breathless quest of an infinite richness which it can never master. There is too much, more than one can say. But nontotalization can also be determined in another way: not from the standpoint of the concept of finitude as assigning us to an empirical view, but from the standpoint of the concept of *freeplay.* If totalization no longer has any meaning, it is not because the infinity of a field cannot be covered by a finite glance or a finite discourse, but because the nature of the field—that is, language and a finite language—excludes totalization. This field is in fact that of *freeplay,* that is to say, a field of infinite substitutions in the closure of a finite ensemble. This field permits these infinite substitutions only because it is finite, that is to say, because instead of being an inexhaustible field, as in the classical hypothesis, instead of being too large, there is something missing from it: a center which arrests and founds the freeplay of substitutions. One could say—rigorously using that word whose scandalous signification is always obliterated in French—that this movement of the freeplay, permitted by the lack, the absence of a center or origin, is the movement of *supplementarity.* One cannot determine the center, the sign which *supplements*[9] it, which takes its place in its absence—because this sign adds itself, occurs in addition, over and above, comes as a *supplement.*[10] The movement of signification adds something, which results in the fact that there is always more, but this addition is a floating one because it comes to perform a vicarious function, to supplement a lack on the part of the signified. Although Lévi-Strauss in his use of the word supplementary never emphasizes as I am doing here the two directions of meaning which are so strangely compounded within it, it is not by chance that he uses this word twice in his "Introduction to the Work of Marcel Mauss,"[11] at the point where he is speaking of the "superabundance of signifier, in relation to the signifieds to which this superabundance can refer":

> In his endeavor to understand the world, man therefore always has at his disposition a surplus of signification (which he portions out amongst things according to the laws of symbolic thought—which it is the task of ethnologists and linguists to study). This distribution of a *supplementary* allowance [*ration supplémentaire*]—if it is permissible to put it that way—is absolutely necessary in order that on the whole the available signifier and the signified it aims at may remain in the relationship of complementarity which is the very condition of the use of symbolic thought (p. xlix).

(It could no doubt be demonstrated that this *ration supplémentaire* of signification is the origin of the *ratio* itself.) The word reappears a little farther on, after Lévi-Strauss has mentioned "this floating signifier, which is the servitude of all finite thought":

> In other words—and taking as our guide Mauss's precept that all social phenomena can be assimilated to language—we see in *mana, Wakau, oranda* and other notions of the same type, the

conscious expression of a semantic function, whose role it is to
permit symbolic thought to operate in spite of the contradiction
which is proper to it. In this way are explained the apparently
insoluble antinomies attached to this notion. . . . At one and the
same time force and action, quality and state, substantive and verb;
abstract and concrete, omnipresent and localized—*mana* is in
effect all these things. But is it not precisely because it is none of
these things that *mana* is a simple form, or more exactly, a symbol
in the pure state, and therefore capable of becoming charged with
any sort of symbolic content whatever? In the system of symbols
constituted by all cosmologies, *mana* would simply be a *valeur
symbolique zéro*, that is to say, a sign marking the necessity of a
symbolic content *supplementary* [my italics] to that with which the
signified is already loaded, but which can take on any value
required, provided only that this value still remains part of the
available reserve and is not, as phonologists put it, a group-term.

Lévi-Strauss adds the note:

Linguists have already been led to formulate hypotheses of this
type. For example: "A zero phoneme is opposed to all the other
phonemes in French in that it entails no differential characters and
no constant phonetic value. On the contrary, the proper function of
the zero phoneme is to be opposed to phoneme absence." (R.
Jakobson and J. Lutz, "Notes on the French Phonemic Pattern,"
Word, vol. 5, no. 2 [August, 1949], p. 155). Similarly, if we
schematize the conception I am proposing here, it could almost be
said that the function of notions like *mana* is to be opposed to the
absence of signification, without entailing by itself any particular
signification (p. 1 and note).

The *superabundance* of the signifier, its *supplementary* character, is
thus the result of a finitude, that is to say, the result of a lack which must
be *supplemented*.

It can now be understood why the concept of freeplay is important in
Lévi-Strauss. His references to all sorts of games, notably to roulette, are
very frequent, especially in his *Conversations*,[12] in *Race and History*,[13]
and in *The Savage Mind*. This reference to the game or freeplay is always
caught up in a tension.

It is in tension with history, first of all. This is a classical problem,
objections to which are now well worn or used up. I shall simply indicate
what seems to me the formality of the problem: by reducing history, Lévi-
Strauss has treated as it deserves a concept which has always been in
complicity with a teleological and eschatological metaphysics, in other
words, paradoxically, in complicity with that philosophy of presence to
which it was believed history could be opposed. The thematic of histor-

icity, although it seems to be a somewhat late arrival in philosophy, has always been required by the determination of being as presence. With or without etymology, and in spite of the classic antagonism which opposes these significations throughout all of classical thought, it could be shown that the concept of *epistème* has always called forth that of *historia*, if history is always the unity of a becoming, as tradition of truth or development of science or knowledge oriented toward the appropriation of truth in presence and self-presence, toward knowledge in consciousness-of-self.[14] History has always been conceived as the movement of a resumption of history, a diversion between two presences. But if it is legitimate to suspect this concept of history, there is a risk, if it is reduced without an express statement of the problem I am indicating here, of falling back into an anhistoricism of a classical type, that is to say, in a determinate moment of the history of metaphysics. Such is the algebraic formality of the problem as I see it. More concretely, in the work of Lévi-Strauss it must be recognized that the respect for structurality, for the internal originality of the structure, compels a neutralization of time and history. For example, the appearance of a new structure, of an original system, always comes about—and this is the very condition of its structural specificity—by a rupture with its past, its origin, and its cause. One can therefore describe what is peculiar to the structural organization only by not taking into account, in the very moment of this description, its past conditions: by failing to pose the problem of the passage from one structure to another, by putting history into parentheses. In this "structuralist" moment, the concepts of chance and discontinuity are indispensable. And Lévi-Strauss does in fact often appeal to them as he does, for instance, for that structure of structures, language, of which he says in the "Introduction to the Work of Marcel Mauss" that it "could only have been born in one fell swoop":

> Whatever may have been the moment and the circumstances of its appearance in the scale of animal life, language could only have been born in one fell swoop. Things could not have set about signifying progressively. Following a transformation the study of which is not the concern of the social sciences, but rather of biology and psychology, a crossing over came about from a stage where nothing had a meaning to another where everything possessed it (p. xlvi).

This standpoint does not prevent Lévi-Strauss from recognizing the slowness, the process of maturing, the continuous toil of factual transformations, history (for example, in *Race and History*). But, in accordance with an act which was also Rousseau's and Husserl's, he must "brush aside all the facts" at the moment when he wishes to recapture the specificity of a structure. Like Rousseau, he must always conceive of the origin of a new structure on the model of catastrophe—an overturning of nature in nature, a natural interruption of the natural sequence, a brushing aside *of* nature.

Besides the tension of freeplay with history, there is also the tension of freeplay with presence. Freeplay is the disruption of presence. The presence of an element is always a signifying and substitutive reference inscribed in a system of differences and the movement of a chain. Freeplay is always an interplay of absence and presence, but if it is to be radically conceived, freeplay must be conceived of before the alternative of presence and absence; being must be conceived of as presence or absence beginning with the possibility of freeplay and not the other way around. If Lévi-Strauss, better than any other, has brought to light the freeplay of repetition and the repetition of freeplay, one no less perceives in his work a sort of ethic of presence, an ethic of nostalgia for origins, an ethic of archaic and natural innocence, of a purity of presence and self-presence in speech[15]—an ethic, nostalgia, and even remorse which he often presents as the motivation of the ethnological project when he moves toward archaic societies—exemplary societies in his eyes. These texts are well known.

As a turning toward the presence, lost or impossible, of the absent origin, this structuralist thematic of broken immediateness is thus the sad, *negative,* nostalgic, guilty, Rousseauist facet of the thinking of freeplay of which the Nietzschean *affirmation*—the joyous affirmation of the freeplay of the world and without truth, without origin, offered to an active interpretation—would be the other side. *This affirmation then determines the non-center otherwise than as loss of the center.* And it plays the game without security. For there is a *sure* freeplay: that which is limited to the *substitution* of *given and existing, present,* pieces. In absolute chance, affirmation also surrenders itself to *genetic* indetermination, to the *seminal* adventure of the trace.[16]

There are thus two interpretations of interpretation, of structure, of sign, of freeplay. The one seeks to decipher, dreams of deciphering, a truth or an origin which is free from freeplay and from the order of the sign, and lives like an exile the necessity of interpretation. The other, which is no longer turned toward the origin, affirms freeplay and tries to pass beyond man and humanism, the name man being the name of that being who, throughout the history of metaphysics or of ontotheology—in other words, through the history of all of his history—has dreamed of full presence, the reassuring foundation, the origin and the end of the game. The second interpretation of interpretation, to which Nietzsche showed us the way, does not seek in ethnography, as Lévi-Strauss wished, the "inspiration of a new humanism" (again from the "Introduction to the Work of Marcel Mauss").

There are more than enough indications today to suggest we might perceive that these two interpretations of interpretation—which are absolutely irreconcilable even if we live them simultaneously and reconcile them in an obscure economy—together share the field which we call, in such a problematic fashion, the human sciences.

For my part, although these two interpretations must acknowledge and accentuate their difference and define their irreducibility, I do not believe that today there is any question of *choosing*—in the first place because here we are in a region (let's say, provisionally, a region of historicity) where the category of choice seems particularly trivial; and in the second, because we must first try to conceive of the common ground, and the *différence* of this irreducible difference.[17] Here there is a sort of question, call it historical, of which we are only glimpsing today the *conception, the formation, the gestation, the labor.* I employ these words, I admit, with a glance toward the business of childbearing—but also with a glance toward those who, in a company from which I do not exclude myself, turn their eyes away in the face of the as yet unnameable which is proclaiming itself and which can do so, as is necessary whenever a birth is in the offing, only under the species of the non-species, in the formless, mute, infant, and terrifying form of monstrosity.

Discussion

JEAN HYPPOLITE: I should simply like to ask Derrida, whose presentation and discussion I have admired, for some explanation of what is, no doubt, the technical point of departure of the presentation. That is, a question of the concept of the center of structure, or what a center might mean. When I take, for example, the structure of certain algebraic constructions [ensembles], where is the center? Is the center the knowledge of general rules which, after a fashion, allow us to understand the interplay of the elements? Or is the center certain elements which enjoy a particular privilege within the ensemble?

My question is, I think, relevant since one cannot think of the structure without the center, and the center itself is "destructured," is it not?—the center is not structured. I think we have a great deal to learn as we study the sciences of man; we have much to learn from the natural sciences. They are like an image of the problems which we, in turn, put to ourselves. With Einstein, for example, we see the end of a kind of privilege of empiric evidence. And in that connection we see a constant appear, a constant which is a combination of space-time, which does not belong to any of the experiments who live the experience, but which, in a way, dominates the whole construct; and this notion of the constant—is this the center? But natural science has gone much further. It no longer searches for the constant. It considers that there are events, somehow improbable, which bring about for a while a structure and an invariability. Is it that everything happens as though certain mutations, which don't come from any author or any hand, and which are, like the poor reading of a manuscript, realized [only] as a defect of a structure, simply exist as mutations? Is this the case? Is it a question of a structure which is in the nature of a genotype produced by chance from an improbable happening, of a meeting which involved a series of chemical molecules and which organized them in a certain way, creating a genotype which will be realized, and whose origin is lost in a mutation? Is that what you are tending toward? Because, for my part, I feel that I am going in that direction and that I find there the example—even when we are talking about a kind of end of history—of the integration of the historic; under the form of *event,* so long as it is improbable, at the very center of the realization of the structure, but a history which no longer has anything to do with eschatological history, a history which loses itself always in its own pursuit, since the origin is perpetually displaced. And you know that the language we are speaking today, *à propos* of language, is spoken about genotypes, and about information theory. Can this sign without sense, this perpetual turning back, be understood in the light of a kind of philosophy of nature in which nature will not only have realized a mutation, but will have realized a perpetual mutant: man? That is, a kind of error of transmission or of malformation would have created a being which is always malformed, whose adaptation is a perpetual aberration, and the problem of man would become part of a much larger field in which what you want to do, what you are in the process of doing, that is, the loss of the center—the fact that there is no privileged or original structure—could be seen under this very form to which man would be restored. Is this what you wanted to say, or were you getting at something else? That is my last question, and I apologize for having held the floor so long.

JACQUES DERRIDA: With the last part of your remarks, I can say that I agree fully—but you were asking a question. I was wondering myself if I know where I am going. So I would answer you by saying, first, that I am trying, precisely, to put myself at a point so that I do not know any longer where I am going. And, as to this loss of the center, I *refuse* to approach an idea of the "non-center" which would no longer be the tragedy of the loss of the center—this sadness is classical. And I don't mean to say that I thought of approaching an idea by which this loss of the center would be an affirmation.

As to what you said about the nature and the situation of man in the products of nature, I think that we have already discussed this together. I will assume entirely with you this partiality which you expressed—with the exception of your [choice of] words, and here the words are more than mere words, as always. That is to say, I cannot accept your precise formulation, although I am not prepared to offer a precise alternative. So, it being understood that I do not know where I am going, that the words which we are using do not satisfy me, with these reservations in mind, I am entirely in agreement with you.

Concerning the first part of your question, the Einsteinian constant is not a constant, is not a center. It is the very concept of variability—it is, finally, the concept of the game. In other words, it is not the concept of some*thing*—of a center starting from which an observer could master the field—but the very concept of the game which, after all, I was trying to elaborate.

HYPPOLITE: It is a constant in the game?

DERRIDA: It is *the* constant of the game ...

HYPPOLITE: It is the rule of the game.

DERRIDA: It is a rule of the game which does not govern the game; it is a rule of the game which does not dominate the game. Now, when the rule of the game is displaced by the game itself, we must find something other than the word *rule*. In what concerns algebra, then, I think that it is an example in which a group of significant figures, if you wish, or of signs, is deprived of a center. But we can consider algebra from two points of view. Either as the example or analogue of this absolutely de-centered game of which I have spoken; or we can try to consider algebra as a limited field of ideal objects, products in the Husserlian sense, beginning from a history, from a *Lebenswelt*, from a subject, etc., which constituted, created its ideal objects, and consequently we should always be able to make substitutions, by reactivating in it the origin—that of which the significants, seemingly lost, are the derivations. I think it is in this way that algebra was thought of classically. One could, perhaps, think of it otherwise as an image of the game. Or else one thinks of algebra as a field of ideal objects, produced by the activity of what we call a subject, or man, or history, and thus, we recover the possibility of algebra in the field of classical thought; or else we consider it as a disquieting mirror of a world which is algebraic through and through.

HYPPOLITE: What is a structure then? If I can't take the example of algebra anymore, how will you define a structure for me?—to see where the center is.

DERRIDA: The concept of structure itself—I say in passing—is no longer satisfactory to describe that game. How to define structure? Structure should be centered. But this center can be either thought, as it was classically, like a creator or being or a fixed and natural place; or also as a deficiency, let's say; or something which makes possible "free play," in the sense in which one speaks of the "jeu dans la machine," of the "jeu des pièces," and which receives—and this is what we call history—a se-

ries of determinations, of signifiers, which have no signifieds [*signifiés*]
finally, which cannot become signifiers except as they begin from this deficiency. So, I think that what I have said can be understood as a criticism
of structuralism, certainly.

RICHARD MACKSEY: I may be off-side [*hors jeu*] in trying to identify
prematurely those players who can join your team in the critique of metaphysics represented by your tentative game-theory. Still, I was struck by
the sympathy with which two contemporary figures might view that formidable prospect which you and Nietzsche invite us to contemplate. I am
thinking, first, of the later career of Eugen Fink, a "reformed" phenome-
nologist with the peculiarly paradoxical relationship to Heidegger. Even
as early as the colloquia at Krefeld and Royaumont he was prepared to argue the secondary status of the conceptual world, to see *Sein, Wahrheit,*
and *Welt* as irreducibly part of a single, primal question. Certainly in his
Vor-Fragen and in the last chapter of the Nietzsche book he advances a
Zarathustrian notion of *game* as the step outside (or behind) philosophy.
It is interesting to contrast his Nietzsche with Heidegger's; it seems to me
that you would agree with him in reversing the latter's primacy of *Sein*
over *Seiendes,* and thereby achieve some interesting consequences for the
post-humanist critique of our announced topic, "les sciences *humaines.*"
For surely, in *Spiel als Weltsymbol* the presiding Worldgame is profoundly
anterior and anonymous, anterior to the Platonic division of being and appearance and dispossessed of a human, personal center.

The other figure is that writer who has made the shifting center of his
fictional poetics the narrative game in "the *unanimous* night," that architect and prisoner of labyrinths, the creator of Pierre Menard.

DERRIDA: You are thinking, no doubt, of Jorge Luis Borges.

CHARLES MORAZÉ: Just a remark. Concerning the dialogue of the
past twenty years with Lévi-Strauss on the possibility of a grammar other
than that of language—I have a great deal of admiration for what Lévi-
Strauss has done in the order of a grammar of mythologies. I would like to
point out that there is also a grammar of the event—that one can make a
grammar of the event. It is more difficult to establish. I think that in the
coming months, in the coming years, we will begin to learn how this
grammar or rather this set of grammars of events can be constituted. And
[this grammar] leads to results, may I say, anyway with regard to my personal experience, which are a little less pessimistic than those you have
indicated.

LUCIEN GOLDMANN: I would like to say that I find that Derrida, with
whose conclusions I do not agree, has a catalytic function in French cultural life, and for that reason I pay him homage. I said once that he brings
to my mind that memory of when I arrived in France in '34. At that time
there was a very strong royalist movement among the students and sud-

denly a group appeared which was equally in defense of royalism, but which demanded a real Merovingian king!

In this movement of negation of the subject or of the center, if you like, which Derrida defines remarkably, he is in the process of saying to all the people who represent this position, "But you contradict yourself; you never carry through to the end. Finally, in criticizing mythologies, if you deny the position, the existence, of the critic and the necessity of saying anything, you contradict yourself, because you are still M. Lévi-Strauss who says something and if you make a new mythology.... " Well, the criticism was remarkable and it's not worth taking it up again. But if I have noted the few words which were added to the text and which were of a destructive character, we could discuss that on the level of semiology. But I would like to ask Derrida a question: "Let us suppose that instead of discussing on the basis of a series of postulates toward which all contemporary currents, irrationalist as well as formalist, are oriented, you have before you a very different position, say the dialectical position. Quite simply, you think that science is something that men make, that history is not an error, that what you call theology is something acceptable, an attempt not to say that the world is ordered, that it is theological, but that the human being is one who places his stake on the possibility of giving a meaning to a word which will eventually, at some point, resist this meaning. And the origin or the fundamental of that which is before a typical state of dichotomy of which you speak (or in grammatology the action which registers before there is a meaning) is something which we are studying today, but which we cannot, which we don't even want to, penetrate from the inside, because it can be penetrated from the inside only in silence, while we want to understand it according to the logic which we have elaborated, with which we try somehow or other to go farther, not to discover a meaning hidden by some god, but to give a meaning to a world in which that is the function of man (without knowing, moreover, where man comes from—we can't be entirely consistent, because if the question is clear, we know, if we say that man comes from God, then somebody will ask "Where does God come from?" and if we say that man comes from nature, somebody will ask "Where does nature come from?" and so on). But we are on the inside and we are in this situation. Is this position before you, then, still contradictory?

JAN KOTT: At one time this famous phrase of Mallarmé seemed to be very significant: "A throw of dice will never abolish chance." ["Un coup de dés n'abolira jamais le hasard."] After this lesson you have given us, isn't it possible to say that: "And chance will never abolish the throw of dice! ["Et le hasard n'abolira jamais le coup de dés."]

DERRIDA: I say "Yes" immediately to Mr. Kott. As to what Mr. Goldmann has said to me, I feel that he has isolated, in what I said, the aspect that he calls destructive. I believe, however, that I was quite explicit about the fact that nothing of what I said had a destructive meaning. Here or there I have used the word *déconstruction,* which has nothing to do with destruction. That is to say, it is simply a question of (and this is a necessity of criticism in the classical sense of the word) being alert to the implications, to the historical sedimentation of the language which we use—and that is not destruction. I believe in the necessity of scientific work in the classical sense, I believe in the necessity of everything which is being done and even of what you are doing, but I don't see why I should renounce or why anyone should renounce the radicality of a critical work under the pretext that it risks the sterilization of science, humanity, progress, the origin of meaning, etc. I believe that the risk of sterility and sterilization has always been the price of lucidity. Concerning the initial anecdote, I take it rather badly, because it defines me as an ultraroyalist, or an "ultra," as they said in my native country not so long ago, whereas I have a much more humble, modest, and classical conception of what I am doing.

Concerning Mr. Morazé's allusion to the grammar of the event, there I must return his question, because I don't know what a grammar of the event can be.

SERGE DOUBROVSKY: You always speak of a *non-center.* How can you, within your own perspective, explain or at least understand what a perception is? For a perception is precisely the manner in which the world appears *centered* to me. And language you represent as flat or level. Now language is something else again. It is, as Merleau-Ponty said, a corporeal intentionality. And starting from this utilization of language, in as much as there is an intention of language, I inevitably find a center again. For it is not "One" who speaks, but "I." And even if you reduce the I, you are obliged to come across once again the concept of intentionality, which I believe is at the base of a whole thought, which, moreover, you do not deny. Therefore I ask how you reconcile it with your present attempts?

DERRIDA: First of all, I didn't say that there was no center, that we could get along without the center. I believe that the center is a function, not a being—a reality, but a function. And this function is absolutely indispensable. The subject is absolutely indispensable. I don't destroy the subject; I situate it. That is to say, I believe that at a certain level both of experience and of philosophical and scientific discourse one cannot get along without the notion of subject. It is a question of knowing where it comes from and how it functions. Therefore I keep the concept of center, which I explained was indispensable, as well as that of subject, and the whole system of concepts to which you have referred.

Since you mentioned intentionality, I simply try to see those who are founding the movement of intentionality—which cannot be conceived in the term intentionality. As to perception, I should say that once I recognized it as a necessary conservation. I was extremely conservative. Now I don't know what perception is and I don't believe that anything like perception exists. Perception is precisely a concept, a concept of an intuition or of a given originating from the thing itself, present itself in its meaning, independently from language, from the system of reference. And I believe that perception is interdependent with the concept of origin and of center and consequently whatever strikes at the metaphysics of which I have spoken strikes also at the very concept of perception. I don't believe that there is any perception.

NOTES

1. "La Structure, le signe et le jeu dans le discours des sciences humaines." The text which follows is a translation of the revised version of M. Derrida's communication. The word "jeu" is variously translated here as "play," "interplay," "game," and "stake," besides the normative translation "freeplay." All footnotes to this article are additions by the translator.
2. *Interdite:* "forbidden," "disconcerted," "confounded," "speechless."
3. " ... qui naît toujours d'une certaine manière d'être impliqué dans le jeu, d'être pris au jeu, d'être comme être d'entrée de jeu dans le jeu."
4. *Le cru et le cuit* (Paris: Plon, 1964).
5. *Les structures élémentaires de la parenté* (Paris: Presses Universitaires de France, 1949).
6. *La pensée sauvage* (Paris: Plon, 1962).
7. A *bricoleur* is a jack-of-all trades, someone who potters about with odds-and-ends, who puts things together out of bits and pieces.
8. Reprinted in: G. Genette, *Figures* (Paris: Editions du Seuil, 1966), p. 145.
9. The point being that the word, both in English and French, means "to supply a deficiency," on the one hand, and "to supply something additional," on the other.
10. " ... ce signe s'ajoute, vient en sus, en *supplément.*"
11. "Introduction à l'oeuvre de Marcel Mauss," in: Marcel Mauss, *Sociologie et anthropologie* (Paris: Presses Universitaires de France, 1950).
12. Presumably: G. Charbonnier, *Entretiens avec Claude Lévi-Strauss* (Paris: Plon-Julliard, 1961).
13. *Race and History* (Paris: UNESCO Publications, 1958).
14. " ... l'unité d'un devenir, comme tradition de la vérité dans la présence et la présence à soi, vers le savoir dans la conscience de soi."
15. " ... de la présence à soi dans la parole."
16. "Tournée vers la présence, perdue ou impossible, de l'origine absente, cette thématique structuraliste de l'immédiateté rompue est donc la face triste, *négative*, nostalgique, coupable, rousseauiste, de la pensée du jeu dont *l'affirmation* nietzschéenne, l'affirmation joyeuse du jeu du monde et de l'in-

nocence du devenir, l'affirmation d'un monde de signes sans faute, sans vérité, sans origine, offert à une interprétation active, serait l'autre face. *Cette
affirmation détermine alors le* non-centre *autrement que comme perte du
centre.* Et elle joue sans sécurité. Car il y a un jeu *sûr:* celui qui se limite à
la *substitution* de pièces *données et existantes, présentes.* Dans le hasard
absolu, l'affirmation se livre aussi à l'indétermination *génétique,* à l'aven-
ture *séminale* de la trace."

17.   From *différer,* in the sense of "to postpone," "put off," "defer." Elsewhere
       Derrida uses the word as a synonym for the German *Aufschub:* "postpone-
       ment," and relates it to the central Freudian concepts of *Verspätung, Nach-
       träglichkeit,* and to the "*détours* to death" of *Beyond the Pleasure Principle*
       by Sigmund Freud (Standard Edition, ed. James Strachey, vol. XIX, London,
       1961), Chap. V.

Two
literature

Yvor Winters

Preliminary Problems

First Problem

Is it possible to say that Poem A (one of Donne's *Holy Sonnets*, or one of the poems of Jonson or of Shakespeare) is better than Poem B (Collins' *Ode to Evening*) or vice versa?

If not, is it possible to say that either of these is better than Poem C (*The Cremation of Sam Magee*, or something comparable)?

If the answer is no in both cases, then any poem is as good as any other. If this is true, then all poetry is worthless; but this obviously is not true, for it is contrary to all our experience.

If the answer is yes in both cases, then there follows the question of whether the answer implies merely that one poem is better than another for the speaker, or whether it means that one poem is intrinsically better than another. If the former, then we are impressionists, which is to say relativists; and are either mystics of the type of Emerson, or hedonists of the type of Stevens and Ransom. If the latter, then we assume that constant principles govern the poetic experience, and that the poem (as likewise the judge) must be judged in relationship to those principles. It is important, therefore, to discover the consequences of assuming each of these positions.

If our answer to the first question is no and to the second yes, then we are asserting that we can distinguish between those poems which are of the canon and those which are not, but that within the canon all judgment is impossible. This view, if adopted, will require serious elucidation, for on the face of it, it appears inexplicable. On the other hand, one cannot deny that within the canon judgment will become more difficult, for the nearer two poems may be to the highest degrees of excellence, the harder it will be to choose between them. Two poems, in fact, might be so excellent that there would be small profit in endeavoring to say that one was better, but one could arrive at this conclusion only after a careful examination of both.

Second Problem

If we accept the view that one poem can be regarded as better than another, the question then arises whether this judgment is a matter of
inexplicable intuition, or whether it is a question of intuition that can be
explained, and consequently guided and improved by rational elucidation.

If we accept the view that the judgment in question is inexplicable,
then we are again forced to confess ourselves impressionists and relativists, unless we can show that the intuitions of all men agree at all times,
or that the intuitions of one man are invariably right and those of all others wrong whenever they differ. We obviously can demonstrate neither of
these propositions.

If we start, then, with the proposition that one poem may be intrinsically superior to another, we are forced to account for differences of opinion regarding it. If two critics differ, it is possible that one is right and the
other wrong, more likely that both are partly right and partly wrong, but
in different respects: neither the native gifts nor the education of any man
have ever been wholly adequate to many of the critical problems he will
encounter, and no two men are ever the same in these respects or in any
others. On the other hand, although the critic should display reasonable
humility and caution, it is only fair to add that few men possess either the
talent or the education to justify their being taken very seriously, even of
those who are nominally professional students of these matters.

But if it is possible by rational elucidation to give a more or less clear
account of what one finds in a poem and why one approves or disapproves,
then communication between two critics, though no doubt imperfect, becomes possible, and it becomes possible that they may in some measure
correct each other's errors and so come more near to a true judgment of
the poem.

Third Problem

If rational communication about poetry is to take place, it is necessary
first to determine what we mean by a poem.

A poem is first of all a statement in words.

But it differs from all such statements of a purely philosophical or
theoretical nature, in that it has by intention a controlled content of feeling. In this respect, it does not differ from many works written in prose,
however.

A poem differs from a work written in prose by virtue of its being
composed in verse. The rhythm of verse permits the expression of more

powerful feeling than is possible in prose when such feeling is needed, and it permits at all times the expression of finer shades of feeling.

A poem, then, is a statement in words in which special pains are taken with the expression of feeling. This description is merely intended to distinguish the poem from other kinds of writing; it is not offered as a complete description.

Fourth Problem

What, however, are words?

They are audible sounds, or their visual symbols, invented by man to communicate his thoughts and feelings. Each word has a conceptual content, however slight; each word, exclusive, perhaps, of the particles, communicates vague associations of feeling.

The word *fire* communicates a concept; it also connotes very vaguely certain feelings, depending on the context in which we happen to place it—depending, for example, on whether we happen to think of a fire on a hearth, in a furnace, or in a forest. These feelings may be rendered more and more precise as we render the context more and more precise; as we come more and more near to completing and perfecting our poem.

Fifth Problem

But if the poem, as compared to prose, pays especial attention to feeling, are we to assume that the rational content of the poem is unimportant to its success?

The rational content cannot be eliminated from words; consequently the rational content cannot be eliminated from poetry. It is there. If it is unsatisfactory in itself, a part of the poem is unsatisfactory; the poem is thus damaged beyond argument. If we deny this, we must surely explain ourselves very fully.

If we admit this, we are faced with another problem: is it conceivable that rational content and feeling-content may both be perfect, and yet that they may be unrelated to each other, or imperfectly related? To me this is inconceivable, because the emotional content of words is generated by our experience with the conceptual content, so that a relationship is necessary.

This fact of the necessity of such relationship may fairly return us for a moment to the original question: whether imperfection of rational content damages the entire poem. If there is a necessary relationship between concept and feeling, and concept is unsatisfactory, then feeling must be damaged by way of the relationship.

Sixth Problem

If there is a relationship between concept and feeling, what is the nature of that relationship?

To answer this, let us return to the basic unit, the word. The concept represented by the word, motivates the feeling which the word communicates. It is the concept of fire which generates the feelings communicated by the word, though the sound of the word may modify these feelings very subtly, as may other accidental qualities, especially if the word be used skillfully in a given context. The accidental qualities of a word, however, such as its literary history, for example, can only modify, cannot essentially change, for these will be governed ultimately by the concept; that is, *fire* will seldom be used to signify *plum-blossom*, and so will have few opportunities to gather connotations from the concept, *plum-blossom*. The relationship, in the poem, between rational statement and feeling, is thus seen to be that of motive to emotion.

Seventh Problem

But has not this reasoning brought us back to the proposition that all poems are equally good? For if each word motivates its own feeling, because of its intrinsic nature, will not any rational statement, since it is composed of words, motivate the feeling exactly proper to it?

This is not true, for a good many reasons, of which I shall enumerate only a few of the more obvious. In making a rational statement, in purely theoretical prose, we find that our statement may be loose or exact, depending upon the relationships of the words to each other. The precision of a word depends to some extent upon its surroundings. This is true likewise with respect to the connotations of words. Two words, each of which has several usably close rational synonyms, may reinforce and clarify each other with respect to their connotations or they may not do so.

Let me illustrate with a simple example from Browning's *Serenade at the Villa:*

> So wore night; the East was gray,
>   White the broad-faced hemlock flowers.

The lines are marred by a crowding of long syllables and difficult consonants, but they have great beauty in spite of the fault. What I wish to point out, for the sake of my argument, is the relationship between the words *wore* and *gray*. The verb *wore* means literally that the night passed, but it carries with it connotations of exhaustion and attrition which belong to the condition of the protagonist; and grayness is a color which we associate with such a condition. If we change the phrase to read: "Thus night passed," we shall have the same rational meaning, and a meter quite as respectable, but no trace of the power of the line: the connotation of *wore* will be lost, and the connotation of *gray* will remain merely in a state of ineffective potentiality. The protagonist in seeing his feeling mirrored in the landscape is not guilty of motivating his feeling falsely, for we know his general motive from the poem as a whole; he is expressing a portion of the feeling motivated by the total situation through a more or less common psychological phenomenon. If the poem were such, however, that we did not know why the night *wore* instead of *passed*, we should have just cause for complaint; in fact, most of the strength of the word would probably be lost. The second line contains other fine effects, immediately with reference to the first line, ultimately with reference to the theme; I leave the reader to analyze them for himself, but he will scarcely succeed without the whole poem before him.

Concepts, as represented by particular words, are affected by connotations due to various and curious accidents. A word may gather connotations from its use in folk-poetry, in formal poetry, in vulgar speech, or in technical prose: a single concept might easily be represented by four words with these distinct histories; and any one of the words might prove to be proper in a given poetic context. Words gain connotation from etymological accidents. Something of this may be seen in the English word *outrage*, in which is commonly felt, in all likelihood, something associated with *rage*, although there is no rage whatever in the original word. Similarly the word *urchin*, in modern English, seldom connotes anything related to hedgehogs, or to the familiars of the witches, by whose intervention the word arrived at its modern meaning and feeling. Yet the connotation proper to any stage in the history of such a word might be resuscitated, or a blend of connotations effected, by skillful use. Further, the connotation of a word may be modified very strongly by its function in the metrical structure, a matter which I shall discuss at length in connection with the theories of Ransom.

This is enough to show that exact motivation of feeling by concept is not inherent in any rational statement. Any rational statement will govern the general possibilities of feeling derivable from it, but the task of the poet is to adjust feeling to motive precisely. He has to select words containing not only the right relationships within themselves, but the right relationships to each other. The task is very difficult; and this is no doubt the reason why the great poetry of a great poet is likely to be very small in bulk.

Eighth Problem

Is it not possible, however, to escape from this relationship of motive to emotion by confining ourselves very largely to those words which denote emotion: love, envy, anger, and the like?

This is not possible, for these words, like others, represent concepts. If we should confine ourselves strictly to such a vocabulary, we should merely write didactic poetry: poetry about love in general, or about anger in general. The emotion communicated would result from our apprehension of the ideas in question. Such poetry is perfectly legitimate, but it is only one kind of poetry, and it is scarcely the kind which the Romantic theorist is endeavoring to define.

Such poetry has frequently been rendered particular by the use of allegory. The playful allegorizing of minor amoristic themes which one encounters in the Renaissance and which is possibly descended from certain neo-Platonic elements in medieval poetry may serve as illustration. Let us consider these and the subsequent lines by Thomas Lodge:

> Love in my bosom like a bee
>   Doth suck his sweet;
> Now with his wings he plays with me,
>   Now with his feet.

Love itself is a very general idea and might include many kinds of experience; the idea is limited by this allegory to the sentimental and sensual, but we still have an idea, the subdivision of the original idea, and the feeling must be appropriate to the concept. The concept is rendered concrete by the image of Cupid, whose actions, in turn, are rendered visible by comparison to the bee: it is these actions which make the poem a kind of anticipatory meditation on more or less sensual love, a meditation which by its mere tone of expression keeps the subject in its proper place as a very minor one. Sometimes the emphasis is on the mere description of the bee, sometimes on the description of Cupid, sometimes on the lover's feeling; but the feeling motivated in any passage is governed by this emphasis. The elements, once they are united in the poem, are never really separated, of course. In so far as the poet departs from his substantial theme in the direction of mere bees and flowers, he will achieve what Ransom calls irrelevance; but if there is much of this the poem will be weakened. Whether he so departs or not, the relation of motive to emotion must remain the same, within each passage. I have discussed this problem in my essay on Ransom.

A common romantic practice is to use words denoting emotions, but to use them loosely and violently, as if the very carelessness expressed emotion. Another is to make a general statement, but seem to refer it to a particular occasion, which, however, is never indicated: the poet thus seems to avoid the didactic, yet he is not forced to understand the particular motive. Both these faults may be seen in these lines from Shelley:

> Out of the day and night
> A joy has taken flight;
>   Fresh spring, and summer, and winter hoar,
> Move my faint heart with grief, but with delight
>   No more—oh, never more.

The poet's intention is so vague, however, that he achieves nothing but stereotypes of a very crude kind.

The Romantics often tried other devices. For example, it would be possible to write a poem on fear in general, but to avoid in some measure the effect of the purely didactic by illustrating the emotion along the way with various experiences which might motivate fear. There is a danger here, though it is merely a danger, that the general idea may not dominate the poem, and that the poem may thus fall apart into a group of poems on particular experiences. There is the alternative danger, that the particular quality of the experiences may be so subordinated to the illustrative function of the experiences, that within each illustration there is merely a stereotyped and not a real relationship of motive to feeling: this occurs in Collins' *Ode to Fear*, though a few lines in the Epode come surprisingly to life. But the methods which I have just described really offer no semblance of an escape from the theory of motivation which I am defending.

Another Romantic device, if it is conscious enough to be called a device, is to offer instead of a defensible motive a false one, usually culled from landscape. This kind of writing represents a tacit admission of the principle of motivation which I am defending, but a bad application of the principle. It results in the kind of writing which I have called pseudo-reference in my volume, *Primitivism and Decadence*. One cannot believe, for example, that Wordsworth's passions were charmed away by a look at the daffodils, or that Shelley's were aroused by the sight of the leaves blown about in the autumn wind. A motive is offered, and the poet wants us to accept it, but we recognize it as inadequate. In such a poem there may be fragments of good description, which motivate a feeling more or less purely appropriate to the objects described, and these fragments may sustain our liking for the poem: this happens in Collins' *Ode to Evening*; but one will find also an account of some kind of emotion essentially irrelevant to the objects described, along with the attempt, more or less explicit, to deduce the emotion from the object.

There remains the method of the Post-Romantics, whether French Symbolists or American Experimentalists: the method of trying to extinguish the rational content of language while retaining the content of association. This method I have discussed in *Primitivism and Decadence*, and I shall discuss it again in this book.

Ninth Problem

The relationship in the poem of rational meaning to feeling we have seen to be that of motive to emotion; and we have seen that this must be a satisfactory relationship. How do we determine whether such a relationship is satisfactory? We determine it by an act of moral judgment. The question then arises whether moral judgments can be made, whether the concept of morality is or is not an illusion.

If morality can be considered real, if a theory of morality can be said to derive from reality, it is because it guides us toward the greatest happiness which the accidents of life permit: that is, toward the fullest realization of our nature, in the Aristotelian or Thomistic sense. But is there such a thing, abstractly considered, as full realization of our nature?

To avoid discussion of too great length, let us consider the opposite question: is there such a thing as obviously unfulfilled human nature? Obviously there is. We need only turn to the feeble-minded, who cannot think and so cannot perceive or feel with any clarity; or to the insane, who sometimes perceive and feel with great intensity, but whose feelings and perceptions are so improperly motivated that they are classed as illusions. At slightly higher levels, the criminal, the dissolute, the unscrupulously selfish, and various types of neurotics are likely to arouse but little disagreement as examples.

Now if we are able to recognize the fact of insanity—if in fact we are forced to recognize it—that is, the fact of the obvious maladjustment of feeling to motive, we are forced to admit the possibility of more accurate adjustment, and, by necessary sequence, of absolutely accurate adjustment, even though we admit the likelihood that most people will attain to a final adjustment but very seldom indeed. We can guide ourselves toward such an adjustment in life, as in art, by means of theory and the critical examination of special instances; but the final act of judgment is in both life and art a unique act—it is a relationship between two elements, the rational understanding and the feeling, of which only one is classificatory and of which the other has infinite possibilities of variation.

Tenth Problem

If the final act of adjustment is a unique act of judgment, can we say that it is more or less right, provided it is demonstrably within the general limits prescribed by the theory of morality which has led to it? The answer to this question is implicit in what has preceded; in fact the answer resembles exactly that reached at the end of the first problem examined. We can say that it is more or less nearly right. If extreme deviation from right judgment is obvious, then there is such a thing as right judgment. The mere fact that life may be conducted in a fairly satisfactory manner, by means of inaccurate judgment within certain limits, and that few people ever bother to refine their judgment beyond the stage which enables them to remain largely within those limits, does not mean that accurate judgment has no reality. Implicit in all that has preceded is the concept that in any moral situation, there is a right judgment as an ultimate possibility; that the human judge, or actor, will approximate it more or less nearly; that the closeness of his approximation will depend upon the accuracy of his rational understanding and of his intuition, and upon the accuracy of their interaction upon each other.

Eleventh Problem

Nothing has thus far been said about human action, yet morality is supposed to guide human action. And if art is moral, there should be a relationship between art and human action.

The moral judgment, whether good, bad, or indifferent, is commonly the prelude and instigation to action. Hastily or carefully, intelligently or otherwise, one arrives at some kind of general idea of a situation calling for action, and one's idea motivates one's feeling: the act results. The part played by will, or the lack of it, between judgment and act, the possibility that action may be frustrated by some constitutional or habitual weakness or tendency, such as cowardice or a tendency to anger, in a person of a fine speculative or poetic judgment, are subjects for a treatise on ethics or psychology; a treatise on poetry stops with the consideration of the speculative judgment, which reaches its best form and expression in poetry. In the situations of daily life, one does not, as a rule, write a poem before acting: one makes a more rapid and simple judgment. But if the poem does not individually lead to a particular act, it does not prevent action. It gives us a better way of judging representative acts than we should otherwise have. It is thus a civilizing influence: it trains our power of judgment, and should, I imagine, affect the quality of daily judgments and actions.

Twelfth Problem

What, then, is the nature of the critical process?

It will consist (1) of the statement of such historical or biographical knowledge as may be necessary in order to understand the mind and method of the writer; (2) of such analysis of his literary theories as we may need to understand and evaluate what he is doing; (3) of a rational critique of the paraphrasable content (roughly, the motive) of the poem; (4) of a rational critique of the feeling motivated—that is, of the details of style, as seen in language and technique; and (5) of the final act of judgment, a unique act, the general nature of which can be indicated, but which cannot be communicated precisely, since it consists in receiving from the poet his own final and unique judgment of his matter and in judging that judgment. It should be noted that the purpose of the first four processes is to limit as narrowly as possible the region in which the final unique act is to occur.

In the actual writing of criticism, a given task may not require all of these processes, or may not require that all be given equal emphasis; or it may be that in connection with a certain writer, whether because of the nature of the writer or because of the way in which other critics have treated him previously, one or two of these processes must be given so much emphasis that others must be neglected for lack of space. These are practical matters to be settled as the occasions arise.

René Wellek

The Mode of Existence of a Literary Work of Art

This abstruse-sounding title[1] is the best name I can think of for a problem which is, in all sorts of disguises, widely discussed and of far-reaching importance both for critical theory and practice. What is meant by saying that a certain person does not understand the real poem? What is the real poem, where should we look for it, how does it exist? A correct answer to these questions must solve several critical problems and open a way to the proper analysis of a work of art. It, at least, will dispose of many pseudo-problems. We shall not, of course, find an answer to the question whether a given poem is good or bad, but we might find an answer which would tell us where to look for the genuine poem and how to avoid the pitfalls into which criticism has frequently fallen because of a lack of clarity on some of these fundamental semi-philosophical questions.

To the question what and where is a poem, or rather a literary work of art in general, several traditional answers have been given which must be criticized and eliminated before we can attempt an answer of our own. One of the most common and oldest answers is the view that a poem is an artifact, an object of the same nature as a piece of sculpture or a painting. Thus the work of art is considered identical with the black lines of ink on white paper or parchment or, if we think of a Babylonian poem, with the grooves in the brick. Obviously this answer is quite unsatisfactory. There is, first of all, the huge oral "literature" (a question-begging term in its etymology). There are poems or stories which have never been fixed in writing and still continue to exist. Thus the lines in black ink are merely a method of recording a poem which must be conceived as existing elsewhere. If we destroy the writing or even all copies of a printed book we still may not destroy the poem, as it might be preserved in oral tradition or in the memory of a man like Macaulay who boasted of knowing *Paradise Lost* and *Pilgrim's Progress* by heart. On the other hand, if we destroy a painting or a piece of sculpture or a building, we destroy it completely, though we may preserve descriptions or records in another medium and might even try to reconstruct what has been lost. But we shall always create a different work of art (however similar), while the mere destruction of the copy of a book or even of all its copies may not touch the work of art at all. That the writing on the paper is not the "real" poem can be demonstrated also by another argument. The printed page contains a great many elements which are extraneous to the poem: the size of the type, the sort of type used (roman, italic), the size of the page and many other factors. If we should take seriously the view that a poem is an artifact, we would have to come to the conclusion that every single copy is a different work of art. There would be no *a priori* reason why copies in different editions should be copies of the same book. Besides, not every printing is considered by us, the readers, a correct printing of a poem. The very fact that we are able to correct printer's errors in a text which we might not have read before or, in some rare cases, restore the genuine meaning of the text shows that we do not consider the printed lines as the genuine poem. In accepting, for instance, Theobald's emendation in the Hostess's story of Falstaff's death from "a table of green fields" to "a babbled of green fields" we do not give rein to our imagination nor do we correct and criticize the author as we should if we would change the color of a painting or chip off a piece of marble from a statue. We know that we have restored the genuine poem and that we have corrected a way of recording. Thus we have shown that the poem (or any literary work of art) can exist outside its printed version and that the printed artifact contains many elements which we all must consider as not included in the genuine poem.

Still, this negative conclusion should not blind us to the enormous practical importance, since the invention of writing and printing, of our methods of recording poetry. There is no doubt that much literature has been lost and thus completely destroyed because its written records have disappeared and the theoretically possible means of oral tradition have failed or have been interrupted. Writing and especially printing have made possible the continuity of literary tradition and must have done much to increase the unity and integrity of works of art. Besides, at least in certain periods of the history of poetry, the graphic picture has become a part of some finished works of art. I am thinking of such poems as the *Altar* or the *Church-floor* of George Herbert or of similar poems of the metaphysicals which can be paralleled on the Continent in Spanish Gongorism, Italian Marinism, in German Baroque poetry and elsewhere. Also modern poetry in America (E. E. Cummings), in Germany (Arno Holz), in France (Apollinaire) and elsewhere, has used graphic devices like unusual line arrangements or even beginnings at the bottom of the page, different colors of printing, etc. In the novel *Tristram Shandy*, Sterne used, as far back as the eighteenth century, blank and marbled pages. All such devices are integral parts of these particular works of art. Though we know that a majority of poetry is independent of them, they cannot and should not be ignored in those cases. Besides, the role of print in poetry is by no means confined to such comparatively rare extravaganzas; the line-ends of verses, the grouping into stanzas, the paragraphs of prose passages, eye-rhymes or puns which are comprehensible only through spelling and many similar devices must be considered integral factors of literary works of art. A purely oral theory tends to exclude all considerations of such devices, but they cannot be ignored in any complete analysis of many works of literary art. Their existence merely proves that print has become very important for the practice of poetry in modern times, that poetry is written for the eye as well as for the ear. Though the use of graphic devices is not indispensable, they are far more frequent in literature than in music, where the printed score is in a position similar to the printed page in poetry. In music such uses are rare, though by no means non-existent. There are many curious optical devices (colors, etc.) in Italian madrigal scores of the sixteenth century. The supposedly "pure" composer Handel wrote a chorus speaking of the Red Sea flood where the "water stood like a wall" and the notes on the printed page of music form firm rows of evenly spaced dots suggesting a phalanx or wall.

We have started with a theory which probably has not many serious adherents today. The second answer to our original question puts the essence of a literary work of art into the sequence of sounds uttered by a speaker or reader of poetry. This is a widely accepted solution favored especially by reciters. But the answer is equally unsatisfactory. Every reading aloud or reciting of a poem is merely a performance of a poem and not the poem itself. It is on exactly the same level as the performance of a piece of music by a musician. There is—to follow the line of our previous argument—a huge written literature which may never be sounded at all. To deny this, we have to subscribe to some such absurd theory as that of some behaviorists that all silent reading is accompanied by movements of the vocal cords. Actually, all experience shows that unless we are almost illiterate or are struggling with the reading of a foreign language or want to articulate the sound whisperingly on purpose we usually read "globally," that is, we grasp printed words as wholes without breaking them up into sequences of phonemes and thus do not pronounce them even silently. In reading quickly we have no time even to articulate the sounds with our vocal cords. To assume besides that a poem exists in the reading aloud leads to the absurd consequence that a poem is nonexistent when it is not sounded and that it is re-created afresh by every reading. Moreover, we could not show how a work like Homer's *Iliad*, or Tolstoy's *War and Peace*, exists as a unity as it can never be read aloud all in one sitting. But most importantly, every reading of a poem is more than the genuine poem: each performance contains elements which are extraneous to the poem and individual idiosyncrasies of pronunciation, pitch, tempo and distribution of stress—elements which are either determined by the personality of the speaker or are symptoms and means of his interpretation of the poem. Moreover, the reading of a poem not only adds individual elements but it always represents only a selection of factors implicit in the text of a poem: the pitch of the voice, the speed in which a passage is read, the distribution and intensity of the stresses, these may be either right or wrong, and even when right may still represent only one version of reading a poem. We must acknowledge the possibility of several readings of a poem: readings which we either consider wrong readings as we feel them as distortions of the true meaning of the poem or readings which we have to consider as correct and admissible, but still may not consider ideal. The reading of the poem is not the poem itself, as we can correct the performance mentally. Even if we hear a recitation which we acknowledge to be excellent or perfect we cannot preclude the possibility that somebody else, or even the same reciter at another time, may give a very different rendering which would bring out other elements of the poem equally well. The analogy to a musical performance is again helpful: the performance of a symphony even by Toscanini is not the symphony itself, as it is inevitably colored by the individuality of the performers and adds concrete details of tempo, rubato, timbre, etc. which may be changed in a next performance, though it would be impossible to deny that the same symphony has been performed for the second time. Thus we have shown that the poem can exist outside its sounded performance, and that the sounded performance contains many elements which we must consider as not included in the poem.

Still, in some literary works of art (especially in lyrical poetry) the vocal side of poetry may be an important factor of the general structure. Attention can be drawn to it by various means like meter, patterns of vowel or consonant sequences, alliteration, assonance, rhyme, etc. This fact explains—or rather helps to explain—the inadequacy of much translating of lyrical poetry, since these potential sound-patterns cannot be transferred into another linguistic system, though a skillful translator may approximate their general effect in his own language. There is, however, an enormous literature which is relatively independent of sound-patterns, as can be shown by the historical effects of many works in even pedestrian translations. But the importance of sound-patterns, in lyrical poetry, has also been frequently overrated for several reasons. One is the fact that most critics in speaking about the sound of poetry actually refer to effects induced by meaning. Apart from the associations aroused by the meaning most sound-structures are, purely as sound, indifferent. Mr. John Crowe Ransom has demonstrated amusingly how much the sound effect of Tennyson's verse depends on the meaning by suggesting a change from "the murmuring of innumerable bees" to "the murdering of innumerable beeves" which, though only slightly different as sound-pattern, completely alters the effect of the sound. Mr. I. A. Richards has made a similar experiment by taking a stanza from Milton's *Ode on Christ's Nativity* and rewriting it into nonsense words while keeping the meter and the vowel patterns as closely as possible. The poetic sound-effect has altogether disappeared. Another argument frequently quoted in support of the paramount importance of sound is the fact that we enjoy the sound of poetry read aloud in a foreign language, though we do not understand its meaning. Actually, in hearing foreign poetry recited we do not hear merely a sound-pattern, but the inflections of the voice, the changes of intonation; the gestures and physiognomy of the speaker convey much information on meaning. All this does not deny that sound may be an important factor in the structure of a poem, but the answer that a poem is a sequence of sounds is as unsatisfactory as the solution which puts faith in the print on the page.

The third, very common answer to our question says that a poem is the experience of the reader. A poem, it is argued, is nothing outside the mental processes of individual readers and is thus identical with the mental state or process which we experience in reading or listening to a poem. Again this "psychological" solution seems unsatisfactory. It is true, of course, that a poem can be known only through individual experiences, but it is not identical with such an individual experience. Every individual experience of a poem contains something idiosyncratic and purely individual. It is colored by our mood and our individual preparation. The education, the personality of every reader, the general cultural climate of a time, the religious or philosophical or purely technical preconceptions of every reader will add something instantaneous and extraneous to every reading of a poem. Two readings at different times by the same individual may vary considerably either because he has matured mentally or is weakened in his alertness by momentary circumstances such as fatigue, worry, or distraction. Every experience of a poem thus both leaves out something or adds something individual. The experience will never be commensurate with the poem: even a good reader will discover new details in poems which he had not experienced during previous readings and it is needless to point out how distorted or shallow may be the reading of a less trained or untrained reader. The view that the mental experience of a reader is the poem itself leads to the absurd conclusion that a poem is nonexistent unless experienced and that it is re-created in every experience. There thus would not be one *Divine Comedy*, but as many Divine Comedies as there are and were and will be readers. We end in complete scepticism and anarchy and arrive at the vicious maxim of *De gustibus non est disputandum*. If we should take this view seriously it would be impossible to explain why one experience of a poem by one reader should be better than the experience of any other reader and why it is possible to correct the interpretation of another reader. It would mean the definite end of all teaching of literature which aims at enhancing the understanding and appreciation of a text. The writings of Mr. I. A. Richards, especially his book on *Practical Criticism*, have shown how much can be done in analyzing the individual idiosyncrasies of readers and how much a good teacher can achieve in rectifying false approaches. Curiously enough, Mr. Richards, who constantly criticizes the experiences of his pupils, holds to an extreme psychological theory which is in flat contradiction to his excellent critical practice. The idea that poetry is supposed to order our impulses and the conclusion that the value of poetry is in some sort of psychical therapy leads him finally to the admission that this goal may be accomplished by a bad as well as a good poem, by a carpet as well as by a sonata. Thus the supposed pattern in our mind is not definitely related to the poem which caused it. The psychology of the reader, however interesting in itself or useful for pedagogical purposes, will always remain outside the object of literary study—the concrete work of art—and is unable to deal with the question of the structure and value of the work of art. Psychological theories must be theories of effect and may lead in extreme cases to such criteria of the value of poetry as that proposed by A. E. Housman in a lecture, *Name and Nature of Poetry* (1933), where he tells us (one hopes with his tongue in his cheek) that good poetry can be recognized by the thrill down our spine. This is on the same level as eighteenth-century theories which measured the quality of a tragedy by the amount of tears shed by the audience or the movie scout's conception of the quality of a comedy on the basis of the number of laughs he has counted in the audience. Thus anarchy, scepticism, a complete confusion of values, is the result of every psychological theory, as it must be unrelated either to the structure or the quality of a poem.

The psychological theory is only very slightly improved by Mr. I. A. Richards when he defines a poem as the "experience of the right kind of reader." Obviously the whole problem is shifted to the conception of the *right* reader—and the meaning of that adjective. But even assuming an ideal condition of mood in a reader of the finest background and the best training, the definition remains unsatisfactory as it is open to all criticism we have made of the psychological method. It puts the essence of the poem into a momentary experience which even the right kind of reader could not repeat unchanged. It will always fall short of the full meaning of a poem at any given instance and will always add the inevitable personal elements to the reading.

A fourth answer has been suggested to obviate this difficulty. The poem, we hear, is the experience of the author. Only in parenthesis, we may dismiss the view that the poem is the experience of the author at any time of his life after the creation of his work, when he rereads it. He then has obviously become simply a reader of his work and is liable to errors and misinterpretations of his own work almost as much as any other reader. Many instances of glaring misinterpretations by an author of his own work could be collected: the old anecdote about Browning professing not to understand his own poem has probably its element of truth. It happens to all of us that we misinterpret or do not fully understand what we have written some time ago. Thus the suggested answer must refer to the experience of the author during the time of creation. By experience of the author we might mean, however, two different things: the conscious experience, the intentions which the author wanted to embody in his work, or the total conscious and unconscious experience during the prolonged time of creation. The view that the genuine poem is to be found in the intentions of an author is widespread even though it is not always explicitly stated. It justifies much historical research and is at the bottom of many arguments in favor of specific interpretations. However, for most works of art we have no evidence to reconstruct the intentions of the author except the finished work itself. Even if we are in possession of contemporary evidence in the form of an explicit profession of intentions, such a profession need not be binding on a modern observer. "Intentions" of the author are always *a posteriori* rationalizations, commentaries which certainly must be taken into account but also must be criticized in the light of the finished work of art. The "intentions" of an author may go far beyond the finished work of art: they may be merely pronouncements of plans and ideals, while the performance may be either far below or far aside the mark. If we could have interviewed Shakespeare he probably would have expressed his intentions in writing *Hamlet* in a way which we should find most unsatisfactory. We would still quite rightly insist on finding meanings in *Hamlet* (and not merely inventing them) which were probably far from clearly formulated in Shakespeare's conscious mind.

Artists may be strongly influenced by a contemporary critical situation and by contemporary critical formulae while giving expression to their intentions, but the critical formulae themselves might be quite inadequate to characterize their actual artistic achievement. The baroque age is an obvious case in point, where a surprisingly new artistic practice found little expression either in the pronouncements of the artists or the comments of the critics. A sculptor such as Bernini could lecture to the Paris Academy expounding the view that his own practice was in strict conformity to that of the ancients, and Daniel Adam Poppelmann, the architect of that highly rococo building in Dresden called the Zwinger, wrote a whole pamphlet in order to demonstrate the strict agreement of his creation with the purest principles of Vitruvius. The metaphysical poets had only a few quite inadequate critical formulae (like "strong lines") which scarcely touch the actual novelty of their practice; and medieval artists frequently had purely religious or didactic "intentions" which do not even begin to give expression to the artistic principles of their practice. Divergence between conscious intention and actual performance is a common phenomenon in the history of literature. Zola sincerely believed in his scientific theory of the experimental novel, but actually produced highly melodramatic and symbolic novels. It is simply impossible to rely on the study of the intentions of an author, as they might not even represent a reliable commentary on his work, and at their best are not more than such a commentary.[2]

But also the alternative suggestion: that the genuine poem is in the total experience, conscious and unconscious, during the time of the creation, is very unsatisfactory. In practice this conclusion has the serious disadvantage of putting the problem into a completely inaccessible and purely hypothetical x which we have no means of reconstructing or even of exploring. Beyond this insurmountable practical difficulty, the solution is also unsatisfactory because it puts the existence of the poem into a subjective experience which already is a thing of the past. The experiences of the author during creation ceased precisely when the poem had begun to exist. If this conception were right, we should never be able to come into direct contact with the work of art itself, but have constantly to make the assumption that our experiences in reading the poem are in some way identical with the long past experiences of the author. Mr. E. M. Tillyard in his book on *Milton* has tried to use the idea that *Paradise Lost* is about the state of the author when he wrote it, and could not, in a long and frequently irrelevant exchange of arguments with C. S. Lewis, acknowledge that *Paradise Lost* is, first of all, about Satan and Adam and Eve and hundreds and thousands of different ideas, representations and concepts, rather than about Milton's state of mind during creation. That the whole content of a poem was once in contact with the conscious and subconscious mind of Milton is perfectly true, but this state of mind is inaccessible and might have been filled, in those particular moments, with millions of experiences of which we cannot find a trace in the poem itself. Taken literally, this whole solution must lead to absurd speculations about the exact duration of the state of mind of the creator and its exact content which might include a toothache at the moment of creation.[3] The whole psychological approach through states of mind whether of the reader or the listener or the speaker or the author raises more problems than it can possibly solve.

A better way is obviously in the direction of defining the work of art in terms of social and collective experience. There are two possibilities of solution which, however, still fall short of solving our problem satisfactorily. We may say that the work of art is the sum of all past and possible ex-

periences of the poem: a solution which leaves us with an infinity of irrelevant individual experiences, bad and false readings, perversions, etc.
In short, it merely gives us the answer that the poem is in the state of
mind of its reader, multiplied by infinity. The other answer I have seen
suggested solves the question by stating that the genuine poem is the experience common to all the experiences of the poem. But this answer
would obviously reduce the work of art to the common denominator of all
these experiences. This denominator must be the *lowest* common denominator, the most shallow, most superficial and trivial experience.
This solution, besides its practical difficulties, would completely impov-
erish the total meaning of a work of art.

II

An answer to our question in terms of individual or social psychology
cannot, I am convinced, be found. A poem, we have to conclude, is not an
individual experience or a sum of experiences, but only a potential cause
of experiences. Definition in terms of states of mind fails because it cannot account for the normative character of the genuine poem, for the simple fact that it might be experienced correctly or incorrectly. In every individual experience only a small part can be considered as adequate to the
true poem. Thus, the real poem must be conceived as a system of norms,
realized only partially in the actual experience of its many readers. Every
single experience (reading, reciting, and so forth) is only an attempt—
more or less successful and complete—to grasp this set of norms or standards.
    The term "norms" as used here should not, of course, be confused
with norms which are either classical or romantic, ethical or political.
The norms we have in mind are implicit norms which have to be extracted
from every individual experience of a work of art and together make up
the genuine work of art as a whole. It is true, that if we compare works of
art among themselves, similarities or differences between these norms
will be ascertained, and from the similarities themselves it ought to be
possible to proceed to a classification of works of art according to the type
of norms they embody. We may finally arrive at theories of genres and ultimately at theories of literature in general. To deny this as it has been denied by those who, with some justification, stress the uniqueness of every
work of art, seems to push the conception of individuality so far that
every work of art would become completely isolated from tradition and
thus finally both incommunicable and incomprehensible. Assuming that
we have to start with the analysis of an individual work of art, we still can
scarcely deny that there must be some links, some similarities, some

common elements or factors which would approximate two or more given works of art and thus would open the door to a transition from the analysis of one individual work of art to a type such as Greek tragedy and hence to tragedy in general, to literature in general, and finally to some all-inclusive structure common to all arts.

But this is a further problem. We, however, have still to decide where and how these norms exist. A closer analysis of a work of art will show that it is best to think of it as not merely one system of norms, but rather a system which is made up of several strata, each implying its own subordinate group. There is a system of norms implied in the sound-structure of a literary work of art and this, in turn, implies units of meaning based on the sentence patterns, and these units in their turn construct a world of objects to which the meaning refers. It is useful to illustrate this conception by the parallel which can be drawn from linguistics. Linguists such as the Geneva school and the Prague Linguistic Circle carefully distinguish between *langue* and *parole,* the system of language and the individual speech-act; and this distinction corresponds to that between the individual experience of the poem and the poem as such. The system of language is a collection of conventions and norms whose workings and relations we can observe and describe as having a fundamental coherence and identity in spite of the very different, imperfect or incomplete pronouncements of individual speakers. In this respect at least, a literary work of art is in exactly the same position as a system of language. We as individuals shall never realize it completely as we shall never use our own language completely and perfectly. The very same situation is actually exhibited in every single act of cognition. We shall never know an object in all its qualities, but still we can scarcely deny the identity of objects even though we may see them from different perspectives. We always grasp some "structure of determination" in the object which makes the act of cognition not an act of arbitrary invention of subjective distinctions, but the recognition of some norms imposed on us by reality. Similarly the structure of a work of art has the character of a "duty which I have to realize." I shall always realize it imperfectly, but in spite of some incompleteness, a certain "structure of determination" remains, just as in any other object of knowledge.

• • •

Just as modern linguists have analyzed the potential sounds as phonemes, they can also analyze morphemes and syntagmas. The sentence, for instance, can be described not merely as an *ad hoc* utterance, but as a syntactic pattern. Outside of phonemics, modern functional linguistics is still comparatively undeveloped, but the problems, though difficult, are not insoluble or completely new: they are rather restatements of the morphological and syntactical questions as they were discussed in older grammars. The analysis of a literary work of art has to cope with parallel problems, with units of meaning and their specific organization towards aesthetic purposes. Such problems as those of poetic semantics and diction and imagery are reintroduced in a new and more careful restatement which avoids the pitfalls of the psychological and impressionist approaches. Units of meaning, sentences and sentence-structures refer to objects, construct imaginative realities such as landscapes, interiors, characters, actions, or ideas. These also can be analyzed in a way which does not confuse them with empirical reality and does not ignore the fact that they inhere in linguistic structures. A figure in a novel or play grows only out of the units of meaning, is made of the sentences either pronounced by the figure or pronounced about it. It has an indeterminate structure in comparison with a biological person who has his coherent past. Thus speculations about Hamlet's studies in Wittenberg or his father's influence on his youth, or the number of Lady Macbeth's children are shown as confusions between fiction and reality, of the same order as if a spectator should try to find the continuation of a picture under its frame. The advantage of all these distinctions of strata is that they supersede the age-old superficial and misleading distinction of content and form. The content will reappear in close contact with the linguistic substratum, in which it is implied and on which it is dependent.

But this conception of the literary work of art as a stratified system of norms still leaves undetermined the actual mode of existence of this system. To deal with this matter properly we should have to solve such questions as those of nominalism versus realism, mentalism versus behaviorism,—in short, all main problems of epistemology. For our purposes it will be, it seems, sufficient to steer clear of two opposite pitfalls, of the Charybdis of Platonism and the Scylla of extreme nominalism as it is advocated today by behaviorists and some positivists. There is no need to hypostatize or "reify" this system of norms to make it a sort of Platonic idea floating in a timeless void of essences. The literary work of art is not of the same ontological status as the idea of a triangle, or of a number, or a quality like "redness." In difference from such "subsistences" the literary work of art is, first of all, created at a certain point in time, and secondly is subject to change and even complete destruction. In this respect it rather resembles the system of language, though the exact moment of creation or death is probably much less clearly definable in the case of language than with the literary work of art which is usually an individual creation. Also language, of course, is no Platonic essence, immutable and indestructible. On the other hand, one should recognize that an extreme nominalism which rejects the concept of a "system of language" and thus of a work of art in our sense, or admits it only as a useful fiction or a "scientific description," misses the whole problem and the point at issue. All these objections are founded on the extremely narrow preconception of behaviorism which declares anything to be "mystical" or "metaphysical" which does not conform to a very limited conception of empirical reality. To call the phoneme a "fiction" or the system of language merely a "scientific description of speech-acts" is to ignore the problem of truth. We recognize norms and deviations from norms and do not merely devise some purely verbal descriptions. The whole behaviorist point of view is, in this respect, based on a bad theory of abstraction. Numbers or norms are what they are whether we construct them or not. Certainly I perform the counting, I perform the reading, but number-presentation or recognition of a norm is not the same as the number or norm itself. The pronouncement of the sound h is not the phoneme h. We recognize some structure of norms within reality and do not simply invent verbal constructs. The objection that we have access to these norms only through individual acts of cognition and that we cannot get out of these acts or beyond them, is only apparently impressive. It is the objection which has been made to Kant's criticism of our cognition and can be refuted with the Kantian arguments. It is true we are ourselves liable to misunderstandings and lack of comprehension of these norms, but this does not mean that the critic assumes a superhuman role of criticizing our comprehension from the outside or that he pretends to grasp the perfect whole of the system of norms in some act of intellectual intuition. We criticize rather a part of our knowledge in the light of the higher standard set by another part. We are not supposed to put ourselves into the position of a man who, in order to test his vision, tries to look at his own eyes, but into the position of a man who compares the objects he sees clearly with those he sees only dimly, makes then generalizations as to the kinds of objects which fall into the two classes, and explains the difference by some theory of vision which takes account of distance, light, and so forth.

Analogously, we can distinguish between right and wrong readings of a poem, or between a recognition or a distortion of the norms implicit in a work of art by acts of comparison, by a study of different false or incomplete realizations. We can study the actual workings, relations, and combinations of these norms, just as the phoneme can be studied. The literary work of art is neither an empirical fact, in the sense of being a state of mind of any given individual or of any group of individuals, nor is it an ideal changeless object such as a triangle. The work of art may become an object of experience; it is, we admit, accessible only through individual experience, but it is not identical with any experience. It differs from ideal objects such as numbers precisely because it is accessible only through the empirical part of its structure, the sound-system, while a triangle or a number can, I presume, be intuited directly. It also differs from ideal objects in one important respect. It has something which can be called

"Life." It arises at a certain point of time, changes in the course of history and may perish. A work of art is "timeless" only in the sense that, if preserved, it has some fundamental structure of identity since its creation, but it is "historical" too. It has a development which can be described. This development is nothing but the series of concretizations of a given work of art in the course of history which we may, to a certain extent, reconstruct from the reports of critics and readers about their experiences and judgments and the effect of a given work of art on other works. Our consciousness of earlier concretizations (readings, criticisms, misinterpretations) will affect our own experience: earlier readings may educate us to a deeper understanding or may cause a violent reaction against the prevalent interpretations of the past. All this shows the importance of the history of criticism, or in linguistics, of historical grammar, and leads to difficult questions about the nature and limits of individuality. How far can a work of art be said to be changed and still remain identical? The *Iliad* still "exists," that is, it can become again and again effective and is thus different from a historical phenomenon like the battle of Waterloo which is definitely past, though its course may be reconstructed and its effects may be felt even today. In what sense can we, however, speak of an identity between the *Iliad* as the contemporary Greeks heard or read it, and the *Iliad* we now read? Even assuming that we know the identical text, our actual experience must be very different. We cannot contrast its language with the everyday language of Greece, and cannot therefore feel the deviations from colloquial language on which much of the poetic effect must depend. We are unable to understand many verbal ambiguities which are an essential part of every poet's meaning. Obviously it requires in addition some imaginative effort, which can have only very partial success, to think ourselves back into the Greek belief in gods, or the Greek scale of moral values. Still, it could scarcely be denied that there is a substantial identity of structure which has remained the same throughout the ages. This structure, however, is dynamic: it changes throughout the process of history while passing through the minds of its readers, critics and fellow artists. Thus the system of norms is growing and changing and will remain, in some sense, always incompletely and imperfectly realized. But this dynamic conception does not mean mere subjectivism and relativism. All the different points of view are by no means equally right. It will always be possible to determine which point of view grasps the subject most thoroughly and deeply. A hierarchy of viewpoints, a criticism of the grasp of norms, is implied in the concept of the adequacy of interpretation. All relativism is ultimately defeated by the recognition that the Absolute is in the relative, though not finally and fully in it.

The work of art, then, appears as an object of knowledge *sui generis* which has a special ontological status. It is neither real (like a statue) nor mental (like the experience of light or pain) nor ideal (like a triangle). It is a system of norms of ideal concepts which are intersubjective. They must be assumed to exist in collective ideology, changing with it, accessible only through individual mental experiences, based on the sound-structure of its sentences.

Our interpretation of the literary work of art as a system of norms has served its purpose if it has suggested an argument against the insidious psychological relativism which must always end in scepticism and finally mental anarchy. It may also have demonstrated the truism—of which we cannot be reminded too frequently—that all problems, pursued far enough, even in such an apparently concrete and limited field as literary criticism, lead to ultimate questions and decisions about the nature of reality and truth, the processes of our cognition and the motives of our actions.

We have avoided the problem of value: no distinction could be made between a good and bad literary work of art in our context. But I am convinced that a profitable discussion of the problem of value and valuation has to begin with the recognition of the work of art as a system of norms.

NOTES

1. Part of this paper is an elaboration of a passage in my "Theory of Literary History" (in the *Travaux du Cercle Linguistique de Prague* VI, 1936, 173–191. There detailed acknowledgements are made to the linguistic theories of the Prague Linguistic Circle as well as to the logical theories of Edmund Husserl and his Polish pupil Roman Ingarden.
2. There can be no objections against the study of "intention," if we mean by it merely a study of the integral work of art which would not ignore some elements and would be directed to the total meaning. But this use of the term "intention" is different and somewhat misleading. [*Author's note.*] See "The Intentional Fallacy," by W. K. Wimsatt, Jr. and M. C. Beardsley: *Sewanee Review,* 54 (Summer, 1946), 458, 488. And "A Note on Intentions" by R. W. Stallman: *College English,* 10 (October, 1948), 40–41. [*Editor's note.*]
3. M. Pierre Audiat, who, in his well-known *Biographie de l'oeuvre littéraire* (1925), has argued that the work of art "represents a period in the life of the writer," actually becomes involved in such impossible and quite unnecessary dilemmas. [*Author's note.*]

Kenneth Burke

The Philosophy of Literary Form

Situations and Strategies

Let us suppose that I ask you: "What did the man say?" And that you answer: "He said 'yes.'" You still do not know what the man said. You would not know unless you knew more about the situation, and about the remarks that preceded his answer.

Critical and imaginative works are answers to questions posed by the situation in which they arose. They are not merely answers, they are *strategic* answers, *stylized* answers. For there is a difference in style or strategy, if one says "yes" in tonalities that imply "thank God" or in tonalities that imply "alas!" So I should propose an initial working distinction between "strategies" and "situations," whereby we think of poetry (I here use the term to include any work of critical or imaginative cast) as the adopting of various strategies for the encompassing of situations. These strategies size up the situations, name their structure and outstanding ingredients, and name them in a way that contains an attitude towards them.

This point of view does not, by any means, vow us to personal or historical subjectivism. The situations are real; the strategies for handling them have public content; and in so far as situations overlap from individual to individual, or from one historical period to another, the strategies possess universal relevance.

Situations do overlap, if only because men now have the same neural and muscular structure as men who have left their records from past ages. We and they are in much the same biological situation. Furthermore, even the concrete details of social texture have a great measure of overlap. And the nature of the human mind itself, with the function of abstraction rooted in the nature of language, also provides us with "levels of generalization" (to employ Korzybski's term) by which situations greatly different in their particularities may be felt to belong in the same class (to have a common substance or essence).

Consider a proverb, for instance. Think of the endless variety of situations, distinct in their particularities, which this proverb may "size up," or attitudinally name. To examine one of my favorites: "Whether the pitcher strikes the stone, or the stone the pitcher, it's bad for the pitcher." Think of some primitive society in which an incipient philosopher, in disfavor with the priests, attempted to criticize their lore. They are powerful, he is by comparison weak. And they control all the channels of power. Hence, whether they attack him or he attacks them, he is the loser. And he could quite adequately size up this situation by saying, "Whether the pitcher strikes the stone, or the stone the pitcher, it's bad for the pitcher." Or Aristophanes could well have used it, in describing his motivation when, under the threats of political dictatorship, he gave up the lampooning of political figures and used the harmless Socrates as his goat instead. Socrates was propounding new values—and Aristophanes, by aligning himself with conservative values, against the materially powerless dialectician, could himself take on the rôle of the stone in the stone-pitcher ratio. Or the proverb could be employed to name the predicament of a man in Hitler's Germany who might come forward with an argument, however well reasoned, against Hitler. Or a local clerk would find the proverb apt, if he would make public sport of his boss. These situations are all distinct in their particularities; each occurs in a totally different texture of history; yet all are classifiable together under the generalizing head of the same proverb.

Might we think of poetry as complex variants and recombinations of such material as we find in proverbs? There are situations typical and recurrent enough for men to feel the need of having a name for them. In sophisticated work, this naming is done with great complexity. Think of how much modern psychology, for instance, might be placed as a highly alembicated way of *seeing through to the end* the formulation now become proverbial: "The wish is father to the thought." Or think of how much in the Hegelian dialectic might be summed up, as an over-all title, in the idealist Coleridge's favorite proverb, "Extremes meet." And in all work, as in proverbs, the naming is done "strategically" or "stylistically," in modes that embody attitudes, of resignation, solace, vengeance, expectancy, etc.

Magic and Religion

In addition to the leads or cues, for the analysis of poetic strategy, that we get from proverbs, with their strongly realistic element, we may get leads from magic and religion.

Magic, verbal coercion, establishment or management by decree, says, in effect: " 'Let there be'—and there was." And men share in the magical resources of some power by speaking "in the name of" that power. As Ogden and Richards remind us in *The Meaning of Meaning,* modern Biblical scholarship has disclosed that we should interpret in this wise the formula, "taking the name of the Lord in vain." The formula referred to the offense of conjuring for malign purposes by uttering one's magical decrees "in the name of" the Lord.

The device, in attenuated and alembicated variants, is not so dead, or even so impotent, as one might at first suppose. Today, for instance, we are facing problems that arise from an attempt to fit private enterprise with the requirements of the citizenry as a whole. Think of the difference in magic if you confront this situation *in the strategic name of* "planned economy" or, employing a different strategy, *in the name of* "regimentation."

The magical decree is implicit in all language; for the mere act of naming an object or situation decrees that it is to be singled out as such-and-such rather than as something-other. Hence, I think that an attempt to *eliminate* magic, in this sense, would involve us in the elimination of vocabulary itself as a way of sizing up reality. Rather, what we may need is *correct* magic, magic whose decrees about the naming of real situations is the closest possible approximation to the situation named (with the greater accuracy of approximation being supplied by the "collective revelation" of testing and discussion).

If magic says, "*Let there be* such and such," religion says, "*Please do* such and such." The decree of magic, the petition of prayer. Freud has discussed the "optative as indicative" in dreams (where "would that it were" is stylistically rephrased: "it is"—as when the dreamer, desiring to be rid of a certain person, dreams that this person is departing). Neopositivism has done much in revealing the secret commands and exhortations in words—as Edward M. Maisel, in *An Anatomy of Literature,* reveals in a quotation from Carnap, noting how the apparent historical creed: "There is only one race of superior men, say the race of Hottentots, and this race alone is worthy of ruling other races. Members of these other races are inferior," should be analytically translated as: "Members of the race of Hottentots! Unite and battle to dominate the other races!" The "facts" of the historical assertion here are but a strategy of inducement (apparently describing the *scene* for the action of a drama, they are themselves a dramatic *act prodding to a further dramatic act*).

It is difficult to keep the magical decree and the religious petition totally distinct. Though the distinction between the coercive command and the conducive request is clear enough in its extremes, there are many borderline cases. Ordinarily, we find three ingredients interwoven in a given utterance: the spell and the counter-spell, the curse; the prayer and the prayer-in-reverse, oath, indictment, invective; the dream, and the dream gone sour, nightmare.

So, taking this ingredient as common to all verbal action, we might make the following three subdivisions for the analysis of an act in poetry:

> dream (the unconscious or subconscious factors in a poem—the factor slighted by the Aristotelians, though by no means left unconsidered, as John Crowe Ransom's chapters on "The Cathartic Principle" and "The Mimetic Principle" in *The World's Body* make apparent),
>
> prayer (the communicative functions of a poem, which leads us into the many considerations of form, since the poet's inducements can lead us to participate in his poem only in so far as his work has a public, or communicative, structure—the factor slighted by the various expressionistic doctrines, the Art for Art's Sake school stressing the work solely as the poet's externalizing of himself, or naming of his own peculiar number),
>
> chart (the realistic sizing-up of situations that is sometimes explicit, sometimes implicit, in poetic strategies—the factor that Richards and the psychoanalysts have slighted).

It may annoy some persons that I take the realistic chart to possess "magical" ingredients. That is, if you size up a situation in the name of regimentation you *decree* it a different essence than if you sized it up in the name of planned economy. The choice here is not a choice between magic and no magic, but a choice between magics that vary in their degree of approximation to the truth. In both these magics, for instance, there is usually an assumption (or implied *fiat*) to the effect that increased industrial production is itself a good. But when we recall that every increase in the *consumption* of natural resources could with equal relevance be characterized as a corresponding increase in the *destruction* of natural resources, we can glimpse the opportunity for a totally different magic here, that would size up the situation by a different quality of namings. And when I read recently of an estimate that more soil had been lost through erosion in the last twenty years than in all the rest of human history, I began to ask whether either the "regimentation" magic or the "planned economy" magic is a close enough approximate for the naming of the situation in which we now are. The "regimentation" magic is on its face by far the worse, since its implicit demand, "Let us have no collective control over production," calls for as much wastage as is possible in an ailing property structure. But this wastage is, ironically, curtailed mainly by the maladjustments of the very property structure that the "regimentation" magic would perpetuate. The "planned economy" magic is much superior, but only when corrected by a criticism of "new needs." It is a menace when combined, as it usually is, with a doctrine that increased industrial output is synonymous with "progress." The irony is that a readjusted property structure would make possible greater wastage (or "consumption") than our present ailing one. Hence, the magic that made greater production possible would be the worst of calamities unless corrected by another magic decreeing that many of our present kinds of industrial output are culturally sinister.

The ideal magic is that in which our assertions (or verbal decrees) as to the nature of the situation come closest to a correct gauging of that situation as it actually is. Any *approximate* chart is a "decree." Only a *completely accurate* chart would dissolve magic, by making the structure of names identical with the structure named. This latter is the kind of chart that Spinoza, in his doctrine of the "adequate idea," selected as the goal of philosophy, uniting free will and determinism, since the "So be it" is identical with the "It must be so" and the "It is so." A completely adequate chart would, of course, be possible only to an infinite, omniscient mind.

"It is (morally or technically) wrong" is a stylized variant of "Don't do it." However, to note this translation of a command into the idiom of realism must not be taken as identical with a "debunking" of the verbal assertion. For a command may be a good command, involving a strategy that is quite accurate for encompassing the situation. Science simultaneously admits and conceals the element of *fiat* in a calculus by Latinistic stylization, as when it explicitly states the commands basic to a calculus but couches these in terms of "postulates" (*postulatum:* command, demand), a kind of "*provisory* command," in keeping with the customary trend towards *attenuation* in scientific stylizations. It replaces "big commands" with a whole lot of "little commands" that fall across one another on the bias, quite as modern poetry has replaced the "big spell" with a lot of "little spells," each work pulling us in a different direction and these directions tending to cancel off one another, as with the conflicting interests of a parliament.

Symbolic Action

We might sum all this up by saying that poetry, or any verbal act, is to be considered as "symbolic action." But though I must use this term, I object strenuously to having the general perspective labeled as "symbolism." I recognize that people like to label, that labeling *comforts* them by *getting things placed.* But I object to "symbolism" as a label, because it suggests too close a link with a particular school of poetry, the Symbolist Movement, and usually implies the unreality of the world in which we live, as though nothing could be what it is, but must always be something else (as though a house could never be a house, but must be, let us say, the concealed surrogate for a woman, or as though the woman one marries could never be the woman one marries, but must be a surrogate for one's mother, etc.).

Still, there is a difference, and a radical difference, between building a house and writing a poem about building a house—and a poem about having children by marriage is not the same thing as having children by marriage. There are *practical* acts, and there are symbolic acts (nor is the distinction, clear enough in its extremes, to be dropped simply because there is a borderline area wherein many practical acts take on a symbolic ingredient, as one may buy a certain commodity not merely to use it, but also because its possession testifies to his enrollment in a certain stratum of society).

The symbolic act is the *dancing of an attitude* (a point that Richards has brought out, though I should want to revise his position to the extent of noting that in Richards' doctrines the attitude is pictured as too sparse in realistic content). In this attitudinizing of the poem, the whole body may finally become involved, in ways suggested by the doctrines of behaviorism. The correlation between mind and body here is neatly conveyed in two remarks by Hazlitt, concerning Coleridge:

> I observed that he continually crossed me on the way by shifting from one side of the foot-path to the other. This struck me as an odd movement; but I did not at that time connect it with any instability of purpose or involuntary change of principle, as I have done since. . . .
> There is a *chaunt* in the recitation both of Coleridge and Wordsworth, which acts as a spell upon the hearer, and disarms the judgment. Perhaps they have deceived themselves by making habitual use of this ambiguous accompaniment. Coleridge's manner is more full, animated, and varied; Wordsworth's more equable, sustained, and internal. The one might be termed more *dramatic*, the other more *lyrical*. Coleridge has told me that he himself liked to compose in walking over uneven ground, or breaking through the straggling branches of a copse-wood; whereas Wordsworth always wrote (if he could) walking up and down a straight gravel-walk, or in some spot where the continuity of his verse met with no collateral interruption.[1]

We might also cite from a letter of Hopkins, mentioned by R. P. Blackmur in *The Kenyon Review* (Winter, 1939):

> As there is something of the "old Adam" in all but the holiest men and in them at least enough to make them understand it in others, so there is an old Adam of barbarism, boyishness, wildness,

rawness, rankness, the disreputable, the unrefined in the refined and educated. It is that that I meant by tykishness (a tyke is a stray sly unowned dog).

Do we not glimpse the labyrinthine mind of Coleridge, the *puzzle* in its pace, "danced" in the act of walking—and do we not glimpse behind the agitated rhythm of Hopkins' verse, the conflict between the priest and the "tyke," with the jerkiness of his lines "symbolically enacting" the mental conflict? So we today seem to immunize ourselves to the arhythmic quality of both traffic and accountancy by a distrust of the lullaby and the rocking cradle as formative stylistic equipment for our children.

The accumulating lore on the nature of "psychogenic illnesses" has revealed that something so "practical" as a bodily ailment may be a "symbolic" act on the part of the body which, in this materialization, *dances* a corresponding state of mind, reordering the glandular and neural behavior of the organism in obedience to mind-body correspondences, quite as the formal dancer reorders his externally observable gesturing to match his attitudes. Thus, I know of a man who, going to a dentist, was proud of the calmness with which he took his punishment. But after the session was ended, the dentist said to him: "I observe that you are very much afraid of me. For I have noted that, when patients are frightened, their saliva becomes thicker, more sticky. And yours was exceptionally so." Which would indicate that, while the man in the dentist's chair was "dancing an attitude of calmness" on the public level, as a social facade, on the purely bodily or biological level his salivary glands were "dancing his true attitude." For he *was* apprehensive of pain, and his glandular secretions "said so." Similarly I have read that there is an especially high incidence of stomach ulcers among taxi drivers—an occupational illness that would not seem to be accounted for merely by poor and irregular meals, since these are equally the lot of workers at other kinds of jobs. Do we not see, rather, a bodily response to the intensely arhythmic quality of the work itself, the irritation in the continual jagginess of traffic, all puzzle and no pace, and only the timing of the cylinders performing with regularity, as if all the *ritual* of the occupational act had been drained off, into the *routine* of the motor's explosions and revolutions?

In such ways, the whole body is involved in an enactment. And we might make up a hypothetical illustration of this sort: imagine a poet who, on perfectly rational grounds rejecting the political and social authority of the powers that be, wrote poems enacting this attitude of rejection. This position we might call his symbolic act on the abstract level. On the personal, or intimate level, he might embody the same attitude in a vindictive style (as so much of modern work, proud of its emancipation from prayer, has got this emancipation dubiously, by simply substituting

prayer-in-reverse, the oath). And on the biological level, this same attitude might be enacted in the imagery of excretion, as with the scene of
vomiting with which Farrell ends the second volume of his Studs Lonigan
trilogy.

Sir Richard Paget's theory of gesture speech gives us inklings of the
way in which such enactment might involve even the selection of words
themselves on a basis of tonality. According to Paget's theory, language
arose in this wise: If a man is firmly gripping something, the muscles of
his tongue and throat adopt a position in conformity with the muscles
with which he performs the act of gripping. He does not merely grip with
his hands; he "grips all over." Thus, in conformity with the act of gripping, he would simultaneously grip with his mouth, by closing his lips
firmly. If, now, he uttered a sound with his lips in this position, the only
sound he could utter would be m. M therefore is the sound you get when
you "give voice" to the posture of gripping. Hence, m would be the proper
tonality corresponding to the act of gripping, as in contact words like
"maul," "mix," "mammae," and "slam." The relation between sound
and sense here would not be an onomatopoetic one, as with a word like
"sizzle," but it would rather be like that between the visual designs on a
sound track and the auditory vibrations that arise when the instrument
has "given voice" to these designs (except that, in the case of human
speech, the designs would be those of the tongue and throat, plastic rather
than graphic).

The great resistance to Paget's theory doubtless arises in large part
from the conservatism of philological specialists. They have an investment in other theories—and only the most pliant among them are likely
to see around the corner of their received ideas (Paget cites remarks by Jes-
persen that hit about the edges of his theory). But some of the resistance,
I think, also arises from an error in Paget's strategy of presentation. He
offers his theory as a *philological* one, whereas it should be offered as a
contribution to *poetics*. Philology, because of its involvement in historicism, really deals with *the ways in which, if Paget's theory were 100 per
cent correct, such linguistic mimesis as he is discussing would become
obscured by historical accretions.*

Let us suppose, for instance, that *f* is an excellent linguistic gesture
for the *p* sound prolonged, and the lips take the posture of *p* in the act of
spitting—hence, the *p* is preserved in the word itself, in "spittle" and
"puke," and in words of re*p*ulsion and re*p*ugnance. The close phonetic relation between *p* and *f* is observed in the German exclamation of repug-
nance, *"pfui."* Mencken, in *The American Language*, cites two synthetic
words by Winchell that perfectly exemplify this faugh-*f:* "phfft" and
"foofff." These are "nonsense syllables" Winchell has invented to convey,
by tonality alone, the idea that is denoted in our word *"pest."* Here, since

the inventor has complete freedom, there are no historical accidents of language to complicate his mimesis, so he can symbolically spit long and hard.

Imagine, however, a new movement arising in history—and, as is so often the case with new movements, imagine that it is named by the enemy (as "liberalism" was named by the Jesuits, to convey connotations of "licentiousness," in contrast with *"servile,"* to convey connotations of "loyal"). If we hypothetically grant the existence of a faugh-*f*, we should discover that the enemy danced the attitude towards this new movement with perfect accuracy in naming the new movement "phfftism" or "foofff-ism." However, as so often happens in history, the advocates of "foofff-ism" accepted the term, and set out to "live it down" (as with "liberal-ism"—and also "nihilism," which was named by the enemy, but in the late nineteenth century recruited nihilistic *heroes*). And let us finally imagine, as so often happens in history, that the new movement, begin-ning in great disrepute, finally triumphs and becomes the norm. Though the attitude towards the name is now changed, the name itself may be re-tained, and so we may find earnest fellows saying, "I hereby solemnly swear allegiance to the flag of foofffism."

Now, philology would deal with these historical developments whereby the originally accurate mimesis became *obscured*—and it is in this sense that, to my way of thinking, Paget's theory should be presented as a contribution not to philology, but to poetics. The greatest attempt at a *poetics* of sound is Dante's *De Vulgari Eloquio,* which is equally con-cerned with a *rational selection* of a poetic language, its systematic iso-lation from a common speech that had developed by the hazards of his-torical accretion. And Paget's theory should, I contend, be viewed as a corresponding enterprise, except that now, given the change of reference from Dante's day to ours, the theory is grounded on a *biological* or *natu-ralistic* base.

A possible way whereby these theories might be empirically tested is this: We should begin by asking whether our system of phonetic recording might be inaccurate. Might there, for instance, be at least *two* sounds of *f*, whereas both were recorded in writing as the same sound (as in French three different sounds of *e* are explicitly indicated, whereas the English ways of recording *e* do not indicate such differences)? Why, in the light of such evidence, should we assume that there is but one *f* simply because our mode of recording this sound indicates but one? Might there, let us say, be a faugh-*f* and a flower-*f* (with the second trying to bring out the smoothness of *f*, as were one to recite sympathetically Coleridge's line, "Flowers are lovely, love is flowerlike," and the other trying to stress its expulsive quality, as when I once heard a reactionary orator, spewing forth a spray of spittle, fulminate against "fiery, frenzied fanatics")? I do not know how accurate the electric recordings of a sound-track are, or how close a microscopic analysis of them could be: but if these recordings are accurate enough, and if microscopic analysis can be refined to the point of discriminating very minute differences in the design of the sound-track, one could select flower-passages and faugh-passages, have them recited by a skilled actor (without telling him of the theory), take an electric recording of his recitation, and then examine the sound-track for *quantitative* evidence (in the design of the sound-track) of a distinction in *f* not indicated by our present conventions of writing. We might perhaps more accurately use *two* symbols, thus: *f'* and *f"*. *It should be noted, however, that such a difference would not be absolute and constant.* That is, one might pronounce a word like "of" differently if it appeared expressively in a "flower" context than if it appeared in a "faugh" context. Which would again take us out of philology into poetics.

Similarly, inasmuch as *b* is midway between mammal *m* and the repulsion *p*, we might expect it to have an *m*-like sound on some occasions and a *p*-like sound on others. Thus, in the lines

O blasphemy! to mingle fiendish deeds
With blessedness!

we could expect "*b*lasphemy" to approximate "*p*lasphemy," and "*b*lessedness" to be more like "*m*lessedness," the explosive possibilities of *b* being purposely coached in the first case and tempered in the second. (Incidentally, no words are more like home to an idealist philosopher than "subject" and "object"—and we are told that when Coleridge had fallen into one of his famous monologues, he pronounced them "sumject" and "omject.")

Our gradual change of emphasis from the spoken to the documentary (with many symbols of mathematics and logic having no tonal associations whatsoever, being hardly other than designs) has made increasingly for a purely ocular style—so that children now are sometimes even trained to read wholly by eye. And there are indeed many essayistic styles that profit greatly if one can master the art of reading them without hearing them at all. For they are as arhythmic as traffic itself, and can even give one a palpitation of the heart if he still reads with an encumbrance of auditory imagery, and so accommodates his bodily responses to their total tonal aimlessness. But whatever may be the value of such styles, for bookkeeping purposes, they have wandered far afield from the gesturing of heard poetic speech. Paradoxically, their greatest accuracy, from the standpoint of mimesis, is in their *very absence* of such, for by this absence they conform with our sedentary trend from the bodily to the abstract (our secular variant of the spiritual). It is the style of men and women whose occupations have become dissociated from the bodily level, and whose expression accordingly does not arise from a physical act as the rhythms of a Negro work song arise from the rhythms of Negroes at work.

In any event, as regards the correlation between mind and body, we may note for future application in this essay, that the poet will naturally tend to write about that which most deeply engrosses him—and nothing more deeply engrosses a man than his *burdens,* including those of a physical nature, such as disease. We win by capitalizing on our debts, by turning our liabilities into assets, by using our burdens as a basis of insight. And so the poet may come to have a "vested interest" in his handicaps; these handicaps may become an integral part of his method; and in so far as his style grows out of a disease, his loyalty to it may reinforce the disease. It is a matter that Thomas Mann has often been concerned with. And it bears again upon the subject of "symbolic action," with the poet's burdens symbolic of his style, and his style symbolic of his burdens. I think we should not be far wrong if, seeking the area where states of mind are best available to empirical observation, we sought for correlations between styles and physical disease (particularly since there is no discomfiture, however mental in origin, that does not have its physiological correlates). So we might look for "dropsical" styles (Chesterton), "asthmatic" (Proust), "phthisic" (Mann), "apoplectic" (Flaubert), "blind" (Milton), etc. The one great objection to such a nosological mode of classification is that it leads to a Max Nordau mode of equating genius with degeneracy. This is not the case, however, if one properly discounts his terminology, reminding himself that the true locus of assertion is not in the *disease,* but in the *structural powers* by which the poet encompasses it. The disease, seen from this point of view, is hardly more than the *caricature* of the man, the oversimplification of his act—hence, most easily observable because it is an oversimplification. This oversimplifying indicator is deceptive unless its obviousness as a caricature is discounted.

Another Word for "Symbolic"

I respect the resistance to the notion of "symbolic action," since this resistance is based upon a healthy distrust of the irrational (the only question being whether we are rational enough in merely trying to outlaw the irrational by magical decree, and whether we might be more rational in confronting it). Respecting the resistance, I want to offer some considerations that may ease the pain. One of the most "rational" of words today is our word *statistical,* as applied for instance to the thorough rationality of an actuarial table. So I want to see whether we might be justified in borrowing this word for our purposes, in considering at least some aspects of "symbolic action." I propose to offer reasons why we might equate the word *symbolic* with the word *statistical*.

Mr. Q writes a novel. He has a score to settle with the world, and he settles it on paper, symbolically. Let us suppose that his novel is about a deserving individual in conflict with an undeserving society. He writes the work from the standpoint of his unique engrossments. However, as Malcolm Cowley has pointed out, there is a whole *class* of such novels. And if we take them all together, in the lump, "statistically," they become about as unique as various objects all going downstream together in a flood. They are "all doing the same"—they become but different individuations of a common paradigm. As so considered, they become "symbolic" of something—they become "representative" of a social trend.

Or consider the matter from another angle. One puts his arms on the table. This is a unique, real act—and one is perfectly conscious of what he is doing. There is, to be sure, a lot that he doesn't know: he is not conscious, for instance, of the infinite muscular and nervous adjustments that accompany the act. But he is perfectly conscious of the overall event: he knows what he is doing. Yet I have heard a portrait-painter exclaim at such a moment, when a man placed his arm on the table: "There—just like that—that's your characteristic posture." Thus, for this painter, the act had become "symbolic," "representative" of the man's character. There was a kind of informal fact-gathering that had been going on, as the painter had observed this man—and his exclamation was a kind of informally statistical conclusion.

But let's make one more try at taking the fearsomeness out of the word "symbolic." John Crowe Ransom, in *The World's Body*, makes some praiseworthy attempts to reaffirm a realistic basis for poetry; as part of his tactics, he would present even the lyric poem as the enactment of a dramatic rôle. The poet is "play-acting"—and so we must not consider his work as merely a symbolization of his private problems. Well and good. But let us suppose that a writer has piled up a considerable body of work; and upon inspecting the lot, we find that there has been great selectivity in his adoption of dramatic rôles. We find that his rôles have not been like "repertory acting," but like "type casting." This "statistical" view of his work, in disclosing a *trend*, puts us upon the track of the ways in which his selection of rôle is a "symbolic act." He is like a man with a tic, who spasmodically blinks his eyes when certain subjects are mentioned. If you kept a list of these subjects, noting what was said each time he spasmodically blinked his eyes, you would find what the tic was "symbolic" of.

Now, the work of every writer contains a set of implicit equations. He uses "associational clusters." And you may, by examining his work, find "what goes with what" in these clusters—what kinds of acts and images and personalities and situations go with his notions of heroism, villainy, consolation, despair, etc. And though he be perfectly conscious of the act of writing, conscious of selecting a certain kind of imagery to reinforce a certain kind of mood, etc., he cannot possibly be conscious of the inter-relationships among all these equations. Afterwards, by inspecting his work "statistically," we or he may disclose by objective citation the struc-ture of motivation operating here. There is no need to "supply" motives. The interrelationships themselves *are* his motives. For they are his *situ-ation;* and *situation* is but another word for *motives.* The motivation out of which he writes is synonymous with the structural way in which he puts events and values together when he writes; and however consciously he may go about such work, there is a kind of generalization about these interrelations that he could not have been conscious of, since the gener-alization could be made by the kind of inspection that is possible only *af-ter the completion* of the work.

At present I am attempting such a "symbolic" analysis of Coleridge's writings. His highly complex mind makes the job of charting difficult. The associational interweavings are so manifold as to present quite a problem in bookkeeping. Thus, even if my method were hypothetically granted to be correct, it is as though one invented a machine for recover-ing the exact course each person had taken on passing through Times Square. Even if one's machine were completely trustworthy, he would have difficulty in trying to present, on a design, the different paths taken. The lines would merge into a blot.

However, there are two advantages about the case of Coleridge that make the job worth trying. In the first place, there is the fact that he left so full a record, and that he employed the same imagery in his poems, lit-erary criticism, political and religious tracts, letters, lectures, and intro-spective jottings. Thus we have objective bridges for getting from one area to another; these images "pontificate" among his various interests, and so provide us with a maximum opportunity to work out a psychology by ob-jective citation, by "scissor work." If you want to say that this equals that, you have the imagery, explicitly shared by this and that in common, to substantiate the claim. In fact, a psychology of poetry, so conceived, is about as near to the use of objective, empirical evidence as even the phys-ical sciences. For though there must be purely theoretical grounds for se-lecting some interrelationships rather than others as more significant, the interrelationships themselves can be shown *by citation* to be there.

The second advantage in the case of Coleridge is that, along with his highly complex mind (perhaps one of the most complex that has left us a full record) you have an easily observable *simplification.* I refer to the bur-den of his drug addiction. Criticism is usually up against a problem of this sort: The critic tries to explain a complexity in terms of a simplicity, and when he is finished, his opponent need but answer: "But you have explained a complexity in terms of a simplicity, and a simplicity is precisely what a complexity is *not*. So you have explained something in terms of what it isn't." Explanation entails simplification; and any simplification is open to the charge of "oversimplification." So we have tried to explain human beings in terms of mechanistic psychology, adults in terms of child psychology, sophisticates in terms of primitive psychology, and the normal in terms of abnormal psychology—with the opponent's categorical refutation of the effort implicit in the nature of the effort itself. In the case of Coleridge's enslavement to his drug, however, you get an observable simplification, a burden the manifestations of which can be trailed through his work—yet at the same time you have him left in all his complexity, and so may observe the complex ways in which this burden becomes interwoven with his many other concerns.

To note the matter of symbolic action, however, is by no means to involve oneself in a purely subjectivist position. There are respects in which the clusters (or "what goes with what") are private, and respects in which they are public. Thus, I think we can, by analysis of the "clusters" in Coleridge's work, find ingredients in the figure of the Albatross slain in "The Ancient Mariner" that are peculiar to Coleridge (i.e., the figure is "doing something for Coleridge" that it is not doing for anyone else); yet the introduction of the Albatross, as victim of a crime to motivate the sense of guilt in the poem, was suggested by Wordsworth. And as Lowes has shown amply, "The Ancient Mariner" also drew upon legends as public as those of the Wandering Jew and the fratricide of Cain. There are many points at which we, as readers, "cut in"—otherwise the poem would not affect us, would not communicate. But to grasp the full nature of the symbolic enactment going on in the poem, we must study the interrelationships disclosable by a study of Coleridge's mind itself. If a critic prefers to so restrict the rules of critical analysis that these private elements are excluded, that is his right. I see no formal or categorical objection to criticism so conceived. But if his interest happens to be in the structure of the poetic act, he will use everything that is available—and would even consider it a kind of vandalism to exclude certain material that Coleridge has left, basing such exclusion upon some conventions as to the ideal of criticism. The main ideal of criticism, as I conceive it, is to use all that is there to use. And merely because some ancient author has left us scant biographical material, I do not see why we should confine our study of a modern author, who has left us rich biographical material, to the same coördinates as we should apply in studying the work of the ancient author. If there is any slogan that should reign among critical precepts, it is that "circumstances alter occasions."

However, I shall try to show, later in this essay, that the perspective which I employ can quite naturally include observations as to the structure of a poem, even considered in isolation, and regardless of the poem's bearing upon symbolic action peculiar to the poet.

Maybe we could clarify the relation between the public act and the private act in this way: Suppose that we began by analyzing the structure of "The Ancient Mariner" as though we did not know one single detail about the author, and had not one single other line written by this author. We would note such events as the peripety in the fourth part, where the water snakes become transubstantiated (removed from the category of the loathsome into the category of the beautiful and blessed). We would note that the Mariner suffered his punishments under the aegis of the Sun, and that his cure was effected under the aegis of the Moon. We would have some "equations" to work on, as the Sun is "like God's own head," and the "loon," whose cure began when "the moving Moon went up the sky," was laved by a curative rain that, in ending the state of drought, filled "silly buckets"; and when the Mariner entered the Pilot's boat the Pilot's boy, "who now doth crazy go," called him the Devil. We may also see inklings of a "problem of marriage," in the setting of the poem, and in the closing explicit statement as to a preference for church over marriage.

If we had other poems, we could trail down these equations farther. For instance, we would find the "guilt, Sun at noon, problem of marriage" equations recurring. If we had the letters and introspective jottings, we could by imagistic bridging disclose the part that Coleridge's struggles with his drug played in the "loon, Moon, silly, crazy" equations (as Coleridge in despair speaks of his addiction as idiocy, talks of going to an asylum to be cured, and also employs the snake image with reference to the addiction). Now, if we had the one poem alone, we could note something like a dramatized "problem of metaphysical evil" (much like the basis of *Moby Dick*). Given other poems, we could make this more precise. Given biographical reference, we could also show the part played by his drug addiction and his marital difficulties in giving this general problem explicit content for Coleridge.

This would not vow us to the assertion that "you cannot understand 'The Ancient Mariner' unless you know of Coleridge's drug addiction and marriage problems." You can give a perfectly accurate account of its structure on the basis of the one poem alone. But in studying the full nature of a symbolic act you are entitled, if the material is available, to disclose also the things that the act is doing for the poet and no one else. Such private goads stimulate the artist, yet we may respond to imagery of guilt from totally different private goals of our own. We do not have to be drug addicts to respond to the guilt of a drug addict. The addiction is private, the guilt public. It is in such ways that the private and public areas of a symbolic act at once overlap and diverge. The recording has omitted some of these private ingredients, quite as it has omitted the exact personal way in which Coleridge recited the poem. If we happened to have liked Coleridge's "chaunt," this necessary omission from the stage directions for its recital is a loss; otherwise, it is a gain.

NOTES

1.   The quotations are lifted from Lawrence Hanson's excellent study, *The Life of S. T. Coleridge.*

Three
author

W. K. Wimsatt, Jr. and Monroe C. Beardsley

The Intentional Fallacy

The claim of the author's "intention" upon the critic's judgment has been challenged in a number of recent discussions, notably in the debate entitled *The Personal Heresy*, between Professors Lewis and Tillyard. But it seems doubtful if this claim and most of its romantic corollaries are as yet subject to any widespread questioning. The present writers, in a short article entitled "Intention" for a *Dictionary*[1] of literary criticism, raised the issue but were unable to pursue its implications at any length. We argued that the design or intention of the author is neither available nor desirable as a standard for judging the success of a work of literary art, and it seems to us that this is a principle which goes deep into some differences in the history of critical attitudes. It is a principle which accepted or rejected points to the polar opposites of classical "imitation" and romantic expression. It entails many specific truths about inspiration, authenticity, biography, literary history and scholarship, and about some trends of contemporary poetry, especially its allusiveness. There is hardly a problem of literary criticism in which the critic's approach will not be qualified by his view of "intention."

"Intention," as we shall use the term, corresponds to *what he intended* in a formula which more or less explicitly has had wide acceptance. "In order to judge the poet's performance, we must know *what he intended.*" Intention is design or plan in the author's mind. Intention has obvious affinities for the author's attitude toward his work, the way he felt, what made him write.

We begin our discussion with a series of propositions summarized and abstracted to a degree where they seem to us axiomatic.

1. A poem does not come into existence by accident. The words of a poem, as Professor Stoll has remarked, come out of a head, not out of a hat. Yet to insist on the designing intellect as a *cause* of a poem is not to grant the design or intention as a *standard* by which the critic is to judge the worth of the poet's performance.

2. One must ask how a critic expects to get an answer to the question about intention. How is he to find out what the poet tried to do? If the poet succeeded in doing it, then the poem itself shows what he was trying to do. And if the poet did not succeed, then the poem is not adequate evidence, and the critic must go outside the poem—for evidence of an intention that did not become effective in the poem. "Only one *caveat* must be borne in mind," says an eminent intentionalist[2] in a moment when his theory repudiates itself; "the poet's aim must be judged at the moment of the creative act, that is to say, by the art of the poem itself."

3. Judging a poem is like judging a pudding or a machine. One demands that it work. It is only because an artifact works that we infer the intention of an artificer. "A poem should not mean but be." A poem can *be* only through its *meaning*—since its medium is words—yet it *is*, simply *is*, in the sense that we have no excuse for inquiring what part is intended or meant. Poetry is a feat of style by which a complex of meaning is handled all at once. Poetry succeeds because all or most of what is said or implied is relevant; what is irrelevant has been excluded, like lumps from pudding and "bugs" from machinery. In this respect poetry differs from practical messages, which are successful if and only if we correctly infer the intention. They are more abstract than poetry.

4. The meaning of a poem may certainly be a personal one, in the sense that a poem expresses a personality or state of soul rather than a physical object like an apple. But even a short lyric poem is dramatic, the response of a speaker (no matter how abstractly conceived) to a situation (no matter how universalized). We ought to impute the thoughts and attitudes of the poem immediately to the dramatic *speaker*, and if to the author at all, only by an act of biographical inference.

5. There is a sense in which an author, by revision, may better achieve his original intention. But it is a very abstract sense. He intended to write a better work, or a better work of a certain kind, and now has done it. But it follows that his former concrete intention was not his intention. "He's the man we were in search of, that's true," says Hardy's rustic constable, "and yet he's not the man we were in search of. For the man we were in search of was not the man we wanted."

"Is not a critic," asks Professor Stoll, "a judge, who does not explore his own consciousness, but determines the author's meaning or intention, as if the poem were a will, a contract, or the constitution? The poem is not the critic's own." He has accurately diagnosed two forms of irresponsibility, one of which he prefers. Our view is yet different. The poem is not the critic's own and not the author's (it is detached from the author at birth and goes about the world beyond his power to intend about it or control it). The poem belongs to the public. It is embodied in language, the peculiar possession of the public, and it is about the human being, an object of public knowledge. What is said about the poem is subject to the same scrutiny as any statement in linguistics or in the general science of psychology.

A critic of our *Dictionary* article, Ananda K. Coomaraswamy, has argued[3] that there are two kinds of inquiry about a work of art: (1) whether the artist achieved his intentions; (2) whether the work of art "ought ever to have been undertaken at all" and so "whether it is worth preserving." Number (2), Coomaraswamy maintains, is not "criticism of any work of art *qua* work of art," but is rather moral criticism; number (1) is artistic criticism. But we maintain that (2) need not be moral criticism: that there is another way of deciding whether works of art are worth preserving and whether, in a sense, they "ought" to have been undertaken, and this is the way of objective criticism of works of art as such, the way which enables us to distinguish between a skillful murder and a skillful poem. A skillful murder is an example which Coomaraswamy uses, and in his system the difference between the murder and the poem is simply a "moral" one, not an "artistic" one, since each if carried out according to plan is "artistically" successful. We maintain that (2) is an inquiry of more worth than (1), and since (2) and not (1) is capable of distinguishing poetry from murder, the name "artistic criticism" is properly given to (2).

II

It is not so much a historical statement as a definition to say that the intentional fallacy is a romantic one. When a rhetorician of the first century A.D. writes: "Sublimity is the echo of a great soul," or when he tells us that "Homer enters into the sublime actions of his heroes" and "shares the full inspiration of the combat," we shall not be surprised to find this rhetorician considered as a distant harbinger of romanticism and greeted in the warmest terms by Saintsbury. One may wish to argue whether Longinus should be called romantic, but there can hardly be a doubt that in one important way he is.

Goethe's three questions for "constructive criticism" are "What did the author set out to do? Was his plan reasonable and sensible, and how far did he succeed in carrying it out?" If one leaves out the middle question, one has in effect the system of Croce—the culmination and crowning philosophic expression of romanticism. The beautiful is the successful intuition-expression, and the ugly is the unsuccessful; the intuition or private part of art is *the* aesthetic fact, and the medium or public part is not the subject of aesthetic at all.

The Madonna of Cimabue is still in the Church of Santa Maria
Novella; but does she speak to the visitor of to-day as to the
Florentines of the thirteenth century?

Historical interpretation labours ... to reintegrate in us the
psychological conditions which have changed in the course of
history. It ... enables us to see a work of art (a physical object) as its
author saw it in the moment of production.[4]

The first italics are Croce's, the second ours. The upshot of Croce's system is an ambiguous emphasis on history. With such passages as a point of departure a critic may write a nice analysis of the meaning or "spirit" of a play by Shakespeare or Corneille—a process that involves close historical study but remains aesthetic criticism—or he may, with equal plausibility, produce an essay in sociology, biography, or other kinds of nonaesthetic history.

III

I went to the poets; tragic, dithyrambic, and all sorts.... I took
them some of the most elaborate passages in their own writings,
and asked what was the meaning of them.... Will you believe me?
... there is hardly a person present who would not have talked better
about their poetry than they did themselves. Then I knew that not
by wisdom do poets write poetry, but by a sort of genius and
inspiration.

That reiterated mistrust of the poets which we hear from Socrates may have been part of a rigorously ascetic view in which we hardly wish to participate, yet Plato's Socrates saw a truth about the poetic mind which the world no longer commonly sees—so much criticism, and that the most inspirational and most affectionately remembered, has proceeded from the poets themselves.

Certainly the poets have had something to say that the critic and professor could not say; their message has been more exciting: that poetry should come as naturally as leaves to a tree, that poetry is the lava of the imagination, or that it is emotion recollected in tranquillity. But it is necessary that we realize the character and authority of such testimony. There is only a fine shade of difference between such expressions and a kind of earnest advice that authors often give. Thus Edward Young, Carlyle, Walter Pater:

I know two golden rules from *ethics*, which are no less golden in
Composition, than in life. 1. *Know thyself*; 2dly, *Reverence thyself*.

This is the grand secret for finding readers and retaining them: let him who would move and convince others, be first moved and convinced himself. Horace's rule, *Si vis me flere,* is applicable in a wider sense than the literal one. To every poet, to every writer, we might say: Be true, if you would be believed.

Truth! there can be no merit, no craft at all, without that. And further, all beauty is in the long run only *fineness* of truth, or what we call expression, the finer accommodation of speech to that vision within.

And Housman's little handbook to the poetic mind yields this illustration:

Having drunk a pint of beer at luncheon—beer is a sedative to the brain, and my afternoons are the least intellectual portion of my life—I would go out for a walk of two or three hours. As I went along, thinking of nothing in particular, only looking at things around me and following the progress of the seasons, there would flow into my mind, with sudden and unaccountable emotion, sometimes a line or two of verse, sometimes a whole stanza at once.

This is the logical terminus of the series already quoted. Here is a confession of how poems were written which would do as a definition of poetry just as well as "emotion recollected in tranquillity"—and which the young poet might equally well take to heart as a practical rule. Drink a pint of beer, relax, go walking, think on nothing in particular, look at things, surrender yourself to yourself, search for the truth in your own soul, listen to the sound of your own inside voice, discover and express the *vraie vérité.*

It is probably true that all this is excellent advice for poets. The young imagination fired by Wordsworth and Carlyle is probably closer to the verge of producing a poem than the mind of the student who has been sobered by Aristotle or Richards. The art of inspiring poets, or at least of inciting something like poetry in young persons, has probably gone further in our day than ever before. Books of creative writing such as those issued from the Lincoln School are interesting evidence of what a child can do.[5] All this, however, would appear to belong to an art separate from criticism—to a psychological discipline, a system of self-development, a yoga, which the young poet perhaps does well to notice, but which is something different from the public art of evaluating poems.

Coleridge and Arnold were better critics than most poets have been, and if the critical tendency dried up the poetry in Arnold and perhaps in Coleridge, it is not inconsistent with our argument, which is that judgment of poems is different from the art of producing them. Coleridge has given us the classic "anodyne" story, and tells what he can about the gen-

esis of a poem which he calls a "psychological curiosity," but his definitions of poetry and of the poetic quality "imagination" are to be found
elsewhere and in quite other terms.

It would be convenient if the passwords of the intentional school,
"sincerity," "fidelity," "spontaneity," "authenticity," "genuineness,"
"originality," could be equated with terms such as "integrity," "relevance," "unity," "function," "maturity," "subtlety," "adequacy," and
other more precise terms of evaluation—in short, if "expression" always
meant aesthetic achievement. But this is not so.

"Aesthetic" art, says Professor Curt Ducasse, an ingenious theorist
of expression, is the conscious objectification of feelings, in which an intrinsic part is the critical moment. The artist corrects the objectification
when it is not adequate. But this may mean that the earlier attempt was
not successful in objectifying the self, or "it may also mean that it was a
successful objectification of a self which, when it confronted us clearly,
we disowned and repudiated in favor of another."[6] What is the standard by
which we disown or accept the self? Professor Ducasse does not say.
Whatever it may be, however, this standard is an element in the definition
of art which will not reduce to terms of objectification. The evaluation of
the work of art remains public; the work is measured against something
outside the author.

IV

There is criticism of poetry and there is author psychology, which when
applied to the present or future takes the form of inspirational promotion;
but author psychology can be historical too, and then we have literary biography, a legitimate and attractive study in itself, one approach, as Professor Tillyard would argue, to personality, the poem being only a parallel
approach. Certainly it need not be with a derogatory purpose that one
points out personal studies, as distinct from poetic studies, in the realm
of literary scholarship. Yet there is danger of confusing personal and
poetic studies; and there is the fault of writing the personal as if it were
poetic.

There is a difference between internal and external evidence for the
meaning of a poem. And the paradox is only verbal and superficial that
what is (1) internal is also public: it is discovered through the semantics
and syntax of a poem, through our habitual knowledge of the language,
through grammars, dictionaries, and all the literature which is the source
of dictionaries, in general through all that makes a language and culture;
while what is (2) external is private or idiosyncratic; not a part of the work
as a linguistic fact: it consists of revelations (in journals, for example, or
letters or reported conversations) about how or why the poet wrote the

poem—to what lady, while sitting on what lawn, or at the death of what friend or brother. There is (3) an intermediate kind of evidence about the character of the author or about private or semiprivate meanings attached to words or topics by an author or by a coterie of which he is a member. The meaning of words is the history of words, and the biography of an author, his use of a word, and the associations which the word had for *him*, are part of the word's history and meaning.[7] But the three types of evidence, especially (2) and (3), shade into one another so subtly that it is not always easy to draw a line between examples, and hence arises the difficulty for criticism. The use of biographical evidence need not involve intentionalism, because while it may be evidence of what the author intended, it may also be evidence of the meaning of his words and the dramatic character of his utterance. On the other hand, it may not be all this. And a critic who is concerned with evidence of type (1) and moderately with that of type (3) will in the long run produce a different sort of comment from that of the critic who is concerned with (2) and with (3) where it shades into (2).

The whole glittering parade of Professor Lowes' *Road to Xanadu*, for instance, runs along the border between types (2) and (3) or boldly traverses the romantic region of (2). " 'Kubla Khan,' " says Professor Lowes, "is the fabric of a vision, but every image that rose up in its weaving had passed that way before. And it would seem that there is nothing haphazard or fortuitous in their return." This is not quite clear—not even when Professor Lowes explains that there were clusters of associations, like hooked atoms, which were drawn into complex relation with other clusters in the deep well of Coleridge's memory, and which then coalesced and issued forth as poems. If there was nothing "haphazard or fortuitous" in the way the images returned to the surface, that may mean (1) that Coleridge could not produce what he did not have, that he was limited in his creation by what he had read or otherwise experienced, or (2) that having received certain clusters of associations, he was bound to return them in just the way he did, and that the value of the poem may be described in terms of the experiences on which he had to draw. The latter pair of propositions (a sort of Hartleyan associationism which Coleridge himself repudiated in the *Biographia*) may not be assented to. There were certainly other combinations, other poems, worse or better, that might have been written by men who had read Bartram and Purchas and Bruce and Milton. And this will be true no matter how many times we are able to add to the brilliant complex of Coleridge's reading. In certain flourishes (such as the sentence we have quoted) and in chapter headings like "The Shaping Spirit," "The Magical Synthesis," "Imagination Creatrix," it may be that Professor Lowes pretends to say more about the actual poems than he does. There is a certain deceptive variation in these fancy chapter titles; one expects to pass on to a new stage in the argument, and one finds—

more and more sources, more and more about "the streamy nature of association."[8]

"Wohin der Weg?" quotes Professor Lowes for the motto of his book. "Kein Weg! Ins Unbetretene." Precisely because the way is *unbetreten*, we should say, it leads away from the poem. Bartram's *Travels* contains a good deal of the history of certain words and of certain romantic Floridian conceptions that appear in "Kubla Khan." And a good deal of that history has passed and was then passing into the very stuff of our language. Perhaps a person who has read Bartram appreciates the poem more than one who has not. Or, by looking up the vocabulary of "Kubla Khan" in the *Oxford English Dictionary*, or by reading some of the other books there quoted, a person may know the poem better. But it would seem to pertain little to the poem to know that *Coleridge* had read Bartram. There is a gross body of life, of sensory and mental experience, which lies behind and in some sense causes every poem, but can never be and need not be known in the verbal and hence intellectual composition which is the poem. For all the objects of our manifold experience, for every unity, there is an action of the mind which cuts off roots, melts away context—or indeed we should never have objects or ideas or anything to talk about.

It is probable that there is nothing in Professor Lowes' vast book which could detract from anyone's appreciation of either *The Ancient Mariner* or "Kubla Khan." We next present a case where preoccupation with evidence of type (3) has gone so far as to distort a critic's view of a poem (yet a case not so obvious as those that abound in our critical journals).

In a well known poem by John Donne appears this quatrain:

> Moving of th' earth brings harmes and feares,
>   Men reckon what it did and meant,
> But trepidation of the spheares,
>   Though greater farre, is innocent.

A recent critic in an elaborate treatment of Donne's learning has written of this quatrain as follows:

> He touches the emotional pulse of the situation by a skillful allusion to the new and the old astronomy. ... Of the new astronomy, the "moving of the earth" is the most radical principle; of the old, the "trepidation of the spheres" is the motion of the greatest complexity. ... The poet must exhort his love to quietness and calm upon his departure; and for this purpose the figure based upon the latter motion (trepidation), long absorbed into the traditional astronomy, fittingly suggests the tension of the moment without arousing the "harmes and feares" implicit in the figure of the moving earth.[9]

The argument is plausible and rests on a well substantiated thesis that Donne was deeply interested in the new astronomy and its repercussions in the theological realm. In various works Donne shows his familiarity with Kepler's *De Stella Nova*, with Galileo's *Siderius Nuncius*, with William Gilbert's *De Magnete*, and with Clavius' commentary on the *De Sphaera* of Sacrobosco. He refers to the new science in his Sermon at Paul's Cross and in a letter to Sir Henry Goodyer. In *The First Anniversary* he says the "new philosophy calls all in doubt." In the *Elegy on Prince Henry* he says that the "least moving of the center" makes "the world to shake."

It is difficult to answer argument like this, and impossible to answer it with evidence of like nature. There is no reason why Donne might not have written a stanza in which the two kinds of celestial motion stood for two sorts of emotion at parting. And if we become full of astronomical ideas and see Donne only against the background of the new science, we may believe that he did. But the text itself remains to be dealt with, the analyzable vehicle of a complicated metaphor. And one may observe: (1) that the movement of the earth according to the Copernican theory is a celestial motion, smooth and regular, and while it might cause religious or philosophic fears, it could not be associated with the crudity and earthiness of the kind of commotion which the speaker in the poem wishes to discourage; (2) that there is another moving of the earth, an earthquake, which has just these qualities and is to be associated with the tear-floods and sigh-tempests of the second stanza of the poem; (3) that "trepidation" is an appropriate opposite of earthquake, because each is a shaking or vibratory motion; and "trepidation of the spheres" is "greater far" than an earthquake, but not much greater (if two such motions can be compared as to greatness) than the annual motion of the earth; (4) that reckoning what it "did and meant" shows that the event has passed, like an earthquake, not like the incessant celestial movement of the earth. Perhaps a knowledge of Donne's interest in the new science may add another shade of meaning, an overtone to the stanza in question, though to say even this runs against the words. To make the geocentric and heliocentric antithesis the core of the metaphor is to disregard the English language, to prefer private evidence to public, external to internal.

V

If the distinction between kinds of evidence has implications for the historical critic, it has them no less for the contemporary poet and his critic. Or, since every rule for a poet is but another side of a judgment by a critic, and since the past is the realm of the scholar and critic, and the future and present that of the poet and the critical leaders of taste, we may say that the problems arising in literary scholarship from the intentional fallacy are matched by others which arise in the world of progressive experiment.

The question of "allusiveness," for example, as acutely posed by the poetry of Eliot, is certainly one where a false judgment is likely to involve the intentional fallacy. The frequency and depth of literary allusion in the poetry of Eliot and others has driven so many in pursuit of full meanings to the *Golden Bough* and the Elizabethan drama that it has become a kind of commonplace to suppose that we do not know what a poet means unless we have traced him in his reading—a supposition redolent with intentional implications. The stand taken by F. O. Matthiessen is a sound one and partially forestalls the difficulty.

> If one reads these lines with an attentive ear and is sensitive to their sudden shifts in movement, the contrast between the actual Thames and the idealized vision of it during an age before it flowed through a megalopolis is sharply conveyed by that movement itself, whether or not one recognizes the refrain to be from Spenser.

Eliot's allusions work when we know them—and to a great extent even when we do not know them, through their suggestive power.

But sometimes we find allusions supported by notes, and it is a nice question whether the notes function more as guides to send us where we may be educated, or more as indications in themselves about the character of the allusions. "Nearly everything of importance ... that is apposite to an appreciation of 'The Waste Land,' " writes Matthiessen of Miss Weston's book, "has been incorporated into the structure of the poem itself, or into Eliot's Notes." And with such an admission it may begin to appear that it would not much matter if Eliot invented his sources (as Sir Walter Scott invented chapter epigraphs from "old plays" and "anonymous" authors, or as Coleridge wrote marginal glosses for *The Ancient Mariner*). Allusions to Dante, Webster, Marvell, or Baudelaire doubtless gain something because these writers existed, but it is doubtful whether the same can be said for an allusion to an obscure Elizabethan:

> The sound of horns and motors, which shall bring
> Sweeney to Mrs. Porter in the spring.

"Cf. Day, *Parliament of Bees:*" says Eliot,

> When of a sudden, listening, you shall hear,
> A noise of horns and hunting, which shall bring
> Actaeon to Diana in the spring,
> Where all shall see her naked skin.

The irony is completed by the quotation itself; had Eliot, as is quite conceivable, composed these lines to furnish his own background, there would be no loss of validity. The conviction may grow as one reads Eliot's next note: "I do not know the origin of the ballad from which these lines are taken: it was reported to me from Sydney, Australia." The important word in this note—on Mrs. Porter and her daughter who washed their feet in soda water—is "ballad." And if one should feel from the lines themselves their "ballad" quality, there would be little need for the note. Ultimately, the inquiry must focus on the integrity of such notes as parts of the poem, for where they constitute special information about the meaning of phrases in the poem, they ought to be subject to the same scrutiny as any of the other words in which it is written. Matthiessen believes the notes were the price Eliot "had to pay in order to avoid what he would have considered muffling the energy of his poem by extended connecting links in the text itself." But it may be questioned whether the notes and the need for them are not equally muffling. F. W. Bateson has plausibly argued that Tennyson's "The Sailor Boy" would be better if half the stanzas were omitted, and the best versions of ballads like "Sir Patrick Spens" owe their power to the very audacity with which the minstrel has taken for granted the story upon which he comments. What then if a poet finds he cannot take so much for granted in a more recondite context and rather than write informatively, supplies notes? It can be said in favor of this plan that at least the notes do not pretend to be dramatic, as they would if written in verse. On the other hand, the notes may look like unassimilated material lying loose beside the poem, necessary for the meaning of the verbal symbol, but not integrated, so that the symbol stands incomplete.

We mean to suggest by the above analysis that whereas notes tend to seem to justify themselves as external indexes to the author's *intention*, yet they ought to be judged like any other parts of a composition (verbal arrangement special to a particular context), and when so judged their reality as parts of the poem, or their imaginative integration with the rest of the poem, may come into question. Matthiessen, for instance, sees that Eliot's titles for poems and his epigraphs are informative apparatus, like the notes. But while he is worried by some of the notes and thinks that Eliot "appears to be mocking himself for writing the note at the same time that he wants to convey something by it," Matthiessen believes that the "device" of epigraphs "is not at all open to the objection of not being sufficiently structural." "The *intention*," he says, "is to enable the poet to secure a condensed expression in the poem itself." "In each case the epigraph is *designed* to form an integral part of the effect of the poem." And Eliot himself, in his notes, has justified his poetic practice in terms of intention.

> The Hanged Man, a member of the traditional pack, fits my purpose in two ways: because he is associated in my mind with the Hanged God of Frazer, and because I associate him with the hooded figure

in the passage of the disciples to Emmaus in Part V. . . . The man
with Three Staves (an authentic member of the Tarot pack) I
associate, quite arbitrarily, with the Fisher King himself.

And perhaps he is to be taken more seriously here, when off guard in a
note, than when in his Norton Lectures he comments on the difficulty of
saying what a poem means and adds playfully that he thinks of prefixing
to a second edition of *Ash Wednesday* some lines from *Don Juan:*

> I don't pretend that I quite understand
> My own meaning when I would be *very* fine;
> But the fact is that I have nothing planned
> Unless it were to be a moment merry.

If Eliot and other contemporary poets have any characteristic fault, it may
be in *planning* too much.

Allusiveness in poetry is one of several critical issues by which we
have illustrated the more abstract issue of intentionalism, but it may be
for today the most important illustration. As a poetic practice allusiveness would appear to be in some recent poems an extreme corollary of the
romantic intentionalist assumption, and as a critical issue it challenges
and brings to light in a special way the basic premise of intentionalism.
The following instance from the poetry of Eliot may serve to epitomize
the practical implications of what we have been saying. In Eliot's "Love
Song of J. Alfred Prufrock," toward the end, occurs the line: "I have heard
the mermaids singing, each to each," and this bears a certain resemblance
to a line in a Song by John Donne, "Teach me to heare Mermaides singing," so that for the reader acquainted to a certain degree with Donne's
poetry, the critical question arises: Is Eliot's line an allusion to Donne's?
Is Prufrock thinking about Donne? Is Eliot thinking about Donne? We
suggest that there are two radically different ways of looking for an answer
to this question. There is (1) the way of poetic analysis and exegesis,
which inquires whether it makes any sense if Eliot-Prufrock *is* thinking
about Donne. In an earlier part of the poem, when Prufrock asks, "Would
it have been worth while, . . . To have squeezed the universe into a ball,"
his words take half their sadness and irony from certain energetic and passionate lines of Marvel "To His Coy Mistress." But the exegetical inquirer
may wonder whether mermaids considered as "strange sights" (to hear
them is in Donne's poem analogous to getting with child a mandrake
root) have much to do with Prufrock's mermaids, which seem to be symbols of romance and dynamism, and which incidentally have literary authentication, if they need it, in a line of a sonnet by Gérard de Nerval. This
method of inquiry may lead to the conclusion that the given resemblance
between Eliot and Donne is without significance and is better not

thought of, or the method may have the disadvantage of providing no certain conclusion. Nevertheless, we submit that this is the true and objective way of criticism, as contrasted to what the very uncertainty of exegesis might tempt a second kind of critic to undertake: (2) the way of biographical or genetic inquiry, in which, taking advantage of the fact that Eliot is still alive, and in the spirit of a man who would settle a bet, the critic writes to Eliot and asks what he meant, or if he had Donne in mind. We shall not here weigh the probabilities—whether Eliot would answer that he meant nothing at all, had nothing at all in mind—a sufficiently good answer to such a question—or in an unguarded moment might furnish a clear and, within its limit, irrefutable answer. Our point is that such an answer to such an inquiry would have nothing to do with the poem "Prufrock"; it would not be a critical inquiry. Critical inquiries, unlike bets, are not settled in this way. Critical inquiries are not settled by consulting the oracle.

Boris Tomaševskij

Literature and Biography*

Diaries as well as curiosity about unpublished documents and biographical "findings" mark an unhealthy sharpening of interest in documentary literary history, that is, history that is concerned with mores, personalities, and with the interrelationship between writers and their milieu. Most of the "documents" are relevant, not to literature or its history, but rather to the study of the author as a man (if not to the study of his brothers and aunts).

In contrast to these biographical studies, there is a concurrent development of critical literature concentrating on the specific poetic elements in verbal art (the contributions of the *Opojaz* and other branches of "Formalism"). Thus at first glance there would appear to be a profound split among literary scholars. These two currents seem to have diverged in a definitive way, and no reconciliation seems possible. To a certain extent this is true: many biographers cannot be made to comprehend an artistic work as anything but a fact of the author's biography; on the other hand, there are those for whom any kind of biographical analysis is unscientific contraband, a "back-door" approach.

Consider Puškin's poem, *Ja pomnju čudnoe mgnoven'e* [I Recall a Wondrous Instant]. Is this an artistic reference to the personal relation of Puškin to A. Kern? Or is it a free lyrical composition which uses the image of Kern as an indifferent "emblem," as structural material having no relationship to biography? Is it possible to take a neutral position on this question? Or would this be sitting down between two chairs? The question itself is very clear: do we need the poet's biography in order to understand his work, or do we not?

Before we can answer this question, however, we must remember that creative literature exists, not for literary historians, but for readers, and we must consider how the poet's biography operates in the reader's

*"Literatura i biografija," *Kniga i revoljucija*, 4 (1923), pp. 6–9. Translated by Herbert Eagle.

consciousness. Here we shall not regard "biography" as a self-sufficient class of historical writing (from this point of view Puškin's biography is no different from the biographies of generals and engineers); instead, we shall consider the "literary functions" of biography as the traditional concomitant of artistic work.

There have been eras during which the personality of the artist was of no interest at all to the audience. Paintings were signed with the donor's name, not the artist's; literary works bore the name of the customer or the printer. There was a great tendency toward anonymity, thus leaving a wide field of investigation for present-day archaeologists and textologists. The name of the master had as much significance as the trademark of a company has today. Thus Rembrandt had no qualms about signing the paintings of his pupil, Maas.

However, during the individualization of creativity—an epoch which cultivated subjectivism in the artistic process—the name and personality of the author came to the forefront. The reader's interest reached beyond the work to its creator. This new relationship toward creativity began with the great writers of the eighteenth century. Before that time the personality of the author was hidden. Bits of gossip and anecdotes about authors did penetrate society, but these anecdotes were not combined into biographical images and considered equally along with authors and personages not connected with literature. In fact, the less gifted the writer, the more numerous the anecdotes about him. Thus anecdotes have come down to us concerning, for example, the Abbé Cotin, a minor eighteenth-century poet—but no one knows his works. At the same time, our information about Molière or about Shakespeare is quite meager, though it is true that nineteenth-century biographers later "created" the biographies of these writers and even projected their plays onto these imagined biographies. However, such biographies did not prevent others from just as successfully attributing the tragedies of Shakespeare to Bacon, Rutland, or others. From a biographical standpoint, Shakespeare remains the "iron mask" of literature.

On the other hand, eighteenth-century writers, especially Voltaire, were not only writers but also public figures. Voltaire made his artistic work a tool for propaganda, and his life, bold and provocative, served this same end. The years of exile, the years of reigning at Ferney, were used as weapons for the ideological battle and for preaching. Voltaire's works were inseparably linked with his life. His audience not only read his work but even went on pilgrimages to him. Those who admired his writings were worshipers of his personality; the adversaries of his writings were his personal enemies. Voltaire's personality linked his literary works together. When his name was mentioned, his literary works were not what first came to mind. Even today, when most of his tragedies and poems have been completely forgotten, the image of Voltaire is still alive; those forgotten works shine with reflected light in his unforgettable biography. Equally unforgettable is the biography of his contemporary, Rousseau, who left his *Confessions* and thus bequeathed to posterity the history of his life.

Voltaire and Rousseau, like many of their contemporaries, were prolific in many genres, from musical comedies to novels and philosophical treatises, from epigrams and epitaphs to theoretical articles on physics and music. Only their lives could have united these various forms of verbal creation into a system. This is why their biographies, their letters and memoirs, have become such an integral part of their literary heritage. In fact, the knowledge that their biographies were a constant background for their works compelled Voltaire and Rousseau to dramatize certain epic motifs in their own lives and, furthermore, to create for themselves an artificial legendary biography composed of intentionally selected real and imaginary events. The biographies of such authors require a Ferney or a Jasnaja Poljana: they require pilgrimages by admirers and condemnations from Sorbonnes or Holy Synods.

Following in the footsteps of these eighteenth-century writers, Byron, the poet of sharp-tempered characters, created the canonical biography for a lyrical poet. A biography of a Romantic poet was more than a biography of an author and public figure. The Romantic poet *was* his own hero. His *life* was poetry, and soon there developed a canonical set of actions to be carried out by the poet. Here, the traditions of the eighteenth century served as a model. The end of that century had produced the stereotype of the "dying poet": young, unable to overcome the adversities of life, perishing in poverty, the fame he merited coming too late. Such were the legendary biographies of two poets, Malfilâtre and Gilbert, later popularized by the Romantics (for example, Alfred de Vigny). The late eighteenth-century poets Parny and Bertin wrote their elegies with a definite orientation toward autobiography. They arranged those elegies in such a way as to convince the reader that their poems were fragments of a real romance, that their Eleonoras and Eucharidas were actual people. Delille in France and our own Xvostov appended footnotes to the feminine names they used, such as "the poet's name for his wife."

The necessity for such "real" commentary was dictated by the style of the period. Readers demanded the complete illusion of life. They made pilgrimages to the final resting places of the heroes of even the most unbelievable novels. For example, near Moscow one can still visit "Liza's Pond," in which Karamzin's sugary heroine drowned herself. They say that at Lermontov's house in Pjatigorsk artifacts which belonged to Princess Mary are exhibited.

The readers' demand for a living hero results in the perennial question: from whom is the character drawn? This is the question which Lermontov contemptuously brushed aside in the introduction to *A Hero of Our Time*. In this connection we should consider the usual commentary to Griboedov's *Gore ot uma* [Woe from Wit]; the Moscow "old-timers" assigned all of Griboedov's heroes to actual people—as is typical of old-timers.

Once the question of copying characters from life has arisen, writers actually *do* begin to copy from life—or at least they pretend to do so. The author becomes a witness to and a living participant in his novels, a living hero. A double transformation takes place: heroes are taken for living personages, and poets become living heroes—their biographies become poems.

In the Puškin era, when the genre of "friendly epistles" flourished, poets paraded before their audience as characters. Now Puškin writes to Baratynskij from Bessarabia, now Jazykov writes to Puškin. And then all three of them become the themes of lyrical poems.

The lyricism of Puškin's long poems is clearly the result of an orientation toward autobiography. The reader had to feel that he was reading, not the words of an abstract author, but those of a living person whose biographical data were at his disposal. Thus the author had to make literary use of his own biography. So Puškin used his southern exile as a poetic banishment. Motifs of exile, of wanderings, run throughout his poetry in many variations. We must assume that Puškin poetically fostered certain facts of his life. For example, he jealously expunged references to *deva junaja* [the young maid] from poems already completed and well-known in print, and from those widely circulated in manuscript. At the same time, he wrote to his friends in an ambiguous and enigmatic tone about unrequited love. In conversation, he became prone to mysteriously incoherent outpourings. And behold, the poetic legend of a "concealed love" was created with its ostentatious devices used for concealing love, when it would have been much simpler to keep silent. However, Puškin was concerned about his "biography," and the image of a young exile with a hidden and unrequited love, set against the background of Crimean nature, fascinated him. He needed this image as a frame for his southern poems. Nonetheless, present-day biographers have dealt mercilessly with this stylish legend. They have been determined to learn at any cost the identity of the woman whom Puškin so hopelessly loved (or pretended to love). Thus they have destroyed the very core of the legend—the unknown. In place of "young maids," they have proposed various respectable society women.

The interrelationships of life and literature became confused during the Romantic era. Romanticism and its mores constitute a problem to which careful investigations have been devoted. It is sometimes difficult to decide whether literature recreates phenomena from life or whether the opposite is in fact the case: that the phenomena of life are the result of the penetration of literary clichés into reality. Such motifs as the duel, the Caucasus, etc., were invariant components both of literature and of the poet's biography.

The poets used their lives to realize a literary purpose, and these literary biographies were necessary for the readers. The readers cried: "Author! author!"—but they were actually calling for the slender youth in a cloak, with a lyre in his hands and an enigmatic expression on his face. This demand for a potentially existing author, whether real or not, gave rise to a special kind of anonymous literature: literature with an invented author, whose biography was appended to the work. We find a literary precedent for this genre in Voltaire's mystifications. He published stories under the name of Guillaume Vadé and appended a letter written by Catherine Vadé (the imaginary first cousin of the imagined author) describing the last days of her cousin Guillaume.

In this connection, we should also consider the stories of Belkin and Rudyj Pan'ko. At the basis of these mystifications lies the very same demand of the public: "Give us a living author!" If the author wanted to hide, then he had to send forth an invented narrator. Biography became an element of literature.

The biographies of real authors, for example of Puškin and Lermontov, were cultivated as oral legends. How many interesting anecdotes the old-timers "knew" about Puškin! Read the reminiscences of the Kišenev inhabitants about the poet. You will find tales that even Puškin wouldn't have dreamt of. In these tales, a tragic love and an exotic lover (a gypsy or a Greek) are absolutely necessary. As fiction, however, all this is far more superior to the recently published anecdote in the notes of Naščokin-Bartenevskij concerning Puškin and the Countess Finkel'mon.

Thus, legends about poets were created, and it was extremely important for the literary historian to occupy himself with the restoration of these legends, i.e., with the removal of later layers and the reduction of the legend to its pure "canonical" form. These biographical legends are the literary conception of the poet's life, and this conception was necessary as a perceptible background for the poet's literary works. The legends are a premise which the author himself took into account during the creative process.

The biographical commentary to a literary work often consists of the curriculum vitae, the genealogy, of the characters mentioned in the work. However, in referring to a given character, the author did not assume that the reader knew the curriculum vitae of that character. However, he did assume that the reader knew the character's anecdotal representation, consisting of actual and invented material, created in the reader's milieu. When Puškin was writing *Mozart and Salieri*, what was important was not the actual historical relationship between these two composers (and here their biographies, based on documents and investigations, would not help anyway), but the fact that there existed a legend about the poisoning of Mozart by Salieri, and that rumors were current that Beaumarchais had poisoned his wives. The question of whether these rumors and legends had any foundation in fact was irrelevant to their function.

In exactly the same way, the poet considers as a premise to his creations not his actual curriculum vitae, but his ideal biographical legend. Therefore, only this biographical legend should be important to the literary historian in his attempt to reconstruct the psychological milieu surrounding a literary work. Furthermore, the biographical legend is necessary only to the extent that the literary work includes references to "biographical" facts (real or legendary) of the author's life.

However, the poet did not always have a biography. Toward the middle of the nineteenth century, the poet-hero was replaced by the professional poet, the businessman-journalist. The writer wrote down his manuscript and gave it to a publisher; he did not allow any glimpses of his personal life. The human face of the author peered out only in pasquinades, in satirical pamphlets, or in monetary squabbles which burst out noisily in public whenever contributors were not satisfied with their royalties. Thus the phenomenon of writers without biographies appeared. All attempts to invent biographies for these writers and to project their work onto these biographies have consistently ended in farce. Nekrasov, for example, appears on the literary scene without a biography, as do Ostrovskij and Fet. Their works are self-contained units. There are no biographical features shedding light on the meaning of their works. Nevertheless, there are scholars who want to imagine literary biographies even for these authors.

It is, of course, obvious that these authors do have *actual* biographies, and that their literary work enters into these biographies as a fact of their lives. Such actual biographies of private individuals may be interesting for cultural history, but not for the history of literature. (I say nothing of those literary historians who classify literary phenomena on the basis of the circumstances of the writer's birth.) No poetic image of the author—except perhaps as a deliberately invented narrator who is introduced into the story itself (like Puškin's Belkin)—can be found in this period. Works did not depend on the presence of a biographical background.

This "cold" nineteenth-century writer, however, did not represent an exclusive type which was to replace "biographically oriented" literature forever. At the very end of the century interest in the author began to arise once again, and this interest has continued to grow to the present day. First, there appeared a timid interest in "good people." We suffered through a period when the writer was necessarily considered "a good person"; we suffered through images of wretched victims, images of oppressed consumptive poets. We suffered through them to the point of nausea.

In the twentieth century there appeared a special type of writer with a demonstrative biography, one which shouted out: "Look at how bad and how impudent I am! Look! And don't turn your head away, because all of you are just as bad, only you are faint-hearted and hide yourselves. But I am bold; I strip myself stark naked and walk around in public without feeling ashamed." This was the reaction to the "sweetness" of the "good man."

Fifteen years ago someone came out with a "calendar of writers," in which the autobiographies of the men of letters fashionable at that time were collected. These writers all vied with one another in crying out that they had no formal education because they had been expelled from high school and from trade school, that they had only torn trousers and a few buttons—and all this because they absolutely didn't care about anything.

However, alongside this petty naughtiness in literature, there emerged a new intimate style. Many writers, of course, still persisted in concealing their private lives from the public. Sologub, for one, systematically refused to provide any information whatsoever about himself. But other and rather different trends were also present in literature. Vasilij Rozanov created a distinctive intimate style. The pages of his books were like "falling leaves," and he strolled through them uncombed, whole, completely himself. He produced a special literature of intimate conversations and confidential confessions. We know, by his own admission, that he was a mystifier. It is the business of cultural historians to judge to what extent the face he carefully drew in his fragments and aphorisms was his own. As a literary legend, Rozanov's image has been drawn, by him, definitively and with complete consistency. This image shows little resemblance either to the "heroic poets" of the beginning of the nineteenth century or to the "good persons" with progressive convictions of the end of the century. However, it is impossible to deny that this image was viable and artistically functional during the years of Rozanov's literary work. Furthermore, the autobiographical devices of Rozanov's literary manner have survived him and are still present today in novelistic or fragmentary memoirs.

Parallel to this prosaic element in the Symbolist movement, there also developed a biographical lyricism. Blok was certainly a poet with a lyrical biography. The numerous memoirs and biographical works on Blok which appeared within a year of his death testify to the fact that his biography was a living and necessary commentary to his works. His poems are lyrical episodes about himself, and his readers always informed themselves (perhaps at third-hand) about the principal events of his life. It would be inaccurate to say that Blok put his life on display. Nonetheless, his poems did arouse an insurmountable desire to know about the author, and they made his readers avidly follow the various twists and turns of his life. Blok's legend is an inescapable concomitant to his poetry. The elements of intimate confession and biographical allusion in his poetry must be taken into account.

Symbolism was superseded by Futurism, which intensified to a hyperbolic clarity those features which had previously appeared only in hidden, mystically masked forms of Symbolism. Intimate confessions and allusions were transformed into demonstrative declarations delivered in a monumental style. Whereas Blok's biography appeared only as a legendary concomitant to his poetry, the Futurist legendary biographies were boldly inserted into the works themselves.

Futurism took the Romantic orientation toward autobiography to its ultimate conclusions. The author really became the hero of his works. We need mention here only the construction of Majakovskij's books: they are an open diary in which intimate feelings are recorded. This type of construction, in fact, intersects the path of the future biographer, who will have to try to construct a different, extraliterary, biography. Today the writer shows his readers his own life and writes his own biography, tightly binding it to the literary cycles of his work. If, for example, Gor'kij drives away importunate idlers, then he does this knowingly, as a demonstration: he knows that this very fact will be taken into account in his biography. Just consider how many of today's poets reminisce about themselves and their friends, how many of them produce memoir literature—memoirs transformed into artistic structures.

Obviously, the question of the role of biography in literary history cannot be solved uniformly for all literatures. There are writers with biographies and writers without biographies. To attempt to compose biographies for the latter is to write satires or denunciations on the alive or the dead as well. On the other hand, for a writer with a biography, the facts of the author's life must be taken into consideration. Indeed, in the works themselves the juxtaposition of the texts and the author's biography plays a structural role. The literary work plays on the potential reality of the author's subjective outpourings and confessions. Thus the biography that is useful to the literary historian is not the author's curriculum vitae or the investigator's account of his life. What the literary historian really needs is the biographical legend created by the author himself. Only such a legend is a *literary fact.*

As far as "documentary biographies" are concerned, these belong to the domain of cultural history, on a par with the biographies of generals and inventors. With regard to literature and its history, these biographies may be considered only as external (even if necessary) reference material of an auxiliary nature.

Michel Foucault

What Is an Author?

In proposing this slightly odd question, I am conscious of the need for an explanation. To this day, the "author" remains an open question both with respect to its general function within discourse and in my own writings; that is, this question permits me to return to certain aspects of my own work which now appear ill-advised and misleading. In this regard, I wish to propose a necessary criticism and reevaluation.

For instance, my objective in *The Order of Things* had been to analyse verbal clusters as discursive layers which fall outside the familiar categories of a book, a work, or an author. But while I considered "natural history," the "analysis of wealth," and "political economy" in general terms, I neglected a similar analysis of the author and his works; it is perhaps due to this omission that I employed the names of authors throughout this book in a naive and often crude fashion. I spoke of Buffon, Cuvier, Ricardo, and others as well, but failed to realize that I had allowed their names to function ambiguously. This has proved an embarassment to me in that my oversight has served to raise two pertinent objections.

It was argued that I had not properly described Buffon or his work and that my handling of Marx was pitifully inadequate in terms of the totality of his thought.[1] Although these objections were obviously justified, they ignored the task I had set myself: I had no intention of describing Buffon or Marx or of reproducing their statements or implicit meanings, but, simply stated, I wanted to locate the rules that formed a certain number of concepts and theoretical relationships in their works.[2] In addition, it was argued that I had created monstrous families by bringing together names as disparate as Buffon and Linnaeus or in placing Cuvier next to Darwin in defiance of the most readily observable family resemblances and natural ties.[3] This objection also seems inappropriate since I had never tried to establish a genealogical table of exceptional individuals, nor was I concerned in forming an intellectual daguerreotype of the scholar or naturalist of the seventeenth and eighteenth century. In fact, I had no intention of forming any family, whether holy or perverse. On the contrary,

I wanted to determine—a much more modest task—the functional conditions of specific discursive practices.

Then why did I use the names of authors in *The Order of Things?* Why not avoid their use altogether, or, short of that, why not define the manner in which they were used? These questions appear fully justified and I have tried to gauge their implications and consequences in a book that will appear shortly.[4] These questions have determined my effort to situate comprehensive discursive units, such as "natural history" or "political economy," and to establish the methods and instruments for delimiting, analyzing, and describing these unities. Nevertheless, as a privileged moment of individualization in the history of ideas, knowledge, and literature, or in the history of philosophy and science, the question of the author demands a more direct response. Even now, when we study the history of a concept, a literary genre, or a branch of philosophy, these concerns assume a relatively weak and secondary position in relation to the solid and fundamental role of an author and his works.

For the purposes of this paper, I will set aside a sociohistorical analysis of the author as an individual and the numerous questions that deserve attention in this context: how the author was individualized in a culture such as ours; the status we have given the author, for instance, when we began our research into authenticity and attribution; the systems of valorization in which he was included; or the moment when the stories of heroes gave way to an author's biography; the conditions that fostered the formulation of the fundamental critical category of "the man and his work." For the time being, I wish to restrict myself to the singular relationship that holds between an author and a text, the manner in which a text apparently points to this figure who is outside and precedes it.

Beckett supplies a direction: "What matter who's speaking, someone said, what matter who's speaking."[5] In an indifference such as this we must recognize one of the fundamental ethical principles of contemporary writing. It is not simply "ethical" because it characterizes our way of speaking and writing, but because it stands as an immanent rule, endlessly adopted and yet never fully applied. As a principle, it dominates writing as an ongoing practice and slights our customary attention to the finished product.[6] For the sake of illustration, we need only consider two of its major themes. First, the writing of our day has freed itself from the necessity of "expression"; it only refers to itself, yet it is not restricted to the confines of interiority. On the contrary, we recognize it in its exterior deployment.[7] This reversal transforms writing into an interplay of signs, regulated less by the content it signifies than by the very nature of the signifier. Moreover, it implies an action that is always testing the limits of its regularity, transgressing and reversing an order that it accepts and manipulates. Writing unfolds like a game that inevitably moves beyond its own rules and finally leaves them behind. Thus, the essential basis of this writing is not the exalted emotions related to the act of composition or the insertion of a subject into language. Rather, it is primarily concerned with creating an opening where the writing subject endlessly disappears.[8]

The second theme is even more familiar: it is the kinship between writing and death. This relationship inverts the age-old conception of Greek narrative or epic, which was designed to guarantee the immortality of a hero. The hero accepted an early death because his life, consecrated and magnified by death, passed into immortality; and the narrative redeemed his acceptance of death. In a different sense, Arabic stories, and *The Arabian Nights* in particular, had as their motivation, their theme and pretext, this strategy for defeating death. Storytellers continued their narratives late into the night to forestall death and to delay the inevitable moment when everyone must fall silent. Scheherazade's story is a desperate inversion of murder; it is the effort, throughout all those nights, to exclude death from the circle of existence.[9] This conception of a spoken or written narrative as a protection against death has been transformed by our culture. Writing is now linked to sacrifice and to the sacrifice of life itself; it is a voluntary obliteration of the self that does not require representation in books because it takes place in the everyday existence of the writer. Where a work had the duty of creating immortality, it now attains the right to kill, to become the murderer of its author. Flaubert, Proust, and Kafka are obvious examples of this reversal.[10] In addition, we find the link between writing and death manifested in the total effacement of the individual characteristics of the writer; the quibbling and confrontations that a writer generates between himself and his text cancel out the signs of his particular individuality. If we wish to know the writer in our day, it will be through the singularity of his absence and in his link to death, which has transformed him into a victim of his own writing. While all of this is familiar in philosophy, as in literary criticism, I am not certain that the consequences derived from the disappearance or death of the author have been fully explored or that the importance of this event has been appreciated. To be specific, it seems to me that the themes destined to replace the privileged position accorded the author have merely served to arrest the possibility of genuine change. Of these, I will examine two that seem particularly important.

To begin with, the thesis concerning a work. It has been understood that the task of criticism is not to reestablish the ties between an author and his work or to reconstitute an author's thought and experience through his works and, further, that criticism should concern itself with the structures of a work, its architectonic forms, which are studied for their intrinsic and internal relationships.[11] Yet, what of a context that questions the concept of a work? What, in short, is the strange unit des-

ignated by the term, work? What is necessary to its composition, if a work
is not something written by a person called an "author?" Difficulties
arise on all sides if we raise the question in this way. If an individual is not
an author, what are we to make of those things he has written or said, left
among his papers or communicated to others? Is this not properly a work?
What, for instance, were Sade's papers before he was consecrated as an author? Little more, perhaps, than roles of paper on which he endlessly un-
ravelled his fantasies while in prison.

Assuming that we are dealing with an author, is everything he wrote
and said, everything he left behind, to be included in his work? This problem is both theoretical and practical. If we wish to publish the complete
works of Nietzsche, for example, where do we draw the line? Certainly,
everything must be published, but can we agree on what "everything"
means? We will, of course, include everything that Nietzsche himself
published, along with the drafts of his works, his plans for aphorisms, his
marginal notations and corrections. But what if, in a notebook filled with
aphorisms, we find a reference, a reminder of an appointment, an address,
or a laundry bill, should this be included in his works? Why not? These
practical considerations are endless once we consider how a work can be
extracted from the millions of traces left by an individual after his death.
Plainly, we lack a theory to encompass the questions generated by a work
and the empirical activity of those who naively undertake the publication
of the complete works of an author often suffers from the absence of this
framework. Yet more questions arise. Can we say that *The Arabian
Nights,* and *Stromates* of Clement of Alexandria, or the *Lives* of Diogenes
Laertes constitute works? Such questions only begin to suggest the range
of our difficulties, and, if some have found it convenient to bypass the individuality of the writer or his status as an author to concentrate on a
work, they have failed to appreciate the equally problematic nature of the
word "work" and the unity it designates.

Another thesis has detained us from taking full measure of the author's disappearance. It avoids confronting the specific event that makes
it possible and, in subtle ways, continues to preserve the existence of the
author. This is the notion of *écriture.*[12] Strictly speaking, it should allow
us not only to circumvent references to an author, but to situate his recent
absence. The conception of *écriture,* as currently employed, is concerned
with neither the act of writing nor the indications, as symptoms or signs
within a text, of an author's meaning; rather, it stands for a remarkably
profound attempt to elaborate the conditions of any text, both the conditions of its spatial dispersion and its temporal deployment.

It appears, however, that this concept, as currently employed, has
merely transposed the empirical characteristics of an author to a transcendental anonymity. The extremely visible signs of the author's empir-

ical activity are effaced to allow the play, in parallel or opposition, of religious and critical modes of characterization. In granting a primordial status to writing, do we not, in effect, simply reinscribe in transcendental terms the theological affirmation of its sacred origin or a critical belief in its creative nature? To say that writing, in terms of the particular history it made possible, is subjected to forgetfulness and repression, is this not to reintroduce in transcendental terms the religious principle of hidden meanings (which require interpretation) and the critical assumption of implicit significations, silent purposes, and obscure contents (which give rise to commentary)? Finally, is not the conception of writing as absence a transposition into transcendental terms of the religious belief in a fixed and continuous tradition or the aesthetic principle that proclaims the survival of the work as a kind of enigmatic supplement of the author beyond his own death?[13]

This conception of *écriture* sustains the privileges of the author through the safeguard of the a priori; the play of representations that formed a particular image of the author is extended within a gray neutrality. The disappearance of the author—since Mallarmé, an event of our time—is held in check by the transcendental. Is it not necessary to draw a line between those who believe that we can continue to situate our present discontinuities within the historical and transcendental tradition of the nineteenth century and those who are making a great effort to liberate themselves, once and for all, from this conceptual framework?[14]

It is obviously insufficient to repeat empty slogans: the author has disappeared; God and man died a common death.[15] Rather, we should reexamine the empty space left by the author's disappearance; we should attentively observe, along its gaps and fault lines, its new demarcations, and the reapportionment of this void; we should await the fluid functions released by this disappearance. In this context we can briefly consider the problems that arise in the use of an author's name. What is the name of an author? How does it function? Far from offering a solution, I will attempt to indicate some of the difficulties related to these questions.

The name of an author poses all the problems related to the category of the proper name. (Here, I am referring to the work of John Searle,[16] among others.) Obviously not a pure and simple reference, the proper name (and the author's name as well) has other than indicative functions. It is more than a gesture, a finger pointed at someone; it is, to a certain extent, the equivalent of a description. When we say "Aristotle," we are using a word that means one or a series of definite descriptions of the type: "the author of the *Analytics*," or "the founder of ontology," and so forth.[17] Furthermore, a proper name has other functions than that of signification: when we discover that Rimbaud has not written *La Chasse spirituelle*, we cannot maintain that the meaning of the proper name or this author's name has been altered. The proper name and the name of an author oscillate between the poles of description and designation, and, granting that they are linked to what they name, they are not totally determined either by their descriptive or designative functions.[18] Yet—and it is here that the specific difficulties attending an author's name appear—the link between a proper name and the individual being named and the link between an author's name and that which it names are not isomorphous and do not function in the same way; and these differences require clarification.

To learn, for example, that Pierre Dupont does not have blue eyes, does not live in Paris, and is not a doctor does not invalidate the fact that the name, Pierre Dupont, continues to refer to the same person; there has been no modification of the designation that links the name to the person. With the name of an author, however, the problems are far more complex. The disclosure that Shakespeare was not born in the house that tourists now visit would not modify the functioning of the author's name, but, if it were proved that he had not written the sonnets that we attribute to him, this would constitute a significant change and affect the manner in which the author's name functions. Moreover, if we establish that Shakespeare wrote Bacon's *Organon* and that the same author was responsible for both the works of Shakespeare and those of Bacon, we would have introduced a third type of alteration which completely modifies the functioning of the author's name. Consequently, the name of an author is not precisely a proper name among others.

Many other factors sustain this paradoxical singularity of the name of an author. It is altogether different to maintain that Pierre Dupont does not exist and that Homer or Hermes Trismegistes have never existed. While the first negation merely implies that there is no one by the name of Pierre Dupont, the second indicates that several individuals have been referred to by one name or that the real author possessed none of the traits traditionally associated with Homer or Hermes. Neither is it the same thing to say that Jacques Durand, not Pierre Dupont, is the real name of X and that Stendhal's name was Henri Beyle. We could also examine the function and meaning of such statements as "Bourbaki is this or that person," and "Victor Eremita, Climacus, Anticlimacus, Frater Taciturnus, Constantin Constantius, all of these are Kierkegaard."

These differences indicate that an author's name is not simply an element of speech (as a subject, a complement, or an element that could be replaced by a pronoun or other parts of speech). Its presence is functional in that it serves as a means of classification. A name can group together a number of texts and thus differentiate them from others. A name also establishes different forms of relationships among texts. Neither Hermes not Hippocrates existed in the sense that we can say Balzac existed, but the fact that a number of texts were attached to a single name implies that relationships of homogeneity, filiation, reciprocal explanation, authentification, or of common utilization were established among them. Finally, the author's name characterizes a particular manner of existence of discourse. Discourse that possesses an author's name is not to be immediately consumed and forgotten; neither is it accorded the momentary attention given to ordinary, fleeting words. Rather, its status and its manner of reception are regulated by the culture in which it circulates.

We can conclude that, unlike a proper name, which moves from the interior of a discourse to the real person outside who produced it, the name of the author remains at the contours of texts—separating one from the other, defining their form, and characterizing their mode of existence. It points to the existence of certain groups of discourse and refers to the status of this discourse within a society and culture. The author's name is not a function of a man's civil status, nor is it fictional; it is situated in the breach, among the discontinuities, which gives rise to new groups of discourse and their singular mode of existence.[19] Consequently, we can say that in our culture, the name of an author is a variable that accompanies only certain texts to the exclusion of others: a private letter may have a signatory, but it does not have an author; a contract can have an underwriter, but not an author; and, similarly, an anonymous poster attached to a wall may have a writer, but he cannot be an author. In this sense, the function of an author is to characterize the existence, circulation, and operation of certain discourses within a society.

In dealing with the "author" as a function of discourse, we must consider the characteristics of a discourse that support this use and determine its difference from other discourses. If we limit our remarks to only those books or texts with authors, we can isolate four different features.

First, they are objects of appropriation; the form of property they have become is of a particular type whose legal codification was accomplished some years ago. It is important to notice, as well, that its status as property is historically secondary to the penal code controlling its appropriation. Speeches and books were assigned real authors, other than mythical or important religious figures, only when the author became subject to punishment and to the extent that his discourse was considered transgressive. In our culture—undoubtedly in others as well—discourse was not originally a thing, a product, or a possession, but an action situated in a bipolar field of sacred and profane, lawful and unlawful, religious and blasphemous. It was a gesture charged with risks long before it became a possession caught in a circuit of property values.[20] But it was at the moment when a system of ownership and strict copyright rules were established (toward the end of the eighteenth and beginning of the nineteenth century) that the transgressive properties always intrinsic to the act of writing became the forceful imperative of literature.[21] It is as if the author, at the moment he was accepted into the social order of property which governs our culture, was compensating for his new status by reviving the older bipolar field of discourse in a systematic practice of transgression and by restoring the danger of writing which, on another side, had been conferred the benefits of property.

Secondly, the "author-function"[22] is not universal or constant in all discourse. Even within our civilization, the same types of texts have not always required authors; there was a time when those texts which we now call "literary" (stories, folk tales, epics, and tragedies) were accepted, circulated, and valorized without any question about the identity of their author. Their anonymity was ignored because their real or supposed age was a sufficient guarantee of their authenticity. Texts, however, that we now call "scientific" (dealing with cosmology and the heavens, medicine or illness, the natural sciences or geography) were only considered truthful during the Middle Ages if the name of the author was indicated. Statements on the order of "Hippocrates said ... " or "Pliny tells us that ... " were not merely formulas for an argument based on authority; they marked a proven discourse. In the seventeenth and eighteenth centuries, a totally new conception was developed when scientific texts were accepted on their own merits and positioned within an anonymous and coherent conceptual system of established truths and methods of verification. Authentification no longer required reference to the individual who had produced them; the role of the author disappeared as an index of truthfulness and, where it remained as an inventor's name, it was merely to denote a specific theorem or proposition, a strange effect, a property, a body, a group of elements, or pathological syndrome.

At the same time, however, "literary" discourse was acceptable only if it carried an author's name; every text of poetry or fiction was obliged to state its author and the date, place, and circumstance of its writing. The meaning and value attributed to the text depended on this information. If by accident or design a text was presented anonymously, every effort was made to locate its author. Literary anonymity was of interest only as a puzzle to be solved as, in our day, literary works are totally dominated by the sovereignty of the author. (Undoubtedly, these remarks are far too categorical. Criticism has been concerned for some time now with aspects of a text not fully dependent on the notion of an individual creator; studies of genre or the analysis of recurring textual motifs and their variations from a norm other than the author. Furthermore, where in mathematics the author has become little more than a handy reference for a particular theorem or group of propositions, the reference to an author in biology and medicine, or to the date of his research has a substantially different bearing. This latter reference, more than simply indicating the source of information, attests to the "reliability" of the evidence, since it entails an appreciation of the techniques and experimental materials available at a given time and in a particular laboratory.)

The third point concerning this "author-function" is that it is not formed spontaneously through the simple attribution of a discourse to an individual. It results from a complex operation whose purpose is to construct the rational entity we call an author. Undoubtedly, this construction is assigned a "realistic" dimension as we speak of an individual's "profundity" or "creative" power, his intentions or the original inspiration manifested in writing. Nevertheless, these aspects of an individual, which we designate as an author (or which comprise an individual as an author), are projections, in terms always more or less psychological, of our way of handling texts: in the comparisons we make, the traits we extract as pertinent, the continuities we assign, or the exclusions we practice. In addition, all these operations vary according to the period and the form of discourse concerned. A "philosopher" and a "poet" are not constructed in the same manner; and the author of an eighteenth-century novel was formed differently from the modern novelist. There are, nevertheless, transhistorical constants in the rules that govern the construction of an author.

In literary criticism, for example, the traditional methods for defining an author—or, rather, for determining the configuration of the author from existing texts—derive in large part from those used in the Christian tradition to authenticate (or to reject) the particular texts in its possession. Modern criticism, in its desire to "recover" the author from a work, employs devices strongly reminiscent of Christian exegesis when it wished to prove the value of a text by ascertaining the holiness of its author. In *De Viris Illustribus*, Saint Jerome maintains that homonymy is not proof of the common authorship of several works, since many individuals could have the same name or someone could have perversely appropriated another's name. The name, as an individual mark, is not sufficient as it relates to a textual tradition. How, then, can several texts be attributed to an individual author? What norms, related to the function of the author, will disclose the involvement of several authors? According to Saint Jerome, there are four criteria: the texts that must be eliminated from the list of works attributed to a single author are those inferior to the others (thus, the author is defined as a standard level of quality); those whose ideas conflict with the doctrine expressed in the others (here the author is defined as a certain field of conceptual or theoretical coherence); those written in a different style and containing words and phrases not ordinarily found in the other works (the author is seen as a stylistic uniformity); and those referring to events or historical figures subsequent to the death of the author (the author is thus a definite historical figure in which a series of events converge). Although modern criticism does not appear to have these same suspicions concerning authentication, its strategies for defining the author present striking similarities. The author explains the presence of certain events within a text, as well as their transformations, distortions, and their various modifications (and this through an author's biography or by reference to his particular point of view, in the analysis of his social preferences and his position within a class or by delineating his fundamental objectives). The author also constitutes a principle of unity in writing where any unevenness of production is ascribed to changes caused by evolution, maturation, or outside influence. In addition, the author serves to neutralize the contradictions that are found in a series of texts. Governing this function is the belief that there must be—at a particular level of an author's thought, of his conscious or unconscious desire—a point where contradictions are resolved, where the incompatible elements can be shown to relate to one another or to cohere around a fundamental and originating contradiction. Finally, the author is a particular source of expression who, in more or less finished forms, is manifested equally well, and with similar validity, in a text, in letters, fragments, drafts, and so forth. Thus, even while Saint Jerome's four principles of authenticity might seem largely inadequate to modern critics, they, nevertheless, define the critical modalities now used to display the function of the author.[23]

However, it would be false to consider the function of the author as a pure and simple reconstruction after the fact of a text given as passive material, since a text always bears a number of signs that refer to the author. Well known to grammarians, these textual signs are personal pronouns, adverbs of time and place, and the conjugation of verbs.[24] But it is important to note that these elements have a different bearing on texts with an author and on those without one. In the latter, these "shifters" refer to a real speaker and to an actual deictic situation, with certain exceptions such as the case of indirect speech in the first person. When discourse is linked to an author, however, the role of "shifters" is more complex and variable. It is well known that in a novel narrated in the first person, neither the first person pronoun, the present indicative tense, nor, for that matter, its signs of localization refer directly to the writer, either to the time when he wrote, or to the specific act of writing; rather, they stand for a "second self"[25] whose similarity to the author is never fixed and undergoes considerable alteration within the course of a single book. It would be as false to seek the author in relation to the actual writer as to the fictional narrator; the "author-function" arises out of their scission—in the division and distance of the two. One might object that this phenomenon only applies to novels or poetry, to a context of "quasi-discourse," but, in fact, all discourse that supports this "author-function" is characterized by this plurality of egos. In a mathematical treatise, the ego who indicates the circumstances of composition in the preface is not identical, either in terms of his position or his function, to the "I" who concludes a demonstration within the body of the text. The former implies a unique individual who, at a given time and place, succeeded in completing a project, whereas the latter indicates an instance and plan of demonstration that anyone could perform provided the same set of axioms, preliminary operations, and an identical set of symbols were used. It is also possible to locate a third ego: one who speaks of the goals of his investigation, the obstacles encountered, its results, and the problems yet to be solved and this "I" would function in a field of existing or future mathematical discourses. We are not dealing with a system of dependencies where a first and essential use of the "I" is reduplicated, as a kind of fiction, by the other two. On the contrary, the "author-function" in such discourses operates so as to effect the simultaneous dispersion of the three egos.[26]

Further elaboration would, of course, disclose other characteristics of the "author-function," but I have limited myself to the four that seemed the most obvious and important. They can be summarized in the following manner: the "author-function" is tied to the legal and institutional systems that circumscribe, determine, and articulate the realm of discourses; it does not operate in a uniform manner in all discourses, at all times, and in any given culture; it is not defined by the spontaneous attribution of a text to its creator, but through a series of precise and complex procedures; it does not refer, purely and simply, to an actual individual insofar as it simultaneously gives rise to a variety of egos and to a series of subjective positions that individuals of any class may come to occupy.

I am aware that until now I have kept my subject within unjustifiable limits; I should also have spoken of the "author-function" in painting, music, technical fields, and so forth. Admitting that my analysis is restricted to the domain of discourse, it seems that I have given the term "author" an excessively narrow meaning. I have discussed the author only in the limited sense of a person to whom the production of a text, a book, or a work can be ligitimately attributed. However, it is obvious that even within the realm of discourse a person can be the author of much more than a book—of a theory, for instance, of a tradition or a discipline within which new books and authors can proliferate. For convenience, we could say that such authors occupy a "transdiscursive" position.

Homer, Aristotle, and the Church Fathers played this role, as did the first mathematicians and the originators of the Hippocratic tradition. This type of author is surely as old as our civilization. But I believe that the nineteenth century in Europe produced a singular type of author who should not be confused with "great" literary authors, or the authors of canonical religious texts, and the founders of sciences. Somewhat arbitrarily, we might call them "initiators of discursive practices."

The distinctive contribution of these authors is that they produced not only their own work, but the possibility and the rules of formation of other texts. In this sense, their role differs entirely from that of a novelist, for example, who is basically never more than the author of his own text. Freud is not simply the author of *The Interpretation of Dreams* or of *Wit and its Relation to the Unconscious* and Marx is not simply the author of the *Communist Manifesto* or *Capital:* they both established the endless possibility of discourse. Obviously, an easy objection can be made. The author of a novel may be responsible for more than his own text; if he acquires some "importance" in the literary world, his influence can have significant ramifications. To take a very simple example, one could say that Ann Radcliffe did not simply write *The Mysteries of Udolpho* and a few other novels, but also made possible the appearance of Gothic Romances at the beginning of the nineteenth century. To this extent, her function as an author exceeds the limits of her work. However, this objection can be answered by the fact that the possibilities disclosed by the initiators of discursive practices (using the examples of Marx and Freud, whom I believe to be the first and the most important) are significantly different from those suggested by novelists. The novels of Ann Radcliffe put into circulation a certain number of resemblances and analogies patterned on her work—various characteristic signs, figures, relationships, and structures that could be integrated into other books. In short, to say that Ann Radcliffe created the Gothic Romance means that there are certain elements common to her works and to the nineteenth-century Gothic romance: the heroine ruined by her own innocence, the secret fortress that functions as a counter-city, the outlaw-hero who swears revenge on the world that has cursed him, etc. On the other hand, Marx and Freud, as "initiators of discursive practices," not only made possible a certain number of analogies that could be adopted by future texts, but, as importantly, they also made possible a certain number of differences. They cleared a space for the introduction of elements other than their own, which, nevertheless, remain within the field of discourse they initiated. In saying that Freud founded psychoanalysis, we do not simply mean that the concept of libido or the techniques of dream analysis reappear in the writings of Karl Abraham or Melanie Klein, but that he made possible a certain number of differences with respect to his books, concepts, and hypotheses, which all arise out of psychoanalytic discourse.

Is this not the case, however, with the founder of any new science or of any author who successfully transforms an existing science? After all, Galileo is indirectly responsible for the texts of those who mechanically applied the laws he formulated, in addition to having paved the way for the production of statements far different from his own. If Cuvier is the founder of biology and Saussure of linguistics, it is not because they were imitated or that an organic concept or a theory of the sign was uncritically integrated into new texts, but because Cuvier, to a certain extent, made possible a theory of evolution diametrically opposed to his own system and because Saussure made possible a generative grammar radically different from his own structural analysis. Superficially, then, the initiation of discursive practices appears similar to the founding of any scientific endeavor, but I believe there is a fundamental difference.

In a scientific program, the founding act is on an equal footing with its future transformations: it is merely one among the many modifications that it makes possible. This interdependence can take several forms. In the future development of a science, the founding act may appear as little more than a single instance of a more general phenomenon that has been discovered. It might be questioned, in retrospect, for being too intuitive or empirical and submitted to the rigors of new theoretical operations in order to situate it in a formal domain. Finally, it might be thought a hasty generalization whose validity should be restricted. In other words, the founding act of a science can always be rechanneled through the machinery of transformations it has instituted.[27]

On the other hand, the initiation of a discursive practice is heterogeneous to its ulterior transformations. To extend psychoanalytic practice, as initiated by Freud, is not to presume a formal generality that was not claimed at the outset; it is to explore a number of possible applications. To limit it is to isolate in the original texts a small set of propositions or statements that are recognized as having an inaugurative value and that mark other Freudian concepts or theories as derivative. Finally, there are no "false" statements in the work of these initiators; those statements considered inessential or "prehistoric," in that they are associated with another discourse, are simply neglected in favor of the more pertinent aspects of the work. The initiation of a discursive practice, unlike the founding of a science, overshadows and is necessarily detached from its later developments and transformations. As a consequence, we define the theoretical validity of a statement with respect to the work of the initiator, whereas in the case of Galileo or Newton, it is based on the structural and intrinsic norms established in cosmology or physics. Stated schematically, the work of these initiators is not situated in relation to a science or in the space it defines; rather, it is science or discursive practice that relate to their works as the primary points of reference.

In keeping with this distinction, we can understand why it is inevitable that practitioners of such discourses must "return to the origin." Here, as well, it is necessary to distinguish a "return" from scientific "rediscoveries" or "reactivations." "Rediscoveries" are the effects of analogy or isomorphism with current forms of knowledge that allow the perception of forgotten or obscured figures. For instance, Chomsky in his book on Cartesian grammar[28] "rediscovered" a form of knowledge that had been in use from Cordemoy to Humboldt. It could only be understood from the perspective of generative grammar because this later manifestation held the key to its construction: in effect, a retrospective codification of an historical position. "Reactivation" refers to something quite different: the insertion of discourse into totally new domains of generalization, practice, and transformations. The history of mathematics abounds in examples of this phenomenon as the work of Michel Serres on mathematical anamnesis shows.[29]

The phrase, "return to," designates a movement with its proper specificity, which characterizes the initiation of discursive practices. If we return, it is because of a basic and constructive omission, an omission that is not the result of accident or incomprehension.[30] In effect, the act of initiation is such, in its essence, that it is inevitably subjected to its own distortions; that which displays this act and derives from it is, at the same time, the root of its divergences and travesties. This nonaccidental omission must be regulated by precise operations that can be situated, analysed, and reduced in a return to the act of initiation. The barrier imposed by omission was not added from the outside; it arises from the discursive practice in question, which gives it its law. Both the cause of the barrier and the means for its removal, this omission—also responsible for the obstacles that prevent returning to the act of initiation—can only be resolved by a return. In addition, it is always a return to a text in itself, specifically, to a primary and unadorned text with particular attention to those things registered in the interstices of the text, its gaps and absences. We return to those empty spaces that have been masked by omission or concealed in a false and misleading plenitude. In these rediscoveries of an essential lack, we find the oscillation of two characteristic responses: "This point was made—you can't help seeing it if you know how to read"; or, inversely, "No, that point is not made in any of the printed words in the text, but it is expressed through the words, in their relationships and in the distance that separates them." It follows naturally that this return, which is a part of the discursive mechanism, constantly introduces modifications and that the return to a text is not a historical supplement that would come to fix itself upon the primary discursivity and redouble it in the form of an ornament which, after all, is not essential. Rather, it is an effective and necessary means of transforming discursive practice. A study of Galileo's works could alter our knowledge of the history, but not the science, of mechanics; whereas, a reexamination of the books of Freud or Marx can transform our understanding of psychoanalysis or Marxism.

A last feature of these returns is that they tend to reinforce the enigmatic link between an author and his works. A text has an inaugurative value precisely because it is the work of a particular author, and our returns are conditioned by this knowledge. The rediscovery of an unknown text by Newton or Cantor will not modify classical cosmology or group theory; at most, it will change our appreciation of their historical genesis. Bringing to light, however, *An Outline of Psychoanalysis,* to the extent that we recognize it as a book by Freud, can transform not only our historical knowledge, but the field of psychoanalytic theory—if only through a shift of accent or of the center of gravity. These returns, an important component of discursive practices, form a relationship between "fundamental" and mediate authors, which is not identical to that which links an ordinary text to its immediate author.

These remarks concerning the initiation of discursive practices have been extremely schematic, especially with regard to the opposition I have tried to trace between this initiation and the founding of sciences. The distinction between the two is not readily discernible; moreover, there is no proof that the two procedures are mutually exclusive. My only purpose in setting up this opposition, however, was to show that the "author-function," sufficiently complex at the level of a book or a series of texts that bear a definite signature, has other determining factors when analysed in terms of larger entities—groups of works or entire disciplines.

Unfortunately, there is a decided absence of positive propositions in this essay, as it applies to analytic procedures or directions for future research, but I ought at least to give the reasons why I attach such importance to a continuation of this work. Developing a similar analysis could provide the basis for a typology of discourse. A typology of this sort cannot be adequately understood in relation to the grammatical features, formal structures, and objects of discourse, because there undoubtedly exist specific discursive properties or relationships that are irreducible to the rules of grammar and logic and to the laws that govern objects. These properties require investigation if we hope to distinguish the larger categories of discourse. The different forms of relationships (or nonrelationships) that an author can assume are evidently one of these discursive properties.

This form of investigation might also permit the introduction of an historical analysis of discourse. Perhaps the time has come to study not only the expressive value and formal transformations of discourse, but its mode of existence: the modifications and variations, within any culture, of modes of circulation, valorization, attribution, and appropriation. Partially at the expense of themes and concepts that an author places in his work, the "author-function" could also reveal the manner in which discourse is articulated on the basis of social relationships.

Is it not possible to reexamine, as a legitimate extension of this kind of analysis, the privileges of the subject? Clearly, in undertaking an internal and architectonic analysis of a work (whether it be a literary text, a philosophical system, or a scientific work) and in delimiting psychological and biographical references, suspicions arise concerning the absolute nature and creative role of the subject. But the subject should not be entirely abandoned. It should be reconsidered, not to restore the theme of an originating subject, but to seize its functions, its intervention in discourse, and its system of dependencies. We should suspend the typical questions: how does a free subject penetrate the density of things and endow them with meaning; how does it accomplish its design by animating the rules of discourse from within? Rather, we should ask: under what conditions and through what forms can an entity like the subject appear in the order of discourse; what position does it occupy; what functions does it exhibit; and what rules does it follow in each type of discourse? In short, the subject (and its substitutes) must be stripped of its creative role and analysed as a complex and variable function of discourse.

The author—or what I have called the "author-function"—is undoubtedly only one of the possible specifications of the subject and, considering past historical transformations, it appears that the form, the complexity, and even the existence of this function are far from immutable. We can easily imagine a culture where discourse would circulate without any need for an author. Discourses, whatever their status, form, or value, and regardless of our manner of handling them, would unfold in a pervasive anonymity. No longer the tiresome repetitions:

"Who is the real author?"
"Have we proof of his authenticity and originality?"
"What has he revealed of his most profound self in his language?"

New questions will be heard:

"What are the modes of existence of this discourse?"
"Where does it come from; how is it circulated; who controls it?"
"What placements are determined for possible subjects?"
"Who can fulfill these diverse functions of the subject?"

Behind all these questions we would hear little more than the murmur of indifference:

"What matter who's speaking?"

This essay originally appeared in the *Bulletin de la Société française de Philosophie*, 63, No. 3 (1969), 73–104. It was delivered as a lecture before the Society at the Collège de France on February 22, 1969, with Jean Wahl presiding. We have omitted Professor Wahl's introductory remarks and also Foucault's response and the debate that followed his lecture. Foucault's initial statement, however, has been interpolated in the first paragraph of the translation. The interest of the discussion that followed Foucault's paper lies in its preoccupation—especially as voiced by Lucien Goldmann—with Foucault's supposed affinity with the structuralist enterprise. As in the conclusion of *The Archaeology of Knowledge* (esp. pp. 200–201), Foucault forcefully denies this connection. This essay is reproduced here by permission of the Society. (All footnotes supplied by the editor.)

NOTES

1. See "Entretiens sur Michel Foucault" (directed by J. Proust), *La Pensée*, No. 137 (1968), pp. 6–7 and 11; and also Sylvie le Bon, "Un Positivisme déses-perée," *Esprit*, No. 5 (1967), pp. 1317–1319.

2. Foucault's purpose, concerned with determining the "codes" of discourse, is explicitly stated in the Preface to *The Order of Things*, p. xx. These objec-tions—see "Entretiens sur Michel Foucault"—are obviously those of spe-cialists who fault Foucault for his apparent failure to appreciate the facts and complexities of their theoretical field.

3. For an appreciation of Foucault's technique, see Jonathan Culler, "The Lin-guistic Basis of Structuralism," *Structuralism: An Introduction*, ed. David Robey (Oxford: Clarendon Press, 1973), pp. 27–28.

4. *The Archaeology of Knowledge*, trans. A. M. Sheridan Smith (London: Tav-istock, 1972) was published in France in 1969; for discussion of the author, see esp. pp. 92–6, 122.

5. Samuel Beckett, *Texts for Nothing*, trans. Beckett (London: Calder & Boyars, 1974), p. 16.

6. Cf. Edward Said, "The Ethics of Language," *Diacritics*, 4 (1974), 32.

7. On "expression" and writing as self-referential, see Jean-Marie Benoist, "The End of Structuralism," *Twentieth Century Studies*, 3 (1970), 39; and Roland Barthes, *Critique et vérité* (Paris: Collection Tel Quel, 1966). As the following sentence implies, the "exterior deployment" of writing relates to Ferdinand de Saussure's emphasis of the acoustic quality of the signifier, an external phenomena of speech which, nevertheless, responds to its own in-ternal and differential articulation.

8. On "transgression," see above, "A Preface to Transgression," p. 42; and "Language to Infinity," p. 56. Cf. Blanchot, *L'Espace littéraire* (Paris, 1955), p. 58; and David P. Funt, "Newer Criticism and Revolution," *Hudson Re-view*, 22 (1969), 87–96.

9. See above, "Language to Infinity," p. 58.

10. The recent stories of John Barth, collected in *Lost in the Funhouse* and *Chi-mera*, supply interesting examples of Foucault's thesis. The latter work in-cludes, in fact, a novelistic reworking of *Arabian Nights*.

11. Plainly a prescription for criticism as diverse as G. Wilson Knight's *The Wheel of Fire* (London, 1930) and Roland Barthes' *On Racine*, trans. Richard Howard (New York: Hill & Wang, 1964).

12. We have kept the French, *écriture*, with its double reference to the act of writing and to the primordial (and metaphysical) nature of writing as an en-tity in itself, since it is the term that best identifies the program of Jacques Derrida. Like the theme of a self-referential writing, it too builds on a theory of the sign and denotes writing as the interplay of presence and absence in

that "signs represent the present in its absence" ("Differance," in *Speech and Phenomena,* trans. David B. Allison [Evanston, Ill.: Northwestern Univ. Press, 1973], p. 138). See J. Derrida, *De la grammatologie* (Paris: Editions de Minuit, 1967).

13. On "supplement," see *Speech and Phenomena,* pp. 88–104.
14. This statement is perhaps the polemical ground of Foucault's dissociation from phenomenology (and its evolution through Sartre into a Marxist discipline) on one side and structuralism on the other. It also marks his concern that his work be judged on its own merits and not on its reputed relationship to other movements. This insistence informs his appreciation of Nietzsche in "Nietzsche, Genealogy, History" as well as his sense of his own position in the Conclusion of *The Archaeology of Knowledge.*
15. Nietzsche, *The Gay Science,* III, 108.
16. John Searle, *Speech Acts: An Essay in the Philosophy of Language* (Cambridge: Cambridge University Press, 1969), pp. 162–174.
17. Ibid., p. 169.
18. Ibid., p. 172.
19. This is a particularly important point and brings together a great many of Foucault's insights concerning the relationship of an author (subject) to discourse. It reflects his understanding of the traditional and often unexamined unities of discourse whose actual discontinuities are resolved in either of two ways: by reference to an originating subject or to a language, conceived as plenitude, which supports the activities of commentary or interpretation. But since Foucault rejects the belief in the presumed fullness of language that underlies discourse, the author is subjected to the same fragmentation which characterizes discourse and he is delineated as a discontinuous series; for example, see *L'Ordre du discours,* pp. 54–55 and 61–62.
20. In a seminar entitled "L'Epreuve et l'enquête," which Foucault conducted at the University of Montreal in the spring of 1974, he centered the debate around the following question: is the general conviction that truth derives from and is sustained by knowledge not simply a recent phenomenon, a limited case of the ancient and widespread belief that truth is a function of events? In an older time and in other cultures, the search for truth was hazardous in the extreme and truth resided in a danger zone, but if this was so and if truth could only be approached after a long preparation or through the details of a ritualized procedure, it was because it represented power. Discourse, for these cultures, was an active appropriation of power and to the extent that it was successful, it contained the power of truth itself, charged with all its risks and benefits.
21. Cf. *The Order of Things,* p. 300; and above, "A Preface to Transgression, pp. 30–33.
22. Foucault's phrasing of the "author-function" has been retained. This concept should not be confused (as it was by Goldmann in the discussion that followed Foucault's presentation) with the celebrated theme of the "death of man" in *The Order of Things* (pp. 342 and 386). On the contrary, Foucault's purpose is to revitalize the debate surrounding the subject by situating the subject, as a fluid function, within the space cleared by archaeology.

23. See Evaristo Arns, *La Technique du livre d'après Saint Jerome* (Paris, 1953).

24. On personal pronouns ("shifters"), see R. Jakobson, *Selected Writings* (Paris: Mouton, 1971), II, 130–32; and *Essais de linguistique générale* (Paris, 1966), p. 252. For its general implications, see Eugenio Donato, "Of Structuralism and Literature," *MLN*, 82 (1967), 556–58. On adverbs of time and place, see Emile Benveniste, *Problèmes de la linguistique générale* (Paris, 1966), pp. 237–50.

25. Cf. Wayne C. Booth, *The Rhetoric of Fiction* (Chicago: Univ. of Chicago Press, 1961), pp. 67–77.

26. This conclusion relates to Foucault's concern in developing a "philosophy of events" as described in *L'Ordre du discours*, pp. 60–61: "I trust that we can agree that I do not refer to a succession of moments in time, nor to a diverse plurality of thinking subjects; I refer to a caesura which fragments the moment and disperses the subject into a plurality of possible positions and functions."

27. Cf. the discussion of disciplines in *L'Ordre du discours*, pp. 31–38.

28. Noam Chomsky, *Cartesian Linguistics* (New York: Harper & Row, 1966).

29. *La Communication: Hermes I* (Paris: Editions de Minuit, 1968), pp. 78–112.

30. For a discussion of the recent reorientation of the sign, see Foucault's "Nietzsche, Freud, Marx." On the role of repetition, Foucault writes in *L'Ordre du discours:* "The new is not found in what is said, but in the event of its return" (p. 28); see also below, "Theatrum Philosophicum," pp. 186–196.

Four
tradition

T. S. Eliot

Tradition and the Individual Talent

I

In English writing we seldom speak of tradition, though we occasionally apply its name in deploring its absence. We cannot refer to "the tradition" or to "a tradition"; at most, we employ the adjective in saying that the poetry of So-and-so is "traditional" or even "too traditional." Seldom, perhaps, does the word appear except in a phrase of censure. If otherwise, it is vaguely approbative, with the implication, as to the work approved, of some pleasing archaeological reconstruction. You can hardly make the word agreeable to English ears without this comfortable reference to the reassuring science of archaeology.

Certainly the word is not likely to appear in our appreciations of living or dead writers. Every nation, every race, has not only its own creative, but its own critical turn of mind; and is even more oblivious of the shortcomings and limitations of its critical habits than of those of its creative genius. We know, or think we know, from the enormous mass of critical writing that has appeared in the French language the critical method or habit of the French; we only conclude (we are such unconscious people) that the French are "more critical" than we, and sometimes even plume ourselves a little with the fact, as if the French were the less spontaneous. Perhaps they are; but we might remind ourselves that criticism is as inevitable as breathing, and that we should be none the worse for articulating what passes in our minds when we read a book and feel an emotion about it, for criticizing our own minds in their work of criticism. One of the facts that might come to light in this process is our tendency to insist, when we praise a poet, upon those aspects of his work in which he least resembles anyone else. In these aspects or parts of his work we pretend to find what is individual, what is the peculiar essence of the man. We dwell with satisfaction upon the poet's difference from his predecessors, especially his immediate predecessors; we endeavour to find something that can be isolated in order to be enjoyed. Whereas if we approach a poet without his prejudice we shall often find that not only the best, but the most individual parts of his work may be those in which the dead poets, his ancestors, assert their immortality most vigorously. And I do not mean the impressionable period of adolescence, but the period of full maturity.

Yet if the only form of tradition, of handing down, consisted in following the ways of the immediate generation before us in a blind or timid adherence to its successes, "tradition" should positively be discouraged. We have seen many such simple currents soon lost in the sand; and novelty is better than repetition. Tradition is a matter of much wider significance. It cannot be inherited, and if you want it you must obtain it by great labour. It involves, in the first place, the historical sense, which we may call nearly indispensable to anyone who would continue to be a poet beyond his twenty-fifth year; and the historical sense involves a perception, not only of the pastness of the past, but of its presence; the historical sense compels a man to write not merely with his own generation in his bones, but with a feeling that the whole of the literature of Europe from Homer and within it the whole of the literature of his own country has a simultaneous existence and composes a simultaneous order. This historical sense, which is a sense of the timeless as well as of the temporal and of the timeless and of the temporal together, is what makes a writer traditional. And it is at the same time what makes a writer most acutely conscious of his place in time, of his contemporaneity.

No poet, no artist of any art, has his complete meaning alone. His significance, his appreciation is the appreciation of his relation to the dead poets and artists. You cannot value him alone; you must set him, for contrast and comparison, among the dead. I mean this as a principle of aesthetic, not merely historical, criticism. The necessity that he shall conform, that he shall cohere, is not one-sided; what happens when a new work of art is created is something that happens simultaneously to all the works of art which preceded it. The existing monuments form an ideal order among themselves, which is modified by the introduction of the new (the really new) work of art among them. The existing order is complete before the new work arrives; for order to persist after the supervention of novelty, the *whole* existing order must be, if ever so slightly, altered; and so the relations, proportions, values of each work of art toward the whole are readjusted; and this is conformity between the old and the new. Whoever has approved this idea of order, of the form of European, of English literature, will not find it preposterous that the past should be altered by the present as much as the present is directed by the past. And the poet who is aware of this will be aware of great difficulties and responsibilities.

In a peculiar sense he will be aware also that he must inevitably be judged by the standards of the past. I say judged, not amputated, by them;

not judged to be as good as, or worse or better than, the dead; and certainly not judged by the canons of dead critics. It is a judgment, a comparison, in which two things are measured by each other. To conform merely would be for the new work not really to conform at all; it would not be new, and would therefore not be a work of art. And we do not quite say that the new is more valuable because it fits in; but its fitting in is a test of its value— a test, it is true, which can only be slowly and cautiously applied, for we are none of us infallible judges of conformity. We say: it appears to conform, and is perhaps individual, or it appears individual, and may conform; but we are hardly likely to find that it is one and not the other.

To proceed to a more intelligible exposition of the relation of the poet to the past; he can neither take the past as a lump, an indiscriminate bolus, nor can he form himself wholly one one or two private admirations, nor can he form himself wholly upon one preferred period. The first course is inadmissible, the second is an important experience of youth, and the third is a pleasant and highly desirable supplement. The poet must be very conscious of the main current, which does not at all flow invariably through the most distinguished reputations. He must be quite aware of the obvious fact that art never improves, but that the material of art is never quite the same. He must be aware that the mind of Europe— the mind of his own country—a mind which he learns in time to be much more important than his own private mind—is a mind which changes, and that this change is a development which abandons nothing *en route,* which does not superannuate either Shakespeare, or Homer, or the rock drawing of the Magdalenian draughtsmen. That this development, refinement perhaps, complication certainly, is not, from the point of view of the artist, any improvement. Perhaps not even an improvement from the point of view of the psychologist or not to the extent which we imagine; perhaps only in the end based upon a complication in economics and machinery. But the difference between the present and the past is that the conscious present is an awareness of the past in a way and to an extent which the past's awareness of itself cannot show.

Some one said: "The dead writers are remote from us because we *know* so much more than they did." Precisely, and they are that which we know.

I am alive to a usual objection to what is clearly part of my programme for the *métier* of poetry. The objection is that the doctrine requires a ridiculous amount of erudition (pedantry), a claim which can be rejected by appeal to the lives of poets in any pantheon. It will even be affirmed that much learning deadens or perverts poetic sensibility. While, however, we persist in believing that a poet ought to know as much as will not encroach upon his necessary receptivity and necessary laziness, it is not desirable to confine knowledge to whatever can be put into

a useful shape for examinations, drawing-rooms, or the still more pretentious modes of publicity. Some can absorb knowledge, the more tardy
must sweat for it. Shakespeare acquired more essential history from Plu-
tarch than most men could from the whole British Museum. What is to
be insisted upon is that the poet must develop or procure the consciousness of the past and that he should continue to develop this consciousness
throughout his career.

What happens is a continual surrender of himself as he is at the moment to something which is more valuable. The progress of an artist is a
continual self-sacrifice, a continual extinction of personality.

There remains to define this process of depersonalization and its relation to the sense of tradition. It is in this depersonalization that art may
be said to approach the condition of science. I shall, therefore, invite you
to consider, as a suggestive analogy, the action which takes place when a
bit of finely filiated platinum is introduced into a chamber containing
oxygen and sulphur dioxide.

II

Honest criticism and sensitive appreciation is directed not upon the poet
but upon the poetry. If we attend to the confused cries of the newspaper
critics and the susurrus of popular repetition that follows, we shall hear
the names of poets in great numbers; if we seek not Blue-book knowledge
but the enjoyment of poetry, and ask for a poem, we shall seldom find it.
In the last article I tried to point out the importance of the relation of the
poem to other poems by other authors, and suggested the conception of
poetry as a living whole of all the poetry that has ever been written. The
other aspect of this Impersonal theory of poetry is the relation of the
poem to its author. And I hinted, by an analogy, that the mind of the mature poet differs from that of the immature one not precisely in any valuation of "personality," not being necessarily more interesting, or having
"more to say," but rather by being a more finely perfected medium in
which special, or very varied, feelings are at liberty to enter into new combinations.

The analogy was that of the catalyst. When the two gases previously
mentioned are mixed in the presence of a filament of platinum, they form
sulphurous acid. This combination takes place only if the platinum is
present; nevertheless the newly formed acid contains no trace of platinum, and the platinum itself is apparently unaffected; has remained in-
ert, neutral, and unchanged. The mind of the poet is the shred of platinum. It may partly or exclusively operate upon the experience of the man
himself; but, the more perfect the artist, the more completely separate in

him will be the man who suffers and the mind which creates; the more perfectly will the mind digest and transmute the passions which are its material.

The experience, you will notice, the elements which enter the presence of the transforming catalyst, are of two kinds: emotions and feelings. The effect of a work of art upon the person who enjoys it is an experience different in kind from any experience not of art. It may be formed out of one emotion, or may be a combination of several; and various feelings, inhering for the writer in particular words or phrases or images, may be added to compose the final result. Or great poetry may be made without the direct use of any emotion whatever: composed out of feelings solely. Canto XV of the *Inferno* (Brunetto Latini) is a working up of the emotion evident in the situation; but the effect, though single as that of any work of art, is obtained by considerable complexity of detail. The last quatrain gives an image, a feeling attaching to an image, which "came," which did not develop simply out of what precedes, but which was probably in suspension in the poet's mind until the proper combination arrived for it to add itself to. The poet's mind is in fact a receptacle for seizing and storing up numberless feelings, phrases, images, which remain there until all the particles which can unite to form a new compound are present together.

If you compare several representative passages of the greatest poetry you see how great is the variety of types of combination, and also how completely any semi-ethical criterion of "sublimity" misses the mark. For it is not the "greatness," the intensity, of the emotions, the components, but the intensity of the artistic process, the pressure, so to speak, under which the fusion takes place, that counts. The episode of Paolo and Francesca employs a definite emotion, but the intensity of the poetry is something quite different from whatever intensity in the supposed experience it may give the impression of. It is no more intense, furthermore, than Canto XXVI, the voyage of Ulysses, which has not the direct dependence upon an emotion. Great variety is possible in the process of transmution of emotion: the murder of Agamemnon, or the agony of Othello, gives an artistic effect apparently closer to a possible original than the scenes from Dante. In the *Agamemnon,*, the artistic emotion approximates to the emotion of an actual spectator; in *Othello* to the emotion of the protagonist himself. But the difference between art and the event is always absolute; the combination which is the murder of Agamemnon is probably as complex as that which is the voyage of Ulysses. In either case there has been a fusion of elements. The ode of Keats contains a number of feelings which have nothing particular to do with the nightingale, but which the nightingale, partly perhaps because of its attractive name, and partly because of its reputation, served to bring together.

The point of view which I am struggling to attack is perhaps related to the metaphysical theory of the substantial unity of the soul: for my meaning is, that the poet has, not a 'personality' to express, but a particular medium, which is only a medium and not a personality, in which impressions and experiences combine in peculiar and unexpected ways. Impressions and experiences which are important for the man may take no place in the poetry, and those which become important in the poetry may play quite a negligible part in the man, the personality.

I will quote a passage which is unfamiliar enough to be regarded with fresh attention in the light—or darkness—of these observations:

> And now methinks I could e'en chide myself
> For doating on her beauty, though her death
> Shall be revenged after no common action.
> Does the silkworm expend her yellow labours
> For thee? For thee does she undo herself?
> Are lordships sold to maintain ladyships
> For the poor benefit of a bewildering minute?
> Why does yon fellow falsify highways,
> And put his life between the judge's lips,
> To refine such a thing—keeps horse and men
> To beat their valours for her? ...

In this passage (as is evident if it is taken in its context) there is a combination of positive and negative emotions: an intensely strong attraction towards beauty and an equally intense fascination by the ugliness which is contrasted with it and which destroys it. This balance of contrasted emotion is in the dramatic situation to which the speech is pertinent, but that situation alone is inadequate to it. This is, so to speak, the structural emotion, provided by the drama. But the whole effect, the dominant tone, is due to the fact that a number of floating feelings, having an affinity to this emotion by no means superficially evident, have combined with it to give us a new art emotion.

It is not in his personal emotions, the emotions provoked by particular events in his life, that the poet is in any way remarkable or interesting. His particular emotions may be simple, or crude, or flat. The emotion in his poetry will be a very complex thing, but not with the complexity of the emotions of people who have very complex or unusual emotions in life. One error, in fact, of eccentricity in poetry is to seek for new human emotions to express; and in this search for novelty in the wrong place it discovers the perverse. The business of the poet is not to find new emotions, but to use the ordinary ones and, in working them up into poetry, to express feelings which are not in actual emotions at all. And emotions which he has never experienced will serve his turn as well as those familiar to him. Consequently, we must believe that "emotion recollected in tranquillity" is an inexact formula. For it is neither emotion, nor recollection, nor, without distortion of meaning, tranquillity. It is a concentration, and a new thing resulting from the concentration, of a very great number of experiences which to the practical and active person would not seem to be experiences at all; it is a concentration which does not happen consciously or of deliberation. These experiences are not "recollected," and they finally unite in an atmosphere which is "tranquil" only in that it is a passive attending upon the event. Of course this is not quite the whole story. There is a great deal, in the writing of poetry, which must be conscious and deliberate. In fact, the bad poet is usually unconscious where he ought to be conscious, and conscious where he ought to be unconscious. Both errors tend to make him "personal." Poetry is not a turning loose of emotion, but an escape from emotion; it is not the expression of personality, but an escape from personality. But, of course, only those who have personality and emotions know what it means to want to escape from these things.

III

δ δζ νοῦς Ισως θεώτεϱόυ τι καὶ δπμθές ἐστω

This essay proposes to halt at the frontier of metaphysics or mysticism, and confine itself to such practical conclusions as can be applied by the responsible person interested in poetry. To divert interest from the poet to the poetry is a laudable aim: for it would conduce to a juster estimation of actual poetry, good and bad. There are many people who appreciate the expression of sincere emotion in verse, and there is a smaller number of people who can appreciate technical excellence. But very few know when there is expression of *significant* emotion, emotion which has its life in the poem and not in the history of the poet. The emotion of art is impersonal. And the poet cannot reach this impersonality without surrendering himself wholly to the work to be done. And he is not likely to know what is to be done unless he lives in what is not merely the present, but the present moment of the past, unless he is conscious, not of what is dead, but of what is already living.

Jurij Tynjanov
(Dedicated to Boris Eixenbaum)

On Literary Evolution*

1. Within the cultural disciplines literary history still retains the status of a colonial territory. On the one hand, individualistic psychologism dominates it to a significant extent, particularly in the West, unjustifiably replacing the problem of literature with the question of the author's psychology, while the problem of literary evolution becomes the problem of the genesis of literary phenomena. On the other hand, a simplified causal approach to a literary order leads to a sharp break between the literary order itself and the point of observation, which always turns out to be the major but also the most remote social orders. The organization of a closed literary order and the examination of the evolution within it sometimes collides with the neighboring cultural, behavioral, and social orders in the broad sense. Thus such an effort is doomed to incompleteness. The theory of value in literary investigation has brought about the danger of studying major but isolated works and has changed the history of literature into a *history of generals*. The blind rejection of a history of generals has in turn caused an interest in the study of mass literature, but no clear theoretical awareness of how to study it or what the nature of its significance is.

Finally, the relationship between the history of literature and living contemporary literature—a relationship useful and very necessary to science—is not always necessary and useful to the development of literature. The representatives of literature are ready to view the history of literature as the codification of certain traditional norms and laws and to confuse the historical character of a literary phenomenon with "historicism." As a result of this conflict, there has arisen an attempt to study isolated works and the laws of their construction on an extrahistorical plane, resulting in the abolition of the history of literature.

*"O literaturnoj èvoljucii," *Arxaisty i novatory* (Leningrad, 1929), pp. 30–47. Translated by C. A. Luplow. The first Russian version was published in 1927.

2. In order to become finally a science, the history of literature must claim reliability. All of its terminology, and first of all the very term, "the history of literature," must be reconsidered. The term proves to be extremely broad, covering both the material history of belles lettres, the history of verbal art, and the history of writing in general. It is also pretentious, since "the history of literature" considers itself a priori a discipline ready to enter into "the history of culture" as a system equipped with a scientific methodology. As yet it has no right to such a claim.

Meanwhile, the historical investigations of literature fall into at least two main types, depending on the points of observation the investigation of the genesis of literary phenomena, and the investigation of the evolution of a literary order, that is, of literary changeability.

The point of view determines not only the significance but also the nature of the phenomenon being studied. In the investigation of literary evolution, the moment of genesis has its own significance and character, which are obviously not the same as in the investigation of the genesis per se.

Furthermore, the study of literary evolution or changeability must reject the theories of naive evaluation, which result from the confusion of points of observation, in which evaluation is carried over from one epoch or system into another. At the same time, evaluation itself must be freed from its subjective coloring, and the "value" of a given literary phenomenon must be considered as having an "evolutionary significance and character."

The same must also apply to such concepts as "epigonism," "dilettantism," or "mass literature," which are for now evaluative concepts.[1]

Tradition, the basic concept of the established history of literature, has proved to be an unjustifiable abstraction of one or more of the literary elements of a given system within which they occupy the same plane and play the same role. They are equated with the like elements of another system in which they are on a different plane, thus they are brought into a seemingly unified, fictitiously integrated system.

The main concept for literary evolution is the *mutation* of systems, and thus the problem of "traditions" is transferred onto another plane.

3. Before this basic problem can be analyzed, it must be agreed that a literary work is a system, as is literature itself. Only after this basic agreement has been established is it possible to create a literary science which does not superficially examine diverse phenomena but studies them closely. In this way the problem of the role of contiguous systems in literary evolution is actually posited instead of being rejected.

The analysis of the separate elements of a work, such as the composition, style, rhythm, and syntax in prose, and the rhythm and semantics in poetry, provides sufficient evidence that these elements, within certain limits, can be abstracted as a *working hypothesis,* although they are interrelated and interacting. The study of rhythm in poetry and prose was bound to show that the role of a given element is different in different systems.

The interrelationship of each element with every other in a literary work and with the whole literary system as well may be called the constructional *function* of the given element.

On close examination, such a function proves to be a complex concept. An element is on the one hand interrelated with similar elements in other works in other systems, and on the other hand it is interrelated with different elements within the same work. The former may be termed the *auto-function* and the latter, the *syn-function.*

Thus, for example, the lexicon of a given work is interrelated with both the whole literary lexicon and the general lexicon of the language, as well as with other elements of that given work. These two components or functions operate simultaneously but are not of equal relevance.

The function of archaisms, for example, depends wholly on the system within which they are used. In Lomonosov's system, in which lexical coloring plays a dominant role, such archaisms function as "elevated" word usage. They are used for their lexical association with Church Slavic. In Tjutčev's work archaisms have a different function. In some instances they are abstract, as in the pair: *fontan-vodomet* [fountain-spout]. An interesting example is the usage of archaisms in an ironical function: *"Pušek grom i musikija"* [Thunder of guns and musicke] is used by a poet who otherwise employs a word such as *musikijskij* [musicall] in a completely different function. The auto-function, although it is not decisive, makes the existence of the syn-function possible and at the same time conditions it. Thus up to the time of Tjutčev, in the eighteenth and nineteenth centuries, there existed an extensive parodic literature in which archaisms had a parodic function. But the semantic and intonational system of the given work finally determines the function of a given expression, in this case determining the word usage to be "ironic" rather than "elevated."

It is incorrect to isolate the elements from one system outside their constructional function and to correlate them with other systems.

4. Is the so-called "immanent" study of a work as a system possible without comparing it with the general literary system? Such an isolated study of a literary work is equivalent to abstracting isolated elements and examining them outside their work. Such abstracting is continuously applied to contemporary works and may be successful in literary criticism, since the interrelationship of a contemporary work with contemporary literature is in advance an established, although concealed, fact. (The interrelationship of a work with other works by the same author, its relationship to genre, and so on, belong here.)

Even in contemporary literature, however, isolated study is impossible. The very existence of a fact *as literary* depends on its differential quality, that is, on its interrelationship with both literary and extraliterary orders. Thus, its existence depends on its function. What in one epoch would be a literary fact would in another be a common matter of social communication, and vice versa, depending on the whole literary system in which the given fact appears.

Thus the friendly letter of Deržavin is a social fact. The friendly letter of the Karamzin and Puškin epoch is a literary fact. Thus one has the literariness of memoirs and diaries in one system and their extraliterariness in another.

We cannot be certain of the structure of a work if it is studied in isolation.

Finally, the auto-function, that is, the interrelationship of an element with similar elements in other systems, conditions the syn-function, that is, the constructionsl function of the element.

Thus, whether or not an element is "effaced" is important. But what is the effacement of a line, meter, plot structure, and so on? What, in other words, is the "automatization" of one or another element?

The following is an example from linguistics. When the referential meaning of a word is effaced, that word becomes the expression of a relationship, a connection, and thus it becomes an auxiliary word. In other words, its function changes. The same is true of the "automatization" of a literary element. It does not disappear. Its function simply changes, and it becomes auxiliary. If the meter of a poem is "effaced," then the other signs of verse and the other elements of the work become more important in its place, and the meter takes on other functions.

Thus the short feuilleton verse of the newspaper uses mainly effaced, banal meters which have long been rejected by poetry. No one would read it as a "poem" related to "poetry." Here the effaced meter is a means of attaching feuilleton material from everyday life to literature. Meter thus has an auxiliary function, which is completely different from its function in a poetic work. This also applied to parody in the verse feuilleton. Parody is viable only in so far as what is being parodied is still alive. What literary significance can the thousandth parody of Lermontov's "When the golden cornfield sways ... " or Puškin's "The Prophet" have today? The verse feuilleton, however, uses such parody constantly. Here again we have the same phenomenon: the function of parody has become auxiliary, as it serves to apply extraliterary facts to literature.

In a work in which the so-called plot is effaced, the story carries out different functions than in a work in which it is not effaced. The story might be used merely to motivate style or as a strategy for developing the material. Crudely speaking, from our vantage point in a particular literary system, we would be inclined to reduce nature descriptions in old

novels to an auxiliary role, to the role of making transitions or retarda-
tion; therefore we would almost ignore them, although from the vantage
point of a different literary system we would be forced to consider nature
descriptions as the main, dominant element. In other words, there are situations in which the story simply provides the motivation for the treatment of "static descriptions."

5. The more difficult and less studied question of literary genres can
be resolved in the same way. The novel, which seems to be an integral
genre that has developed in and of itself over the centuries, turns out to be
not an integral whole but a variable. Its material changes from one literary
system to another, as does its method of introducing extraliterary language materials into literature. Even the features of the genre evolve. The
genres of the "short story" and the "novella" were defined by different features in the system of the twenties to forties than they are in our time, as
is obvious from their very names. We tend to name genres according to
secondary features or, crudely speaking, by size. For us the labels, short
story, novella, and novel, are adequate only to define the quantity of
printed pages. This proves not so much the "automatization" of genres in
our literary system as the fact that we define genres by other features. The
size of a thing, the quantity of verbal material, is not an indifferent feature; we cannot, however, define the genre of a work if it is isolated from
the system. For example, what was called an ode in the 1820s or by Fet was
so labeled on the basis of features different from those used to define an
ode in Lomonosov's time.

Consequently, we may conclude that the study of isolated genres outside the features characteristic of the genre system with which they are
related is impossible. The historical novel of Tolstoj is not related to the
historical novel of Zagoskin, but to the prose of his contemporaries.

6. Strictly speaking, one cannot study literary phenomena outside of
their interrelationships. Such, for example, is the problem of prose and poetry. We tacitly consider metrical prose to be prose, and nonmetrical free
verse to be poetry, without considering the fact that in another literary
system we would thus be placed in a difficult position. The point is that
prose and poetry are interrelated and that there is a mutually shared function of prose and poetry. (Note the interrelationship of prose and poetry in
their respective development, as established by Boris Èjxenbaum.)

The function of poetry in a particular literary system was fulfilled by
the formal element of meter; but prose displays differentiation and develops, and so does poetry. The differentiation of one interrelated type leads
to, or better, is connected with, the differentiation of another interrelated
type. Thus metrical prose arises, as in the works of Adrej Belyj. This is
connected with the transfer of the verse function in poetry from meter

onto other features which are in part secondary and resultant. Such features may be rhythm, used as the feature of verse units, a particular syntax or particular lexicon, and so on. The function of prose with regard to verse remains, but the formal elements fulfilling this function are different. In the course of centuries the further evolution of forms may consolidate the function of verse with regard to prose, transfer it onto a whole series of other features, or it may infringe upon it and make it unessential. And just as in contemporary literature the interrelationship of genres is hardly essential and is established according to secondary signs, so a period may come in which it will be unessential whether a work is written in prose or poetry.

7. The evolutionary relationship of function and formal elements is a completely uninvestigated problem. An example is given above of how the evolution of forms results in a change of function. There are also many examples of how a form with an undetermined function creates or defines a new one, and there are also others in which a function seeks its own form. I will give an example in which both occurred together.

In the archaist trend of the 1820s the function of the combined elevated and folk verse epos arises. *The interrelationship of literature with the social order led to the large verse form.* But there were no formal elements, and the demands of the social system turned out to be unequal to the demands of literature. Then the search for formal elements began. In 1824 Katenin advocated the octave as the formal element of the poetic epopea. The passionate quarrels concerning the seemingly innocent octave were appropriate to the tragic "orphanhood" of function without form. The epos of the archaists failed. Six years later Ševyrev and Puškin used the form in a different function: to break with the whole iambic tetrameter epos and create a new, "debased" (as opposed to "elevated"), prosaicized epos, such as Puškin's *Little House in Kolomna*.

The relationship between form and function is not accidental. The comparable combination of a particular lexicon with a particular meter by Katenin and then twenty or thirty years later by Nekrasov, who probably did not know about Katenin, was not accidental.

The variability of the functions of a given formal element, the rise of some new function of a formal element, and the attaching of a formal element to a function are all important problems of literary evolution; but there is no room to study or resolve these problems here. I would like to say only that the whole problem of literature as a system depends on further investigation.

8. The assumption that the interrelationship of literary phenomena occurs when a work enters into a synchronic literary system and there "acquires" a function is not entirely correct. The very concept of a con-

tinuously evolving synchronic system is contradictory. A literary system is first of all a *system of the functions of the literary order which are in continual interrelationship with other orders.* Systems change in their composition, but the differentiation of human activities remains. The evolution of literature, as of other cultural systems, does not coincide either in tempo or in character with the systems with which it is interrelated. This is owing to the specificity of the material with which it is concerned. The evolution of the structural function occurs rapidly; the evolution of the literary function occurs over epochs; and the evolution of the functions of a whole literary system in relation to neighboring systems occurs over centuries.

9. Since a system is not an equal interaction of all elements but places a group of elements in the foreground—the "dominant"—and thus involves the deformation of the remaining elements, a work enters into literature and takes on its own literary function through this dominant. Thus we correlate poems with the verse category, not with the prose category, not on the basis of all their characteristics, but only of some of them. The same is true concerning genres. We relate a novel to "the novel" on the basis of its size and the nature of its plot development, while at one time it was distinguished by the presence of a love intrigue.

Another interesting fact from an evolutionary point of view is the following. A work is correlated with a particular literary system depending on its deviation, its "difference" as compared with the literary system with which it is confronted. Thus, for example, the unusually sharp argument among the critics of the 1820s over the genre of the Puškin narrative poem arose because the Puškin genre was a combined, mixed, new genre without a ready-made "name." The sharper the divergence or differentiation from a particular literary system, the more that system from which the derivation occurs is accentuated. Thus, free verse emphasized the verse principle of *nonmetrical* features, while Sterne's novel emphasized the compositional principle of *nonplot* features (Sklovskij). The following is an analogy from linguistics: "The variability of the word stem makes it the center of maximum expressiveness and thus extricates it from the net of prefixes which do not change" (Vendryes).

10. What constitutes the interrelationship of literature with neighboring orders? What, moreover, are these neighboring orders? The answer is obvious: social conventions.

Yet, in order to solve the problem of the interrelationship of literature with social conventions, the question must be posited: *how and by what means* are social conventions interrelated with literature? Social conventions are by nature many-sided and complex, and only the function of all their aspects is specific in it. Social conventions are correlated with literature first of all in its verbal aspect. This interrelationship is realized through language. That is, literature in relation to social conventions has a verbal function.

We use the term "orientation." It denotes approximately the "creative intention of the author." Yet it happens that "the intention may be good, but the fulfillment bad." Furthermore, the author's intention can only be a catalyst. In using a specific literary material, the author may yield to it, thus departing from his first intention. Thus Griboedov's *Wit Works Woe* was supposed to be "elevated" and even "grandiose," according to the author's terminology. But instead it turned out to be a political publicistic comedy of the archaist school. *Evgenij Onegin* was first meant to be a "satiric narrative poem" in which the author would be "brimming over with bitterness." However, while working on the fourth chapter, Puškin had already said, "Where is my satire? There's not a trace of it in *Evgenij Onegin*."

The structural function, that is, the interrelationship of elements within a work, changes the "author's intention" into a catalyst, but does nothing more. "Creative freedom" thus becomes an optimistic slogan which does not correspond to reality, but yields instead to the slogan "creative necessity."

The literary function, that is, the interrelationship of a work with the literary order, completes the whole thing. If we eliminate the teleological, goal-oriented allusion, the "intention," from the word "orientation," what happens? The "orientation" of a literary work then proves to be its verbal function, its interrelationship with the social conventions.

The "orientation" of the Lomonosov ode, its verbal function, is oratorical. The word is oriented on *pronunciation*. and to carry further the associations with actual life, the orientation is on declamation in the large palace hall. By the time of Karamzin, the ode was literarily "worn out." The "orientation" had died out or narrowed down in significance and had been transferred onto other forms related to life. Congratulatory odes, as well as others, became "uniform verses," i.e., what are purely real-life phenomena. Ready-made literary genres did not exist. Everyday verbal communication took their place. The verbal function, or orientation, was seeking its forms and found them in the romance, the joking play with rhymes, *bouts rimés*, charades, and so on. And here the moment of genesis, the presence of certain forms of everyday speech, received evolutionary significance. These speech phenomena were found in the salon of Karamzin's epoch. And the salon, a fact of everyday life, at this time became a literary fact. In this way the forms of social life acquired a literary function.

Similarly, the semantics of the intimate domestic circle always exists, but in particular periods it takes on a literary function. Such, too, is the application of *accidental results*. The rough drafts of Puškin's verse programs and the drafts of his "scenarios" became his finished prose. This is possible only through the evolution of a whole system—through the evolution of its orientation.

An analogy from our own time of the struggle between two orientations is seen in the mass orientation of Majakovskij's poetry ("the ode") in competition with the romance, chamber-style orientation of Esenin ("the elegy").

11. The verbal function must also be taken into consideration in dealing with the problem of the reverse expansion of literature into actual life. The *literary personality,* or the *author's personality,* or at various times the *hero,* becomes the verbal orientation of literature. And from there it enters into real life. Such are the lyric heroes of Byron in relationship to his "literary personality," i.e., to the personality which came to life for the readers of his poems and which was thus transferred into life. Such is the "literary personality" of Heine, which is far removed from the real biographical Heine. In given periods, biography becomes oral, apocryphal literature. This happens naturally, in connection with the speech orientation of a given system. Thus, one had Puškin, Tolstoj, Blok, Majakovskij, and Esenin as opposed to the absence of a literary personality in Leskov, Turgenev, Fet, Majkov, Gumilev, and others. This corresponds to the absence of a speech orientation on "the literary personality." Obviously, special real-life conditions are necessary for the expansion of literature into life.

12. Such is the immediate social function of literature. It can be established and investigated only through the study of closely related conditions, without the forcible incorporation of remote, though major, causal orders.

Finally, the concept of the "orientation" of a speech function is applicable to a literary order but not to an individual work. A separate work must be related to a literary order before one can talk about its orientation. The law of large numbers does not apply to small numbers. In establishing the distant causal orders for separate works and authors, we study not the evolution of literature but its modification, not how literature changes and evolves in correlation with other orders, but how neighboring orders deform it. This problem too is worth studying, but on a completely different plane.

The direct study of the author's psychology and the construction of a causal "bridge" from the author's environment, daily life, and class to his works is particularly fruitless. The erotic poetry of Batjuškov resulted from his work on the poetic language—note his speech, "On the Influence of Light Poetry on Language"—and Vjazemskij refused to seek its genesis in Batjuškov's psychology. The poet, Polonskij, who was never a theoretician but who as a poet and master of his craft understood this, wrote of Benediktov,

> It is possible that the severity of nature, the forests, the fields
> ... influenced the impressionable soul of the child and future poet,
> but how did they influence it? This is a difficult question, and no
> one will resolve it without straining the point. It is not nature,
> which is the same for everyone, that plays the major role here.

Sudden changes in artists which are unexplainable in terms of their personal changes are typical. Such are the sudden changes in Deržavin and Nekrasov, in whose youth "elevated" poetry went side by side with "low" satiric poetry, but later under objective conditions were merged, thus creating new phenomena. Clearly, the problem here is not one of individual psychological conditions, but of objective, evolving functions of the literary order in relation to the adjacent social order.

13. It is therefore necessary to reexamine one of the most complex problems of literary evolution, the problem of "influence." There are deep psychological and personal influences which are not reflected on the literary level at all, as with Čaadaev and Puškin. There are influences which modify and deform literature without having any evolutionary significance, as with Mixajlovskij and Gleb Uspenskij. Yet what is most striking of all is the fact that you can have an extrinsic indication of an influence where no such influence has occurred. I have already cited the examples of Katenin and Nekrasov. There are other examples as well. The South American tribes created the myth of Prometheus without the influence of classical mythology. These facts point to a convergence or coincidence. They have proved to be so significant that they completely obscure the psychological approach to the problem of influence and make chronology ("Who said it first?") unessential. "Influence" can occur at such a time and in such a direction as literary conditions permit. In the case of functional coincidence, whatever influences him provides the artist with elements which permit the development and strengthening of the function. If there is no such "influence," then an analogous function may result in analogous formal elements without any influence.

14. It is now time to pose the problem of the main term with which literary history operates, namely, "tradition." If we agree that evolution is the change in interrelationships between the elements of a system—between functions and formal elements—then evolution may be seen as the "mutations" of systems. These changes vary from epoch to epoch, occurring sometimes slowly, sometimes rapidly. They do not entail the sudden and complete renovation or the replacement of formal elements, but rather the *new function of these formal elements*. Thus the very compar-

ison of certain literary phenomena must be made on the basis of functions, not only forms. Seemingly dissimilar phenomena of diverse functional systems may be similar in function, and vice versa. The problem is obscured here by the fact that each literary movement in a given period seeks its supporting point in the preceding systems. This is what may be called "traditionalism."

Thus, perhaps, the functions of Puškin's prose are closer to the functions of Tolstoj's prose than the functions of Puškin's verse are to those of his imitators in the 1830s or those of Majkov.

15. To summarize, the study of literary evolution is possible only in relation to literature as a system, interrelated with other systems and conditioned by them. Investigation must go from constructional function to literary function; from literary function to verbal function. It must clarify the problem of the evolutionary interaction of functions and forms. The study of evolution must move from the literary system to the nearest correlated systems, not the distant, even though major, systems. In this way the prime significance of major social factors is not at all discarded. Rather, it must be elucidated to its full extent through the problem of the evolution of literature. This is in contrast to the establishment of the direct "influence" of major social factors, which replaces the study of *evolution* of literature with the study of the *modification* of literary works— that is to say, of their deformation.

NOTES

1.   One need only examine the mass literature of the 1820s and 1830s to be convinced of their colossal evolutionary difference. In the 1830s, years of the automatization of preceding traditions, years of work on dusty literary material, "dilettantism" suddenly received a tremendous evolutionary magnificence. It is from dilettantism, from the atmosphere of "verse notes written on the margins of books," that a new phenomenon emerged—Tjutčev, who transformed poetic language and genres by his intimate intonations. The relationship of social conventions to literature, which seems to be its degeneration from an evaluative point of view, transforms the literary system. In the 1820s, the years of the "masters" and the creation of new poetic genres, dilettantism and mass literature were called "graphomania." The poets, who from the point of view of evolutionary significance were the leading figures of the 1830s, appeared to be determined as the "dilettantes" (Tjutčev, Poležaev) or the "epigones" and "pupils" (Lermontov) in their struggle with the preceding norms. In the period of the 1830s, however, even the secondary poets appeared like leading masters; note, for example, the universality and grandioseness of the genres used by such mass poets as Olin. It is clear that the evolutionary significance of such phenomena as dilettantism or epigonism is different from period to period. Supercilious, evaluative treatment of these phenomena is the heritage of the old history of literature.

Harold Bloom

The Dialectics of Poetic Tradition

Emerson chose three mottos for his most influential essay, "Self-Reliance." The first, from the *Satires* of Persius: "Do not seek yourself outside yourself." The second, from Beaumont and Fletcher:

Man is his own star; and the soul that can
Render an honest and a perfect man,
Commands all light, all influence, all fate;
Nothing to him falls early or too late. . . .

The third, one of Emerson's own gnomic verses, is prophetic of much contemporary shamanism:

Cast the bantling on the rocks,
Suckle him with the she-wolf's teat,
Wintered with the hawk and fox,
Power and speed be hands and feet.

Like the fierce, rhapsodic essay they precede, these mottos are addressed to young Americans, men and women, of 1840, who badly needed to be told that they were not latecomers. But we, in fact, *are* latecomers (as indeed they were), and we are better off for consciously knowing it, at least right now. Emerson's single aim was to awaken his auditors to a sense of their own potential *power of making*. To serve his tradition now, we need to counsel a *power of conserving*.

"The hint of the dialectic is more valuable than the dialectic itself," Emerson once remarked, but I intend to contradict him on that also, and to sketch some aspects of the dialects of literary tradition. Modernism in literature has not passed; rather, it has been exposed as never having been there. Gossip grows old and becomes myth; myth grows older, and becomes dogma. Wyndham Lewis, Eliot and Pound gossiped with one another; the New Criticism aged them into a myth of Modernism; now the antiquarian Hugh Kenner has dogmatized this myth into the Pound Era, a canon of accepted titans. Pretenders to godhood Kenner roughly reduces to their mortality; the grand triumph of Kenner is his judgment that Wallace Stevens represented the culmination of the poetics of Edward Lear.

Yet this is already dogma grown antique: Post-Modernism also has its canons and its canonizers; and I find myself surrounded by living classics, in recently dead poets of strong ambition and hysterical intensity, and in hyperactive novelist non-novelists, who are I suppose the proper seers for their armies of student non-students. I discover it does little good these days to remind literary students that Cowley, Cleveland, Denham and Waller were for generations considered great poets, or that much of the best contemporary opinion preferred Campbell, Moore and Rogers to John Keats. And I would fear to tell students that while I judge Ruskin to have been the best critic of the nineteenth century, he did proclaim *Aurora Leigh* by Mrs. Browning to be the best long poem of that century. Great critics nod, and entire generations go wrong in judging their own achievements. Without what Shelley called a being washed in the blood of the Great Redeemer, Time, literary tradition appears powerless to justify its own selectivities. Yet if tradition cannot establish its own centrality, it becomes something other than the liberation from time's chaos it implicitly promised to be. Like all convention, it moves from an idealized function to a stifling or blocking tendency.

I intend here to reverse Emerson (though I revere him) and to assert for literary tradition its currently pragmatic as opposed to idealized function: it is now valuable precisely because it partly blocks, because it stifles the weak, because it represses even the strong. To study literary tradition today is to achieve a dangerous but enabling act of the mind that works against all ease in fresh "creation." Kierkegaard could afford to believe that he became great in proportion to striven-with greatness, but we come later. Nietzsche insisted that nothing was more pernicious than the sense of being a latecomer, but I want to insist upon the contrary: nothing is now more salutary than such a sense. Without it, we cannot distinguish between the energy of humanistic performance and merely organic energy, which never alas needs to be saved from itself.

I remember, as a young man setting out to be a university teacher, how afflicted I was by my sense of uselessness, my not exactly vitalizing fear that my chosen profession reduced to an incoherent blend of antiquarianism and culture-mongering. I recall also that I would solace myself by thinking that while a scholar-teacher of literature could do no good, at least he could do no harm, or anyway not to others, whatever he did to himself. But that was at the very start of the decade of the fifties, and after more than twenty years I have come to understand that I underrated my profession, as much in its capacity for doing harm as in its potential for good works. Even our treasons, our betrayals of our implicit trusts, are treasons of something more than of the intellectuals, and most directly damage our immediate students, our Oedipal sons and daughters. Our profession is not genuinely akin any longer to that of the historians or the philosophers. Without willing the change, our theoretical critics have become negative theologians, our practical critics are close to being Agaddic commentators, and all of our teachers, of whatever generation, teach how to live, what to do, in order to avoid the damnation of death-in-life. I do not believe that I am talking about an ideology, nor am I acknowledging any shade whatsoever of the recent Marxist critiques of our profession. Whatever the academic profession of letters now is on the Continent (shall we say an anthropology half-Marxist, half-Buddhist?) or in Britain (shall we say a middle-class amateurism displacing an aristocratic amateurism?), it is currently in America a wholly Emersonian phenomenon. Emerson abandoned his church to become a secular orator, rightly trusting that the lecture, rather than the sermon, was the proper and luminous melody for Americans. We have institutionalized Emerson's procedures, while abandoning (understandably) his aims, for the burden of his prophecy is already carried by our auditors.

Northrop Frye, who increasingly looks like the Proclus or Iamblichus of our day, has Platonized the dialectics of tradition, its relation to fresh creation, into what he calls the Myth of Concern, which turns out to be a Low Church version of T. S. Eliot's Anglo-Catholic myth of Tradition and the Individual Talent. In Frye's reduction, the student discovers that he becomes something, and thus uncovers or demystifies himself, by first being persuaded that tradition is inclusive rather than exclusive, and so makes a place for him. The student is a cultural assimilator who *thinks* because he has *joined* a larger body of thought. Freedom, for Frye as for Eliot, is the change, however slight, that any genuine single consciousness brings about in the order of literature simply by joining the simultaneity of such order. I confess that I no longer understand this simultaneity, except as a fiction that Frye, like Eliot, passes upon himself. This fiction is a noble idealization, and as a lie against time will go the way of every noble idealization. Such positive thinking served many purposes during the sixties, when continuities, of any kind, badly required to be summoned, even if they did not come to our call. Wherever we are bound, our dialectical development now seems invested in the interplay of repetition and discontinuity, and needs a very different sense of what our stance is in regard to literary tradition.

All of us now have been pre-empted, as I think we are all quite uneasily aware. We are rueful that we are asked ("compelled" might be more accurate) to pay for the discontents not only of the civilization we enjoy, but of the civilization of all previous generations from whom we have inherited. Literary tradition, once we even contemplate entering its academies, now insists upon being our "family history," and inducts us into its "family romance" in the unfortunate role prefigured by Browning's Childe Roland, a candidate for heroism who aspired only to fail at least as miserably as his precursors failed. There are no longer any archetypes to displace; we have been ejected from the imperial palace whence we came, and any attempt to find a substitute for it will not be a benign displacement but only another culpable trespass, neither more nor less desperate than any Oedipal return to origins. For us, creative emulation of literary tradition leads to images of inversion, incest, sado-masochistic parody, of which the great, gloriously self-defeating master is Pynchon, whose *Gravity's Rainbow* is a perfect text for the sixties, Age of Frye and Borges, but already deliberately belated for the seventies. Substitute-gratifications and myths-of-displacement turn out to be an identity in Pynchon's book.

Gershom Scholem has an essay on "Tradition and New Creation in the Ritual of the Kabbalists" that reads like a prescription for Pynchon's novel, and I suspect Pynchon found another source in it. The magical formula of the Kabbalistic view of ritual, according to Scholem, is as follows: "everything not only *is in* everything else but also *acts upon* everything else." Remind yourself that Kabbalah literally means "tradition," that which has been received, and reflect on the extraordinary over-determination and stupefying over-organization that a Kabbalistic book like *Gravity's Rainbow* is condemned to manifest. I will mention Kabbalism and its overrelevances again later in this chapter, but need first to demythologize and de-esotericize my own view of literary tradition. The proper starting point for any de-mystification has to be a return to the commonal. Let me ask then: what is literary tradition? What is a classic? What is a canonical view of tradition? How are canons of accepted classics formed, and how are they unformed? I think that all these quite traditional questions can take one simplistic but still dialectical question as their summing-up: do we choose a tradition or does it choose us, and why is it necessary that a choosing take place, or a being chosen? What happens if one tries to write, or to teach, or to think, or even to read without the sense of a tradition?

Why, nothing at all happens, just nothing. You cannot write or teach or think or even read without imitation, and what you imitate is what another person has done, that person's writing or teaching or thinking or reading. Your relation to what informs that person *is* tradition, for tradition is influence that extends past one generation, a carrying-over of influence. Tradition, the Latin *traditio*, is etymologically a handing-over or a giving-over, a delivery, a giving-up and so even a surrender or a betrayal. *Traditio* in our sense is Latin only in language; the concept deeply derives from the Hebraic *Mishnah*, an oral handing-over, or transmission of oral precedents, of what has been found to work, of what has been instructed successfully. Tradition is good teaching, where "good" means pragmatic, instrumental, fecund. But how primal is teaching, in comparison to writing? Necessarily, the question is rhetorical; whether or not the psychic Primal Scene is the one where we were begotten, and whether or not the societal Primal Scene is the murder of a Sacred Father by rival sons, I would venture that the artistic Primal Scene *is* the trespass of teaching. What Jacques Derrida calls the Scene of Writing itself depends upon a Scene of Teaching, and poetry is crucially pedagogical in its origins and function. Literary tradition begins when a fresh author is simultaneously cognizant not only of his own struggle against the forms and presence of a precursor, but is compelled also to a sense of the Precursor's place in regard to what came before *him*.

Ernst Robert Curtius, in the best study of literary tradition I have ever read, his definitive *European Literature and the Latin Middle Ages* (1948), concluded that "like all life, tradition is a vast passing away and renewal." But even Curtius, who could accept his own wisdom, cautioned us that Western literary tradition could be apprehended clearly "only" for the twenty-five centuries from Homer to Goethe; for the two centuries after Goethe we still could not know what was canonical or not. The later Enlightenment, Romanticism, Modernism, Post-Modernism; all these, by implication, are one phenomenon and we still cannot know precisely whether or not that phenomenon possesses continuity rather than primarily discontinuity in regard to the tradition between Homer and Goethe. Nor are there Muses, nymphs who *know*, still available to tell us the secrets of continuity, for the nymphs certainly are now departing. I prophesy though that the first true break with literary continuity will be brought about in generations to come, if the burgeoning religion of Liberated Woman spreads from its clusters of enthusiasts to dominate the West. Homer will cease to be the inevitable precursor, and the rhetoric and forms of our literature then may break at last from tradition.

It remains not arbitrary nor even accidental to say that everyone who now reads and writes in the West, of whatever racial background, sex or ideological camp, is still a son or daughter of Homer. As a teacher of literature who prefers the morality of the Hebrew Bible to that of Homer, indeed who prefers the Bible aesthetically to Homer, I am no happier about this dark truth than you are, if you happen to agree with William Blake when he passionately cries aloud that it is Homer and Virgil, the Classics, and not the Goths and Vandals that fill Europe with wars. But how did this truth, whether dark or not, impose itself upon us?

All continuities possess the paradox of being absolutely arbitrary in their origins, and absolutely inescapable in their teleologies. We know this so vividly from what we all of us oxymoronically call our love lives that its literary counterparts need little demonstration. Though each generation of critics rightly re-affirms the aesthetic supremacy of Homer, he is so much part of the aesthetic *given* for them (and us) that the re-affirmation is a redundancy. What we call "literature" is inescapably connected to education by a continuity of twenty-five hundred years, a continuity that began in the sixth century B.C. when Homer first became a schoolbook for the Greeks, or as Curtius says simply and definitively: "Homer, for them, was the 'tradition.' " When Homer became a schoolbook, literature became a school subject quite permanently. Again, Curtius makes the central formulation: "Education becomes the medium of the literary tradition: a fact which is characteristic of Europe, but which is not necessarily so in the nature of things."

This formulation is worth considerable dialectical investigation, particularly in a time as educationally confused as ours recently has been. Nothing in the literary world even sounds quite so silly to me as the passionate declarations that poetry must be liberated from the academy, declarations that would be absurd at any time, but peculiarly so some twenty-five hundred years after Homer and the academy first became indistinguishable. For the answer to the question "What is literature?" must begin with the word "literature," based on Quintilian's word *litteratura* which was his translation of the Greek *grammatike*, the art of reading and writing conceived as a dual enterprise. Literature, and the study of literature, were in their origin a single, unified concept. When Hesiod and Pindar invoke the Muses, they do so *as students*, so as to enable themselves *to teach their readers*. When the first literary scholars wholly distinct from poets created their philology in Alexandria, they began by classifying and then selecting authors, canonizing according to secular principles clearly ancestral in relation to our own. The question we go on asking—"What is a classic?"—they first answered for us by reducing the tragedians initially to five, and later to three. Curtius informs us that the name *classicus* first appears very late, under the Antonine emperors, meaning literary citizens of the first class, but the concept of classification was itself Alexandrian. We are Alexandrians still, and we may as well be proud of it, for it is central to our profession. Even "Modernism," a shibboleth many of us think we may have invented, is necessarily an Alexandrian inheritance also. The scholar Aristarchus, working at the Museion in Alexandria, first contrasted the *neoteroi* or "moderns" with Homer, in defense of a latecomer poet like Callimachus. *Modernus*, based on the word *modo*, for "now," first came into use in the sixth century A.D., and it is worth remembering that "Modernism" always means "For Now."

Alexandria, which thus founded our scholarship, permanently set the literary tradition of the school, and introduced the secularized notion of the canon, though the actual term of canon for "catalogue" of authors was not used until the eighteenth century. Curtius, in his wonderfully comprehensive researches, ascribes the first canon-formation in a modern vernacular, secular literature to the sixteenth-century Italians. The French in the seventeenth century followed, establishing their permanent version of classicism, a version that the English Augustans bravely but vainly tried to emulate before they were flooded out by that great English renaissance of the English Renaissance we now call the Age of Sensibility or the Sublime, and date fairly confidently from the mid-1740's. This renaissance of the Renaissance was and is Romanticism, which is of course *the* tradition of the last two centuries. Canon-formation, for us, has become a part of Romantic tradition, and our still-current educational crisis in the West is rather clearly only another Romantic epicycle, part of the continuity of upheaval that began with revolution in the West Indies and America, spread to France and through her to the Continent, and thence to Russia, Asia and Africa in our time. Just as Romanticism and Revolution became one composite form, so the dialectic of fresh canon-formation joining itself to a gradual ideological reversal endures into this current decade.

But Romantic tradition differs vitally from earlier forms of tradition, and I think this difference can be reduced to a useful formula. Romantic tradition is *consciously late,* and Romantic literary psychology is therefore necessarily a *psychology of belatedness.* The romance-of-trespass, of violating a sacred or daemonic ground, is a central form in modern literature, from Coleridge and Wordsworth to the present. Whitman follows Emerson by insisting that he strikes up for a new world, yet the guilt of belatedness haunts him and all of his American literary descendants. Yeats was early driven into Gnostic evasions of nature by a parallel guilt, and even the apocalyptic Lawrence is most persuasive when he follows his own analyses of Melville and Whitman to trumpet the doom of what he calls our white race with its hideously belated aversion from what he oddly insisted upon calling blood-consciousness. Romanticism, more than any other tradition, is appalled by its own overt continuities, and vainly but perpetually fantasizes some end to repetitions.

This Romantic psychology of belatedness, from which Emerson failed to save us, his American descendants, is the cause, in my judgment, of the excessively volatile senses-of-tradition that have made canon-formation so uncertain a process during the last two centuries, and particularly during the last twenty years. Take some contemporary examples. A quick way to start a quarrel with any current group of critics would be to express my conviction that Robert Lowell is anything but a permanent poet, that he has been mostly a maker of period-pieces from his origins until now. Similarly, as violent a quarrel would ensue if I expressed my judgment that Norman Mailer is so flawed a writer that his current enshrinement among academics is the largest single index to our current sense of belatedness. Lowell and Mailer, however I rate them, are at least conspicuous literary energies. It would lead to something more intense than quarrels if I expressed my judgment upon "black poetry" or the "literature of Women's Liberation." But quarrels, or even abuse, is all such *obiter dicta* could lead to, for our mutual sense of canonical standards has undergone a remarkable dimming, a fading into the light of a common garishness. Revisionism, always a Romantic energizer, has become so much a norm that even rhetorical standards seem to have lost their efficacy. Literary tradition has become the captive of the revisionary impulse, and I think we must go past viewing-with-alarm if we are to understand this quite inescapable phenomenon, the subsuming of tradition by belatedness.

The revisionary impulse, in writing and in reading, has a directly inverse relationship to our psychological confidence in what I am calling the Scene of Instruction. Milton's Satan, who remains the greatest really Modern or Post-Enlightenment poet in the language, can give us a paradigm of this inverse relationship. The ultimate Scene of Instruction is described by Raphael in Book V of *Paradise Lost*, where God proclaims to the Angels that "This day I have begot whom I declare/My only son" and provocatively warns that "him who disobeys/Mee disobeys ... /and ... falls/Into utter darkness." We can describe this as an imposition of the psychology of belatedness, and Satan, like any strong poet, declines to be merely a latecomer. His way of returning to origins, of making the Oedipal trespass, is to become a rival creator to God-as-creator. He embraces Sin as his Muse, and begets upon her the highly original poem of Death, the only poem that God will permit him to write.

Let me reduce my own allegory, or my allegorical interpretation of Satan, by invoking a wonderful poem of Emily Dickinson's, "The Bible is an antique Volume—" (no. 1545), in which she calls Eden "the ancient Homestead," Satan "the Brigadier," and Sin "a distinguished Precipice/Others must resist." As a heretic whose orthodoxy was Emersonianism, Dickinson recognized in Satan a distinguished precursor gallantly battling against the psychology of belatedness. But then, Dickinson and Emerson wrote in an America that needed, for a while, to battle against the European exhaustions of history. I am temperamentally a natural revisionist, and I respond to Satan's speeches more strongly than to any other poetry I know, so it causes some anguish in me to counsel that currently we need Milton's sense of tradition much more than Emerson's revisionary tradition. Indeed, the counsel of necessity must be taken further: most simply, we need Milton, and not the Romantic return of the repressed Milton but the Milton who made his great poem identical with the process of repression that is vital to literary tradition. But a resistance even in myself is set up by my counsel of necessity, because even I want to know: what do I mean by "we"? Teachers? Students? Writers? Readers?

I do not believe that these are separate categories, nor do I believe that sex, race, social class can narrow this "we" down. If we are human, then we depend upon a Scene of Instruction, which is necessarily also a scene of authority and of priority. If you will not have one instructor or another, then precisely by rejecting all instructors, you will condemn yourself to the earliest Scene of Instruction that imposed itself upon you. The clearest analogue is necessarily Oedipal; reject your parents vehemently enough, and you will become a belated version of them, but compound with their reality, and you may partly free yourself. Milton's Satan failed, particularly as poet, after making a most distinguished beginning, because he became only a parody of the bleakest aspects of Milton's God. I greatly prefer Pynchon to Mailer as a writer because a voluntary parody is more impressive than an involuntary one, but I wonder if our aesthetic possibilities need to be reduced now to just such a choice. Do the dialectics of literary tradition condemn us, at this time, either to an affirmation of belatedness, via Kabbalistic inversion, or to a mock-vitalistic lie-against-time, via an emphasis upon the self-as-performer?

I cannot answer this hard question, because I am uneasy with the current alternatives to the ways of Pynchon and of Mailer, at least in fictional or quasi-fictional prose. Saul Bellow, with all his literary virtues, clearly shows the primal exhaustions of being a latecomer rather more strenuously in his way than Pynchon or Mailer do in theirs. I honestly don't enjoy Bellow more, and I would hesitate to find anything universal in such enjoyment even if I had it. Contemporary American poetry seems healthier to me, and provides alternatives to the voluntary parodies that Lowell has given us, or the involuntary parodies at which Ginsberg is so prominent. Yet even the poets I most admire, John Ashbery and A. R. Ammons, are rendered somewhat problematic by a cultural situation of such belatedness that literary survival itself seems fairly questionable. As Pynchon says in the closing pages of his uncanny book: "You've got much older. ... Fathers are carriers of the virus of Death, and sons are the infected. ... " And he adds a little further on in his Gospel of Sado-anarchism that this time we "*will* arrive, my God, too late."

I am aware that this must seem a Gospel of Gloom, and no one ought to be asked to welcome a kakangelist, a bearer of ill-tidings. But I cannot see that evasions of Necessity benefit anyone, least of all educationally. The teacher of literature now in America, far more than the teacher of history or philosophy or religion, is condemned to teach the presentness of the past, because history, philosophy and religion have withdrawn as agents from the Scene of Instruction, leaving the bewildered teacher of literature alone at the altar, terrifiedly wondering whether he is to be sacrifice or priest. If he evades his burden by attempting to teach only the supposed presence of the present, he will find himself teaching only some simplistic, partial reduction that wholly obliterates the present in the name of one or another historicizing formula, or past injustice, or dead faith, whether secular or not. Yet how is he to teach a tradition now grown so wealthy and so heavy that to accommodate it demands more strength than any single consciousness can provide, short of the parodistic Kabbalism of a Pynchon?

All literary tradition has been necessarily élitist, in every period, if only because the Scene of Instruction always depends upon a primal choosing and a being chosen, which is what "élite" means. Teaching, as Plato knew, is necessarily a branch of erotics, in the wide sense of desiring what we have not got, of redressing our poverty, of compounding with our fantasies. No teacher, however impartial he or she attempts to be, can avoid choosing among students, or being chosen by them, for this is the very nature of teaching. Literary teaching is precisely like literature itself; no strong writer can choose his precursors until first he is chosen by them, and no strong student can fail to be chosen by his teachers. Strong students, like strong writers, will find the sustenance they must have. And strong students, like strong writers, will rise in the most unexpected places and times, to wrestle with the internalized violence pressed upon them by their teachers and precursors.

Yet our immediate concern, as I am aware, is hardly with the strong, but with the myriads of the many, as Emersonian democracy seeks to make its promises a little less deceptive than they have been. Do the dialectics of literary tradition yield us no wisdom that can help with the final burden of the latecomer, which is the extension of the literary franchise? What is the particular inescapability of literary tradition for the teacher who must go out to find himself as a voice in the wilderness? Is he to teach *Paradise Lost* in preference to the Imamu Amiri Baraka?

I think these questions are self-answering, or rather will be, with the passage of only a few more years. For the literary teacher, more than ever, will find he is teaching *Paradise Lost,* and the other central classics of Western literary tradition, whether he is teaching them overtly or not. The psychology of belatedness is unsparing, and the Scene of Instruction becomes ever more primal as our society sags around us. Instruction, in our late phase, becomes an antithetical process almost in spite of itself, and for antithetical teaching you require antithetical texts, that is to say, texts antithetical to your students as well as to yourself and to other texts. Milton's Satan may stand as representative of the entire canon when he challenges us to challenge Heaven with him, and he will provide the truest handbook for all those, of whatever origin, who as he says "with ambitious mind/Will covet more." Any teacher of the dispossessed, of those who assert *they* are the insulted and injured, will serve the deepest purposes of literary tradition and meet also the deepest needs of his students when he gives them possession of Satan's grand opening of the Debate in Hell, which I cite now to close this chapter on the dialectics of tradition:

> With this advantage then
> To union, and firm Faith, and firm accord,
> More than can be in Heav'n, we now return
> To claim our just inheritance of old,
> Surer to prosper than prosperity
> Could have assur'd us; and by what best way,
> Whether of open War or covert guile,
> We now debate; who can advise, may speak.

Five
conventions

Ludwig Wittgenstein

Philosophical Investigations I

156. This will become clearer if we interpolate the consideration of another word, namely "reading." First I need to remark that I am not counting the understanding of what is read as part of 'reading' for purposes of this investigation: reading is here the activity of rendering out loud what is written or printed; and also of writing from dictation, writing out something printed, playing from a score, and so on.

The use of this word in the ordinary circumstances of our life is of course extremely familiar to us. But the part the word plays in our life, and therewith the language-game in which we employ it, would be difficult to describe even in rough outline. A person, let us say an Englishman, has received at school or at home one of the kinds of education usual among us, and in the course of it has learned to read his native language. Later he reads books, letters, newspapers, and other things.

Now what takes place when, say, he reads a newspaper?—His eye passes—as we say—along the printed words, he says them out loud—or only to himself; in particular he reads certain words by taking in their printed shapes as wholes; others when his eye has taken in the first syllables; others again he reads syllable by syllable, and an occasional one perhaps letter by letter.—We should also say that he had read a sentence if he spoke neither aloud nor to himself during the reading but was afterwards able to repeat the sentence word for word or nearly so.—He may attend to what he reads, or again—as we might put it—function as a mere reading-machine: I mean, read aloud and correctly without attending to what he is reading; perhaps with his attention on something quite different (so that he is unable to say what he has been reading if he is asked about it immediately afterwards).

Now compare a beginner with this reader. The beginner reads the words by laboriously spelling them out.—Some however he guesses from the context, or perhaps he already partly knows the passage by heart. Then his teacher says that he is not really *reading* the words (and in certain cases that he is only pretending to read them).

If we think of *this* sort of reading, the reading of a beginner, and ask ourselves what *reading* consists in, we shall be inclined to say: it is a special conscious activity of mind.

We also say of the pupil: "Of course he alone knows if he is really reading or merely saying the words off by heart." (We have yet to discuss these propositions: "He alone knows. . . . ")

But I want to say: we have to admit that—as far as concerns uttering any *one* of the printed words—the same thing may take place in the consciousness of the pupil who is 'pretending' to read, as in that of the practised reader who is 'reading' it. The word "to read" is applied *differently* when we are speaking of the beginner and of the practised reader.—Now we should of course like to say: What goes on in that practised reader and in the beginner when they utter the word *can't* be the same. And if there is no difference in what they happen to be conscious of there must be one in the unconscious workings of their minds, or, again, in the brain.—So we should like to say: There are at all events two different mechanisms at work here. And what goes on in them must distinguish reading from not reading.—But these mechanisms are only hypotheses, models designed to explain, to sum up, what you observe.

157. Consider the following case. Human beings or creatures of some other kind are used by us as reading-machines. They are trained for this purpose. The trainer says of some that they can already read, of others that they cannot yet do so. Take the case of a pupil who has so far not taken part in the training: if he is shewn a written word he will sometimes produce some sort of sound, and here and there it happens 'accidentally' to be roughly right. A third person hears this pupil on such an occasion and says: "He is reading." But the teacher says: "No, he isn't reading; that was just an accident."—But let us suppose that this pupil continues to react correctly to further words that are put before him. After a while the teacher says: "Now he can read!"—But what of that first word? Is the teacher to say: "I was wrong, and he *did* read it"—or: "He only began really to read later on"?—When did he begin to read? Which was the first word that he *read?* This question makes no sense here. Unless, indeed, we give a definition: "The first word that a person 'reads' is the first word of the first series of 50 words that he reads correctly" (or something of the sort).

If on the other hand we use "reading" to stand for a certain experience of transition from marks to spoken sounds, then it certainly makes sense to speak of the *first* word that he really read. He can then say, e.g. "At this word for the first time I had the feeling: 'now I am reading.' "

Or again, in the different case of a reading machine which translated marks into sounds, perhaps as a pianola does, it would be possible to say: "The machine *read* only after such-and-such had happened to it—after such-and-such parts had been connected by wires; the first word that it read was.... "

But in the case of the living reading-machine "reading" meant reacting to written signs in such-and-such ways. This concept was therefore quite independent of that of a mental or other mechanism.—Nor can the teacher here say of the pupil: "Perhaps he was already reading when he said that word." For there is no doubt about what he did.—The change when the pupil began to read was a change in his *behaviour*; and it makes no sense here to speak of 'a first word in his new state.'

158. But isn't that only because of our too slight acquaintance with what goes on in the brain and the nervous system? If we had a more accurate knowledge of these things we should see what connexions were established by the training, and then we should be able to say when we looked into his brain: "Now he has *read* this word, now the reading connexion has been set up."—And it presumably *must* be like that—for otherwise how could we be so sure that there was such a connexion? That it is so is presumably a priori—or is it only probable? And how probable is it? Now, ask yourself: what do you *know* about these things?—But if it is a priori, that means that it is a form of account which is very convincing to us.

159. But when we think the matter over we are tempted to say: the one real criterion for anybody's *reading* is the conscious act of reading, the act of reading the sounds off from the letters. "A man surely knows whether he is reading or only pretending to read!"—Suppose A wants to make B believe he can read Cyrillic script. He learns a Russian sentence by heart and says it while looking at the printed words as if he were reading them. Here we shall certainly say that A knows he is not reading, and has a sense of just this while pretending to read. For there are of course many more or less characteristic sensations in reading a printed sentence; it is not difficult to call such sensations to mind: think of sensations of hesitating, of looking closer, of misreading, of words following on one another more or less smoothly, and so on. And equally there are characteristic sensations in reciting something one has learnt by heart. In our example A will have none of the sensations that are characteristic of reading, and will perhaps have a set of sensations characteristic of cheating.

160. But imagine the following case: We give someone who can read fluently a text that he never saw before. He reads it to us—but with the sensation of saying something he has learnt by heart (this might be the effect of some drug). Should we say in such a case that he was not really reading the passage? Should we here allow his sensations to count as the criterion for his reading or not reading?

Or again: Suppose that a man who is under the influence of a certain drug is presented with a series of characters (which need not belong to any existing alphabet). He utters words corresponding to the number of the characters, as if they were letters, and does so with all the outward signs, and with the sensations, of reading. (We have experiences like this in dreams; after waking up in such a case one says perhaps: "It seemed to me as if I were reading a script, though it was not writing at all.") In such a case some people would be inclined to say the man was *reading* those marks. Others, that he was not.—Suppose he has in this way read (or interpreted) a set of five marks as A B O V E—and now we shew him the same marks in the reverse order and he reads E V O B A; and in further tests he always retains the same interpretation of the marks: here we should certainly be inclined to say he was making up an alphabet for himself *ad hoc* and then reading accordingly.

161. And remember too that there is a continuous series of transitional cases between that in which a person repeats from memory what he is supposed to be reading, and that in which he spells out every word without being helped at all by guessing from the context or knowing by heart.

Try this experiment: say the numbers from 1 to 12. Now look at the dial of your watch and *read* them.—What was it that you called "reading" in the latter case? That is to say: what did you do, to make it into *reading*?

162. Let us try the following definition: You are reading when you *derive* the reproduction from the original. And by "the original" I mean the text which you read or copy; the dictation from which you write; the score from which you play; etc. etc.—Now suppose we have, for example, taught someone the Cyrillic alphabet, and told him how to pronounce each letter. Next we put a passage before him and he reads it, pronouncing every letter as we have taught him. In this case we shall very likely say that he derives the sound of a word from the written pattern by the rule that we have given him. And this is also a clear case of *reading*. (We might say that we had taught him the 'rule of the alphabet.')

But why do we say that he has *derived* the spoken from the printed words? Do we know anything more than that we taught him how each letter should be pronounced, and that he then read the words out loud? Perhaps our reply will be: the pupil shews that he is using the rule we have given him to pass from the printed to the spoken words.—How this can be *shewn* becomes clearer if we change our example to one in which the pupil has to write out the text instead of reading it to us, has to make the transition from print to handwriting. For in this case we can give him the rule in the form of a table with printed letters in one column and cursive letters in the other. And he shews that he is deriving his script from the printed words by consulting the table.

163. But suppose that when he did this he always wrote *b* for *A*, *c* for *B*, *d* for *C*, and so on, and *a* for *Z?*—Surely we should call this too a derivation by means of the table.—He is using it now, we might say, according to the second schema in §86 instead of the first.

It would still be a perfectly good case of derivation according to the table, even if it were represented by a schema of arrows without any simple regularity.

Suppose, however, that he does not stick to a *single* method of transcribing, but alters his method according to a simple rule: if he has once written *n* for *A*, then he writes *o* for the next *A*, *p* for the next, and so on.—But where is the dividing line between this procedure and a random one?

But does this mean that the word "to derive" really has no meaning, since the meaning seems to disintegrate when we follow it up?

164. In case (162) the meaning of the word "to derive" stood out clearly. But we told ourselves that this was only a quite special case of deriving; deriving in a quite special garb, which had to be stripped from it if we wanted to see the essence of deriving. So we stripped those particular coverings off; but then deriving itself disappeared.—In order to find the real artichoke, we divested it of its leaves. For certainly (162) was a special case of deriving; what is essential to deriving, however, was not hidden beneath the surface of this case, but his 'surface' was one case out of the family of cases of deriving.

And in the same way we also use the word "to read" for a family of cases. And in different circumstances we apply different criteria for a person's reading.

165. But surely—we should like to say—reading is a quite particular process! Read a page of print and you can see that something special is going on, something highly characteristic.—Well, what does go on when I read the page? I see printed words and I say words out loud. But, of course, that is not all, for I might see printed words and say words out loud and still not be reading. Even if the words which I say are those which, going by an existing alphabet, are *supposed* to be read off from the printed ones.—And if you say that reading is a particular experience, then it becomes quite unimportant whether or not you read according to some generally recognized alphabetical rule.—And what does the characteristic thing about the experience of reading consist in?—Here I should like to say: "The words that I utter *come* in a special way." That is, they do not come as they would if I were for example making them up.—They come of themselves.—But even that is not enough; for the sounds of words may *occur* to me while I am looking at printed words, but that does not mean that I have read them.—In addition I might say here, neither do the spoken words occur to me as if, say, something reminded me of them. I should for

example not wish to say: the printed word "nothing" always reminds me of the sound "nothing"—but the spoken words as it were slip in as one reads. And if I so much as look at a German printed word, there occurs a peculiar process, that of hearing the sound inwardly.

166. I said that when one reads the spoken words come 'in a special way': but in what way? Isn't this a fiction? Let us look at individual letters and attend to the way the sound of the letter comes. Read the letter A.—Now, how did the sound come?—We have no idea what to say about it.—Now write a small Roman a.—How did the movement of the hand come as you wrote? Differently from the way the sound came in the previous experiment?—All I know is, I looked at the printed letter and wrote the cursive letter.—Now look at the mark ⌒ and let a sound occur to you as you do so; utter it. The sound 'U' occurred to me; but I could not say that there was any essential difference in the kind of way that sound *came.* The difference lay in the difference of situation. I had told myself beforehand that I was to let a sound occur to me; there was a certain tension present before the sound came. And I did not say 'U' automatically as I do when I look at the letter U. Further, that mark was not *familiar* to me in the way the letters of the alphabet are. I looked at it rather intently and with a certain interest in its shape; as I looked I thought of a reversed sigma.—Imagine having to use this mark regularly as a letter; so that you got used to uttering a particular sound at the sight of it, say the sound "sh." Can we say anything but that after a while this sound comes automatically when we look at the mark? That is to say: I no longer ask myself on seeing it "What sort of letter is that?"—nor, of course, do I tell myself "This mark makes me want to utter the sound 'sh,' " nor yet "This mark somehow reminds me of the sound 'sh.' "

(Compare with this the idea that memory images are distinguished from other mental images by some special characteristic.)

167. Now what is there in the proposition that reading is 'a quite particular process'? It presumably means that when we read *one* particular process takes place, which we recognize.—But suppose that I at one time read a sentence in print and at another write it in Morse code—is the mental process really the same?—On the other hand, however, there is certainly some uniformity in the experience of reading a page of print. For the process is a uniform one. And it is quite easy to understand that there is a difference between this process and one of, say, letting words occur to one at the sight of arbitrary marks.—For the mere look of a printed line is itself extremely characteristic—it presents, that is, a quite special appearance, the letters all roughly the same size, akin in shape too, and always recurring; most of the words constantly repeated and enormously familiar to us, like well-known faces.—Think of the uneasiness we feel when the spelling of a word is changed. (And of the still stronger feelings that questions about the spelling of words have aroused.) Of course, not

all signs have impressed themselves on us so *strongly.* A sign in the algebra of logic for instance can be replaced by any other one without exciting a strong reaction in us.—

Remember that the look of a word is familiar to us in the same kind of way as its sound.

197. "It's as if we could grasp the whole use of a word in a flash."— And that is just what we say we do. That is to say: we sometimes describe what we do in these words. But there is nothing astonishing, nothing queer, about what happens. It becomes queer when we are led to think that the future development must in some way already be present in the act of grasping the use and yet isn't present.—For we say that there isn't any doubt that we understand the word, and on the other hand its meaning lies in its use. There is no doubt that I now want to play chess, but chess is the game it is in virtue of all its rules (and so on). Don't I know, then, which game I want to play until I *have* played it? or are all the rules contained in my act of intending? Is it experience that tells me that this sort of game is the usual consequence of such an act of intending? so is it impossible for me to be certain what I am intending to do? And if that is nonsense—what kind of super-strong connexion exists between the act of intending and the thing intended?—Where is the connexion effected between the sense of the expression "Let's play a game of chess" and all the rules of the game?—Well, in the list of rules of the game, in the teaching of it, in the day-to-day practice of playing.

198. "But how can a rule shew me what I have to do at *this* point? Whatever I do is, on some interpretation, in accord with the rule."—That is not what we ought to say, but rather: any interpretation still hangs in the air along with what it interprets, and cannot give it any support. Interpretations by themselves do not determine meaning.

"Then can whatever I do be brought into accord with the rule?"—Let me ask this: what has the expression of a rule—say a sign-post—got to do with my actions? What sort of connexion is there here?—Well, perhaps this one: I have been trained to react to this sign in a particular way, and now I do so react to it.

But that is only to give a causal connexion; to tell how it has come about that we now go by the sign-post; not what this going-by-the-sign really consists in. On the contrary; I have further indicated that a person goes by a sign-post only in so far as there exists a regular use of sign-posts, a custom.

199. Is what we call "obeying a rule" something that it would be possible for only *one* man to do, and to do only *once* in his life?—This is of course a note on the grammar of the expression "to obey a rule."

It is not possible that there should have been only one occasion on which someone obeyed a rule. It is not possible that there should have been only one occasion on which a report was made, an order given or understood; and so on.—To obey a rule, to make a report, to give an order, to play a game of chess, are *customs* (uses, institutions).

To understand a sentence means to understand a language. To understand a language means to be master of a technique.

200. It is, of course, imaginable that two people belonging to a tribe unacquainted with games should sit at a chess-board and go through the moves of a game of chess; and even with all the appropriate mental accompaniments. And if *we* were to see it we should say they were playing chess. But now imagine a game of chess translated according to certain rules into a series of actions which we do not ordinarily associate with a *game*—say into yells and stamping of feet. And now suppose those two people to yell and stamp instead of playing the form of chess that we are used to; and this in such a way that their procedure is translatable by suitable rules into a game of chess. Should we still be inclined to say they were playing a game? What right would one have to say so?

201. This was our paradox: no course of action could be determined by a rule, because every course of action can be made out to accord with the rule. The answer was: if everything can be made out to accord with the rule, then it can also be made out to conflict with it. And so there would be neither accord nor conflict here.

It can be seen that there is a misunderstanding here from the mere fact that in the course of our argument we give one interpretation after another; as if each one contented us at least for a moment, until we thought of yet another standing behind it. What this shews is that there is a way of grasping a rule which is *not* an *interpretation*, but which is exhibited in what we call "obeying the rule" and "going against it" in actual cases.

Hence there is an inclination to say: every action according to the rule is an interpretation. But we ought to restrict the term "interpretation" to the substitution of one expression of the rule for another.

202. And hence also 'obeying a rule' is a practice. And to *think* one is obeying a rule is not to obey a rule. Hence it is not possible to obey a rule 'privately': otherwise thinking one was obeying a rule would be the same thing as obeying it.

203. Language is a labyrinth of paths. You approach from *one* side and know your way about; you approach the same place from another side and no longer know your way about.

Raymond Williams

Conventions

The meaning of convention was originally an assembly and then, by derivation, an agreement. Later the sense of agreement was extended to tacit agreement and thence to custom. An adverse sense developed, in which a convention was seen as no more than an old rule, or somebody else's rule, which it was proper and often necessary to disregard. The meaning of 'convention' in art and literature is still radically affected by this varying history of the word.

Yet the point is not to choose between the relatively favourable and unfavourable senses. Within any social theory of art and literature, a convention is an established relationship, or ground of a relationship, through which a specific shared practice—the making of actual works—can be realized. It is the local or general indicator, both of the situations and occasions of art, and of the means of an art. A social theory, with its emphasis on distinct and contrasting traditions, institutions, and formations, related to but not identical with distinct and opposing social classes, is thus well placed to understand the shifting evaluations of conventions and of the reality of conventions. Negatively it can uncover the characteristic belief of certain classes, institutions, and formations that their interests and procedures are not artificial and limited but universally valid and applicable, their methods then being 'true,' 'real,' or 'natural' as distinct from the limited and limiting 'conventions' of others. Positively it can show the real grounds of the inclusions and exclusions, the styles and the ways of seeing, that specific conventions embody and ratify. For a social theory insists on seeing, within all established relationships and procedures, the specific substance and its methods, rather than an assumed or claimed 'self-evidence' or universality.

Conventions are in this sense inherent, and by definition are historically variable. This does not mean, however, that certain kinds of convention do not extend beyond their period, class, or formation. Some fundamental literary conventions do so extend, and are crucial to problems of genre and form. Moreover, we need to define the complex relation between conventions and notations. For while all notations are conventional, not all conventions are specific notations. Notations, while obviously more specific, are also more limited than conventions, which can include, for example, conventions of the absence or the setting aside of certain procedures and substance which other conventions include. Indeed, without such conventions, many notations would be incomplete or even incomprehensible.

Certain basic conventions become in effect naturalized within a particular cultural tradition. This is true, for example, of the basic convention of dramatic performance, with its assigned distribution of actors and spectators. Within a culture in which drama is now conventional, the distribution seems self-evident and the restraints are normally respected. Outside such a culture, or at its edges, the represented dramatic action may be taken as a 'real' act, or spectators may try to intervene, beyond the conventional restraints. Even within a culture with a long tradition of drama, comparable responses, putting the conventions under pressure, are common. For dramatic performance is a convention instituted in specific periods within specific cultures, rather than any kind of 'natural' behaviour. Similar deep conventions, involving agreed relationships, apply to most kinds of oral narrative and address. Authorial identification, in drama and in printed books, is similarly subject to historically variable conventions which determine the whole concept of composition.

Moreover, within these fundamental conventions, every element of composition is also conventional, with significant historical variations in different periods and cultures, both between conventions and between their relative unity and relative diversity. Thus *basic modes of 'speech'*— from choral to individual singing to recitative to declamation to rehearsed conversation—*or of writing*—from the range of verse forms to the forms of prose, and from the 'monologic' to the 'collective'—and then the diversity of each in relation to contemporary 'everyday' spoken forms, are radically conventional. They are in many cases but not all indicated by specific notations. All these are separable as 'formal' elements; yet the conventions of real forms extend beyond them, with significant but not regular relations to them.

Thus the *presentation of persons ('characters')* has significantly variable conventions. Consider two standard variables in such presentation: personal appearance and social situation. Almost every conceivable combination of these elements, but also the exclusion of one or even both, has been conventionally practised in drama and narrative. Moreover, within each, there is a significant conventional range: from briefly typical presentation to exhaustive analysis. Further, the conventional variations in the presentation of 'personal appearance' correspond to deep variations in the effective perception and valuation of others, often in close relation to variations in the effective significance of family (lineage), social status, and social history, which are variable contexts of the essential definition of presented individuals. The difference of presentation between the undelineated medieval Everyman and the nineteenth-century fictional character whose appearance, history, and situation are described in sustained significant detail is an obvious example. What may be less obvious is the kind of absence, ratified by convention, in literature nearer our own time, where the conventions may appear to be not 'literary' or indeed not conventions at all, but self-defining criteria of significance and relevance. Thus the inclusion or exclusion of specific family or social history, or indeed of any detailed identity 'before the event,' represents basic conventions of the nature of individuals and their relationships.

The selection of individuals, presented in any of these ways, is again evidently conventional. There is hierarchical selection by status, as in the old limitation of tragic status to persons of rank, a convention consciously discarded in bourgeois tragedy. In modern class societies the selection of characters almost always indicates an assumed or conscious class position. The conventions of selection are more intricate when hierarchy is less formal. Without formal ratification, all other persons may be conventionally presented as instrumental (servants, drivers, waiters), as merely environmental (other people in the street), or indeed as essentially absent (not seen, not relevant). Any such presentation depends on the acceptance of its convention, but it is always more than a 'literary' or 'aesthetic' decision. The social hierarchy or social norms that are assumed or invoked are substantial terms of relationship which the conventions are intended (often, in the confidence of a form, not consciously) to carry. They are no less terms of social relationship when the hierarchy or selection is not manifestly social but is based on the assignment of different orders of significant being to the selected few and the irrelevant many. Gogol's satirical account of this fundamental problem of the writer of modern internal consciousness—where, if the problem is taken literally, nobody can move without contact with another being whose internal consciousness demands similar priority and who will therefore cancel the chosen first person singular—highlights the selective internal convention through which this problem is temporarily solved, though beyond the convention the basic issue of significance of being remains.

Other conventions control the specification of such matters as work or income. In certain presentations these are crucial, and in all relationships they are evidently available facts. The convention which allows them to be treated as unimportant, or indeed to be absent, in the interest of what is taken as primary identity or an alternatively significant social

character, is as evidently general as that less common but still important
converse convention through which people are specified only at the level
of general social and economic facts, with no individuation beyond them.

Significant facts of real relationships are thus included or excluded,
assumed or described, analysed or emphasized by variable conventions
which can be identified by formal analysis but can be understood only by
social analysis. Variable conventions of *narrative stance* (from 'omniscience' to the necessarily limited 'personal' account) interact with these
conventions of selection and exclusion in very complex ways. They interact also with significant conventions of the *wholeness of an account*,
which involve radical questions of the nature of events. Certain stories require, conventionally, a pre-history and a projected ('after' or 'ever after')
history, if their reading of cause, motive, and consequence is to be understood. The exclusion of such elements, like their inclusion, is not an 'aesthetic' choice—the 'way to tell a story'—but a variable convention involving radical social assumptions of causation and consequence.
(Compare the final 'settlement' chapter in early Victorian English novels—e.g. Gaskell's *Mary Barton*—and the final 'breakaway' chapter in
English novels between 1910 and 1940—e.g. Lawrence's *Sons and Lovers*.) Similarly, variable conventions of temporal sequence, while serving
other ends—altered perceptions of event and memory, for example—in-
terlock with these basic assumptions of causation and consequence, and
thus with the conventional processes through which these are understood and the conventional criteria of relevant evidence.

Again, the presentation of *place* depends on variable conventions
from a deliberate unlocation to a simple naming to a brief sketch to variably detailed description, up to the point where, as it is said, the place itself becomes a 'character' or 'the character.' Radically variable assumptions of the relations between people and places, and between 'man' and
'nature,' are conveyed in these apparently self-evident ways. Other conventions assume or indicate variable relations between places and societies—'environments'—over a range from the abstraction of place from
people, through the perception of people as symptoms of places, to the active apprehension of places as made by people. Descriptions of great
houses, of rural landscapes, of cities, or of factories are evident examples
of these variable conventions, where the 'point of view' may be experienced as an 'aesthetic' choice but where any point of view, including that
which excludes persons or converts them into landscape, is social.

There are similar conventions for the description of *action*. Variations in direct and indirect presentation, and of focus within direct presentation, are especially marked in three kinds of human action: killing,
the sexual act, and work. It is often said that these are matters of taste and
fashion. But in each case the convention adopted assumes a specific (if of-

ten complex) relation of the event to other events and to more general organizations of significance. Thus violent death is 'central' in Greek tragedy, yet it is never presented but is reported or subsequently displayed. Other presentations are relatively formal, within speech or song, or within formal situations which are intended to define the act. At another extreme the detail of the event is predominant. It is not a question of abstract 'appropriateness.' It is often a question of whether the killing is significant primarily in its motivation or consequence, or whether these are secondary or irrelevant to the event and to the intended experience of the event itself. (Compare descriptions of the corpse in detective stories, where the convention indicates the occasion for an investigation and no more—in a context of rational control rather than of general or metaphysical reference—yet where a contradictory convention, a bloody immediacy, is often employed. As in all cases of confused or overlapping conventions there is ground here for an investigation of problems of consciousness which cannot be reduced to the abstract methods of a particular kind of story.) Again, changing levels of description of sexual intercourse and of its preliminaries and variants involve general conventions of social discourse and its inclusions and exclusions, but also specific conventions which follow from variable relations of the act to changing institutions and relationships. Thus specific conventions of 'subjective' experience (the act as experienced by one partner with the other conventionally excluded; the act as consumed; the act as verbalized for pseudo-consumption) can be contrasted with conventions within which the act is habitual or even indifferent, abstracted, distanced, or merely summarized or implied in concentration on its 'objective' social effect. The variable levels of physical description can be interestingly compared with the variable levels of the description of work. There is a similar range of 'subjective' and 'objective' conventions, from work as experienced in physical or other detail to work as a simple indicator of social position. Of course in much of our received literature an earlier convention had operated, the persons chosen being relieved from the necessity to work at all, in the class-situation that corresponds to their selection as interesting. Thus, at a more overt level than in the case of sexuality, the distinction is not only between abstract 'subjective' and 'objective' viewpoints. The conventions rest, ultimately, on variations in the perception of work as an agent or condition of general consciousness, and thus, not only in work but in sexuality and in public action, on radically variable assumptions of human nature and identity: assumptions that are usually not argued but, through literary conventions, presented as 'natural' or self-evident.

A range of conventions in the presentation of *speech* has been closely studied, especially by the formalists (and it is significant that speech has received more attention than character, action, or place). There has been important analysis of the formal modes of presentation, representation, direct and indirect report, and reproduction. The relation between the styles of narrative and of directly represented speech is especially important in fictional conventions. One significant social distinction is between an integrity of style, based on a real or assumed social identity between narrator and characters (as in Jane Austen), through various hierarchical differentiations, to the break or even formal contrast between narrated and spoken language (as in George Eliot or Hardy). Conventional orthographies of variation, for foreign or regional speech, and crucially, in bourgeois literature, as class indications, are local examples of a range which establishes overt or, as often, displaced and covert social relationships which, except in these 'isolable' forms, are usually not seen as parts of the substantial human composition.

There is important variation between historical periods in the range of available conventions. Some periods have comparatively few; others, like our own, have comparatively many and permit substantial variations, themselves ultimately related to different real positions and formations. In certain periods of relative stability the conventions are themselves stable and may be seen as no more than formal, the 'rules' of a particular art. In other periods the variation and indeed uncertainty of conventions have to be related to changes, divisions, and conflicts in the society, all normally going deeper (beyond what are still, in certain privileged areas, taken as 'rules' or as neutrally variable aesthetic methods) than can be seen without analysis. For it is of the essence of a convention that it ratifies an assumption or a point of view, so that the work can be made and received. The modern controversy about conventions, or the cases of deliberate exposure or reversal of older or inherent conventions in an attempt to create new relations with audiences, thus relate directly to the whole social process, in its living flux and contestation. But the reality of conventions as the mode of junction of social position and literary practice remains central. It is then necessary to consider the relation of conventions, over the range indicated, to the concepts of genre and of form.

Tzvetan Todorov

Literary Genres

"The Fantastic" is a name given to a kind of literature, to a literary genre. When we examine works of literature from the perspective of genre, we engage in a very particular enterprise: we discover a principle operative in a number of texts, rather than what is specific about each of them. To study Balzac's *The Magic Skin* in the context of the fantastic as a genre is quite different from studying this book in and of itself, or in the canon of Balzac's works, or in that of contemporary literature. Thus the concept of genre is fundamental to the discussion which follows, and we must first clarify and define it, even if such an endeavor apparently diverts us from the fantastic itself.

The notion of genre immediately raises several questions; fortunately, some of these vanish once we have formulated them explicitly. The first question is: are we entitled to discuss a genre without having studied (or at least read) all the works which constitute it? The graduate student who asks this question might add that a catalogue of the fantastic would include thousands of titles. Whence it is only a step to the image of the diligent student buried under books he must read at the rate of three a day, obsessed by the idea that new ones keep being written and that he will doubtless never manage to absorb them all. But one of the first characteristics of scientific method is that it does not require us to observe every instance of a phenomenon in order to describe it; scientific method proceeds rather by deduction. We actually deal with a relatively limited number of cases, from them we deduce a general hypothesis, and we verify this hypothesis by other cases, correcting (or rejecting) it as need be. Whatever the number of phenomena (of literary works, in this case) studied, we are never justified in extrapolating universal laws from them; it is not the quantity of observations, but the logical coherence of a theory that finally matters. As Karl Popper writes:

> It is far from obvious, from a logical point of view, that we are
> justified in inferring universal statements from singular ones, no

matter how numerous; for any conclusion drawn in this way may always turn out to be false: no matter how many instances of white swans we have observed, this does not justify the conclusion that all swans are white.

On the other hand, a hypothesis which is based on the observation of a limited number of swans but which also informs us that their whiteness is the consequence of an organic characteristic would be perfectly legitimate. To return from swans to novels, this general scientific truth applies not only to the study of genres, but also to that of a writer's entire *oeuvre*, or to that of a specific period, etc. Let us leave exhaustiveness, then, to those who have no other recourse.

The level of generality on which a genre is to be located raises a second question. Are there only a few genres (i.e., lyric, epic, dramatic), or many more? Are genres finite in number or infinite? The Russian formalists tended toward a relativist answer. According to Tomashevsky:

> Works are divided into large classes which are subdivided into types and species. In this way, moving down the ladder of genres, we move from abstract classes to concrete historical distinctions (the poem by Byron, the short story by Chekhov, the novel by Balzac, the religious ode, proletarian poetry) and even to specific works.

This passage certainly raises more problems than it solves, and we shall return to it shortly: but we may already accept the idea that genres exist at different levels of generality, and that the content of this notion is defined by the point of view we have chosen.

A third problem is a matter of aesthetics. We are told that it is pointless to speak of genres (tragedy, comedy, etc.), for the work of art is essentially unique, valuable because of what is original about it that distinguishes it from all other works, and not because of whatever in it may resemble them. If I like *The Charterhouse of Parma*, I do so not because it is a novel (genre) but because it is a novel different from all other novels (an individual work). This response implies a romantic attitude with regard to the material under observation. Such a position is not, strictly speaking, false; it is simply extraneous. We may certainly like a work for one reason or another; this is not what defines it as an object of study. The motive of an intellectual enterprise need not dictate the form which that enterprise ultimately assumes. As for the aesthetic problem in general, it will not be dealt with here: not because it does not exist, but because it far exceeds our present means.

However, this same objection can be formulated in different terms, whereupon it becomes much more difficult to refute. The concept of genre (or species) is borrowed from the natural sciences. It is no accident, moreover, that the pioneer structural analyst of narrative, Vladimir Propp, employed analogies with botany or zoology. Now there is a qualitative difference as to the meanings of the terms "genre" and "specimen," depending on whether they are applied to natural beings or to works of the mind. In the former case, the appearance of a new example does not necessarily modify the characteristics of the species; consequently, the properties of the new example are for the most part entirely deducible from the pattern of the species. Being familiar with the species tiger, we can deduce from it the properties of each individual tiger; the birth of a new tiger does not modify the species in its definition. The impact of individual organisms on the evolution of the species is so slow that we can discount it in practice. Similarly in the case of linguistic utterances (though to a lesser degree): an individual sentence does not modify the grammar of the language, and the grammar must permit us to deduce the properties of the sentence.

The same is not the case in the realm of art or of science. Here evolution operates with an altogether different rhythm: *every* work modifies the sum of possible works, each new example alters the species. We might say that in art we are dealing with a language of which every utterance is agrammatical at the moment of its performance. More exactly, we grant a text the right to figure in the history of literature or of science only insofar as it produces a change in our previous notion of the one activity or the other. Texts that do not fulfill this condition automatically pass into another category: that of so-called "popular" or "mass" literature in the one case; in the other, that of the academic exercise or unoriginal experiment. (Hence the unavoidable comparison of the artisanal product, the unique example, on the one hand, and of mass production, the mechanical stereotype, on the other.) To return to our subject, only "popular" literature (detective stories, serialized novels, science fiction, etc.) would approach fulfilling the requirements of genre in the sense the word has in natural science; for the notion of genre in that sense would be inapplicable to strictly literary texts.

Such a position obliges us to make our own theoretical assumptions explicit. Dealing with any text belonging to "literature," we must take into account a double requirement. First, we must be aware that it manifests properties that it shares with all literary texts, or with texts belonging to one of the sub-groups of literature (which we call, precisely, genres). It is inconceivable, nowadays, to defend the thesis that everything in the work is individual, a brand-new product of personal inspiration, a creation with no relation to works of the past. Second, we must understand that a text is not only the product of a pre-existing combinatorial system (constituted by all that is literature *in posse*); it is also a transformation of that system.

We can already say, then, that every literary study must participate in a double movement: from the particular work to literature generally (or genre), and from literature generally (from genre) to the particular work.

To grant a temporary privilege to one direction or the other—to difference or to resemblance—is a perfectly legitimate transaction. Further, it is of the very nature of language to move within abstraction and within the "generic." The individual cannot exist *in* language, and our formulation of a text's specificity automatically becomes the description of a genre, whose particular characteristic is that the work in question is its first and unique example. Any description of a text, by the very fact that it is made by means of words, is a description of genre. Moreover, this is not a purely theoretical assertion; we are repeatedly given examples by literary history, whenever epigones imitate precisely what was specific in the initiator.

There can therefore be no question of "rejecting the notion of genre," as Croce, for example, called for. Such a rejection would imply the renunciation of language and could not, by definition, be formulated. It is important, on the other hand, to be aware of the degree of abstraction that one assumes, and of the position of this abstraction with regard to any real development; such development will thereby be kept within a system of categories which establish and at the same time depend on it.

The fact remains that literature now seems to be abandoning the division into genres. Over a decade ago, Maurice Blanchot wrote:

> Only the book matters, as it stands, far from genres, apart from the labels—prose, poetry, novel, reportage—by which it refuses to be categorized and to which it denies the power to assign its place and determine its form. A book no longer belongs to a genre, every book proceeds only from literature, as if literature held in advance, in their generality, the secrets and formulas which alone permit giving what is written the reality of a book [*Le Livre à Venir*].

Why then raise these outdated problems? Gérard Genette has answered perfectly: "Literary discourse is produced and developed according to structures it can transgress only because it finds them, even today, in the field of its language and style" (*Figures*, II). For there to be a transgression, the norm must be apparent. Moreover, it is doubtful that contemporary literature is entirely exempt from generic distinctions; it is only that these distinctions no longer correspond to the notions bequeathed by the literary theories of the past. We are of course not obliged to abide by such notions now; indeed there is a growing necessity to elaborate abstract categories that could be applied to contemporary work. More generally, failing to recognize the existence of genres is equivalent to claiming that a literary work does not bear any relationship to already existing works. Genres are precisely those relay-points by which the work assumes a relation with the universe of literature.

In order to take a step forward, let us select a contemporary theory of genres for closer scrutiny. Thus, starting from a single model, we can get a better sense of what positive principles must guide our work, what dangers are to be avoided. Which is not to say that new principles will not arise from our own discourse, as we proceed, or that unsuspected obstacles will not appear at many points.

The theory of genres to be discussed in detail here is that of Northrop Frye, especially as it is formulated in his *Anatomy of Criticism*. Nor is this choice arbitrary: Frye today occupies a preeminent place among Anglo-American critics, and his book is undoubtedly one of the most remarkable works of criticism published since the Second World War. *Anatomy of Criticism* is at once a theory of literature (and therefore of genres) and a theory of criticism. More precisely, this book is composed of two kinds of texts, one of a theoretical order (the introduction, the conclusion, and the second essay: "Ethical Criticism: Theory of Symbols"), the other, more descriptive, in which Frye sets forth his system of genres. But in order to be understood, this system cannot be isolated from the whole; therefore we shall begin with the theoretical part.

Here are its chief characteristics:

1. Literary studies are to be undertaken with the same seriousness, the same rigor evinced by the other sciences:

> If criticism exists, it must be an examination of literature in terms of a conceptual framework derivable from an inductive survey of the literary field. ... There may be a scientific element in criticism which distinguishes it from literary parasitism on the one hand, and the superimposed critical attitude on the other.

2. A consequence of this first postulate is the necessity of removing from literary study any value judgment concerning the works in question. Frye is quite severe on this point. We may ease his verdict and say that evaluation will have its place in the field of poetics, but that for the moment to refer to evaluation would be to complicate matters to no purpose.

3. The literary work, like literature in general, forms a system; nothing in it is due to chance. Or as Frye puts it: "The first postulate of this inductive leap is the same as that of any science: the assumption of total coherence."

4. Synchrony is to be distinguished from diachrony: literary analysis requires us to take synchronic soundings in history, and it is within these that we must *begin* by seeking the system. As Frye writes in *Fables of Identity*, "When a critic deals with a work of literature, the most natural thing for him to do is to freeze it, to ignore its movement in time and look at it as a completed pattern of words, with all its parts existing simultaneously."

5. The literary text does not enter into a referential relation with the "world," as the sentences of everyday speech often do; it is not "representative" of anything but itself. In this, literature resembles mathemat-

ics rather than ordinary language: literary discourse cannot be true or false, it can only be valid in relation to its own premises. "The poet, like the pure mathematician, depends not on descriptive truth, but on conformity to his hypothetical postulates. ... Literature, like mathematics, is a language, and a language in itself represents no truth, though it may provide the means for expressing any number of them." Thus the literary text participates in tautology: it signifies itself: "the poetic symbol means primarily itself in relation to the poem." The poet's answer as to what any element of his work means must always be: "I meant it to form a part of the play."

6. Literature is created from literature, not from reality, whether that reality is material or psychic; every literary work is a matter of convention. "Poetry can only be made out of other poems, novels out of other novels. Literature shapes itself and is not shaped externally. ... Everything that is new in literature is a reworking of what is old. ... Self-expression in literature is something which has never existed."

None of these ideas is entirely original (though Frye rarely gives his sources): they can be found on the one hand in Mallarmé or Valéry, as well as in a tendency of contemporary French criticism which continues their tradition (Blanchot, Barthes, Genette); on the other hand, very abundantly, in the Russian formalists; and finally in authors such as T. S. Eliot. The sum of these postulates, as valid for literary studies as for literature itself, constitutes our own point of departure. But all this has taken us quite far from genres. Let us turn to the part of Frye's book which interests us more directly. Throughout the *Anatomy* (which consists, we must recall, of texts which first appeared separately), Frye proposes several sets of categories, all of which can be subdivided into genres (though Frye applies the term "genre" to only one of these sets). I do not intend to discuss them in detail here. Concentrating on a purely methodological discussion, I shall retain only the logical articulation of his classifications without giving his examples.

1. The first classification defines the "modes of fiction." They are constituted by the relation between the hero of the work and ourselves or the laws of nature, and are five in number:

i The hero is by *nature* superior to the reader *and* to the laws of nature; this genre is called *myth.*

ii The hero is by *degree* superior to the reader *and* to the laws of nature; this genre is that of *legend* or *fairy tale.*

iii The hero is by *degree* superior to the reader *but not* to the laws of nature; this is the *high mimetic genre.*

iv The hero is *on a basis of equality with* the reader *and* the laws of nature; this is the *low mimetic genre.*

v The hero is *inferior to* the reader; this is the genre of *irony.*

2. Another fundamental category is that of verisimilitude. The two poles of literature are here constituted by the plausible narrative and the narrative whose characters can do anything.

3. A third category emphasizes two principal tendencies of literature: the comic, which reconciles the hero with society; and the tragic, which isolates him from it.

4. The classification which appears to be most important for Frye is the one which defines the archetypes. There are four of these (four *mythoi*, to use a term Frye employs as a synonym for "archetypes"), based on the opposition of the real and the ideal. Thus Frye characterizes *romance* (based on the ideal), *irony* (based on reality), comedy (which involves a transition from reality to the ideal), and tragedy (which involves a transition from the ideal to reality).

5. Next comes the division into genres strictly speaking, based on the type of audience for which the works are intended. The genres are: *drama* (works to be performed), *lyric poetry* (works to be sung), epic poetry (works to be recited), prose (works to be read). To which is added the following specification: "The chief distinction is involved with the fact that *epos* is episodic and fiction continuous."

6. A final classification is articulated in terms of oppositions between intellectual and personal, introvert and extrovert, and may be presented schematically as follows:

	intellectual	*personal*
introvert	confession	romance
extrovert	anatomy	novel

These are some of the categories (we may also say, some of the genres) proposed by Frye. His boldness is apparent and praiseworthy; it remains to be seen what it contributes.

I

The first remarks we shall formulate, and the easiest, are based on logic, if not on common sense (their usefulness for the study of the fantastic will appear, it is to be hoped, later on). Frye's classifications are not logically coherent, either among themselves or individually. In his critique of Frye, Wimsatt has already, and justifiably, pointed out the impossibility of coordinating the two chief classifications, the first and the fourth summarized above. As for the internal inconsistencies, they appear as soon as we make even cursory analysis of the first classification.

In that classification, a unit, the hero, is compared both with the reader ("ourselves") and with the laws of nature. The relation (of superiority), moreover, can be either qualitative (of nature) or quantitative (of degree). But by schematizing this classification, we discover that many possible combinations are missing from Frye's enumeration. Let us say straight off that there is an asymmetry: only one category of inferiority corresponds to the three categories of the hero's superiority; further, the distinction of nature as opposed to degree is applied only once, whereas we might produce it apropos of each category. Doubtless we might avoid the reproach of incoherence by postulating additional restrictions which would reduce the number of possibilities. For example, we could say that the relation of the hero to the laws of nature functions between a whole and an element, not between two elements: if the hero obeys these laws, there can no longer be a question of difference between quality and quantity. In the same way, we could specify that if the hero is inferior to the laws of nature, he can be superior to the reader, but that the converse is not true. These additional restrictions would permit us to avoid inconsistencies: but it is absolutely necessary to formulate them; otherwise we are employing a system which is not explicit and we remain in the realm of faith—unless it is the realm of superstitions.

An objection to our own objections might be: if Frye enumerates only five genres (modes) out of the thirteen possibilities that are theoretically available, it is because these five genres have existed, which is not true of the eight others. This remark leads to an important distinction between two meanings given to the word genre. In order to avoid all ambiguity, we should posit, on the one hand, *historical genres*; on the other, *theoretical genres*. The first would result from an observation of literary reality; the second from a deduction of a theoretical order. What we learn in school about genres always relates to historical genres: we are told about classical tragedy because there have been, in France, works which manifested their relation to this literary form. We find examples of theoretical genres, on the other hand, in works of the ancient writers on poetics. Thus Diomedes, in the fourth century, follows Plato in dividing all works into three categories: those in which only the narrator speaks; those in which only the characters speak; and those in which both speak. This classification is not based on a comparison of works to be found in the history of literature (as in the case of historical genres), but on an abstract hypothesis which postulates that the performer of the speech act is the most important element of the literary work, and that according to the nature of this performer, we can distinguish a logically calculable number of theoretical genres. Lessing proceeds in the same fashion when he "calculates" in advance the sub-genres of the epigram, which consists, he asserts, of an expectation and an explanation: "Of course there may be only two sub-genres of the epigram, the first, which awakens expectation without affording a solution; the second, which affords the solution without having created expectations."

Now Frye's system, like that of the ancient writers or Lessing's, is composed of *theoretical* genres and not historical ones. There are a certain number of genres not because more have not been observed, but because the principle of the system imposes that number. It is therefore necessary to deduce all the possible combinations from the categories chosen. We might even say that if one of these combinations had in fact never been manifested, we should describe it even more deliberately: just as in Mendeleev's system one could describe the properties of elements not yet discovered, similarly we shall describe here the properties of genres—and therefore of works—still to come.

To this first observation, we may add two other remarks. First, any theory of genres is based on a conception of the work, on an image of the work, which involves on one hand a certain number of abstract properties, on the other a certain number of laws governing the relation of these properties. If Diomedes divides genres into three categories, it is because he postulates, within the work, a certain feature: the existence of a performer of the speech act; furthermore, by basing his classification on this feature, he testifies to the primary importance he grants it. Similarly, if Frye bases his classification on the relation of superiority or inferiority between the hero and ourselves, it is because he regards this relation as an element of the work and, further, as one of its fundamental elements.

We may, to proceed a step further, introduce an additional distinction within the theoretical genres, and speak of *elementary genres* and *complex* ones. The first would be defined by the presence or absence of a single characteristic, as in Diomedes; the second, by the coexistence of several characteristics. For instance, we might define the complex genre "sonnet" as uniting the following properties: (1) certain prescriptions as to rhymes; (2) certain prescriptions as to meter; (3) certain prescriptions as to theme. Such a definition presupposes a theory of meter, of rhyme, and of themes (in other words, a total theory of literature). It thus becomes obvious that historical genres form a part of the complex theoretical genres.

II

By noting certain formal incoherences in Frye's classifications, we have already been led to an observation which no longer bears on the logical form of his categories but on their content. Frye never makes explicit his conception of the work (which, as we have seen, must serve as the point of departure for any classification into genres) and he devotes remarkably few pages to the theoretical discussion of his categories. Let us attempt to do so in his place.

First let us enumerate some of them: superior/inferior; verisimilitude/fantasy; reconciliation/exclusion (in relation to society); real/ideal; introvert/extrovert; intellectual/personal. What is striking in this list from the very first is its arbitrariness: why are these categories and not others useful in describing a literary text? One looks for a closely reasoned argument which would prove this importance; but there is no trace of such an argument. Further, we cannot fail to notice a characteristic common to these categories: their non-literary nature. They are all borrowed from philosophy, from psychology, or from a social ethic, and moreover not from just any psychology or philosophy. Either these terms are to be taken in a special, strictly literary sense; or—and since we are told nothing about such a sense, this is the only possibility available to us—they lead us outside of literature. Whereupon literature becomes no more than a means of expressing philosophical categories. Its autonomy is thus profoundly contested—and we again contradict one of the theoretical principles stated, precisely, by Frye himself.

Even if these categories applied only to literature, they would require a more extended explanation. Can we speak of the hero as if this notion were self-explanatory? What is the precise meaning of this word? And what is verisimilitude? Is its contrary (fantasy) only the property of stories in which the characters "can do anything"? Frye himself, moreover, gives another interpretation of verisimilitude which contests this first sense of the word: "An original painter knows, of course, that when the public demands likeness to an object, it generally wants the exact opposite, likeness to the pictorial conventions it is familiar with."

III

When we press Frye's analyses still more closely, we discover another postulate which, though unformulated, plays a leading role in his system. The points we have hitherto criticized could be readily accommodated without altering the system itself: we could avoid the logical incoherences and find a theoretical basis for the choice of categories. The consequences of this new postulate are much more serious, for it involves a fundamental option, the very one by which Frye clearly opposes the structuralist attitude, attaching himself instead to a tradition that includes such names as Jung, Gaston Bachelard, Gilbert Durand (however different their works).

This is the postulate: the *structures* formed by literary phenomena *manifest themselves at the level of these phenomena*—i.e., these structures are directly observable. Lévi-Strauss writes, on the contrary: "The fundamental principle is that the notion of social structure is not related to empirical reality but to the model constructed according to that reality." To simplify, we might say that in Frye's view, the forest and the sea form an elementary structure; for a structuralist, on the contrary, these two phenomena manifest an abstract structure which is a mental construction and which sets in opposition, let us say, the static and the dynamic. Hence we see why certain images such as the four seasons, or the four times of day, or the four elements play such an important role for Frye: as he himself asserts in his preface to a translation of Bachelard: "earth, air, fire, and water are still the four elements of imaginative experience, and always will be." While the "structure" of the structuralists is above all an abstract principle or rule, Frye's "structure" is reduced to an arrangement in space. Frye is explicit on the point: "Very often a 'structure' or 'system' of thought can be reduced to a diagrammatic pattern—in fact both words are to some extent synonyms of diagram."

A postulate has no need of proofs; but its effectiveness can be measured by the results we reach by accepting it. Since the formal organization cannot be apprehended, we believe, on the level of the images themselves, all that we can say about the latter will remain only approximate. We must be content with probabilities, instead of dealing with certainties and impossibilities. To return to our example of the most elementary kind, the forest and the sea *can* often be found in opposition, thus forming a "structure"; but they do not *have to;* while the static and the dynamic necessarily form an opposition, which can be manifested in that of the forest and the sea. Literary structures are so many systems of rigorous rules, and it is only their manifestations which conform to probabilities. If we seek the structures on the level of the observable images, we thereby refuse all certain knowledge.

This is certainly what happens in Frye's case. One of the words most often encountered in the *Anatomy* is surely the word *often* and its synonyms. Some examples:

> This myth is *often* associated with a flood, the regular symbol of the beginning and the end of a cycle.... The infant hero is *often* placed in an ark *or* chest floating on the sea.... On dry land the infant *may* be rescued *either* from *or* by an animal.... Its *most common* settings are the mountaintop, the island, the tower, the lighthouse, and the ladder or staircase.... He *may* also be a ghost, like Hamlet's father; *or* it *may* not be a person at all, but simply an invisible force known only by its effects.... *Often,* as in the revenge-tragedy, it is an event previous to the action of which the tragedy itself is the consequence [my italics].

The postulate of a direct manifestation of structures produces a sterilizing effect in several other directions. First we must remark that Frye's hypothesis cannot go further than a taxonomy, a classification (according to his explicit declarations). But to say that the elements of a whole can be classified is to formulate the weakest possible hypothesis about these elements.

Moreover, Frye's *Anatomy* constantly suggests a catalogue in which countless literary images might be inventoried; but a catalogue is of course only one of the tools of knowledge, not knowledge itself. It might even be said that the man who merely classifies cannot do his job so well: his classification is arbitrary, for it does not rest on an explicit theory—it is a little like those pre-Linnaean classifications of living organisms which readily constructed a category of all animals which scratch themselves...

If we admit, with Frye, that literature is a language, we are entitled to expect that the critic should be quite close, in what he does, to the linguist. But the author of *Anatomy of Criticism* rather puts one in mind of those dialect-lexicographers of the nineteenth century who combed remote villages for rare or unknown words. No matter how many thousands of words are collected, one does not thereby discover the principles, even the most elementary ones, of the functioning of a language. The work of the dialect-collectors has not been useless, yet it is misleading: for language is not a stockpile of words but a mechanism. In order to understand this mechanism, it suffices to start from the most ordinary words, the simplest sentences. Even in criticism: we can approach the essential problems of literary theory without necessarily possessing the scintillating erudition of a Northrop Frye.

It is time to close this long digression, whose usefulness for the study of the fantastic as a literary genre may have appeared problematical. It has, at least, allowed us to reach certain precise conclusions, which may be summarized as follows:

1. Every theory of genres is based on a hypothesis concerning the nature of literary works. We must therefore begin by presenting our own point of departure, even if subsequent efforts lead us to abandon it.

In short, we shall distinguish three aspects of the literary work: the verbal, the syntactical, and the semantic.

The verbal aspect resides in the concrete sentences which constitute the text. We may note here two groups of problems. The first is linked to the properties of the utterance itself. The second group is linked to its performance, to the person who emits the text and to the person who receives it: in each case, what is involved is an image implicit in the text, not a real author or reader. (These problems have hitherto been studied in terms of "points of view.")

By the syntactic aspect, we account for relations which the parts of the work sustain among themselves (the old expression for this was "composition"). These relations can be of three types: logical, temporal, and spatial, as I have had occasion to discuss elsewhere.

There remains the semantic aspect, or the "themes" of a literary text. With respect to this third aspect we posit, at the outset, no general hypothesis; we do not know how literary themes are articulated. Yet we may safely assume that there exists some universal semantics of literature, comprehending the themes which are to be met with always and everywhere and which are limited in number; their transformations and combinations produce the apparent multitude of literary themes.

These three aspects of the work are manifested in a complex interrelation; they are to be found in isolation only in our analysis.

2. A preliminary choice must be made as to the level on which to locate literary structures. We have decided to consider all the immediately observable elements of the literary universe as the manifestation of an abstract and isolated structure, a mental construction, and to establish an organization on this level alone. Here a fundamental cleavage occurs.

3. The concept of genre must be qualified. We have set in opposition, on the one hand, historical and theoretical genres: historical genres are the result of an observation of literary phenomena; theoretical genres are deduced from a theory of literature. Further, we have distinguished, within theoretical genres, between elementary and complex genres: the former are characterized by the presence or absence of a single structural feature; the latter by the presence or absence of a conjunction of such features. Everything suggests that historical genres are a sub-group of complex theoretical genres.

Abandoning now the analyses by Frye which have guided us thus far, we must finally, with their help, formulate a more general and more cautious view of the objectives and limits of any study of genres. Such a study must constantly satisfy requirements of two orders: practical and theoretical, empirical and abstract. The genres we deduce from the theory must be verified by reference to the texts: if our deductions fail to correspond to any work, we are on a false trail. On the other hand, the genres which we encounter in literary history must be subject to the explanation of a coherent theory; otherwise, we remain imprisoned by prejudices transmitted from century to century, and according to which (an imaginary example) there exists a genre such as comedy, which is in fact a pure illusion. The definition of genres will therefore be a continual oscillation between the description of phenomena and abstract theory.

Such are our objectives; but upon closer inspection, we cannot help doubting the success of the enterprise. Consider the first requirement, that of the conformity of the theory to the phenomena. We have postulated that literary structures, hence genres themselves, be located on an abstract level, separate from that of concrete works. We would have to say that a given work manifests a certain genre, not that this genre exists in the work. But this relation of manifestation between the abstract and the concrete is of a probabilistic nature; in other words, there is no necessity that a work faithfully incarnate its genre, there is only a probability that it will do so. Which comes down to saying that no observation of works can strictly confirm or invalidate a theory of genres. If I am told: a certain work does not fit any of your categories, hence your categories are wrong, I could object: your "hence" has no reason to exist: works need not coincide with categories, which have merely a constructed existence; a work can, for example, manifest more than one category, more than one genre. We are thus led to an exemplary methodological impasse: how to prove the descriptive failure of any theory of genres whatever? The reproach we made to Frye appears to apply to any work, ours included.

Consider now the other side, the conformity of known genres to theory. The theoretical test will be no easier than the empirical one. The danger is nonetheless of a different nature: it is that our categories will tend to lead us outside of literature. Every theory of literary themes, for example (up till now, in any case), tends to reduce these themes to a complex of categories borrowed from psychology or philosophy or sociology (witness Frye). Were these categories to be borrowed from linguistics, the situation would not be qualitatively different. Further: by the very fact that we must use ordinary language in order to speak of literature, we imply that literature transmits something which could be designated by other means. But if this were true, why should literature exist at all? Its only reason for being is that it says what non-literary language does not and cannot say. Therefore some of the best critics tend to become writers themselves in order to avoid the violence wrought upon literature by non-literature; but it is a hopeless effort. A new literary work has been created, the previous one has not been matched. Literature says what it alone can say. When the critic has said everything in his power about a literary text, he has still said nothing; for the very existence of literature implies that it cannot be replaced by non-literature.

These skeptical reflections need not discourage us; they merely oblige us to become aware of limits we cannot transcend. The goal of knowledge is an approximate truth, not an absolute one. If descriptive science claimed to speak *the* truth, it would contradict its reason for being. (Indeed, a certain form of physical geography no longer exists since all the continents have been correctly described.) Imperfection is, paradoxically, a guarantee of survival.

Six

style

Leo Spitzer

Linguistics and Literary History[1]

The title of this book is meant to suggest the ultimate unity of linguistics and literary history. Since my activity, throughout my scholarly life, has been largely devoted to the rapprochement of these two disciplines, I may be forgiven if I preface my remarks with an autobiographic sketch of my first academic experiences: What I propose to do is to tell you only my own story, how I made my way through the maze of linguistics, with which I started, toward the enchanted garden of literary history—and how I discovered that there is as well a paradise in linguistics as a labyrinth in literary history; that the methods and the degree of certainty in both are basically the same; and, that if today the humanities are under attack (and, as I believe, under an unwarranted attack, since it is not the humanities themselves that are at fault but only some so-called humanists who persist in imitating an obsolete approach to the natural sciences, which have themselves evolved toward the humanities)—if, then, the humanities are under attack, it would be pointless to exempt any one of them from the verdict: if it is true that there is no value to be derived from the study of language, we cannot pretend to preserve literary history, cultural history—or history.

I have chosen the autobiographical way because my personal situation in Europe forty years ago was not, I believe, essentially different from the one with which I see the young scholar of today (and in this country) generally faced. I chose to relate to you my own experiences also because the basic approach of the individual scholar, conditioned as it is by his first experiences, by his *Erlebnis*, as the Germans say, determines his method: *Methode ist Erlebnis*, Gundolf has said. In fact, I would advise every older scholar to tell his public the basic experiences underlying his methods, his *Mein Kampf*, as it were—without dictatorial connotations, of course.

I had decided, after college had given me a solid foundation in the classical languages, to study the Romance languages and particularly French philology, because, in my native Vienna, the gay and orderly, skeptic and sentimental, Catholic and pagan Vienna of yore was filled with adoration of the French way of life. I had always been surrounded by a French atmosphere and, at that juvenile stage of experience, had acquired a picture, perhaps overgeneralized, of French literature, which seemed to me definable by an Austrianlike mixture of sensuousness and reflection, of vitality and discipline, of sentimentality and critical wit. The moment when the curtain rose on a French play given by a French troupe, and the valet, in a knowing accent of psychological alertness, with his rich, poised voice, pronounced the words "Madame est servie," was a delight to my heart.

But when I attended the classes of French linguistics of my great teacher Meyer-Lübke no picture was offered us of the French people, or of the Frenchness of their language: in these classes we saw Latin *a* moving, according to relentless phonetic laws, toward French *e* (*pater* > *père*); there we saw a new system of declension spring up from nothingness, a system in which the six Latin cases came to be reduced to two, and later to one—while we learned that similar violence had been done to the other Romance languages and, in fact, to many modern languages. In all this, there were many facts and much rigor in the establishment of facts, but all was vague in regard to the general ideas underlying these facts. What was the mystery behind the refusal of Latin sounds or cases to stay put and behave themselves? We saw incessant change working in language— but why? I was a long while realizing that Meyer-Lübke was offering only the *pre*-history of French (as he established it by a comparison with the other Romance languages), not its history. And we were never allowed to contemplate a phenomenon in its quiet being, to look into its face: we always looked at its neighbors or at its predecessors—we were always looking over our shoulder. There were presented to us the relationships of phenomenon *a* and phenomenon *b*; but phenomenon *a* and phenomenon *b* did not exist in themselves, nor did the historical line *a-b*. In reference to a given French form, Meyer-Lübke would quote Old Portuguese, Modern Bergamesque and Macedo-rumanian, German, Celtic, and paleo-Latin forms; but where was reflected in this teaching my sensuous, witty, disciplined Frenchman, in his presumably 1000 years of existence? He was left out in the cold while we talked about his language; indeed, French was not the language of the Frenchman, but an agglomeration of unconnected, separate, anecdotic, senseless evolutions: a French historical grammar, apart from the word-material, could as well have been a Germanic or a Slav grammar: the leveling of paradigms, the phonetic evolutions occur there just as in French.

When I changed over to the classes of the equally great literary historian Philipp August Becker, that ideal Frenchman seemed to show some faint signs of life—in the spirited analyses of the events in the *Pèlerinage de Charlemagne,* or of the plot of a Molière comedy; but it was as if the treatment of the contents were only subsidiary to the really scholarly work, which consisted in fixing the dates and historical data of these works of art, in assessing the amount of autobiographical elements and written sources which the poets had supposedly incorporated into their artistic productions. Had the *Pèlerinage* to do with the Xth crusade? Which was its original dialect? Was there any epic poetry, Merovingian or other, which preceded Old French epic poetry? Had Molière put his own matrimonial disillusionment into the *Ecole des femmes?* (While Becker did not insist on an affirmative conclusion, he considered such a question to be a part of legitimate literary criticism.) Did the medieval farce survive in the Molière comedy? The existing works of art were stepping-stones from which to proceed to other phenomena, contemporary or previous, which were in reality quite heterogeneous. It seemed indiscrete to ask what made them works of art, what was expressed in them, and why these expressions appeared in France, at that particular time. Again, it was prehistory, not history, that we were offered, and a kind of materialistic prehistory, at that. In this attitude of positivism, exterior events were taken thus seriously only to evade the more completely the real question: Why did the phenomena *Pèlerinage* and *Ecole des femmes* happen at all? And, I must admit, in full loyalty to Meyer-Lübke, that he taught more of reality than did Becker: it was unquestionable that Latin *a* had evolved to French *e;* it was untrue that Molière's experience with the possibly faithless Madeleine Béjart had evolved to the work of art *Ecole des femmes.* But, in both fields, that of linguistics as well as that of literary history (which were separated by an enormous gulf: Meyer-Lübke spoke only of language and Becker only of literature), a meaningless industriousness prevailed: not only was this kind of humanities not centered on a particular people in a particular time, but the subject matter itself had got lost: Man.[2] At the end of my first year of graduate studies, I had come to the conclusion, not that the science offered *ex cathedra* was worthless but that I was not fit for such studies as that of the irrational vowel -*i*- in Eastern French dialects, or of the *Subjektivismusstreit* in Molière: never would I get a Ph.D.! It was the benignity of Providence, exploiting my native Teutonic docility toward scholars who knew more than I, which kept me faithful to the study of Romance philology. By not abandoning prematurely this sham science, by seeking, instead, to appropriate it, I came to recognize its true value as well as my own possibilities of work—and to establish my life's goal. By using the tools of science offered me, I came to see under their dustiness the fingerprints of a Friedrich Diez and of the Romantics, who had created these tools; and henceforth they were not dusty any more, but ever radiant and ever new. And I had learned to handle many and manifold facts: training in handling facts, brutal facts, is perhaps the best education for a wavering, youthful mind.

And now let me take you, as I promised to do, on the path that leads from the most routinelike techniques of the linguist toward the work of the literary historian. The different fields will appear here in the ascending order, as I see them today, while the concrete examples, drawn from my own activity, will not respect the chronological order of their publication.

Meyer-Lübke, the author of the comprehensive and still final etymological dictionary of Romance languages, had taught me, among many other things, how to find etymologies; I shall now take the liberty of inflicting upon you a concrete example of this procedure—sparing you none of the petty drudgery involved. Since my coming to America, I have been curious about the etymology of two English words, characterized by the same "flavor": *conundrum* "a riddle the answer to which involves a pun; a puzzling question," and *quandary* "a puzzling situation." The NED attests conun*drum* first in 1596; early variants are *conimbrum*, *quonundrum*, *quadrundum*. The meaning is "whim" or "pun." In the seventeenth century it was known as an Oxford term: preachers were wont to use in their sermons the baroque device of puns and conundrums, e.g. "Now all House is turned into an Alehouse, and a pair of dice is made a Paradice; was it thus in the days of Noah? Ah no." This baroque technique of interlarding sermons with puns is well known from the *Kapuziner-Predigt*, inspired by Abraham a Santa Clara, in Schiller's *Wallenstein's Lager:* "Der *Rheinstrom* ist worden zu einem *Peinstrom*," etc.

The extraordinary instability (reflecting the playfulness of the concept involved) of the phonetic structure: *conundrum—conimbrum—quadrundrum*, points to a foreign source, to a word which must have been (playfully) adapted in various ways. Since the English variants include among them a -*b*- and a -*d*- which are not easily reducible to any one basic sound, I propose to submit a French word-family which, in its different forms, contains both -*b*- and -*d*-: the French *calembour* is exactly synonymous with *conundrum* "pun." This *calembour* is evidently related to *calembredaine* "nonsensical or odd speech," and we can assume that *calembour*, too, had originally this same general reference. This word-family goes back probably to Fr. *bourde* "tall story" to which has been added the fanciful, semipejorative prefix *cali*, that can be found in *à califourchon* "straddling" (from Latin *quadrifurcus*, French *carrefour* "crossroads": the *qu*- of the English variants points to this Latin etymon). The French ending -*aine* of *calembredaine* developed to -*um*: *n* becomes *m* as in *ransom* from French *rançon*; *ai* becomes *o* as in *mitten* (older *mitton*) from French *mitaine*. Thus *calembourdane*, as a result of various assimilations and shortenings which I will spare you, becomes

colundrum, *columbrum* and then *conundrum, conimbrum*, etc. Unfortunately, the French word-family is attested rather late, occurring for
the first time in a comic opera of Vadé in 1754. We do find, however, an
équilbourdie "whim" as early as 1658 in the *Muse normande*, a dialectal
text. The fact is that popular words of this sort have, as a rule, little
chance of turning up in the (predominantly idealistic) literature of the
Middle Ages; it is, therefore, a mere accident that English *conundrum* is
attested in 1596 and French *calembour* only in 1757; at least, the chance
appearance of *équilbourdie* in the dialectal text of 1658 gives us an earlier
attestation of the French word-family. That the evidently popular medieval words emerge so late in literature is a fact explainable by the currents
prevalent in literature; the linguist must take his chances with what literature offers him in the way of attestation. In view of the absolute evidence of the equation *conundrum* = *calembredaine* we need not be
intimidated by chronological divergencies—which the older school
of etymologists (as represented by the editors of the NED) seem to have
overrated.

After *conundrum* had ceased to be a riddle to me, I was emboldened
to ask myself whether I could not now solve the etymology of the word
quandary—which also suggested to me a French origin. And, lo and behold: this word, of unknown origin, which is attested from about 1580 on,
revealed itself etymologically identical with *conundrum!* There are English dialect forms such as *quándorum quóndorum* which serve to establish an uninterrupted chain: *calembredaine* becomes *conimbrum conundrum quonundrum quandorum* and these give us *quandary.*[8]

Now what can be the humanistic, the spiritual value of this (as it
may have seemed to you) juggling with word forms? The particular etymology of *conundrum* is an inconsequential fact; that an etymology can
be found by man is a miracle. An etymology introduces meaning into the
meaningless: in our case, the evolution of two words in time—that is, a
piece of linguistic history—has been cleared up. What seemed an agglomeration of mere sounds now appears motivated. We feel the same "inner click" accompanying our comprehension of this evolution in time as
when we have grasped the meaning of a sentence or a poem—which then
become more than the sum total of their single words or sounds (*poem*
and *sentence* are, in fact, the classical examples given by Augustine and
Bergson in order to demonstrate the nature of a stretch of *durée réelle:*
the parts aggregating to a whole, time filled with contents). In the problem
which we chose, two words which seemed erratic and fantastic, with no
definite relationships in English, have been unified among themselves
and related to a French word-family.

The existence of such a loan-word is another testimony to the well-
known cultural situation obtaining when medieval England was in the
sway of French influence: the English and French word-families, al-

though attested centuries after the Middle Ages, must have belonged to one Anglo-French word-family during that period, and their previous existence is precisely proved by proving their family relationship. And it is not by chance that English borrows words for "pun" or "whim" from the witty French, who have also given *carriwitchet* "quibble," and (perhaps: see the NED) *pun* itself to English. But, since a loan-word rarely feels completely at home in its new environment, we have the manifold variations of the word, which fell apart into two word-groups (clearly separated, today, by the current linguistic feeling): *conundrum-quandary*. The instability and disunity of the word-family is symptomatic of its position in the new environment.

But the instability apparent in our English words had already been characteristic of *calembredaine–calembour*, even in the home environment: this French word-family, as we have said, was a blend of at least two word-stems. Thus we must conclude that the instability is also connected with the semantic content: a word meaning "whim, pun" easily behaves whimsically—just as, in all languages throughout the world, the words for "butterfly" present a kaleidoscopic instability. The linguist who explains such fluttery words has to juggle, because the speaking community itself (in our case, the English as well as the French) has juggled. This juggling in itself is psychologically and culturally motivated: language is not, as the behavioristic, antimentalistic, mechanistic or materialistic school of linguists, rampant in some universities, would have it: a meaningless agglomeration of corpses: dead word-material, automatic "speech habits" unleashed by a trigger motion. A certain automatism may be predicated of the use of *conundrum* and *quandary* in contemporary English, and of *calembour, calembredaine* in contemporary French (though, even today, this automatism is not absolute, since all these words have still a connotation of whimsicality or fancifulness and are, accordingly, somewhat motivated). But this is certainly not true for the history of the words: the linguistic creation is always meaningful and, yes, clear-minded: it was a feeling for the appositeness of nomenclature which prompted the communities to use, in our case, two-track words. They gave a playful expression to a playful concept, symbolizing in the word their attitude toward the concept. It was when the creative, the Renaissance, phase had passed that English let the words congeal, petrify, and split into two. This petrification is, itself, due to a decision of the community which, in eighteenth-century England, passed from the Renaissance attitude to the classicistic attitude toward language, which would replace creativity by standardization and regulation. Another cultural climate, another linguistic style. Out of the infinity of word-histories which could be imagined we have chosen only one, one which shows quite individual circumstances, such as the borrowing of a foreign word

by English, the original French blend, the subsequent alterations and restrictions; every word has its own history, not to be confused with that of
any other. But what repeats itself in all word-histories is the possibility of
recognizing the signs of a people at work, culturally and psychologically.
To speak in the language of the homeland of philology: *Wortwandel ist
Kulturwandel und Seelenwandel;* this little etymological study has been
humanistic in purpose.

If we accept the equation: *conundrum* and *quandary* = *calembredaine*—how has this been found? I may say, by quite an orthodox technique which would have been approved by Meyer-Lübke—though he
would not, perhaps, have stopped to draw the inferences on which I have
insisted. First, by collecting the material evidence about the English
words, I was led to seek a French origin. I had also observed that the great
portion of the English vocabulary which is derived from French has not
been given sufficient attention by etymologists; and, of course, my familiarity with the particular behavior of "butterfly words" in language was
such as to encourage a relative boldness in the reconstruction of the etymon. I had first followed the inductive method—or rather a quick intuition—in order to identify *conundrum* with *calembredaine;* later, I had to
proceed deductively, to verify whether my assumed etymon concorded
with all the known data, whether it really explained all the semantic and
phonetic variations; while following this path I was able to see that *quandary* must also be a reflection of *calembredaine*. (This to-and-fro movement is a basic requirement in all humanistic studies, as we shall see
later.) For example, since the French word-family is attested later than is
the English, it seemed necessary to dismiss the chronological discrepancies; fortunately—or, as I would say, providentially—the Normandian
équilbourdie of 1658 turned up! In this kind of gentle blending together
of the words, of harmonizing them and smoothing out difficulties, the
linguist undoubtedly indulges in a propensity to see things as shifting and
melting into each other—an attitude to which you may object: I cannot
contend more than that this change was *possible* in the way I have indicated, since it contradicts no previous experience; I can say only that two
unsolved problems (the one concerning the prehistory of *conundrum*, the
other that of *calembredaine*) have, when brought together, shed light on
each other, thereby enabling us to see the common solution. I am reminded here of the story of the Pullman porter to whom a passenger com-
plained in the morning that he had got back one black shoe and one tan;
the porter replied that, curiously enough, a similar discovery had been
made by another passenger. In the field of language, the porter who has
mixed up the shoes belonging together is language itself, and the linguist
is the passenger who must bring together what was once a historical unit.
To place two phenomena within a framework adds something to the

knowledge about their common nature. There is no mathematical demonstrability in such an equation, only a feeling of inner evidence; but this feeling, with the trained linguist, is the fruit of observation combined with experience, of precision supplemented by imagination—the dosage of which cannot be fixed a priori, but only in the concrete case. There is underlying such a procedure the belief that this is the way things happened; but there is always a belief underlying the humanist's work (similarly, it cannot be demonstrated that the Romance languages form a unity going back to Vulgar Latin; this basic assumption of the student in Romance languages, first stated by Diez, cannot be proved to the disbeliever).[4] And who says belief, says suasion: I have, deliberately and tendentiously, grouped the variants of *conundrum* in the most plausible order possible for the purpose of winning your assent. Of course, there are more easily believable etymologies, reached at the cost of less stretching and bending: no one in his senses would doubt that French *père* comes from Latin *pater*, or that this, along with English *father*, goes back to an Indo-European prototype. But we must not forget that these smooth, standard equations are relatively rare—for the reason that a word such as "father" is relatively immune to cultural revolutions or, in other words, that, in regard to the "father," a continuity of feeling, stretching over more than 4000 years, exists in Indo-European civilization.

Thus our etymological study has illuminated a stretch of linguistic history, which is connected with psychology and history of civilization; it has suggested a web of interrelations between language and the soul of the speaker. This web could have been as well revealed by a study of a syntactical, a morphological evolution—even a phonetic evolution of the type "*a* becomes *e*," wherein Meyer-Lübke had failed to see the *durée réelle*, exclusively concerned as he was with *l'heure de la montre*; his historical "clock time."

Now, since the best document of the soul of a nation is its literature, and since the latter is nothing but its language as this is written down by elect speakers, can we perhaps not hope to grasp the spirit of a nation in the language of its outstanding works of literature? Because it would have been rash to compare the whole of a national literature to the whole of a national language (as Karl Vossler has prematurely tried to do) I started, more modestly, with the question: "Can one distinguish the soul of a particular French writer in his particular language?" It is obvious that literary historians have held this conviction, since, after the inevitable quotation (or misquotation) of Buffon's saying: *"Le style c'est l'homme,"* they generally include in their monographs a chapter on the style of their author. But I had in mind the more rigorously scientific definition of an individual style, the definition of a linguist which should replace the casual, impressionistic remarks of literary critics. Stylistics, I thought, might bridge the gap between linguistics and literary history. On the other hand, I was warned by the scholastic adage: *individuum est ineffabile*; could it be that any attempt to define the individual writer by his style is doomed to failure? The individual stylistic deviation from the general norm must represent a historical step taken by the writer, I argued: it must reveal a shift of the soul of the epoch, a shift of which the writer has become conscious and which he would translate into a necessarily new linguistic form; perhaps it would be possible to determine the historical step, psychological as well as linguistic? To determine the beginning of a linguistic innovation would be easier, of course, in the case of contemporary writers, because their linguistic basis is better known to us than is that of past writers.

In my reading of modern French novels, I had acquired the habit of underlining expressions which struck me as aberrant from general usage, and it often happened that the underlined passages, taken together, seemed to offer a certain consistency. I wondered if it would not be possible to establish a common denominator for all or most of these deviations; could not the common spiritual etymon, the psychological root, of several individual "traits of style" in a writer be found, just as we have found an etymon common to various fanciful word formations?[5] I had, for example, noticed in the novel *Bubu de Montparnasse* of Charles-Louis Philippe (1905), which moves in the underworld of Parisian pimps and prostitutes, a particular use of *à cause de*, reflecting the spoken, the unliterary language: "Les réveils de midi sont lourds et poisseux. ... On éprouve un sentiment de déchéance *à cause* des réveils d'autrefois." More academic writers would have said "'en se rappelant des réveils d'autrefois ...,'" "'à la suite du souvenir. ... '" This, at first glance, prosaic and commonplace *à cause de* has nevertheless a poetic flavor, because of the unexpected suggestion of a causality, where the average person would see only coincidence: it is, after all, not unanimously accepted that one awakes with a feeling of frustration from a noon siesta *because* other similar awakenings have preceded; we have here an assumed, a poetic reality, but one expressed by a prosaic phrase. We find this *à cause de* again in a description of a popular celebration of the 14th of July: "[le peuple], *à cause de* l'anniversaire de sa délivrance, laisse ses filles danser en liberté." Thus, one will not be surprised when the author lets this phrase come from the mouth of one of his characters: "Il y a dans mon coeur deux ou trois cent petites émotions qui brûlent *à cause de toi*." Conventional poetry would have said "qui brûlent pour toi"; "qui brûlent *à cause de toi*" is both less and more: more, since the lover speaks his heart better in this sincere, though factual manner. The causal phrase, with all its semipoetic implications, suggests rather a commonplace speaker, whose speech and whose habits of thought the writer seems to endorse in his own narrative.

Our observation about *à cause de* gains strength if we compare the use, in the same novel, of other causal conjunctions, such as *parce que:* for example, it is said of the pimp's love for his sweetheart Berthe: "[il aimait] sa volupté particulière, quand elle appliquait son corps contre le sien. . . . Il aimait cela qui la distinguait de toutes les femmes qu'il avait connues *parce que* c'était plus doux, *parce que* c'était plus fin, et *parce que* c'était sa femme à lui, qu'il avait eue vierge. Il l'aimait *parce qu'*elle était honnête et qu'elle en avait l'air, et pour toutes les raisons qu'ont les bourgeois d'aimer leur femme." Here, the reasons why Maurice loved to embrace his sweetheart (*parce que c'était doux, fin, parce que c'était sa femme a lui*) are outspokenly classified or censored by the writer as being *bourgeois;* and yet, in Philippe's narrative, the *parce que* is used as if he considered these reasons to be objectively valid.

The same observation holds true for the causal conjunction *car:* in the following passage which describes Maurice as a being naturally loved by women: "Les femmes l'entouraient d'amour comme des oiseaux qui chantent le soleil et la force. Il était un de ceux que nul ne peut assujettir, *car* leur vie, plus forte et plus belle, comporte l'amour du danger."

Again, it can happen that a causal relationship is implied without the use of a conjunction, a relationship due to the gnomic character adherent, at least in that particular milieu, to a general statement—the truth of which is, perhaps, not so fully accepted elsewhere: "Elle l'embrassa à pleine bouche. *C'est une chose hygiénique* et bonne entre un homme et sa femme, qui vous amuse un petit quart d'heure avant de vous endormir." (Philippe could as well have written "car . . .," "parce que c'est une chose hygiénique. . . . ") Evidently this is the truth only in that particular world of sensuous realism which he is describing. At the same time, however, the writer, while half-endorsing these bourgeois platitudes of the underworld, is discreetly but surely suggesting his criticism of them.

Now I submit the hypothesis that all these expansions of causal usages in Philippe cannot be due to chance: there must be "something the matter" with his conception of causality. And now we must pass from Philippe's style to the psychological etymon, to the radix in his soul. I have called the phenomenon in question "pseudo-objective motivation": Philippe, when presenting causality as binding for his characters, seems to recognize a rather objective cogency in their sometimes awkward, sometimes platitudinous, sometimes semipoetic reasonings; his attitude shows a fatalistic, half-critical, half-understanding, humorous sympathy with the necessary errors and thwarted strivings of these underworld beings dwarfed by inexorable social forces. The pseudo-objective motivation, manifest in his style, is the clue to Philippe's *Weltan-schauung;* he sees, as has also been observed by literary critics, without revolt but with deep grief and a Christian spirit of contemplativity, the world functioning wrongly with an appearance of rightness, of objective logic. The different word-usages, grouped togeher (just as was done with the different forms of *conundrum* and *quandary*) lead toward a psychological etymon, which is at the bottom of the linguistic as well as of the literary inspiration of Philippe.

Thus we have made the trip from language or style to the soul. And on this journey we may catch a glimpse into a historical evolution of the French soul in the twentieth century: first we are given insight into the soul of a writer who has become conscious of the fatalism weighing on the masses, then, into that of a section of the French nation itself, whose faint protest is voiced by our author. And in this procedure there is, I think, no longer the timeless, placeless philology of the older school, but an explanation of the concrete *hic et nunc* of a historical phenomenon. The to-and-fro movement we found to be basic with the humanist has been followed here, too: first we grouped together certain causal expressions, striking with Philippe, then hunted out their psychological explanation, and finally, sought to verify whether the element of "pseudo-objective motivation"[6] concorded with what we know, from other sources, about the elements of his inspiration. Again, a belief is involved—which is no less daring than is the belief that the Romance languages go back to one invisible, basic pattern manifest in them all: namely, the belief that the mind of an author is a kind of solar system into whose orbit all categories of things are attracted: language, motivation, plot, are only satellites of this mythological entity (as my antimentalistic adversaries would call it): *mens Philippina*. The linguist as well as his literary colleague must always ascend to the etymon which is behind all those particular so-called literary or stylistic devices which the literary historians are wont to list. And the individual *mens Philippina* is a reflection of the *mens Franco-gallica* of the twentieth century; its ineffability consists precisely in Philippe's anticipatory sensitivity for the spiritual needs of the nation.

Now, it is obvious that a modern writer such as Philippe, faced with the social disintegration of humanity in the twentieth century, must show more patent linguistic deviations, of which the philologist may take stock in order to build up his "psychogram" of the individual artist. But does Philippe, a stranded being broken loose from his moorings, transplanted, as it were, into a world from which he feels estranged—so that he must, perforce, indulge in arbitrary whimsicality—represent only a modern phenomenon? If we go back to writers of more remote times, must it not be that we will always find a balanced language, with no deviations from common usage?

It suffices to mention the names of such dynamic writers of older times as Dante or Quevedo or Rabelais to dispel such a notion. Whoever has thought strongly and felt strongly has innovated in his language; mental creativity immediately inscribes itself into the language, where it becomes linguistic creativity; the trite and petrified in language is never sufficient for the needs of expression felt by a strong personality. In my first publication, "Die Wortbildung als stilistisches Mittel" (a thesis written in 1910), I dealt with Rabelais' comic word-formations, a subject to which I was attracted because of certain affinities between Rabelaisian and Viennese (Nestroy!) comic writing, and which offered the opportunity of bridging the gap between linguistic and literary history. Be it said to the eternal credit of the scholarly integrity of Meyer-Lübke that he, in contrast to the antimentalists who would suppress all expressions of opposition to their theories, recommended for publication a book with an approach so aberrant from his own. In this work I sought to show, for example, that a neologism such as *pantagruélisme,* the name given by Rabelais to his stoic-epicurean philosophy ("certaine gayeté d'esprict, conficte en mépris des choses fortuites") is not only a playful outburst of a genuine gaiety, but a thrust from the realm of the real into that of the unreal and the unknown—as is true, in fact, of any nonce-word. On the one hand, a form with the suffix -*ism* evokes a school of serious philosophic thought (such as *Aristotelianism, scholasticism,* etc.); on the other, the stem, *Pantagruel,* is the name of a character created by Rabelais, the half-jocular, half-philosophical giant and patriarchal king. The coupling of the learned philosophical suffix with the fanciful name of a fanciful character amounts to positing a half-real, half-unreal entity: "the philosophy of an imaginary being." The contemporaries of Rabelais who first heard this coinage must have experienced the reactions provoked by any nonce-word: a moment of shock followed by a feeling of reassurance: to be swept toward the unknown frightens, but realization of the benignly fanciful result gives relief: laughter, our physiological reaction on such occasions, arises precisely out of a feeling of relief following upon a temporary breakdown of our assurance. Now, in a case such as that of the creation *pantagruelisme,* the designation of a hitherto unknown but, after all, innocuous philosophy, the menacing force of the neologism is relatively subdued. But what of such a list of names as that concocted by Rabelais for the benefit of his hated adversaries, the reactionaries of the Sorbonne: *sophistes, sorbillans, sorbonagres, sorbonigenes, sorbonicoles, sorboniformes, sorboniseques, niborcisans, sorbonisans, saniborsans.* Again, though differently, there is an element of realism present in these coinages: the Sorbonne is an existing reality, and the formations are explainable by well-known formative processes. The edition of Abel Lefranc, imbued with his positivistic approach, goes to the trouble of explaining each one of these formations: *sorboniforme* is after *uniforme, sorbonigene* after *homogène*, while *niborcisans, saniborsans* offer what, in the jargon of the linguists, is called a metathesis. But by explaining every coinage separately, by dissolving the forest into trees, the commentators lose sight of the whole phenomenon: they no longer see the forest—or rather the jungle which Rabelais must have had before his eyes, teeming with viper-like, hydralike, demonlike shapes. Nor is it enough to say that the scholarly Rabelais indulges in humanistic word lists with a view to enriching the vocabulary—in the spirit of an Erasmus who prescribed the principle of *copia verborum* to students of Latin—or that Rabelais' rich nature bade him make the French language rich; the aesthetics of richness is, in itself, a problem; and why should richness tend toward the frightening, the bottomless? Perhaps Rabelais' whole attitude toward language rests upon a vision of imaginary richness whose support is the bottomless. He creates word-families, representative of gruesome fantasy-beings, copulating and engendering before our eyes, which have reality only in the world of language, which are established in an intermediate world between reality and irreality, between the nowhere that frightens and the "here" that reassures. The *niborcisans* are as yet an entity vaguely connected with the *sorbonisans*, but at the same time so close to nothingness that we laugh—uneasily; it is *le comique grotesque* which skirts the abyss. And Rabelais will shape grotesque word-families (or families of word-demons) not only by altering what exists: he may leave intact the forms of his word material and create by juxtaposition: savagely piling epithet upon epithet to an ultimate effect of terror, so that, from the well known emerges the shape of the unknown—a phenomenon the more startling with the French, who are generally considered to inhabit an orderly, clearly regulated, well-policed language. Now, of a sudden, we no longer recognize this French language, which has become a chaotic word-world situated somewhere in the chill of cosmic space. Just listen to the inscription on the *abbaye de Thélème*, that Renaissance convent of his shaping, from which Rabelais excludes the hypocrites:

> Cy n'entrez pas, hypocrites, bigots,
> Vieux matagotz, marmiteux, borsoufles,
> Torcoulx, badaux, plus que n'estoient les Gotz,
> Ny Ostrogotz, precurseurs des magotz,
> Haires, cagotz, cafars empantouflez,
> Gueux mitoufles, frapars escorniflez,
> Befflez, enflez, fagoteurs de tabus;
> Tirez ailleurs pour vendre vos abus.

The prosaic commentators of the Lefranc edition would explain that this kind of rather mediocre poetry is derived from the popular genre of the *cry* (the harangue of a barker), and overloaded with devices of the *rhétoriqueur* school. But I can never read these lines without being frightened, and I am shaken in this very moment by the horror emanating from this accumulation of -fl- and -got- clusters—of sounds which, in themselves, and taken separately, are quite harmless, of words grouped together, bristling with Rabelais' hatred of hypocrisy—that greatest of all crimes against life. A cry, yes, but in a more extensive meaning of the word: it is the gigantic voice of Rabelais which cries to us directly across the gulf of the centuries, as shattering now as at the hour when Rabelais begot these word-monsters.

If, then, it is true that Rabelais' word-formation reflects an attitude somewhere between reality and irreality, with its shudders of horror and its comic relief, what of Lanson's famous statement on Rabelais in general, which is repeated in thousands of French schools and in most of the Lanson-imbued seminars of French throughout the world: "Jamais réalisme plus pur, plus puissant et plus triomphant ne s'est vu"? Well, it is simply wrong. I have not time to develop here the conclusions which would round out the utterly antirealistic picture of Rabelais that stands out in his work; it could be shown that the whole plot of Rabelais' epic, the fantastic voyage of fantastic people to the oracle of the priestess Bacbuc (whose ambiguous response: "Trinc!" is just a nowhere word) as well as the invention of detail (e.g. Panurge's speech on debtors and lenders, in which the earthy Panurge drives forward, from his astute egoistic refusal to live without debts, to a cosmic, utopian vision of a paradoxical world resting on the universal law of indebtedness)—that everything in Rabelais' work tends toward the creation of a world of irreality.

Thus, what has been disclosed by the study of Rabelais' language, the literary study would corroborate; it could not be otherwise, since language is only one outward crystallization of the "inward form," or, to use another metaphor: the lifeblood of the poetic creation[7] is everywhere the same, whether we tap the organism at "language" or "ideas," at "plot" or at "composition." As regards the last, I could as well have begun with a study of the rather loose literary composition of Rabelais' writings and only later have gone over to his ideas, his plot, his language. Because I happened to be a linguist it was from the linguistic angle that I started, to fight my way to his unity. Obviously, no fellow scholar must be required to do the same. What he must be asked to do, however, is, I believe, to work from the surface to the "inward life-center" of the work of art: first observing details about the superficial appearance of the particular work (and the "ideas" expressed by a poet are, also, only one of the superficial traits in a work of art);[8] then, grouping these details and seeking to integrate them into a creative principle which may have been present in the soul of the artist; and, finally, making the return trip to all the other groups of observations in order to find whether the "inward form" one has tentatively constructed gives an account of the whole. The scholar will surely be able to state, after three or four of these "fro voyages," whether he has found the life-giving center, the sun of the solar system (by then he will know whether he is really permanently installed in the center, or whether he finds himself in an "excentric" or peripheric position). There is no shadow of truth in the objection raised not long ago by one of the representatives of the mechanist Yale school of linguists against the "circularity of arguments" of the mentalists: against the "explanation of a linguistic fact by an assumed psychological process for which the only evidence is the fact to be explained."[9] I could immediately reply that my school is not satisfied with psychologizing one trait but bases its assumptions on several traits carefully grouped and integrated; one should, in fact, embrace *all* the linguistic traits observable with a given author (I myself have tried to come as close as possible to this requirement of completeness in my studies on Racine, Saint-Simon, Quevedo [in *RSL*]). And the circle of which the adversary just quoted speaks is not a vicious one; on the contrary, it is the basic operation in the humanities, the *Zirkel im Verstehen* as Dilthey has termed the discovery, made by the Romantic scholar and theologian Schleiermacher, that cognizance in philology is reached not only by the gradual progression from one detail to another detail, but by the anticipation or divination of the whole—because "the detail can be understood only by the whole and any explanation of detail presupposes the understanding of the whole."[10] Our to-and-fro voyage from certain outward details to the inner center and back again to other series of details is only an application of the principle of the "philological circle." After all, the concept of the Romance languages as based on one Vulgar Latin substratum, and reflected in them although identical with none—this has been reached by the founder of Romance philology, Diez, the pupil of the Romantics, precisely by means of this "philological circle," which allowed him to sit installed in the center of the phenomenon "Romance Languages," whereas Raynouard, his predecessor, by identifying one of the Romance varieties, Provençal, with Proto-Romance, found himself in an excentric position, from which point it was impossible to explain satisfactorily all the outward traits of Romance. To proceed from some exterior traits of Philippe's or Rabelais' language to the soul or mental center of Philippe and Rabelais, and back again to the rest of the exterior traits of Philippe's and Rabelais' works of art, is the same *modus operandi* as that which proceeds from some details of the Romance languages to a Vulgar Latin prototype and then, in reverse order, explains other details by this assumed prototype—or even, from that which infers from some of the outward, phonetic and semantic appearances of the English word *conundrum* to its medieval French soul, and back to all its phonetic and semantic traits.

To posit a soul of Rabelais which creates from the real in the direction of the unreal is, of course, not yet all that is desirable in order to understand the whole phenomenon: the Rabelaisian entity must be integrated into a greater unit and located somewhere on a historical line, as Diez, in a grandiose way, did with Romance—as we have tried to do, on a minor scale, with *calembredaine–conundrum*. Rabelais may be a solar system which, in its turn, forms part of a transcending system which embraces others as well as himself, others around, before, and after him; we must place him, as the literary historians would say, within the framework of the history of ideas, or *Geistesgeschichte*. The power of wielding the word as though it were a world of its own between reality and irreality, which exists to a unique degree with Rabelais, cannot have sprung out of nothingness, cannot have entirely ebbed after him. Before him there is, for example, Pulci, who, in his *Morgante Maggiore*, shows a predilection for wordlists, especially when he has his facetious knights indulge in name-calling. And, with Pulci, the Rabelaisian tendency to let language encroach on reality, is also to be found: when he retells, in half-facetious vein, the story immortalized by Turoldus of the battle of Roncevaux, we learn that the Saracens fell under the blows of the Christian knights in a trice: they stayed not upon the order of their dying but died at once: not tomorrow, or the day after tomorrow, nor the day after the day after tomorrow, nor the day after the day after the day after tomorrow: not *crai e poscrai, o poscrilla, o posquacchera*. In this sequel of gurgling and guttural sounds, the words *crai* and *poscrai* are genuine Italian reflections of the Latin words *cras* and *posteras*; but *poscrilla, posquacchera* are popular fantasy words.[11] The onomatopoeias with which popular language likes to juggle have here been used by a reflective poet for purposes of grotesque art: we can see here the exact point of transition of popular language into literature. Pulci believes in the ideals of Christian orthodox knighthood less full-heartedly than did Turoldus, for whom the heroic and religious values were real, and who must needs subordinate his language to the expression of these values. The word-world, admitted to a work of art by Pulci, was not yet available to Turoldus, or even to Dante (the "etymological puns" of the *Vita nuova* are quite another matter: they are only "illustrations," just as had been true of the puns of the Church Fathers).[12] The appearance of this intermediate world is conditioned by a belief in the reality of words, a belief which would have been condemned by the "realists" of the Middle Ages. The belief in such vicarious realities as words is possible only in an epoch whose belief in the *universalia realia* has been shaken. It is this phantasmagoric climate, casually evoked by Pulci, in which Rabelais will move easily and naturally, with a kind of cosmic independence. It is the belief in the autonomy of the word which made possible the whole movement of Humanism, in which so much importance was given to the word of the ancients and of the Biblical writers; it is this belief which will in part explain the extraordinary development of mathematics in the sixteenth and seventeenth centuries—i.e. of the most autonomous language that man has ever devised.

Now, who are the descendants of Rabelais? French classical literature, with its ideal of the *mot juste*, of the *mot mis à sa place*, broke away from the Renaissance tradition of the autonomy of the word. But undercurrents persisted, and I would say that Balzac, Flaubert (in his Letters), Théophile Gautier (in his *grotesqueries*), Victor Hugo (in his *William Shakespeare*), and Huysmans are, to a certain extent, descendants of Rabelais in the nineteenth century. In our own time, with Ferdinand Céline, who can build a whole book out of invectives against the Jews ("Bagatelles pour un massacre"), we may see language exceed its boundaries: this book, in the words of André Gide, is a "chevauchée de Don Quichotte en plein ciel ... "; "ce n'est pas la réalité que peint Céline; c'est l'hallucination que la réalité provoque." The following sample of Celinian inspiration makes a pseudo-Rabelaisian effect, and can be compared with the apocalyptic inscription over the portal of Thélème: "Penser 'sozial!' cela veut dire dans la pratique, en termes bien crus: 'penser juif! pour les juifs! par les juifs, sous les juifs!' Rien d'autre! Tout le surplus immense des mots, le vrombissant verbiage socialitico-humanitaro-scientifique, tout le cosmique carafouillage de l'impératif despotique juif n'est que l'enrobage mirageux, le charabia fatras poussif, la sauce orientale pour ces enculés d'aryens, la fricassée terminologique pour rire, pour l'adulation des aveulis blancs,' ivrognes rampants, intouchables, qui s'en foutrent, à bite que veux-tu, s'en mystifient, s'en baffrent à crever."

Here, evidently, the verbal creation, itself a *vrombissant verbiage* (to use the alliterative coinage of Céline), has implications more eschatological than cosmic: the word-world is really only a world of noisy words, clanking sounds, like so many engines senselessly hammering away, covering with their noise the fear and rage of man lonely in the doomed modern world. Words and reality fall apart. This is really a *voyage au bout du monde:* not to the oracle of Bacbuc but to chaos, to the end of language as an expression of thought.

The historical line we have drawn (we may call it the evolution of an idea: the idea of "language become autonomous"), which is marked by the stages Pulci–Rabelais–Victor Hugo–Céline, is paralleled or crossed by other historical lines with other names located on the historical ladder. Victor Hugo is not Rabelais, although there may be Hugoesque traits in Rabelais, Rabelaisian traits in Hugo. We must not confuse a historical line with a solar system resting in itself: what appeared to us central in Rabelais may be peripheric in Victor Hugo, and the reverse. Every solar system, unique in itself, undefinable (*"ineffabile"*) to a certain extent, is traversed by different historical lines of "ideas," whose intersection pro-

duces the particular climate in which the great literary work matures—
just as the system of a language is made up of the intersections of different
historical lines of the *calembredaine–conundrum* variety.

Thus we started with a particular historical line, the etymology of a
particular word-family, and found therein evidences of a change of historical climate. Then we considered the change of a whole historical climate
as expressed in the innovations, linguistic and literary, of writers of two
different epochs (the twentieth and the sixteenth), finally to arrive at the
point of positing theoretically self-sufficient systems: the great works of
art, determined by different historical developments and reflecting in all
their outward details, linguistic as well as literary, their respective central "sun." It is obvious that, in this paper, I have been able to give you
only scattered samples, the conclusions from which I have loaded, and
perhaps overloaded, with an experience resulting from hundreds of such
to-and-fro voyages—all directed by the same principles, but each one
bound for an unpredictable goal. My personal way has been from the observed detail to ever broadening units which rest, to an increasing degree,
on speculation. It is, I think, the philological, the inductive way, which
seeks to show significance in the apparently futile, in contrast to the deductive procedure which begins with units assumed as given—and
which is rather the way followed by the theologians who start from on
high, to take the downward path toward the earthly maze of detail, or by
the mathematicians, who treat their axioms as if these were God-given.
In philology, which deals with the all-too-human, with the interrelated
and the intertwined aspects of human affairs, the deductive method has
its place only as a verification of the principle found by induction—which
rests on observation.

But, of course, the attempt to discover significance in the detail,[13] the
habit of taking a detail of language as seriously as the meaning of a work
of art—or, in other words, the attitude which sees all manifestations of
man as equally serious—this is an outgrowth of the preestablished firm
conviction, the "axiom," of the philologian, that details are not an in-
choate chance aggregation of dispersed material through which no light
shines. The philologian must believe in the existence of some light from
on high, of some *post nubila Phoebus*. If he did not know that at the end
of his journey there would be awaiting him a life-giving draught from
some *dive bouteille,* he would not have commenced it: "Tu ne me cher-
cherais pas si tu ne m'avais pas déjà trouvé," says Pascal's God. Thus, humanistic thought, in spite of the methodological distinction just made, is
not so completely divorced from that of the theologian as is generally believed; it is not by chance that the "philological circle" was discovered by
a theologian, who was wont to harmonize the discordant, to retrace the
beauty of God in this world. This attitude is reflected in the word coined

by Schleiermacher: *Weltanschauung:*[14] "die Welt anschauen": "to see, to cognize the universe *in its sensuous detail.*" The philologian will then continue the pursuit of the microscopic because he sees therein the microcosmic; he will practice that *"Andacht zum Kleinen"* which Jacob Grimm has prescribed; he will go on filling his little cards with dates and examples, in the hope that supernal light will shine over them and bring out the clear lines of truth. The Humanist believes in the power bestowed on the human mind of investigating the human mind. When, with scholars whose goal and whose tool are thus identical, the faith in the human mind, as a tool and as a goal, is broken, this can only mean a crisis in the humanities—or, should I say, in the *Divinities?* And this is the situation today. A man without belief in the human mind is a stunted human being—how can he be a Humanist? The humanities will be restored only when the Humanists shed their agnostic attitudes, when they become human again, and share the belief of Rabelais' humanistic and religious king: "sapience n'entre point en ame malivole; et science sans conscience n'est que ruine de l'ame"—or, to go back to the Augustinian wording: "Non intratur in veritatem nisi per charitatem."[15]

In the essays to follow I have made an attempt to apply the principle of the "philological circle" to various authors of different nations and periods, applying it in varying degree and manner and in combination with other methods. But these articles are conceived not only as illustrations of my procedure, but as independent contributions to the understanding of the writers treated therein: contributions which should prove readable for any cultured person interested in the style of works of art.[16] For if my procedure should have any value, this must be revealed in the new results, the scholarly progress, attained by its means: the philological circle should not imply that one moves complacently in the circle of the already-known, in a *piétinement sur place.* Thus each single essay is intended to form a separate, independent unit: I hope that the repetitions of theoretical and historical statements which are the unavoidable consequence of this manner of presentation, will be felt by the reader rather as recurrent *leitmotifs* or *refrains* destined to emphasize a constancy and unity of approach.

Before putting to the test the method of the "philological circle" already delineated, I should like to warn the reader that he must not expect to find, in my demonstration of this method, the systematic step-by-step procedure which my own description of it may have seemed to promise.[17] For, when I spoke in terms of a series of back-and-forth movements (first the detail, then the whole, then another detail, etc.), I was using a linear and temporal figure in an attempt to describe states of apperception

which, in the mind of the humanist, only too often co-exist. This gift, or
vice (for it has its dangers), of seeing part and whole together, at any moment, and which, to some degree, is basic to the operation of the philological mind, is, perhaps, in my own case, developed to a particular degree, and has aroused objections from students and readers—in Germany,
where the synthetic capacities of the public are, in general, superior to
their analytic capacities, as well as in America where the opposite ob-
tains. A very understanding but critical ex-student of mine, an American,
once wrote me: "To establish a behavioristic technique which would reveal the application of your method is, it seems to me, beyond your possibilities. You know the principles that motivate you, rather than any
'technique' that you rigorously follow. Here, it may be a memory from
boyhood, there an inspiration you got from another poem; here, there and
everywhere it is an urge in you, an instinct backed up by your experience,
that tells you immediately: 'this is not important; this is.' At every second you are making choices, but you hardly know that you make them:
what seems right to you must be immediately right. And you can only
show by doing; you see the meaning as a whole from the beginning; there
are almost no steps in your mental processes; and, writing from the midst
of your thoughts you take it for granted that the reader is with you and that
what is self-evident to you as the next step (only, it's not the next step,
even: it's already included, somehow) will also be so to him."

These words, obviously, offer a picture of the limitations of a particular individual temperament. But much of what my correspondent says is
given with the operation of the circle—when this is applied, not to routine reading, on the one hand, or to the deductions of schematic linguistics on the other, but to a work of art: the solution attained by means of
the circular operation cannot be subjected to a rigorous rationale because,
at its most perfect, this is a negation of steps: once attained, it tends to
obliterate the steps leading up to it (one may remember the lion of medieval bestiaries who, at every step forward, wiped out his footprints with
his tail, in order to elude his pursuers!).

Why do I insist that it is impossible to offer the reader a step-by-step
rationale to be applied to a work of art? For one reason, that the first step,
on which all may hinge, can never be planned: it must already have taken
place. This first step is the awareness of having been struck by a detail,
followed by a conviction that this detail is connected basically with the
work of art; it means that one has made an "observation,"—which is the
starting point of a theory, that one has been prompted to raise a question—which must find an answer. To begin by omitting this first step
must doom any attempt at interpretation—as was the case with the dissertation (mentioned in note I of my article on Diderot) devoted to the
"imagery" of Diderot, in which the concept "imagery" was based on no

preliminary observation but on a ready-made category applied from without to the work of art.

Unfortunately, I know of no way to guarantee either the "impression" or the conviction just described: they are the results of talent, experience, and faith. And, even then, the first step is not to be taken at our own volition: how often, with all the theoretical experience of method accumulated in me over the years, have I stared blankly, quite similar to one of my beginning students, at a page that would not yield its magic. The only way leading out of this state of unproductivity is to read and reread,[18] patiently and confidently, in an endeavor to become, as it were, soaked through and through with the atmosphere of the work. And suddenly, one word, one line, stands out, and we realize that, now, a relationship has been established between the poem and us. From this point on, I have usually found that, what with other observations adding themselves to the first, and with previous experiences of the circle intervening, and with associations given by previous education building up before me (all of this quickened, in my own case, by a quasi-metaphysical urge toward solution) it does not seem long until the characteristic "click" occurs, which is the indication that detail and whole have found a common denominator—which gives the etymology of the writing.[19] And looking back on this process (whose end, of course, marks only the conclusion of the *preliminary* stage of analysis), how can we say when exactly it began? (Even the "first step" was preconditioned.) We see, indeed, that to read is to have read, to understand is equivalent to having understood.[20]

I have just spoken of the importance of past experience in the process of understanding the work of art—but as only one of the intervening factors. For experience with the "circle" is not, itself, enough to enable one to base thereupon a program applicable to all cases. For every poem the critic needs a separate inspiration, a separate light from above (it is this constant need which makes for humility, and it is the accumulation of past enlightenments that encourages a sort of pious confidence). Indeed, a Protean mutability is required of the critic, for the device which has proved successful for one work of art cannot be applied mechanically to another: I could not expect that the "trick of the five *grands*" (which I shall apply to an ode of Claudel's) would work for the "récit de Théramène," or that proper names, which will serve as a point of departure in my article on Cervantes, would play any part in the study on Diderot. It is, indeed, most trying for the experienced teacher to have to watch a beginner re-use and consequently mis-use, a particular clue that had served the teacher when he was treating a quite different writer—as though a young actor were to use the leer of Barrymore's Richard III for his performance of Othello. The mutability required of the critic can be gained only by repeated experiences with totally different writers; the "click" will come oftener and more quickly after several experiences of "clicks" have been realized by the critic. And, even then, it is not a foregone conclusion that it will inevitably come; nor can one ever foretell just when and where it will materialize ("The Spirit bloweth ... ").

The reason that the clues to understanding cannot be mechanically transferred from one work of art to another lies in the fact of artistic expressivity itself: the artist lends to an outward phenomenon of language an inner significance (thereby merely continuing and expanding the basic fact of human language: that a meaning is quite arbitrarily—arbitrarily, at least, from the point of view of the current usage of the language—associated with an acoustic phenomenon); just *which* phenomena the literary artist will choose for the embodiment of his meaning is arbitrary from the point of view of the "user" of the work of art. To overcome the impression of an arbitrary association in the work of art, the reader must seek to place himself in the creative center of the artist himself—and recreate the artistic organism. A metaphor, an anaphora, a staccato rhythm may be found anywhere in literature; they may or may not be significant. What tells us that they are important is only the feeling, which we must have already acquired, for the whole of the particular work of art.

And the capacity for this feeling is, again, deeply anchored in the previous life and education of the critic, and not only in his scholarly education: in order to keep his soul ready for his scholarly task he must have already made choices, in ordering his life, of what I would call a moral nature; he must have chosen to cleanse his mind from distraction by the inconsequential, from the obsession of everyday small details—to keep it open to the synthetic apprehension of the "wholes" of life, to the symbolism in nature and art and language. I have sometimes wondered if my "explication de texte" in the university classroom, where I strive to create an atmosphere suitable for the appreciation of the work of art, would not have succeeded much better if that atmosphere had been present at the breakfast table of my students.

NOTES

1. Text of an address, originally entitled "Thinking in the Humanities," delivered to the Department of Modern Languages and Literatures of Princeton University, to which some notes and an epilogue have been added.

    It is paradoxical that professors of literature who are too superficial to immerse themselves in a text and who are satisfied with stale phrases out of a manual, are precisely those who contend that it is superfluous to teach the aesthetic value of a text of Racine or Victor Hugo: the student will, in some way or another, come to grasp its beauty without any direction—or, if he is incapable of doing so, it is useless to talk about it. But there are hidden beauties which do not reveal themselves at the first exploratory attempts (as the apologetic theologians know); in fact, all beauty has some mysterious quality which does not appear at first glance. But there is no more reason for dodging the description of the aesthetic phenomenon than of any natural phenomenon. Those who oppose the aesthetic analysis of poetic works seem to affect at times the susceptibility of a sensitive plant: if one is to believe them, it is because they cherish so deeply the works of art, it is because they respect their chastity, that they would not deflower, by means of intellectual formulas, the virginal and ethereal quality of works of art, they would not brush off the shimmering dust from the wings of these poetic butterflies! I would maintain, on the contrary, that to formulate observations by means of words is not to cause the artistic beauty to evaporate in vain intellectualities; rather, it makes for a widening and a deepening of the aesthetic taste. Love, whether it be love for God, love for one's fellow men, or the love of art, can only gain by the effort of the human intellect to search for the reasons of its most sublime emotions, and to formulate them. It is only a frivolous love that cannot survive intellectual definition; great love prospers with understanding.

2. The presentation of so great a scholar as Meyer-Lübke from the only anglo which concerns us here is necessarily one-sided; for a more complete evaluation of his scholarship, as well as for a picture of his personality, I may refer the reader to my paper, "Mes souvenirs sur Meyer-Lübke" in *Le français moderne*, VI, 213. As for Philipp August Becker, my few remarks have given no real idea of his exuberant personality—which seldom penetrated into his scholarship; his was an orgiastic nature which somehow did not fit into the traditional pattern of a scholar. A story told me by Walther von Wartburg may illustrate this: Becker, who was rather given to the worship of Bacchus-Dionysos, used to invite his colleagues at Leipzig to a certain popular inn for copious libations. One night, after many hours of merrymaking, he realized that the bourgeois patrons sitting around him were shocked by his exuberance; immediately turning to his colleagues, he remarked: "And now I want to tell you something about early Christian hymns!" For almost an hour he talked, to the delight, not only of his colleagues but also of the crowd of *Spiessbürger* who had gradually drawn closer to him, enthralled by the eloquence of this greybeard bard who was reviving the spirit of Saint Ambrosius in a tavern.

3. These etymologies have appeared in the *Journal of English and Germanic Philology*, XLII, 405; there I suggested also the possibility of a * *calembourdon* as etymon, but today I prefer *calembredaine* to that unattested formation.

4. In fact, Ernst Lewy would destroy the unity of "Romance Languages" by placing French and Spanish, along with Basque and Irish, in an Atlantic group of languages, and Rumanian within the Balkan group (see my discussion in *Anales de l'Inst. de lingüística de Cuyo*, II). Again, there is the Russian school of "Japhetists" who believe not in "families" but in "systems" of languages, and who make bold to discover in any given language certain

primeval basic "elements" of the prelogical period in human speech (see Malkiel's article in *Language*, XX, 157).

5. Perhaps the transition from a particular historical line in language, as traced by an etymology, to the self-contained system of a work of literature, may seem violent to the reader: in the first case the "etymon" is the "soul of the nation" at the moment of the creation of the word; in the second, it is the "soul of one particular author." The difference, as Professor Singleton has pointed out to me, is that between the unconscious will of the nation that creates its language, and the conscious will of one member of the nation who creates wilfully and more or less systematically. But, apart from the fact that there are rational elements in popular linguistic creations, and irrational ones in those of the creative artist—what I would point out here is the relationship, common to both, between the linguistic detail and the soul of the speaker(s), and the necessity, in both cases, of the to-and-fro philological movement.

Perhaps a better parallel to the system of a work of art would be the system of a language at a definite moment of its evolution. I attempted just such a characterization of a linguistic system in my article on Spanish in *Stilstudien*, I.

6. This study has been published in *Stilstudien*, II.

The method I have been describing in the text is, of course, one that is followed by all of us when we must interpret the correspondence of someone with whom we are not well acquainted. For several years I had been in correspondence with a German emigrant in France whom I did not know personally and whose letters had given me the impression of a rather self-centered person who craved a cozy and congenial environment. When she was finally rescued to another country, she published a book of memoirs, a copy of which was sent me. On the cover of the book I saw pictured the window of the room she had occupied in Paris; behind this window, in the foreground, was a great cat looking out upon the Cathedral of Notre Dame. A great part of the book itself was taken up with this cat, and I had not read far before I found—without great surprise—several sentences such as "blottie dans un fauteuil, j'éprouvai un tel bonheur, je me sentis si bien à mon aise sous ce soleil doux qui me faisait ronronner à la manière des chats." Evidently a catlike existence was the deep-felt aspiration of this emigrant who, in the midst of world catastrophe, had lost the feeling of protectedness and had had to seek protection in herself.

7. We could here also be reminded of Goethe's simile (in *Die Wahlverwandtschaften*, II, 2): "We have learned about a special arrangement of the English Navy: all ropes of the Royal Fleet, from the strongest to the thinnest, have a red thread woven into them in such a way that it cannot be taken out without completely raveling the rope, so that even the smallest particle is stamped as the property of the Crown. Similarly, Ottilia's diary is pervaded by a thread of affection and attachment which connects every part and characterizes the whole of it." In this passage Goethe has formulated the principle of inner cohesion as it exists in a sensitive writer. It is the recognition of this principle which enabled Freud to apply his psychoanalytical finds to

works of literature. While I do not wish to disavow the Freudian influence in my earlier attempts at explaining literary texts, my aim today is to think, not so much in terms of the all-too-human "complexes" which, in Freud's opinion, are supposed to color the writing of the great figures of literature, but of "ideological patterns," as these are present in the history of the human mind.

Mr. Kenneth Burke, in his book *Philosophy of Literary Form* (Louisiana, 1940), has worked out a methodology of what he calls the "symbolic" or "strategic" approach to poetry—an approach which comes very close to the Freudian one (and to my own, as far as it was influenced by Freud), and which consists of establishing emotional clusters. When Mr. Burke finds such clusters in Coleridge, for example, and observes their constancy in the writings of this poet, he will claim to have found a factual, observable, irrefutable basis for the analysis of the structure of the work of art in general.

What I would object to in this method is that it can, obviously, be applied only to those poets who do, in fact, reveal such associational clusters— which is to say, only to those poets who do allow their phobias and idiosyncrasies to appear in their writing. But this must exclude all writers before the eighteenth century, the period in which the theory of the "original genius" was discovered and applied. Before this period, it is very difficult to discover, in any writer, "individual" associations, that is to say, associations not prompted by a literary tradition. Dante, Shakespeare, Racine are great literary "individuals," but they did not (or could not) allow their style to be permeated by their personal phobias and idiosyncrasies (even Montaigne, when portraying himself, thought of himself as "l'homme"). When a student of mine, working on the style of Agrippa d'Aubigné, was influenced by Professor Burke's book to apply the method of "emotional clusters" to that sixteenth-century epic poet, and was able, indeed, to find a series of antithetical associations, such as "milk-poison," "mother-serpent," "nature-unnatural" used in reference to pairs represented by the Catholic Catherine de Medicis and her Protestant opponents, I had to point out to him that these particular associational patterns (which had reminded him of Joyce) were all given by classical and Scriptural tradition: D'Aubigné merely gave powerful expression to age-old ideological motifs that transcended his personal, nervous temperament: the starting point for his "mère non-mère" was, obviously, the Greek μήτηρ ἀμήτωρ. Recently, I have had occasion also to point out the same truth in regard to the sixteenth-century poet Guevara, whose style has been explained by Freudian frustration.

8. Under the noble pretext of introducing "history of ideas" into literary criticism, there have appeared in recent times, with the approval of the departments of literary history, academic theses with such titles as "Money in Seventeenth-Century French (English, Spanish etc.) Comedy," "Political Tendencies in Nineteenth-Century French (English, Spanish etc.) Literature." Thus we have come to disregard the philological character of the discipline of literary history, which is concerned with ideas couched in linguistic and literary form, not with ideas in themselves (this is the field of history of philosophy) or with ideas as informing action (this is the field of history

and the social sciences). Only in the linguistico-literary field are we philologians competent qua scholars. The type of dissertations cited above reveals an unwarranted extension of the (in itself commendable) tendency toward breaking down departmental barriers, to such a degree that literary history becomes the gay sporting ground of incompetence. Students of the department of literature come to treat the complex subjects of a philosophical, political, or economic nature with the same self-assurance that once characterized those Positivists who wrote on "The Horse in Medieval Literature." But while it is possible for the average person to know "what a horse is" (if less so what "a horse in literature" is), it is much more difficult for a student of literature to know "what money is" (and still more so what "money in literature" is). In fact, this new type of thesis is only an avatar of the old positivistic thesis; but, while the original positivism was motivated by a sincere respect for competence, the neo-positivists now would administer the death-blow to scholarly competence.

9. Cf. my article in *Modern Philological Quarterly:* "Why Does Language Change?" and the polemics resulting therefrom in *Language,* XX, 45 and 245.

10. Cf. Schleiermacher, *Sämtl. Werke,* III, 3, p. 343. "Über den Begriff der Hermeneutik mit Bezug auf F. A. Wolfs Andeutungen und Arts Lehrbuch"—a speech delivered in 1829. Schleiermacher distinguishes between the "comparative" and the "divinatory" methods, the combination of which is necessary in "hermeneutics," and since hermeneutics falls into two parts, a "grammatical" and a "psychological" part, both methods must be used in both parts of hermeneutics. Of the two methods, it is the divinatory which requires the "Zirkelschluss." We have been dealing here with the *Zirkelschluss* in the "divination" of the psychology of authors; as for "grammatical divination," any college student who attempts to parse a Ciceronian period is constantly using it: he cannot grasp the construction except by passing continuously from the parts to the whole of the sentence and back again to its parts.

Dr. Ludwig Edelstein has called my attention to the Platonic origin of Schleiermacher's discovery: it is in *Phaedo* that Socrates states the importance of the whole for the cognition of the parts. Accordingly, it would appear that I err in adopting Schleiermacher's "theological" approach and that I am undiplomatic in asking for an approach so at variance with that which is traditional in the humanities (when Dewey reproved the Humanists for the residues of theology in their thinking, they made haste to disavow any theological preoccupation—while I take the stand of saying: "Yes, we Humanists are theologians!"); would it not, I am asked, be better to show the irrationalism inherent in any rational operation in the humanities, than to demand the overt irrationalism of religion which our secular universities must thoroughly abhor? My answer is that Socrates himself was a religious genius and that, through Plato, he is present in much of Christian thought. As concerns the necessity, for the scholar, of having recourse to religion, cf. the conclusive reasoning of Erich Frank in his book *Philosophical Understanding and Religious Truth* (1945).

The traditional view of the "viciousness" of the philological circle is unfortunately held in an otherwise brilliant attack against "the biographical fashion in literary criticism" (University of California Publications, in *Classical Philology*, XII, 288) by Professor Harold Cherniss: in his argument against the philologians of the Stefan George school who, though not dealing with the outward biography of artists, believe that the inner form of the artist's personality can be grasped in his works by a kind of intuition, Cherniss writes: "The intuition which discovers in the writings of an author the 'natural law' and 'inward form' of his personality, is proof against all objections, logical and philological; but, while one must admit that a certain native insight, call it direct intelligence or intuition as you please, is required for understanding any text, it is, all the same, a vicious circle to intuit the nature of the author's personality from his writings and then to interpret those writings in accordance with the 'inner necessity' of that intuited personality. Moreover, once the intuition of the individual critic is accepted as the ultimate basis of all interpretation, the comprehension of a literary work becomes a completely private affair, for the intuition of any one interpreter has no more objective validity than that of any other."

I believe that the word "intuition" with its deliberate implication of extraordinary mystic qualities on the part of the critic, vitiates not only the reasoning of the Stefan George school but also that of their opponents. The "circle" is vicious only when an uncontrolled intuition is allowed to exercise itself upon the literary works; the procedure from details to the inner core and back again is not in itself at all vicious; in fact, the "intelligent reading" which Professor Cherniss advocates without defining it (though he is forced to grant rather uncomfortably that it is "a certain native insight, call it direct intelligence or intuition as you please") is based precisely on that very philological circle. To understand a sentence, a work of art, or the inward form of an artistic mind involves to an increasing degree, irrational moves — which must, also to an increasing degree, be controlled by reason.

Heidegger, in *Sein und Zeit*, I, 32 ("Verstehen und Auslegung"), shows that all "exegesis" is circular, i.e. is a catching up with the "understanding," which is nothing else than an anticipation of the whole that is "existentially" given to man: "Zuhandenes wird immer schon aus der Bewandtnisganzheit der verstanden. ... Die Auslegung gründet jeweils in einer *Vorsicht*, die das in Vorhabe Genommene auf eine bestimmte Auslegbarkeit hin 'anschnèidet.' ... Auslegung ist nie ein voraussetzungsloses Erfassen eines Vorgegebenen. ... Alle Auslegung, die Verständnis beistellen soll, muss schon das Auszulegende verstanden haben. ... *Aber in diesem Zirkel ein vitiosum sehen und nach Wegen Ausschau halien, ihn zu vermeiden, ja ihn auch nur als unvermeidliche Unvollkommenheit 'empfinden,' heisst das Verstchen von Grund aus missverstehen* [the italics are the author's]. ... Das Entscheidende ist nicht aus dem Zirkel heraus-, sondern in ihn nach der rechten Weise hineinzukommen. ... In ihm verbirgt sich eine positive Möglichkeit ursprünglichsten Erkennens, die freilich in echter Weise nur dann ergriffen ist, wenn die Auslegung verstanden hat, dass ihre erste, ständige und letzte Aufgabe bleibt, sich jeweils Vorhabe, Vorsicht und Vorgriff nicht durch Einfälle und Volksbegriffe vorgeben zu lassen, sondern in deren Ausarbeitung aus den Sachen selbst her das wissenschaftliche Thema zu sichern. Der 'Zirkel' im Verstehen gehört zur Struktur des Sinnes, welches Phänomen in der existenzialen Verfassung des Daseins, im auslegenden Verstehen verwurzelt ist."

This "Vorsicht," this anticipation of the whole, is especially necessary for the understanding of philosophical writing. Franz Rosenzweig, "Das neue Denken" (in *Kleinere Schriften*, 1937) writes: "The first pages of philosophical books are held by the reader in special respect. . . . He thinks they [such books] ought to be 'especially logical,' and by this he means that each sentence depends on the one that precedes it, so that if the famous one stone is pulled, 'the whole tumbles.' Actually, this is nowhere less the case than in philosophical books. Here a sentence does not follow from its predecessor, but much more probably from its successor. . . . Philosophical books refuse such methodical ancien-régime strategy; they must be conquered à la Napoleon, in a bold thrust against the main body of the enemy; and after the victory at this point, the small fortresses will fall of themselves." (I owe this quotation to Kurt H. Wolf's article, "The Sociology of Knowledge" in *Philosophy of Science*, X; Wolf calls the anticipatory understanding of wholes a "central attitude": "In our everyday social interaction we constantly practice the central-attitude approach without which we could not 'know' how to behave toward other persons, or how to read a book, to see a picture, or to play or listen to a piece of music. . . . ") What Heidegger, Rosenzweig, and Wolf describe is the method of the humanities which Pascal has called the "esprit de finesse" (as contrasted to the "esprit géométrique").

For the students in Romance Gröber formulated the idea of the philological circle (without mentioning the "circle" itself) in *Gröber's Grundriss* 1/3 (1888): "Absichtslose Wahrnehmung, unscheinbare Anfänge gehen dem zielbewussten Suchen, dem allseitigen Erfassen des Gegenstandes voraus. Im sprungweisen Durchmessen des Raumes hascht dann der Suchende nach dem Ziel, Mit einem Schema unfertiger Ansichten über ähnliche Gegenstände scheint er das Ganze erfassen zu können, ehe Natur und Teile gekannt sind. Der vorschnellen Meinung folgt die Einsicht des Irrtums, nur langsam der Entschluss, dem Gegenstand in kleinen und kleinsten vorsichtigen Schritten nahe zu kommen, Teil und Teilchen zu beschauen und nicht zu ruhen, bis die Überzeugung gewonnen ist, dass sie nur so und nicht anders aufgefasst werden müssen."

It is also true of the comparative linguist who establishes his "phonetic laws" on the basis of "evident etymologies," which themselves are based on those "phonetic laws," that he moves in a circle, in the words of Zupitza, *Zeitschr. f. vergl. Sprachwissenschaft*, XXXVII (1904) p. 387: "Unsere wissenschaft kommt aus einem kreislauf nicht heraus: sie geht von evidenten gleichungen aus, entnimmt diesen ihre gesetze und prüft an diesen gesetzen jene gleichungen, die ihre grundlage bilden." And even elementary language teaching must move in a circle: R. A. Hall in *Bull. of the American University Professors*, XXXI, 6, advocating the modern "direct method" as preferable to the old "reading method," writes: "When he [the student] has learnt a sufficient number of examples, the linguistic analysis becomes simply a series of obvious deductions from what he has learned; it helps him to perceive the patterns inherent in what he already knows, and tells him how far he can go in extending these patterns to new material." The inference from "patterns" is nothing but an anticipation of a whole deduced from the known examples.

11. This point has been entirely overlooked in the treatment of the passage by an antimentalist; see my article in *Italica*, XXI, 154.

12. This is not to say that the puns and repetitions used by Rabelais do not historically develop from the same devices used by the Fathers and the medieval writers. Rabelais' facetious etymology *Beauce* = "[je trouve] beau ce," and his repetition of words, such as *moine moinant de moinerie*, are scholastic devices—only that they are used by him in an antimedieval manner, informed by a worldly spirit and, most important of all, by the consciousness of the autonomy of a "word world."

13. I have often wondered how historians of literature could make such sweeping statements, as they are wont to do, on the whole of the literary work of a poet, or of a period, without descending into the detail of texts (and into the linguistic detail). Goethe speaks pertinently ("Einleitung in die Propyläen") of the "Anschauung" necessary for the concrete apperception of works of art: "Um von Kunstwerken eigentlich und mit wahrem Nutzen für sich und andere zu sprechen, sollte es freilich nur in Gegenwart derselben geschehen. Alles kommt aufs Anschauen an; es kommt darauf an, dass bei dem Worte, wodurch man ein Kunstwerk zu erläutern hofft, das Bestimmteste gedacht werde, weil sonst gar nichts gedacht wird. Daher geschieht es so oft, dass derjenige, der über Kunstwerke schreibt, bloss im Allgemeinen verweilt...."

The same seems to have been felt by Santayana in regard to the field of philosophy; in *The Middle Span*, p. 155, he has the following to say about the habits of his Harvard students during the last decades of the nineteenth century: "I doubt that the texts were much studied directly in those days at Harvard. The undergraduates were thinking only of examinations and relied on summaries in the histories of philosophy and on lecture notes.... Philosophy can be communicated only by being evoked: the pupil's mind must be engaged dialectically in the discussion. Otherwise, all that can be taught is the literary history of philosophy, that is, the *phrases* that various philosophers have rendered famous. To conceive what those phrases meant or could mean would require a philosophical imagination in the public which cannot be demanded. All that usually exists is familiarity with current phrases, and a shock, perhaps of pleased curiosity but more often of alarm and repulsion, due to the heterodoxy of any different phrases." It is needless to add that a "literary history" which is satisfied with enumerating the "phrases" (whether famous or not) used by a writer (philosophical or otherwise), without establishing any connection between them and the mainspring of the writer's inspiration, is sham literary history.

14. According to Gundolf, in his essay on Schleiermacher. According to A. Götze, *Euphorion* 1924, however, the word was not previously coined by him, but is a creation of his period.

15.   Even with philologians (who are not by nature apt to be insensitive to liter-
      ary values, as are so many of the so-called "linguists") one can discern "un-
      humanistic" prejudices. For example, Professor Entwistle ("Idealistic Exten-
      sions of Linguistics" in *Miscel-lania Fabra*, Buenos Aires, 1943) maintains
      that the linguistic interpretation of poetry implies the crossing of an intel-
      lectual frontier: the philologian has to deal not with "science" which treats
      of things that can be measured and weighed, not with "unambiguous facts"
      which can be tested by anyone, but with "knowledge" irreducible to "sci-
      entific" treatment—to which belongs hermeneutics, the study of the poet's
      meaning: this meaning cannot be treated in the "old assertive language" of
      the positivistic linguist, and still less can be the elusive significance of a po-
      etic text, which transcends the poet's conscious intention. By such distinc-
      tions Professor Entwistle is perpetuating the nineteenth-century rift be-
      tween positivistic science and wisdom. As concerns what Entwistle
      considers to be the purely scientific part of philology—such as the phonetic
      laws, which he ranks with the facts testable by everyone—I wonder if the
      formulation of a phonetic law is not as much of a speculation as is the at-
      tempt to discover the significance of a poetic passage; and is it really true
      that a phonetic law can be tested by anyone who has not had a preparation for
      this type of study? It can be done only to the same extent, I should think,
      which would hold true for the establishment of the meaning of a poetic pas-
      sage. And as for the unconscious intentions of the poet, I simply would not
      advise the interpreter to concern himself with them. As a matter of fact, the
      example of "unconscious poetic intention" offered by Mr. Entwistle seems
      to me to show how little he has grasped the purpose of philological studies:
      of the passage from the *Aeneid* in which Aeneas sees depicted on the walls
      of Carthage the Trojan war and his father's deeds:

> En Priamus! Sunt hic etiam sua praemia laudi;
> sunt lacrimae rerum, et mentem mortalia tangunt.
> Solve metus; feret haec aliquam tibi fama salutem.

Entwistle writes: "The sense of the second last line, in its context, seems to
be encouraging [he has translated it: "tears are shed for his misfortunes and
his death moves men's minds to pity"]: it is better to be remembered sor-
rowfully than to be forgotten altogether. Yet *sunt lacrimae rerum* means
something other and more moving than that. There is music and intensity
in the line beyond anything Vergil may have consciously meant.... 'Nature's
tears and the mortal sadness of mankind' has been discovered in that music
by posterity, and, I think, justly so." But it can be *proved* by the philologist
that Vergil *meant* (and it is only with conscious meaning that the philologian is concerned) the first, the "lesser" of the two meanings mentioned (as
is indicated by the two anaphoric *sunt*'s which suggest a parallelism of arguments leading to the encouraging final line). The second meaning which
has been attached to the line by posterity is an error due to its isolated consideration out of context (which led to the misinterpretation of *rerum* as
"Nature" instead of "misfortunes," an error comparable to the famous misinterpretation of Buffon's "le style c'est l'homme même"—or even to many

witty or punning misinterpretations of certain poetic lines (e.g. when the line of Schiller's Maid of Orleans: "Johanna geht und nimmer kehrt sie wieder" is facetiously interpreted to mean that never again will she sweep the floor). To the philologian this secondary graft or palimpsest imposed upon the original text may be historically quite interesting, but it has to be discarded from his interpretation of the given work of art. There is no music in Vergil's poetry but that which he put in it—but, by the same token, it is also necessary that this music be retained and not destroyed, as it is by such a translation as "tears are shed for *his* misfortunes and *his* death": the indefinite quality of "misfortune" and "death" should be preserved. Vergil's poetic music consists in the procedure of expanding the particular example of Priam's fate to that of man (and, similarly, *mortalia* should not be concretized to "death" but left as "the mortal fate"); it is the general gnome, so indissolubly linked by Vergil with the particular case, that posterity has arbitrarily detached (and, in addition to this antipoetic first move, has misinterpreted—this time poetically, in the manner mentioned above).

In this, as in the following studies, the reader will find me polemizing against the views of fellow scholars. I have sometimes been accused of raising up straw men just to knock them down, instead of being satisfied with offering my own picture of the phenomenon in question. My answer is that, in matters stylistic as well as in factual questions of literary history or linguistics, the *consensus omnium* is a desideratum, the only path to which is the discussion of the pros and cons of theories different from one's own, which enable us to vindicate the relative superiority of our own theory. The greater the objective certainty that a stylistic explanation can claim, the more we will have overcome that impressionism which, until recently, has seemed the only alternative to the positivistic treatment of literature.

16. The frequent occurrence, in my text, of quotations in the original foreign language (or languages) may prove a difficulty for the English reader. But since it is my purpose to take the word (and the wording) of the poets seriously, and since the convincingness and rigor of my stylistic conclusions depends entirely upon the minute linguistic detail of the original texts, it was impossible to offer translations.

17. Perhaps I should make it clear that I am using the word "method" in a manner somewhat aberrant from common American use: it is for me much more a "habitual procedure of the mind" (Lalande, *Vocabulaire de la philosophie,* s.v. *méthode* 1) than a "program regulating beforehand a series of operations ... in view of reaching a well-defined result" (*ibid.* 2). As used by me it is nearly synonymous with *Erlebnis,* and consequently would correspond relatively to what is called in America "approach," were it not for the volitional and even "strategic" nuance, in this word, of military siege or of tracking down a quarry, by which it may be historically explained.

In this connection I may quote a passage from a letter of Descartes to Mersenne (*Oeuvres,* ed. Adam-Tannery, I, 347): "Mais ie n'ay sceu bien entendre ce que vous objectez touchant le titre [Discours de la Méthode]; car ie ne mets pas *Traité de la Methode,* mais *Discours de la Methode,* ce qui est le mesme que *Preface ou Advis touchant la Methode,* pour monstrer que ie n'ay pas dessein de l'enseigner, mais seulement d'en parler. Car comme on peut voir de ce que i'en dis, elle consiste plus en Pratique qu'en Theorie, & ie nomme les Traitez suivans des *Essais de cette Methode*, pource que ie pretens que les choses qu'ils contiennent n'ont pû estre trouvées sans elle, & qu'on peut connoistre par eux ce qu'elle vaut."

18. If I were to give one piece of advice to our students of literary history, it would be substantially the same as that which Lanson, touring the United States forty years ago, gave to the students of his time who were then, as they are now, only too eager to rush to their big libraries to find in the many books of "secondary literature" an alibi for getting away from the "primary" texts they should study: *"Read your texts!"* My "circular method" is, in fact, nothing but an expansion of the common practice of "reading books": reading at its best requires a strange cohabitation in the human mind of two opposite capacities: contemplativity on the one hand and, on the other, a Protean mimeticism. That is to say: an undeflected patience that "stays with" a book until the forces latent in it unleash in us the recreative process.

19. Sometimes it may happen that this "etymology" leads simply to a characterization of the author that has been long accepted by literary historians (who have not needed, apparently, to follow the winding path I chose), and which can be summed up in a phrase which smacks of a college handbook. But, to make our own way to an old truth is not only to enrich our own understanding; it produces inevitably new evidence, of objective value, for this truth—which is thereby renewed. A *comédie-proverbe* of Musset is based, after all, on a commonplace saying: was it a waste of time to illustrate so wittily "il faut qu'une porte soit ouverte ou fermée"?

20. The requirement at St. John's for the Hundred Great Books is good, I believe, in so far as it may encourage the "click" to repeat itself in an accelerated manner—if, of course, it has come about in the first experiences: to have read these hundred books "without click" would be equivalent to not having read a single book.

Cleanth Brooks

The Heresy of Paraphrase

The ten poems that have been discussed were not selected because they happened to express a common theme or to display some particular style or to share a special set of symbols. It has proved, as a matter of fact, somewhat surprising to see how many items they do have in common: the light symbolism as used in "L'Allegro-Il Penseroso" and in the "Intimations" ode, for example; or, death as a sexual metaphor in "The Canonization" and in *The Rape of the Lock;* or the similarity of problem and theme in the "Intimations" ode and "Among School Children."

On reflection, however, it would probably warrant more surprise if these ten poems did not have much in common. For they are all poems which most of us will feel are close to the central stream of the tradition. Indeed, if there is any doubt on this point, it will have to do with only the first and last members of the series—poems whose relation to the tradition I shall, for reasons to be given a little later, be glad to waive. The others, it will be granted, are surely in the main stream of the tradition.

As a matter of fact, a number of the poems discussed in this book were not chosen by me but were chosen for me. But having written on these, I found that by adding a few poems I could construct a chronological series which (though it makes no pretension to being exhaustive of periods or types) would not leave seriously unrepresented any important period since Shakespeare. In filling the gaps I tried to select poems which had been held in favor in their own day and which most critics still admire. There were, for example, to be no "metaphysical" poems beyond the first exhibit and no "modern" ones other than the last. But the intervening poems were to be read as one has learned to read Donne and the moderns. One was to attempt to see, in terms of this approach, what the masterpieces had in common rather than to see how the poems of different historical periods differed—and in particular to see whether they had anything in common with the "metaphysicals" and with the moderns.

The reader will by this time have made up his mind as to whether the readings are adequate. (I use the word advisedly, for the readings do not pretend to be exhaustive, and certainly it is highly unlikely that they are not in error in one detail or another.) If the reader feels that they are seriously inadequate, then the case has been judged; for the generalizations that follow will be thoroughly vitiated by the inept handling of the particular cases on which they depend.

If, however, the reader does feel them to be adequate, it ought to be readily apparent that the common goodness which the poems share will have to be stated, not in terms of "content" or "subject matter" in the usual sense in which we use these terms, but rather in terms of structure. The "content" of the poems is various, and if we attempt to find one *quality* of content which is shared by all the poems—a "poetic" subject matter or diction or imagery—we shall find that we have merely confused the issues. For what is it to be poetic? Is the schoolroom of Yeats's poem poetic or unpoetic? Is Shakespeare's "new-borne babe/Striding the blast" poetic whereas the idiot of his "Life is a tale tolde by an idiot" is unpoetic? If Herrick's "budding boy or girl" is poetic, then why is not that monstrosity of the newspaper's society page, the "society bud," poetic too?

To say this is not, of course, to say that all materials have precisely the same potentialities (as if the various pigments on the palette had the same potentialities, any one of them suiting the given picture as well as another). But what has been said, on the other hand, requires to be said: for, if we are to proceed at all, we must draw a sharp distinction between the attractiveness or beuty of any particular item taken as such and the "beauty" of the poem considered as a whole. The latter is the effect of a total pattern, and of a kind of pattern which can incorporate within itself items intrinsically beautiful or ugly, attractive or repulsive. Unless one asserts the primacy of the pattern, a poem becomes merely a bouquet of intrinsically beautiful items.

But though it is in terms of structure that we must describe poetry, the term "structure" is certainly not altogether satisfactory as a term. One means by it something far more internal than the metrical pattern, say, or than the sequence of images. The structure meant is certainly not "form" in the conventional sense in which we think of form as a kind of envelope which "contains" the "content." The structure obviously is everywhere conditioned by the nature of the material which goes into the poem. The nature of the material sets the problem to be solved, and the solution is the ordering of the material.

Pope's *Rape of the Lock* will illustrate: the structure is not the heroic couplet as such, or the canto arrangement; for, important as is Pope's use of the couplet as one means by which he secures the total effect, the heroic couplet can be used—has been used many times—as an instrument in securing very different effects. The structure of the poem, furthermore, is not that of the mock-epic convention, though here, since the term "mock-epic" has implications of attitude, we approach a little nearer to the kind of structure of which we speak.

The structure meant is a structure of meanings, evaluations, and interpretations; and the principle of unity which informs it seems to be one of balancing and harmonizing connotations, attitudes, and meanings. But even here one needs to make important qualifications: the principle is not one which involves the arrangement of the various elements into homogeneous groupings, pairing like with like. It unites the like with the unlike. It does not unite them, however, by the simple process of allowing one connotation to cancel out another nor does it reduce the contradictory attitudes to harmony by a process of subtraction. The unity is not a unity of the sort to be achieved by the reduction and simplification appropriate to an algebraic formula. It is a positive unity, not a negative; it represents not a residue but an achieved harmony.

The attempt to deal with a structure such as this may account for the frequent occurrence in the preceding chapters of such terms as "ambiguity," "paradox," "complex of attitudes," and—most frequent of all, and perhaps most annoying to the reader—"irony." I hasten to add that I hold no brief for these terms as such. Perhaps they are inadequate. Perhaps they are misleading. It is to be hoped in that case that we can eventually improve upon them. But adequate terms—whatever those terms may turn out to be—will certainly have to be terms which do justice to the special kind of structure which seems to emerge as the common structure of poems so diverse on other counts as are *The Rape of the Lock* and "Tears, Idle Tears."

The conventional terms are much worse than inadequate: they are positively misleading in their implication that the poem constitutes a "statement" of some sort, the statement being true or false, and expressed more or less clearly or eloquently or beautifully; for it is from this formula that most of the common heresies about poetry derive. The formula begins by introducing a dualism which thenceforward is rarely overcome, and which at best can be overcome only by the most elaborate and clumsy qualifications. Where it is not overcome, it leaves the critic lodged upon one or the other of the horns of a dilemma: the critic is forced to judge the poem by its political or scientific or philosophical truth; or, he is forced to judge the poem by its form as conceived externally and detached from human experience. Mr. Alfred Kazin, for example, to take an instance from a recent and popular book, accuses the "new formalists"—his choice of that epithet is revealing—of accepting the latter horn of the dilemma because he notices that they have refused the former. In other words, since they refuse to rank poems by their messages, he assumes that they are compelled to rank them by their formal embellishments.

The omnipresence of this dilemma, a false dilemma, I believe, will also account for the fact that so much has been made in the preceding chapters of the resistance which any good poem sets up against all attempts to paraphrase it. The point is surely not that we cannot describe adequately enough for many purposes what the poem in general is "about" and what the general effect of the poem is: *The Rape of the Lock* is *about* the foibles of an eighteenth-century belle. The effect of "Corinna's going a-Maying" is one of gaiety tempered by the poignance of the fleetingness of youth. We can very properly use paraphrases as pointers and as shorthand references provided that we know what we are doing. But it is highly important that we know what we are doing and that we see plainly that the paraphrase is not the real core of meaning which constitutes the essence of the poem.

For the imagery and the rhythm are not merely the instruments by which this fancied core-of-meaning-which-can-be-expressed-in-a-paraphrase is directly rendered. Even in the simplest poem their mediation is not positive and direct. Indeed, whatever statement we may seize upon as incorporating the "meaning" of the poem, immediately the imagery and the rhythm seem to set up tensions with it, warping and twisting it, qualifying and revising it. This is true of Wordsworth's "Ode" no less than of Donne's "Canonization." To illustrate: if we say that the "Ode" celebrates the spontaneous "naturalness" of the child, there is the poem itself to indicate that Nature has a more sinister aspect—that the process by which the poetic lamb becomes the dirty old sheep or the child racing over the meadows becomes the balding philosopher is a process that is thoroughly "natural." Or, if we say that the thesis of the "ode" is that the child brings into the natural world a supernatural glory which acquaintance with the world eventually and inevitably quenches in the light of common day, there is the last stanza and the drastic qualifications which it asserts: it is significant that the thoughts that lie too deep for tears are mentioned in this sunset stanza of the "Ode" and that they are thoughts, not of the child, but of the man.

We have precisely the same problem if we make our example *The Rape of the Lock*. Does the poet assert that Belinda is a goddess? Or does he say that she is a brainless chit? Whichever alternative we take, there are elaborate qualifications to be made. Moreover, if the simple propositions offered seem in their forthright simplicity to make too easy the victory of the poem over any possible statement of its meaning, then let the reader try to formulate a proposition that will say what the poem "says." As his proposition approaches adequacy, he will find, not only that it has increased greatly in length, but that it has begun to fill itself up with reservations and qualifications—and most significant of all—the formulator will find that he has himself begun to fall back upon metaphors of his own in his attempt to indicate what the poem "says." In sum, his proposition, as it approaches adequacy, ceases to be a proposition.

Consider one more case, "Corinna's going a-Maying." Is the doctrine preached to Corinna throughout the first four stanzas true? Or is it damnably false? Or is it a "harmlesse follie"? Here perhaps we shall be tempted to take the last option as the saving mean—what the poem really *says*—and my account of the poem at the end of the third chapter is perhaps susceptible of this interpretation—or misinterpretation. If so, it is high time to clear the matter up. For we mistake matters grossly if we take the poem to be playing with opposed extremes, only to point the golden mean in a doctrine which, at the end, will correct the falsehood of extremes. The reconcilement of opposites which the poet characteristically makes is not that of a prudent splitting of the difference between antithetical overemphases.

It is not so in Wordsworth's poem nor in Keats's nor in Pope's. It is not so even in this poem of Herrick's. For though the poem reflects, if we read it carefully, the primacy of the Christian mores, the pressure exerted throughout the poem is upon the pagan appeal; and the poem ends, significantly, with a reiteration of the appel to Corinna to go a-Maying, an appeal which, if qualified by the Christian view, still, in a sense, has been deepened and made more urgent by that very qualification. The imagery of loss and decay, it must be remembered, comes in this last stanza after the admission that the May-day rites are not a real religion but a "harmless follie."

If we are to get all these qualifications into our formulation of what the poem says—and they are relevant—then, our formulation of the "statement" made by Herrick's poem will turn out to be quite as difficult as that of Pope's mock-epic. The truth of the matter is that all such formulations lead away from the center of the poem—not toward it; that the "prose-sense" of the poem is not a rack on which the stuff of the poem is hung; that it does not represent the "inner" structure or the "essential" structure or the "real" structure of the poem. We may use—and in many connections must use—such formulations as more or less convenient ways of referring to parts of the poem. But such formulations are scaffoldings which we may properly for certain purposes throw about the building: we must not mistake them for the internal and essential structure of the building itself.

Indeed, one may sum up by saying that most of the distempers of criticism come about from yielding to the temptation to take certain remarks which we make *about* the poem—statements about what it says or about what truth it gives or about what formulations it illustrates—for the essential core of the poem itself. As W. M. Urban puts it in his *Language and Reality*: "The general principle of the inseparability of intuition and expression holds with special force for the aesthetic intuition. Here it means that form and content, or content and medium, are inseparable. The artist does not first intuit his object and then find the appropriate medium. It is rather in and through his medium that he intuits the object."

So much for the process of composition. As for the critical process: "To pass from the intuitible to the nonintuitible is to negate the function and meaning of the symbol." For it "is precisely because the more universal and ideal relations cannot be adequately expressed directly that they are indirectly expressed by means of the more intuitible." The most obvious examples of such error (and for that reason those which are really least dangerous) are those theories which frankly treat the poem as propaganda. The most subtle (and the most stubbornly rooted in the ambiguities of language) are those which, beginning with the "paraphrasable" elements of the poem, refer the other elements of the poem finally to some role subordinate to the paraphrasable elements. (The relation between all the elements must surely be an organic one—there can be no question about that. There is, however, a very serious question as to whether the paraphrasable elements have primacy.)

Mr. Winters' position will furnish perhaps the most respectable example of the paraphrastic heresy. He assigns primacy to the "rational meaning" of the poem. "The relationship, in the poem, between rational statement and feeling," he remarks in his latest book, "is thus seen to be that of motive to emotion." He goes on to illustrate his point by a brief and excellent analysis of the following lines from Browning:

So wore night; the East was gray,
  White the broad-faced hemlock flowers. . . .

"The verb *wore*," he continues, "means literally that the night passed, but it carries with it connotations of exhaustion and attrition which belong to the condition of the protagonist; and grayness is a color which we associate with such a condition. If we change the phrase to read: 'Thus night passed,' we shall have the same rational meaning, and a meter quite as respectable, but no trace of the power of the line: the connotation of *wore* will be lost, and the connotation of *gray* will remain in a state of ineffective potentiality."

But the word *wore* does not mean *literally* "that the night passed," it means literally "that the night *wore*"—whatever *wore* may mean, and as Winters' own admirable analysis indicates, *wore* "means," whether *rationally* or *irrationally*, a great deal. Furthermore, "So wore night" and "Thus night passed" can be said to have "the same rational meaning" only if we equate "rational meaning" with the meaning of a loose paraphrase. And can a loose paraphrase be said to be the "motive to emotion"? Can it be said to "generate" the feelings in question? (Or, would Mr. Winters not have us equate "rational statement" and "rational meaning"?)

Much more is at stake here than any quibble. In view of the store which Winters sets by rationality and of his penchant for poems which make their evaluations overtly, and in view of his frequent blindness to those poems which do not—in view of these considerations, it is important to see that what "So wore night" and "Thus night passed" have in common as their "rational meaning" is not the "rational meaning" of each but the lowest common denominator of both. To refer the structure of the poem to what is finally a paraphrase of the poem is to refer it to something outside the poem.

To repeat, most of our difficulties in criticism are rooted in the heresy of paraphrase. If we allow ourselves to be misled by it, we distort the relation of the poem to its "truth," we raise the problem of belief in a vicious and crippling form, we split the poem between its "form" and its "content"—we bring the statement to be conveyed into an unreal competition with science or philosophy or theology. In short, we put our questions about the poem in a form calculated to produce the battles of the last twenty-five years over the "use of poetry."[1]

If we allow ourselves to be misled by the heresy of paraphrase, we run the risk of doing even more violence to the internal order of the poem itself. By taking the paraphrase as our point of stance, we misconceive the function of metaphor and meter. We demand logical coherences where they are sometimes irrelevant, and we fail frequently to see imaginative coherences on levels where they are highly relevant. Some of the implications of the paraphrastic heresy are so stubborn and so involved that I have thought best to relegate them to an appendix. There the reader who is interested may find further discussion of the problem and, I could hope, answers to certain misapprehensions of the positive theory to be adumbrated here.

But what would be a positive theory? We tend to embrace the doctrine of a logical structure the more readily because, to many of us, the failure to do so seems to leave the meaning of the poem hopelessly up in the air. The alternative position will appear to us to lack even the relative stability of an Ivory Tower: it is rather commitment to a free balloon. For, to deny the possibility of pinning down what the poem "says" to some "statement" will seem to assert that the poem really says nothing. And to point out what has been suggested in earlier chapters and brought to a head in this one, namely, that one can never measure a poem against the scientific or philosophical yardstick for the reason that the poem, when laid along the yardstick, is never the "full poem" but an abstraction from the poem—such an argument will seem to such readers a piece of barren logic-chopping—a transparent dodge.

Considerations of strategy then, if nothing more, dictate some positive account of what a poem is and does. And some positive account can be given, though I cannot promise to do more than suggest what a poem is, nor will my terms turn out to be anything more than metaphors.[2]

The essential structure of a poem (as distinguished from the rational or logical structure of the "statement" which we abstract from it) resembles that of architecture or painting: it is a pattern of resolved stresses.

Or, to move closer still to poetry by considering the temporal arts, the structure of a poem resembles that of a ballet or musical composition. It is a pattern of resolutions and balances and harmonizations, developed through a temporal scheme.[3]

Or, to move still closer to poetry, the structure of a poem resembles that of a play. This last example, of course, risks introducing once more the distracting element, since drama, like poetry, makes use of words. Yet, on the whole, most of us are less inclined to force the concept of "statement" on drama than on a lyric poem; for the very nature of drama is that of something "acted out"—something which arrives at its conclusion through conflict—something which builds conflict into its very being. The dynamic nature of drama, in short, allows us to regard it as *an action* rather than as a formula for action or as a statement about action. For this reason, therefore, perhaps the most helpful analogy by which to suggest the structure of poetry is that of the drama, and for many readers at least, the least confusing way in which to approach a poem is to think of it as a drama.

The general point, of course, is not that either poetry or drama makes no use of ideas, or that either is "merely emotional"—whatever *that* is— or that there is not the closest and most important relationship between the intellectual materials which they absorb into their structure and other elements in the structure. The relationship between the intellectual and the nonintellectual elements in a poem is actually far more intimate than the conventional accounts would represent it to be: the relationship is not that of an idea "wrapped in emotion" or a "prose-sense decorated by sensuous imagery."

The dimension in which the poem moves is not one which excludes ideas, but one which does include attitudes. The dimension includes ideas, to be sure; we can always abstract an "idea" from a poem—even from the simplest poem—even from a lyric so simple and unintellectual as

Western wind, when wilt thou blow
That the small rain down can rain?
Christ, that my love were in my arms
And I in my bed again?

But the idea which we abstract—assuming that we can all agree on what that idea is—will always be *abstracted:* it will always be the projection of a plane along a line or the projection of a cone upon a plane.

If this last analogy proves to be more confusing than illuminating, let us return to the analogy with drama. We have argued that any proposition asserted in a poem is not to be taken in abstraction but is justified, in terms of the poem, if it is justified at all, not by virtue of its scientific or historical or philosophical truth, but is justified in terms of a principle analogous to that of dramatic propriety. Thus, the proposition that "Beauty is truth, truth beauty" is given its precise meaning and significance by its relation to the total context of the poem.

This principle is easy enough to see when the proposition is asserted overtly in the poem—that is, when it constitutes a specific detail of the poem. But the reader may well ask: is it not possible to frame a proposition, a statement, which will adequately represent the total meaning of the poem; that is, is it not possible to elaborate a summarizing proposition which will "say," briefly and in the form of a proposition, what the poem "says" as a poem, a proposition which will say it fully and will say it exactly, no more and no less? Could not the poet, if he had chosen, have framed such a proposition? Cannot we as readers and critics frame such a proposition?

The answer must be that the poet himself obviously did not—else he would not have had to write his poem. We as readers can attempt to frame such a proposition in our effort to understand the poem; it may well help toward an understanding. Certainly, the efforts to arrive at such propositions can do no harm *if we do not mistake them for the inner core of the poem*—if we do not mistake them for "what the poem *really* says." For, if we take one of them to represent the essential poem, we have to disregard the qualifications exerted by the total context as of no account, or else we have assumed that we can reproduce the effect of the total context in a condensed prose statement.[4]

But to deny that the coherence of a poem is reflected in a logical paraphrase of its "real meaning" is not, of course, to deny coherence to poetry; it is rather to assert that its coherence is to be sought elsewhere. The characteristic unity of a poem (even of those poems which may accidentally possess a logical unity as well as this poetic unity) lies in the unification of attitudes into a hierarchy subordinated to a total and governing attitude. In the unified poem, the poet has "come to terms" with his experience. The poem does not merely eventuate in a logical conclusion. The conclusion of the poem is the working out of the various tensions—set up by whatever means—by propositions, metaphors, symbols. The unity is achieved by a dramatic process, not a logical; it represents an equilibrium of forces, not a formula. It is "proved" as a dramatic conclusion is proved: by its ability to resolve the conflicts which have been accepted as the *données* of the drama.

Thus, it is easy to see why the relation of each item to the whole context is crucial, and why the effective and essential structure of the poem has to do with the complex of attitudes achieved. A scientific preposition can stand alone. If it is true, it is true. But the expression of an attitude, apart from the occasion which generates it and the situation which it encompasses, is meaningless. For example, the last two lines of the "Intimations" ode,

> To me the meanest flower that blows can give
> Thoughts that do often lie too deep for tears,

when taken in isolation—I do not mean quoted in isolation by one who is even vaguely acquainted with the context—makes a statement which is sentimental if taken in reference to the speaker, and one which is patent nonsense if taken with a general reference. The man in the street (of whom the average college freshman is a good enough replica) knows that the meanest flower that grows does not give *him* thoughts that lie too deep for tears; and, if he thinks about the matter at all, he is inclined to feel that the person who can make such an assertion is a very fuzzy sentimentalist.

We have already seen the ease with which the statement "Beauty is truth, truth beauty" becomes detached from its context, even in the hands of able critics; and we have seen the misconceptions that ensue when this detachment occurs. To take one more instance: the last stanza of Herrick's "Corinna," taken in isolation, would probably not impress the average reader as sentimental nonsense. Yet it would suffer quite as much by isolation from its context as would the lines from Keats's "Ode." For, as mere statement, it would become something flat and obvious—of course our lives are short! And the conclusion from the fact would turn into an obvious truism for the convinced pagan, and, for the convinced Christian, equally obvious, though damnable, nonsense.

Perhaps this is why the poet, to people interested in hard-and-fast generalizations, must always seem to be continually engaged in blurring out distinctions, effecting compromises, or, at the best, coming to his conclusions only after provoking and unnecessary delays. But this last position is merely another variant of the paraphrastic heresy: to assume it is to misconceive the end of poetry—to take its meanderings as negative, or to excuse them (with the comfortable assurance that the curved line is the line of beauty) because we can conceive the purpose of a poem to be only the production, in the end, of a proposition—of a statement.

But the meanderings of a good poem (they are meanderings only from the standpoint of the prose paraphrase of the poem) are not negative, and they do not have to be excused; and most of all, we need to see what their positive function is; for unless we can assign them a positive function, we shall find it difficult to explain why one divergence from "the prose line of the argument" is not as good as another. The truth is that the apparent irrelevancies which metrical pattern and metaphor introduce do become relevant when we realize that they function in a good poem to modify, qualify, and develop the total attitude which we are to take in coming to terms with the total situation.

If the last sentence seems to take a dangerous turn toward some special "use of poetry"—some therapeutic value for the sake of which poetry is to be cultivated—I can only say that I have in mind no special ills which poetry is to cure. Uses for poetry are always to be found, and doubtless will continue to be found. But my discussion of the structure of poetry is not being conditioned at this point by some new and special role which I expect poetry to assume in the future or some new function to which I would assign it. The structure described—a structure of "gestures" or attitudes—seems to me to describe the essential structure of both the *Odyssey* and *The Waste Land*. It seems to be the kind of structure which the ten poems considered in this book possess in common.

If the structure of poetry is a structure of the order described, that fact may explain (if not justify) the frequency with which I have had to have recourse, in the foregoing chapters, to terms like "irony" and "paradox." By using the term irony, one risks, of course, making the poem seem arch and self-conscious, since irony, for most readers of poetry, is associated with satire, *vers de société*, and other "intellectual" poetries. Yet, the necessity for some such term ought to be apparent; and irony is the most general term that we have for the kind of qualification which the various elements in a context receive from the context. This kind of qualification, as we have seen, is of tremendous importance in any poem. Moreover, irony is our most general term for indicating that recognition of incongruities—which, again, pervades all poetry to a degree far beyond what our conventional criticism has been heretofore willing to allow.

Irony in this general sense, then, is to be found in Tennyson's "Tears, Idle Tears" as well as in Donne's "Canonization." We have, of course, been taught to expect to find irony in Pope's *Rape of the Lock*, but there is a profound irony in Keats's "Ode on a Grecian Urn"; and there is irony of a very powerful sort in Wordsworth's "Intimations" ode. For the thrusts and pressures exerted by the various symbols in this poem are not avoided by the poet: they are taken into account and played, one against the other. Indeed, the symbols—from a scientific point of view—are used perversely: it is the child who is the best philosopher; it is from a kind of darkness—from something that is "shadowy"—that the light proceeds; growth into manhood is viewed, not as an extrication from, but as an incarceration within, a prison.

There should be no mystery as to why this must be so. The terms of science are abstract symbols which do not change under the pressure of the context. They are pure (or aspire to be pure) denotations; they are defined in advance. They are not to be warped into new meanings. But where is the dictionary which contains the terms of a poem? It is a truism that the poet is continually forced to remake language. As Eliot has put it, his task is to "dislocate language into meaning." And, from the standpoint of a scientific vocabulary, this is precisely what he performs: for, rationally considered, the ideal language would contain one term for each meaning, and the relation between term and meaning would be constant. But the word, as the poet uses it, has to be conceived of, not as a discrete particle of meaning, but as a potential of meaning, a nexus or cluster of meanings.

What is true of the poet's language in detail is true of the larger wholes of poetry. And therefore, if we persist in approaching the poem as primarily a rational statement, we ought not to be surprised if the statements seems to be presented to us always in the ironic mode. When we consider the statement immersed in the poem, it presents itself to us, like the stick immersed in the pool of water, warped and bent. Indeed, whatever the statement, it will always show itself as deflected away from a positive, straightforward formulation.

It may seem perverse, however, to maintain, in the face of our revived interest in Donne, that the essential structure of poetry is not logical. For Donne has been appealed to of late as the great master of metaphor who imposes a clean logic on his images beside which the ordering of the images in Shakespeare's sonnets is fumbling and loose. It is perfectly true that Donne makes a great show of logic; but two matters need to be observed. In the first place, the elaborated and "logical" figure is not Donne's only figure or even his staple one. "Telescoped" figures like "Made one anothers hermitage" are to be found much more frequently than the celebrated comparison of the souls of the lovers to the legs of a pair of compasses. In the second place, where Donne uses "logic," he regularly uses it to justify illogical positions. He employs it to overthrow a conventional position or to "prove" an essentially illogical one.

Logic, as Donne uses it, is nearly always an ironic logic to state the claims of an idea or attitude which we have agreed, with our everyday logic, is false. This is not to say, certainly, that Donne is not justified in using his logic so, or that the best of his poems are not "proved" in the only senses in which poems can be proved.

But the proof is not a logical proof. "The Canonization" will scarcely prove to the hard-boiled naturalist that the lovers, by giving up the world, actually attain a better world. Nor will the argument advanced in the poem convince the dogmatic Christian that Donne's lovers are really saints.

In using logic, Donne as a poet is fighting the devil with fire. To adopt Robert Penn Warren's metaphor (which, though I lift it somewhat scandalously out of another context, will apply to this one): "The poet, somewhat less spectacularly [than the saint], proves his vision by submitting it to the fires of irony—to the drama of the structure—in the hope that the fires will refine it. In other words, the poet wishes to indicate that his vision has been earned, that it can survive reference to the complexities and contradictions of experience."

The same principle that inspires the presence of irony in so many of our great poems also accounts for the fact that so many of them seem to be built around paradoxes. Here again the conventional associations of the term may prejudice the reader just as the mention of Donne may prejudice him. For Donne, as one type of reader knows all too well, was of that group of poets who wished to impress their audience with their cleverness. All of us are familiar with the censure passed upon Donne and his followers by Dr. Johnson, and a great many of us still retain it as our own, softening only the rigor of it and the thoroughness of its application, but not giving it up as a principle.

Yet there are better reasons than that of rhetorical vain-glory that have induced poet after poet to choose ambiguity and paradox rather than plain, discursive simplicity. It is not enough for the poet to analyse his experience as the scientist does, breaking it up into parts, distinguishing part from part, classifying the various parts. His task is finally to unify experience. He must return to us the unity of the experience itself as man knows it in his own experience. The poem, if it be a true poem is a simulacrum of reality—in this sense, at least, it is an "imitation"—by *being* an experience rather than any mere statement about experience or any mere abstraction from experience.

Tennyson cannot be content with *saying* that in memory the poet seems both dead *and* alive; he must dramatize its life-in-death for us, and his dramatization involves, necessarily, ironic shock and wonder. The dramatization demands that the antithetical aspects of memory be coalesced into one entity which—if we take it on the level of statement—is a paradox, the assertion of the union of opposites. Keats's Urn must express a life which is above life and its vicissitudes, but it must also bear witness to the fact that its life is not life at all but is a kind of death. To put it in other terms, the Urn must, in its role as historian, assert that myth is truer than history. Donne's lovers must reject the world in order to possess the world.

Or, to take one further instance: Wordsworth's light must serve as the common symbol for aspects of man's vision which seem mutually incompatible—intuition and analytic reason. Wordsworth's poem, as a matter of fact, typifies beautifully the poet's characteristic problem itself. For even this poem, which testifies so heavily to the way in which the world is split up and parceled out under the growing light of reason, cannot rest in this fact as its own mode of perception, and still be a poem. Even after the worst has been said about man's multiple vision, the poet must somehow prove that the child is father to the man, that the dawn light is still somehow the same light as the evening light.

If the poet, then, must perforce dramatize the oneness of the experience, even though paying tribute to its diversity, then his use of paradox and ambiguity is seen as necessary. He is not simply trying to spice up, with a superficially exciting or mystifying rhetoric, the old stale stockpot (though doubtless this will be what the inferior poet does generally and what the real poet does in his lapses). He is rather giving us an insight which preserves the unity of experience and which, at its higher and more serious levels, triumphs over the apparently contradictory and conflicting elements of experience by unifying them into a new pattern.

Wordsworth's "Intimations" ode, then, is not only a poem, but, among other things, a parable about poetry. Keats's "Ode on a Grecian Urn" is quite obviously such a parable. And, indeed, most of the poems which we have discussed in this study may be taken as such parables.

In one sense, Pope's treatment of Belinda raises all the characteristic problems of poetry. For Pope, in dealing with his "goddess," must face the claims of naturalism and of common sense which would deny divinity to her. Unless he faces them, he is merely a sentimentalist. He must do an even harder thing: he must transcend the conventional and polite attributions of divinity which would be made to her as an acknowledged belle. Otherwise, he is merely trivial and obvious. He must "prove" her divinity against the common-sense denial (the brutal denial) and against the conventional assertion (the polite denial). The poetry must be wrested from the context: Belinda's lock, which is what the rude young man wants and which Belinda rather prudishly defends and which the naturalist asserts is only animal and which displays in its curled care the style of a particular era of history, must be given a place of permanence among the stars.

NOTES

1. I do not, of course, intend to minimize the fact that some of these battles have been highly profitable, or to imply that the foregoing paragraphs could have been written except for the illumination shed by the discussions of the last twenty-five years.

2. For those who cannot be content with metaphors (or with the particular metaphors which I can give) I recommend Rene Wellek's excellent "The Mode of Existence of a Literary Work of Art" (*The Southern Review*, Spring, 1942). I shall not try to reproduce here as a handy, thumb-nail definition his account of a poem as "a stratified system of norms," for the definition would be relatively meaningless without the further definitions which he assigns to the individual terms which he uses. I have made no special use of his terms in this chapter, but I believe that the generalizations about poetry outlined here can be thoroughly accommodated to the position which his essay sets forth.

3. In recent numbers of *Accent*, two critics for whose work I have high regard have emphasized the dynamic character of poetry. Kenneth Burke argues that if we are to consider a poem as a poem, we must consider it as a "mode of action." R. P. Blackmur asks us to think of it as gesture, "the outward and dra-

matic play of inward and imagined meaning." I do not mean to commit either of these critics to my own interpretation of dramatic or symbolic action; and I have, on my own part, several rather important reservations with respect to Mr. Burke's position. But there are certainly large areas of agreement among our positions. The reader might also compare the account of poetic structure given in this chapter with the following passage from Susanne Langer's *Philosophy in a New Key:* "... though the *material* of poetry is verbal, its import is not the literal assertion made in the words, but *the way the assertion is made,* and this involves the sound, the tempo, the aura of associations of the words, the long or short sequences of ideas, the wealth or poverty of transient imagery that contains them, the sudden arrest of fantasy by pure fact, or of familiar fact by sudden fantasy, the suspense of literal meaning by a sustained ambiguity resolved in a long-awaited key-word, and the unifying, all-embracing artifice of rhythm."

4. We may, it is true, be able to adumbrate what the poem says if we allow ourselves enough words, and if we make enough reservations and qualifications, thus attempting to come nearer to the meaning of the poem by successive approximations and refinements, gradually encompassing the meaning and pointing to the area in which it lies rather than realizing it. The earlier chapters of this book, if they are successful, are obviously illustrations of this process. But such adumbrations will lack, not only the tension—the dramatic force—of the poem; they will be at best crude approximations of the poem. Moreover—and this is the crucial point—they will be compelled to resort to the methods of the poem—analogy, metaphor, symbol, etc.—in order to secure even this near an approximation.

Urban's comment upon this problem is interesting: he says that if we expand the symbol, "we lose the 'sense' or value of the symbol *as symbol.* The solution ... seems to me to lie in an adequate theory of interpretation of the symbol. It does not consist in substituting *literal* for symbol sentences, in other words substituting 'blunt' truth for symbolic truth, but rather in deepending and enriching the meaning of the symbol."

Nelson Goodman

The Status of Style

1. Exceptions Taken

Obviously, subject is what is said, style is how. A little less obviously, that
formula is full of faults. Architecture and nonobjective painting and most
of music have no subject. Their style cannot be a matter of how they say
something, for they do not literally say anything; they do other things,
they mean in other ways. Although most literary works say something,
they usually do other things, too; and some of the ways they do some of
these things are aspects of style. Moreover, the what of one sort of doing
may be part of the how of another. Indeed, even where the only function
in question is saying, we shall have to recognize that some notable features of style are features of the matter rather than the manner of the saying. In more ways than one, subject is involved in style. For this and other
reasons, I cannot subscribe to the received opinion[1] that style depends
upon an artist's conscious choice among alternatives. And I think we
shall also have to recognize that not all differences in ways of writing or
painting or composing or performing are differences in style.

My quarrels, though, are not with the practice of critics and art historians but with their definitions and theories of style, so often at odds
with that practice.

2. Style and Subject

Plainly, when something is said, some aspects of the way it is said are
matters of style. So far as the descriptive, narrative, or expository function of literature goes, variations in style are variations in how this function is performed by texts. Form varies while content remains constant—
but there are difficulties with even this dictum. Graham Hough writes:
" ... the more we reflect on it, the more doubtful it becomes how far we
can talk about different ways of saying; is not each different way of saying

254

in fact the saying of a different thing?"[2] More recently, E. D. Hirsch, Jr., starting from the premise that style and stylistics depend upon there being alternative ways of saying exactly the same thing, strives to defend and define synonymy.[3]

Synonymy is a suspect notion; and a study of my own suggests that no two terms have exactly the same meaning.[4] But distinctness of style from content requires not that exactly the same thing may be said in different ways but only that what is said may vary nonconcomitantly with ways of saying. Pretty clearly there are often very different ways of saying things that are very nearly the same. Conversely, and often more significantly, very different things may be said in much the same way—not, of course, by the same text but by texts that have in common certain characteristics that constitute a style. Many works on many matters may be in the same style; and much discussion of styles is carried on without regard to subject. Styles of saying—as of painting or composing or performing—may often be compared and contrasted irrespective of what the subjects are and even of whether there are any. Even without synonymy, style and subject do not become one.[5]

So far our results are negative and nearly nil. Not only is style not subject; but where there is no subject, style is not at all delimited by not being subject. Even this is a risky statement. For sometimes style *is* a matter of subject. I do not mean merely that subject may influence style but that some differences in style consist entirely of differences in what is said. Suppose one historian writes in terms of military conflicts, another in terms of social changes; or suppose one biographer stresses public careers, another personal lives. The differences between the two histories of a given period, or between the two biographies of a given person, here lie not in the character of the prose but in what is said. Nevertheless, these are differences in literary style no less pronounced than are differences in wording. I have purposely picked examples of descriptive or expository literature, but part of a poet's style as well may consist of what he says—of whether he focuses on the fragile and transcendent or the powerful and enduring, upon sensory qualities or abstract ideas, and so on.

The prospect of paradox looms here. If what is said is sometimes an aspect of style, and style is a way of saying what is said, a tactless logician might point to the unwelcome consequence that what is said is sometimes an aspect of a way of saying what is said—a formula with the ambivalent aroma of a self-contradictory truism.

The remedy looks at first sight even more weird. What is said, rather than being a way of saying what is said, may be a way of talking about something else; for example, writing about Renaissance battles and writing about Renaissance arts are not different ways of writing about the battles or about the arts but different ways of writing about the Renaissance. Saying different things may count as different ways of talking about something more comprehensive that embraces both. Thus without departing from the principle that style pertains to ways of saying we can, for example, recognize as aspects of style both writing about the battles rather than the arts and writing in Latinate rather than Anglo-Saxon prose. But then we give up what seemed the very point of that principle; the contrast between ways of saying and what is said, between style and subject. If both packaging and contents are matters of style, what isn't?

Looking once more and harder, we may notice that differences in style dependent upon differences in subject do not arise from the mere fact that what is said is not the same. When the military-minded historian writes about two different periods, his style may remain the same even though what he says is very different—at least as different as what he and the arts-minded historian write about a given period. To say that style is a matter of subject is thus vague and misleading. Rather, only *some* features of what is said count as aspects of style; only certain characteristic differences in what is said constitute differences in style.

Likewise, of course, only certain features of the wording, and not others, constitute features of style. That two texts consist of very different words does not make them different in style. What count as features of style here are such characteristics as the predominance of certain kinds of words, the sentence structure, and the use of alliteration and rhyme.

Thus we need not have worried about the difficulty of distinguishing form from content; for that distinction, insofar as it is clear, does not coincide with but cuts across the distinction between what is style and what is not. Style comprises certain characteristic features both of what is said and of how it is said, both of subject and of wording, both of content and of form. The distinction between stylistic and nonstylistic features has to be drawn on other grounds.

3. Style and Sentiment

Have we by any chance, in our struggle so far, left out the very essence of style? Some say that style enters where fact stops and feeling starts; that style is a matter of the "affective and expressive"[6] as against the logical, intellectual, cognitive aspects of art; that neither what is said nor what says it have anything to do with style except as they participate in expressing emotion. Two reports of a walk in the rain that use different words and describe different incidents may be in the same style, but they are in different styles if one is glum and the other gleeful. Style in general on this view consists of such, and much more subtle, qualities of feeling expressed.

As a criterion for distinguishing stylistic from nonstylistic features, this proposal has obvious limitations. Under any plausible sorting of properties into emotive and cognitive, some stylistic properties are emotive and some are not. Tight or loose construction, brevity or verbosity, plain or ornate vocabulary may arouse but hardly express admiration or antipathy and are surely not themselves emotional properties. Accordingly, "emotion" in this context comes to be replaced by the vaguer term "feeling"; and each plainly nonemotive stylistic property is held to have its peculiar feel. Periodic sentences feel different from loose sentences; we can feel the difference between a Latinate and an Anglo-Saxon vocabulary. Moreover, we are often aware of these qualities of feeling before we discern the underlying factual properties, as we often feel a pain before perceiving the wound. And it is just these feelings rather than their vehicles that count as aspects of style. Such is the claim.

In this version, the thesis is attenuated to the point of evaporation. In any sense that the cited features of a text have their peculiar feeling qualities, so it seems does every other—indeed every word and sequence of words. That we can feel such properties seems to mean little more than that we can perceive them without analysis into component traits, just as we recognize a face; but this surely is true of most properties, and useless for distinguishing style. Making the theory broad enough is making it too broad to work.

Furthermore, definition of style in terms of feelings expressed goes wrong in overlooking not only structural features that are neither feelings nor expressed but also features that though not feelings *are* expressed. Although the Sturgis drawing and the Pollaiuolo engraving illustrated below (pp. 804 and 805) both represent men in physical conflict, the Sturgis expresses flashing action while the Pollaiuolo expresses poised power.[7] A Daumier lithograph may express weight, a passage from Vivaldi express visual patterns of sakters, and Joyce's *Ulysses* express an infinite cycling of time.

Thus style is confined neither to what is expressed nor to feelings. Nevertheless, expressing is at least as important a function of many works as is saying: and what a work expresses is often a major ingredient of its style. The differences between sardonic, sentimental, savage, and sensual writing are stylistic. Emotions, feelings, and other properties expressed in the saying are part of the way of saying; what is expressed is an aspect of how what is said is said, and as in music and abstract painting may be an aspect of style even when nothing is said.

All this is plain enough, and yet plainly not enough. For since expression is a function of works of art, *ways* of expressing as well as ways of saying must be taken into account. And as differences in what is expressed may count as differences in style of saying, so differences in what is said may count as differences in style of expressing. Gloominess may

be typical of a writer's way of describing outdoor activities; emphasis on
rainy weather may be typical of his way of expressing gloom. What is said,
how it is said, what is expressed, and how it is expressed are all intimately
interrelated and involved in style.

4. Style and Structure

That features of what is said and of what is expressed must be taken into
account does not at all diminish the central importance of sentence structure, rhythmic pattern, use of iteration and antithesis, and so on. Nor, as
illustrated by certain characteristics of vocabulary (Latinate or Anglo-
Saxon, collegiate or colloquial) in prose and of color in painting, are all
features of style that are not properties of what is said or expressed 'formal' or 'structural' in any but an overstretched sense.

We are tempted to classify all such properties as intrinsic or internal
on the ground that unlike properties of something—subject or feeling—
that a text or picture refers to by way of denotation (description, representation, etc.) or expression, these belong to, are possessed by, are inherent
in, the text or picture itself. But philosophers have had trouble trying to
draw any clear line between internal and external properties. After all,
what a text says or expresses is a property of the text, not of something
else; and on the other hand, properties possessed by the text are different
from and are not enclosed within it, but relate it to other texts sharing
these properties.

Can this class of not exclusively formal and not clearly intrinsic features be better defined in terms of the difference between what a work
does and what it *is?* Saying the earth is round or expressing gloom is doing
so; being tautly written or freely painted is just being so. I am afraid this
does not quite work either. In the first place, the gloom expressed by a
poem or picture is in my view possessed by it, albeit metaphorically
rather than literally; that is, the poem or picture expressing gloom *is*
(metaphorically) gloomy.[8] In the second place, I think the so-called intrinsic stylistic features of a work are never merely possessed but are among
those possessed properties that are manifested, shown forth, *exemplified*
just as color and texture and weave, but not shape or size, are exemplified
by the tailor's swatch he uses as a sample. Thus, expressing and exemplifying alike are matters of being and doing, of possessing properties *and*
referring to them. This, indeed, provides a clue to the distinction we have
been trying to make: the features here in question, whether structural or
nonstructural, are all properties literally exemplified by a work.

Exemplification, though one of the most frequent and important functions of works of art, is the least noticed and understood. Not only some troubles about style but many futile debates over the symbolic character of art can be blamed on ignoring the lessons, readily learned from everyday cases of the relation of being-a-sample-of, that mere possession of a property does not amount to exemplification, that exemplification involves reference by what possesses to the property possessed, and thus that exemplification though obviously different from denotation (or description or representation) is no less a species of reference.

In summary so far, a feature of style may be a feature of what is said, of what is exemplified, or of what is expressed. Goya and El Greco characteristically differ in all three ways: in subject matter, drawing, and feeling. Features of any of these kinds may also be ways of performing one or more of the three functions. For example, shapes exemplified in a painting of drapery may at once constitute a way of representing costume and a way of expressing bulk or agitation or dignity; the drapery "can curl, it can swirl, it can billow, it can melt; or it can resist the eye with a structure of humps and hollows as durable as a rock modelled by the waves," can become "an instrument of harmonious certainty."[9] In other cases, differences in what is expressed—say in the character of the risen Christ in Mantegna's engraving and Piero della Francesca's painting—may be different ways of depicting the same subject. Again, features of what is said may be ways of saying or expressing; Whitman's choice of detail is both an aspect of his way of describing human beings and his way of celebrating vitality, and the different subjects chosen by Vermeer and de Heem and van der Heyden and van Everdingen are at once different ways of depicting life in seventeenth-century Holland and different ways of expressing its domestic quality. Sometimes, features of what is exemplified, such as color organizations, are ways of exemplifying other features, such as a spatial pattern; witness the differently colored impressions from a single silk-screen design by Albers, and more recently by Patrick Heron. And a given structure, such as the sonnet form, may of course be exemplified in poems having quite different subjects, so that features of a subject matter count as ways of exemplifying a form.

But we need not ring all the changes here or argue over particular examples. My purpose has not been to impose an elaborate and rigid system of classification upon features of style, but rather to free the theory of style from the warping constraints of prevalent dogma—from the misleading opposition of style and subject, of form and content, of what and how, of intrinsic and extrinsic. Far from claiming that the tripartite taxonomy outlined is mandatory or the best possible or even altogether adequate, I am urging explicit recognition of aspects of style that, while often considered by critics, are shortchanged by traditional theory. This does

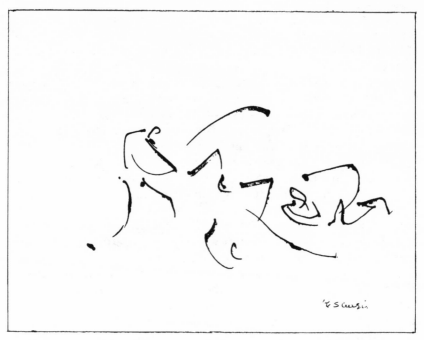

Katharine Sturgis, Drawing from a hockey series, Ink, Courtesy of the artist.

not answer but only underlines the question what in general distinguishes stylistic features from others. Identifying the properties of a literary—or pictorial or musical—style matters more than further classifying them into ways of saying, exemplifying, and expressing.

5. Style and Signature

Yet while style embraces features of the several sorts described, such features are not always stylistic. If a work is in a given style, only certain among all the aspects of the subject, form, and feeling of the work are elements of that style.

In the first place, a property—whether of statement made, structure displayed, or feeling conveyed—counts as stylistic only when it associates a work with one rather than another artist, period, region, school, etc. A style is a complex characteristic that serves somewhat as an individual or group signature—that bespeaks Resnais or Whistler or Borodin, that distinguishes early from late Corot, Baroque from Rococo, Baoulé from Pahouin. By extension, we may speak of a work by one author as being in the style of another, or of a passage being or not being in the style of other

Antonio Pollaiuolo, *Battle of Naked Men*, Engraving, Courtesy of the Cleveland Museum of Art, Purchase, J. H. Wade Fund.

passages in the same or another work; but in general stylistic properties help answer the questions: who? when? where? A feature that is nonindicative by itself may combine with others to place a work; a property common to many works may be an element of style for some but stylistically irrelevant for others; some properties may be only usual rather than constant features of a given style; and some may be stylistically significant not through appearing always or even often in works of a given author or period but through appearing never or almost never in other works. No fixed catalogue of the elementary properties of style can be compiled; and we normally come to grasp a style without being able to analyze it into component features. The test of our grasp lies in the sureness and sensitivity of our sorting of works.

In the second place, not even every property that helps determine the maker or period or provenance of a work is stylistic. The label on a picture, a listing in a catalogue raisonné, a letter from the composer, a report of excavation may help place a work; but being so labelled or documented or excavated is not a matter of style. Nor are the chemical properties of pigments that help identify a painting. Even being signed by Thomas Eakins or Benjamin Franklin is an identifying property that is not stylistic. Although a style is metaphorically a signature, a literal signature is no feature of style.

Why do such properties, even though plainly who-when-where relevant, fail to qualify as stylistic? Briefly, because they are not properties of the functioning of the work as a symbol. In contrast, such typical stylistic qualities as a concentration upon setting, a peculiar elaboration of curved forms, a subtle quality of bittersweet feeling, are aspects of what the poem or picture or piano sonata says or exemplifies or expresses. Style has to do exclusively with the symbolic functioning of a work as such.[10] Earlier we saw that any, and now we see that only, aspects of such symbolic functioning may enter into a style.

The lineaments of a definition of style are thus before us. Basically, style consists of those features of the symbolic functioning of a work that are characteristic of author, period, place, or school. If this definition does not seem notably novel, still its divergence from some prevalent views must not be overlooked. According to this definition, style is not exclusively a matter of how as contrasted with what, does not depend either upon synonymous alternatives or upon conscious choice among alternatives, and comprises only but not all aspects of how and what a work symbolizes.

Throughout, I have been speaking of style of works of art. But need style, as conceived here, be confined to works, or might the term "work" in our definition be as well replaced by "object" or by "anything"? Unlike some other definitions, ours does not rest upon an artist's intentions. What counts are properties symbolized, whether or not the artist chose or is even aware of them; and many things other than works of art symbolize. Insofar as the properties in question are characteristic of an author or maker, style indeed pertains only to artefacts, unless "maker" covers also the person who presents an *objet trouvé* as art. But natural objects and events may function otherwise as symbols, and properties of what they symbolize may be characteristic of time or place of origin or occurrence. A Mandalay sunrise may be not merely a sunrise in Mandalay but a sunrise expressing the suddenness of thunder—a sunrise in Mandalay style. Nevertheless, in the present context we may do well to restrict style to works and performances and objects of art.[11]

Some stylistic features are more prominent and more telling than others; but the line between trivial stylistic features and features like those cited earlier that are not stylistic at all has seldom been clearly drawn. Consider some fussy statistical characteristic of the novels of a given author, such as that more than the usual proportion of second words of his sentences begin with consonants. Is the difference between this and an important genuine feature of style categorical or comparative? This property is statistical, but so are many plainly stylistic properties such as the frequency of rhyme or alliteration. This property is determinable only by long labor; but some of the most significant properties of style are so subtle as to be discovered only at great pains. Finally, that this property is too ad hoc to be interesting is a matter of degree; just as generalizations in science are the more ad hoc the fewer and weaker their connections with the theoretical background, so stylistic properties are the more ad hoc the fewer and weaker their connections with the network of other stylistic concepts.

So far, then, nothing distinguishes our preposterous property from unmistakably stylistic properties. Nevertheless, our definition of style discloses a categorical difference here. Though our property indeed belongs to the novels in question and even identifies them as by the given author, it is hardly exemplified or symbolized in any way by them as works. In this it is like the size and shape of a tailor's swatch that serves as a sample not of these properties but of color and texture. Since our property is not symbolized by the novels, it does not satisfy our definition of style. In contrast with even the strangest or most negligible stylistic properties, this is not a stylistic property at all.

Now admittedly, while what is or is not exemplified by a tailor's swatch is evident enough, just which properties are exemplified by a work of art or a performance is often difficult to determine. The distinction drawn in the definition may sometimes be hard to apply. But likewise, we often find it hard to tell just what a work says or expresses. That we have trouble making a determination implies that there is something to be determined: that the work in fact does or in fact does not say so-and-so, does or does not exemplify (or express) a given property. Whether a property is stylistic depends no more than what a work says either upon the difficulty of determining or upon the importance of what is exemplified or said.

6. The Significance of Style

Stylistics, plainly, is a narrow part of criticism. Criticism may incorporate discussion not only of historical, biographical, psychological, and sociological factors, but of any properties whatever of the works studied. Stylistics, in contrast, is confined to features of what and how the works symbolize, and still further to such of these features as are characteristic of a given author, period, region, school, etc.

Does this mean that concepts of style are mere instruments for the literary or art historian, curatorial devices for sorting works according to origin? Are styles, like catalogue listings and excavation reports, simply aids in filing or have they aesthetic significance? Is stylistics merely part of the mechanics of scholarship or does it concern works as art?

The question as framed is misleading. It assumes that attribution is alien to aesthetics, that the 'mere' identification of artist, period, place, or school is aesthetically irrelevant, that history and criticism are entirely independent pursuits. This is a mistake. As I have argued elsewhere,[12] knowledge of the origin of a work, even if obtained by chemical analysis or other purely scientific means, informs the way the work is to be looked at or listened to or read, providing a basis for the discovery of nonobvious ways the work differs from and resembles other works. Indeed, the perceptual discovery of a style must usually start from prior identification of works representing an artist or school. Thus attributions however effected contribute to the understanding of works as art.

The question really at issue here is different: whether stylistic properties have any more direct aesthetic significance than do nonstylistic properties that aid attribution. The answer is implicit in what has already been said. Placing a work is itself aesthetically significant insofar as it makes for discovery of such qualities as those of style. That style is by definition characteristic of an author or period or region or school does not reduce it to a device for attribution; rather, so far as aesthetics is concerned, attribution is a preliminary or auxiliary to or a byproduct of the perception of style. History and criticism differ not in having separate subject matters or unrelated tasks but in exchanging ends for means. Where the historian uses his grasp of style to identify a picture as by Rembrandt or a poem as by Hopkins, the critic uses the identification of authorship as a step toward discerning the Rembrandt properties or the Hopkins properties of the work.

Why, though, should style matter more than some quality that might be discerned, with enough study, as characteristic of works in a random selection? Partly for the same reason that ad hoc stylistic properties count for little: lack of interesting interrelationships with the ever-developing fabric of other features involved in organizing our aesthetic experience; and partly because, in the absence of any claimed correlation with such projectible factors as authorship or school, our tentative perception cannot be reinforced, refined, or extended by testing against further cases. Nothing here is incompatible with the familiar fact that interesting qualities are sometimes revealed through the juxtaposition of works in a mixed anthology, exhibition, collection, or concert, or even a storeroom jumble.

The style of Haydn or Hardy or Holbein does not proclaim itself to the casual listener or reader or museum goer, and is seldom to be recognized by following explicit instructions. Styles are normally accessible only to the knowing eye or ear, the tuned sensibility, the informed and inquisitive mind. This is not surprising, or even peculiar to styles. No feature of anything is so central or so potentially prominent as not to be overlooked even under close and repeated scrutiny. What we find is heavily dependent on how and what we seek. We fail to see the face in the woods in a child's picture puzzle. We may miss form and feeling as we focus upon what is said, or miss what is said as we listen to rhyme and rhythm. People equally at home in two languages may, when learning lists or tests in a mixture of the two, hardly notice and quickly forget which words are in which language. Overall design may be ignored for or distract attention from fine detail. The perception of any pattern not fitting the structure of the search often takes great trouble.

Yet the more complicated and elusive the style, the more does it stimulate exploration and reward success with illumination. An obvious style, easily identified by some superficial quirk, is properly decried as a mere mannerism. A complex and subtle style, like a trenchant metaphor, resists reduction to a literal formula. We usually perceive the style or the sadness of a picture or a poem without being able to analyze either property into elements or specify necessary and sufficient conditions for it. Just for this reason, the perception when achieved increases the dimensions of our comprehension of the work. And the less accessible a style is to our approach and the more adjustment we are forced to make, the more insight we gain and the more our powers of discovery are developed. The discernment of style is an integral aspect of the understanding of works of art.

Originally delivered, in an earlier version, as a Miller Lecture at the University of Illinois at Urbana-Champaign in April 1974. Useful suggestions have been made by Howard Gardner, Vernon Howard, David Perkins, Sheldon Sacks, and Paolo Valesio.

NOTES

1. E.g., Stephen Ullmann, in *Style in the French Novel* (Cambridge, 1957), p. 6, writes: "There can be no question of style unless the speaker or writer has the possibility of choosing between alternative forms of expression. Synonymy, in the widest sense of the term, lies at the root of the whole problem of style." This passage is quoted, with apparent approval, by E. H. Gombrich in "Style" (*International Encyclopedia of the Social Sciences*, vol. 15), p. 353.
2. Graham Hough, in his admirable and useful *Style and Stylistics* (London, 1969), p. 4. I concur also with his skepticism about resurrecting the notion of synonymy through transformational linguistics.
3. E. D. Hirsch, Jr., "Stylistics and Synonymity," *Critical Inquiry* 1 (March 1975): 559–579.
4. Nelson Goodman, "On Likeness of Meaning," *Analysis* 10, no. 1 (October 1949): 1–7; reprinted in Goodman, *Problems and Projects* (Indianapolis, 1972), pp. 231–38. This challenge to synonymy was by no means the first but (1) went further than earlier ones by showing that even under an analysis de-

pendent solely on the extensions of terms, every two terms differ in meaning, and (2) suggested a criterion for comparative likeness of meaning, thus providing a basis for distinguishing style from content.

5. "Subject" is rather ambiguoug as between topic and what is said about a topic; and some remarks below bear on the relationship between the two. But for purposes of the present paper, differences among topic, subject, subject matter, content, what is said, and what is named or described or depicted usually count for less than the shared differences from other features discussed below.

6. E.g., C. Bally; see the account of his view in Hough, esp. p. 23.

7. Both works, of course, express much else.

8. Even though a metaphorical statement may be literally false, metaphorical truth differs from metaphorical falsity much as literal truth differs from literal falsity. This and other matters—pertaining to metaphor, to denotation and exemplification and expression, and to symbolization or reference in general—that are essential to but can only be briefly summarized in the present paper are more fully explained in Nelson Goodman, *Languages of Art: An Approach to a Theory of Symbols* (Indianapolis, 1968).

9. Quotations are from Kenneth Clark, *Piero della Francesca,* 2d ed. (London, 1969), p. 14.

10. And only as such; not, for example, with the symbolic functioning of a poem as a message in some military code.

11. Although my examples in the present paper are works, what I say of styles applied equally to performances. The much-abused question "What is art?"—that is how, or better when, anything qualifies as a work of art, good or bad—and related questions concerning the *objet trouvé* and conceptual art are explored once more in my lecture "When is Art?" now being prepared for publication.

12. Goodman, *Languages of Art,* pp. 99–111.

Seven
narrative

Wayne C. Booth

Distance and Point-of-View: An Essay in Classification

> 'But he [the narrator] little knows what
> surprises lie in wait for him, if someone were to
> set about analysing the mass of truths and
> falsehoods which he has collected here.'
> —'Dr. S.,' in *Confessions of Zeno*

Like other notions used in talking about fiction, point-of-view has proved less useful than was expected by the critics who first brought it to our attention. When Percy Lubbock hailed the triumph of Henry James's dramatic use of the 'central intelligence,' and told us that 'the whole intricate question of method, in the craft of fiction,' is governed by 'the relation in which the narrator stands to the story,' he might have predicted that many critics would, like E. M. Forster, disagree with him. But he could hardly have predicted that his converts would produce, in forty years of elaborate investigations of point-of-view, so little help to the author or critic who must decide whether this or that technique in a particular work is appropriate to this or that effect. On the one hand we have been given classifications and descriptions which leave us wondering why we have bothered to classify and describe; the author who counted the number of times the word 'I' appears in each of Jane Austen's novels may be more obviously absurd than the innumerable scholars who have traced in endless detail the *'Ich-Erzählung,'* or *'erlebte Rede,'* or *'monologue intérieur'* from Dickens to Joyce or from James to Robbes-Grillet. But he is no more irrelevant to literary judgment. To describe particulars may be interesting but it is only the preliminary to the kind of knowledge that might help us explain the success or failure of individual works.

On the other hand, our efforts at formulating useful principles have been of little more use because they have been overtly prescriptive. If to count the number of times 'I' occurs tells us nothing about how many times 'I' should occur, to formulate abstract appeals for more 'showing' and less 'telling,' for less authorial commentary and more drama, for more realistic consistency and fewer arbitrary shifts which remind the reader that he is reading a book, gives us the illusion of having discovered criteria when we really have not. While it is certainly true that some effects are best achieved by avoiding some kinds of telling, too often our prescriptions have been for 'the novel' entire, ignoring what James himself knew well: there are '5,000,000 ways to tell a story,' depending on one's overall

269

purposes. Too many Jamesians have tried to establish in advance the precise degree of realistic intensity or irony or objectivity or 'aesthetic distance' his work should display.

It is true that dissenting voices are now heard more and more frequently, perhaps the most important being Kathleen Tillotson's recent inaugural lecture at The University of London, *The Tale and the Teller.* But the clichés about the superiority of dramatic showing over mere telling are still to be found everywhere: in scholarly journals, in the literary quarterlies, in the weekly reviews, in the latest book on how to read a novel, and in dust-jacket blurbs. 'The author does not tell you directly but you find out for yourself from their [the characters] every word, gesture, and act,' a Modern Library jacket tells us about Salinger's *Nine Stories.* That this is praise, that Salinger would be in error if he were found telling us anything directly, is taken for granted.

Since the novelist's choices are in fact practically unlimited, in judging their effectiveness we can only fall back on the kind of reasoning used by Aristotle in the *Poetics: if* such-and-such an effect is desired, *then* such-and-such points-of-view will be good or bad. We all agree that point-of-view is in some sense a technical matter, a means to larger ends; whether we say that technique is the artist's way of discovering his artistic meaning or that it is his way of working his will upon his audience, we still can judge it only in the light of the larger meanings or effects which it is designed to serve. Though we all at times violate our own convictions, most of us are convinced that we have no right to impose on the artist abstract criteria derived from other kinds of work.

But even when we have decided to put our judgments in the hypothetical 'if-then' form, we are still faced with an overwhelming variety of choices. One of the most striking features of our criticism is the casual way in which we allow ourselves to reduce this variety, thoughtlessly, carelessly, to simple categories, the impoverishment of which is evident whenever we look at any existing novel. On the side of effect critics at one time had a fairly large number of terms to play with—terms like tragedy, comedy, tragi-comedy, epic, farce, satire, elegy, and the like. Though the neo-classical kinds were often employed in inflexible form, they did provide a frame of discourse which allowed the critic and artist to communicate with each other: 'if the effect you want is what we have traditionally expected under the concept "tragedy," then your technique here is inadequate.' If what we are working for is a first-rate comedy, Dryden tells us in 'An Essay of Dramatic Poesy,' then here are some rules we can count on; they may be difficult to apply, they may require painstaking discussion, and they will certainly require genius if they are to be made to work, but they can still be of help to artist and critic because they are based on an agreement about a recognised literary effect.

In place of the earlier kinds, we have generally substituted a criticism based on qualities that are supposed to be sought in all works. All novels are said to be aiming for a common degree of realistic intensity; ambiguity and irony are discussed as if they were always beauties, never blemishes. Point-of-view should always be used 'consistently,' because otherwise the realistic illusion will be destroyed.

When technical means are related to such simplified ends, it is hardly surprising that they are themselves simplified. Yet we all know that our experience of particular works is more complex than the simple terminology suggests. The prescriptions against 'telling' cannot satisfy any reader who has experienced *Tom Jones, The Egoist, Light in August,* or *Ulysses* (the claim that the author does not address us directly in the last of these is one of the most astonishingly persistent myths in modern criticism). They explicitly contradict our experience of dozens of good novels of the past fifteen years which, like Joyce Cary's posthumous *The Captive and the Free,* have rediscovered for us how lively 'telling' can be. We all know, of course, that 'too much' of the author's voice is, as Aristotle said, unpoetic. But how much is too much? Is there an abstract rule applicable to 'the novel,' quite aside from the needs of particular works or kinds?

Our experience with the great novels tells us that there is not. Most novels, like most plays, cannot be purely dramatic, entirely shown as taking place in the moment. There are always what Dryden called 'relations,' narrative summaries of action that takes place 'off-stage.' And try as we will to ignore the troublesome fact, 'some parts of the action are more fit to be represented, some to be related.' But related by whom? When? At what length? The dramatist must decide, and his decision will be based in large part on the particular needs of the work in hand. The novelist's case is different mainly in that he has more devices to choose from; he may speak with all of the voices available to the dramatist, and he may also choose—some would say he is also tempted by—some forms of telling not easily adapted to the stage.

Unfortunately our terminology for the author's many voices has been inadequate. If we name over three or four of the great narrators—say Cervantes' Cid Hamete Benengeli, Tristram Shandy, the 'author' of *Middlemarch* and Strether in *The Ambassadors* (with his nearly effaced 'author' using his mind as a reflector of events)—we find again that to describe any of them with conventional terms like 'first-person' and 'omniscient' tells us little about how they differ from each other, and consequently it tells us little about why they succeed while others, described in the same terms, fail. Some critics do, indeed, talk about the problem of 'authority,' showing that first-person tales produce difficulties in stories which do not allow any one person to know all that goes on: having made this point, which seems so obvious, they are often then driven to find fault with stories like *Moby Dick*, in which the author allows his narrator to know of events that happen outside his designated sphere of authority.

We can never be sure that enriching our terms will improve our criticism. But we can be quite sure that the terms with which we have long been forced to work cannot help us in discriminating among effects too subtle—as are all actual literary effects—to be caught in such loose-meshed nets. Even at the risk of pedantry, then, it should be worth our while to attempt a richer tabulation of the forms the author's voice can take.

(1) Perhaps the most overworked distinction is that of 'person.' To say that a story is told in the first or the third person, and to group novels into one or the other kind, will tell us nothing of importance unless we become more precise and describe how the particular qualities of the narrators relate to specific desired effects. It is true that choice of the first person is sometimes unduly limiting; if the 'I' has inadequate access to necessary information, the author may be led into improbabilities. But we can hardly expect to find useful criteria in a distinction that would throw all fiction into two, or at most three, heaps. In *this* pile we see *Henry Esmond*, 'A Cask of Amontillado,' *Gulliver's Travels* and *Tristram Shandy*. In *that* we have *Vanity Fair*, *Tom Jones*, *The Ambassadors*, and *Brave New World*. But the commentary in *Vanity Fair* and *Tom Jones* is in the first person, often resembling more the intimate effect of *Tristram Shandy* than that of many third person works. And again, the effect of *The Ambassadors* is much closer to that of the great first-person novels, since Strether in large parts 'narrates' his own story, even though he is always referred to in the third person.

Further evidence that this distinction is ordinarily overemphasised is seen in the fact that all of the following functional distinctions apply to both first and third-person narration alike.

(2) There are *dramatised* narrators and *undramatised* narrators. The former are always and the latter are usually distinct from the implied author who is responsible for their creation.

(a) The Implied Author (the author's 'second self').

Even the novel in which no narrator is dramatised creates an implicit picture of an author who stands behind the scenes, whether as stage-manager, as puppeteer, or as an indifferent God, silently paring his fingernails. This implied author is always distinct from the 'real man'—whatever we may take him to be—who creates a superior version of himself as he creates his work; any successful novel makes us believe in an 'author' who amounts to a kind of 'second self.' This second self is usually a highly refined and selected version, wiser, more sensitive, more perceptive than any real man could be.

In so far as a novel does not refer directly to this author, there will be no distinction between him and the implied, undramatized narrator; for example, in Hemingway's *The Killers* there is no narrator other than the implicit second self that Hemingway creates as he writes.

(b) Undramatised Narrators.

Stories are usually not as rigorously scenic as *The Killers*; most tales are presented as passing through the consciousness of a teller, whether an 'I' or a 'he.' Even in drama much of what we are given is narrated by someone, and we are often as much interested in the effect on the narrator's own mind and heart as we are in learning what *else* the author has to tell us. When Horatio tells of his first encounter with the ghost in *Hamlet*, his own character, though never mentioned explicitly as part of the narrative event, is important to us as we listen. In fiction, as soon as we encounter an 'I' we are conscious of an experiencing mind whose views of the experience will come between us and the event. When there is no such 'I,' as in *The Killers*, the inexperienced reader may make the mistake of thinking that the story comes to him unmediated. But even the most naïve reader must recognise that something mediating and transforming has come into a story from the moment that the author explicitly places a narrator into the tale, even if he is given no personal characteristics whatever.

One of the most frequent reading faults comes from a naïve identification of such narrators with the authors who create them. But in fact there is always a distinction, even though the author himself may not have been aware of it as he wrote. The created author, the 'second self,' is built up in our minds from our experience with all of the elements of the presented story. When one of those elements is an explicit reference to an experiencing narrator, our view of the author is derived in part from our notion of how the presented 'I' relates to what he claims to present. Even when the 'I' or 'he' thus created is ostensibly the author himself—Fielding, Jane Austen, Dickens, Meredith—we can always distinguish between the narrator and the created author who presents him. But though the distinction is always present, it is usually important to criticism only when the narrator is explicitly dramatised.

(c) Dramatised Narrators.

In a sense even the most reticent narrator has been 'dramatised' as soon as he refers to himself as 'I,' or, like Flaubert, tells us that 'we' were in the classroom when Charles Bovary entered. But many novels dramatise their narrators with great fullness. In some works the narrator becomes a major person of great physical, mental and moral vividness (*Tristram Shandy*, *Remembrance of Things Past*, and *Dr. Faustus*); in such works the narrator is often radically different from the implied author who creates him, and whose own character is built up in our minds partly by the way in which the narrator is made to differ from him. The range of

human types that have been dramatised as narrators is almost as great as
the range of other fictional characters—one must say 'almost' because
there are some characters who are unqualified to narrate or reflect a story.

We should remind ourselves that many dramatised narrators are
never explicitly labelled as narrators at all. In a sense, every speech, every
gesture, narrates; most works contain disguised narrators who, like Molière's *raisonneurs*, are used to tell the audience what it needs to know,
while seeming merely to act out their roles. The most important unac-
knowledged narrators are, however, the third-person 'centres of consciousness' through whom authors filter their narrative. Whether such
'reflectors,' as James sometimes called them, are highly-polished, lucid
mirrors reflecting complex mental experience, or the rather turbid, sense-
bound 'camera eyes' of much fiction since James, they fill precisely the
function of avowed narrators.

> 'Gabriel had not gone to the door with the others. He was in a dark
> part of the hall gazing up the staircase. A woman was standing near
> the top of the first flight, in the shadow also. He could not see her
> face but he could see the terracotta and salmon-pink panels of her
> skirt which the shadow made appear black and white. It was his
> wife. She was leaning on the banisters, listening to something.
> Gabriel was surprised at her stillness and strained his ear to listen
> also. But he could hear little save the noise of laughter and dispute
> on the front steps, a few chords struck on the piano and a few notes
> of a man's voice singing ... He asked himself what is a woman
> standing on the stairs in the shadow, listening to distant music, a
> symbol of.'

The very real advantages of this method, for some purposes, have been a
dominant note in modern criticism. Indeed, so long as our attention is on
such qualities as naturalness and vividness, the advantages seem overwhelming. It is only as we break out of the fashionable assumption that
all good fiction seeks these qualities in the same degree that we are forced
to recognise disadvantages. The third-person reflector is only one mode
among many, suitable for some effects but cumbersome and even harmful
when other effects are desired.

(3) Among dramatised narrators, whether first-person or third-person reflectors, there are mere *observers* (The 'I' of *Tom Jones, The Egoist,
Troilus and Criseyde*), and there are *narrator-agents* who produce some
measurable effect on the course of events (ranging from the minor involvement of Nick in *The Great Gatsby* to the central role of Tristram
Shandy, Moll Flanders, Huckleberry Finn, and—in the third-person—
Paul Morel in *Sons and Lovers*). Clearly any rules we might discover
about observers may or may not apply to narrator-agents, yet the distinction is seldom made in talk about point-of-view.

(4) All narrators and observers, whether first or third-person, can relay their tales to us primarily as *Scene* ('The Killers,' *The Awkward Age*), primarily as *summary* or what Lubbuck called 'picture' (Addison's almost completely non-scenic tales in *The Spectator*) or, most commonly, as a combination of the two.

Like Aristotle's distinction between dramatic and narrative manners, the somewhat different modern distinction between telling and showing does cover the ground. But the trouble is that it pays for broad coverage with gross imprecision. Narrators of all shapes and shades must either report dialogue alone or support it with 'stage directions' and description of setting. But when we think of the radically different effect of a scene reported by Huck Finn and a scene reported by Poe's Montresor, we see that the quality of being 'scenic' suggests very little about literary effect. And compare the delightful summary of twelve years given in two pages of *Tom Jones* (III, i), with the tedious showing of even ten minutes of uncurtailed conversation in the hands of a Sartre when he allows his passion for 'durational realism' to dictate a scene when summary is called for. We can only conclude that the contrast between scene and summary, between showing and telling—indeed, between any two dialectical terms that try to cover so much ground—is not prescriptive or normative but loosely descriptive only. And as description, it is likely to tell us very little until we specify the kind of narrator who is providing the scene or the summary.

(5) Narrators who allow themselves to tell as well as show vary greatly depending on the amount and king of *commentary* allowed in addition to a direct relating of events in scene and summary. Such commentary can, of course, range over any aspect of human experience, and it can be related to the main business in innumerable ways and degrees. To treat of it as if it were somehow a single device is to ignore important differences between commentary that is merely ornamental, commentary that serves a rhetorical purpose but is not part of the dramatic structure, and commentary that is integral to the dramatic structure, as in *Tristram Shandy*.

(6) Cutting across the distinction between observers and narrator-agents of all these kinds is the distinction between *self-conscious narrators*, aware of themselves as writers (*Tom Jones, Tristram Shandy, Barchester Towers, The Catcher in the Rye, Remembrance of Things Past, Dr. Faustus*), and narrators or observers who rarely if ever discuss their writing chores (*Huckleberry Finn*) or who seem unaware that they are writing, thinking, speaking, or 'reflecting' a literary work (Camus' *The Stranger*, Lardner's *Haircut*, Bellow's *The Victim*).

(7) Whether or not they are involved in the action as agents, narrators and third-person reflectors differ markedly according to the degree and

kind of *distance* that separates them from the author, the reader, and the other characters of the story they relate or reflect. Such distance is often discussed under terms like 'irony,' or 'tone,' but our experience is in fact much more diverse than such terms are likely to suggest. 'Aesthetic distance' has been especially popular in recent years as a catch-all term for any lack of identification between the reader and the various norms in the work. But surely this useful term should be reserved to describe the degree to which the reader or spectator is asked to forget the artificiality of the work and 'lose himself' in it; whatever makes him aware that he is dealing with an aesthetic object and not real life increases 'aesthetic distance,' in this sense. What I am dealing with is more complex and more difficult to describe, and it includes 'aesthetic distance' as one of its elements.

In any reading experience there is an implied dialogue among author, narrator, the other characters, and the reader. Each of the four can range, in relation to each of the others, from identification to complete opposition, on any axis of value or judgment; moral, intellectual, aesthetic, and even physical (does the reader who stammers react to the stammering of H. C. Earwicker as I do? Surely not). The elements usually discussed under 'aesthetic distance' enter in of course; distance in time and space, differences of social class or conventions of speech or dress—these and many others serve to control our sense that we are dealing with an aesthetic object, just as the paper moons and other unrealistic stage effects of some modern drama have had an 'alienation' effect. But we must not confuse these effects with the equally important effects of personal beliefs and qualities, in author, narrator, reader, and all others in the cast of characters. Though we cannot hope to deal with all of the varieties of control over distance that narrative technique can achieve, we can at least remind ourselves that we deal here with something more than the question of whether the author attempts to maintain or destroy the illusion of reality.

(a) The *narrator* may be more or less distant from the *implied author*. The distance may be moral (Jason vs. Faulkner; the barber vs. Lardner, the narrator vs. Fielding in *Jonathan Wild*). It may be intellectual (Twain and Huck Finn, Sterne and Tristram Shandy in the matter of bigotry about the influence of noses, Richardson and Clarissa). It may be physical or temporal: most authors are distant from even the most knowing narrator in that they presumably know how 'everything turns out in the end'; and so on.

(b) The *narrator* also may be more or less distant from the *characters* in the story he tells. He may differ, for example, morally, intellectually and temporally (the mature narrator and his younger self in *Great Expectations* or *Redburn*), morally and intellectually (Fowler the narrator and Pyle the American in Greene's *The Quiet American*, both departing rad-

ically from the author's norms but in different directions), morally and emotionally (Maupassant's 'The Necklace,' and Huxley's 'Nuns at Luncheon,' in which the narrators affect less emotional involvement than Maupassant and Huxley clearly expect from the reader).

(c) The *narrator* may be more or less distant from the *reader's* own norms, e.g., physically and emotionally (Kafka's *The Metamorphosis*); morally and emotionally (Pinkie in *Brighton Rock*, the miser in Mauriac's *Knot of Vipers*; the many moral degenerates that modern fiction has managed to make into convincing human beings).

One of the standard sources of plot in modern fiction—often advanced in the name of repudiating plot—is the portrayal of narrators whose characteristics change in the course of the works they narrate. Ever since Shakespeare taught the modern world what the Greeks had overlooked in neglecting character change (compare *Macbeth* and *Lear* with *Oedipus*), stories of character development or degeneration have become more and more popular. But it was not until we had discovered the full uses of the third-person reflector that we found how to show a narrator changing *as he narrates*. The mature Pip, in *Great Expectations*, is presented as a generous man whose heart is where the reader's is supposed to be; he watches his young self move away from the reader, as it were, and then back again. But the third-person reflector can be shown, technically in the past tense but in effect present before our eyes, moving toward or away from values that the reader holds dear. The twentieth-century has proceeded almost as if determined to work out all of the permutations and combinations on this effect: start far and end near; start near and end far; start far, move close, but lose the prize and end far; start near, like Pip, move away but see the light and return close; start far and move farther (many modern 'tragedies' are so little tragic because the hero is too distant from us at the beginning for us to care that he is, like Macbeth, even further at the end); start near and end nearer . . . I can think of no theoretical possibilities that haven't been tried; anyone who has read widely in modern fiction can fill in examples.

(d) The *implied author* may be more or less distant from the *reader*. The distance may be intellectual (the implied author of *Tristram Shandy*, not of course to be identified with Tristram, is more interested in and knows more about recondite classical lore than any of his readers), moral (the works of Sade), and so on. From the author's viewpoint, a successful reading of his book will reduce to zero the distance between the essential norms of his implied author and the norms of the postulated reader. Often enough there is very little distance to begin with; Jane Austen does not have to convince us that pride and prejudice are undesirable. A bad book, on the other hand, is often a book whose implied author clearly asks that we judge according to norms we cannot accept.

(e) The *implied author* (and reader) may be more or less distant from *other characters*, ranging from Jane Austen's complete approval of Jane Fairfax in *Emma* to her contempt for Wickham in *Pride and Prejudice*. The complexity that marks our pleasure in all significant literature can be seen by contrasting the kinds of distance in these two situations. In *Emma*, the *narrator* is non-committal toward Jane Fairfax, though there is no sign of disapproval. The *author* can be inferred as approving of her almost completely. But the chief *reflector, Emma*, who has the largest share of the job of narration, is definitely disapproving of Jane Fairfax for most of the way. In *Pride and Prejudice*, on the other hand, the narrator is non-committal toward Wickham for as long as possible, hoping to mystify us; the author is secretly disapproving; and the chief reflector, Elizabeth, is definitely approving for the first half of the book.

It is obvious that on each of these scales my examples do not begin to cover the possibilities. What we call 'involvement' or 'sympathy' or 'identification,' is usually made up of many reactions to author, narrators, observers, and other characters. And narrators may differ from their authors or readers in various kinds of involvement or detachment, ranging from deep personal concern (Nick in *The Great Gatsby*, MacKellar in *The Master of Ballantrae*, Zeitblom in *Dr. Faustus*) to a bland or mildly amused or merely curious detachment (Waugh's *Decline and Fall*).

In talk about point-of-view in fiction, the most seriously neglected of these kinds of distance is that between the fallible or unreliable narrator and the implied author who carries the reader with him as against the narrator. If the reason for discussing point-of-view is to find how it related to literary effects, then surely the moral and intellectual qualities of the narrator are more important to our judgment than whether he is referred to as 'I' or 'he,' or whether he is privileged or limited, and so on. If he is discovered to be untrustworthy, then the total effect of the work he relays to us is transformed.

Our terminology for this kind of distance in narrators is almost hopelessly inadequate. For lack of better terms, I shall call a narrator *reliable* when he speaks for or acts in accordance with the norms of the work (which is to say, the implied author's norms), *unreliable* when he does not. It is true that most of the great reliable narrators indulge in large amounts of incidental irony, and they are thus 'unreliable' in the sense of being potentially deceptive. But difficult irony is not sufficient to make a narrator unreliable. We should reserve the term unreliable for those narrators who are presented as if they spoke *throughout* for the norms of the book and who do not in fact do so. Unreliability is not ordinarily a matter of lying, although deliberately deceptive narrators have been a major resource of some modern novelists (Camus' *The Fall*, Calder Willingham's

Natural Child, etc.). It is most often a matter of what James calls *inconscience;* the narrator is mistaken, or he pretends to qualities which the author denies him. Or, as in *Huckleberry Finn,* the narrator claims to be naturally wicked while the author silently praises his virtues, as it were, behind his back.

Unreliable narrators thus differ markedly depending on how far and in what direction they depart from their author's norms: the older term 'tone,' like the currently fashionable 'distance,' covers many effects that we should distinguish. Some narrators, like Barry Lyndon, are placed as far 'away' from author and reader as possible, in respect to every virtue except a kind of interesting vitality. Some, like Fleda Vetch, the reflector in James's *The Spoils of Poynton,* come close to representing the author's ideal of taste, judgment, and moral sense. All of them make stronger demands on the reader's powers of inference than does reliable narration.

(8) Both reliable and unreliable narrators can be *isolated,* unsupported or uncorrected by other narrators (Gully Jimson in *The Horse's Mouth,* Henderson in Bellow's *Henderson the Rain King*) or supported or corrected (*The Sound and the Fury*). Sometimes it is almost impossible to infer whether or to what degree a narrator is fallible; sometimes explicit corroborating or conflicting testimony makes the inference easy. Support or correction differs radically, it should be noted, depending on whether it is provided from within the action, so that the narrator-agent might benefit (Faulkner's *Intruder in the Dust*) or is simply provided externally, to help the reader correct or reinforce his own views *as against the narrator's* (Graham Green's *The Power and the Glory*). Obviously the effects of isolation will be radically different in the two cases.

(9) Observers and narrator-agents, whether self-conscious or not, reliable or not, commenting or silent, isolated or supported, can be either *privileged* to know what could not be learned by strictly natural means or *limited* to realistic vision and inference. Complete privilege is what we usually call omniscience. But there are many kinds of privilege and very few 'omniscient' narrators are allowed to know or show as much as their authors know.

We need a good study of the varieties of limitation and their function. Some limitations are only temporary, or even playful, like the ignorance Fielding sometimes imposes on his 'I' (as when he doubts his own powers of narration and invokes the Muses for aid, e.g. *Tom Jones* XIII, i). Some are more nearly permanent but subject to momentary relaxation, like the generally limited, humanly realistic Ishmael in *Moby Dick,* who can yet break through his human limitations when the story requires (' "He waxes brave, but nevertheless obeys; most careful bravery that!" murmured Ahab'—with no one present to report to the narrator.) And some are confined to what their literal condition would allow them to know (first person, Huck Finn; third person, Miranda and Laura in Katherine Anne Porter's stories).

The most important single privilege is that of obtaining an inside view, because of the rhetorical power that such a privilege conveys upon a narrator. A curious ambiguity in our notions of 'omniscience' is ordinarily hidden by our terminology. Many modern works that we usually classify as narrated dramatically, with everything relayed to us through the limited views of the characters, postulate fully as much omniscience in the silent author as Fielding claims for himself. Our roving visitation into the minds of sixteen characters in Faulkner's *As I Lay Dying*, seeing nothing but what those minds contain, may seem in one sense not to depend on an omniscient narrator. But this method is omniscience with teeth in it: the implied author demands our absolute faith in his powers of divination. We must never for a moment doubt that he knows everything about each of these sixteen minds, or that he has chosen correctly how much to show of each. In short the choice of the most rigorously limited point-of-view is really no escape from omniscience—the true narrator is as "unnaturally' all-knowing as he ever was. If evident artificiality were a fault—which it is not—modern narration would be as faulty as Trollope's.

Another way of suggesting the same ambiguity is to look closely at the concept of 'dramatic' story-telling. The author can present his characters in a dramatic situation without in the least presenting them in what we normally think of as a dramatic manner. When Joseph Andrews, who has been stripped and beaten by thieves, is overtaken by a stagecoach. Fielding presents the scene in what by some modern standards must seem an inconsistent and undramatic mode. 'The poor wretch, who lay motionless a long time, just began to recover his senses as a stagecoach cambe by. The postilion hearing a man's groans, stopped his horses, and told the coachman he was certain there was a dead man lying in the ditch ... A lady, who heard what the postilion said, and likewise heard the groan, called eagerly to the coachman to stop and see what was the matter. Upon which he bid the postilion alight, and look into the ditch. He did so, and returned, "That there was a man sitting upright, as naked as ever he was born." ' There follows a splendid description, hardly meriting the name of *scene*, in which the selfish reactions of each passenger are recorded. A young lawyer points out that they might be legally liable if they refuse to take Joseph up. 'These words had a sensible effect on the coachman, who was well acquainted with the person who spoke them; and the old gentleman above mentioned, thinking the naked man would afford him frequent opportunities of showing his wit to the lady, offered to join with the company in giving a mug of beer for his fare; till partly alarmed by the threats of the one, and partly by the promises of the other, and being perhaps a little moved with compassion at the poor creature's condition, who stood bleeding and shivering with the cold, he at length agreed.' Once Joseph is in the coach, the same kind of indirect reporting of the 'scene' continues, with frequent excursions, however superficial, into the minds and hearts of the assembly of fools and knaves, and occasional guesses when complete knowledge seems inadvisable. If to be dramatic is to show characters dramatically engaged with each other, motive clashing with motive, the outcome depending upon the resolution of motives, then this scene is dramatic. But if it is to give the impression that the story is taking place by itself, with the characters existing in a dramatic relationship vis-a-vis the spectator, unmediated by a narrator and decipherable only through inferential matching of word to word and word to deed, then this is a relatively undramatic scene.

On the other hand, an author can present a character in this latter kind of dramatic relationship with the reader without involving that character in any internal drama at all. Many lyric poems are dramatic in this sense and totally undramatic in any other. 'That is no country for old men—' Who says? Yeats, or his 'mask,' says. To whom? To us. How do we know that it is Yeats and not some character as remote from him as Caliban is remote from Browning in "Caliban upon Setebos'? We infer it as the dramatised statement unfolds; the need for the inference is what makes the lyric *dramatic* in this sense. Caliban, in short, is dramatic in two senses; he is in a dramatic situation with other characters and he is in a dramatic situation over-against us. Yeats, or if we prefer 'Yeats' mask,' is dramatic in only one sense.

The ambiguities of the word dramatic are even more complicated in fiction that attempts to dramatise states of consciousness directly. Is *A Portrait of the Artist as a Young Man* dramatic? In some respects, yes. We are not told about Stephen. He is placed on the stage before us, acting out his destiny with only disguised helps or comments from his author. But it is not his actions that are dramatised directly, not his speech that we hear unmediated. What is dramatised is his mental record of everything that happens. We see his consciousness at work on the world. Sometimes what it records is itself dramatic, as when Stephen observes himself in a scene with other characters. But the report itself, the internal record, is dramatic in the second sense only. The report we are given of what goes on in Stephen's mind is a monologue uninvolved in any modifying dramatic context. And it is an *infallible* report, even less subject to critical doubts than the typical Elizabethan soliloquy. We accept, by convention, the claim that what is reported as going on in Stephen's mind really goes on there, or in other words, that Joyce knows how Stephen's mind works. 'The equation of the page of his scribbler began to spread out a widening tail, eyed and starred like a peacock's; and, when the eyes and stars of its indices had been eliminated, began slowly to fold itself together again. The indices appearing and disappearing were eyes opening and closing; the eyes opening and closing were stars ... ' Who says so? Not Stephen, but the omniscient, infallible author. The report is direct, and it is clearly unmodified by any 'dramatic' context—that is, unlike a speech in a dramatic scene, we do not suspect that the report has here been in any way aimed at an effect on anyone but the reader. We are thus in a dramatic relation with Stephen only in a limited sense—the sense in which a lyrical poem is dramatic.

Indeed if we compare the act of reporting in *Tom Jones* with the act of reporting in *Portrait*, the former is in one sense considerably more dramatic; Fielding dramatises himself and his telling, and even though he is essentially reliable we must be constantly on our toes in comparing word to word and word to deed. 'It is an observation sometimes made, that to indicate our idea of a simple fellow, we say, he is easily to be seen through: nor do I believe it a more improper denotation of simple book. Instead of applying this to any particular performance, we choose rather to remark the contrary in this history, where the scene opens itself by small degrees; and he is a sagacious reader who can see two chapters before him.' Our running battle to keep up with these incidental ironies in Fielding's narration is matched, in *Portrait*, with an act of absolute, unquestioning credulity.

We should note finally that the author who eschews both forms of artificiality, both the traditional omniscience and the modern manipulation of inside views, confining himself to 'objective' surfaces only, is not necessarily identical with the 'undramatised author' under (2) above. In *The Awkward Age*, for example, James allows himself to comment frequently, but only to conjecture about the meaning of surfaces; the author is dramatised, but dramatised as partially ignorant of what is happening.

(10) Finally, narrators who provide inside views differ in the depth and the axis of their plunge. Boccaccio can give inside views, but they are extremely shallow. Jane Austen goes relatively deep morally, but scarcely skims the surface psychologically. All authors of stream-of-consciousness narration attempt to go deep psychologically, but some of them deliberately remain shallow in the moral dimension. We should remind ourselves that any sustained inside view, of whatever depth, temporarily turns the character whose mind is shown into a narrator; inside views are thus subject to variations in all of the qualities we have described above, and most importantly in the degree of unreliability. Generally speaking, the deeper our plunge, the more unreliability we will accept without loss of sympathy. The whole question of how inside views and moral sympathy interrelate has been seriously neglected.

Narration is an art, not a science, but this does not mean that we are necessarily doomed to fail when we attempt to formulate principles about it. There are systematic elements in every art, and criticism of fiction can never avoid the responsibility of trying to explain technical successes and failures by reference to general principles. But the question is that of where the general principles are to be found. Fiction, the novel, point-of-view—these terms are not in fact subject to the kind of definition that alone makes critical generalisations and rules meaningful. A given technique cannot be judged according to its service to 'the novel,' or 'fiction,' but only according to its success in particular works or kinds of work.

It is not surprising to hear practising novelists report that they have never had help from critics about point-of-view. In dealing with point-of-view the novelist must always deal with the individual work: which particular character shall tell this particular story, or part of a story, with what precise degree of reliability, privilege, freedom to comment, and so on. Shall he be given dramatic vividness? Even if the novelist has decided on a narrator who will fit one of the critic's classifications—'omniscient,' 'first-person,' 'limited omniscient,' 'objective,' 'roving,' 'effaced,' and so on—his troubles have just begun. He simply cannot find answers to his immediate, precise, practical problems by referring to statements that the 'omniscient is the most flexible method,' or 'the objective the most rapid or vivid,' or whatever. Even the soundest of generalisations at this level will be of little use to him in his page-by-page progress through his novel. As Henry James's detailed records show, the novelist discovers his narrative technique as he tries to achieve for his readers the potentialities of his developing idea. The majority of his choices are consequently choices of degree, not kind. To decide that your narrator shall not be omniscient decides practically nothing. The hard question is, just hos *inconscient* shall he be? To decide that you will use first-person narration decides again almost nothing. What kind of first-person? How fully characterised? How much aware of himself as a narrator? How reliable? How much confined to realistic inference, how far privileged to go beyond realism? At what points shall he speak truth and at what points utter no judgment or even utter falsehood?[1]

There are no doubt *kinds* of effect to which the author can refer— e.g., if he wants to make a scene more amusing, poignant, vivid, or ambiguous, or if he wants to make a character more sympathetic or more convincing, such-and-such practices may be indicated. But it is not surprising that in his search for help in his decisions, he should find the practice of his peers more helpful than the abstract rules of the textbooks: the sensitive author who reads the great novels finds in them a storehouse of precise examples, examples of how *this* effect, as distinct from all other possible effects, was heightened by the proper narrative choice. In dealing

with the tyes of narration, the critic must always limp behind, referring
constantly to the varied practice which alone can correct his temptations
to overgeneralise.

NOTE

1. I try to deal with some of these questions in *The Rhetoric of Fiction*. This
   article is an expanded version of one chapter from that book.

Mixail Baxtin

Discourse Typology in Prose[*]

A set of certain verbal devices used in literary art has recently attracted the special attention of investigators. This set comprises stylization, parody, *skaz* (in its strict sense, the oral narration of a narrator), and dialogue.

Despite the fundamental differences among them, all these devices have one feature in common: in all of them discourse maintains a double focus, aimed at the referential object of speech, as in ordinary discourse, and simultaneously at a second context of discourse, a second speech act by another addresser. If we remain ignorant of this second context, if we accept stylization or parody as we accept ordinary speech with its single focus on its referential object, then we shall fail to grasp these devices for what they really are; we shall take stylization for straight style and read parody as poor writing.

Skaz and dialogue, restricted to the single "reply" of one participant, are the less obvious cases of this double orientation. *Skaz* may indeed have sometimes only one focus—a focus on its own referential object. Likewise, a single line of dialogue may well refer directly to the object without any mediation. In the majority of cases, however, both are oriented toward another speech act, one which *skaz* stylizes and which the line of dialogue reflects upon, or replies to, or anticipates.

Stylization, parody, *skaz*, and dialogue are phenomena of the most fundamental importance; they call for a thoroughly new approach to the analysis of discourse—an approach unamenable to the usual framework of stylistic and lexicological study. The fact is that the usual approach treats word-usage within the bounds of a single monologic context, defining each lexical item in relation to its referential object (the study of tropes) or in relation to the other words of the same context, of the same speech act (stylistics, in the narrow sense). It is true that lexicology does know a somewhat different approach to word usage. The lexical tint of a

[*] "Tipy prozaičeskogo slova," in *Problemy tvorčestva Dostoevskogo* (Leningrad, 1929), pp. 105–135. Translated by Richard Balthazar and I. R. Titunik.

word, for instance, an archaism or a provincialism, points to some other context, in which it normally functions (as in ancient literary monuments, or regional speech). In such a case, however, we are dealing with a language system, not a concrete context of speech; the words in question are not utterances from another speech act, but are impersonal language material not implemented in any concrete utterance. If, however, the lexical tint is individualized, even slightly, if it points to some speech act from which it was borrowed or after which it was patterned, then we are already dealing with stylization, or parody, or some analogous phenomenon. Thus lexicology also remains restricted to a single monologic context, recognizing only the direct, unmediated relationship between word and referent, without consideration of any other speech act, any second context.

The very fact that instances do exist of doubly oriented discourse in which a relationship with another speech act is the essential factor makes it incumbent upon us to furnish a complete and thorough-going classification of types of word usage in accordance with the new principle we have suggested, a principle that neither stylistics, nor lexicology, nor semantics has taken into account. There is no trouble in seeing that, besides a word usage carrying out direct referential aims and a word usage focusing on another speech act, there yet must be a third type. But even within this third type of doubly oriented word usage (in which another speech act is a factor), differentiation is necessary, since it embraces such disparate phenomena as stylization, parody, and dialogue. The fundamental variants of these phenomena have to be brought to light from the vantage point of this same new principle. Inevitably there will arise the question as to whether, and how, heterogeneous types of word-usage may be combined within a single context. On these grounds, a whole set of new stylistic problems arises, problems which until now stylistics has failed to take into account. As concerns style in prose, it is precisely these problems that have a paramount significance.[1]

On the one hand, we observe discourse of a direct, unmediated, intentional nature, which names, or communicates, or expresses something, and which involves a comprehension of the same nature (the first type of word usage); and on the other hand, discourse which is represented or objectified (the second type). The most typical and extensive variety of represented or objectified word usage is the direct speech of characters. Such speech has its own immediate referential object, yet it does not occupy a position on the same plane with the direct speech of the author; instead, it stands at a certain remove from the author's speech, as if in perspective. It is meant not only to be understood in terms of its own referential object, but, by virtue of its character-defining capacity, or its typicality, or its colorfulness, it also appears as the object of another (the author's) intention.

Whenever we have the direct speech of a single character within the context of the author's speech, we confront, within that one context, two speech centers and two speech complexes: the complex of the author's message, and the complex of the character's message. The second complex, however, is not independent of the first; it is subordinated to it and figures as one of its components. The stylistic handling of each of the two messages is different. The character's utterance is handled precisely as the words of another addresser—as words belonging to a personage of a certain specific individuality or type, that is, it is handled as an object of the author's intentions, and not at all in terms of its own proper referential aim. The author's speech, on the contrary, is handled stylistically as speech aimed at its direct referential denotation: it must be adequate to its object (of whatever nature, discursive, poetic, or other); it must be expressive, forceful, pithy, elegant, and so on, from the point of view of its direct referential mission—to denote, express, convey or depict something; and its stylistic treatment is concurrently oriented toward the comprehension of the referent. However, should the author's speech be so treated as to display the individual or typical features of a particular person, or of a particular social status, or of a particular literary manner, then what we are dealing with is already stylization, either the usual kind of literary stylization or that of a stylized *skaz*. Such an instance belongs to the third type of discourse. We shall come to this type later.

Discourse that is directly intentional in nature knows only itself and its referential object, and it aims to be maximally adequate to the latter. If in the course of carrying out its mission it shows that it has imitated or learned something from someone, that does not in the least change things—all that is merely the scaffolding, which the builder could hardly do without but which does not become part of the architectural structure. The fact of imitation itself and the evidence of all sorts of influences (easily detectible by the literary historian or by any competent reader) do not enter into the mission the discourse carries out. If this were the case—if the discourse itself clearly marked its reference to another speech act— then once again we would be dealing with discourse of the third (not the first) type.

The stylistic handling of objectified discourse—the discourse of the characters—is subsumed under and becomes part of the stylistic missions of the author's context, which bears the ultimate, the highest, authority. This fact gives rise to a number of stylistic problems having to do with the introduction and the organic incorporation of the directly reported speech of the character into the author's context. The ultimate conceptual authority and consequently the ultimate stylistic authority are lodged in the author's direct speech.

The ultimate conceptual authority, which calls directly for a concurring comprehension of the referent, occurs as a matter of course in any literary work, but it is not always presented in the author's direct speech. The author's direct speech may be altogether absent—the speech of a narrator functioning as its compositional replacement, or, if the instance is a play, without any compositional equivalent in the work. In all these cases, the entire verbal material of the work belongs to either the second or third type of discourse. A play is almost always made up of represented, objectified utterances. But in certain stories, for instance, Puškin's *Tales of Belkin*, the narrative (Belkin's words) is made up of utterances of the third type; the utterances of the other characters belong to the second type. The absence of discourse carrying out the direct auctorial intent is a common phenomenon. The ultimate conceptual authority (the author's intention) is brought out, not in the author's direct speech, but by manipulating the utterances of another addresser, utterances intentionally created and deployed as belonging to someone other than the author.

The degree to which the represented utterance of a character is objectified may vary considerably. One need only point to the contrast between, say, the words of Tolstoj's Prince Andrej and those of any of Gogol's characters, Akakij Akakijevič, for instance. As the force of direct referential intentionality in a character's words increases and as, correspondingly, objectification decreases, the relationship between the author's speech and that of the character begins to approach the relationship between the two sides in a dialogue. The perspective between them diminishes, and they may come to occupy the same plane. However, this may be postulated only as a tendency toward an extreme never actually reached.

We have an instance of a dialogic relationship among directly intentional utterances within a single context in the typical scholarly article in which statements by various writers are cited, some for the purpose of refutation, others for the purpose of corroboration or supplementation. These binary relations (agreement vs. disagreement, assertion vs. supplementation, question vs. answer) are purely dialogic in nature. Moreover, these relations are not, of course, between separate words, or sentences, or other segments of a statement, but between whole statements. In dramatic dialogue, or in dramatized dialogue presented within the author's context, these relations coordinate represented, objectified utterances, and therefore they are themselves objectified. What occurs here is not the confrontation of two ultimate conceptual authorities but the objectified (plotted) confrontation of two represented positions—a confrontation wholly subordinated to the supreme, ultimate authority of the author. In this situation, the monologic context does not weaken or disintegrate.

The weakening or destruction of a monologic context comes about only when two directly intentional statements converge. Two directly intentional utterances of equal rank within a single context cannot occur together without interacting as a dialogue; it makes no difference in what specific way (by corroborating, or mutually supplementing each other, or by engaging in some other dialogic form of relationship, as, for instance, the question-answer form of colloquy). Two statements of equal weight on the same subject, once they come together, cannot line up in a row like two objects—they must make an inner contact, that is, they must enter into a conceptual bond.

The unmediated, intentional utterance is focused on its referential object, and it constitutes the ultimate conceptual authority within the given context. The objectified utterance is likewise focused only on its referential object, but at the same time it is itself the object of another, the author's, intention. Still, this other intention does not penetrate the objectified utterance; it takes that utterance as a whole and, without altering its meaning or tone, subordinates it to its own purposes. It does not impose upon the objectified utterance a different referential meaning. An utterance which becomes objectified does so, as it were, without knowing it, like a man who goes about his business unaware that he is being watched. An objectified utterance sounds just as if it were a direct, intentional utterance. Utterances both of the first and the second type of discourse have each one intention, each one voice: they are single-voiced utterances.

Yet an author may utilize the speech act of another in pursuit of his own aims and in such a way as to impose a new intention on the utterance, which nevertheless retains its own proper referential intention. Under these circumstances and in keeping with the author's purpose, such an utterance must be recognized as originating from another addresser. Thus, within a single utterance there may occur two intentions, two voices. Such is the nature of parody, stylization, and stylized *skaz*. We now come to a characterization of the third type of discourse.

Stylization presupposes style; it presupposes that the set of stylistic devices it reproduces had at one time a direct and immediate intentionality and expressed the ultimate conceptual authority. Only discourse of the first type can be the object of stylization. Stylization forces another intention (an artistic-thematic intention) to serve its aims, its own new intentions. The stylizer makes use of another speech act as such and in that way casts a somewhat objectified tint over it. In fact, however, that speech act does not become an objectified utterance. After all, what is uppermost for the stylizer is another person's set of devices precisely as the expression of a special point of view. He operates with this other point of view. Therefore, a certain tint of objectification does fall on that point of view, on that other intention, and, as a consequence, it becomes conventional. The objectified speech of a character is never conventional. A character's speech is always seriously spoken. The author's intention does not penetrate the character's speech but observes it from without.

A conventionalized utterance is always a double-voiced utterance. Only what was once perfectly serious and nonrelative to another point of view can become conventional. What was once a straightforward and nonconventional value now serves new aims, aims which take possession of it from inside and render it conventional. That is what distinguishes stylization from imitation. Imitation does not make a form conventional, owing to the simple fact that it takes the object of imitation seriously, makes it its own, directly appropriates the other speech act, and assimilates it to itself. The voices in this case merge completely. If we hear another voice, then we hear something which did not figure in the imitator's plan.

Though a sharp conceptual dividing line separates stylization and imitation, as has just been established, historically a set of extremely subtle and sometimes subliminal transitions does exist between them. The weaker the original seriousness of a style becomes in the hands of its epigone-imitators, the more nearly its devices become conventionalized—imitation thus becoming semi-stylization. Stylization in turn may become imitation, should the stylizer's fascination with his model destroy the distance between them and undermine the deliberate marking of the reproduced style as the style belonging to another writer. What, after all, creates conventionality is, in fact, distance.

A narrator's narration, which compositionally replaces the author's discourse, is analogous to stylization. Such narration may take the form of the standard written language (Puškin's Belkin or Dostoevskij's narrator-chroniclers) or the form of oral speech (*skaz*, in the direct sense of the word). Here, too, the verbal manner of another addresser is utilized by the author as a point of view, a position, essential to the way the author wants to conduct the story. But here the tint of objectification in the narrator's speech is much heavier, and the conventionality much weaker, than in stylization. Needless to say, the degrees involved vary substantially. Still, the narrator's discourse can never become purely objectified discourse, even when he himself is one of the cast of characters and assumes only a part of the narration. After all, his importance to the author is not only a matter of his individual or typical manner of thinking, experiencing, and speaking, but is above all a matter of his seeing and depicting, for it is in this area that his direct designation as a narrator replacing the author consists. Thus the author's intentions, just as in stylization, penetrate the narrator's utterances, making them to a greater or lesser degree conventional. The author does not exhibit the narrator's speech to us (as he does exhibit the objectified utterances of the characters) but manipulates it from within for his own purposes, forcing us to be keenly aware of the distance between himself and this other speech act.

The element of *skaz* in the direct sense (an orientation toward oral speech) is a factor necessarily inherent in any storytelling. Even if the narrator is represented as writing his story and giving a certain literary polish to it, all the same he is not a literary professional; what he commands is not a specific style but only a socially or individually defined manner of storytelling, a manner that gravitates toward oral *skaz*. If, on the other hand, he does command a certain specific literary style, a style which the author reproduces in the narrator's name, then we are dealing with stylization, not with narrator's narration—there are, indeed, various ways of introducing and motivating stylization.

Both narrator's narration and even pure *skaz* may drop all their conventionality and become the author's direct speech expressing his intentions without any mediation. Such is almost always the nature of Turgenev's *skaz:* when Turgenev introduces his narrator, he does not in most instances stylize a distinct individual and social manner of storytelling. For instance, in "Andrej Kolosov," the story is told by the intelligent and cultured kind of man of Turgenev's own circle. He himself would have spoken thus about matters of the greatest seriousness in his own life. There is no effort here that is directed toward creating a socially different "*skaz*ified" tone or a socially different manner of observing and reporting observations; nor is there any effort to create an individually characteristic manner. Turgenev's *skaz* is unequivocally referential and contains only one voice, directly expressing the author's intentions. Here *skaz* is a simple compositional device. The nature of the *skaz* in the narration of *First Love* is identical (there presented by the narrator in written form).[2]

It is impossible to say the same thing about Belkin as a narrator. He is important to Puškin as a different, separate voice, above all, as a socially distinct person with a spiritual diapason and an approach to the world appropriate to him, and next in order of importance, he is a figure of certain individual characteristics. Consequently, the author's intentions in this case are refracted in the speech of the narrator; discourse here is double-voiced.

The problem of *skaz* was brought forward for the first time by B. M. Ejxenbaum.[3] He saw *skaz* exclusively as oriented toward the oral form of narration, orientation toward oral speech and its concomitant linguistic features (the special intonation, the syntactic arrangement, the lexicon, etc., of oral speech). He completely failed to consider the fact that in the majority of cases *skaz* consists above all in an orientation toward another speech act, and only in turn, and as a consequence, toward oral speech.

Our conception of *skaz* seems to us far more to the point in treating the problem in its literary historical dimensions. We believe that in the majority of cases *skaz* is brought in precisely for the sake of a different voice, one which is socially distinct and carries with it a set of viewpoints and evaluations which are just what the author needs. In point of fact, it is a storyteller who is brought in, and a storyteller is not a literary man; he usually belongs to the lower social strata, to the common people (precisely the quality the author values in him), and he brings with him oral speech.

Direct auctorial discourse is not possible in every literary period; not every period commands a style, since style presupposes the presence of authoritative points of view and authoritative, durable, social evaluations. Such styleless periods either go the way of stylization or revert to extraliterary forms of narration which command a particular manner of observing and depicting the world. When there is no adequate form for an unmediated expression of an author's intentions, it becomes necessary to refract them through another's speech. Moreover, the tasks facing literature are sometimes such that there is no other way open to implement them than by means of double-voiced discourse. That was exactly the case with Dostoevskij.

We believe that Leskov resorted to a narrator primarily for the sake of socially different speech and world outlook, and only secondarily for the sake of the oral quality in *skaz* (since he was interested in folk speech). Conversely, Turgenev looked to a narrator precisely for the sake of an oral form of narration which would directly express his own intentions. An orientation toward oral speech, not toward another speech act, was indeed characteristic of him. Turgenev could not refract his intentions through another speech act, nor did he like to do so. He managed very poorly with double-voiced discourse (for instance, in the satiric and parodic passages in *Smoke*). For this reason he chose a narrator from his own social circle. Since a narrator inevitably had to speak in the literary language, he could not sustain the oral quality of the narration throughout; for Turgenev it was important only to enliven his literary speech with oral intonations. In contrast, the attraction to *skaz* in contemporary literature is, as we see it, an attraction to another speech act. Direct auctorial speech is at present undergoing a socially conditioned crisis.

This is not the place to go into the proofs of all our assertions concerning literary history. Let them remain simply suppositions. One thing, however, we must insist on: that the strict distinction within *skaz* of an orientation toward another speech act and an orientation toward oral speech is absolutely essential. To see in *skaz* only oral speech is to miss the main point. Moreover, a large number of intonational, syntactic, and other linguistic phenomena are to be explained in *skaz* (given the author's orientation toward another speech act) precisely by its double-voiced quality, the intersecting of two voices and two accents within it. There are no similar phenomena in Turgenev, for instance, though his narrators show a much stronger tendency to oral speech than do those of Dostoev-skij.

Ich-Erzählung is analogous to narrator's narration: sometimes it is marked by orientation toward another speech act, and sometimes (as in Turgenev's narration) it will approach and finally merge with the author's direct speech, that is, operate with the single-voiced discourse of the first type.

One must keep in mind that compositional forms do not of themselves decide the question of what type of discourse will be used. Such descriptive terms as *Ich-Erzählung*, "narrator's narration," "author's narration," and so on, are purely compositional terms. These compositional types of narration do gravitate, it is true, toward specific types of discourse, but they are not in obligatory bond with them.

All the instances of the third type of discourse thus far investigated—stylization, narrator's narration, and *Ich-Erzählung*—have a common feature sufficient to class them as a special (first) variety of that type. The common feature is that the author manipulates another speech act in the direction of his own intentions. Stylization stylizes another style in the direction of its own projects. All it does is make those projects conventional. Similarly, the narrator's narration, through which the author's intentions are refracted, does not deviate from its straight path but is sustained in the tones and intonations which really do belong to it. The author's intention, having penetrated the other speech act and having become embedded in it, does not clash with another intention; it follows that intention in the latter's own direction, only making that direction conventional.

The case is different with parody. Here, too, as in stylization, the author employs the speech of another, but, in contradistinction to stylization, he introduces into that other speech an intention which is directly opposed to the original one. The second voice, having lodged in the other speech, clashes antagonistically with the original, host voice and forces it to serve directly opposite aims. Speech becomes a battlefield for opposing intentions. Thus the merger of voices which is possible in stylization or in a narrator's narration (in Turgenev, for instance) is not possible in parody; the voices in parody are not only distinct and set off from one another but are also antagonistically opposed. That is why the other speech act in parody must be so very clearly and sharply marked and why the author's intentions must be individualized to a higher degree and given the fullest substance. It is possible to parody another style from different angles and to bring to bear in it a wide variety of new accents, whereas it can be stylized only, by and large, in one direction—in accordance with the task proper to stylization.

Parody allows considerable variety: one can parody another's style as a style, or parody another's socially typical or individually characteristic manner of observing, thinking, and speaking. Furthermore, the depth of parody may vary: one can limit parody to the forms that make up the verbal surface, but one can also parody even the deepest principles of the other speech act. Moreover, the parodic speech act itself may be variously utilized by the author: parody may be a goal in itself (for example, literary parody as a genre), or it may serve to achieve other, positive goals (as Ariosto's parodic style, or Puškin's). But in all the varieties of parodic discourse possible the relationship between the author's intention and that of the other speech remains the same: the two intentions are at odds, are vari-directional, as against the uni-directional orientation of intentions in stylization, narrator's narration, and analogous forms.

Thus the difference between simple *skaz* and parodic *skaz* is a very fundamental one. The struggle between two intentions in parodic *skaz* gives rise to the extremely distinctive linguistic phenomena mentioned above. If we ignore the orientation toward another speech act in *skaz* and, consequently, its double-voiced nature, we preclude any understanding of those complex relationships into which the voices within *skaz* discourse can enter when their orientation becomes vari-directional. *Skaz* in contemporary literature for the most part has parodic coloring. Zoščenko's *skaz*, for instance, is parodic *skaz*. In Dostoevskij's stories parodic elements of a special type are always present.

Parodic word usage is analogous to an ironic or any other ambivalent use of another addresser's words, since in these cases, too, the other person's words are utilized to convey antagonistic intentions. In our everyday speech such a use of another person's words is extremely common, particularly in dialogue. There one speaker very often repeats literally an assertion made by another speaker, investing it with a new intention and enunciating it in his own way: with an expression of doubt, indignation, irony, mockery, derision, or the like.

Leo Spitzer, in his book on the special features of conversational Italian, makes the following remark:

> When we reproduce in our own speech a portion of what our conversational partner said, a change of tone inevitably occurs if for no other reason than that the addressers have been shifted around: the words of the "other" in our mouths always sound like something foreign, very often with a mocking, exaggerated, or derisive intonation. ... In this connection I should like to make a special point of the funny or sharply ironic repetition of the verb of our partner's question in our subsequent reply. In such a situation it may be seen that we often resort, not only to grammatically incorrect, but even to very daring, sometimes completely impossible constructions for the sole purpose of somehow repeating a part of our partner's speech and giving it an ironic twist.[4]

Someone else's words introduced into our speech inevitably assume a new (our own) intention, that is, they become double-voiced. It is only the relationship between these two voices that may vary. Even the transmission of another's assertion in the form of a question leads to a clash of the two intentions in one utterance: we not only question his assertion, we make a problem out of it. Our everyday speech is full of other people's words: with some of them our voice is completely merged, and we forget whose words they were; we use others that have authority, in our view, to substantiate our own words; and in yet others we implant our different, even antagonistic intentions.

Let us proceed to the final variety of the third type of discourse. In both of the preceding varieties, exemplified by stylization and parody, respectively, the author utilizes what are distinctly another person's words for the expression of his own particular intentions. In the third variety, the other speech act remains outside the bounds of the author's speech, but is implied or alluded to in that speech. The other speech act is not reproduced with a new intention, but shapes the author's speech while remaining outside its boundaries. Such is the nature of discourse in hidden polemic and equally, as a rule, in a single line of dialogue.

In hidden polemic the author's discourse is oriented toward its referential object, as is any other discourse, but at the same time each assertion about that object is constructed in such a way that, besides its referential meaning, the author's discourse brings a polemical attack to bear against another speech act, another assertion, on the same topic. Here one utterance focused on its referential object clashes with another utterance on the grounds of the referent itself. That other utterance is not reproduced; it is understood only in its import; but the whole structure of the author's speech would be completely different, if it were not for this reaction to another's unexpressed speech act. In stylization, the actual model reproduced (the other style) also remains outside the author's context, its existence being merely understood. Likewise, in parody the existence of the actual, particular speech being parodied is only understood. In these instances, however, the author's speech itself either poses as someone else's speech (stylization) or lays claim to someone else's speech as its own (parody). In any case, it operates directly with another speech act, the implied model (the other actual speech act) only supplying the material and functioning as a document proving that the author is really reproducing another particular speech act. In the hidden polemic, on the other hand, the other speech act is reacted to, and this reaction, no less than the topic of discussion, determines the author's speech. This radically changes the semantics of the discourse involved: alongside its referential meaning, a second meaning—the fact of its taking bearings on another speech act—comes into play. One cannot completely and properly understand such speech when only its direct referential denotation is considered. The polemical shading of the discourse also shows up in other purely linguistic features: in intonation and in syntactic construction.

To draw a distinct dividing line between the hidden and the overt, open polemic in a concrete case sometimes proves quite difficult, but the conceptual differences are essential. Overt polemic is simply directed toward the other speech act, the one being refuted, as its own referential object. Hidden polemic is usually focused on some referential object which it denotes, depicts, expresses—and only obliquely does it strike at the other speech act, somehow clashing with it on the grounds of the referent itself. As a result, the latter begins to influence the author's speech from within. It is for that reason we call hidden polemic double-voiced, although the relationship of the two voices here is special. The other intention does not enter explicitly into the discourse but is only reflected in it, determining its tone and meaning. One speech act acutely senses another speech act close by, one addressed to the same topic, and this recognition determines its entire internal structure.

Internally polemical speech—speech that is aware of another and an antagonistic speech act—is especially widespread in everyday as well as literary speech, and it has an enormous significance in the formation of style. In everyday speech, instances of internal polemics are all "barbed" words and words used as "brickbats." This category also includes any speech that is servile or overblown, any speech that has determined beforehand not to be itself, any speech replete with reservations, concessions, loopholes, and so on. Such speech seems to cringe in the presence, or at the presentiment of, some other persons's statement, reply, objection. The individual manner of a person's own speech construction is determined to a considerable degree by his own peculiar feeling for the speech of other people and by his means of reacting to it.

In literary speech the significance of hidden polemic is enormous. In every style, properly speaking, there is an element of internal polemic, the difference being only in its degree and character. Any literary discourse more or less keenly senses its listener, reader or critic, and reflects anticipated objections, evaluations, points of view. Moreover, literary discourse senses other literary discourse, other style, alongside it. An element of the so-called reaction against a previous literary style which is present in every new style is just such an internal polemic; it is a hidden antistylization, so to speak, of another style, which often unites with an outright parody of that other style. The significance of the internal polemic for the formation of style is especially great in autobiographies and in forms of *Ich-Erzählung* of the confessional sort. Rousseau's *Confession* is a sufficient example.

Analogous to the hidden polemic is the single line of dialogue (assuming the dialogue to be of some weight and substance). In such a line every utternace, while focused on its referential object, at the same time displays an intensive reaction to another utterance, either replying to it or anticipating it. This feature of reply and anticipation penetrates deeply into the intensively dialogic utterance. Such an utterance appears to be taking in, sucking into itself, the utterances and intentions of the speaker and intensively reworking them. The semantics of dialogic discourse is of a completely special kind. All those subtle alterations in meaning which occur in the heat of a dialogic exchange unfortunately still remain totally unstudied. Once the counterstatement (*Gegenrede*) is taken into consideration, certain specific changes in the structure of dialogic discourse come into play: dialogue becomes an arena of events within itself and its very topic of discourse is seen in a new light, disclosing new facets inaccessible to monologic discourse.

Especially significant and important for our subsequent aims is hidden dialogue (not to be identified with hidden polemic). Imagine a dialogue between two persons in which the statements of the second speaker are deleted, but in such a way that the general sense is not disrupted. The second speaker's presence is not shown; his actual words are not given, but the deep impression of these words has a determining effect on all the utterances made by the only one who does speak. We feel that this is a conversation of the most intense kind, because each uttered word, in all its fiber, responds and reacts to the invisible partner, referring to something outside itself, beyond its limits, to the unspoken word of the other speaker. In Dostoevskij's works this hidden dialogue occupies a very important place and is extremely subtle and profoundly elaborated.

The third variety of the third type, as we see, differs sharply from the two preceding varieties of this type. We may call this third variety the active one, in distinction from the others, which are more passive. It is indeed a fact that in stylization, narrator's narration, and parody the other speech act is completely passive in the hands of the author who avails himself of it. He, so to speak, takes someone else's speech act, which is defenseless and submissive, and implants his own intentions in it, making it serve his new aims. Contrastingly, in hidden polemic and dialogue, the other speech act actively influences the author's speech and forces it to change shape in whatever ways its influence and initiative dictate.

It is possible, however, for the role of the other speech act to become more active in all occurrences of the second variety of the third type. When parody becomes aware of substantial resistance, a certain forcefulness and profundity in the speech act it parodies, it takes on a new dimension of complexity via the tones of the hidden polemic. Such a parody already "sounds" quite different: the speech act being parodied sounds more active and brings a counteraction to bear on the author's intention. A process of inner dialogization takes place within the parodic speech act.

Similar phenomena also occur when hidden dialogue combines with narrator's narration—in general, in all manifestations of the third type wherever the author's intentions and those of the other speech act diverge.

With a decrease in the objectification of the other speech act (objectification being, as we know, an inherent trait, to one or another degree, of the third type) in all the instances of uni-directional discourse (stylization, uni-directional narrator's narration) there occurs a merging together of the author's voice and the other voice. The distance between the two is lost; stylization becomes style; the narrator is transformed into a simple compositonal convention. In the case of vari-directional discourse, a decrease in objectification and a corresponding increase in the active role of the intentions belonging to the other speech act lead inevitably to the internal dialogization of discourse. In such discourse the author's intention no longer retains its dominant hold over the other intention; it loses its composure and assuredness, becomes perturbed, internally indecisive and ambiguous. Such speech is not only double-voiced, but also double-accented. It would be difficult to sound such speech aloud, because any actual enunciation would overmonologize it and fail to do justice to the other intention present in it.

This internal dialogization—connected with a decrease in objectification in vari-directional variants of the third type—does not, of course, constitute a new category of that type. It is only a tendency, one inherent in every occurrence of the given type (provided that it is vari-directionally oriented). At its upper limit this tendency leads to the splitting of double-voiced discourse into two speech acts, into two entirely separate and autonomous voices. Conversely, the tendency with the variants of uni-directional discourse, given a decrease in the objectification of the other speech act, leads at its upper limit to a complete fusion of voices and consequently to single-voiced discourse of the first type. All occurrences of the third type fluctuate between these two limits.

We have by no means exhausted all the possible occurrences of double-voiced discourse or all the possible means of orientation with respect to another speech act which gives the usual referential orientation of normal speech a new complexity. A more profound and refined classification, with a larger collection of varieties, even perhaps of types, might be possible. However, for our aims the given classification appears to be sufficient. The following is its schematic representation.

The classification outlined below naturally bears a purely conceptual, abstract character. A concrete instance of discourse may belong simultaneously to different varieties, and even to different types. Also, relationships with another speech act in a concrete, continuing context do not have a static, but rather a dynamic character. The relationship of voices in discourse may change sharply: uni-directional utterances may turn vari-directional; internal dialogization may become stronger or weaker; a passive type may undergo activization, and so on.

1
Direct unmediated discourse, focused solely on its referential object, as expression of the speaker's ultimate conceptual authority.

2
Objectified discourse (the speech of a person represented).

1. With a predominance of so-ciotypical determinations.	Various degrees of objectification.
2. With a predominance of indi-vidually characteristic deter-minations.	

3.
Discourse with emphasis on another speech act (double-voiced discourse).

1. Uni-directional variants.	With reduced objectification,
a. Stylization.	these variants approach a fusion
b. Narrator's narration.	of voices, i.e., approach the first
c. Unobjectified speech of a character who carries out the author's intentions (in part).	type of discourse.
d. *Ich-Erzählung.*	
2. Vari-directional variants.	With reduced objectification of
a. Parody with all its shadings.	the other intention, these var-
b. Parodic narration.	iants become internally dialog-
c. Parodic *Ich-Erzählung.*	ized to some degree and ap-
d. Speech of a character who is parodically represented.	proach a division into two speech acts (two voices) of the
e. Any reportage of someone else's speech with an altered accent.	first type.
3. Active type (another speech act reflected).	The other speech act exerts an
a. Hidden, internal polemic.	influence from within; the
b. Polemically colored autobiog-raphy and confession.	forms of relationship between the two voices may vary widely,
c. Any speech with an aware-ness of another's speech.	as may ghe degree of the deform-ing influence of the other speech
d. The single line of dialogue.	act.
e. Hidden dialogue.	

The plane of the investigation of discourse we have proposed, with its focal point on the relationship of one speech act with another, has, we believe, exceptionally important meaning for the understanding of artistic prose. The speech of poetry in the narrow sense requires a unified usage of all words, their reduction to a common denominator of intention, that denominator either being discourse of the first type or belonging to certain watered-down varieties of the other types. Of course, poetic works in which not all the speech material is reduced to a common denominator are possible, but these are rare occurrences, such as, for example, the "prosaic" lyrics of Heine, Barbier, Nekrasov, and others. One of the essential peculiarities of prose fiction is the possibility it allows of using different types of discourse, with their distinct expressiveness intact, on the plane of a single work without reduction to a common denominator. Here resides the profound difference between style in prose and style in poetry. Yet even in poetry a whole series of crucial problems cannot be solved without considering the system of investigation here proposed, because different types of discourse require a different stylistic treatment in poetry.

Contemporary stylistics, which ignores this plane of investigation, is in fact stylistics of the first type of discourse alone, that is, the author's direct referent-oriented speech. Contemporary stylistics, with its roots going back to the poetics of Neoclassicism, cannot to the present day give up Neoclassicist norms and schemes. Neoclassicist poetics was oriented on direct intentional discourse somewhat slanted toward conventionalized stylized speech. Semiconventionalized, semistylized discourse sets the tone in classical poetics. And stylistics up to the present day has taken for its orientation just such semiconventionalized direct speech, which in fact it has identified with poetic speech per se. For Classicism discourse belongs to the level of language; words are common property, objects which go to make up the poetic lexicon, and any item taken from the storehouse of poetic language is transferred directly into the monologic context of the given poetic expression. Thus, a stylistics nurtured on Classicism recognizes only the existence and viability of discourse in a single closed context. It ignores those changes which come about in discourse during the process of shifting words from one concrete utterance to another and during the process of the mutual orientation of those utterances. It recognizes only those changes which come about when words are shifted from the language system into a monologic poetic utterance. The viability and function of words in the style of a concrete utterance is assumed to be the face value of their viability and function in the language system. The inner dialogic relationship that may exist between a word in one context and the same word in the context of another speech act, on someone else's lips, is ignored. Stylistics has operated within this framework up to the present time.

Romanticism brought with it direct-intentional words with no deviation toward conventionality. Direct, expressive auctorial speech, untempered by any sort of refraction through the verbal medium of any other speech act, was characteristic of Romanticism to the point of utter distraction. In Romantic poetics considerable significance was attached to variants of the second and, particularly, of the last categories of the third type,[5] but all the same directly intentional discourse, discourse of the first type, extended to its limits, dominated to such a degree that no alterations with any real bearing on the problem under discussion could come about in Romanticism. In this respect the poetics of Classicism was hardly affected. Nevertheless, contemporary stylistics is far from being sufficient even to deal with Romanticism.

Prose fiction, especially the novel, is completely beyond the reach of such stylistics. It treats with some degree of success only minor areas of the art of prose, those areas least characteristic and least crucial for prose. To the prose writer the world is full of other people's speech acts; he orients himself among these, and he must have a keen ear for perceiving and identifying their peculiarities. He has to incorporate them on the plane of his own speech, but in such a way that that plane will not be destroyed.[6] He works with a very rich speech palette, and he works exceptionally well with it. And we, while we are reading prose, must also orient ourselves very sensitively among all the types and varieties of discourse analyzed above. What is more, even in ordinary life, that same sensitivity enables us to hear distinctly all these shades in the speech of people surrounding us; and we ourselves work with all these colors on the speech palette. We are quick to detect the smallest deviation in intention, the faintest counterpoint of voices in whatever of interest is said to us by another person in the ordinary business of life. All those verbal side-glances, reservations, loopholes, insinuations, thrusts do not escape our hearing and are not alien to our own usage. This makes it all the more astonishing that until now this whole situation has not found a clear-cut theoretical cognizance, a due evaluation. In theory, we analyze only the stylistic relationship of elements within a closed message, against a background of abstract linguistic categories. Only such single-voiced phenomena are within the reach of that superficial linguistic stylistics which until now, for all its linguistic worth, has been capable of registering in literary creation only the traces and outcroppings of artistic aims (of which it is ignorant) on the verbal periphery of literary works. The actual living nature of discourse in prose is not amenable to such a framework. That framework is even too narrow for poetry.

The problem of the orientation of speech toward another utterance also has a sociological significance of the highest order. The speech act by its nature is social. The word is not a tangible object, but an always shifting, always changing means of social communication. It never rests with one consciousness, one voice. Its dynamism consists in movement from speaker to speaker, from one context to another, from one social community to another, from one generation to another. Through it all the word does not forget its path of transfer and cannot completely free itself from the power of those concrete contexts into which it had entered. By no means does each member of the community apprehend the word as a neutral element of the language system, free from intentions and untenanted by the voices of its previous users. Instead, he receives the word from another voice, a word full of that other voice. The word enters his context from another context and is permeated with the intentions of other speakers. His own intention finds the word already occupied.

Thus the orientation of the word among words, the various perceptions of other speech acts, and the various means of reacting to them are perhaps the most crucial problems in the sociology of language usage, any kind of language usage, including the artistic. Each social group in each historical period has its own individual perception of the word, its own range of verbal possibilities. By no means can the ultimate conceptual authority of the artist always be expressed in direct, unrefracted, nonconventionalized auctorial speech in every social situation. When one does not have one's own proper "ultimate word," any creative intention, any thought, feeling, or experience must be refracted through the medium of another speech act, another style, another manner, with which it cannot immediately merge without reservation, distance, refraction. If a given social group has at its disposal an authoritative and durable medium of refraction, then conventionalized discourse in one or another of its varieties will hold sway, and to one or another degree of conventionality. If there is no such medium, then vari-directional, double-voiced discourse will hold sway: parodic speech in all its varieties, or a special type of semiconventionalized, semi-ironic speech (that of late Classicism). In such periods, especially when conventionalized discourse is dominant, directly intentional, reservationless, unrefracted speech appears to be a barbaric, coarse, bizarre kind of speech. Cultured speech is speech refracted through the authoritative canonical medium.

Which type of discourse dominates in a given period in a given social setting, which forms of speech refraction exist, and what serves as the medium of refraction—all these are questions of paramount significance for the sociology of artistic speech.

NOTES

1. The classification of the types and varieties of discourse offered below is without examles, since in the following chapter [of Baxtin's book] extensive material from the works of Dostoevskij is given for each case discussed.

2. Boris Èjxenbaum quite correctly, but from a different point of view, remarks
    on this peculiarity of Turgenev's narration: "The form of the author's moti-
    vated introduction of a special narrator to whom the narration is entrusted is
    especially common. However, very often this form has a completely conven-
    tional character (as in Maupassant or Turgenev), evincing only the vitality of
    the tradition of the narrator as a special personage in the story. In such cases
    the narrator remains the same as the author, and the motivation for his inser-
    tion plays the role of a simple introduction." (Boris Èjxenbaum, *Literature:
    teorija, kritika, polemika,* Leningrad, 1927), p. 217.
3. First in the article "Kak sdelana 'Šinel' " " in the collection, *Poètika* (1919).
    Then in particular in the article "Leskov i sovremennaja proza," *ibid.* pp. 210
    ff.
4. Leo Spitzer, *Italienische Umgangssprache* (Leipzig, 1922), pp. 175–176.
5. In connection with the interest in folkways (not as an ethnographic category),
    an enormous significance in Romanticism was attached to different forms of
    skaz as another speech act used as refractor with a weak degree of objectifi-
    cation. For Classicism, "folk speech" (in the sense of another type of speech
    that was socially typical and individually characteristic) was purely objecti-
    fied speech (in the low genres). Among the variants of the third type, polem-
    ical *Ich-Erzählung* (particularly the confessional type) was especially impor-
    tant.
6. The majority of prose genres, particularly the novel, are constructive in na-
    ture: they are structures of elements that are whole utterances, though these
    utterances are not fully authoritative and are subordinated to the monologic
    unity.

A. J. Greimas
Translated by Catherine Porter

Elements of a Narrative Grammar

1. Narrativity and Semiotic Theory*

1.1 HISTORICAL BACKGROUND

The widening interest in narrativity studies in recent years parallels the emergence of a general semiotics whose aspirations are becoming increasingly specific.

At an early stage, the comparison of the results of research undertaken independently—by V. Propp on folklore [*Morphology of the Folktale*, tr. C. Scott (Bloomington: Linguistics Center, 1958)], by Claude Lévi-Strauss [*Structural Anthropology*, tr. C. Jacobson) New York: Basic Books, 1963)] on the structure of myth, by Etienne Souriau [*Les Deux cent mille situations dramatiques* (Paris: Flammarion, 1950)] on the theatre—made it possible to establish the existence of an autonomous area of inquiry. Later, new methodological investigations, such as that of Claude Bremond interpreting narration from the perspective of decisional logic [*Logique du récit* (Paris: Seuil, 1973)], or that of Alan Dundes seeking to describe the organization of narrative in the form of a narrative grammar [*The Morphology of North American Indian Folktales* (Helsinki: Suomalainen Tiedenkatemia, 1964)], contributed to a diversification of the theoretical approaches. Our own concern, during this period, was both to extend as far as possible the field of application of narrative analysis, and to pursue the formalization of the partial models which had emerged from the ongoing research on narrative [1966a, pp. 192–221]: it seemed important to us to insist first and foremost on the semio-linguistic character of the categories used in the elaboration of these models, so as to ensure their universal applicability and to provide for the integration of narrative structures into a general semiotic theory.

---

*All notes and intra-textual references are provided by the editors. References indicated by dates will be found in the bibliography of Greimas's works at the end of the text.

1.2 NARRATIVITY AND ITS MANIFESTATION

One consequence of the methodological enrichment of narrative analysis and the possibility of applying it to areas other than folklore or mythology has been to bring to light some important problems, calling back into question the most widely accepted ideas in linguistics.

It was first necessary to acknowledge that narrative structures can be identified outside of the manifestations of meaning that occur in the natural languages: in the languages of cinema and of dream, in figurative painting, etc. [cf. Christian, *Film Language,* tr. M. Taylor (New York: Oxford University Press, 1974); J.-L. Schefer, *Scénographie d'un tableau* (Paris: Seuil, 1969); and Louis Marin, *Etudes sémiologiques* (Paris: Klinksieck, 1972)]. But this amounted to recognizing and accepting the necessity of a fundamental distinction between two levels of representation and analysis: an *apparent level* of narration, at which the manifestations of narration are subject to the specific exigencies of the linguistic substances through which they are expressed, and an *immanent level,* constituting a sort of common structural trunk, at which narrativity is situated and organized prior to its manifestation. A common semiotic level is thus distinct from the linguistic level and is logically prior to it, whatever the language chosen for the manifestation.

On the other hand, if narrative structures are anterior to their manifestation, the latter, in order to take place, has to utilize linguistic units whose dimensions are larger than those of the utterance [*énoncé*], units which would constitute "a comprehensive syntagmatics," as Ch. Metz put it in speaking of the semiotics of cinema. Thus, corresponding to *narrative structures* one finds, at the level of manifestation, *linguistic structures of narrative* and narrative analysis has discourse analysis as its corollary.

1.3 NARRATIVITY AND SEMIOTICS

It is thus apparent that, if we acknowledge that signification[1] is indifferent to the modes of its manifestation [1970 b, p. 13], we are obliged to recognize an autonomous structural level or region where vast fields of signification are organized. This level will have to be integrated into any general semiotic theory precisely insofar as the latter aims to account for the articulation and the manifestation of the semantic universe as a totality of meaning that is cultural or personal in nature. By the same token, the general economy of such a theory is overturned: previously, for example, one could suppose that linguistic inquiry consisted in setting up a mechanism, combinatory or generative in character, which would account, on the basis of simple elements and primitive kernels, for the production of an unlimited number of utterances, and that, in turn, the transformation and combination of these utterances would produce the strings of utterances constituting discourse. Now, on the contrary, we have to imagine instances[2] *ab quo* of the generation of signification such that, starting with minimally articulated agglomerations of meaning we may obtain, as we move down from level to level, meaning-bearing articulations that are more and more refined, in order to achieve, simultaneously, the two goals that meaning pursues as it becomes manifest: to appear as *articulated meaning*, i.e., as signification, and as *discourse on meaning*, i.e., as a vast paraphrase developing in its own way all the prior articulations of meaning. Put another way, *the generation of signification does not pass first through the production of utterances and their combination in discourse; it is relayed, in following its course [parcours], by narrative structures, and these are the structures which produce meaningful discourse articulated in utterances.*

Hence it is apparent that the elaboration of a theory of narrativity which would justify and establish narrative analysis theoretically as a methodologically self-sufficient area of research does not consist simply in the perfecting and formalizing of the narrative models obtained by ever more numerous and varied descriptions, nor in a typology of these models which would subsume them all, but also, and especially, it consists in the positioning of narrative structures as an *autonomous instance* within the general economy of semiotics, conceived as the science of signification.

1.4 THE INSTANCES OF A GENERAL SEMIOTICS

For this to be done, semiotic theory must be conceived in such a way as to ensure that between the fundamental instances *ab quo*, in which semantic substance receives its first articulations and constitutes itself in signifying form, and the ultimate [surface] instances *ad quem*, in which signification is manifested through multiple languages, a broad space is reserved for the installation of an instance of mediation in which semiotic structures possessing an autonomous status would be found. Among these semiotic structures the narrative structures would be construed as areas for the elaboration of complementary articulations of contents and a sort of grammar, at once general and fundamental, presiding over the establishment of articulated discourse. The structural project relative to this instance of mediation is thus two-fold: on the one hand, it is a question of sketching the construction of models for content articulation, as these can be imagined at this level of the course of meaning; on the other hand, it is a question of setting up the formal models which may be capable of manipulating these contents and arranging them in such a way that they can govern the production and the segmentation of discourse, can organize, under certain conditions, the manifestation of narrativity. In other words, semiotic theory will be satisfying only if it succeeds in staking out at its core a place for a *fundamental semantics and a fundamental grammar.*

1.5 TOWARD A FUNDAMENTAL SEMANTICS

The project of a fundamental semantics, different from the semantics of linguistic manifestation, can only be based upon theory of meaning. This project is thus directly linked to the explicitation of the conditions in which meaning can be grasped and to the *elementary structure of signification* which may be deduced from it, and which will be presented thereafter as an axiomatics. This elementary structure, previously analyzed and described [1968], must be conceived as the logical development of a binary semic category, of the type *white vs. black;* the relation of the terms of this category is that of mutual contraries, each one being at the same time capable of projecting a new term which would be its contradictory; the contradictory terms capable in turn of entering into a relationship of presupposition with respect to the opposed contrary terms:[3]

(→ marks presupposition; ↔ marks contradiction)

The subsequent assumption is that this elementary structure of signification furnishes a semiotic model adequate to account for initial articulations of meaning within a *semantic micro-universe.*

A clarification is necessary here regarding our conception of the semantic universe. At a first stage [cf. 1966, pp. 25–27, 102–16], we had proposed to consider it as the totality of the "semantic substance" that can only signify through the net of articulations by which it is covered, meaning being grasped only if it is articulated. These articulations of meaning could be explained, we thought, as the result of a combinatorial operation carried out on the basis of a limited inventory of semic categories. One further step could be taken today, suggesting a somewhat more refined representation of this net of articulations. For we can imagine that each of the constitutive categories of the combinatorial (which, as we have seen, can be rendered at any moment as an elementary structure) may be transformed into a *constitutive semiotic model,* and, subordinating to itself other categories from the same inventory that serve as its sub-articulations, may thus subsume a vast field of signification, may serve as a covering for a semantic micro-universe. Therefore the fundamental inventory of semic categories necessary for the articulation of the semantic universe in its totality is at the same time the virtual inventory of all possible micro-universes, since each culture, each personality can favor, through privileged articulations, one particular micro-universe [cf. 1966, pp. 126–27] at the expense of another (the culture of wine in France, the exploitation of spring water in Turkey).

Hence the constitutive model is none other than the elementary structure of signification used, as a form, for the articulation of the semantic substance of a micro-universe. We might say that the isotopy[4] of the terms of the elementary structure grounds and secures the micro-universe as a unit of meaning, and makes it possible to consider, within our elaboration of axioms, the constitutive model as a canonical form, as an inaugural instance for a fundamental semantics.

To examine the conditions of such a semantics would take us beyond the scope of this proposal. We are concerned here simply with distinguishing clearly the two levels—semantic and grammatical—of the exploration we are undertaking. Thus it would perhaps be preferable to mark this distinction with a terminological division, by speaking of *content values* each time we are dealing with semic units isolated within a micro-universe by means of the articulations of the constitutional model, and reserving the expression "structural *term*" for the formal units of the semiotic model.

1.6 TOWARD A FUNDAMENTAL GRAMMAR

But if the elementary structure serves thus as a model for the structuring of the contents (i.e., the semantic substances), if it is capable of enabling meaning to signify, it remains nonetheless a semiotic form which may be considered apart from any investment. This structure is the "semiotic principle" which, according to Hjelmslev [*Prolegomena to a Theory of Language*, trans. F. J. Whitfield (Madison: Univ. of Wisconsin Press, 1961)], institutes and organizes all language, in the most general sense. This explains why, even though as a constitutive model it lies at the basis of the organization of contents, the elementary structure is at the same time the formal model which, owing to its constitutive categories, manipulates the contents organized without being identified with them. We have already noted, moreover, that the categories necessary to the formalization of the elementary structure of signification are the same epistemological categories used for the construction of any semiotic theory. It is with these "universals of language," established as a semiotic model, as a primitive instance of any manipulation of meaning, that we may envisage the elaboration of the first premises of a fundamental grammar.

2. Elements of a Fundamental Grammar

2.1 THE TAXONOMIC CORE

It is difficult, at the present time, to elaborate an axiomatics on which narrative structures would be based: a complete semiotic theory would be a prerequisite. Thus one can do no more than sketch in, by referring to the global conception of such a semiotics, the principal articulatory instances and the predictable operational sequences of a projected narrative grammar.

All grammars include, more or less explicitly, two components, a morphology and a syntax. The nature of the morphology is that of a taxonomy whose terms are interdefined, the syntax consists in a set of operational rules or else in means of manipulating the terms of the morphology.

To illustrate what a taxonomic model of this type might be, we may refer to the structural analysis of the Oedipal myth carried out as early as 1955 by Claude Lévi-Strauss [in *Structural Anthropology;* cf. Greimas, 1956, 1965, 1966], an analysis which resulted in the construction of a simple achronic model on the basis of which, according to the author, all the Oedipal myths, including Freud's, can be generated. This model, the result of a paradigmatic reading of the mythic discourse, can be defined— we have examined it elsewhere—as the establishment of a correlation of coupled contradictory terms.

It is easy to see that such a model is in every respect comparable to the constitutional model to which we have already referred, and that it may be interpreted by application of the same relational categories. Thus by calling a *schema* the structure which includes two terms joined by the relations of contradiction $(s \leftrightarrow \bar{s}_1 \text{ or } s \leftrightarrow \bar{s}_2)$, and by calling a *correlation* the relation between two schemas whose terms, taken one by one, are in the relation of contrariety with the corresponding terms of the other schema (cf. 1.5), we can say that the taxonomic model is a *structure with four terms* which are mutually interdefined by a network of precise relations describable as *the correlation between two schemas.*

For Lévi-Strauss, as we have seen, such a model accounts for the achronic apprehension of the signification of all the possible narratives belonging to a certain semantic micro-universe. It is a formal model: it does no more than articulate the invested content. Moreover, it is independent of its mode of manifestation: the discourse which manifests it may be a mythic narrative, but it may also be the didactic discourse of Freud; it can just as well be present, in a diffuse form, in interminable anthropological or psychoanalytical discourses.

In other words, it is on the basis of this first taxonomic instance that value-systems, or *axiologies,* and the recurrent processes of value-creation, or *ideologies,* can be articulated and manifested in a static mode. Even though it is capable of generating non-narrative discursive forms, the taxonomic instance is just as much a necessary base for any dynamic process generative of *narrative syntax.*

2.2 THE NARRATIVIZATION OF THE TAXONOMY

It is evident that the taxonomic model, owing to the stability of the relations which define its structural terms, may be taken as the initial nucleus of an elementary morphology. However, examining the conditions of the apprehension of meaning, we see clearly that if signification, to the extent that one attempts to find it in the object, appears as an articulation of fundamental stable relations, it is at the same time capable of a dynamic representation as soon as it is considered either as an apprehension or as a production of meaning by the subject. Taking this dynamic aspect into account, one can establish a network of equivalences between the fundamental *relations* constitutive of the taxonomic model, and the projections of these same relations, or *operations,* bearing this time on already-established terms of this elementary morphology. The regulation of these operations would constitute syntax. Thus contradicition, inasmuch as it is a relation, serves, at the taxonomic level, for the establishment of binary schemas: inasmuch as it is an operation of contradiction, it will consist, at the syntactic level, in negating one of the terms of the schema and in affirming at the same time its contradictory term. Such an operation, when it is carried out on terms already invested with value, results in the transformation of contents by negating those which have been posited and by replacing them with new contents which are asserted.

Consequently, we can place the first cornerstone, a provisional one, of a fundamental syntax by saying that it consists in setting the taxonomic model into motion through transformations of contents invested in the taxonomic terms on which that fundamental syntax operates.

Note: We have seen that the apprehension of myth called achronic is an unstable instance, that its "dogmatic" structure is at every moment ready to develop into narrative. The studies carried out on certain minor genres (proverbs, wellerisms, headlines of news items, etc.) which seem at first glance to be pure axiological manifestations how on the contrary their thoroughgoing instability and a pronounced tendency toward narrativization.

2.3 THE ORIENTATION OF THE SYNTACTIC OPERATIONS

The representation of syntax as a sequence of operations carried out on the defined terms of a taxonomic structure makes it possible to infer from them more easily a new property: *the syntactic operations are oriented.*

Thus in the framework of a single taxonomic schema one can foresee two possible syntactic operations, and two possible transformations of content:

$$\text{either } s_1 \rightarrow \bar{s}_1$$
$$\text{or } \bar{s}_1 \rightarrow s_1$$

Furthermore, since the taxonomic model is made up of two schemas, the question of the logical priority of the syntactic operations cannot fail to arise. The oriented operations may begin

$$\text{either with the first schema: } s_1 \rightarrow \bar{s}_1, \text{ or } \bar{s}_1 \rightarrow s_1,$$
$$\text{or with the second schema: } s_2 \rightarrow \bar{s}_2, \text{ or } \bar{s}_2 \rightarrow s_2;$$

this already gives rise, as is apparent, to a first combinatorial of syntactic operations.

Finally, knowledge of the relational properties of the elementary structure—which are at the same time those of the syntactic operations—prescribes the following: the operation of contradiction which, in negating for example the term s_1, poses at the same time the term $\bar{s}_1$, and must be followed by a new operation of presupposition giving rise to the new term, s_2, which is conjoined to $\bar{s}_1$. Thus the syntactic operations are not only oriented, but are also organized in logical series.

2.4 THE CHARACTERISTICS OF A FUNDAMENTAL GRAMMAR

The characteristics which we have just specified and which can serve as a basis for the elaboration of a fundamental grammar can be summarized as follows:

1. Narrative grammar is composed of an *elementary morphology,* furnished by the taxonomic model, and of a *fundamental syntax which operates on the taxonomic terms* interdefined at the outset.

2. Narrative syntax consists in operations carried out upon the terms subject to being invested with content values; owing to this fact it transforms them and manipulates them, by negating them and affirming them, or—what amounts to the same thing—by *disjoining* and *conjoining* them.

3. The syntactic operations, situated in the established taxonomic framework, are oriented, and therefore predictable and calculable.

4. The operations, moreover, are *ordered in series* and constitute processes which can be segmented into *operational syntactic units.*

These minimal determinations, conditions of a fundamental grammar, even though incomplete, allow us to approach the problems relating to the construction of a surface narrative grammar.

3. Elements of a Surface Narrative Grammar

3.1 THE PROBLEM OF LEVELS OF GRAMMAR

If we possessed a fundamental grammar it would be possible to imagine "lower" levels of grammar which, by making more specific the categories used or by transcribing them in a more complex manner, would progressively move closter to grammar as it is manifested for example in the natural languages. Thus, by simplifying considerably, we may say that the fundamental grammar, which is *concepetual* in nature, must first receive, at an intermediate semiotic level, an *anthropomorphic* but non-figurative representation, in order to be able to produce narratives manifested in a *figurative* form (where human or personaified actors would accomplish tasks, undergo trials, reach goals). It is this anthropomorphic level which we shall designate by the term *surface narrative grammar*, specifying that the adjective "surface," with no pejorative connotations, indicates only that we are dealing with a semiotic level whose definitions and grammatical rules are capable, with the help of a final transcoding, of passing directly into discourse and into linguistic utterances.

The term *grammatical level* needs to be defined first. If we say that a grammar can be constructed at two different levels, that means that it is possible to construct two different meta-languages accounting for one and the same linguistic phenomenon present at a third level, in our case that of manifestation. We shall say likewise that these two metalanguages are *equivalent*, because they are isotopic but not isomorphic, indicating thereby that a determined segment of one metalanguage can be transcoded into an isotopic segment of another, even though the constitutive elements of the two languages are not by this token formally identical.

The constitutive categories of such a surface grammar are distinguished, as we were saying, by their anthropomorphic character, from the logical character proper to the categories of the fundamental grammar.

3.2 NARRATIVE UTTERANCES

3.2.1 The Anthropomorphic Practice

If, in consequence, one of the basic concepts of the fundamental grammar is that of the syntactic *operation*, it will correspond, on the surface level, to syntactic *practice*.

The establishment of equivalence between operation and practice [*le faire*] is in fact what brings the anthropomorphic dimension into grammar. This fact can be interpreted in different ways:

a) Whereas a logical operation is conceived as an autonomous metalinguistic process, allowing the subject of the operation to be bracketed (or allowing the use of any operator whatsoever), a practice, whether practical or mythical, implies as an activity—a *human subject* (or at least an anthropomorphosized one: "the pencil writes"). In other words, the practice is an operation defined by the adjunction of the classeme "human."

b) When we speak of the practice, it is evident that we are not thinking of the "real" practice situated at the level of the semiotics of the natural world, but of the linguistic *practice* (whatever the language, natural or not, in which it is manifested), a practice transcoded as message. Whether it is a question, with respect to the semiotic system that serves as the frame of reference, of an *enacted practice* or of a *spoken practice*, its status as meta-semiotic practice (because it is described) makes it a message-object, situated within the process of communication, implying an addresser and an addressee.

The *practice* is thus a double anthropomorphic operation: as activity, it presupposes a subject; as message, it is objectivized and implies the axis of transmission between sender and receiver.

3.2.2 Simple Narrative Utterances

Conversion—the passage from one grammatical level to another—can thus be defined as an equivalence between the operation and the practice, by giving to the implications of the concept of practice the form of a simple narrative utterance (NU):

$$NU = F(A)$$

in which the practice, as a process of actualization, is labeled *function* (F) and in which the subject of the practice, as a potentiality of the process, is designated *actant* (A). Thus we shall say that any operation of the fundamental grammar can be converted into a narrative utterance whose minimal canonic form is F(A). It is still understood that narrative utterances are syntactic utterances, that is, independent of the content which may be invested in any given practice, and that the constitutive elements of the utterance F and A, are isotopes: any semantic restriction of F will necessarily have repercussions on A, and vice versa. The actant is, to give one example, an isotope of its function, in the same way that the name of the agent is of its verb (cf. hunter-hunt).

3.2.3 Modal Utterances and Descriptive Utterances

Thus a typology of narrative utterances—and, at the same time, of actants—can be constructed through the progressive introduction of determined semantic restrictions. If, for example, we find that a certain class of functions is defined by the adjunction of the classeme "want" [*vouloir*][5], the actants, isotopes of these functions, will constitute a restrictive class which can be designated as that of subject-actants. In fact, *wanting* is an anthropomorphic (but not necessarily figurative: cf. "this rule requires that ... ") classeme which institutes the actant as subject, i.e., as possible operator of the practice [*faire*]. And on this basis one can constitute, alongside the descriptive utterances (DU) a new type of narrative utterance: the modal utterances (MU).

In fact, from the linguistic point of view, *to want* is a modal predicate which governs properly descriptive utterances. For example:

(1) John wants Peter to leave.
(2) Peter wants to leave.

Once transcribed as semantic utterances, these linguistic utterances appear as follows:

(1) F: want/S: John; O (F: departure; A: Peter)/
(2) F: want/S: Peter; O (F: departure; A: Peter)/

It is clear that, linguistically, the introduction of the classeme "want" is something other than an overdetermination of the predicate, that it necessitates the construction of two distinct utterances of which the first is modal and the second descriptive; the latter, hypotaxic with respect to the former, serves as its *Object-Actant*. If for the moment we do not take into account the fact that, in the first example, the semantic subjects of the two utterances are different and in the second case identical, we can interpret the modal utterance as "the desire to realize" a program which is present in the form of a descriptive utterance and is at the same time, given its status as object, part of the modal utterance. This allows us already to provide a formal description of modal utterances, as follows:

$$MU = F: desire/S; O/$$

These are enunciations of virtual programs made explicit in the framework of object-actants, it being understood that the object-actant of the modal utterance may can at all times be converted into any descriptive utterance whatsoever.

If we now introduce a supplementary restriction, postulating that the semantic subject of the descriptive utterance must be the same as that of the modal utterance, we can say, after a fashion, that the syntactic practice consists in the transformation of a virtual program into an actualized one.

As the descriptive utterance conceived as a program remains unchanged, the transformation can be interpreted as the substitution, for the modal utterance with the function "want," of a modal utterance of existence which is recognized as an implicit presupposition of every descriptive utterance.

3.2.4 Attributive Utterances

Our statement that the Object of desire, presented as Object-Actant, is in reality a program-utterance, requires some further attention. Other examples will allow us to introduce new characteristics of these descriptive utterances:

(3) Peter wants an apple
(4) Peter wants to be good

These linguistic utterances may be represented semantically as [O = object]:

(3) F: want/S: Peter; O (F: acquisition; A: Peter; O: apple)/
(4) F: want/S: Peter; O (F: acquisition; A: Peter; O: goodness)/

The semantic explicitation, as we can see, allows us to establish, alongside of already-mentioned utterances whose function belongs to the order of practice, the existence of two other types of descriptive utterances characterized by their functions, which are at times of *the order of having*, at other times of *the order of being*. As a subclass of descriptive utterances they can be designated as attributive utterances (AU). What differentiates these two types of utterances, at the level of semantic description, is less the specification of their functions—we are dealing in both cases with a relation of attribution between the subject and the semantic object—than the specification of the external or internal nature of attributable objects. To the extent that by bringing together in order to interpret them the functions of the two utterances, modal and descriptive, we can say that the desire for possession institutes the object of a virtual possession as a *value*, we can see that *apple* is an external value with respect to the subject of the desire, while *goodness* is a value internal to the subject. We can state this difference in syntactic terms by saying that the relation between subject and object of the attributive utterance is, in the first case, *hypotaxis* and, in the second, *hyponomic* [cf. 1966, pp. 28–29].

Let us then offer the following points in summary:

a) The introduction into the surface grammar of the *modality* of wanting permits the construction of modal utterances with *two actants:* the *subject* and the *object*. The axis of desire which unites them permits us, in turn, to interpret them semantically as a virtual *performing subject* and as an *object instituted as value*.

b) If the modality of wanting valorizes the object, this object, as an actant of the modal utterance, may be converted either into an utterance *descriptive of practice* (examples 1 and 2)—and practice as such is found to be valorized—or into *attributive* utterances (examples 3 and 4)—and the actualization of wanting is then expressed through the possession of object-values indicated in the attributive utterances.

c) The distinction of two types of attribution of object-values (*hypotaxic* and *hyponomic* (must be maintained: it offers a formal criterion for distinguishing two orders of value (objective and subjective) of capital importance for the understanding of narrative structure.

3.2.5 Modal Utterances as Functions of Attributive Utterances

We have yet to complete our list of examples of narrative utterances with the following:

(5) Peter wants to know [something]
(6) Peter wants to be able [to do something]

It is immediately apparent, without a semantic transcription, that the distinguishing feature of this type of utterance lies in the fact that a modal utterance can have as its object not a simple descriptive utterance, but another modal utterance, functioning as a descriptive utterance, and thereby subject to being valorized in turn.

A certain number of remarks are pertinent in this regard:

1. Our present knowledge of these matters would suggest [cf. 1976d] that only the modalities of *knowing* [*savoir*] and of *being able* [*pouvoir*] must be taken into consideration in the construction of the superficial grammar.

2. From among the properties of these modalities we shall retain:
a) the possibility of forming modal canonical utterances:

MU (kn or ab) = F: to know or to be able/S; O(F: to do; O)/

b) the possibility of being objects of modal utterances of wanting:

MU (w) = F: to want/S; O (F: to know or to be able; A; O)/

c) the possibility of being objects of attributive utterances

AU = F: attribution/S; O: a knowledge or an ability/

3.3 NARRATIVE UNITS

3.3.1 Performance and Its Polemical Nature

In order to complete the positing of the elementary units of the surface grammar equivalent to those of the fundamental grammar and to pass on to the construction of larger units, we must insist on the polemical representation which the relation of contradiction receives at this surface level. The axis of contradiction which we have designated as *schema* is known to be the locus of negation and assertion of contradictory terms.[6] If we admit that the anthropomorphic representation of contradiction is polemical in nature, the syntagmatic string—which corresponds to the transformation of content values resulting, at the level of the fundamental grammar, from the operations of negation and assertion—will have to appear here as a string of narrative utternaces whose semantic restrictions will assume the function of conferring upon it a character of confrontation and struggle. Constitution of this syntagmatic string requires us to postulate:

a) the existence of *two subjects* S_1 and S_2 (or that of a Subject and an Anti-Subject) which correspond to the two contradictory *practices*, the relation of contradiction being recognized as a non-oriented one;

b) the semantic restriction of the syntactic practice through the establishment of equivalence between the operation of *negation* and the function of *domination*, result of the polemical antagonism;

c) the recognition of the principle of *orientation* valid for the two levels of grammar: to a given orientation of logical operations corresponds a given arbitrary choice of the negating subject and of the domination of one of the subjects over the other.

d) the admission that the dialectical procedure according to which the negation of a term is *at the same time* the assertion of the contradictory term is represented, at the level of the surface syntax, by two independent narrative utterances: the first, with its function of domination, corresponds to the instance of negation, and the second, with the function of attribution, to the instance of assertion.

The syntagmatic string known as *performance* can be represented as follows:

$$NU_1 = F: \text{confrontation } (S \leftrightarrow S_2)$$

Note: this narrative utterance expressing anthropomorphically the relation of contradiction between two terms is in reality the syncretism of two modal utterances belonging to each of the subjects.

$$NU_2 = F: \text{domination } (S_1 \leftrightarrow S_2)$$

Note: The utterance corresponds to the triggering of the operation of oriented negation, in which S_1 negates S_2, or vice versa; negation, as we have seen, consists in the transformation of the virtual to the actualized or, what amounts to the same thing, in the substitution of the MU of existence for the MU of wanting, of domination for the desire to dominate.

$$NU_3 = F: \text{attribution } (S_1 \leftarrow O)$$

Note: The latter utterance corresponds to the instance of assertion: this is expressed anthropomorphically by the attribution of an Object-value.

3.3.2 The Constitutive Elements of Performance

In this sketch of surface grammar we have placed the emphasis—by taking, as an example, a single syntagm—on the establishment of term-for-term correspondences between the two grammatical levels, on the bringing to light as well of the anthropomorphic categories which substitute for the logical terms and operations. The result is the construction of a particular narrative unit, that of performance; owing to the fact that it constitutes the operatory schema of the transformation of content, it is probably *the most characteristic unit of narrative syntax.*

Performance thus defined is a syntactic unit, a formal schema apt to receive the most varied contents. From another standpoint, the two subjects of the performance are interchangeable, each able to dominate or be dominated; likewise, the class of objects is subject to variation according to the distinct modes of syntactic attribution.

From the viewpoint of its syntactic status, performance has the form of a series of narrative utterances constructed according to the canonical formula: the narrative utterance is a relation among actants. This relation, designated a function, is capable of receiving certain semantic specifications which are transmitted, owing to the isotopy of the whole, to the actants and which go so far as to determine their number.

If the functions and the actants are the constitutive *elements* of this narrative grammar, if the *narrative utterances* are its basic syntactic forms, the *narrative units*—an example of which is represented here by *performance*—are syntagmatic strings of narrative utterances.

3.3.3 The Constitutive Relations of Performance

The problem of the relations between utterances which are constituted as narrative units does not fail to arise here. We have seen that performance, taken as a narrative unit, corresponds to the taxonomic schema and that, because of this, the utterances which constitute it are equivalent to the logical operations situated inside the schema. We have also seen that the logical operations constitutive of the schema were oriented.

Now it must be remarked that to this *orientation*, which is a rule of basic grammar, corresponds the relation of *implication* on the level of superficial grammar, with the difference however that if orientation follows the order of utterances,

$$NU_1 \rightarrow NU_2 \rightarrow NU_3$$

implication, for its part, is oriented in the other direction:

$$NU_3 \mid NU_2 \mid NU_1.$$

This conversion, which allows us to define the narrative unit as a sequence of implications among utterances, has a certain practical importance when narrative analysis is undertaken at the level of manifestation, where it grounds the rules for ellipsis and catalysis: the narrative utterances logically implied in the framework of a performance may be elliptical in the manifestation; the presence of the last link in the chain of implications (NU_3) suffices for us to proceed, working toward a reconstruction of the narrative unit, to a catalysis which reestablishes it in its integrity.

3.3.4 The Modalization of Performances

A step backward and a reflection on the properties of modal utterances will permit us to establish the distinction between two possible types of performances. Let us recall that the modal utterances having "want" as their function institute the subject as a virtuality of the practice, while two other modal utterances, characterized by the modalities of knowledge and ability, determine this potential practice in two different ways: as a practice derived from knowledge, or as one based solely upon ability.

These two different modalizations of practice can then be recognized in performances. Thus we shall distinguish performances modalized by knowledge of how to do [something] [*le savoir-faire*] (P_{kn})—in which the performing subject will act, at the level of manifestation, through ruse and deceit—from performances carried out by dint of *ability to do* [something] [*le pouvoir-faire*] (P_{ab})—in which the performing subject uses only its energy and its force, real or magical.

3.4 PERFORMANCIAL STRINGS

3.4.1 A Syntax of Communication

Up to now we have considered the terminal narrative utterances of performance (NU_3)—which is the equivalent, on the superficial level, of the logical assertion in the fundamental grammar—to be an attributive utterance (AU). We may ask however whether such a formulation is satisfactory.

Such an attribution—or the acquisition, by the subject, of the object—seems to present itself as a reflexive practice: the performing subject attributes itself to itself, considering itself as subject of the descriptive utterance, an object-value. If this is the case, the reflexive attribution is only a particular case of a much more general structure of attribution, well-known in linguistics as the *schema of communication* or, still more generally, as the *structure of exchange:* it is represented, in its canonical form, as an utterance with three actants: the addresser the addressee, and the object of communication:

$$TU = F: \text{transfer } (A_1 \rightarrow O \rightarrow A_2)$$

The possibility of using a very general schema is an initial advantage of this formulation. The latter allows us, furthermore, to distinguish clearly between two different syntactic levels: a) the level at which is situated the syntactic operator of the assertion, translated in surface grammar as the subject performing the attribution (in reality it is a meta-subject and the cause of the transfers which are accomplished) and b) the level at which the transfers themselves occur. The terms addresser and addressee merely camouflage the distinction.

The second level—which is descriptive and not operational—can now receive an anthropomorphosized topological representation: the actants are no longer conceived as operators but as loci where the object-values may be situated, places to which they may be brought and from which they may be removed. The transfer is, in this case, capable of being interpreted *at one and the same time* as a deprivation (at the surface level) or as a disjunction (at the fundamental level) and as an attribution (at the surface level) or as a conjunction (at the fundamental level).

Such an interpretation, which replaces the attributive utterances by the *translative utterances* (TU), appears to provide a more correct representation of performance: the consequence of the latter (NU_3) is no longer a simple acquisition of value, it is a transfer of value: if the object-value is *attributed* to the dominant subject, this is because the dominated subject is at the same time *deprived* of this object value; the two logical operations are thus summed up in a single utterance.

3.4.2 The Topological Syntax of Objective Values

Such a topological representation of the circulation of object-values [cf. 1976a] amounts to identifying the deixes of the transfers to the terms of the taxonomic model, considered as morphological units capable of being invested with content. We have already seen that investments of content values were distributed according to two correlated schemas. We can say now that at the anthropomorphic level, the schemas correspond to the *isotopic spaces* which are the places where performances occur, and that each space is made up of two deixes[8] which are *conjoined* (because they correspond to the same axis of contradiction), but are not *conformal;* they are equivalent, at the fundamental level, to the contradictory terms:

On the other hand, the hypotaxic axes $\bar{d}_2 \to d_1$ and $\bar{d}_1 \to d_2$ constitute *heterotopic spaces* whose deixes are disjunctive, because they do not belong to the same schemas, but *conformal,* since they are linked by the relation of presupposition.

Hence the circulation of value, interpreted as a string of transfers of objects-values, can take two courses:

$$(1) \ F \ (d_1 \rightarrow O \rightarrow d_1) \rightarrow F(d_1 \rightarrow O \rightarrow d_2)$$

This in the particular case of the Russian tales studied by Propp, can be interpreted as follows: society (d_1) experiences a lack, the villain (d_1) ravishes the king's daughter (O) and moves her elsewhere to hide her (d_2).

$$(2) \ F \ (d_2 \rightarrow O \rightarrow d_2) \rightarrow F \ (d_2 \rightarrow O \rightarrow d_1)$$

This will mean: the hero (d_2) finds somewhere (d_2) the king's daughter (O) and returns here to her parents (d_1).

Thus the Russian tale manifests a circular transmission of values by utilizing, successively, two performing subjects and by valorizing one of the conformal spaces (that of the hero) at the expense of the other (that of the villain) [1973]. It is clear, however, that here we have nothing more than a simple doubling of the narrative. Myths of origin generally consider the absence of a given object of value as an original situation and the acquisition of values follows a single course (2). This is perfectly understandable, moreover: what is acquisition of value for the deixis d_1 is necessarily and simultaneously deprivation of value for the deixis d_2, and vice versa. According to the perspective adopted, the same trajectory of value-transfers is subject to two interpretations: the narrative is at once a story of victory and a story of defeat. What determines the choice of one of these two interpretations does not stem from the narrative syntax but from the axiological articulation of content values: given the two *conformal spaces*, the investment of the one is given initially as *euphoric* and that of the other as *dysphoric* [cf. 1966].

Limiting ourselves for the moment to objective values, we may say that the topological syntax of transfers, doubling the courses of meaning apprehension described as logical operations at the level of the fundamental grammar, organizes the narration as a value-creating process. It is consequently this topological syntax which has the task of providing meaning to the narrative and it constitutes the latter's principal armature. Thus from the formal viewpoint, just as the translative utterances are the terminal utterances of performances and imply them logically, the syntactic trajectories expressed in the form of transfers constitute in fact *syntagmatic strings of performances:* that is, syntactic units of a higher order.

3.4.3 The Installation [Institution] of Syntactic Operators

Such a topological syntax is however purely descriptive: we have insisted on this point in denying any operational character to the actants of the translative utterances, which we have designated, in order to avoid any confusion, as deixes and not as addressers or addressees. This is because a *syntax of operators* has to be constructed independently of a *syntax of operations:* a meta-semiotic level must be put in place in order to justify the transfers of value.

The syntactic operators are conceived here as subjects endowed with the virtual capacity for particularizing that which will make them capable of accomplishing the transfer operation envisaged. This virtuality of the practice is nothing other than a modality: knowledge of ability; it can be formulated, as we have already seen, in two different ways: either as a modal utterance representing the subject's knowing-how-to-do or his ability-to-do; or as an attributive utterance, signalling the acquisition of a modal value by the subject.

If the subjects are transformed into operators following the attribution of a modal value (an attribution which we have just replaced by the more satisfying function of transfer), then the installation of operators can be established according to the same model of topological syntax of transfer, with this difference that the loci of transfers are no longer deixes here, but subject-actants. The operator thus established and endowed with a knowing-how-to-do or an ability-to-do becomes only then capable of realizing the performance for which it has just been created.

Two series of performances can then be distinguished: (a) performances allowing for the acquisition and the transmission of modal values and (b) performances characterized by the acquisition and the transfer of objective values. The first install the subjects as operators, the second then effect the operations; the former create virtualities, the latter realize them.

Thus alongside a topological course foreseen for the transfer of objective values and which institutes, as we have seen, a first syntagmatic string of performances, a second course of the same type can be predicted for the transfer of modal values.

We cannot elaborate here on the origin of the first operator-actant which initiates the syntactic trajectory: that would entail close examination of a particular narrative unit, the contract that institutes the subject of desire by the attribution of the modality of wanting [*vouloir*] (cf. 1966, pp. 195–96), the probable realization of a "causing-to-want" skimming from the original sender. It will suffice to note for the moment that it is the wanting of the subject which makes the subject prone to carry out the first performance, marked by the attribution of the modal value of the knowledge or ability.

A first hierarchy of modal values may be indicated; it orients as follows the syntactic trajectory,

$$want \rightarrow know \rightarrow be\ able \rightarrow do$$

and serves as a basis for the organization of the syntagmatic string of performances. Certain implications of such an orientation are immediately visible:

a) only the acquisition of the modal value of ability makes operative subject prone to carry out the performance which attributes objective value to that subject;

b) it follows that the acquisition of the modal value of knowledge has as its consequence the attribution of the ability-to-do (the mediation of this capacity-for-practice is necessary for the actualization of the practice);

c) on the other hand, the mediation of knowledge does not seem necessary for the acquisition of the ability-to-do. This latter feature allows us to distinguish two sorts of subjects: "knowing" subjects whose aptitude for carrying out the performances stems from a knowing-how-to-do initially *acquired,* and the subjects which are "powerful" [*puissants*] by nature.

Note: The acquisition of a modal value by the subject (or the anti-subject), which is manifested, for example, through the obtaining of a magical agent or of a message-object of knowledge, institutes the subject as *adjuvant* (or as *opponent*) capable of moving on to the following performance.

Such a syntagmatic string, established outside of the formal framework of tranlative utterances, that is, without considering the actants implied, makes it possible already to specify the nature of the relationship between two different types of performances: a string of performances is *oriented,* since the performance instituting the syntactic operator is followed by the performance which effects the syntactic operation; at the same time, the objective performance *implies* the modal performance.

3.4.4 The Topological Syntax of Modal Values

Given the polemical nature of narrativity, two syntactic operators are necessary in order to establish a narrative syntax: we have, for this reason, already envisaged two subjects (S_1 and S_2) for the construction of the performance. It is consequently the axis of exchange between these two subjects which constitutes the locus of modal value transfers: the attribution of a modal value to S_1 supposes that S_2 is simultaneously deprived of this value.

Two courses for the transfer of modal values will then be envisaged, according to whether we are dealing with a "knowing" or an "able" subject, i.e., according to the priority accorded to the acquisition of one or the other of the two modalities in question.

a) In the first case, the syntagmatic string will be oriented as follows:

$$TU_1 (S_1 \rightarrow O:\ know \rightarrow S_2) \rightarrow TU_2 (S_1 \rightarrow O:\ be\ able \rightarrow S_2)$$

It can be interpreted as the acquisition, by S_2, of a capability deriving from a knowledge previously obtained; and at the same time as the loss, by S_1, of all capability owing to the loss of knowledge.

b) In the second case, the orientation will be reversed:

$$TU_1 \; (S_2 \rightarrow O: \; \text{be able} \rightarrow S_1) \rightarrow TU_2 \; (S_2 \rightarrow O: \; \text{know} \rightarrow S_1)$$

The string can be interpreted as the acquisition by S_1 of a knowledge that derives from a recognized capability, and inversely as the loss, by S_2, of all knowledge following upon the loss of capability.

One of the two strings suffices to constitute, in combination with the string of transfers of objective values, the completed narrative. If however we have chosen as addressees of modal values two different subjects for each of the two courses (S_2 and S_1) [this is clearly an arbitrary choice], it is in order to account at the same time for the particular organization of the doubled narrative, such as it is presented, for example, in the form of a Russian folktale studied by Propp. Here we see, in fact, first the subject S_2, axiologically labeled *villain*, acquiring modal values at the expense of S_1:

$$S_2 = O_1: \; \text{know} \rightarrow O_2: \; \text{be able}$$

S_2 then gives up its place to the subject S_1, labeled *hero:* S_2 takes over the previously acquired values, progressively depriving S_2 of them.

$$S_1 = O_1: \; \text{be able} \rightarrow O_2: \; \text{know}$$

3.4.5 The General Form of the Narrative Grammar

We have just traced the broad outlines of a surface narrative syntax, or rather, only a part of this syntax relative to the body of the narrative itself. What is lacking in this sketch and what we can only indicate briefly here is the examination and the establishment of syntactic units for the framework of the narrative, corresponding to the initial and final sequences of manifested narrative.

It would be a question, in this regard, of accounting for the syntactic units corresponding to what are, at the level of deep grammar, the hypotaxic relations of the taxonomic model, i.e., to the relations that can be established in this model between the terms s_1 and $\bar{s}_2$ on the one hand, and between the terms s_2 and $\bar{s}_1$ on the other. The starting point of the narration would be represented as the establishment of a *conjunctive* contractual relation between an addresser and an addressee, followed by a spatial disjunction between the two actants. The completion of the narrative would be marked, on the contrary, by a spatial conjunction and a final transfer of values, instituting a new contract through a new distribution of values, objective as well as modal.

Even though remaining incomplete, our attempt should give at least some idea of what a syntactic organization of narrativity might be. We have recognized two sorts of *oriented syntagmatic strings* organizing the transfer of values, modal as well as objective, in the framework of a syntax which is topological in nature. The object-values are situated in the framework of terminal narrative utterances representing the consequences of performances and implying them logically; these syntagmatic strings are thus in reality arrangements of performances which, as syntactic units, are recurrent and formally identical. Another principle of syntagmatic organization has likewise been recognized: the performances are arranged in such a way that the first, characterized by the attribution of a modal value which institutes the *subject-operator*, must be followed by a second which actualizes the *operation*.

As for the typical syntactic unit, we have seen that it can be conceived as a string of three narrative utterances which are linked by implications. In examining the narrative utterances, we have been able to sketch out a summary typology; by introducing the supplementary semantic determinations of their functions and by varying the number and the specifications of their actants, we have distinguished three principal types of narrative utterances: descriptive, modal, and translative; every utterance represents, on the level of surface narrative grammar, either a relation or an operation of a fundamental grammar.

Such a narrative grammar, once achieved, would have both a deductive and an analytical form. It would trace a set of itineraries for the manifestation of meaning; on the basis of the elementary operations of the fundamental grammar which would take the paths of the process by which meaning is actualized through the combinations of syntagmatic strings of the superficial grammar which are only anthropomorphic representations of these operations, the contents are invested, through the intermediary of the performances, in the narrative utterances, organized in linear strings of canonical utterances linked among themselves, like the links in a single chain, by a series of logical implications. When we have such strings of narrative utterances, we shall be able to conceive— with the help of a rhetoric, of a stylistics, but also of a linguistic grammar—of the linguistic manifestations of narrativized signification.

Bibliography: Works by A. J. Greimas

1949: *Le vocabulaire de la mode romantique,* thesis. [Paris: Sorbonne]
1956a: "L'actualité du saussurisme," *Le Francais Moderne,* 24.
1956b: "Pour une sociologie du language," *Arguments,* 1.
1960: "Idiotismes, proverbes, dictons," *Cahiers de Lexicologie,* 2 (reprinted in part in 1970b)

1962–63: "Linguistique statistique et linguistique structurale," *Le Francais Moderne*, 30, 31.

1963a: "La description de la signification et la mythologie comparée," *l'Homme*, 3 (also in 1970b); trans. *Mythology*, P. Marenda ed. [London: Penguin Books, 1972]

1963b: "Comment définir les indéfinis," *Etudes de Linguistique Appliquée*, II.

1964a: "La structure élémentaire de la signification en linguistique," *l'Homme*, 4 (also in 1966b).

1964b: "Les Topologiques," *Cahiers de Lexicologie*, 4, 1.

1964c: "La signification et sa manifestation dans le discours," *Cahiers de Lexicologie*, No. 5, 2

1965: "Le conte populaire russe, analyse fonctionnelle," *International Journal of Slavic Linguistics and Poetics*, IX (also in 1966b).

1966a: "Structure et Histoire," *Les Temps Modernes*, 246 (also in 1970b).

1966b: *Sémantique Structurale*. [Paris: Larousse].

1966c: "Eléments pour une théorie de l'interprétation du récit mythique," *Communications* No. 8 (also in 1970b); trans. as *Structural Analysis and Oral Tradition*, Pierre & Elie Maranda, ed. [Philadelphia: Univ. of Pennsylvania Press, 1971]

1967a: "La linguistique structurale et la poétique," *Revue Internationale des Sciences Sociales*, XIX (also in 1970b).

1967b: "Approche générative de l'analyse des actants," *Word*, 23, 1-2-3 (also in 1970b)

1967c: "L'Ecriture Cruciverbiste," *To Honor Roman Jakobson* [The Hague: Mouton]. (also in 1970b).

1967d: "Le problème des ad'dad et les niveaux de signification," *L'Ambivalence dans la Culture Arabe*, J. Berque & J. P. Charney ed. [Paris: Anthropos].

1967e: *Modelli semiologici*. [Urbino: Argalia].

1968a: "Conditions d'une sémiotique du monde naturel," *Languages*, 10 (also in 1970b).

1968b: "Réflexions sur la théorie du langage," in *Travaux de la Conférence Internationale de Sémiotique* (also in 1970b).

1968c: "The interactions of semiotic contraints," with Francois Rastier, *Yale French Studies*, 41 (French translation in 1970b).

1969a: "Eléments d'une grammaire narrative," *l'Homme*, IX (also in 1970b)

1969b: "La Structure sémantique," *Symposium on Cognitive Studies and Artificial Intelligence* (also in 1970b).

1969c: "Des modeles theoriques en socio-linguistique," *International Days of Socio-Linguistics* (also in 1970b).

1969d: *Dictionnaire de l'Ancien Francais* [Paris: Larousse].

1970a: "Sémantique, sémiotique et sémiologie," *Sign, Language, Culture*, ed. A. J. Greimas & al [The Hague: Mouton] (also in 1970b).

1970b: *Du sens* [Paris: Seuil].

1970d: "Sémiotique et communications sociales," *Annuario* of A. Gemmeli Institute Milano (also in 1976b).

1970e: "Analyse d'un discours juridique," with Eric Landowski, *Prepublications of Urbino University* (also in 1976b).

1970f: "La Littérature ethnique," *Colloque de Palerme sur la Littérature Ethnique* (avril 1970) (also in 1976b).

1971: "Narrative Grammar: Units and Levels," *Modern Language Notes*, 86.

1972a: *Essais de Sémiotique Poétique*, ed. (Paris: Larousse)

1972b: "Pour une sémiotique topologique," *Colloque sur la sémiotique de l'espace* (also in 1976b).

1973a: "Sur l'histoire événementielle," *Geschichte: Ereignis und Erzählung*, R. Kosellek, ed. [Munich: W. Fink].

1973b: "Réflexions sur les objets ethno-sémiotiques," *Congrès International d'Ethnologie européenne*, (also in 1976b).

1973c: "Les actants, les acteurs, et les figures," in *Sémiotique narrative et textuelle*, ed. Cl. Chabrol [Paris: Larousse].

1973d: "Un problème de sémiotique narrative: les objets de valeur," *Languages*, 31.

1974a: "Interview,"; by H. Parret, *Discussing Language*, H. Parret ed. (the Hague: Mouton).

1974b: "Des Accidents dans les sciences dites Humaines," *Versus* [Milan: Bompiani] (mimeograph).

1975: "Cendrillon va au bal," with J. Courtes, to be published in *Hommage à Germaine Duteurlein* [Paris: Hermann, 1977].

1975: "Cendrillon va au bal" with J. Courtès (mimeograph)

1976a: "Entretien avec Frederic Nef," *Structures Elémentaires de la* Signification, ed. F. Nef [Bruxelles: Complexe].

1976b: *Semiotique et Sciences sociales* [Paris: Seuil].

1976c: *Maupassant. La sémiotique du texte: Exercices Pratiques* [Paris: Seuil].

1976d: "Pour une theorie des modalités," *Languages*, 43.

1976e: *Semiotica do discurso científico. Da modalidaire* [Sao Paulo: Difel].

1976f: "Le contrat de veridiction," *Langages* vol. 5, No. 11, Tokyo (in Japanese).

1976g: "Entretien," *Pratiques*, 11-12

1976h: "Les acquis et les projets," *Introduction à la sémiotique narrative et discursive*, J. Courtés ed., [Paris: Hachette].

1976i: "The cognitive dimension of narrative discourses," with J. Courtès, *New Literary History*, VII, 3.

1977: "Essai sur la vie sentimentale des Hippopotames," with Frederic Nef *Grammars and Descriptions*, ed. Petofi & van Dyck [Berlin: De Gruyter] (in press).

NOTES

1. "Signification is then only this transposition from one language-level to another, of one language into a different language, and meaning [*sens*] is simply this possibility of transcoding" [1970b, p. 13].

2. Instance. The use of instance in contemporary French to convey at once a moment of occurrence or intervention and a state or status of insistency is increasingly widespread. Rather than translate it variously by terms such as level, moment, modality, import, etc., according to the context, we have de-

cided to use systematically the English cognate, instance (from the Latin *in-stantia*, a standing upon or near, being present). Cf. J. Lacan, "L'Instance de la lettre dans l'inconscient" in *Ecrits* [Paris: Seuil, 1965].

3. This semiotic square is not exactly the same as that of 1968. The shift is discussed in F. Nef, ed., *Structures élémentaires de la signification* [Bruxelles: Editions Complexe, 1976].

4. On the notion of isotopy (cf. hereafter 3.2.2), see Greimas, 1966, pp. 69–72; F. Rastier, "Vers une systématique des isotopies," in Greimas, 1972; and Rastier, *Essais de sémiotique discursive* [Paris: Mame, 1973]. The reader can compare this abstract notion with her/his intuitive experience of a level of reading.

5. English provides no adequate equivalent for this use of *vouloir* (wanting in the sense of volition), which is a verb (infinitive) used as a substantive. The same remark will apply to *le faire* (the doing) hereafter; contextual considerations have led us to translate *le faire* by the noun *practice*.

6. Concerning the terms "schema," "deixis," and "axis," cf. 1968:

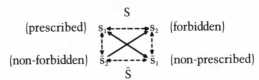

Here S and $\bar{S}$ are the axis; $s_1 + \bar{s}_1$ and $s_2 + \bar{s}_2$ are the schemas; $s_1 + \bar{s}_2$ and $s_2 + \bar{s}_1$ are the deixis. [cf. 1970, p. 140].

7. The problem of the number of actants is discussed in 1966, pp. 172–89, and also in René Thom, *Stabilité structurelle el morphogénèse* [Paris: Benjamin, 1972].

8. I.e., s_1—$\bar{s}_2$ and s_2—$\bar{s}_1$.

Eight
interpretation

Paul Ricoeur

What Is a Text? Explanation and Understanding

This essay will be devoted primarily to the debate between two fundamental attitudes which may be adopted in regard to a text. These two attitudes were summed up, in the period of Wilhelm Dilthey at the end of
the last century, by the two words 'explanation' and 'interpretation.' For
Dilthey, 'explanation' referred to the model of intelligibility borrowed
from the natural sciences and applied to the historical disciplines by positivist schools; 'interpretation,' on the other hand, was a derivative form
of understanding, which Dilthey regarded as the fundamental attitude of
the human sciences and as that which could alone preserve the fundamental difference between these sciences and the sciences of nature. Here
I propose to examine the fate of this opposition in the light of conflicts
between contemporary schools. For the notion of explanation has since
been displaced, so that it derives no longer from the natural sciences but
from properly linguistic models. As regards the concept of interpretation,
it has undergone profound transformations which distance it from the
psychological notion of understanding, in Dilthey's sense of the word. It
is this new position of the problem, perhaps less contradictory and more
fecund, which I should like to explore. But before unfolding the new concepts of explanation and understanding, I should like to pause at a preliminary question which in fact dominates the whole of our investigation.
The question is this: what is a text?

I. What Is a Text?

Let us say that a text is any discourse fixed by writing. According to this
definition, fixation by writing is constitutive of the text itself. But what
is fixed by writing? We have said: any discourse. Is this to say that discourse had to be pronounced initially in a physical or mental form? that
all writing was initially, at least in a potential way, speaking? In short,
what is the relation of the text to speech?

To begin with, we are tempted to say that all writing is added to some anterior speech. For if by speech [*parole*] we understand, with Ferdinand de Saussure, the realisation of language [*langue*] in an event of discourse, the production of an individual utterance by an individual speaker, then each test is in the same position as speech with respect to language. Moreover, writing as an institution is subsequent to speech, and seems merely to fix in linear script all the articulations which have already appeared orally. The attention given almost exclusively to phonetic writings seems to confirm that writing adds nothing to the phenomenon of speech other than the fixation which enables it to be conserved. Whence the conviction that writing is fixed speech, that inscription, whether it be graphics or recording, is inscription of speech—an inscription which, thanks to the subsisting character of the engraving, guarantees the persistence of speech.

The psychological and sociological priority of speech over writing is not in question. It may be asked, however, whether the late appearance of writing has not provoked a radical change in our relation to the very statements of our discourse. For let us return to our definition: the text is a discourse fixed by writing. What is fixed by writing is thus a discourse which could be said, of course, but which is written precisely because it is not said. Fixation by writing takes the very place of speech, occurring at the site where speech could have emerged. This suggests that a text is really a text only when it is not restricted to transcribing an anterior speech, when instead it inscribes directly in written letters what the discourse means.

This idea of a direct relation between the meaning of the statement and writing can be supported by reflecting on the function of reading in relation to writing. Writing calls for reading in a way which will enable us shortly to introduce the concept of interpretation. For the moment, let us say that the reader takes the place of the interlocutor, just as writing takes the place of speaking and the speaker. The writing-reading relation is thus not a particular case of the speaking-answering relation. It is not a relation of interlocution, not an instance of dialogue. It does not suffice to say that reading is a dialogue with the author through his work, for the relation of the reader to the book is of a completely different nature. Dialogue is an exchange of questions and answers; there is no exchange of this sort between the writer and the reader. The writer does not respond to the reader. Rather, the book divides the act of writing and the act of reading into two sides, between which there is no communication. The reader is absent from the act of writing; the writer is absent from the act of reading. The text thus produces a double eclipse of the reader and the writer. It thereby replaces the relation of dialogue, which directly connects the voice of one to the hearing of the other.

The substitution of reading for a dialogue which has not occurred is so manifest that when we happen to encounter an author and to speak to him (about his book, for example), we experience a profound disruption of the peculiar relation that we have with the author in and through his work. Sometimes I like to say that to read a book is to consider its author as already dead and the book as posthumous. For it is when the author is dead that the relation to the book becomes complete and, as it were, intact. The author can no longer respond; it only remains to read his work.

The difference between the act of reading and the act of dialogue confirms our hypothesis that writing is a realisation comparable and parallel to speech, a realisation which takes the place of it and, as it were, intercepts it. Hence we could say that what comes to writing is discourse as intention-to-say and that writing is a direct inscription of this intention, even if, historically and psychologically, writing began with the graphic transcription of the signs of speech. This emancipation of writing, which places the latter at the site of speech, is the birth of the text.

Now, what happens to the statement itself when it is directly inscribed instead of being pronounced? The most striking characteristic has always been emphasised: writing preserves discourse and makes it an archive available for individual and collective memory. It may be added that the linearisation of symbols permits an analytic and distinctive translation of all the successive and discrete features of language and thereby increases its efficacy. Is that all? Preservation and increased efficacy still only characterise the transcription of oral language in graphic signs. The emancipation of the text from the oral situation entails a veritable upheaval in the relations between language and the world, as well as in the relation between language and the various subjectivities concerned (that of the author and that of the reader). We glimpsed something of this second upheaval in distinguishing reading from dialogue; we shall have to go still further, but this time beginning from the upheaval which the referential relation of language to the world undergoes when the text takes the place of speech.

What do we understand by the referential relation or referential function? In addressing himself to another speaker, the subject of discourse says something about something; that about which he speaks is the referent of his discourse. As is well known, this referential function is supported by the sentence, which is the first and the simplest unit of discourse. It is the sentence which intends to say something true or something real, at least in declarative discourse. The referential function is so important that it compensates, as it were, for another characteristic of language, namely the separation of signs from things. By means of the referential function, language 'pours back into the universe' (according to an expression of Gustave Guillaume) those signs which the symbolic function, at its birth, divorced from things. All discourse is, to some extent, thereby reconnected to the world. For if we did not speak of the world, of what should we speak?

When the text takes the place of speech, something important occurs. In speech, the interlocutors are present not only to one another, but also to the situation, the surroundings and the circumstantial milieu of discourse. It is in relation to this circumstantial milieu that discourse is fully meaningful; the return to reality is ultimately a return to this reality, which can be indicated 'around' the speakers, 'around,' if we may say so, the instance of discourse itself. Language is, moreover, well equipped to secure this anchorage. Demonstratives, adverbs of time and place, personal pronouns, verbal tenses, and in general all the 'deictic' and 'ostensive' indicators serve to anchor discourse in the circumstantial reality which surrounds the instance of discourse. Thus, in living speech, the *ideal* sense of what is said turns towards the *real* reference, towards that 'about which' we speak. At the limit, this real reference tends to merge with an ostensive designation where speech rejoins the gesture of pointing. Sense fades into reference and the latter into the act of showing.

This is no longer the case when the text takes the place of speech. The movement of reference towards the act of showing is intercepted, at the same time as dialogue is interrupted by the text. I say intercepted and not suppressed; it is in this respect that I shall distance myself from what may be called henceforth the ideology of the absolute text. On the basis of the sound remarks which we have just made, this ideology proceeds, by an unwarranted hypostasis, through a course that is ultimately surreptitious. As we shall see, the text is not without reference; the task of reading, *qua* interpretation, will be precisely to fulfil the reference. The suspense which defers the reference merely leaves the text, as it were, 'in the air,' outside or without a world. In virtue of this obliteration of the relation to the world, each text is free to enter into relation with all the other texts which come to take the place of the circumstantial reality referred to by living speech. This relation of text to text, within the effacement of the world about which we speak, engenders the quasi-world of texts or *literature.*

Such is the upheaval which affects discourse itself, when the movement of reference towards the act of showing is intercepted by the text. Words cease to efface themselves in front of things; written words become words for themselves.

The eclipse of the circumstantial world by the quasi-world of texts can be so complete that, in a civilisation of writing, the world itself is no longer what can be shown in speaking but is reduced to a kind of 'aura' which written works unfold. Thus we speak of the Greek world or the Byzantine world. This world can be called 'imaginary,' in the sense that it is *represented* by writing in lieu of the world *presented* by speech; but this imaginary world is itself a creation of literature.

The upheaval in the relation between the text and its world is the key to the other upheaval of which we have already spoken, that which affects the relation of the text to the subjectivities of the author and the reader. We think that we know what the author of a text is because we derive the notion of the author from that of the speaker. The subject of speech, according to Benveniste, is what designates itself in saying 'I.' When the text takes the place of speech, there is no longer a speaker, at least in the sense of an immediate and direct self-designation of the one who speaks in the instance of discourse. This proximity of the speaking subject to his own speech is replaced by a complex relation of the author to the text, a relation which enables us to say that the author is instituted by the text, that he stands in the space of meaning traced and inscribed by writing. The text is the very place where the author appears. But does the author appear otherwise than as first reader? The distancing of the text from its author is already a phenomenon of the first reading which, in one move, poses the whole series of problems that we are now going to confront concerning the relations between explanation and interpretation. These relations arise at the time of reading.

II. Explanation or Understanding?

As we shall see, the two attitudes which we have initially placed under the double title of explanation and interpretation will confront one another in the act of reading. This duality is first encountered in the work of Dilthey. For him, these distinctions constituted an alternative wherein one term necessarily excluded the other: either you 'explain' in the manner of the natural scientist, or you 'interpret' in the manner of the historian. This exclusive alternative will provide the point of departure for the discussion which follows. I propose to show that the concept of the text, such as we have formulated it in the first part of this essay, demands a renewal of the two notions of explanation and interpretation and, in virtue of this renewal, a less contradictory conception of their interrelation. Let us say straightaway that the discussion will be deliberately oriented towards the search for a strict complementarity and reciprocity between explanation and interpretation.

The initial opposition in Dilthey's work is not exactly between explanation and interpretation, but between explanation and understanding, interpretation being a particular province of understanding. We must therefore begin from the opposition between explanation and understanding. Now if this opposition is exclusive, it is because, in Dilthey's work, the two terms designate two spheres of reality which they serve to separate. These two spheres are those of the natural sciences and the human sciences. Nature is the region of objects offered to scientific observation, a region subsumed since Galileo to the enterprise of mathematisation and since John Stuart Mill to the canons of inductive logic. Mind is the region of psychological individualities, into which each mental life is capable of transposing itself. Understanding is such a transference into another mental life. To ask whether the human sciences can exist is thus to ask whether a scientific knowledge of individuals is possible, whether this understanding of the singular can be objective in its own way, whether it is susceptible of universal validity. Dilthey answered affirmatively, because inner life is given in external signs which can be perceived and understood as signs of another mental life: 'Understanding,' he says in the famous article on 'The development of hermeneutics,' 'is the process by which we come to know something of mental life through the perceptible signs which manifest it.'[1] This is the understanding of which interpretation is a particular province. Among the signs of another mental life, we have the 'manifestations fixed in a durable way,' the 'human testimonies preserved by writing,' the 'written monuments.' Interpretation is the art of understanding applied to such manifestations, to such testimonies, to such monuments, of which writing is the distinctive characteristic. Understanding, as the knowledge through signs of another mental life, thus provides the basis in the pair understanding-interpretation; the latter element supplies the degree of objectification, in virtue of the fixation and preservation which writing confers upon signs.

Although this distinction between explanation and understanding seems clear at first, it becomes increasingly obscure as soon as we ask ourselves about the conditions of scientificity of interpretation. Explanation has been expelled from the field of the human sciences; but the conflict reappears at the very heart of the concept of interpretation between, on the one hand, the intuitive and unverifiable character of the psychologising concept of understanding to which interpretation is subordinated, and on the other hand the demand for objectivity which belongs to the very notion of human science. The splitting of hermeneutics between its psychologising tendency and its search for a logic of interpretation ultimately calls into question the relation between understanding and interpretation. Is not interpretation a species of understanding which explodes the genre? Is not the specific difference, namely fixation by writing, more important here than the feature common to all signs, that of presenting inner life in an external form? What is more important: the inclusion of hermeneutics in the sphere of understanding or its difference therefrom? Schleiermacher, before Dilthey, had witnessed this internal splitting of the hermeneutical project and had overcome it through a happy marriage

of *romantic genius* and *philological virtuosity*. With Dilthey, the epistemological demands are more pressing. Several generations separate him
from the scholar of Romanticism, several generations well versed in epistemological reflection; the contradiction now explodes in full daylight.
Listen to Dilthey commenting upon Schleiermacher: 'The ultimate aim
of hermeneutics is to understand the author better than he understands
himself.' So much for the psychology of understanding. Now for the logic
of interpretation: 'The function of hermeneutics is to establish theoretically, against the constant intrusion of romantic whim and sceptical subjectivism into the domain of history, the universal validity of interpretation, upon which all certitude in history rests.'[2] Thus hermeneutics
fulfils the aim of understanding only by extricating itself from the immediacy of understanding others—from, let us say, dialogical values. Understanding seeks to coincide with the inner life of the author, to liken
itself to him (*sich gleichsetzen*), to reproduce (*nachbilden*) the creative
processes which engendered the work. But the signs of this intention, of
this creation, are to be found nowhere else than in what Schleiermacher
called the 'exterior' and 'interior form' of the work, or again, the 'intercon-
nection' (*Zusammenhang*) which makes it an organised whole. The last
writings of Dilthey ('The construction of the historical world in the human sciences') further aggravated the tension. On the one hand, the objective side of the work was accentuated under the influence of Husserl's
Logical Investigations (for Husserl, as we know, the 'meaning' of a statement constitutes an 'ideality' which exists neither in mundane reality
nor in psychic reality: it is a pure unity of meaning without a real local-
isation). Hermeneutics similarly proceeds from the objectification of the
creative energies of life in works which come in between the author and
us; it is mental life itself, its creative dynamism, which calls for the mediation by 'meanings,' 'values' or 'goals.' The scientific demand thus
presses towards an ever greater depsychologisation of interpretation, of
understanding itself and perhaps even of introspection, if it is true that
memory itself follows the thread of meanings which are not themselves
mental phenomena. The exteriorisation of life implies a more indirect and
mediate characterisation of the interpretation of self and others. But it is
a self and another, posed in psychological terms, that interpretation pursues; interpretation always aims at a reproduction, a *Nachbildung*, of
lived experiences.

This intolerable tension, which the later Dilthey bears witness to,
leads us to raise two questions which guide the following discussion:
Must we not abandon once and for all the reference of interpretation to understanding and cease to make the interpretation of written monuments
a particular case of understanding the external signs of an inner mental
life? But if interpretation no longer seeks its norm of intelligibility in un-

derstanding others, then does not its relation to explanation, which we have set aside hitherto, now demand to be reconsidered?

III. The Text and Structural Explanation

Let us begin again from our analysis of the text and from the autonomous status which we have granted it with respect to speech. What we have called the eclipse of the surrounding world by the quasi-world of texts engenders two possibilities. We can, as readers, remain in the suspense of the text, treating it as a worldless and authorless object; in this case, we explain the text in terms of its internal relations, its structure. On the other hand, we can lift the suspense and fulfil the text in speech, restoring it to living communication; in this case, we interpret the text. These two possibilities both belong to reading, and reading is the dialectic of these two attitudes.

Let us consider them separately, before exploring their articulation. We can undertake a first type of reading which formally records, as it were, the text's interception of all the relations to a world that can be pointed out and to subjectivities that can converse. This transference into the 'place'—a place which is a non-place—constitutes a special project with respect to the text, that of prolonging the suspense concerning the referential relation to the world and to the speaking subject. By means of this special project, the reader decides to situate himself in the 'place of the text' and in the 'closure' of this place. On the basis of this choice, the text has no outside but only an inside; it has no transcendent aim, unlike a speech which is addressed to someone about something.

This project is not only possible but legitimate. For the constitution of the text as text and of the body of texts as literature justifies the interception of the double transcendence of discourse, towards the world and towards someone. Thus arises the possibility of an explanatory attitude in regard to the text.

In contrast to what Dilthey thought, this explanatory attitude is not borrowed from a field of knowledge and an epistemological model other than that of language itself. It is not a naturalistic model subsequently extended to the human sciences. The nature-mind opposition plays no role here at all. If there is some form of borrowing, it occurs within the same field, that of signs. For it is possible to treat the text according to the explanatory rules that linguistics successfully applies to the simple system of signs which constitute language [langue] as opposed to speech [parole]. As is well known, the language-speech distinction is the fundamental distinction which gives linguistics an homogenous object; speech belongs to physiology, psychology and sociology, whereas language, as rules of the game of which speech is the execution, belongs only to linguistics. As is equally well known, linguistics considers only systems of units devoid of proper meaning, each of which is defined only in terms of its difference from all of the others. These units, whether they be purely distinctive like those of phonological articulation or significant like those of lexical articulation, are oppositive units. The interplay of oppositions and their combinations within an inventory of discrete units is what defines the notion of structure in linguistics. This structural model furnishes the type of explanatory attitude which we are now going to see applied to the text.

Even before embarking upon this enterprise, it may be objected that the laws which are valid only for language as distinct from speech could not be applied to the text. Although the text is not speech, is it not, as it were, on the same side as speech in relation to language? Must not discourse, as a series of statements and ultimately of sentences, be opposed in an overall way to language? In comparison to the language-discourse distinction, is not the speaking-writing distinction secondary, such that speaking and writing occur together on the side of discourse? These remarks are perfectly legitimate and justify us in thinking that the structural model of explanation does not exhaust the field of possible attitudes which may be adopted in regard to a text. But before specifying the limits of this explanatory model, it is necessary to grasp its fruitfulness. The working hypothesis of any structural analysis of texts is this: in spite of the fact that writing is on the same side as speech in relation to language—namely, on the side of discourse—the specificity of writing in relation to speech is based on structural features which can be treated as analogues of language in discourse. This working hypothesis is perfectly legitimate; it amounts to saying that under certain conditions the larger units of language [*langage*], that is, the units of a higher order than the sentence, display organisations comparable to those of the smaller units of language, that is, the units which are of a lower order than the sentence and which belong to the domain of linguistics.

In *Structural Anthropology*, Claude Lévi-Strauss formulates this working hypothesis for one category of texts, the category of myths:

> Like every linguistic entity, myth is made up of constitutive units. These units imply the presence of those which normally enter into the structure of language, namely the phonemes, the morphemes and the semantemes. The constituent units of myth are in the same relation to semantemes as the latter are to morphemes, and as the latter in turn are to phonemes. Each form differs from that which precedes it by a higher degree of complexity. For this reason, we shall call the elements which properly pertain to myth (and which are the most complex of all): large constitutive units.[3]

By means of this working hypothesis, the large units which are minimally the size of the sentence, and which placed together constitute the narrative proper to the myth, can be treated according to the same rules that are applied to the smaller units familiar to linguistics. To indicate this analogy, Lévi-Strauss speaks of 'mythemes' in the same way that one speaks of phonemes, morphemes and semantemes. But in order to remain within the limits of the analogy between mythemes and the linguistic units of a lower level, the analysis of texts will have to proceed to the same sort of abstraction as that practised by the phonologist. For the latter, the phoneme is not a concrete sound, to be taken absolutely in its sonorous substance; it is a function defined by the commutative method and its oppositive value is determined by the relation to all other phonemes. In this sense it is not, as Saussure would say, a 'substance' but a 'form,' an interplay of relations. Similarly, a mytheme is not one of the sentences of the myth but an oppositive value which is shared by several particular sentences, constituting, in the language of Lévi-Strauss, a 'bundle of relations.' 'Only in the form of combinations of such bundles do the constituent units acquire a signifying function.'[4] What is called here the 'signifying function' is not at all what the myth means, its philosophical or existential import, but rather the arrangement or disposition of mythemes, in short, the structure of the myth.

I should like to recall briefly the analysis which, according to this method, Lévi-Strauss offers of the Oedius myth. He divides the sentences of the myth into four columns. In the first column he places all the sentences which speak of overrated blood relations (for example, Oedipus marries Jocasta, his mother; Antigone buries Polynices, her brother, in spite of the order forbidding it). In the second column, we find the same relation, but modified by the inverse sign: underrated or devalued blood relations (Oedipus kills his father, Laios; Eteocles kills his brother, Polynices). The third column concerns monsters and their destruction; the fourth groups together all those proper names whose meaning suggests a difficulty in walking straight (lame, clumsy, swollen foot). The comparison of the four columns reveals a correlation. Between the first and second columns we have blood relations overrated or underrated in turn; between the third and fourth we have an affirmation and then a negation of the autochtony of man. 'It follows that the fourth column is related to the third column as the first is to the second ... ; the overrating of blood relations is to their underrating as the attempt to escape from autochtony is to the impossibility of succeeding in it.' The myth thus appears as a kind of logical instrument which brings together contradictions in order to overcome them: 'the impossibility of connecting the groups of relations is overcome (or, more exactly, replaced) by the assertion that two contradictory relations are identical, insofar as each is, like the other, self-contradictory.'[5] We shall return shortly to this conclusion; let us restrict ourselves here to stating it.

We can indeed say that we have thereby explained the myth, but not that we have interpreted it. We have brought out, by means of structural analysis, the logic of the operations which interconnect the packets of relations; this logic constitutes 'the structural law of the myth concerned.'[6] We shall not fail to notice that this law is, *par excellence*, the object of reading and not at all of speech, in the sense of a recitation whereby the power of the myth would be reactivated in a particular situation. Here the text is only a text and the reading inhabits it only as such, while its meaning for us remains in suspense, together with any realisation in present speech.

I have just taken an example from the domain of myths; I could take another from a nearby domain, that of folklore. This domain has been explored by the Russian formalists of the school of Propp and by the French specialists in the structural analysis of narratives, Roland Barthes and A. J. Greimas. In the work of these authors, we find the same postulates as those employed by Lévi-Strauss: the units above the sentence have the same composition as the units below the sentence; the sense of the narrative consists in the very arrangement of the elements, in the power of the whole to integrate the sub-units; and conversely, the sense of an element is its capacity to enter in relation with other elements and with the whole of the work. These postulates together define the closure of the narrative. The task of structural analysis will be to carry out the segmentation of the work (horizontal aspect), then to establish the various levels of integration of the parts in the whole (hierarchical aspect). Thus the units of action isolated by the analyst will not be psychological units capable of being experienced, nor will they be units of behaviour which could be subsumed to a behaviourist psychology. The extremities of these sequences are only the switching points of the narrative, such that if one element is changed, all the rest is different. Here we recognise the transposition of the method of commutation from the phonological level to the level of narrative units. The logic of action thus consists in an interconnected series of action kernels which together constitute the structural continuity of the narrative. The application of this technique ends up by 'dechronologising' the narrative, in a way that brings out the logic underlying narrative time. Ultimately the narrative would be reduced to a combination [*combinatoire*] of a few dramatic units (promising, betraying, hindering, aiding, etc.) which would be the paradigms of action. A sequence is thus a succession of nodes of action, each closing off an alternative opened up by the preceding one. Just as the elementary units are linked together, so too they fit into larger units; for example, an encounter is comprised of elementary actions like approaching, calling out, greeting, etc. To explain a narrative is to grasp this entanglement, this fleeting structure of interlaced actions.

Corresponding to the nexus of actions are relations of a similar nature between the 'actants' of the narrative. By that we understand, not at all the characters as psychological subjects endowed with their own existence, but rather the roles correlated with formalised actions. Actants are defined entirely by the predicates of action, by the semantic axes of the sentence and the narrative: the actant is the one by whom, to whom, with whom, ... the action is done; it is the one who promises, who receives the promise, the giver, the receiver, etc. Structural analysis thus brings out a hierarchy of *actants* correlative to the hierarchy of *actions*.

The narrative remains to be assembled as a whole and put back into narrative communication. It is then a discourse which a narrator addresses to an audience. For structural analysis, however, the two interlocutors must be sought only in the text. The narrator is designated by the signs of narrativity, which belong to the very constitution of the narrative. Beyond the three levels of actions, actants and narration, there is nothing else that falls within the scope of the science of semiology. There is only the world of narrative users, which can eventually be dealt with by other semiological disciplines (those analysing social, economic and ideological systems); but these disciplines are no longer linguistic in nature. This transposition of a linguistic model to the theory of the narrative fully confirms our initial remark: today, explanation is no longer a concept borrowed from the natural sciences and transferred to the alien domain of written artefacts; rather, it stems from the very sphere of language, by analogical transference from the small units of language (phonemes and lexemes) to the units larger than the sentence, such as narratives, folklore and myth. Henceforth, interpretation—if it is still possible to give a sense to this notion—will no longer be confronted by a model external to the human sciences. It will, instead, be confronted by a model of intelligibility which belongs, from birth so to speak, to the domain of the human sciences, and indeed to a leading science in this domain: linguistics. Thus it will be upon the same terrain, within the same sphere of language [*langage*], that explanation and interpretation will enter into debate.

IV. Towards a New Concept of Interpretation

Let us consider now the other attitude that can be adopted in regard to the text, the attitude which we have called interpretation. We can introduce this attitude by initially opposing it to the preceding one, in a manner still close to that of Dilthey. But as we shall see, it will be necessary to proceed gradually to a more complementary and reciprocal relation between explanation and interpretation.

Let us begin once again from reading. Two ways of reading, we said, are offered to us. By reading we can prolong and reinforce the suspense which affects the text's reference to a surrounding world and to the audience of speaking subjects: that is the explanatory attitude. But we can also lift the suspense and fulfil the text in present speech. It is this second attitude which is the real aim of reading. For this attitude reveals the true nature of the suspense which intercepts the movement of the text towards meaning. The other attitude would not even be possible if it were not first apparent that the text, as writing, awaits and calls for a reading. If reading is possible, it is indeed because the text is not closed in on itself but opens out onto other things. To read is, on any hypothesis, to conjoin a new discourse to the discourse of the text. This conjunction of discourses reveals, in the very constitution of the text, an original capacity for renewal which is its open character. Interpretation is the concrete outcome of conjunction and renewal.

In the first instance, we shall be led to formulate the concept of interpretation in opposition to that of explanation. This will not distance us appreciably from Dilthey's position, except that the opposing concept of explanation has already gained strength by being derived from linguistics and semiology rather than being borrowed from the natural sciences.

According to this first sense, interpretation retains the feature of appropriation which was recognised by Schleiermacher, Dilthey and Bultmann. In fact, this sense will not be abandoned; it will only be mediated by explanation, instead of being opposed to it in an immediate and even naive way. By 'appropriation,' I understand this: that the interpretation of a text culminates in the self-interpretation of a subject who thenceforth understands himself better, understands himself differently, or simply begins to understand himself. This culmination of the understanding of a text in self-understanding is characteristic of the kind of reflective philosophy which, on various occasions, I have called 'concrete reflection.' Here hermeneutics and reflective philosophy are correlative and reciprocal. On the one hand, self-understanding passes through the detour of understanding the cultural signs in which the self documents and forms itself. On the other hand, understanding the text is not an end in itself; it mediates the relation to himself of a subject who, in the short circuit of immediate reflection, does not find the meaning of his own life. Thus it must be said, with equal force, that reflection is nothing without the mediation of signs and works, and that explanation is nothing if it is not incorporated as an intermediary stage in the process of self-understanding. In short, in hermeneutical reflection—or in reflective hermeneutics— the constitution of the *self* is contemporaneous with the constitution of *meaning*.

The term 'appropriation' underlines two additional features. One of the aims of all hermeneutics is to struggle against cultural distance. This struggle can be understood in purely temporal terms as a struggle against secular estrangement, or in more genuinely hermeneutical terms as a struggle against the estrangement from meaning itself, that is, from the system of values upon which the text is based. In this sense, interpretation 'brings together,' 'equalises,' renders 'contemporary and similar,' thus genuinely making one's *own* what was initially *alien*.

Above all, the characterisation of interpretation as appropriation is meant to underline the 'present' character of interpretation. Reading is like the execution of a musical score; it marks the realisation, the enactment, of the semantic possibilities of the text. This final feature is the most important because it is the condition of the other two (that is, of overcoming cultural distance and of fusing textual interpretation with self-interpretation). Indeed, the feature of realisation discloses a decisive aspect of reading, namely that it fulfils the discourse of the text in a dimension similar to that of speech. What is retained here from the notion of speech is not the fact that it is uttered but that it is an event, an instance of discourse, as Benveniste says. The sentences of a text signify *here and now*. The 'actualised' text finds a surrounding and an audience; it resumes the referential movement—intercepted and suspended—towards a world and towards subjects. This world is that of the reader, this subject is the reader himself. In interpretation, we shall say, reading becomes like speech. I do not say 'becomes speech,' for reading is never equivalent to a spoken exchange, a dialogue. But reading culminates in a concrete act which is related to the text as speech is related to discourse, namely as event and instance of discourse. Initially the text had only a sense, that is, internal relations or a structure; now it has a meaning, that is, a realisation in the discourse of the reading subject. By virtue of its sense, the text had only a semiological dimension; now it has, by virtue of its meaning, a semantic dimension.

Let us pause here. Our discussion has reached a critical point where interpretation, understood as appropriation, still remains external to explanation in the sense of structural analysis. We continue to oppose them as if they were two attitudes between which it is necessary to choose. I should like now to go beyond this antithetical opposition and to bring out the articulation which would render structural analysis and hermeneutics complementary. For this it is important to show how each of the two attitudes which we have juxtaposed refers back, by means of its own peculiar features, to the other.

Consider again the examples of structural analysis which we have borrowed from the theory of myth and narrative. We tried to adhere to a notion of sense which would be strictly equivalent to the arrangement of the elements of a text, to the integration of the segments of action and the actants within the narrative treated as a whole closed in upon itself. In fact, no one stops at so formal a conception of sense. For example, what Lévi-Strauss calls a 'mytheme'—in his eyes, the constitutive unit of myth—is expressed in a sentence which has a specific meaning: Oedipus kills his father, Oedipus marries his mother, etc. Can it be said that structural explanation neutralises the specific meaning of sentences, retaining only their position in the myth? But the bundle of relations to which Lévi-Strauss reduces the mytheme is still of the order of the sentence; and the interplay of oppositions which is instituted at this very abstract level is equally of the order of the sentence and of meaning. If one speaks of 'overrated' or 'underrated blood relations,' of the 'autochtony' or 'non-autochtony' of man, these relations can still be written in the form of a sentence: the blood relation is the highest of all, or the blood relation is not as high as the social relation, for example in the prohibition of incest, etc. Finally, the contradiction which the myth attempts to resolve, according to Lévi-Strauss, is itself stated in terms of meaningful relations. Lévi-Strauss admits this, in spite of himself, when he writes: 'The reason for these choices becomes clear if we recognise that mythical thought proceeds from the consciousness of certain oppositions and tends towards their progressive mediation';[7] and again, 'the myth is a kind of logical tool intended to effect a mediation between life and death.'[8] In the background of the myth there is a question which is highly significant, a question about life and death: 'Are we born from one or from two?' Even in its formalised version, 'Is the same born from the same or from the other?,' this question expresses the anguish of origins: whence comes man? Is he born from the earth or from his parents? There would be no contradiction, nor any attempt to resolve contradiction, if there were not significant questions, meaningful propositions about the origin and the end of man. It is this function of myth as a narrative of origins that structural analysis seeks to place in parentheses. But such analysis does not succeed in eluding this function: it merely postpones it. Myth is not a logical operator between any propositions whatsoever, but involves propositions which point towards limit situations, towards the origin and the end, towards death, suffering and sexuality.

Far from dissolving this radical questioning, structural analysis reinstates it at a more radical level. Would not the function of structural analysis then be to impugn the surface semantics of the recounted myth in order to unveil a depth semantics which is, if I may say so, the living semantics of the myth? If that were not the function of structural analysis, then it would, in my opinion, be reduced to a sterile game, to a derisory combination [*combinatoire*] of elements, and myth would be deprived of the function which Lévi-Strauss himself recognises when he

asserts that mythical thought arises from the awareness of certain oppositions and tends towards their rogressive mediation. This awareness is a
recognition of the *aporias* of human existence around which mythical
thought gravitates. To eliminate this meaningful intention would be to reduce the theory of myth to a necrology of the meaningless discourses of
mankind. If, on the contrary, we regard structural analysis as a stage—
and a necessary one—between a naive and a critical interpretation, between a surface and a depth interpretation, then it seems possible to situate explanation and interpretation along a unique *hermeneutical arc*
and to integrate the opposed attitudes of explanation and understanding
within an overall conception of reading as the recovery of meaning.

We shall take another step in the direction of this reconciliation between explanation and interpretation if we now turn towards the second
term of the initial contradiction. So far we have worked with a concept of
interpretation which remains very subjective. To interpret, we said, is to
appropriate *here and now* the intention of the text. In saying that, we remain enclosed within Dilthey's concept of understanding. Now what we
have just said about the depth semantics unveiled by the structural analysis of the text invites us to say that the intended meaning of the text is not
essentially the presumed intention of the author, the lived experience of
the writer, but rather what the text means for whoever complies with its
injunction. The text seeks to place us in its meaning, that is—according
to another acceptation of the word *sens*—in the same direction. So if the
intention is that of the text, and if this intention is the direction which it
opens up for thought, then depth semantics must be understood in a fundamentally dynamic way. I shall therefore say: to explain is to bring out
the structure, that is, the internal relations of dependence which constitute the statics of the text; to interpret is to follow the path of thought
opened up by the text, to place oneself *en route* towards the *orient* of the
text. We are invited by this remark to correct our initial concept of interpretation and to search—beyond a subjective process of interpretation as
an act *on* the text—for an objective process of interpretation which
would be the act *of* the text.

I shall borrow an example from a recent study which I made of the
exegesis of the sacerdotal story of creation in Genesis 1–2, 4a.[9] This exegesis reveals, in the interior of the text, the interplay of two narratives: a
Tatbericht in which creation is expressed as a narrative of action ('God
made . . . '), and a *Wortbericht*, that is, a narrative of speech ('God said, and
there was . . . '). The first narrative could be said to play the role of tradition
and the second of interpretation. What is interesting here is that interpretation, before being the act of the exegete, is the act of the text. The relation between tradition and interpretation is a relation internal to the text;

for the exegete, to interpret is to place himself in the meaning indicated by the relation of interpretation which the text itself supports.

This objective and, as it were, intra-textual concept of interpretation is by no means unusual. Indeed, it has a long history rivalling that of the concept of subjective interpretation which is linked, it will be recalled, to the problem of understanding others through the signs that others give of their conscious life. I would willingly connect this new concept of interpretation to that referred to in the title of Aristotle's treatise *On Interpretation*. Aristotle's *hermenetia*, in contrast to the hermeneutical technique of seers and oracles, is the very action of language on things. Interpretation, for Aristotle, is not what one does in a second language with regard to a first; rather, it is what the first language already does, by mediating through signs our relation to things. Hence interpretation is, according to the commentary of Boethius, the work of the *vox significativa per se ipsam aliquid significans, sive complexa, sive incomplexa*. Thus it is the noun, the verb, discourse in general, which interprets in the very process of signifying.

It is true that interpretation in Aristotle's sense does not exactly prepare the way for understanding the dynamic relation between several layers of meaning in the same text. For it presupposes a theory of speech and not a theory of the text: 'The sounds articulated by the voice are symbols of states of the soul, and written words are symbols of words uttered in speech' (*On Interpretation*, para. 1). Hence interpretation is confused with the semantic dimension of speech: interpretation is discourse itself, it is any discourse. Nevertheless, I retain from Aristotle the idea that interpretation is interpretation *by* language before being interpretation *of* lnaguage.

I would look in the work of Charles Sanders Peirce for a concept of interpretation which is closer to that required by an exegesis which relates interpretation to tradition in the very interior of a text. According to Peirce, the relation of a 'sign' to an 'object' is such that another relation, that between 'interpretant' and 'sign,' can be grafted onto the first. What is important for us is that this relation between interpretant and sign is an open relation, in the sense that there is always another interpretant capable of mediating the first relation. G.-G. Granger explains this very well in his *Essai d'une philosophie du style:*

> The interpretant which the sign evokes in the mind could not be the result of a pure and simple deduction which would extract from the sign something already contained therein ... The interpretant is a commentary, a definition, a gloss on the sign in its relation to the object. The interpretant is itself symbolic expression. The sign—interpretant association, realised by whatever psychological

processes, is rendered possible only by the community, more or less imperfect, of an experience between speaker and hearer ... It is always an experience which can never be perfectly reduced to the idea or object of the sign of which, as we said, it is the structure. Whence the indefinite character of Peirce's series of interpretants.[10]

We must, of course, exercise a great deal of care in applying Peirce's concept of interpretant to the interpretation of texts. His interpretant is an interpretant of signs, whereas our interpretant is an interpretant of statements. But our use of the interpretant, transposed from small to large units, is neither more nor less analogical than the structuralist transfer of the laws of organisation from units of levels below the sentence to units of an order above or equal to the sentence. In the case of structuralism, it is the phonological structure of language which serves as the coding model of structures of higher articulation. In our case, it is a feature of lexical units which is transposed onto the plane of statements and texts. So if we are perfectly aware of the analogical character of the transposition, then we can say that the open series of interpretants, which is grafted onto the relation of a sign to an object, brings to light a triangular relation of object—sign—interpretant; and that the latter relation can serve as a model for another triangle which is constituted at the level of the text. In the new triangle, the object is the text itself; the sign is the depth semantics disclosed by structural analysis; and the series of interpretants is the chain of interpretations produced by the interpreting community and incorporated into the dynamics of the text, as the work of meaning upon itself. Within this chain, the first interpretants serve as tradition for the final interpretants, which are the interpretation in the true sense of the term.

Thus informed by the Aristotelian concept of interpretation and above all by Peirce's concept, we are in a position to 'depsychologise' as far as possible our notion of interpretation, and to connect it with the process which is at work in the text. Henceforth, for the exegete, to interpret is to place himself within the sense indicated by the relation of interpretation supported by the text.

The idea of interpretation as appropriation is not, for all that, eliminated; it is simply postponed until the termination of the process. It lies at the extremity of what we called above the *hermeneutical arc:* it is the final brace of the bridge, the anchorage of the arch in the ground of lived experience. But the entire theory of hermeneutics consists in mediating this interpretation-appropriation by the series of interpretants which belong to the work of the text upon itself. Appropriation loses its arbitrariness insofar as it is the recovery of that which is at work, in labour, within the text. What the interpreter says is a re-saying which reactivates what is said by the text.

At the end of our investigation, it seems that reading is the concrete act in which the destiny of the text is fulfilled. It is at the very heart of reading that explanation and interpretation are indefinitely opposed and reconciled.

NOTES

1. W. Dilthey, 'Origine et développement de l'herméneutiqué (1900) in *Le Monde de l'Esprit* I (Paris: Aubier, 1947), p. 320 [English translation: 'The development of hermeneutics' in *Selected Writings*, edited and translated by H. P. Rickman (Cambridge: Cambridge University Press, 1976), p. 248].†

2. Ibid., p. 333 [pp. 259–60].†

3. Claude Lévi-Strauss, *Anthropologie structurale* (Paris: Plon, 1958) p. 233 [English translation: *Structural Anthropology,* translated by Claire Jacobson and Brooke Grundfest Schoepf (Harmondsworth: Penguin Books, 1968), pp. 210–11].†

4. Ibid., p. 234 [p. 211].†

5. Ibid., p. 239 [p. 216].†

6. Ibid., p. 241 [p. 217].†

7. Ibid., p. 248 [p. 224].†

8. Ibid., p. 243 [p. 220].†

9. See Paul Ricoeur, 'Sur l'exégèse de Genèse 1, 1–2, 4a' in Roland Barthes et al., *Exégèse et herméneutique* (Paris: Seuil, 1971), pp. 67–84.

10. G.-G. Granger, *Essai d'une philosophie du style* (Paris: A. Colin, 1968), p. 115.

Stanley Fish

Demonstration vs. Persuasion: Two Models of Critical Activity

By asserting, as I did at the close of my last lecture, that interpretation is the only game in town, I may have seemed only to confirm the fears of those who argue for the necessity of determinate meaning: for, one might say, if interpretation covers the field, there is nothing to constrain its activities and no way to prevent, or even to recognize, its irresponsible exercise. But this is to think of interpretation as something external to the center it supposedly threatens, whereas I have been arguing that interpretation is constitutive of the center—of what will count as a fact, as a text, as a piece of evidence, as a reasonable argument—and thus defines its own limits and boundaries. The mistake is to think of interpretation as an activity in need of constraints, when in fact interpretation is a *structure* of constraints. The field interpretation covers comes complete with its own internal set of rules and regulations, its list of prescribed activities which is also, and at the same time, a list of activities that are proscribed. That is, within a set of interpretive assumptions, to know what you can do is, *ipso facto,* to know what you can't do; indeed, you can't know one without the other; they come together in a diacritical package, indissolubly wed. So that while irresponsible behavior certainly exists (in that one can always recognize it), it exists not as a threat to the system but as a component within it, as much defining responsible behavior as responsible behavior defines it.

That is why the fear of interpretation that is anarchic or totally relativistic will never be realized; for in the event that a fringe or off-the-wall interpretation makes its way into the center, it will merely take its place in a new realignment in which *other* interpretations will occupy the position of being off-the-wall. That is, off-the-wallness is not a property of interpretations that have been judged inaccurate with respect to a freestanding text but a property of an interpretive system within whose confines the text is continually being established and reestablished. It is not a pure but a relational category; an off-the-wall interpretation is simply one that exists in a reciprocally defining relationship with interpretations that are on the wall (you know it by what it is not, and you know what it is not by it); and since the stipulation of what is and is not off the wall is a matter of dispute (the system is precisely a mechanism for the endless negotiation of what will be authorized or nonauthorized) there is always the possibility, and indeed the certainty, that the shape of the stipulation will change. What is not a possibility, however, is that there be *only* off-the-wall interpretation (that "anything goes") because the category only has meaning by virtue of its binary opposite, which is, of course, no less dependent on it. The conclusion is paradoxical, but only superficially so: there is no such thing as an off-the-wall interpretation if by that one means an interpretation that has nothing to do with the text; and yet there is always an off-the-wall interpretation if by that one means an interpretation constitutive of the boundaries within which the text can emerge.

The further conclusion is that off-the-wallness is not inimical to the system but essential to it and to its operation. The production and perception of off-the-wall interpretations is no less a learned and conventional activity than the production and perception of interpretations that are judged to be acceptable. They are, in fact, the same activities enabled by the same set of in-force assumptions about what one can say and not say as a certified member of a community. It is, in short, no easier to disrupt the game (by throwing a monkey wrench into it) than it is to get away from it (by performing independently of it), and for the same reasons. One cannot disrupt the game because any interpretation one puts forward, no matter how "absurd," will already be *in* the game (otherwise one could not even conceive of it as an interpretation); and one cannot get away from the game because anything one does (any account of a text one offers) will be possible and recognizable only within the conditions the game has established.

It is because one can neither disrupt the game nor get away from it that there is never a rupture in the practice of literary criticism. Changes are always produced and perceived within the rules of the game, that is, within its stipulations as to what counts as a successful performance, what claims can be made, what procedures will validate or disconfirm them; and even when some of these stipulations are challenged, others must still be in place in order for the challenge to be recognized. Continuity in the practice of literary criticism is assured not despite but because of the absence of a text that is independent of interpretation. Indeed, from the perspective I have been developing, the fear of discontinuity is an incoherent one. The irony is that discontinuity is only a danger within the model erected to guard against it; for only if there is a free-standing text is there the possibility of moving away from it. But in the system I have been describing any movement away from the text is simultaneously a movement toward it, that is, toward its reappearance as an extension of whatever interpretation has come to the fore.

It could be objected that the continuity I have demonstrated is purchased at its own price, the price of an even greater incoherence attaching to the rationale for engaging in the activity at all; for if changes are to be explained with reference to the conventions of criticism rather than to the ideal of more accurately presenting an independent text, then their succession is pointless, and there is no reason, except for the opportunities made available by the conventions, to argue for one interpretation rather than another. Criticism thus becomes a supremely cynical activity in which one urges a point of view only because it is likely to win points or because it is as yet unsponsored by anyone else. In this view, while all developments are related and therefore not random, in the absence of any extrainstitutional goal such as the progressive clarification of the text, they are empty.

Not only is such a view disturbing but it seems counterintuitive given the very real sense we all have, both as critics and teachers, of advancing toward a clearer sight of our object. Jonathan Culler speaks for all of us when he declares that "often one feels that one has indeed been shown the way to a fuller understanding of literature," and, as he points out, "the time and effort devoted to literary education by generations of students and teachers creates a strong presumption that there is something to be learned, and teachers do not hesitate to judge their pupils' progress toward a general literary competence."[1] Of all the objections to the denial of determinate meaning, this is the most powerful because it trades on the fear, as Culler expresses it, "that the whole institution of literary education is but a gigantic confidence trick." That is to say, if we really believe that a text has no determinate meaning, then how can we presume to judge our students' approximations of it, and, for that matter, how can we presume to teach them anything at all? The question is the one posed by E. D. Hirsch in 1967—"On what ground does [the teacher of literature] claim that his 'reading' is more valid than that of any pupil?"—and common sense as well as professional self-respect are on the side of asserting that the ground must be something other than the accidental fact of a teacher's classroom authority.

The issue is not simply the basis of the confidence we ask our students to have in us but the basis of the confidence we might have in ourselves. How can someone who believes that the force and persuasiveness of an interpretation depends on institutional circumstances (rather than any normative standard of correctness), and that those circumstances are continually changing, argue with conviction for the interpretation he happens to hold at the present time? The answer is that the general or metacritical belief (to which I am trying to persuade you in these lectures) does not in any way affect the belief or set of beliefs (about the nature of literature, the proper mode of critical inquiry, the forms of literary evidence, and so on) which yields the interpretation that now seems to you (or me) to be inescapable and obvious. I may, in some sense, *know* that my present reading of *Paradise Lost* follows from assumptions that I did not always hold and may not hold in a year or so, but that "knowledge" does not prevent me from knowing that my present reading of *Paradise Lost* is the correct one. This is because the reservation with which I might offer my reading amounts to no more than saying "of course I may someday change my mind," but the fact that my mind may someday be other than it now is does not alter the fact that it *is* what it now is; no more than the qualifying "as far as I know" with which someone might preface an assertion means that he doesn't know what he knows—he may someday know something different, and when he does, that something will *then* be as far as he knows and he will know it no less firmly than what he knows today. An awareness that one's perspective is limited does not make the facts yielded by that perspective seem any less real; and when that perspective has given way to another, a new set of facts will occupy the position of the real ones.

Now one might think that someone whose mind had been changed many times would at some point begin to doubt the evidence of his sense, for, after all, "this too may pass," and "what I see today I may not see tomorrow." But doubting is not something one does outside the assumptions that enable one's consciousness; rather doubting, like any other mental activity, is something that one does *within* a set of assumptions that cannot at the same time be the object of doubt. That is to say, one does not doubt in a vacuum but from a perspective, and that perspective is itself immune to doubt until it has been replaced by another which will then be similarly immune. The project of radical doubt can never outrun the necessity of being situated; in order to doubt *everything*, including the ground one stands on, one must stand somewhere else, and that somewhere else will then be the ground on which one stands. This infinite regress could be halted only if one could stand free of any ground whatsoever, if the mind could divest itself of all prejudices and presuppositions and start, in the Cartesian manner, from scratch; but then of course you would have nothing to start *with* and anything with which you *did* start (even "I think, therefore I am") would be a prejudice or a presupposition. To put the matter in a slightly different way: radical skepticism is a possibility only if the mind exists independently of its furnishing, of the categories of understanding that inform it; but if, as I have been arguing, the mind is constituted by those categories, there is no possibility of achieving the distance from them that would make them available to a skpetical inquiry. In short, one cannot, properly speaking, *be* a skeptic, and one cannot be a skeptic for the same reason that one cannot be a relativist, because one cannot achieve the distance from his own beliefs and assumptions that would result in their being no more authoritative *for him* than the beliefs and assumptions held by others or the beliefs and assumptions he himself used to hold. The conclusion is tautological but inescapable: one believes what one believes, and one does so without reservation. The reservation inherent in the general position I have been arguing— that one's beliefs and therefore one's assumptions are always subject to change—has no real force, since until a change occurs the interpretation that seems self-evident to me will continue to seem so, no matter how many previous changes I can recall.

This does not mean that one is always a prisoner of his present perspective. It is always possible to entertain beliefs and opinions other than one's own; but that is precisely how they will be seen, as beliefs and opinions *other than one's own*, and therefore as beliefs and opinions that are false, or mistaken, or partial, or immature, or absurd. That is why a revolution in one's beliefs will always feel like a progress, even though, from the outside, it will have the appearance merely of a change. If one believes what one believes, then one believes that what one believes is *true*, and conversely, one believes that what one doesn't believe is not true, even if that is something one believed a moment ago. We can't help thinking that our present views are sounder than those we used to have or those professed by others. Not only does one's current position stand in a privileged relation to positions previously held, but previously held positions will always have the status of false or imperfect steps, of wrongly taken directions, of clouded or deflected perceptions. In other words, the idea of progress is inevitable, not, however, because there *is* a progress in the sense of a clearer and clearer sight of an independent object but because the *feeling* of having progressed is an inevitable consequence of the firmness with which we hold our beliefs, or, to be more precise, of the firmness with which our beliefs hold us.[2]

That firmness does not preclude a certain nostalgia for the beliefs we used to hold; the sense of progress that attends belief is not always a comfortable one. Quite often we find it inconvenient to believe the things we currently believe, but we find too that it is impossible not to believe them. The recent history of formal linguistics provides a nice example. Whatever judgment history will finally make on the "Chomsky revolution," there can be no doubt of its effects on the practitioners of the discipline. The promise, held out by the generative model, that linguistic behavior could be reduced to a set of abstract formal rules with built-in recursive functions united linguists in a sustained and exhilarating search for those rules. Not only did success seem just around the corner but the generality of the model (it seemed to offer no less than a picture of the operations of the human mind) was such that it recommended itself to a succession of neighboring and not so neighboring disciplines—anthropology, philosophy, sociology, psychology, educational theory, literary criticism. Suddenly in each of these fields one heard the increasingly familiar talk of transformations, deep and surface structures, the distinction between competence and performance, and so on. Linguistics, which had occupied a position in the intellectual world not unlike that of Classics—well thought of but little attended to—suddenly found itself at the center of discussion and debate. In the late sixties, however, a group of Chomsky's best students mounted a disquieting and finally successful challenge to the model within whose assumptions researchers were working by pointing to data that could not be accommodated within those assumptions. In a classic instance of a Kuhnian paradigm shift, the now orthodox Chomskians (defending what they called, significantly, the "standard theory") responded by either ignoring the data, or consigning them to the wastebasket of "performance," or declaring them to be assimilable within the standard model given a few minor revisions or refinements (here a key phrase was "notational variant"). In time, however, the weight of the unassimilable data proved too much for the model, and it more or less collapsed, taking with it much of the euphoria and optimism that had energized the field for a brief but glorious period. The workers in the field (or at least many of them) were in the position of no longer being able to believe in something they would have liked to believe in.

One sees this clearly, for example, in the opening paragraph of Barbara Partee's survey, in 1971, of linguistic metatheory:

> It was much easier to teach a course in syntax in 1965 or 1966 than it is now. In 1965 we had Chomsky's *Aspects* model, and if one didn't pay too much attention to disquieting things like Lakoff's thesis and Postal's underground *Linguistic anarchy notes,* one could present a pretty clear picture of syntax with a well understood phonological component tacked on one end and a not-yet-worked-out imaginable semantic component tacked on the other end. There were plenty of unsolved problems to work on, but the *paradigm* (in Kuhn's sense) seemed clear. But now we're in a situation where there is no theory which is both worked out in a substantial and presentable form and compatible with all the data considered important.[3]

In the face of this situation, Professor Partee finds herself still teaching the *Aspects* model, but only as an "elegant solution" to some syntactic problems; she spends most of her time, she reports, showing her students the "data which doesn't seem amenable to treatment in the framework at all" (p. 652). This is not what she would like to do, but what she *has* to do. "I'm by now sure," she declares regretfully, "that the Katz-Postal-*As-*

pects model can't work, and I consider that a great pity" (p. 675). Pity or not, she can't help herself. No matter how convenient it would be if she still believed in the *Aspects* model—convenient for her teaching, for her research, for her confidence in the very future of the discipline—she can only believe what she believes. That is, she can't *will* a belief in the *Aspects* model any more than she can will a disbelief in the arguments that persuaded her that it was unworkable. (Willing, like doubting, is an action of the mind, and like doubting, it cannot be performed outside the beliefs that are the mind's furniture.)

In literary studies the analogous situation would be one in which a critic or teacher felt compelled (against his wishes, if not his will) to give up an interpretation because it no longer seemed as self-evident as it once did. I myself am now precisely in that position with respect to Spenser's *Shepheardes Calender.* For more than fifteen years I have taught the *Calender* as a serious exploration of pastoral attitudes and possibilities, as a sequence more or less preliminary to Milton's "Lycidas"; but recently I have been persuaded to a different idea of pastoral, one less serious (in the sense of solemn) and more informed by a spirit of play and playful inquiry. As a result when I now look at the *Calender,* I no longer see what I used to see and things that I never saw before now seem obvious and indisputable. Moreover, my sense of which eclogues are central, and in what ways, has changed entirely so that I am now (self-) deprived of some of the set pieces with which I used to adorn my teaching. Instead, I spend most of my time talking about eclogues to which I had previously paid no attention at all, and fielding questions that sound disconcertingly like objections from my former self.

Of course everyone will have had similar experiences, and they will all point to the same conclusion: not only does one believe what one believes but one *teaches* what one believes even if it would be easier and safer and more immediately satisfying to teach something else. No one ever tells a class that he will not teach the interpretation he believes in because he thinks that the interpretation he used to believe in is better. If he thought that his former interpretation was better, he would still believe in it, because to believe in an interpretation is to think that it is better. And since you will always believe in something, there will always be something to teach, and you will teach that something with all the confidence and enthusiasm that attends belief, even if you know, as I do, that the belief which gives you that something, and gives it to you so firmly, may change. The question sometimes put to me—"If what you are saying is true, what is the point of teaching or arguing for anything?"—misses *my* point, which is not that there is no perspective within which one may proceed confidently but that one is always and already proceeding within just such a perspective because one is always and already proceeding within a structure of beliefs. The fact that a standard of truth is never available independently of a set of beliefs does not mean that we can never know for certain what is true but that we *always* know for certain what is true (because we are always in the grip of some belief or other), even though what we certainly know may change if and when our beliefs change. Until they do, however, we will argue *from* their perspective and *for* their perspective, telling our students and readers what it is that we certainly see and trying to alter their perceptions so that, in time, they will come to see it too.

In short, we try to persuade others to our beliefs because if they believe what we believe, they will, as a consequence of those beliefs, see what we see; and the facts to which we point in order to support our interpretations will be as obvious to them as they are to us. Indeed, this is the whole of critical activity, an attempt on the part of one party to alter the beliefs of another so that the evidence cited by the first will be seen *as* evidence by the second. In the more familiar model of critical activity (codified in the dogma and practices of New Criticism) the procedure is exactly the reverse: evidence available apart from any particular belief is brought in to judge between competing beliefs, or, as we call them in literary studies, interpretations. This is a model derived from an analogy to the procedures of logic and scientific inquiry, and basically it is a model of *demonstration* in which interpretations are either confirmed or disconfirmed by facts that are independently specified. The model I have been arguing for, on the other hand, is a model of *persuasion* in which the facts that one cites are available only because an interpretation (at least in its general and broad outlines) has already been assumed. In the first model critical activity is controlled by free-standing objects in relation to which its accounts are either adequate or inadequate; in the other model critical activity is constitutive of its object. In one model the self must be purged of its prejudices and presuppositions so as to see clearly a text that is independent of them; in the other, prejudicial or perspectival perception is all there is, and the question is from which of a number of equally interested perspectives will the text be constituted. In one model change is (at least ideally) progressive, a movement toward a more accurate account of a fixed and stable entity; in the other, change occurs when one perspective dislodges another and brings with it entities that had not before been available.

Obviously the stakes are much higher in a persuasion than in a demonstration model, since they include nothing less than the very conditions under which the game, in all of its moves (description, evaluation, validation, and so on), will be played. That is why Jonathan Culler is only half right when he says that "the possibility of bringing someone to see that a particular interpretation is a good one assumes shared points of departure and common notions of how to read" (p. 28). Culler is right to insist that notions of correctness and acceptability are institution-specific and that knowledge of these "shared points of departure" is a prerequisite of what he calls "literary competence." But he is wrong to imply (as he does here and elsewhere) that literary competence is an unchanging set of rules or operations to which critics must submit in order to be recognized as players in the game. Culler's model of critical activity is one that will hold for the majority of critical performances; for it is certainly true that most of the articles we read and write do little more than confirm or extend assumptions that are already in place. But the activity that is most highly valued by the institution (even if it is often resisted) is more radically innovative. The greatest rewards of our profession are reserved for those who challenge the assumptions within which ordinary practices go on, not so much in order to eliminate the category of the ordinary but in order to redefine it and reshape its configurations. This act of challenging and redefining can occur at any number of levels: one can seek to overturn the interpretation of a single work, or recharacterize the entire canon of an important author, or argue for an entirely new realignment of genres, or question the notion of genre itself, or even propose a new definition of literature and a new account of its function in the world. At any of these levels one will necessarily begin, as Culler says, "with shared points of departure and common notions of how to read," but the goal of the performance will be the refashioning of those very notions and the establishments of new points of departure. That is why, as I said, the stakes in a persuasion model are so high. In a demonstration model our task is to be adequate to the description of objects that exist independently of our activities; we may fail or we may succeed, but whatever we do the objects of our attention will retain their ontological separateness and still be what they were before we approached them. In a model of persuasion, however, our activities are directly constitutive of those objects, and of the terms in which they can be described, and of the standards by which they can be evaluated. The responsibilities of the critic under this model are very great indeed, for rather than being merely a player in the game, he is a maker and unmaker of its rules.

That does not, however, mean that he (or you or I) is ever without rules or texts or standards or "shared points of departure and common notions of how to read." It has been my strategy in these lectures to demonstrate how little we lose by acknowledging that it is persuasion and not demonstration that we practice. We have everything that we always had— texts, standards, norms, criteria of judgment, critical histories, and so on. We can convince others that they are wrong, argue that one interpretation is better than another, cite evidence in support of the interpretations we prefer; it is just that we do all those things within a set of institutional assumptions that can themselves become the objects of dispute. This in turn means that while we still have all the things we had before (texts, standards, norms, criteria of judgment), we do not always have them in the same form. Rather than a loss, however, this is a gain, because it provides us with a principled account of change and allows us to explain to ourselves and to others why, if a Shakespeare sonnet is only 14 lines long, we haven't been able to get it right after four hundred years.

It also allows us to make sense of the history of literary criticism, which under the old model can only be the record of the rather dismal performances of men—like Sidney, Dryden, Pope, Coleridge, Arnold—who simply did not understand literature and literary values as well as we do. Now we can regard those performances not as unsuccessful attempts to approximate our own but as extensions of a literary culture whose assumptions were not inferior but merely different. That is, once we give up the essentialist notions that inform a demonstration model—the notion that literature is a monolith and that there is a single set of operations by which its characteristics are discovered and evaluated—we are free to consider the various forms the literary institution has taken and to uncover the interpretative strategies by which its canons have been produced and understood. But perhaps the greatest gain that falls to us under a persuasion model is a greatly enhanced sense of the importance of our activities. (In certain quarters of course, where the critical ideal is one of self-effacement, this will be perceived to be the greatest danger.) No longer is the critic the humble servant of texts whose glories exist independently of anything he might do; it is what he does, within the constraints embedded in the literary institution, that brings texts into being and makes them available for analysis and appreciation. The practice of literary criticism is not something one must apologize for; it is absolutely essential not only to the maintenance of, but to the very production of, the objects of its attention.

Two questions remain and they are both concerned with what the poststructuralists would term "the status of my own discourse." I have been saying that all arguments are made within assumptions and presuppositions that are themselves subject to challenge and change. Well, isn't that also an argument, and one therefore that is no more securely based than the arguments it seeks to dislodge? The answer, of course, is yes; but the answer is also "so what?" According to the position presented here, no one can claim privilege for the point of view he holds and therefore everyone is obliged to practice the art of persuasion. This includes me, and persuasion is the art that I have been trying to practice here. I have not merely presented my position; I have been arguing for it, and I have been arguing for it in a way that can serve as an example (not necessarily a successful one) of how one must proceed if one operates within a model of persuasion. The first thing that one must do is not assume that he is preaching to the converted. That means that whatever the point of view you wish to establish, you will have to establish it in the face of anticipated objections. In general, people resist what you have to say when it seems to them to have undesirable or even disastrous consequences. With respect to what I have been saying, those consequences include the absence of any standards by which one could determine error, the impossibility of preferring one interpretation to another, an inability to explain the mechanisms by which interpretations are accepted and rejected, or the source of the feeling we all have of progressing, and so on. It has been my strategy to speak to these fears, one by one, and to remove them by showing that dire consequences do not follow from the position I espouse and that in fact it is only within that position that one can account for the phenomena my opponents wish to preserve. In short, I have been trying to persuade you to believe what I believe because it is in your own best interests as *you* understand them. (Notice that the determination of what would count as being persuasive is a function of what is understood to be at stake. That is, the mechanisms of persuasion, like everything else, are context-specific; what will be persuasive in any argument depends on what the parties have agreed to in advance; there must be some shared assumption about what is important and necessary and undesirable, for if there were not, neither party could make a point that would be recognized by the other as telling.)

Of course there is always the possibility that it could happen the other way around: you could persuade me that everything I want to preserve depends on a position other than the one I hold, and if you did that, your position would then be mine and I would believe what you believe; but until that happens I will argue for my position with all the confidence that attends belief even though I know that under certain conditions at some time in the future I might believe something else. Another way to put this is to say that the fact that I am subject to the same challenge I have put to my predecessors is not a weakness in my position but a restatement of it. The idea of a position that was invulnerable to challenge makes sense only if you believe in the possibility of a position innocent of assumptions; this of course is exactly what I do not believe and therefore the fact that my assumptions are capable of being dislodged does not refute my argument but confirms it, because it is an extension of it.

The final question concerns the practical consequences of that argument. Since it is primarily a literary argument, one wonders what implications it has for the practice of literary criticism. The answer is, none whatsoever. That is, it does not follow from what I have been saying that you should go out and do literary criticism in a certain way or refrain from doing it in other ways. The reason for this is that the position I have been presenting is not one that you (or anyone else) could live by. Its thesis is that whatever seems to you to be obvious and inescapable is only so within some institutional or conventional structure, and that means that you can never operate outside some such structure, even if you are persuaded by the thesis. As soon as you descend from theoretical reasoning about your assumptions, you will once again inhabit them and you will inhabit them without any reservations whatsoever; so that when you are called on to talk about Milton or Wordsworth or Yeats, you will do so from within whatever beliefs you held about these authors. The fear that one consequence of this position might be that you would be unable to do practical criticism depends on the possibility of your not believing anything at all about them; but it is impossible even to think about them independently of some or other belief, and so long as you can think about them, there is no danger of your being without something to say or without the confidence to say it. That is why this is not a position you can live by, because to live by it you would have to be forever analyzing beliefs, without ever being committed to any, and that is not a position any of us can occupy. It is, however, a position that we are all living *out*, as one set of firmly held beliefs gives way to another, bringing with them an endless succession of practical activities that we are always able to perform.

I can imagine someone saying at this point that if your argument will have no effect on the way I read and teach poetry, why should I be interested in it? What does it matter? There are two answers to this question. The first is to point out that the question itself assumes that in order for something to be interesting, it must directly affect our everyday experience of poetry; and that assumption is in turn attached to a certain antitheoretical bias built into the ideology of New Criticism. In other words, the fact that a thesis has no consequences for practical criticism is damning only from a parochial point of view and it is that point of view I have been challenging. The other answer to the question is institutional, as it must be. The elaboration of this position is something that matters because the issues it takes up are considered central to the institution's concerns. The status of the text, the source of interpretive authority, the relationship between subjectivity and objectivity, the limits of interpretation—these are topics that have been discussed again and again; they are basic topics, and anyone who is able to advance the discussion of them will automatically be accorded a hearing and be a candidate for the profession's highest rewards. One incontestable piece of evidence in support of this assertion is the fact that I have been here speaking to you for an entire week, and that you have been listening; and for that, and for very much more, I thank you.

That last has the ring of a concluding sentence, but before we adjourn I must remember to tell you the end of the story with which this series of lectures began. You will recall that my colleague was finally able to recognize his student as one of my victims and to hear her question ("Is there a text in this class?") as an inquiry into his theoretical beliefs and therefore as an inquiry into the nature of the standards and accepted practices that would be in force in his classroom. I have deliberately withheld his final reply because if I had reported it earlier you might have heard in it a ringing defense of determinate meaning as something available independently of social and institutional circumstances. But if I have been at all persuasive, you will now be able to hear it as a testimony to the power of social and institutional circumstances to establish norms of behavior not despite, but because of, the absence of transcendental norms. He said: "Yes, there *is* a text in this class; what's more, it has meanings; and I am going to tell you what they are."

NOTES

1. *Structuralist Poetics* (Ithaca: Cornell University Press, 1975), p. 121.
2. To the objection that this condemns everyone to a state of mass delusion I would answer, "mass delusion in relation to what?" Presumably, in relation to a truth independent of anyone's particular set of beliefs; but if there is no one (with the exception of God) who occupies a position independent of belief, no one, that is, who is not a particular, situated, one, then the objection loses its force because the notion "mass delusion" has no operational validity.
3. "Linguistic Metatheory," in *A Survey of Linguistic Science*, ed. W. Dingwall (College Park: University of Maryland Press, 1971), p. 651.

Julia Kristeva
Translated by Margaret Waller

Psychoanalysis and the Polis

> Up until now philosophers have only interpreted
> the world. The point now is to change it.
> —Karl Marx and Friedrich Engels, *Theses on*
> *Feuerbach*

> The delusions [*Wahnbildungen*] of patients appear
> to me to be the equivalents of the [interpretive]
> constructions which we build up in the course of
> an analytic treatment—attempts at explanation
> and cure.
> —Sigmund Freud, "Constructions in Analysis"

The essays in this volume convince me of something which, until now, was only a hypothesis of mine. Academic discourse, and perhaps American university discourse in particular, possesses an extraordinary ability to absorb, digest, and neutralize all of the key, radical, or dramatic moments of thought, particularly, a fortiori, of contemporary thought. Marxism in the United States, though marginalized, remains deafly dominant and exercises a fascination that we have not seen in Europe since the Russian *Proletkult* of the 1930s. Post-Heideggerian "deconstructivism," though esoteric, is welcomed in the United States as an antidote to analytic philosophy or, rather, as a way to valorize, through contrast, that philosophy. Only one theoretical breakthrough seems consistently to *mobilize* resistances, rejections, and deafness: psychoanalysis—not as the "plague" allowed by Freud to implant itself in America as a "commerce in couches" but rather as that which, with Freud and after him, has led the psychoanalytic decentering of the speaking subject to the very foundations of language. It is this latter direction that I will be exploring here, with no other hope than to awaken the resistances and, perhaps, the attention of a concerned few, after the event (*après coup*).

For I have the impression that the "professionalism" discussed throughout the "Politics of Interpretation" conference is never as strong as when professionals denounce it. In fact, the same preanalytic rationality unites them all, "conservatives" and "revolutionaries"—in all cases, jealous guardians of their academic "chairs" whose very existence, I am sure, is thrown into question and put into jeopardy by psychoanalytic discourse. I would therefore schematically summarize what is to follow in this way:

1. There are political implications inherent in the act of interpretation itself, whatever meaning that interpretation bestows. What is the meaning, interest, and benefit of the interpretive position itself, a position from which I wish to give meaning to an enigma? To give a political meaning to something is perhaps only the ultimate consequence of the epistemological attitude which consists, simply, of the desire *to give meaning*. This attitude is not innocent but, rather, is rooted in the speaking subject's need to reassure himself of his image and his identity faced with an object. Political interpretation is thus the apogee of the obsessive quest for A Meaning.

2. The psychoanalytic intervention within Western knowledge has a fundamentally deceptive effect. Psychoanalysis, critical and dissolvant, cuts through political illusions, fantasies, and beliefs to the extent that they consist in providing only one meaning, an uncriticizable ultimate Meaning, to human behavior. If such a situation can lead to despair within the polis, we must not forget that it is also a source of lucidity and ethics. The psychoanalytic intervention is, from this point of view, a counterweight, an antidote, to political discourse which, without it, is free to become our modern religion: the final explanation.

3. The political interpretations of our century have produced two powerful and totalitarian results: fascism and Stalinism. Parallel to the socioeconomic reasons for these phenomena, there exists as well another, more intrinsic reason: the simple desire to give a meaning, to explain, to provide the answer, to interpret. In that context I will briefly discuss Louis Ferdinand Céline's texts insofar as the ideological interpretations given by him are an example of political delirium in avant-garde writing.

I would say that interpretation as an epistemological and ethical attitude began with the Stoics. In other words, it should not be confused with *theory* in the Platonic sense, which assumes a prior knowledge of the ideal Forms to which all action or creation is subordinate. Man, says Epictetus, is "born to contemplate God and his works, and not only to contemplate them but also to interpret them [kai ou monon teatin, ala kai exegetin auton]." "To interpret" in this context, and I think always means "to make a connection." Thus the birth of interpretation is considered the birth of semiology, since the semiological sciences relate a sign (an event-sign) to a signified in order to *act* accordingly, consistently, consequently.[1]

Much has been made of the circularity of this connection which, throughout the history of interpretive disciplines up to hermeneutics, consists in enclosing the enigmatic (interpretable) object within the interpretive theory's preexistent system. Instead of creating an object, however, this process merely produces what the interpretive theory had preselected as an object within the enclosure of its own system. Thus it seems that one does not interpret something outside theory but rather that theory harbors its object within its own logic. Theory merely projects that object onto a theoretical place at a distance, outside its grasp, thereby eliciting the very possibility of interrogation (Heidegger's *Sachverhalt*).

We could argue at length about whether interpretation is a circle or a spiral: in other words, whether the interpretable object it assigns itself is simply constituted by the interpretation's own logic or whether it is recreated, enriched, and thus raised to a higher level of knowledge through the unfolding of interpretive discourse. Prestigious work in philosophy and logic is engaged in this investigation. I will not pursue it here. Such a question, finally seems to me closer to a Platonic idea of interpretation (i.e., theorization) than it does to the true innovation of the Stoics' undertaking. This innovation is the reduction, indeed the elimination, of the distance between theory and action as well as between model and copy. What permits this elimination of the distance between nature (which the Stoics considered interpretable) and the interpreter is the extraordinary opening of the field of subjectivity. The person who does the interpretation, the subject who makes the connection between the sign and the signified, is the Stoic sage displaying, on the one hand, the extraordinary architectonics of his *will* and, on the other, his mastery of *time* (both momentary and infinite).

I merely want to allude to this Stoic notion of the primordial interdependence of *interpretation*, subjective *will*, and mastery of *time*. For my own interest is in contemporary thought which has rediscovered, in its own way, that even if interpretation does no more than establish a simple logical connection, it is nevertheless played out on the scene of speaking subjectivity and the moment of speech. Two great intellectual ventures of our time, those of Marx and Freud, have broken through the hermeneutic tautology to make of it a *revolution* in one instance and, in the other, a *cure*. We must recognize that all contemporary political thought which does not deal with technocratic administration—although technocratic purity is perhaps only a dream—uses interpretation in Marx's and Freud's sense: as transformation and as cure. Whatever *object* one selects (a patient's discourse, a literary or journalistic text, or certain sociopolitical behavior), its interpretation reaches its full power, so as to tip the object toward the *unknown* of the interpretive theory or, more simply, toward the theory's *intentions,* only when the interpreter *confronts* the interpretable object.

It is within this field of confrontation between the object and the subject of interpretation that I want to pursue my investigation. I assume that at its resolution there are two major outcomes. First, the object may succumb to the interpretive intentions of the interpreter, and then we have the whole range of domination from suggestion to propaganda to revolution. Or second, the object may reveal to the interpreter the unknown of his theory and permit the constitution of a new theory. Discourse in this case is renewed; it can begin again: it forms a new object and a new interpretation in this reciprocal transference.

Before going any further, however, I would like to suggest that another path, posthermeneutic and perhaps even postinterpretive, opens up for us within the lucidity of contemporary discourse. Not satisfied to stay within the interpretive place which is, essentially, that of the Stoic sage, the contemporary interpreter renounces the game of *indebtedness, proximity,* and *presence* hidden within the connotations of the concept of interpretation. (*Interpretare* means "to be mutually indebted"; *prêt:* from popular Latin *praestus,* from the classical adverb *praesto,* meaning "close at hand," "nearby"; *praesto esse:* "to be present, attend"; *praestare:* "to furnish, to present [as an object, e.g., money].") The modern interpreter avoids the presentness of subjects to themselves and to things. For in this presentness a strange object appears to speaking subjects, a kind of currency they grant themselves—interpretation—to make certain that they are really there, close by, within reach. Breaking out of the enclosure of the presentness of meaning, the *new* "interpreter" no longer interprets: he speaks, he "associates," because there is no longer an object to interpret; there is, instead, the setting off of semantic, logical, phantasmatic, and indeterminable sequences. As a result, a fiction, an uncentered discourse, a subjective polytopia come about, canceling the metalinguistic status of the discourses currently governing the postanalytic fate of interpretation.

The Freudian position on interpretation has the immense advantage of being midway between a classic interpretive attitude—that of providing meaning through the connection of two terms from a stable place and theory—and the questioning of the subjective and theoretical stability of the interpretant which, in the act of interpretation itself, establishes the theory and the interpreter himself as interpretable objects. The dimension of *desire,* appearing for the first time in the citadel of interpretive will, steals the latform from the Stoic sage, but at the same time it opens up time, suspends Stoic suicide, and confers not only an interpretive power but also a transforming power to these new, unpredictable signifying effects which must be called *an imaginary.* I would suggest that the wise interpreter give way to delirium so that, out of his desire, the imaginary may join interpretive closure, thus producing a perpetual interpretive creative force.

1. What Is Delirium?

Delirium is a discourse which has supposedly strayed from a presumed reality. The speaking subject is presumed to have known an object, a relationship, an experience that he is henceforth incapable of reconstituting accurately. Why? Because the knowing subject is also a *desiring* subject, and the paths of desire ensnarl the paths of knowledge.

Repressed desire pushes against the repression barrier in order to impose its contents on consciousness. Yet the resistance offered by consciousness, on the one hand, and the pressure of desire, on the other, leads to a displacement and deformation of that which otherwise could be reconstituted unaltered. This dynamic of delirium recalls the constitution of the dream or the phantasm. Two of its most important moments are especially noteworthy here.

First, we normally assume the opposite of delirium to be an objective reality, objectively perceptible and objectively knowable, as if the speaking subject were only a simple knowing subject. Yet we must admit that, given the cleavage of the subject (conscious/unconscious) and given that the subject is also a subject of desire, perceptual and knowing apprehension of the original object is only a theoretical, albeit undoubtedly indispensable, hypothesis. More importantly, the system Freud calls perception-knowledge (subsequently an object of interpretation or delirium) is always already marked by a *lack:* for it shelters within its very being the nonsignifiable, the nonsymbolized. This "minus factor," by which, even in perception-knowledge, the subject signifies himself as subject of the desire of the Other, is what provokes, through its insistence on acceding to further significations, those deformations and displacements which characterize delirium. Within the nucleus of delirious construction, we must retain this hollow, this void, this "minus 1," as the instinctual drive's insistence, as the unsymbolizable condition of the desire to speak and to know.

Yet delirium holds; it asserts itself to the point of procuring for the subject both *jouissance* and stability which, without that adhesive of delirium, would disintegrate rapidly into a somatic symptom, indeed, into the unleashing of the death drive. It can do so, however, only because the discourse of delirium "owes its convincing power to the element of historical truth which it inserts in the place of the rejected reality."[2] In other words, delirium masks reality or spares itself from a reality while at the same time saying a truth about it. More true? Less true? Does delirium know a truth which is true in a different way than objective reality because it speaks a certain subjective truth, instead of a presumed objective truth? Because it presents the state of the subject's desire? This "mad truth" (*folle vérité*) of delirium is not evoked here to introduce some kind of relativism or epistemological skepticism.³ I am insisting on the part played by truth in delirium to indicate, rather, that since the displacement and deformation peculiar to delirium are moved by desire, they are not foreign to the passion for knowledge, that is, the subject's subjugation to the desire to know. Desire and the desire to know are not strangers to each other, up to a certain point. What is that point?

Desire, the discourse of desire, moves toward its object through a connection, by displacement and deformation. The discourse of desire becomes a discourse of delirium when it forecloses its object, which is always already marked by that "minus factor" mentioned earlier, and when it establishes itself as the complete locus of *jouissance* (full and without exteriority). In other words, no other exists, no object survives in its irreducible alterity. On the contrary, he who speaks, Daniel Schreber, for example, identifies himself with the very place of alterity, he merges with the Other, experiencing *jouissance* in and through the place of otherness. Thus in delirium the subject himself is so to speak the Phallus, which implies that he has obliterated the primordial object of desire—the mother—either because he has foreclosed the mother, whom he finds lacking, or because he has submerged himself in her, exaggerating the totality thus formed, as if it were the Phallus. Delirium's structure thus constitutes the foreclosure of the paternal function because of the place it reserves for the maternal—but also feminine—object which serves to exclude, moreover, any other consideration of objectality.

By contrast, if it is true that the discourse of knowledge leads its enigmatic preobject, that which solicits interpretation—its *Sachverhalt*—inside its own circle and as such brings about a certain hesitation of objectness, it does not take itself for the Phallus but rather places the Phallus outside itself in what is to be known: object, nature, destiny. That is why the person through whom knowledge comes about is not mad, but (as the Stoics have indicated) he is (subject to) death. The time of accurate interpretation, that is, an interpretation in accordance with destiny (or the Other's Phallus), is a moment that includes and completes eternity; interpretation is consequently both happiness and death of time and of the subject: suicide. The transformation of sexual desire into the desire to know an object deprives the subject of this desire and abandons him or reveals him as subject to death. Interpretation, in its felicitous accuracy, expurgating passion and desire, reveals the interpreter as master of his will but at the same time as slave of death. Stoicism is, and I'll return to this point, the last great pagan ideology, tributary of nature as mother, raised to the phallic rank of Destiny to be interpreted.

2. Analytic Interpretation

Like the delirious subject, the psychoanalyst builds, by way of interpretation, a construction which is true only if it triggers other associations on the part of the analysand, thus expanding the boundaries of the analyzable. In other words, this analytic interpretation is only, in the best of cases, *partially true,* and its truth, even though it operates with the past, is demonstrable only by its *effects in the present.*

In a strictly Stoic sense, analytic interpretation aims to correspond to a (repressed) event or sign in order to *act.* In the same sense, it is a *connection* between disparate terms of the patient's discourse, thereby reestablishing the causes and effects of desire; but it is especially a connection of the signifiers peculiar to the analyst with those of the analysand. This second circulation, dependent on the analyst's desire and operative only with him, departs from interpretive mastery and opens the field to suggestion as well as to projection and indeterminable drifts. In this way, the analyst approaches the vertigo of delirium and, with it, the phallic *jouissance* of a subject subsumed in the dyadic, narcissistic construction of a discourse in which the *Same* mistakes itself for the *Other.* It is, however, only by detaching himself from such a vertigo that the analyst derives both his *jouissance* and his efficacy.

Thus far, we have seen that analytic interpretation resembles delirium in that it introduces desire into discourse. It does so by giving narcissistic satisfaction to the subject (the analyst or the analysand), who, at the risk of foreclosing any true object, derives phallic jubilation from being the author/actor of a connection that leaves room for desire or for death in discourse.

Yet the analytic position also has counterweights that make delirium work on behalf of analytic truth. The most obvious, the most often cited, of these is the *suspension* of interpretation: silence as frustration of meaning reveals the ex-centricity of desire with regard to meaning. Madness/meaninglessness *exists*—this is what interpretive silence suggests. Second, the analyst, constantly tracking his own desire, never stops analyzing not only his patients' discourse but also his own attitude toward it which is his own countertransference. He is not fixed in the position of the classical interpreter, who interprets by virtue of stable meanings derived from a solid system or morality or who at least tries to restrict the range of his delirium through a stable theoretical counterweight. This is not to say that analytic theory does not exist but rather that, all things considered, its consistency is rudimentary when compared to the countertransferential operation which is always specific and which sets the interpretive machine in motion differently every time. If I know that my desire can make me delirious in my interpretive constructions, my return to this delirium allows me to dissolve its meaning, to displace by one or more notches the quest for meaning which I suppose to be *one* and *one only* but which I can *only* indefinitely approach. *There is meaning, and I am supposed to know it to the extent that it escapes me.*

Finally, there is what I will call the *unnameable:* that which is necessarily enclosed in every questionable, interpretable, enigmatic object. The analyst does not exclude the unnameable. He knows that every interpretation will float over that shadowy point which Freud in *The Interpretation of Dreams* calls the dreams' "umbilical." The analyst knows that delirium, in its phallic amibition, consists precisely in the belief that light can rule everywhere, without a shadow. Yet the analyst can sight and hear the unnameable, which he preserves as the condition of interpretation, *only if he sees it as a phantasm.* As origin and condition of the interpretable, the unnameable is, perhaps, the primordial phantasm. What analysis reveals is that the human being does not speak and that, a fortiori, he does not interpret *without* the phantasm of a return to the origin, without the hypothesis of an unnameable, of a *Sachverhalt.*

Furthermore, analysis reveals that interpretive speech, like all speech which is concerned with an object, is acted upon by the desire to return to the archaic mother who is resistant to meaning. Interpretive speech does this so as to place the archaic mother within the order of language—where the subject of desire, insofar as he is a speaking subject, is immediately displaced and yet, henceforth, situated. The return to the unnameable mother may take the form of narcissistic and masochistic delirium, in which the subject merely confronts an idealized petrification of himself in the form of an interpretive Verb, interpretation becoming, in this case, Everything, subject and object. This is what analytic interpretation confronts, undergoes, and, also, displaces.

For, in short, the analyst-interpreter or the interpreter turned analyst derives the originality of his position from his capacity for displacement, from his mobility, from his polytopia. From past to present, from frustration to desire, from the parameter of pleasure to the parameter of death, and so on—he dazes the analysand with the unexpectedness of his interpretation; even so, however, the unexpectedness of the analysis is in any case sustained by a constant: the desire for the Other. ("If you want me to interpret, you are bound in my desire.")

Since Edward Glover's *Technique of Psychoanalysis* (1928), a highly regarded work in its time, analytic theory has appreciably refined its notion of interpretation.[4] The criteria for sound interpretation may undoubtedly vary: "good adpatation" of the analysand, "progress," appearance of remote childhood memories, encounter with the analyst's transference, and so on. Or criteria for a sound interpretation may even disappear, leaving only the need for a temporary sanction (which may be on the order of the parameters already outlined) within an essentially open interpretive process. In this process, *one* meaning and *one meaning alone* is always specifiable for a particular moment of transference; but, given the vast storehouse of the unknown from which analytic interpretation proceeds, this meaning must be transformed.

If it seems that analytic interpretation, like all interpretation in the strong sense of the word, is therefore an action, can we say that this interpretation aims to change the analysand? Two extreme practices exist. In one, the analysis suggests interpretations; in the other, it assumes a purist attitude: by refusing to interpret, the analysis leaves the patient, faced with the absolute silence of the interpreter, dependent on his own capacity for listening, interpreting, and eventually changing. Faced with these excesses, one could argue that in the vast majority of analyses a psychotherapeutic moment occurs which consists in compensating for previous traumatic situations and allowing the analysand to construct another transference, another meaning of his relationship to the Other, the analyst. In the analytic interpretation, however, such a therapeutic moment has, ultimately, no other function than to effect a transference which would otherwise remain doubtful. Only from that moment does true analytic work (i.e., *dissolving*) begin. Basically, this work involves removing obvious, immediate, realistic meaning from discourse so that the meaninglessness/madness of desire may appear and, beyond that, so that every phantasm is revealed as an attempt to return to the unnameable.

I interpret, the analyst seems to say, because Meaning exists. But my interpretation is infinite because Meaning is made infinite by desire. I am not therefore a dead subject, a wise interpreter, happy and self-annihilated in a uniform totality. I am subject to Meaning, a non-Total Meaning, which escapes me.

Analytic interpretation finally leads the analyst to a fundamental problem which I believe underlies all theory and practice of interpretation: the heterogeneous in meaning, the limitation of meaning, its incompleteness. Psychoanalysis, the only modern interpretive theory to hypothesize the heterogeneous in meaning, nevertheless makes that heterogeneity so interdependent with language and thought as to be its very condition, indeed, its driving force. Furthermore, psychoanalysis gives heterogeneity an operative and analyzable status by designating it as sexual desire and/or as death wish.

3. Can Political Interpretation Be True?

The efficacy of interpretation is a function of its transferential truth: this is what political man learns from the analyst, or in any case shares with him. Consider, for example, those political discourses which are said to reflect the desires of a social group or even of large masses. There is always a moment in history when those discourses obtain a general consensus not so much because they interpret the situation correctly (i.e., in accordance with the exigencies of the moment and developments dictated by the needs of the majority) but rather because they correspond to the essentially utopian desires of that majority. Such political interpretation interprets *desires;* even if it lacks reality, it contains the truth of desires. It is, for that very reason, utopian and ideological.

Yet, as in analysis, such an interpretation can be a powerful factor in the mobilization of energies that can lead social groups and masses beyond a sadomasochistic ascesis to change real conditions. Such a mobilizing interpretation can be called revolution or demagogy. By contrast, a more objective, neutral, and technocratic interpretation would only solidify or very slowly modify the real conditions.

All political discourse that wants to be and is efficacious shares that dynamic. Unlike the analytic dynamic, however, the dynamic of political interpretation does not lead its subjects to an elucidation of their own (and its own) truth. For, as I pointed out earlier, analytic interpretation uses desire and transference, but only to lead the subject, faced with the erosion of meaning, to the economy of his own speaking. It does so by deflating the subject's phantasms and by showing that all phantasms, like any attempt to give meaning, come from the phallic *jouissance* obtained by usurping that unnameable object, that *Sachverhalt,* which is the archaic mother.

Of course, no political discourse can pass into nonmeaning. Its goal, Marx stated explicitly, is to reach the goal of interpretation: interpreting the world in order to transform it according to our needs and desires. Now, from the position of the post-Freudian, post-phenomenological analyst— a position which is really an untenable locus of rationality, a close proximity of meaning and nonmeaning—it is clear that there is no World (or that the World is not all there is) and that *to transform* it is only one of the circles of the interpretation—be it Marxist—which refuses to perceive that it winds around a *void.*

Given this constant factor of the human psyche confirmed by the semiotician and the psychoanalyst when they analyze that ordeal of discourse which is the discourse of delirium, what becomes of interpretive discourse? Indeed, what happens to interpretive discourse in view of the void which is integral to meaning and which we find, for example, in the "arbitrariness of the sign" (the unmotivated relation between signifier and signified in Saussure), in the "mirror stage" (where the subject perceives his own image as essentially split, foreign, other), or in the various forms of psychic alienation? Clearly, interpretive discourse cannot be merely a hermeneutics or a politics. Different variants of sacred discourse assume the function of interpretation at this point.

Our cultural orb is centered around the axion that "the Word became flesh." Two thousand years after a tireless exploration of the comings and goings between discourse and the object to be named or interpreted, an object which is the solicitor of interrogation, we have finally achieved a discourse on discourse, an interpretation of interpretation. For the psychoanalyst, this vertigo in abstraction is, nevertheless, a means of protecting us from a masochistic and jubilatory fall into nature, into the full and pagan mother, a fall which is a tempting and crushing enigma for anyone who has not gained some distance from it with the help of an interpretive device. However, and this is the second step post-phenomenological analytic rationality has taken, we have also perceived the incompleteness of interpretation itself, the incompleteness characteristic of all language, sign, discourse. This perception prevents the closure of our interpretation as a self-sufficient totality, which resembles delirium, and at the same time this perception of interpretation constitutes the true life of interpretations (in the plural).

4. Literature as Interpretation: The Text

Philosophical interpretation as well as literary criticism therefore and henceforth both have a tendency to be written as *texts*. They openly assume their status as fiction without, however, abandoning their goal of stating One meaning, The True Meaning, of the discourse they interpret.

The fate of interpretation has allowed it to leave behind the protective enclosure of a metalanguage and to approach the imaginary, without necessarily confusing the two. I would now like to evoke some specifics and some dangers of openly fictional interpretation in literary discourse itself. So as not to simplify the task, I will take as my example a modern French novelist, Louis Ferdinand Céline (1894–1961), whose popular and musical style represents the height of twentieth-century French literature and whose anti-Semitic and para-Nazi pamphlets reveal one of the blackest aspects of contemporary history.

I consider all fiction (poetic language or narrative) already an interpretation in the broad sense of the speaking subject's implication in a transposition (connection) of a presupposed object. If it is impossible to assign to a literary text a preexisting "objective reality," the critic (the interpreter) can nevertheless find the mark of the interpretive function of writing in the transformation which that writing inflicts on the language of everyday communication. In other words, *style* is the mark of interpretation in literature. To quote Céline, "I am not a man of ideas. I am a man of style. . . . This involves taking sentences, I was telling you, and unhinging them."[5] Such an interpretive strategy is clearly an enunciative strategy, and, in Célinian language, it uses two fundamental techniques: *segmentation* of the sentence, characteristic of the first novels; and the more or less recuperable *syntactical ellipses* which appear in the late novels.

The peculiar segmentation of the Célinian phrase, which is considered colloquial, is a cutting up of the syntactic unit by the projected or rejected displacement of one of its components. As a result, the normally descending modulation of the phrasal melody becomes an intonation with two centers. Thus: "I had just discovered war in its entirety. . . . Have to be almost in front of it, like I was then, to really see it, the bitch, face on and in profile."[6]

An analysis of this utterance, not as a syntactic structure but as a *message* in the process of enunciation between a speaking subject and his addressee, would show that the aim of this ejection is to *thematize* the displaced element, which then acquires the status not merely of a theme but of an emphatic theme. "La vache" ("the bitch") is the vehicle for the primary information, the essential message which the speaker emphasizes. From this perspective, the ejected element is desyntacticized, but it is charged with supplementary semantic value, bearing the speaker's emotive attitude and his moral judgment. Thus, the ejection emphasizes the informative kernel at the expense of the syntactic structure and makes the logic of the message (theme/rheme, support/apport, topic/comment, presupposed/posed) dominate over the logic of syntax (verb-object); in other words, the logic of enunciation dominates over that of the enunciated. In fact, the terminal intonational contour of the rheme (along two modalities: assertive and interrogative) indicates the very point at which the modality of enunciation is most profoundly revealed. The notable preponderance of this contour with the bipartition theme/rheme in children's acquisition of syntax or in the emotive or relaxed speech of popular or everyday discourse is added proof that it is a *deeper* organizer of the utterance than syntactic structures.

This "binary shape" in Céline's first novels has been interpreted as an indication of his uncertainty about self-narration in front of the Other. Awareness of the Other's existence would be what determines the phenomena of recall and excessive clarity, which then produces segmentation. In this type of sentence, then, the speaking subject would occupy two places: that of his own identity (when he goes straight to the information, to the rheme) and that of objective expression, for the Other (when he goes back, recalls, clarifies). Given the prevalence of this type of construction in the first phases of children's acquisition of syntax, we can state that this binomial, which is both intonational and logical, coincides with a fundamental stage in the constitution of the speaking subject: his autonomization with respect to the Other, the constitution of his own identity.

To Freud's and René Spitz's insistence that "no" is the mark of man's access to the symbolic and the founding of a distinction between the pleasure principle and the reality principle, one could add that the "binarism" of the message (theme/rheme and vice versa) is another step, a fundamental step, in the symbolic integration of negativism, rejection, and the death drive. It is even a decisive step: with the binarism of the message and before the constitution of syntax, the subject not only differentiates pleasure from reality—a painful and ultimately impossible distinction—but he also distinguishes between the statements: "I say by presupposing" and "I say by making explicit," that is, "I say what matters to me" versus "I say to be clear" or even, "I say what I like" versus "I say for you, for us, so that we can understand each other." In this way, the binary message effects a slippage from the *I* as the pole of pleasure to the *you* as addressee and to the impersonal *one*, he, which is necessary to establish a true universal syntax. This is how the subject of enunciation is born. And it is in remembering this path that the subject rediscovers, if not his origin, at least his originality. The "spoken" writing of Céline achieves just such a remembering.

In addition, in Céline's last novels, *D'un château l'autre, Nord,* and *Rigodon,* he repeatedly uses the famous "three dots" (suspension points) and the exclamations which sometimes indicate an ellipsis in the clause but serve more fundamentally to make the clause overflow into the larger whole of the message. This technique produces a kind of long syntactic period, covering a half-page, a full page, or more. In contrast to Proustian fluctuation, it avoids subordinations, is not given as a logical-syntactic unit, and proceeds by brief utterances: clauses pronounceable in one breath which cut, chop, and give rhythm. Laconism (nominal sentences), exclamations, and the predominance of intonation over syntax reecho (like segmentation but in another way) the archaic phases of the subject of enunciation. On the one hand, these techniques, because of the influx of nonmeaning, arouse the nonsemanticized emotion of the reader. On the other hand, they give an infrasyntactical, intonational inscription of that same emotion which transverses syntax but integrates the message (theme/rheme and subject-addressee).[7]

From this brief linguistico-stylistic discussion, I would like to stress the following: style is interpretation in the sense that it is a connection between the logic of utterance and the logic of enunciation, between syntax and message and their two corresponding subjective structures. The unobjectifiable, unnameable "object" which is thereby caught in the text is what Céline calls an *emotion*. "Drive," and its most radical component, the death drive, is perhaps an even better term for it. "You know, in Scriptures, it is written: 'In the beginning was the Word.' No! In the beginning was emotion. The Word came afterwards to replace emotion as the trot replaced the gallop."[8] And again: "Slang is a language of hatred that knocks the reader over for you ... annihilates him! ... at your mercy! ... he sits there like an ass."[9]

It is as if Céline's stylistic adventure were an aspect of the eternal return to a place which escapes naming and which can be named only if one plays on the whole register of language (syntax, but also message, intonation, etc.). This locus of emotion, of instinctual drive, of non-semanticized hatred, resistant to logico-syntactic naming, appears in Céline's work, as in other great literary texts, as a locus of the ab-ject. The abject, not yet object, is anterior to the distinction between subject and object in normative language. But the abject is also the nonobjectality of the archaic mother, the locus of needs, of attraction and repulsion, from which an object of forbidden desire arises. And finally, abject can be understood in the sense of the horrible and fascinating abomination which is connoted in all cultures by the feminine or, more indirectly, by every partial object which is related to the state of abjection (in the sense of the nonseparation subject/object). It becomes what culture, the *sacred*, must purge, separate, and banish so that it may establish itself as such in the universal logic of catharsis.

Is the abject, the ultimate object of style, the archetype of the *Sachverhalt*, of what solicits interpretation? Is it the archi-interpretable? This is, as I said earlier, something analytic interpretation can argue. Meaning, and the interpretation which both posits and lives off meaning, are sustained by that *elsewhere* which goes beyond them and which fiction, style (other variants of interpretation), never stops approaching—and dissolving.

For this is in fact the central issue in Céline as in the great writers of all times. By their themes (evil, idiocy, infamy, the feminine, etc.) and their styles, they immerse us in the ab-ject (the unnameable, the *Sachverhalt*), not in order to name, reify, or objectify them once and for all but to dissolve them and to displace us. In what direction? Into the harmony of the Word and into the fundamental incompleteness of discourse constituted by a cleavage, a void: an effervescent and dangerous beauty, the fragile obverse of a radical nihilism that can only fade away in "those sparkling depths which [say] that nothing exists any more."[10]

Yet this pulverization of the abject, the ultimate case of interpretation by style, remains fragile. Because it does not always satisfy desire, the writer is tempted to give one interpretation and one only to the outer limit of the nameable. The *Sachverhalt*, the abject, is then embodied in the figure of a maleficent agent, both feminine and phallic, miserable and all-powerful, victim and satrap, idiot and genius, bestial and wily. What once defied discourse now becomes the ultimate object of one and only one interpretation, the source and acme of a polymorphous *jouissance* in which the interpreter, this time in his delirium, is finally reunited with what denies, exceeds, and excites him. He blends into this abject and its feminine-maternal resonance which threatens identity itself. This interpretive delirium—writing's weak moment—found in Céline the Jew as its privileged object in the context of Hitlerism. The historical and social causes of Céline's anti-Semitism can be sought in monotheism, or, rather, in its denials, and in the history of France and the reality of the Second World War. His anti-Semitism also has a more subtle foundation, more intrinsically linked to the psychic instability of the writer and the speaking subject in general: it is the fascination with the wandering and elusive other, who attracts, repels, puts one literally beside oneself. This other, before being another subject, is an object of discourse, a nonobject, an abject. This abject awakens in the one who speaks archaic conflicts with his own improper objects, his ab-jects, at the edge of meaning, at the limits of the interpretable. And it arouses the paranoid rage to dominate those objects, to transform them, to exterminate them.

I do not presume to elucidate in this brief presentation the many causes and aspects of Céline's anti-Semitism. A lengthier consideration of the subject can be found in my *Pouvoirs de l'horreur.* I have broached this difficult and complex subject here to indicate by a *paroxysm,* which we could take as a *hyperbole,* the dangerous paths of interpretive passion, fascinated by an enigma that is beyond discourse. For the psychoanalyst, it recalls a desiring indebtedness to the maternal continent.

I would like the above remarks to be taken both as a "free association" and as the consequence of a certain position. I would want them to be considered not only an epistemological discussion but also a personal involvement (need I say one of desire?) in the dramas of thought, personality, and contemporary politics. Such a vast theme ("the politics of interpretation") cannot help but involve a multiplicity of questions. If their conjunction in my paper seems chaotic, inelegant, and nonscientific to a positivist rationality, this conjunction is precisely what defines for me the originality and the difficulty of psychoanalytic interpretation. The task is not to make an interpretive summa in the name of a system of truths—for that attitude has always made interpretation a rather poor cousin of theology. The task is, instead, to record the *crisis* of modern interpretive systems without smoothing it over, to affirm that this crisis is inherent in the symbolic function itself, and to perceive as symptoms all constructions, including totalizing interpretation, which try to deny this crisis: to dissolve, to displace indefinitely, in Kafka's words, "temporarily and for a lifetime."

Perhaps nothing of the wise Stoic interpreter remains in the analyst except his function as *actor:* he accepts the text and puts all his effort and desire, his passion and personal virtuosity, into reciting it, while remaining indifferent to the events that he enacts. This "indifference," called "benevolent neutrality," is the modest toga with which we cover our interpretive desire. Yet by shedding it, by implicating ourselves, we bring to life, to meaning, the dead discourses of patients which summon us. The ambiguity of such an interpretive position is both untenable and pleasurable. Knowing this, knowing that he is constantly in abjection and in neutrality, in desire and in indifference, the analyst builds a strong ethics, not normative but directed, which no transcendence guarantees. That is where, it seems to me, the modern version of liberty is being played out, threatened as much by a single, total, and totalitarian Meaning as it is by delirium.

Translator's note.—I would like to thank Domna Stanton and Alice Jardine for their help on an earlier version of this translation.

NOTES

1. See Victor Goldschmidt, *Le Système stoïcien et l'idée de temps* (Paris, 1953).
2. Sigmund Freud, "Constructions in Analysis," *The Standard Edition of the Complete Psychological Works of Sigmund Freud,* trans. and ed. James Strachey, 24 vols. (London, 1953–74), 23:268.
3. See in my *Folle vérité* (Paris, 1979) the texts presented in my seminar at l'Hôpital de la Cité Universitaire, Service de psychiatrie.
4. See esp. Jacques Lacan, "De l'interpretation au transfert," *Le Séminaire de Jacques Lacan,* vol. 11, *Les Quatre Concepts fondamentaux de la psychanalyse* (Paris, 1973), pp. 221 ff.
5. Louis Ferdinand Céline, "Louis Ferdinand Céline vous parle," *Oeuvres complètes,* 2 vols. (Paris, 1966–69), 2:934.
6. "Je venais de découvrir la guerre toute entière. . . . Faut être à peu près devant elle comme je l'étais à ce moment-là pour bien la voir, *la vache,* en face et de profil" (Céline, *Voyage au bout de la nuit, Oeuvres complètes,* 1:8).
7. For a lengthier discussion of Céline's style and its interpretation, see my *Pouvoirs de l'horreur: Essai sur l'abjection* (Paris, 1980).
8. Céline, "Céline vous parle," p. 933.
9. Céline, *Entretiens avec le professeur Y* (1955; Paris, 1976), p. 72.
10. Céline, *Rigodon, Oeuvres complètes,* 2:927.

Nine
reception

Wolfgang Iser

The Reading Process: A Phenomenological Approach

I

The phenomenological theory of art lays full stress on the idea that, in considering a literary work, one must take into account not only the actual text but also, and in equal measure, the actions involved in responding to that text. Thus Roman Ingarden confronts the structure of the literary text with the ways in which it can be *konkretisiert* (realized).[1] The text as such offers different 'schematised views'[2] through which the subject matter of the work can come to light, but the actual bringing to light is an action of *Konkretisation*. If this is so, then the literary work has two poles, which we might call the artistic and the aesthetic: the artistic refers to the text created by the author, and the aesthetic to the realization accomplished by the reader. From this polarity it follows that the literary work cannot be completely identical with the text, or with the realization of the text, but in fact must lie halfway between the two. The work is more than the text, for the text only takes on life when it is realized, and furthermore the realization is by no means independent of the individual disposition of the reader—though this in turn is acted upon by the different patterns of the text. The convergence of text and reader brings the literary work into existence, and this convergence can never be precisely pinpointed, but must always remain virtual, as it is not to be identified either with the reality of the text or with the individual disposition of the reader.

It is the virtuality of the work that gives rise to its dynamic nature, and this in turn is the precondition for the effects that the work calls forth. As the reader uses the various perspectives offered him by the text in order to relate the patterns and the "schematised views" to one another, he sets the work in motion, and this very process results ultimately in the awakening of responses within himself. Thus, reading causes the literary work to unfold its inherently dynamic character. That this is no new discovery is apparent from references made even in the early days of the

381

novel. Laurence Sterne remarks in *Tristram Shandy:* "... no author, who understands the just boundaries of decorum and good-breeding, would presume to think all: The truest respect which you can pay to the reader's understanding, is to halve this matter amicably, and leave him something to imagine, in his turn, as well as yourself. For my own part, I am eternally paying him complimends of this kind, and do all that lies in my power to keep his imagination as busy as my own."[3] Sterne's conception of a literary text is that it is something like an arena in which reader and author participate in a game of the imagination. If the reader were given the whole story, and there were nothing left for him to do, then his imagination would never enter the field, the result would be the boredom which inevitably arises when everything is laid out cut and dried before us. A literary text must therefore be conceived in such a way that it will engage the reader's imagination in the task of working things out for himself, for reading is only a pleasure when it is active and creative. In this process of creativity, the text may either not go far enough, or may go too far, so we may say that boredom and overstrain form the boundaries beyond which the reader will leave the field of play.

The extent to which the "unwritten" part of a text stimulates the reader's creative participation is brought out by an observation of Virginia Woolf's in her study of *Jane Austen:* "Jane Austen is thus a mistress of much deeper emotion than appears upon the surface. She stimulates us to supply what is not there. What she offers is, apparently, a trifle, yet is composed of something that expands in the reader's mind and endows with the most enduring form of life scenes which are outwardly trivil. Always the stress is laid upon character.... The turns and twists of the dialogue keep us on the tenterhooks of suspense. Our attention is half upon the present moment, half upon the future.... Here, indeed, in this unfinished and in the main inferior story, are all the elements of Jane Austen's greatness."[4] The unwritten aspects of apparently trivial scenes, and the unspoken dialogue within the "turns and twists," not only draw the reader into the action, but also lead him to shade in the many outlines suggested by the given situations, so that these take on a reality of their own. But as the reader's imagination animates these "outlines," they in turn will influence the effect of the written part of the text. Thus begins a whole dynamic process: the written text imposes certain limits on its unwritten implications in order to prevent these from becoming too blurred and hazy, but at the same time these implications, worked out by the reader's imagination, set the given situation against a background which endows it with far greater significance than it might have seemed to possess on its own. In this way, trivial scenes suddenly take on the shape of an "enduring form of life." What constitutes this form is never named, let alone explained, in the text, although in fact it is the end product of the interaction between text and reader.

II

The question now arises as to how far such a process can be adequately described. For this purpose a phenomenological analysis recommends itself, especially since the somewhat sparse observations hitherto made of the psychology of reading tend mainly to be psychoanalytical, and so are restricted to the illustration of predetermined ideas concerning the unconscious. We shall, however, take a closer look later at some worthwhile psychological observations.

As a starting point for a phenomenological analysis we might examine the way in which sequent sentences act upon one another. This is of especial importance in literary texts in view of the fact that they do not correspond to any objective reality outside themselves. The world presented by literary texts is constructed out of what Ingarden has called *intentionale Satzkorrelate* (intentional sentence correlatives):

> Sentences link up in different ways to form more complex units of meaning that reveal a very varied structure giving rise to such entities as a short story, a novel, a dialogue, a drama, a scientific theory.... In the final analysis, there arises a particular world, with component parts determined in this way or that, and with all the variations that may occur within these parts—all this as a purely intentional correlative of a complex of sentences. If this complex finally forms a literary work, I call the whole form of sequent intentional sentence correlatives the 'world presented' in the work.[5]

This world, however, does not pass before the reader's eyes like a film. The sentences are "component parts" insofar as they make statements, claims, or observations, or convey information, and so establish various perspectives in the text. But they remain only "component parts"—they are not the sum total of the text itself. For the intentional correlatives disclose subtle connections which individually are less concrete than the statements, claims, and observations, even though these only take on their real meaningfulness through the interaction of their correlatives.

How is one to conceive the connection between the correlatives? It marks those points at which the reader is able to "climb aboard" the text. He has to accept certain given perspectives, but in doing so he inevitably causes them to interact. When Ingarden speaks of intentional sentence correlatives in literature, the statements made, or information conveyed in the sentence are already in a certain sense qualified: the sentence does not consist solely of a statement—which, after all, would be absurd, as one can only make statements about things that exist—but aims at something beyond what it actually says. This is true of all sentences in literary works, and it is through the interaction of these sentences that their common aim is fulfilled. This is what gives them their own special quality in literary texts. In their capacity as statements, observations, purveyors of information, etc., they are always indications of something that is to come, the structure of which is foreshadowed by their specific content.

They set in motion a process out of which emerges the actual content of the text itself. In describing man's inner consciousness of time, Husserl once remarked: "Every originally constructive process is inspired by pre-intentions, which construct and collect the seed of what is to come, as such, and bring it to fruition."[6] For this bringing to fruition, the literary text needs the reader's imagination, which gives shape to the interaction of correlatives foreshadowed in structure by the sequence of the sentences. Husserl's observation draws our attention to a point that plays a not insignificant part in the process of reading. The individual sentences not only work together to shade in what is to come; they also form an expectation in this regard. Husserl calls this expectation "pre-intentions." As this structure is characteristic of *all* sentence correlatives, the interaction of these correlatives will not be a fulfilment of the expectation so much as a continual modification of it.

For this reason, expectations are scarcely ever fulfilled in truly literary texts. If they were, then such texts would be confined to the individualization of a given expectation, and one would inevitably ask what such an intention was supposed to achieve. Strangely enough, we feel that any confirmative effect—such as we implicitly demand of expository texts, as we refer to the objects they are meant to present—is a defect in a literary text. For the more a text individualizes or confirms an expectation it has initially aroused, the more aware we become of its didactic purpose, so that at best we can only accept or reject the thesis forced upon us. More often than not, the very clarity of such texts will make us want to free ourselves from their clutches. But generally the sentence correlatives of literary texts do not develop in this rigid way, for the expectations they evoke tend to encroach on one another in such a manner that they are continually modified as one reads. One might simplify by saying that each intentional sentence correlative opens up a particular horizon, which is modified, if not completely changed, by succeeding sentences. While these expectations arouse interest in what is to come, the subsequent modification of them will also have a retrospective effect on what has already been read. This may now take on a different significance from that which it had at the moment of reading.

Whatever we have read sinks into our memory and is foreshortened. it may later be evoked again and set against a different background with the result that the reader is enabled to develop hitherto unforeseeable connections. The memory evoked, however, can never reassume its original shape, for this would mean that memory and perception were identical, which is manifestly not so. The new background brings to light new aspects of what we had committed to memory; conversely these, in turn, shed their light on the new background, thus arousing more complex anticipations. Thus, the reader, in establishing these interrelations between past, present and future, actually causes the text to reveal its potential multiplicity of connections. These connections are the product of the reader's mind working on the raw material of the text, though they are not the text itself—for this consists just of sentences, statements, information, etc.

This is why the reader often feels involved in events which, at the time of reading, seem real to him, even though in fact they are very far from his own reality. The fact that completely different readers can be differently affected by the "reality" of a particular text is ample evidence of the degree to which literary texts transform reading into a creative process that is far above mere perception of what is written. The literary text activates our own faculties, enabling us to recreate the world it presents. The product of this creative activity is what we might call the virtual dimension of the text, which endows it with its reality. This virtual dimension is not the text itself, nor is it the imagination of the reader: it is the coming together of text and imagination.

As we have seen, the activity of reading can be characterized as a sort of kaleidoscope of perspectives, preintentions, recollections. Every sentence contains a preview of the next and forms a kind of view-finder for what is to come; and this in turn changes the "preview" and so becomes a "viewfinder" for what has been read. This whole process represents the fulfilment of the potential, unexpressed reality of the text, but it is to be seen only as a framework for a great variety of means by which the virtual dimension may be brought into being. The process of anticipation and retrospection itself does not by any means develop in a smooth flow. Ingarden has already drawn attention to this fact, and ascribes a quite remarkable significance to it:

> Once we are immersed in the flow of *Satzdenken* (sentence-thought), we are ready, after completing the thought of one sentence, to think out the 'continuation,' also in the form of a sentence—and that is, in the form of a sentence that connects up with the sentence we have just thought through. In this way the process of reading goes effortlessly forward. But if by chance the following sentence has no tangible connection whatever with the sentence we have just thought through, there then comes a blockage in the stream of thought. This hiatus is linked with a more or less active surprise, or with indignation. This blockage must be overcome if the reading is to flow once more.[7]

The hiatus that blocks the flow of sentences is, in Ingarden's eyes, the product of chance, and is to be regarded as a flaw; this is typical of his adherence to the classical idea of art. If one regards the sentence sequence as a continual flow, this implies that the anticipation aroused by one sentence will generally be realized by the next, and the frustration of one's expectations will arouse feelings of exasperation. And yet literary texts are full of unexpected twists and turns, and frustration of expectations. Even in the simplest story there is bound to be some kind of blockage, if only for the fact that no tale can ever be told in its entirety. Indeed, it is only through inevitable omissions that a story will gain its dynamism. Thus whenever the flow is interrupted and we are led off in unexpected directions, the opportunity is given to us to bring into play our own faculty for establishing connections—for filling in the gaps left by the text itself.[8]

These gaps have a different effect on the process of anticipation and retrospection, and thus on the "gestalt" of the virtual dimension, for they may be filled in different ways. For this reason, one text is potentially capable of several different realizations, and no reading can ever exhaust the full potential, for each individual reader will fill in the gaps in his own way, thereby excluding the various other possibilities; as he reads, he will make his own decision as to how the gap is to be filled. In this very act the dynamics of reading are revealed. By making his decision he implicitly acknowledges the inexhaustibility of the text; at the same time it is this very inexhaustibility that forces him to make his decision. With "traditional" texts this process was more or less unconscious, but modern texts frequently exploit it quite deliberately. They are often so fragmentary that one's attention is almost exclusively occupied with the search for connections between the fragments; the object of this is not to complicate the "spectrum" of connections, so much as to make us aware of the nature of our own capacity for providing links. In such cases, the text refers back directly to our own preconceptions—which are revealed by the act of interpretation that is a basic element of the reading process. With all literary texts, then, we may say that the reading process is selective, and the potential text is infinitely richer than any of its individual realizations. This is borne out by the fact that a second reading of a piece of literature often produces a different impression from the first. The reasons for this may lie in the reader's own change of circumstances, still, the text must be such as to allow this variation. On a second reading familiar occurrences now tend to appear in a new light and seem to be at times corrected, at times enriched.

In every text there is a potential time-sequence which the reader must inevitably realize, as it is impossible to absorb even a short text in a single moment. Thus the reading process always involves viewing the text through a perspective that is continually on the move, linking up the different phases, and so constructing what we have called the virtual dimension. This dimension, of course, varies all the time we are reading. However, when we have finished the text, and read it again, clearly our extra knowledge will result in a different time-sequence; we shall tend to establish connections by referring to our awareness of what is to come, and so certain aspects of the text will assume a significance we did not attach to them on a first reading, while others will recede into the background. It is a common enough experience for a person to say that on a second reading he noticed things he had missed when he read the book for the first time, but this is scarcely surprising in view of the fact that the second time he is looking at the text through a different perspective. The time-sequence that he realized on his first reading cannot possibly be repeated on a second reading and this unrepeatability is bound to result in modifications of his reading experience. This is not to say that the second reading is "truer" than the first—they are, quite simply, different: the reader establishes the virtual dimension of the text by realizing a new time-sequence. Thus even on repeated viewings a text allows and, indeed, induces innovative reading.

In whatever way, and under whatever circumstances, the reader may link the different phases of the text together, it will always be the process of anticipation and retrospection that leads to the formation of the virtual dimension, which in turn transforms the text into an experience for the reader. The way in which this experience comes about through a process of continual modification is closely akin to the way in which we gather experience in life. And thus the "reality" of the reading experience can illuminate basic patterns of real experience:

> We have the experience of a world, not understood as a system of relations which wholly determine each event, but as an open totality the synthesis of which is inexhaustible.... From the moment that experience—that is, the opening on to our de facto world—is recognized as the beginning of knowledge, there is no longer any way of distinguishing a level of a prioir truths and one of factual ones, what the world must necessarily be and what it actually is.[9]

The manner in which the reader experiences the text will reflect his own disposition, and in this respect the literary text acts as a kind of mirror; but at the same time, the reality which this process helps to create is one that will be *different* from his own (since, normally, we tend to be bored by texts that present us with things we already know perfectly well ourselves). Thus we have the apparently paradoxical situation in which the reader is forced to reveal aspects of himself in order to experience a reality which is different from his own. The impact this reality makes on him will depend largely on the extent to which he himself actively provides the unwritten part of the text, and yet in supplying all the missing links, he must think in terms of experiences different from his own; indeed, it is only by leaving behind the familiar world of his own experience that the reader can truly participate in the adventure the literary text offers him.

III

We have seen that, during the process of reading, there is an active inter-weaving of anticipation and retrospection, which on a second reading may turn into a kind of advance retrospection. The impressions that arise as a result of this process will vary from individual to individual, but only within the limits imposed by the written as opposed to the unwritten text. In the same way, two people gazing at the night sky may both be looking at the same collection of stars, but one will see the image of a plough, and the other will make out a dipper. The "stars" in a literary text are fixed; the lines that join them are variable. The author of the text may, of course, exert plenty of influence on the reader's imagination—he has the whole panoply of narrative techniques at his disposal—but no author worth his salt will ever attempt to set the *whole* picture before his reader's eyes. If he does, he will very quickly lose his reader, for it is only by activating the reader's imagination that the author can hope to involve him and so realize the intentions of his text.

Gilbert Ryle, in his analysis of imagination, asks: "How can a person fancy that he sees something, without realizing that he is not seeing it?" He answers as follows:

Seeing Helvellyn (the name of a mountain) in one's mind's eye does not entail, what seeing Helvellyn and seeing snapshots of Helvellyn entail, the having of visual sensations. It does involve the thought of having a view of Helvellyn and it is therefore a more sophisticated operation than that of having a view of Helvellyn. It is one utilization among others of the knowledge of how Helvellyn should look, or, in one sense of the verb, it is thinking how it should look. The expectations which are fulfilled in the recognition at sight of Helvellyn are not indeed fulfilled in picturing it, but the picturing of it is something like a rehearsal of getting them fulfilled. So far from picturing involving the having of faint sensations, or wraiths of sensations, it involves missing just what one would be due to get, if one were seeing the mountain.[10]

If one sees the mountain, then of course one can no longer imagine it, and so the act of picturing the mountain presupposes its absence. Similarly, with a literary text we can only picture things which are not there; the written part of the text gives us the knowledge, but it is the unwritten part that gives us the opportunity to picture things; indeed without the elements of indeterminacy, the gaps in the text, we should not be able to use our imagination.[11]

The truth of this observation is borne out by the experience many people have on seeing, for instance, the film of a novel. While reading *Tom Jones*, they may never have had a clear conception of what the hero actually looks like, but on seeing the film, some may say, "That's not how I imagined him." The point here is that the reader of *Tom Jones* is able to visualize the hero virtually for himself, and so his imagination senses the vast number of possibilities; the moment these possibilities are narrowed down to one complete and immutable picture, the imagination is put out of action, and we feel we have somehow been cheated. This may perhaps be an oversimplification of the process, but it does illustrate plainly the vital richness of potential that arises out of the fact that the hero in the novel must be pictured and cannot be seen. With the novel the reader must use his imagination to synthesize the information given him, and so his perception is simultaneously richer and more private; with the film he is confined merely to physical perception, and so whatever he remembers of the world he had pictured is brutally cancelled out.

IV

The "picturing" that is done by our imagination is only one of the activities through which we form the "gestalt" of a literary text. We have already discussed the process of anticipation and retrospection, and to this we must add the process of grouping together all the different aspects of a text to form the consistency that the reader will always be in search of. While expectations may be continually modified, and images continually expanded, the reader will still strive, even if unconsciously, to fit everything together in a consistent pattern. "In the reading of images, as in the hearing of speech, it is always hard to distinguish what is given to us from what we supplement in the process of projection which is triggered off by recognition ... it is the guess of the beholder that tests the medley of forms and colours for coherent meaning, crystallizing it into shape when a consistent interpretation has been found."[12] By grouping together the written parts of the text, we enable them to interact, we observe the direction in which they are leading us, and we project onto them the consistency which we, as readers, require. This "gestalt" must inevitably be colored by our own characteristic selection process. For it is not given by the text itself; it arises from the meeting between the written text and the individual mind of the reader with its own particular history of experience, its own consciousness, its own outlook. The "gestalt" is not the true meaning of the text; at best it is a configurative meaning; " ... comprehension is an individual act of seeing-things-together, and only that."[13] With a literary text such comprehension is inseparable from the reader's expectations, and where we have expectations, there too we have one of the most potent weapons in the writer's armory—illusion.

Whenever "consistent reading suggests itself ... illusion takes over."[14] Illusion, says Northrop Frye, is "fixed or definable, and reality is at best understood as its negation."[15] The "gestalt" of a text normally takes on (or, rather, is given) this fixed or definable outline, as this is essential to our own understanding, but on the other hand, if reading were to consist of nothing but an uninterrupted building up of illusions, it would be a suspect, if not downright dangerous, process: instead of bringing us into contact with reality, it would wean us away from realities. Of course, there is an element of "escapism" in all literature, resulting from this very creation of illusion, but there are some texts which offer nothing but a harmonious world, purified of all contradiction and deliberately excluding anything that might disturb the illusion once established, and these are the texts that we generally do not like to classify as literary. Women's magazines and the brasher forms of detective story might be cited as examples.

However, even if an overdose of illusion may lead to triviality, this does not mean that the process of illusion-building should ideally be dispensed with altogether. On the contrary, even in texts that appear to resist the formation of illusion, thus drawing our attention to the cause of this resistance, we still need the abiding illusion that the resistance itself is the consistent pattern underlying the text. This is especially true of modern texts, in which it is the very precision of the written details which increases the proportion of indeterminacy; one detail appears to contradict another, and so simultaneously stimulates and frustrates our desire to "picture," thus continually causing our imposed "gestalt" of the text to disintegrate. Without the formation of illusions, the unfamiliar world of the text would remain unfamiliar; through the illusions, the experience offered by the text becomes accessible to us, for it is only the illusion, on its different levels of consistency, that makes the experience "readable." If we cannot find (or impose) this consistency, sooner or later we will put the text down. The process is virtually hermeneutic. The text provokes certain expectations which in turn we project onto the text in such a way that we reduce the polysemantic possibilities to a single interpretation in keeping with the expectations aroused, thus extracting an individual, configurative meaning. The polysemantic nature of the text and the illusion-making of the reader are opposed factors. If the illusion were complete, the polysemantic nature would vanish; if the polysemantic nature were all-powerful, the illusion would be totally destroyed. Both extremes are conceivable, but in the individual literary text we always find some form of balance between the two conflicting tendencies. The formation of illusions, therefore, can never be total, but it is this very incompleteness that in fact gives it its productive value.

With regard to the experience of reading, Walter Pater once observed: "For to the grave reader words too are grave; and the ornamental word, the figure, the accessory form or colour or reference, is rarely content to die to thought precisely at the right moment, but will inevitably linger awhile, stirring a long 'brainwave' behind it of perhaps quite alien associations."[16] Even while the reader is seeking a consistent pattern in the text, he is also uncovering other impulses which cannot be immediately integrated or will even resist final integration. Thus the semantic possibilities of the text will always remain far richer than any configurative meaning formed while reading. But this impression is, of course, only to be gained through reading the text. Thus the configurative meaning can be nothing but a *pars pro toto* fulfilment of the text, and yet this fulfilment gives rise to the very richness which it seeks to restrict, and indeed in some modern texts, our awareness of this richness takes precedence over any configurative meaning.

This fact has several consequences which, for the purpose of analysis, may be dealt with separately, though in the reading process they will all be working together. As we have seen, a consistent, configurative meaning is essential for the apprehension of an unfamiliar experience, which through the process of illusion-building we can incorporate in our own imaginative world. At the same time, this consistency conflicts with the many other possibilities of fulfillment it seeks to exclude, with the result that the configurative meaning is always accompanied by "alien associations" that do not fit in with the illusions formed. The first consequence, then, is the fact that in forming our illusions, we also produce at the same time a latent disturbance of these illusions. Strangely enough, this also applies to texts in which our expectations are actually fulfilled—though one would have thought that the fulfilment of expectations would help to complete the illusion. "Illusion wears off once the expectation is stepped up; we take it for granted and want more."[17]

The experiments in "gestalt" psychology referred to by Gombrich in *Art and Illusion* make one thing clear: " ... though we may be intellectually aware of the fact that any given experience must be an illusion, we cannot, strictly speaking, watch ourselves having an illusion."[18] Now, if illusion were not a transitory state, this would mean that we could be, as it were, permanently caught up in it. And if reading were exclusively a matter of producing illusion—necessary though this is for the understanding of an unfamiliar experience—we should run the risk of falling victim to a gross deception. But it is precisely during our reading that the transitory nature of the illusion is revealed to the full.

As the formation of illusions is constantly accompanied by "alien associations" which cannot be made consistent with the illusions, the reader constantly has to lift the restrictions he places on the "meaning" of the text. Since it is he who builds the illusions, he oscillates between involvement in and observation of those illusions; he opens himself to the unfamiliar world without being imprisoned in it. Through this process the reader moves into the presence of the fictional world and so experiences the realities of the text as they happen.

In the oscillation between consistency and "alien associations," between involvement in and observation of the illusion, the reader is bound to conduct his own balancing operation, and it is this that forms the aesthetic experience offered by the literary text. However, if the reader were to achieve a balance, obviously he would then no longer be engaged in the process of establishing and disrupting consistency. And since it is this very process that gives rise to the balancing operation, we may say that the inherent non-achievement of balance is a prerequisite for the very dynamism of the operation. In seeking the balance we inevitably have to start out with certain expectations, the shattering of which is integral to the aesthetic experience.

> Furthermore, to say merely that "our expectations are satisfied" is to be guilty of another serious ambiguity. At first sight such a statement seems to deny the obvious fact that much of our enjoyment is derived from surprises, from betrayals of our expectations. The solution of this paradox is to find some ground for a distinction between "surprise" and "frustration." Roughly, the distinction can be made in terms of the effects which the two kinds of experiences have upon us. Frustration blocks or checks activity. It necessitates new orientation for our activity, if we are to escape the *cul de sac*. Consequently, we abandon the frustrating object and return to blind impulsive activity. On the other hand, surprise merely causes a temporary cessation of the exploratory phase of the experience, and a recourse to intense contemplation and scrutiny. In the latter phase the surprising elements are seen in their connection with what has gone before, with the whole drift of the experience, and the enjoyment of these values is then extremely intense. Finally, it appears that there must always be some degree of novelty or surprise in all these values if there is a progressive specification of the direction of the total act . . . and any aesthetic experience tends to exhibit a continuous interplay between "deductive" and "inductive" operation.[19]

It is this interplay between "deduction" and "induction" that gives rise to the configurative meaning of the text, and not the individual expectations, surprises, or frustrations arising from the different perspectives. Since this interplay obviously does not take place in the text itself, but can only come into being through the process of reading, we may conclude that this process formulates something that is unformulated in the text, and yet represents its "intention." Thus, by reading, we uncover the unformulated part of the text, and this very indeterminacy is the force that drives us to work out a configurative meaning while at the same time giving us the necessary degree of freedom to do so.

As we work out a consistent pattern in the text, we will find our "interpretation" threatened, as it were, by the presence of other possibilities of "interpretation," and so there arise new areas of indeterminacy (though we may only be dimly aware of them, if at all, as we are continually making "decisions" which will exclude them). In the course of a novel, for instance, we sometimes find that characters, events, and backgrounds seem to change their significance; what really happens is that the other "possibilities" begin to emerge more strongly, so that we become more directly aware of them. Indeed, it is this very shifting of perspectives that makes us feel a novel is that much more "true-to-life." Since it is we ourselves who establish the levels of interpretation and switch from one to another as we conduct our balancing operation, we ourselves impart to the text the dynamic lifelikeness which, in turn, enables us to absorb an unfamiliar experience into our personal world.

As we read, we oscillate to a greater or lesser degree between the building and the breaking of illusions. In a process of trial and error, we organize and reorganize the various data offered us by the text. These are the given factors, the fixed points on which we base our "interpretation," trying to fit them together in the way we think the author meant them to be fitted. "For to perceive, a beholder must create his own experience. And his creation must include relations comparable to those which the original producer underwent. They are not the same in any literal sense. But with the perceiver, as with the artist, there must be an ordering of the elements of the whole that is in form, although not in details, the same as the process of organization the creator of the work consciously experienced. Without an act of recreation the object is not perceived as a work of art."[20]

The act of recreation is not a smooth or continuous process, but one which, in its essence, relies on *interruptions* of the flow to render it efficacious. We look forward, we look back, we decide, we change our decisions, we form expectations, we are shocked by their nonfulfilment, we question, we muse, we accept, we reject; this is the dynamic process of recreation. This process is steered by two main structural components within the text: first, a repertoire of familiar literary patterns and recurrent literary themes, together with allusions to familiar social and historical contexts; second, techniques or strategies used to set the familiar against the unfamiliar. Elements of the repertoire are continually backgrounded or foregrounded with a resultant strategic overmagnification, trivialization, or even annihilation of the allusion. This defamiliarization of what the reader thought he recognized is bound to create a tension that will intensify his expectations as well as his distrust of those expectations. Similarly, we may be confronted by narrative techniques that establish links between things we find difficult to connect, so that we are forced to reconsider data we at first held to be perfectly straightforward. On need only mention the very simple trick, so often employed by novelists, whereby the author himself takes part in the narrative, thus establishing perspectives which would not have arisen out of the mere narration of the events described. Wayne Booth once called this the technique of the "unreliable narrator,"[21] to show the extent to which a literary device can counter expectations arising out of the literary text. The figure of the narrator may act in permanent opposition to the impressions we might otherwise form. The question then arises as to whether this strategy, opposing the formation of illusions, may be integrated into a consistent pattern, lying, as it were, a level deeper than our original impressions. We may find that our narrator, by opposing us, in fact turns us against him and thereby strengthens the illusion he appears to be out to destroy; alternatively, we may be so much in doubt that we begin to question all the processes that lead us to make interpretative decisions. Whatever the cause may be, we will find ourselves subjected to this same interplay of illusion-forming and illusion-breaking that makes reading essentially a recreative process.

We might take, as a simple illustration of this complex process, the incident in Joyce's *Ulysses* in which Bloom's cigar alludes to Ulysses's spear. The context (Bloom's cigar) summons up a particular element of the repertoire (Ulysses's spear); the narrative technique relates them to one another as if they were identical. How are we to "organize" these divergent elements, which, through the very fact that they are put together, separate one element so clearly from the other? What are the prospects here for a consistent pattern? We might say that it is ironic—at least that is how many renowned Joyce readers have understood it.[22] In this case, irony would be the form of organization that integrates the material. But if this is so, what is the object of the irony? Ulysses's spear, or Bloom's cigar? The uncertainty surrounding this simple question already puts a strain on the consistency we have established, and indeed begins to puncture it, especially when other problems make themselves felt as regards the remarkable conjunction of spear and cigar. Various alternatives come to mind, but the variety alone is sufficient to leave one with the impression that the consistent pattern has been shattered. And even if, after all, one can still believe that irony holds the key to the mystery, this irony must be of a very strange nature; for the formulated text does not merely mean the opposite of what has been formulated. It may even mean something that cannot be formulated at all. The moment we try to impose a consistent pattern on the text, discrepancies are bound to arise. These are, as it were, the reverse side of the interpretative coin, an involuntary product of the process that creates discrepancies by trying to avoid them. And it is their very presence that draws us into the text, compelling us to conduct a creative examination not only of the text, but also of ourselves.

This entanglement of the reader is, of course, vital to any kind of text, but in the literary text we have the strange situation that the reader cannot know what his participation actually entails. We know that we share in certain experiences, but we do not know what happens to us in the course of this process. This is why, when we have been particularly impressed by a book, we feel the need to talk about it; we do not want to get away from it by talking about it—we simply want to understand more clearly what it is that we have been entangled in. We have undergone an experience, and now we want to know consciously *what* we have experienced. Perhaps this is the prime usefulness of literary criticism—it helps to make conscious those aspects of the text which would otherwise remain concealed in the subconscious; it satisfies (or helps to satisfy) our desire to talk about what we have read.

The efficacy of a literary text is brought about by the apparent evocation and subsequent negation of the familiar. What at first seemed to be an affirmation of our assumpetions leads to our own rejection of them, thus tending to prepare us for a re-orientation. And it is only when we have outstripped our preconceptions and left the shelter of the familiar that we are in a position to gather new experiences. As the literary text involves the reader in the formation of illusion and the simultaneous formation of the means whereby the illusion is punctured, reading reflects the process by which we gain experience. Once the reader is entangled, his own preconceptions are continually overtaken, so that the text becomes his "present" whilst his own ideas fade into the "past"; as soon as this happens he is open to the immediate experience of the text, which was impossible so long as his preconceptions were his "present."

V

In our analysis of the reading process so far, we have observed three important aspects that form the basis of the relationship between reader and text: the process of anticipation and retrospection, the consequent unfolding of the text as a living event, and the resultant impression of life-likeness.

Any "living event" must, to a greater or lesser degree, remain open. In reading, this obliges the reader to seek continually for consistency, because only then can he close up situations and comprehend the unfamiliar. But consistency-building is itself a living process, in which one is constantly forced to make selective decisions—and these decisions in their turn give a reality to the possibilities which they exclude, insofar as they may take effect as a latent disturbance of the consistency established. This is what causes the reader to be entangled in the text "gestalt" that he himself has produced.

Through this entanglement the reader is bound to open himself up to the workings of the text, and so leave behind his own preconceptions. This gives him the chance to have an experience in the way George Bernard Shaw once described it: "You have learnt something. That always feels at first as if you had lost something."[23] Reading reflects the structure of experience to the extent that we must suspend the ideas and attitudes that shape our own personality before we can experience the unfamiliar world of the literary text. But during this process, something happens to us.

This "something" needs to be looked at in detail, especially as the incorporation of the unfamiliar into our own range of experience has been to a certain extent obscured by an idea very common in literary discussion: namely, that the process of absorbing the unfamiliar is labelled as the *identification* of the reader with what he reads. Often the term "identification" is used as if it were an explanation, whereas in actual fact it is nothing more than a description. What is normally meant by "identification" is the establishment of affinities between oneself and someone outside oneself—a familiar ground on which we are able to experience the unfamiliar. The author's aim, though, is to convey the experience and, above all, an attitude towards that experience. Consequently, "identification" is not an end in itself, but a stratagem by means of which the author stimulates attitudes in the reader.

This of course is not to deny that there does arise a form of participation as one reads; one is certainly drawn into the text in such a way that one has the feeling that there is no distance between oneself and the events described. This involvement is well summed up by the reaction of a critic to reading Charlotte Brontë's *Jane Eyre:* "We took up *Jane Eyre* one winter's evening, somewhat piqued at the extravagant commendations we had heard, and sternly resolved to be as critical as Croker. But as we read on we forgot both commendations and criticism, identified ourselves with Jane in all her troubles, and finally married Mr. Rochester about four in the morning."[24] The question is how and why did the critic identify himself with Jane?

In order to understand this "experience," it is well worth considering Georges Poulet's observations on the reading process. He says that books only take on their full existence in the reader.[25] It is true that they consist of ideas thought out by someone else, but in reading the reader becomes the subject that does the thinking. Thus there disappears the subject-object division that otherwise is a prerequisite for all knowledge and all observation, and the removal of this division puts reading in an apparently unique position as regards the possible absorption of new experiences. This may well be the reason why relations with the world of the literary text have so often been misinterpreted as identification. From the idea that in reading we must think the thoughts of someone else, Poulet draws the following conclusion: "Whatever I think is a part of *my* mental world. And yet here I am thinking a thought which manifestly belongs to another mental world, which is being thought in me just as though I did not exist. Already the notion is inconceivable and seems even more so if I reflect that, since every thought must have a subject to think it, this *thought* which is alien to me and yet in me, must also have in me a *subject* which is alien to me. . . . Whenever I read, I mentally pronounce an I, and yet the I which I pronounce is not myself."[26]

But for Poulet this idea is only part of the story. The strange subject that thinks the strange thought in the reader indicates the potential presence of the author, whose ideas can be "internalized" by the reader: "Such is the characteristic condition of every work which I summon back into existence by placing my consciousness at its disposal. I give it not only existence, but awareness of existence."[27] This would mean that consciousness forms the point at which author and reader converge, and at the same time it would result in the cessation of the temporary self-alienation that occurs to the reader when his consciousness brings to life the ideas formulated by the author. This process gives rise to a form of communication which, however, according to Poulet, is dependent on two conditions: the life-story of the author must be shut out of the work, and the individual disposition of the reader must be shut out of the act of reading. Only then can the thoughts of the author take place subjectively in the reader, who thinks what he is not. It follows that the work itself must be thought of as a consciousness, because only in this way is there an adequate basis for the author-reader relationship—a relationship that can only come about through the negation of the author's own life-story and the reader's own disposition. This conclusion is actually drawn by Poulet when he describes the work as the self-presentation or materialization of consciousness: "And so I ought not to hesitate to recognize that so long as it is animated by this vital inbreathing inspired by the act of reading, a work of literature becomes (at the expense of the reader whose own life it suspends) a sort of human being, that it is a mind conscious of itself and constituting itself in me as the subject of its own objects."[28] Even though it is difficult to follow such a substantialist conception of the consciousness that constitutes itself in the literary work, there are, nevertheless, certain points in Poulet's argument that are worth holding onto. But they should be developed along somewhat different lines.

If reading removes the subject-object division that constitutes all perception, it follows that the reader will be "occupied" by the thoughts

of the author, and these in their turn will cause the drawing of new
"boundaries." Text and reader no longer confront each other as object and
subject, but instead the "division" takes place within the reader himself.
In thinking the thoughts of another, his own individuality temporarily re-
cedes into the background since it is supplanted by these alien thoughts,
which now become the theme on which his attention is focussed. As we
read, there occurs an artificial division of our personality because we take
as a theme for ourselves something that we are not. Consequently when
reading we operate on different levels. For although we may be thinking
the thoughts of someone else, what we are will not disappear completely—it will merely remain a more or less powerful virtual force.
Thus, in reading there are these two levels—the alien "me" and the real,
virtual "me"—which are never completely cut off from each other. Indeed, we can only make someone else's thoughts into an absorbing theme
for ourselves, provided the virtual background of our own personality can
adapt to it. Every text we read draws a different boundary within our personality, so that the virtual background (the real "me") will take on a different form, according to the theme of the text concerned. This is inevitable, if only for the fact that the relationship between alien theme and
virtual background is what makes it possible for the unfamiliar to be
understood.

In this context there is a revealing remark made by D. W. Harding,
arguing against the idea of identification with what is read: "What is
sometimes called wish-fulfilment in novels and plays can ... more plausibly be described as wish-formulation or the definition of desires. The
cultural levels at which it works may vary widely; the process is the same
... It seems nearer the truth ... to say that fictions contribute to defining
the reader's or spectator's values, and perhaps stimulating his desires,
rather than to suppose that they gratify desire by some mechanism of vicarious experience."[29] In the act of reading, having to think something
that we have not yet experienced does not mean only being in a position
to conceive or even understand it; it also means that such acts of conception are possible and successful to the degree that they lead to something
being formulated in us. For someone else's thoughts can only take a form
in our consciousness if, in the process, our unformulated faculty for deciphering those thoughts is brought into play—a faculty which, in the act
of deciphering, also formulates itself. Now since this formulation is carried out on terms set by someone else, whose thoughts are the theme of
our reading, it follows that the formulation of our faculty for deciphering
cannot be along our own lines of orientation.

Herein lies the dialectical structure of reading. The need to decipher
gives us the chance to formulate our own deciphering capacity—i.e., we
bring to the fore an element of our being of which we are not directly con-

scious. The production of the meaning of literary texts—which we discussed in connection with forming the "gestalt" of the text—does not merely entail the discovery of the unformulated, which can then be taken over by the active imagination of the reader; it also entails the possibility that we may formulate ourselves and so discover what had previously seemed to elude our consciousness. These are the ways in which reading literature gives us the chance to formulate the unformulated.

NOTES

1. Cf. Roman Ingarden, *Vom Erkennen des literarischen Kunstwerks* (Tübingen, 1968), pp. 49 ff.
2. For a detailed discussion of this term see Roman Ingarden, *Das literarische Kunstwerk* (Tübingen, 1960), pp. 270 ff.
3. Laurence Sterne, *Tristram Shandy* (London, 1956), II, chap. 11, 79.
4. Virginia Woolf, *The Common Reader*, First Series (London, 1957), p. 174.
5. Ingarden, *Vom Erkennen des literarischen Kunstwerks*, p. 29.
6. Edmund Husserl, *Zur Phänomenologie des inneren Zeitbewusstseins, Gesammelte Werke* 10 (Haag, 1966), 52.
7. Ingarden, *Vom Erkennen des literarischen Kunstwerks*, p. 32.
8. For a more detailed discussion of the function of "gaps" in literary texts see Wolfgang Iser, "Indeterminacy and the Reader's Response in Prose Fiction," *Aspects of Narrative*, English Institute Essays, ed. by J. Hillis Miller (New York, 1971), pp. 1–45.
9. M. Merleau-Ponty, *Phenomenology of Perception*, trans. Colin Smith (New York, 1962), pp. 219, 221.
10. Gilbert Ryle, *The Concept of Mind* (Harmondsworth, 1968), p. 255.
11. Cf. Iser, pp. 11ff., 42ff.
12. E. H. Gombrich, *Art and Illusion* (London, 1962), p. 204.
13. Louis O. Mink, "History and Fiction as Modes of Comprehension," *New Literary History*, 1 (1970), 553.
14. Gombrich, p. 278.
15. Northrop Frye, *Anatomy of Criticism* (New York, 1967), pp. 169 f.
16. Walter Pater, *Appreciations* (London, 1920), p. 18.
17. Gombrich, p. 54.
18. *Ibid.*, p. 5.
19. B. Ritchie, "The Formal Structure of the Aesthetic Object," *The Problems of Aesthetics*, ed. by Eliseo Vivas and Murray Krieger (New York, 1965), pp. 230.
20. John Dewey, *Art as Experience* (New York, 1958), p. 54.
21. Cf. Wayne C. Booth, *The Rhetoric of Fiction* (Chicago, 1963), pp. 211 ff., 339 ff.
22. Richard Ellmann, "Ulysses. The Divine Nobody," *Twelve Original Essays on Great English Novels*, ed. by Charles Shapiro (Detroit 1960), p. 247, classified this particular allusion as "mock-heroic."

23. G. B. Shaw, *Major Barbara* (London, 1964), p. 316.
24. William George Clark, *Fraser's*, December, 1849, 692, quoted by Kathleen Tillotson, *Novels of the Eighteen-Forties* (Oxford, 1961), pp. 19 f.
25. Cf. Georges Poulet, "Phenomenology of Reading," *New Literary History*, 1 (1969), 54.
26. *Ibid.*, 56.
27. *Ibid.*, 59.
28. *Ibid.*, p. 59.
29. D. W. Harding, "Psychological Processes in the Reading of Fiction," *Aesthetics in the Modern World*, ed. by Harold Osborne (London, 1968), pp. 313 ff.

Walter J. Ong, S. J.

The Writer's Audience Is Always a Fiction[*]

Epistola ... non erubescit.
— Cicero *Epistolae ad familiares* v.12.1.

Ubi nihil erit quae scribas, id ipsum scribes.
— Cicero *Epistolae ad Atticum* iv.8.4.

I

Although there is a large and growing literature on the differences between oral and written verbalization, many aspects of the differences have not been looked into at all, and many others, although well known, have not been examined in their full implications. Among these latter is the relationship, of the so-called "audience" to writing as such, to the situation that inscribed communication establishes and to the roles that readers as readers are consequently called on to play. Some studies in literary history and criticism at times touch near this subject, but none, it appears, take it up in any detail.

The standard locus in Western intellectual tradition for study of audience responses has been rhetoric. But rhetoric originally concerned oral communication, as is indicated by its name, which comes from the Greek word for public speaking. Over two millennia, rhetoric has been gradually extended to include writing more and more, until today, in highly technological cultures, this is its principal concern. But the extension has come gradually and has advanced pari passu with the slow and largely unnoticed emergence of markedly chirographic and typographic styles out of those originating in oral performance, with the result that the differentiation between speech and writing has never become a matter of urgent concern for the rhetoric of any given age: when orality was in the ascendancy, rhetoric was oral-focused; as orality yielded to writing, the focus of rhetoric was slowly shifted, unreflectively for the most part, and without notice.

[*] In a briefer adaptation, this paper was read at Cambridge Univ., 24 Aug. 1972, at the Twelfth International Congress of the International Federation for Modern Languages and Literatures. At the Center for Advanced Study in the Behavioral Sciences at Stanford, California, I have profited from conversations with Albert Cook of the State Univ. of New York, Buffalo, and Robert Darnton of Princeton Univ., concerning matters in this final version.

Histories of the relationship between literature and culture have something to say about the status and behavior of readers, before and after reading given materials, as do mass media studies, readership surveys, liberation programs for minorities or various other classes of persons, books on reading skills, works of literary criticism, and works on linguistics, especially those addressing differences between hearing and reading. But most of these studies, except perhaps literary criticism and linguistic studies, treat only perfunctorily, if at all, the roles imposed on the reader by a written or printed text not imposed by spoken utterance. Formalist or structuralist critics, including French theorists such as Paul Ricoeur as well as Roland Barthes, Jacques Derrida, Michel Foucault, Philippe Sollers, and Tsvetan Todorov, variously advert to the immediacy of the oral as against writing and print and occasionally study differences between speech and writing, as Louis Lavelle did much earlier in *La Parole et l'écriture* (1942). In treating of masks and "shadows" in his *Sociologie du théâtre* (1965), Jean Duvignaud brilliantly discusses the projections of a kind of collective consciousness on the part of theater audiences. But none of these appear to broach directly the question of readers' roles called for by a written text, either synchronically as such roles stand at present or diachronically as they have developed through history. Linguistic theorists such as John R. Searle and John L. Austin treat "illocutionary acts" (denoted by "warn," "command," "state," etc.), but these regard the speaker's or writer's need in certain instances to secure a special hold on those he addresses,[1] not any special role imposed by writing.

Wayne Booth in *The Rhetoric of Fiction* and Walker Gibson, whom Booth quotes, come quite close to the concerns of the present study in their treatment of the "mock reader," as does Henry James, whom Booth also cites, in his discussion of the way an author makes "his reader very much as he makes his character."[2] But this hint of James is not developed—there is no reason why it should be—and neither Booth nor Gibson discusses in any detail the history of the ways in which readers have been called on to relate to texts before them. Neither do Robert Scholes and Robert Kellogg in their invaluable work, *The Nature of Narrative:* they skirt the subject in their chapter on "The Oral Heritage of Written Narrative,"[3] but remain chiefly concerned with the oral performer, the writer, and techniques, rather than with the recipient of the message. Yet a great many of the studies noted here as well as many others, among which might be mentioned Norman N. Holland's *The Dynamics of Literary Response* (1968), suggest the time is ripe for a study of the history of readers and their enforced roles, for they show that we have ample phenomenological and literary sophistication to manage many of the complications involved.

So long as verbal communication is reduced to a simplistic mechanistic model which supposedly moves corpuscular units of something labeled "information" back and forth along tracks between two termini, there is of course no special problem with those who assimilate the written or printed word. For the speaker, the audience is in front of him. For the writer, the audience is simply further away, in time or space or both. A surface inscribed with information can neutralize time by preserving the information and conquer space by moving the information to its recipient over distances that sound cannot traverse. If, however, we put aside this alluring but deceptively neat and mechanistic mock-up and look at verbal communication in its human actuality, noting that words consist not of corpuscular units but of evanescent sound and that, as Maurice Merleau-Ponty has pointed out,[4] words are never fully determined in their abstract signification but have meaning only with relation to man's body and to its interaction with its surroundings, problems with the writer's audience begin to show themselves. Writing calls for difficult, and often quite mysterious, skills. Except for a small corps of highly trained writers, most persons could get into written form few if any of the complicated and nuanced meanings they regularly convey orally. One reason is evident: the spoken word is part of present actuality and has its meaning established by the total situation in which it comes into being. Context for the spoken word is simply present, centered in the person speaking and the one or ones to whom he addresses himself and to whom he is related existentially in terms of the circumambient actuality.[5] But the meaning caught in writing comes provided with no such present circumambient actuality, at least normally. (One might except special cases of written exchanges between persons present to one another physically but with oral channels blocked: two deaf persons, for example, or two persons who use different variants of Chinese and are orally incomprehensible to one another but can communicate through the same written characters, which carry virtually the same meanings though they are sounded differently in the different varieties of Chinese.)

Such special cases apart, the person to whom the writer addresses himself normally is not present at all. Moreover, with certain special exceptions such as those just suggested, he must not be present. I am writing a book which will be read by thousands, or, I modestly hope, by tens of thousands. So, please, get out of the room. I want to be alone. Writing normally calls for some kind of withdrawal.

How does the writer give body to the audience for whom he writes? It would be fatuous to think that the writer addressing a so-called general audience tries to imagine his readers individually. A well-known novelist friend of mine only laughed when I asked him if, as he was writing a novel, he imagined his real readers—the woman on the subway deep in his book, the student in his room, the businessman on a vacation, the scholar in his study. There is no need for a novelist to feel his "audience" this way at all. It may be, of course, that at one time or another he imagines himself addressing one or another real person. But not all his readers in their particularities. Practically speaking, of course, and under the insistent urging of editors and publishers, he does have to take into consideration the real social, economic, and psychological state of possible readers. He has to write a book that real persons will buy and read. But I am speaking— or writing—here of the "audience" that fires the writer's imagination. If it consists of the real persons who he hopes will buy his book, they are not these persons in an untransmuted state.[6]

Although I have thus far followed the common practice in using the term "audience," it is really quite misleading to think of a writer as dealing with an "audience," even though certain considerations may at times oblige us to think this way. More properly, a writer addresses readers— only, he does not quite "address" them either: he writes to or for them. The orator has before him an audience which is a true audience, a collectivity. "Audience" is a collective noun. There is no such collective noun for readers, nor, so far as I am able to puzzle out, can there be. "Readers" is a plural. Readers do not form a collectivity, acting here and now on one another and on the speaker as members of an audience do. We can devise a singularized concept for them, it is true, such as "readership." We can say that the *Reader's Digest* has a readership of I don't know how many millions—more than it is comfortable to think about, at any rate. But "readership" is not a collective noun. It is an abstraction in a way that "audience" is not.

The contrast between hearing and reading (running the eye over signals that encode sound) can be caught if we imagine a speaker addressing an audience equipped with texts. At one point, the speaker asks the members of the audience all to read silently a paragraph out of the text. The audience immediately fragments. It is no longer a unit. Each individual retires into his own microcosm. When the readers look up again, the speaker has to gather them into a collectivity once more. This is true even if he is the author of the text they are reading.

To sense more fully the writer's problem with his so-called audience let us envision a class of students asked to write on the subject to which schoolteachers, jaded by summer, return compulsively every autumn: "How I Spent My Summer Vacation." The teacher makes the easy assumption, inviting and plausible but false, that the chief problem of a boy and a girl in writing is finding a subject actually part of his or her real life. In-close subject matter is supposed to solve the problem of invention. Of course it does not. The problem is not simply what to say but also whom to say it to. Say? The student is not talking. He is writing. No one is listening. There is no feedback. Where does he find his "audience"? He has to make his readers up, fictionalize them.

If the student knew what he was up against better than the teacher giving the assignment seemingly does, he might ask, "Who wants to know?" The answer is not easy. Grandmother? He never tells grandmother. His father or mother? There's a lot he would not want to tell them, that's sure. His classmates? Imagine the reception if he suggested they sit down and listen quietly while he told them how he spent his summer vacation. The teacher? There is no conceivable setting in which he could imagine telling his teacher how he spent his summer vacation other than in writing this paper, so that writing for the teacher does not solve his problems but only restates them. In fact, most young people do not tell anybody how they spent their summer vacation, much less write down how they spent it. The subject may be in-close; the use it is to be put to remains unfamiliar, strained, bizarre.

How does the student solve the problem? In many cases, in a way somewhat like the following. He has read, let us say, *The Adventures of Tom Sawyer.* He knows what this book felt like, how the voice in it addressed its readers, how the narrator hinted to his readers that they were related to him and he to them, whoever they may actually have been or may be. Why not pick up that voice and, with it, its audience? Why not make like Samuel Clemens and write for whomever Samuel Clemens was writing for? This even makes it possible to write for his teacher—itself likely to be a productive ploy—whom he certainly has never been quite able to figure out. But he knows his teacher has read *Tom Sawyer*, has heard the voice in the book, and could therefore obviously make like a *Tom Sawyer* reader. His problem is solved, and he goes ahead. The subject matter now makes little difference, provided that it is something like Mark Twain's and that it interests him on some grounds or other. Material in-close to his real life is not essential, though, of course, it might be welcome now that he has a way to process it.

If the writer succeeds in writing, it is generally because he can fictionalize in his imagination an audience he has learned to know not from daily life but from earlier writers who were fictionalizing in their imagination audiences they had learned to know in still earlier writers, and so on back to the dawn of written narrative. If and when he becomes truly adept, an "original writer," he can do more than project the earlier audience, he can alter it. Thus it was that Samuel Clemens in *Life on the Mississippi* could not merely project the audience that the many journalistic writers about the Midwestern rivers had brought into being, but could also shape it to his own demands. If you had read Isaiah Sellers, you could read Mark Twain, but with a difference. You had to assume a part in a less owlish, more boisterous setting, in which Clemens' caustic humor masks the uncertainty of his seriousness. Mark Twain's reader is asked to take a special kind of hold on himself and on life.

II

These reflections suggest, or are meant to suggest, that there exists a tradition in fictionalizing audiences that is a component part of literary tradition in the sense in which literary tradition is discussed in T. S. Eliot's "Tradition and the Individual Talent." A history of the ways audiences have been called on to fictionalize themselves would be a correlative of the history of literary genres and literary works, and indeed of culture itself.

What do we mean by saying the audience is a fiction? Two things at least. First, that the writer must construct in his imagination, clearly or vaguely, an audience cast in some sort of role—entertainment seekers, reflective sharers of experience (as those who listen to Conrad's Marlow), inhabitants of a lost and remembered world of prepubertal latency (readers of Tolkien's hobbit stories), and so on. Second, we mean that the audience must correspondingly fictionalize itself. A reader has to play the role in which the author has cast him, which seldom coincides with his role in the rest of actual life. An office worker on a bus reading a novel of Thomas Hardy is listening to a voice which is not that of any real person in the real setting around him. He is playing the role demanded of him by this person speaking in a quite special way from the book, which is not the subway and is not quite "Wessex" either, though it speaks of Wessex. Readers over the ages have had to learn this game of literacy, how to conform themselves to the projections of the writers they read, or at least how to operate in terms of these projections. They have to know how to play the game of being a member of an audience that "really" does not exist. And they have to adjust when the rules change, even though no rules thus far have ever been published and even though the changes in the unpublished rules are themselves for the most part only implied.

A history of literature could be written in terms of the ways in which audiences have successively been fictionalized from the time when writing broke away from oral performance, for, just as each genre grows out of what went before it, so each new role that readers are made to assume is related to previous roles. Putting aside for the moment the question of what fictionalizing may be called for in the case of the audience for oral performance, we can note that when script first came on the scene, the fictionalizing of readers was relatively simple. Written narrative at first was merely a transcription of oral narrative, or what was imagined as oral narrative, and it assumed some kind of oral singer's audience, even when being read. The transcribers of the *Iliad* and the *Odyssey* presumably imagined an audience of real listeners in attendance on an oral singer, and readers of those works to this day do well if they can imagine themselves hearing a singer of tales.[7] How these texts and other oral performances were in fact originally set down in writing remains puzzling, but the transcribers certainly were not composing in writing, but rather recording with minimal alteration what a singer was singing or was imagined to be singing.

Even so, a scribe had to fictionalize in a way a singer did not, for a real audience was not really present before the scribe, so it would seem, although it is just possible that at times one may have been (Lord, pp. 125–28). But, as transcription of oral performance or imagined oral performance gave way gradually to composition in writing, the situation changed. No reader today imagines *Second Skin* as a work that John Hawkes is reciting extempore to a group of auditors, even though passages from it may be impressive when read aloud.

III

We have noted that the roles teachers are called on to play evolve without any explicit rules or directives. How readers pick up the implicit signals and how writers change the rules can be illustrated by examining a passage from a specialist in unpublished directives for readers, Ernest Hemingway. The passage is the opening of *A Farewell to Arms*. At the start of my comment on the passage, it will be clear that I am borrowing a good deal from Walker Gibson's highly discerning book on modern American prose styles, *Tough, Sweet, and Stuffy.*[8] The Hemingway passage follows:

> In the late summer of that year we lived in a house in a village that looked across the river and the plain to the mountains. In the bed of the river there were pebbles and boulders, dry and white in the sun, and the water was clear and swiftly moving and blue in the channels.

Hemingway's style is often characterized as straightforward, unadorned, terse, lacking in qualifiers, close-lipped; and it is all these things. But none of them were peculiar to Hemingway when his writing began to command attention. A feature more distinctive of Hemingway here and elsewhere is the way he fictionalizes the reader, and this fictionalizing is often signaled largely by his use of the definite article as a special kind of qualifier or of the demonstrative pronoun "that," of which the definite article is simply an attenuation.

"The late summer of that year," the reader begins. What year? The reader gathers that there is no need to say. "Across the river." What river? The reader apparently is supposed to know. "And the plain." What plain? "*The* plain"—remember? "To the mountains." What mountains? Do I have to tell you? Of course not. *The* mountains—*those* mountains we know. We have somehow been there together. Who? You, my reader, and I. The reader—every reader—is being cast in the role of a close companion of the writer. This is the game he must play here with Hemingway, not always exclusively or totally, but generally, to a greater or lesser extent. It is one reason why the writer is tight-lipped. Description as such would bore a boon companion. What description there is comes in the guise of pointing, in verbal gestures, recalling humdrum, familiar details. "In the bed of the river there were pebbles and boulders, dry and white in the sun." The known world, accepted and accepting. Not presentation, but recall. The writer needs only to point, for what he wants to tell you about is not the scene at all but his feelings. These, too, he treats as something you really had somehow shared, though you might not have been quite aware of it at the time. He can tell you what was going on inside him and count on sympathy, for you were there. You *know.* The reader here has a well-marked role assigned him. He is a companion-in-arms, somewhat later become a confidant. It is a flattering role. Hemingway readers are encouraged to cultivate high self-esteem.

The effect of the definite article in Hemingway here is quite standard and readily explicable. Normally, in English, we are likely to make an initial reference to an individual object by means of the indefinite article and to bring in the definite only subsequently. "Yesterday on the street *a* man came up to me, and when I stopped in my stride *the* man said. . . . " "A" is a modified form of the term "one," a kind of singular of "some." "A man" means "one man" (of many real or possible men). The indefinite article tacitly acknowledges the existence or possibility of a number of individuals beyond the immediate range of reference and indicates that from among them one is selected. Once we have indicated that we are concerned not with all but with one-out-of-many, we train the definite article or pointer article on the object of our attention.[9] The definite article thus commonly signals some previous, less definite acquaintanceship. Hemingway's exclusion of indefinite in favor of definite articles signals the reader that he is from the first on familiar ground. He shares the author's familiarity with the subject matter. The reader must pretend he has known much of it before.

Hemingway's concomitant use of the demonstrative distancing pronoun "that" parallels his use of "the." For "the" is only an attenuated "that." It is a modified form of the demonstrative pronoun that replaced the original Old English definite article "seo." Both hold their referents at a distance, "that" typically at a somewhat greater distance than "the."

That mountain you see ten miles away is indicated there on *the* map on *the* wall. If we wish to think of the map as close, we would say, *"This* map on this wall."* In distancing their objects, both "that" and "the" can tend to bring together the speaker and the one spoken to. "That" commonly means that-over-there at a distance from you-and-me here, and "the com-monly means much the same. These terms thus can easily implement the Hemingway relationship: you-and-me.

This you-and-me effect of the distancing demonstrative pronoun and the definite article can be seen perhaps more spectacularly in romance etymology. The words for "the" in the romance languages come from the Latin word *ille, illa, illud,* which yields in various romance tongues *il, le, la, el, lo,* and their cognates. *Ille* is a distancing demonstrative in Latin: it means "that-over-there-away-from-you-and-me" and stands in contras-tive opposition to another Latin demonstrative which has no counterpart in English, *iste, ista, istud,* which means "that-over-there-by-you" (and thus can readily become pejorative—"that-little-no-account-thing-of-yours"). *Ille* brings together the speaker and the one spoken to by contrast with the distanced object; *iste* distances from the speaker the one spoken to as well as the object. *Ille* yields the romance definite articles, which correspond quite closely in function to the English "the," and thus adver-tises the close tie between "the" and "that."

Could readers of an earlier age have managed the Hemingway rela-tionship, the you-and-me relationship, marked by tight-lipped empathy based on shared experience? Certainly from antiquity the reader or hearer of an epic was plunged in medias res. But this does not mean he was cast as the author's boon companion. It means rather that he was plunged into the middle of a narrative sequence and told about antecedent events only later. A feeling of camaraderie between companions-in-arms is conveyed in epics, but the companions-in-arms are fictional characters; they are not the reader or hearer and the narrator. *"Forsan et haec olim meminisse iucabit"*—these words in the *Aeneid,* "perhaps some day it will help to recall these very things," are spoken by Aeneas to his companions when they are undergoing a period of hardships. They are one character's words to other characters, not Virgil's words to his hearer or reader. One might urge further that, like Hemingway's reader, the reader or hearer of an epic—most typically, of an oral folk epic—was hearing stories with which he was already acquainted, that he was thus on familiar ground. He was, but not in the sense that he was forced to pretend he had somehow lived as an alter ego of the narrator. His familiarity with the material was not a pretense at all, not a role, but a simple fact. Typically, the epic audi-ence had heard the story, or something very much like it, before.

The role in which Hemingway casts the reader is somewhat different not only from anything these situations in early literature demand but also from anything in the time immediately before Hemingway. This is what makes Hemingway's writing interesting to literary historians. But Hemingway's demands on the reader are by no means entirely without antecedents. The existence of antecedents is indicated by the fact that Hemingway was assimilated by relatively unskilled readers with very little fuss. He does not recast the reader in a disturbingly novel role. By contrast, the role in which Faulkner casts the reader is a far greater departure from preceding roles than is Hemingway's. Faulkner demands more skilled and daring readers, and consequently had far fewer at first, and has relatively fewer even today when the Faulkner role for readers is actually taught in school. (Perhaps we should say the Faulkner roles.)

No one, so far as I know, has worked up a history of the readers' roles that prepared for that prescribed by Hemingway. But one can discern significantly similar demands on readers beginning as early as Addison and Steele, who assume a new fashionable intimacy among readers themselves and between all readers and the writer, achieved largely by casting readers as well as writer in the role of coffeehouse habitués. Defoe develops in his own way comparable author-reader intimacy. The roots of these eighteenth-century intimacies are journalistic, and from earlier journalism they push out later in Hemingway's own day into the world of sportswriters and war correspondents, of whom Hemingway himself was one. With the help of print and the near instantaneousness implemented by electronic media (the telegraph first, later radio teletype and electronic transmission of photography), the newspaper writer could bring his reader into his own on-the-spot experience, availing himself in both sports and war of the male's strong sense of camaraderie based on shared hardships. Virgil's *forsan et haec olim meminisse iucabit* once more. But Virgil was telling a story of the days of old and, as has been seen, the camaraderie was among characters in the story, Aeneas and his men. Sports and war journalism are about the here and now, and, if the story can be got to the reader quickly, the camaraderie can be easily projected between the narrator and the reader. The reader is close enough temporally and photographically to the event for him to feel like a vicarious participant. In journalism Hemingway had an established foundation on which to build, if not one highly esteemed in snobbish literary circles. And he in turn has been built upon by those who have come later. Gibson has shown how much the style of *Time* magazine is an adaptation of Hemingway (pp. 48–54). To Hemingway's writer-reader camaraderie *Time* adds omniscience, solemnly "reporting," for example, in eyewitness style, the behavior and feelings of a chief of state in his own bedroom as he answers an emergency night telephone call and afterward returns to sleep. Hemingway encouraged his readers in high self-esteem. *Time* provides its readers, on a regular weekly basis, companionship with the all-knowing gods.

When we look the other way down the corridors of time to the period before the coffeehouses and the beginnings of intimate journalism, we find that readers have had to be trained gradually to play the game Hemingway engages them in. What if, *per impossibile,* a Hemingway story projecting the reader's role we have attended to here had turned up in Elizabethan England? It would probably have been laughed out of court by readers totally unable to adapt to its demands upon them. It would certainly have collided with representative literary theory, as propounded for example by Sir Philip Sidney in *The Defense of Poesie.* For Sidney and most of his age, poetry—that is to say, literature generally—had as its aim to please, but even more basically to teach, at least in the sense that it gave the reader to know what he did not know before. The Hemingway convention that the reader had somehow been through it all before with the writer would have been to Sidney's age at best confusing and at worst wrongheaded. One could argue that the Hemingway narrator would be telling the reader at least something he did not know before—that is, largely, the feelings of the narrator. But even this revelation, as we have seen, implies in Hemingway a covert awareness on the part of the reader, a deep sympathy or empathy of a basically romantic, nonpublic sort, grounded in intimacy. Sidney would have sent Hemingway back to his writing table to find something newer to write about, or to find a way of casting his material in a fresher-sounding form.

Another, and related, feature of the Hemingway style would have repelled sixteenth-century readers: the addiction to the "the" and "that" to the calculated exclusion of most descriptive qualifiers. There is a deep irony here. For in the rhetorical world that persisted from prehistoric times to the age of romanticism, descriptive qualifiers were commonly epithetic, expected qualifiers. The first chapter of Sidney's *Arcadia* (1590) presents the reader with "the hopeless shepheard," the "friendly rival," "the necessary food," "natural rest," "flowery fields," "the extreme heat of summer," and countless other souvenirs of a country every rhetorician had trod many times before. Is this not making the reader a recaller of shared experience much as Hemingway's use of "the" and "that" does? Not at all in the same way. The sixteenth-century reader recalls the familiar accouterments of literature, which are the familiar accouterments or commonplaces also of sculpture, painting, and all art. These are matters of shared public acquaintanceship, not of private experience. The sixteenth-century reader is walking through land all educated men know. He is not made to pretend he knows these familiar objects because he once shared their presence with this particular author, as a Hemingway reader is made to pretend. In Sidney, there is none of the you-and-I-know-even-if-others-don't ploy.

IV

To say that earlier readers would have been nonplussed at Hemingway's demands on them is not to say that earlier readers did not have special roles to play or that authors did not have their own problems in devising and signaling what the roles were. A few cases might be instanced here.

First of all, it is only honest to admit that even an oral narrator calls on his audience to fictionalize itself to some extent. The invocation to the Muse is a signal to the audience to put on the epic-listener's cap. No Greek, after all, ever talked the kind of language that Homer sang, although Homer's contemporaries could understand it well enough. Even today we do not talk in other contexts quite the kind of language in which we tell fairy stories to children. "Once upon a time," we begin. The phrase lifts you out of the real world. Homer's language is "once upon a time" language. It establishes a fictional world. But the fictionalizing in oral epic is directly limited by live interaction, as real conversation is. A real audience controls the narrator's behavior immediately. Students of mine from Ghana and from western Ireland have reported to me what I have read and heard from many other sources: a given story may take a skilled or "professional" storyteller anywhere from ten minutes to an hour and a half, depending on how he finds the audience relates to him on a given occasion. "You always knew ahead of time what he was going to say, but you never knew how long it would take him to say it," my Irish informant reported. The teller reacts directly to audience response. Oral storytelling is a two-way street.

Written or printed narrative is not two-way, at least in the short run. Readers' reactions are remote and initially conjectural, however great their ultimate effects on sales. We should think more about the problems that the need to fictionalize audiences creates for writers. Chaucer, for example, had a problem with the conjectural readers of the *Canterbury Tales*. There was no established tradition in English for many of the stories, and certainly none at all for a collection of such stories. What does Chaucer do? He sets the stories in what, from a literary-structural point of view, is styled a frame. A group of pilgrims going to Canterbury tell stories to one another: the pilgrimage frames the individual narratives. In terms of signals to his readers, we could put it another way: Chaucer simply tells his readers how they are to fictionalize themselves. He starts by telling them that there is a group of pilgrims doing what real people do, going to a real place, Canterbury. The reader is to imagine himself in their company and join the fun. Of course this means fictionalizing himself as a member of a nonexistent group. But the fictionalizing is facilitated by Chaucer's clear frame-story directives. And to minimize the fiction by maximizing real life, Chaucer installs himself, the narrator, as one of the pilgrims. His reader-role problem is effectively solved. Of course, he got the idea pretty much from antecedent writers faced with similar problems, notably Boccaccio. But he naturalizes the frame in the geography of southeast England.

The frame story was in fact quite common around Europe at this period. Audience readjustment was a major feature of mature medieval culture, a culture more focused on reading than any earlier culture had been. Would it not be helpful to discuss the frame device as a contrivance all but demanded by the literary economy of the time rather than to expatiate on it as a singular stroke of genius? For this it certainly was not, unless we define genius as the ability to make the most of an awkward situation. The frame is really a rather clumsy gambit, although a good narrator can bring it off pretty well when he has to. It hardly has widespread immediate appeal for ordinary readers today.

In the next period of major audience readjustment, John Lyly's *Euphues* and even more Thomas Nashe's *The Unfortunate Traveler* can be viewed as attempts to work out a credible role in which Elizabethan readers could cast themselves for the new medium of print. Script culture had preserved a heavy oral residue signaled by its continued fascination with rhetoric, which had always been orally grounded, a fascination that script culture passed on to early print culture. But the new medium was changing the noetic economy, and, while rhetoric remained strong in the curriculum, strain was developing. Lyly reacts by hyperrhetoricizing his text, tongue-in-cheek, drowning the audience and himself in the highly controlled gush being purveyed by the schools. The signals to the reader are unmistakable, if unconsciously conveyed: play the role of the rhetorician's listener for all you are worth (*Euphues* is mostly speeches), remembering that the response the rhetorician commands is a serious and difficult one—it takes hard work to assimilate the baroque complexity of Lyly's text—but also that there is something awry in all the isocola, apophonemata, and antisagogai, now that the reader is so very much more a reader than a listener. Such aural iconographic equipment had been functional in oral management of knowledge, implementing storage and recall, but with print it was becoming incidental—which is, paradoxically, why it could be so fantastically elaborated.

Nashe shows the same uneasiness, and more, regarding the reader's role. For in the phantasmagoria of styles in *The Unfortunate Traveler* he tries out his reader in every role he can think of: whoever takes on Nashe's story must become a listener bending his ear to political orations, a participant in scholastic disputations, a hanger-on at goliardic Woodstocks, a camp follower fascinated by merry tales, a simpering reader of Italian revenge stories and sixteenth-century true confessions, a fellow conspirator in a world of picaresque cheats, and much more.

Nashe gives a foretaste of other trial-and-error procedures by which recipes were to be developed for the reader of the narrative prose works we now call novels. Such recipes were being worked out in other languages, too: in French notably by Rabelais, whose calls for strenuous shifts in the reader's stance Nashe emulated, and in Spanish by Cervantes, who explores all sorts of ironic possibilities in the reader's relationship to the text, incorporating into the second part of *Don Quixote* the purported reactions of readers and of the tale's characters to the first part of the work. Picaresque travels, well known at least since Apuleius' *Golden Ass*, multiplied, with major audience adjustments, in English down through *Tom Jones*: the unsettled role of the reader was mirrored and made acceptable by keeping the hero himself on the move. Samuel Richardson has his readers pretend they have access to other persons' letters, out of which a story emerges. Journals and diaries also multiplied as narrative devices: the reader becoming a snooper or a collector of seeming trivia that turn out not to be trivia at all. Ultimately, Laurence Sterne is able to involve his reader not only in the procreation of his hero Tristram Shandy but also in the hero's writing of his autobiography, in which pages are left blank for the reader to put his "own fancy in." The audience-speaker interaction of oral narrative here shows the reader in a new ironic guise—somewhat destructive of the printed book, toward which, as an object obtruding in the person-to-person world of human communication, the eighteenth century was feeling some ambiguous hostilities, as Swift's work also shows.

The problem of reader adjustment in prose narrative was in great part due to the difficulty that narrators long had in feeling themselves as other than oral performers. It is significant that, although the drama had been tightly plotted from classical antiquity (the drama is the first genre controlled by writing, and by the same token, paradoxically, the first to make deliberate use of colloquial speech), until the late eighteenth century there is in the whole Western world (and I suspect in the East as well) no sizable prose narrative, so far as I know, with a tidy structure comparable to that known for two millenia in the drama, moving through closely controlled tensions to a climax, with reversal and denouement. This is not to say that until the modern novel emerged narrative was not organized, or that earlier narrators were trying to write modern novels but regularly fell short of their aims. (Scholes and Kellogg have warned in *The Nature of Narrative* against this retroactive analysis of literary history.) But it is to say that narrative had not fully accommodated itself to print or, for that matter, to writing, which drama had long before learned to exploit. *Tom Jones* is highly programed, but in plot it is still episodic, as all prose narrative had been all the way back through the Hellenic romances. With Jane Austen we are over the hurdle: but Jane Austen was a woman, and women were not normally trained in the Latin-based, academic, rhetorical, oral tradition. They were not trained speechmakers who had turned belatedly to chirography and print.

Even by Jane Austen's time, however, the problem of the reader's role in prose narrative was by no means entirely solved. Nervousness regarding the role of the reader registers everywhere in the "dear reader" regularly invoked in fiction well through the nineteenth century. The reader had to be reminded (and the narrator, too) that the recipient of the story was indeed a reader—not a listener, not one of the crowd, but an individual isolated with a text. The relationship of audience-fictionalizing to modern narrative prose is very mysterious, and I do not pretend to explain it all here, but only to point to some of the strange problems often so largely overlooked in the relationship. Tightly plotted prose narrative is the correlative of the audiences fictionalized for the first time with the aid of print, and the demands of such narrative on readers were new.

V

The present reflections have focused on written fictional narrative as a kind of paradigm for the fictionalizing of writers' "audiences" or readers. But what has been said about fictional narrative applies ceteris paribus to all writing. With the possible[10] exception noted above of persons in the presence of one another communicating by writing because of inability to communicate orally, the writer's audience is always a fiction. The historian, the scholar or scientist, and the simple letter writer all fictionalize their audiences, casting them in a made-up role and calling on them to play the role assigned.

Because history is always a selection and interpretation of those incidents the individual historian believes will account better than other incidents for some explanation of a totality, history partakes quite evidently of the nature of poetry. It is a making. The historian does not make the elements out of which he constructs history, in the sense that he must build with events that have come about independently of him, but his selection of events and his way of verbalizing them so that they can be dealt with as "facts," and consequently the overall pattern he reports, are all his own creation, a making. No two historians say exactly the same thing about the same given events, even though they are both telling the truth. There is no *one* thing to say about anything; there are many things that can be said.

The oral "historian" captures events in terms of themes (the challenge, the duel, the arming of the hero, the battle, and so on), and formulas (the brave soldier, the faithful wife, the courageous people, the suffering people), which are provided to him by tradition and are the only ways he knows to talk about what is going on among men. Processed through these conventions, events become assimilable by his auditors and "interesting" to them. The writer of history is less reliant on formulas (or it may be he has such a variety of them that it is hard to tell that is what they are). But he comes to his material laden with themes in much vaster quantity than can be available to any oral culture. Without themes, there would be no way to deal with events. It is impossible to tell everything that went on in the Pentagon even in one day: how many stenographers dropped how many sheets of paper into how many wastebaskets when and where, what they all said to each other, and so on ad infinitum. These are not the themes historians normally use to write what really "happened." They write about material by exploiting it in terms of themes that are "significant" or "interesting." But what is "significant" depends on what kind of history you are writing—national political history, military history, social history, economic history, personal biography, global history. What is significant and, perhaps even more, what is "interesting" also depends on the readers and their interaction with the historian. This interaction in turn depends on the role in which the historian casts his readers. Although so far as I know we have no history of readers of history, we do know enough about historiography to be aware that one could well be worked out. The open-faced way the reader figures in Samuel Eliot Morison's writings is different from the more conspiratorial way he figures in Perry Miller's and both are quite different from the way the reader figures in Herodotus.

Scholarly works show comparable evolution in the roles they enforce on their readers. Aristotle's works, as has often been pointed out, are an agglomerate of texts whose relationship to his own holographs, to his students' notes, and to the work of later editors will remain always more or less a puzzle. Much of Aristotle consists of school logia or sayings, comparable to the logia or sayings of Jesus to his followers of which the Gospels chiefly consist. Aristotle's logia were addressed to specific individuals whom he knew, rather than simply to the wide world. Even his more patently written compositions retain a personal orientation: his work on ethics is the *Nicomachean Ethics,* named for his son. This means that the reader of Aristotle, if he wants to understand his text, will do well to cast himself in the role of one of Aristotle's actual listeners.

The practice of orienting a work, and thereby its readers, by writing it at least purportedly for a specific person or persons continues well through the Renaissance. The first edition of Peter Ramus' *Dialectic* was the French *Dialectique de Pierre de la Ramée à Charles de Lorraine Cardinal, son Mécène* (Paris, 1555), and the first edition of the far more widely used Latin version preserved the same personal address: *Dialectici Libri Duo ... ad Carolum Lotharingum Cardinalem* (Paris, 1556).

Sidney's famous romance or epic is *The Countess of Pembroke's Arcadia.* Often in Renaissance printed editions a galaxy of prefaces and dedicatory epistles and poems establishes a whole cosmos of discourse which, among other things, signals the reader what roles he is to assume. Sidney's, Spenser's, and Milton's works, for example, are heavily laden with introductory material—whole books have been devoted to the study of Sidney's introductory matter alone.

Until recent times the rhetorical tradition, which, with the allied dialectical or logical tradition, dominated most written as well as oral expression, helped in the fictionalizing of the audience of learned works in a generic but quite real way. Rhetoric fixed knowledge in agonistic structures.

For this reason, the roles of the reader of learned works until fairly recent times were regularly more polemic than those demanded of the reader today. Until the age of romanticism reconstituted psychological structures, academic teaching of all subjects had been more or less polemic, dominated by the ubiquitous rhetorical culture, and proceeding typically by proposing and attacking theses in highly partisan fashion. (The academic world today preserves much of the nomenclature, such as "thesis" and "defense" of theses, but less of the programed fighting spirit, which its members let loose on the social order more than on their subject matter or colleagues.) From Augustine through St. Thomas Aquinas and Christian Wolff, writers of treatises generally proceeded in adversary fashion, their readers being cast as participants in rhetorical contests or in dialectical scholastic disputations.

Today the academic reader's role is harder to describe. Some of its complexities can be hinted at by attending to certain fictions which writers of learned articles and books generally observe and which have to do with reader status. There are some things the writer must assume that every reader knows because virtually every reader does. It would be intolerable to write, "Shakespeare, a well-known Elizabethan playwright," not only in a study on Renaissance drama but even in one on marine ecology. Otherwise the reader's role would be confused. There are other things that established fiction holds all readers must know, even though everyone is sure all readers do not know them: these are handled by writing, "as everyone knows," and then inserting what it is that not quite everyone really does know. Other things the reader can safely be assumed not to know without threatening the role he is playing. These gradations of admissible ignorance vary from one level of scholarly writing to another, and since individual readers vary in knowledge and competence, the degree to which they must fictionalize themselves to match the level of this or that reading will vary. Knowledge of the degrees of admissible ignorance for readers is absolutely essential if one is to publish successfully.

This knowledge is one of the things that separates the beginning graduate student or even the brilliant undergraduate from the mature scholar. It takes time to get a feel for the roles that readers can be expected comfortably to play in the modern academic world.

Other kinds of writing without end could be examined in our reflections here on the fictionalizing of readers' roles. For want of time and, frankly, for want of wider reflection, I shall mention only two others. These are genres that do not seem to fall under the rule that the writer's audience is always a fiction since the "audience" appears to be simply one clearly determined person, who hardly need fictionalize himself. The first of the genres is the familiar letter and the second the diary.

The case of the letter reader is really simple enough. Although by writing a letter you are somehow pretending the reader is present while you are writing, you cannot address him as you do in oral speech. You must fictionalize him, make him into a special construct. Whoever saluted a friend on the street with "Dear John"? And if you try the informal horrors, "Hi!" or "Greetings!" or whatever else, the effect is not less but more artificial. You are reminding him that you wish you were not writing him a letter, but, then, why are you? There is no way out. The writer has to set up another relationship to the reader and has to set the reader in a relationship to the writer different from that of nonchirographical personal contact.

The dimensions of fiction in a letter are many. First, you have no way of adjusting to the friend's real mood as you would be able to adjust in oral conversation. You have to conjecture or confect a mood that he is likely to be in or can assume when the letter comes. And, when it does come, he has to put on the mood that you have fictionalized for him. Some of this sort of adjustment goes on in oral communication, too, but it develops in a series of exchanges: a tentative guess at another's mood, a reaction from him, another from yourself, another from him, and you know about where you are. Letters do not have this normal give-and-take: they are one-way movements. Moreover, the precise relationships of writer to reader in letters vary tremendously from age to age even in intensively role-playing correspondence. No one today can capture exactly the fiction in Swift's *Journal to Stella*, though it is informative to try to reconstruct it as fully as possible, for the relationships of children to oldsters and even of man to woman have subtly altered, as have also a vast mesh of other social relationships which the *Journal to Stella* involves.

The epistolary situation is made tolerable by conventions, and learning to write letters is largely a matter of learning what the writer-reader conventions are. The paradoxes they involve were well caught some years ago in a Marx Brothers movie—if I recall correctly where the incident occurred. Letters start with "Dear Sir." An owlish, bemused businessman calls his secretary in. "Take this letter to Joseph Smithers," he directs. "You know his address. 'Dear Sir: You dirty rat. . . . ' " The fiction of the exordium designed to create the *lector benerolens* is first honored and then immediately wiped out.

The audience of the diarist is even more encased in fictions. What is easier, one might argue, than addressing oneself? As those who first begin a diary often find out, a great many things are easier. The reasons why are not hard to unearth. First of all we do not normally talk to ourselves— certainly not in long, involved sentences and paragraphs. Second, the diarist pretending to be talking to himself has also, since he is writing, to pretend he is somehow not there. And to what self is he talking? To the self he imagines he is? Or would like to be? Or really thinks he is? Or thinks other people think he is? To himself as he is now? Or as he will probably or ideally be twenty years hence? If he addresses not himself but "Dear Diary," who in the world is "Dear Diary"? What role does this imply? And why do more women than men keep diaries? Or if they don't (they really do—or did), why do people think they do? When did the diary start? The history of diaries, I believe, has yet to be written. Possibly more than the history of any other genre, it will have to be a history of the fictionalizing of readers.

The case of the diary, which at first blush would seem to fictionalize the reader least but in many ways probably fictionalizes him or her most, brings into full view the fundamental deep paradox of the activity we call writing, at least when writing moves from its initial account-keeping purposes to other more elaborate concerns more directly and complexly involving human persons in their manifold dealings with one another. We are familiar enough today with talk about masks—in literary criticism, psychology, phenomenology, and elsewhere. Personae, earlier generally thought of as applying to characters in a play or other fiction (dramatis personae), are imputed with full justification to narrators and, since all discourse has roots in narrative, to everyone who uses language. Often in the complexities of present-day fiction, with its "unreliable narrator" encased in layer after layer of persiflage and irony, the masks within masks defy complete identification. This is a game fiction writers play, harder now than ever.

But the masks of the narrator are matched, if not one-for-one, in equally complex fashion by the masks that readers must learn to wear. To whom is *Finnegans Wake* addressed? Who is the reader supposed to be? We hesitate to say—certainly I hesitate to say—because we have thought so little about the reader's role as such, about his masks, which are as manifold in their own way as those of the writer.

Masks are inevitable in all human communication, even oral. Role playing is both different from actuality and an entry into actuality: play and actuality (the world of "work") are dialectically related to one another. From the very beginning, an infant becomes an actual speaker by playing at being a speaker, much as a person who cannot swim, after developing some ancillary skills, one day plays at swimming and finds that he is swimming in truth. But oral communication, which is built into existential actuality more directly than written, has within it a momentum that works for the removal of masks. Lovers try to strip off all masks. And in all communication, insofar as it is related to actual experience, there must be a movement of love. Those who have loved over many years may reach a point where almost all masks are gone. But never all. The lover's plight is tied to the fact that every one of us puts on a mask to address himself, too. Such masks to relate ourselves to ourselves we also try to put aside, and with wisdom and grace we to some extent succeed in casting them off. When the last mask comes off, sainthood is achieved, and the vision of God. But this can only be with death.

No matter what pitch of frankness, directness, or authenticity he may strive for, the writer's mask and the reader's are less removable than those of the oral communicator and his hearer. For writing is itself an indirection. Direct communication by script is impossible. This makes writing not less but more interesting, although perhaps less noble than speech. For man lives largely by indirection, and only beneath the indirections that sustain him is his true nature to be found. Writing, alone, however, will never bring us truly beneath to the actuality. Present-day confessional writing—and it is characteristic of our present age that virtually all serious writing tends to the confessional, even drama—likes to make an issue of stripping off all masks. Observant literary critics and psychiatrists, however, do not need to be told that confessional literature is likely to wear the most masks of all. It is hard to bare your soul in any literary genre. And it is hard to write outside a genre. T. S. Eliot has made the point that so far as he knows, great love poetry is never written solely for the ear of the beloved (p. 97), although what a lover speaks with his lips is often indeed for the ear of the beloved and of no other. The point is well made, even though it was made in writing.

NOTES

1. See, e.g., J. R. Searle, *The Philosophy of Language* (London: Oxford Univ. Press, 1971), pp. 24–28, where Austin is cited, and Searle's bibliography, pp. 146–48.
2. *The Rhetoric of Fiction* (Chicago: Univ. of Chicago Press, 1961), pp. 49–52, 138, 363–64.
3. *The Nature of Narrative* (New York: Oxford Univ. Press, 1966), pp. 17–56. Among recent short studies exhibiting concerns tangent to but not the same

as those of the present article might be mentioned three from *New Literary History:* Georges Poulet, "Phenomenology of Reading," 1 (1969–70), 53–68; Geoffrey H. Hartman, "History-Writing as Answerable Style," 2 (1970–71), 73–84; and J. Hillis Miller, "The Still Heart: Poetic Form in Wordsworth," 2 (1970–71), 297–310, esp. p. 310; as well as Gerald Prince, "Introduction à l'étude du narrataire," *Poétique,* No. 14 (1973), pp. 178–96, which is concerned with the "narrataire" only in novels ("narratee" in a related English-language study by the same author as noted by him here) and with literary taxonomy more than history. See also Paul Ricoeur, "What Is a Text? Explanation and Interpretation," Appendix, pp. 135–50, in David Rasmussen, *Mythic-Symbolic Language and Philosophical Anthropology: A Constructive Interpretation of the Thought of Paul Ricoeur* (The Hague: Martinus Nijhoff, 1971).

4. *Phenomenology of Perception,* trans. Colin Smith (London: Routledge, 1962), pp. 181–84.

5. See my *The Presence of the Word* (New Haven and London: Yale Univ. Press, 1967), pp. 116–17.

6. T. S. Eliot suggests some of the complexities of the writer-and-audience problem in his essay on "The Three Voices of Poetry," by which he means (1) "the voice of the poet talking to himself—or to nobody," (2) "the voice of the poet addressing an audience," and (3) "the voice of the poet when he attempts to create a dramatic character speaking" (*On Poetry and Poets,* New York: Noonday Press, 1961, p. 96). Eliot, in the same work, states that these voices often mingle and indeed, for him, "are most often found together" (p. 108). The approach I am here taking cuts across Eliot's way of enunciating the problem and, I believe, brings out some of the built-in relationships among the three voices which help account for their intermingling. The "audience" addressed by Eliot's second voice not only is elusively constituted but also, even in its elusiveness, can determine the voice of the poet talking to himself or to nobody (Eliot's first sense of "voice"), because in talking to oneself one has to objectify oneself, and one does so in ways learned from addressing others. A practiced writer talking "to himself" in a poem has a quite different feeling for "himself" than does a complete illiterate.

7. See Albert B. Lord, *The Singer of Tales,* Harvard Studies in Comparative Literature, No. 24 (Cambridge, Mass.: Harvard Univ. Press, 1964), pp. 124–38.

8. *Tough, Sweet, and Stuffy* (Bloomington and London: Indiana Univ. Press, 1966), pp. 28–54. In these pages, Gibson gets very close to the concern of the present article with readers' roles.

9. The present inclination to begin a story without the initial indefinite article, which tacitly acknowledges a range of existence beyond that of the immediate reference, and to substitute for the indefinite article a demonstrative pronoun of proximity, "this," is one of many indications of the tendency of present-day man to feel his lifeworld—which is now more than ever the whole world—as in-close to him, and to mute any references to distance. It is not uncommon to hear a conversation begin, "Yesterday on the street this man came up to me, and...." A few decades ago, the equivalent would very likely have been, "Yesterday on the street a man came up to me, and...."

This widespread preference, which Hemingway probably influenced little if at all, does show that Hemingway's imposition of fellowship on the reader was an indication, perhaps moderately precocious, of a sweeping trend.

10. "Possible," because there is probably a trace of fictionalizing even when notes are being exchanged by persons in one another's presence. It appears unlikely that what is written in such script "conversations" is exactly the same as what it would be were voices used. The interlocutors are, after all, to some extent pretending to be talking, when in fact they are not talking but writing.

Umberto Eco

The Role of the Reader

0.1. How to Produce Texts by Reading Them

0.1.1. THE TEXT AND ITS INTERPRETER

The very existence of texts that can not only be freely interpreted but also cooperatively generated by the addressee (the 'original' text constituting a flexible *type* of which many *tokens* can be legitimately realized) posits the problem of a rather peculiar strategy of communication based upon a flexible system of signification. "The Poetics of the Open Work" (1959)[1] was already haunted by the idea of unlimited semiosis that I later borrowed from Peirce and that constitutes the philosophical scaffolding of *A Theory of Semiotics* (1976) (hereafter *Theory*). But at the same time, "The Poetics of the Open Work" was presupposing a problem of pragmatics.[2] An 'open' text cannot be described as a communicative strategy if the role of its addressee (the reader, in the case of verbal texts) has not been envisaged at the moment of its generation *qua* text. An open text is a paramount instance of a syntactic-semanticopragmatic device whose foreseen interpretation is a part of its generative process.

When "The Poetics of the Open Work" appeared in 1965 in French as the first chapter of my book *L'oeuvre ouverte*,[3] in a structuralistically oriented milieu, the idea of taking into account the role of the addressee looked like a disturbing intrusion, disquietingly jeopardizing the notion of a semiotic texture to be analyzed in itself and for the sake of itself. In 1967, discussing structuralism and literary criticism with an Italian interviewer, Claude Lévi-Strauss said that he could not accept the perspective of *L'oeuvre ouverte* because a work of art "is an object endowed with precise properties, that must be analytically isolated, and this work can be entirely defined on the grounds of such properties. When Jakobson and myself tried to make a structural analysis of a Baudelaire sonnet, we did not approach it as an 'open work' in which we could find everything that has been filled in by the following epochs; we approached it as an object which, once created, had the stiffness—so to speak—of a crystal; we confined ourselves to bringing into evidence these properties."[4]

It is not necessary to quote Jakobson (1958) and his well-known theory of the functions of language to remind ourselves that, even from a structuralistic point of view, such categories as sender, addressee, and context are indispensable to the understanding of every act of communication. It is enough to consider two points (picked almost at random) from the analysis of Baudelaire's "Les Chats" to understand the role of the reader in the poetic strategy of that sonnet: "Les chats ... ne figurent en nom dans le texte qu'une seule fois ... dès le troisième vers, les chats deviennent un sujet sous-entendu ... remplacé par les pronoms anaphoriques *ils, les, leurs* ... etc."[5] Now, it is absolutely impossible to speak apropos of the anaphorical role of an expression without invoking, if not a precise and empirical reader, at least the 'addressee' as an abstract and constitutive element in the process of actualization of a text.

In the same essay, two pages later, it is said that there is a semantic affinity between the *Erèbe* and the *horreur des ténèbres*. This semantic affinity does not lie in the text as an explicit linear linguistic manifestation; it is the result of a rather complex operation of textual inference based upon an intertextual competence. If this is the kind of semantic association that the poet wanted to arouse, to forecast and to activate such a cooperation from the part of the reader was part of the generative strategy employed by the author. Moreover, it seems that this strategy was aiming at an imprecise or undetermined response. Through the above semantic affinity the text associated the cats to the *coursiers funèbres*. Jakobson and Lévi-Strauss ask: "S'agit-il d'un désir frustré, ou d'une fausse reconnaissance? La signification de ce passage, sur la quelle les critiques se sont interrogés, reste à dessein ambigue."

That is enough, at least for me, to assume that "Les Chats" is a text that not only calls for the cooperation of its own reader, but also wants this reader to make a series of interpretive choices which even though not infinite are, however, more than one. Why not, then, call "Les Chats" an 'open' text? To postulate the cooperation of the reader does not mean to pollute the structural analysis with extratextual elements. The reader as an active principal of interpretation is a part of the picture of the generative process of the text.

There is only one tenable objection to my objection to the objection of Lévi-Strauss: if one considers even anaphorical activations as cases of cooperation on the part of the reader, there is no text escaping such a rule. I agree. So-called open texts are only the extreme and most provocative exploitation—for poetic purposes—of a principle which rules both the generation and the interpretation of texts in general.

0.1.2. SOME PROBLEMS OF THE PRAGMATICS OF COMMUNICATION

As is clearly maintained in *Theory* (2.15), the standard communication model proposed by information theorists (Sender, Message, Addressee— in which the message is decoded on the basis of a Code shared by both the virtual poles of the chain) does not describe the actual functioning of communicative intercourses. The existence of various codes and sub-codes, the variety of sociocultural circumstances in which a message is emitted (where the codes of the addressee can be different from those of the sender), and the rate of initiative displayed by the addressee in making presuppositions and abductions—all result in making a message (insofar as it is received and transformed into the *content* of an *expression*) an empty form to which various possible senses can be attributed. Moreover, what one calls 'message' is usually a *text*, that is, a network of different messages depending on different codes and working at different levels of signification. Therefore the usual communication model should be re-written (even though to a still extremely simplified extent) as in Figure 0.1.

A more reasonable picture of the whole semantico-pragmatic process would take the form (Figure 0.2) already proposed in *Theory,* where, even disregarding both the rightmost quarter of the square (all the 'aberrant' presuppositions) and the lower components (circumstances orienting or deviating the presuppositions), the notion of a crystal-like textual object is abundantly cast in doubt.

It should be clear that Figure 0.2 is not depicting any specially 'open' process of interpretation. It represents a semantico-pragmatic process in general. It is just by playing upon the prerequisites of such a general pro-cess that a text can succeed in being more or less open or closed. As for aberrant presuppositions and deviating circumstances, they are not real-izing any openness but, instead, producing mere states of indeterminacy. What I call open texts are, rather, reducing such as indeterminacy, whereas closed texts, even though aiming at eliciting a sort of 'obedient' cooperation, are in the last analysis randomly open to every pragmatic ac-cident.

0.2. The Model Reader

0.2.1. PRODUCING THE MODEL READERS

To organize a text, its author has to rely upon a series of codes that assign given contents to the expressions he uses. To make his text communica-tive, the author has to assume that the ensemble of codes he relies upon

is the same as that shared by his possible reader. The author has thus to
foresee a model of the possible reader (hereafter Model Reader) supposedly
able to deal interpretatively with the expressions in the same way as the
author deals generatively with them.

At the minimal level, every type of text explicitly selects a very general model of possible reader through the choice (i) of a specific linguistic
code, (ii) of a certain literary style, and (iii) of specific specialization-
indices (a text beginning with / According to the last developments of the
TeSWeST ... / immediately excludes any reader who does not know the
technical jargon of text semiotics). Other texts give explicit information
about the sort of readers they presuppose (for example, children's books,
not only by typographical signals, but also by direct appeals; in other
cases a specific category of addressee is named: /Friends, Romans, Coun-
trymen ... /). Many texts make evident their Model Readers by implicitly
presupposing a specific encyclopedic competence. For instance, the author of *Waverley* opens his story by clearly calling for a very specialized
kind of reader, nourished on a whole chapter of intertextual encyclopedia:

> (1) What could my readers have expected from the chivalrous
> epithets of Howard, Mordaunt, Mortimer or Stanley, or from the
> softer and more sentimental sounds of Belmore, Belville, Belfield
> and Belgrave, but pages of inanity, similar to those which have been
> so christened for half a century past?

But at the same time text (1) *creates* the competence of its Model
Reader. After having read this passage, whoever approaches *Waverley*
(even one century later and even—if the book has been translated into another language—from the point of view of a different intertextual competence) is asked to *assume* that certain epithets are meaning "chivalry"
and that there is a whole tradition of chivalric romances displaying certain deprecatory stylistic and narrative properties.

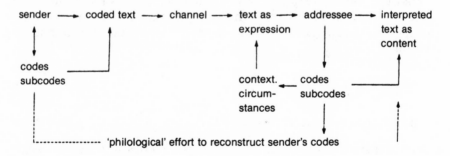

Figure 0.1

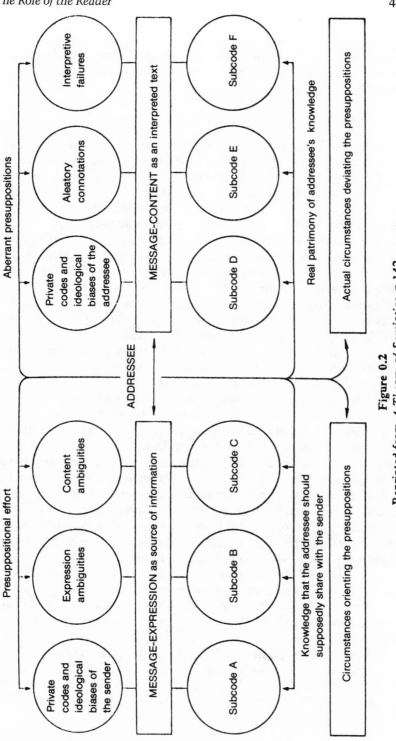

Figure 0.2
Reprinted from *A Theory of Semiotics*, p.142.

Thus it seems that a well-organized text on the one hand presupposes a model of competence coming, so to speak, from outside the text, but on the other hand works to build up, by merely textual means, such a competence (see Riffaterre, 1973).

0.2.2. MODEL READERS FOR CLOSED TEXTS

We have seen that, pragmatically speaking, this situation is a very abstract and optimal one. In the process of communication, a text is frequently interpreted against the background of codes different from those intended by the author. Some authors do not take into account such a possibility. They have in mind an average addressee referred to a given social context. Nobody can say what happens when the actual reader is different from the 'average' one. Those texts that obsessively aim at arousing a precise response on the part of more or less precise empirical readers (be they children, soap-opera addicts, doctors, law-abiding citizens, swingers, Presbyterians, farmers, middle-class women, scuba divers, effete snobs, or any other imaginable sociopsychological category) are in fact open to any possible 'aberrant' decoding. A text so immoderately 'open' to every possible interpretation will be called a *closed* one.

Superman comic strips or Sue's and Fleming's novels belong to this category. They apparently aim at pulling the reader along a predetermined path, carefully displaying their effects so as to arouse pity or fear, excitement or depression at the due place and at the right moment. Every step of the 'story' elicits just the expectation that its further course will satisfy. They seem to be structured according to an inflexible project. Unfortunately, the only one not to have been 'inflexibly' planned is the reader. These texts are potentially speaking to everyone. Better, they presuppose an average reader resulting from a merely intuitive sociological speculation—in the same way in which an advertisement chooses its possible audience. It is enough for these texts to be interpreted by readers referring to other conventions or oriented by other presuppositions, and the result is incredibly disappointing (or exciting—it depends on the point of view). This was the case of Sue's *Les Mystères de Paris*, which, written initially in a dandyish mood to please cultivated readers, aroused as a result a passionate process of identification on the part of an illiterate audience; when, on the contrary, it was written to educate such a "dangerous" audience to a moderate vision of social harmony, it produced as a side effect a revolutionary uprising.

For the saga of Superman and for the *acta sanctorum* of James Bond, we lack comparable sociopsychological evidence, but it is clear that they can give rise to the most unforeseeable interpretations, at least at the ideological level. My ideological reading was only one among the possible:

the most feasible for a smart semiotician who knows very well the 'codes' of the heavy industry of dreams in a capitalistic society. But why not read Superman stories only as a new form of romance that is free from any pedagogical intention? Doing so would not betray the nature of the saga. Superman comic strips are *also* this. And much more. They can be read in various ways, each way being independent from the others.

0.2.3. MODEL READERS FOR OPEN TEXTS

This cannot happen with those I call 'open' texts: they work at their peak revolutions per minute only when each interpretation is reechoed by the others, and vice versa.

Consider, in the essay on the semantics of metaphor (Chapter 2), the interplay of possible interpretations foreseen by Joyce apropos of the trial of Shaun. Consider, even at the reduced scale of a laboratory model of poetic language (in Chapter 3, on Edenic language) the way in which a productively ambiguous message leaves Adam and Eve free to reconsider the whole of their semantic universe, but, at the same time, makes them bound to the indecomposable unity of their alternative interpretations.

An author can foresee an 'ideal reader affected by an ideal insomnia' (as happens with *Finnegans Wake*), able to master different codes and eager to deal with the text as with a maze of many issues. But in the last analysis what matters is not the various issues in themselves but the mazelike structure of the text. You cannot use the text as you want, but only as the text wants you to use it. An open text, however 'open' it be, cannot afford whatever interpretation.

An open text outlines a 'closed' project of its Model Reader as a component of its structural strategy.

When reading a Fleming novel or a Superman comic strip, one can at most guess what kind of reader their authors had in mind, not which requirements a 'good' reader whould meet. I was not the kind of reader foreseen by the authors of Superman, but I presume to have been a 'good' one (I would be more prudent apropos of the intentions of Fleming). On the contrary, when reading *Ulysses* one can extrapolate the profile of a 'good *Ulysses* reader' from the text itself, because the pragmatic process of interpretation is not an empirical accident independent of the text *qua* text, but is a structural element of its generative process.[6] As referred to an unsuitable reader (to a negative Model Reader unable to do the job he has just been postulated to do), *Ulysses qua Ulysses* could not stand up. At most it becomes another text.

It is possible to be smart enough to interpret the relationship between Nero Wolfe and Archie Goodwin as the umpteenth variation of the Oedipus myth without destroying Rex Stout's narrative universe. It is possible to be stupid enough to read Kafka's *Trial* as a trivial criminal novel, but at this point the text collapses—it has been burned out, just as a 'joint' is burned out to produce a private euphoric state.

The 'ideal reader' of *Finnegans Wake* cannot be a Greek reader of the second century B.C. or an illiterate man of Aran. The reader is strictly defined by the lexical and the syntactical organization of the text: the text is nothing else but the semantic-pragmatic production of its own Model Reader.

We shall see in the last essay of this book (Chapter 8) how a story by Alphonse Allais, *Un drame bien parisien,* can be read in two different ways, a naive way and a critical way, but both types of readers are inscribed within the textual strategy. The naive reader will be unable to enjoy the story (he will suffer a final uneasiness), but the critical reader will succeed only by enjoying the defeat of the former. In both cases—anyway—it will be only the text itself—such as it is made—that tells us which kind of reader it postulates. The exactness of the textual project makes for the freedom of its Model Reader. If there is a "jouissance du texte" (Barthes, 1973), it cannot be aroused and implemented except by a text producing all the paths of its 'good' reading (no matter how many, no matter how much determined in advance).

0.2.4. AUTHOR AND READER AS TEXTUAL STRATEGIES

In a communicative process there are a sender, a message, and an addressee. Frequently, both sender and addressee are grammatically manifested by the message: "*I* tell *you* that...."

Dealing with messages with a specific indexical purpose, the addressee is supposed to use the grammatical clues as referential indices (/I/ must designate the empirical subject of that precise instance of utterance, and so on). The same can happen even with very long texts, such as a letter or a private diary, read to get information about the writer.

But as far as a text is focused *qua* text, and especially in cases of texts conceived for a general audience (such as novels, political speeches, scientific instructions, and so on), the sender and the addressee are present in the text, not as mentioned poles of the utterance, but as 'actantial roles' of the sentence (not as *sujet de l'énonciation,* but as *sujet de l'énonceé*) (see Jakobson, 1957).

In these cases the author is textually manifested only (i) as a recognizable *style* or textual *idiolect*—this idiolect frequently distinguishing not an individual but a genre, a social group, a historical period (*Theory,* 3.7.6); (ii) as mere actantial roles (/I/ = "the subject of the present sentence"); (iii) as an illocutionary signal (/I swear that/) or as a perlocutionary operator (/suddenly something *horrible* happened ... /). Usually this conjuring up of the 'ghost' of the sender is ordered to a symmetrical conjuring up of the 'ghost' of the addressee (Kristeva, 1970). Consider the following expressions from Wittgenstein's *Philosophical Investigations,* 66:

> (2) Consider for example the proceedings that we call "games." I mean board-games, card-games, ball-games.... *Look and see* whether there is anything common to all. For if you look at them you will not see something that is common to *all*, but similarities, relationships, and a whole series of them at that.

All the personal pronouns (whether explicit or implicit) are not indicating a person called Wittgenstein or any empirical reader: they are textual strategies. The intervention of a speaking subject is complementary to the activation of a Model Reader whose intellectual profile is determined only by the sort of interpretive operations he is supposed to perform (to detect similarities, to consider certain games ...). Likewise the 'author' is nothing else but a textual strategy establishing semantic correlations and activating the Model Reader: /I mean board-games/ and so on, means that, within the framework of that text, the word /game/ will assume a given semantic value and will become able to encompass board-games, card-games, and so on.

According to this text Wittgenstein is nothing else but *a philosophical style,* and his Model Reader is nothing else but his capability to co-operate in order to reactualize that philosophical style.

In the following paragraphs I shall renounce the use of the term /author/ if not as a mere metaphor for "textual strategy," and I shall use the term Model Reader in the terms stipulated above.

In other words, the Model Reader is a textually established set of felicity conditions (Austin, 1962) to be met in order to have a macrospeech act (such as a text is) fully actualized.

NOTES

1. This article was published later as the first chapter of *Opera Aperta—Forma e indeterminazione nelle poetiche contemporanee* (Milan: Bompiani, 1962).
2. I take the term 'pragmatics' in its current sense. Thus pragmatics concerns itself not only with the interpretation of indexical expressions but with the "essential dependence of communication in natural languages on speaker and hearer, on linguistic context and extralinguistic context ... on the availability of background knowledge, on readiness to obtain this background knowledge and on the good will of the participants in a communication act" (Bar-Hillel, 1968:271; see also Montague, 1968, Petöfi, 1974).
3. *L'oeuvre ouverte* (Paris: Seuil, 1966).

4. Interview by Paolo Caruso in *Paese sera-Libri* (January 20, 1967). Reprinted in *Conversazioni con Lévi-Strauss, Foucault, Lacan,* ed. Paolo Caruso (Milan: Mursia, 1969).
5. Roman Jakobson and Claude Lévi-Strauss, "'Le Chats' de Charles Baudelaire," *L'Homme* (January 1962).
6. This notion of the Model Reader can be extrapolated also from other text theories. See, for example, Barthes (1966), Riffaterre (1971), Schmidt (1973, 1976), and van Dijk (1976c). This 'dialogical' nature of texts has already been advocated by Baxtin.

BIBLIOGRAPHY

Austin, J. L.
    1962   *How to Do Things with Words.* Oxford: Clarendon Press.
Bar-Hillel, Yehoshua
    1968   "Communication and Argumentation in Pragmatic Languages." In
            AA VV, *Linguaggi nella società e nella tecnica.* Milan: Comunita, 1970
            (Convegno promosso della Ing. C. Olivetti & C., Spa, per il centenario della
            nascita di C. Olivetti, Milan, October 1968).
Barthes, Roland
    1966   "Introduction à l'analyse structurale des récits." *Communications*
            8.
    1973   *Le plaisir du texte.* Paris: Seuil.
Dijk, van, Teun A.
    1976c   "Pragmatics and Poetics." In van Dijk, ed., 1976.
Dijk, van, T. A., ed.
    1976   *Pragmatics of Language and Literature.* Amsterdam-Oxford:
            North Holland and American Elsevier.
Eco, Umberto
    1962   *Opera aperta—Forma e indeterminazione nelle poetiche contemporanee.* Milan: Bompiani. 4th ed., 1976 (contains the first version of Eco, 1966).
    1976   *A Theory of Semiotics.* Bloomington: Indiana University Press.
Jakobson, Roman
    1957   *Shifters, Verbal Categories, and the Russian Verb.* Russian Language Project, Department of Slavic Languages and Literatures, Harvard University.
    1958   "Closing Statements: Linquistics and Poetics." In *Style in Language.* Edited by T. A. Sebeok. Cambridge: M.I.T. Press, 1960.
Kristeva, Julia
    1970   *Le texte du roman.* The Hague: Mouton.
Montague, Richard
    1968   "Pragmatics." In *Contemporary Philosophy: A Survey.* Edited by
            Raymond Klibansky. Florence: Nuova Italia.
Petöfi, Janos S.
    1974   *Semantics, Pragmatics, Text Theory.* Urbino, Centro Internazionale
            di semiotica e linguistics. Working Papers, A, 36.

Riffaterre, Michael
    1971   *Essais de stylistique structurale.* Paris: Flammarion.
    1973   "The Self-Sufficient Text." *Diacritics* (fall 1973).
Schmidt, Siegfred J.
    1973   "Texttheorie/Pragmalinguistik." In *Lexicon der germanistischen Linguistik.* Edited by H. P. Althaus, H. Heune and H. E. Wiegand. Tübingen: Niemayer.
    1976   "Towards a Pragmatic Interpretation of Fictionality." In van Dijk, ed., 1976.

Ten
evaluation

Benedetto Croce

Taste and the Reproduction of Art

When the entire aesthetic and externalizing process has been completed, when a beautiful expression has been produced and fixed in a definite physical material, what is meant by *judging it? To reproduce it in oneself*, answer the critics of art, almost with one voice. Very good. Let us try thoroughly to understand this fact, and with that object in view, let us represent it schematically.

The individual A is seeking the expression of an impression, which he feels or has a presentiment of, but has not yet expressed. Behold him trying various words and phrases, which may give the sought-for expression, which must exist, but which he does not know. He tries the combination *m*, but rejects it as unsuitable, inexpressive, incomplete, ugly: he tries the combination *n*, with a like result. *He does not see anything, or he does not see clearly.* The expression still flies from him. After other vain attempts, during which he sometimes approaches, sometimes leaves the sign that offers itself, all of a sudden (almost as though formed spontaneously of itself) he creates the sought-for expression, and *lux facta est.* He enjoys for an instant aesthetic pleasure or the pleasure of the beautiful. The ugly, with its correlative displeasure, was the aesthetic activity, which had not succeeded in conquering the obstacle; the beautiful is the expressive activity, which now displays itself triumphant.

We have taken this example from the domain of speech, as being nearer and more accessible, and because we all talk, though we do not all draw or paint. Now if another individual, whom we shall term B, desire to judge this expression and decide whether it be beautiful or ugly, he *must of necessity place himself at A's point of view,* and go through the whole process again, with the help of the physical sign, supplied to him by A. If A has seen clearly, then B (who has placed himself at A's point of view) will also see clearly and will find this expression beautiful. If A has not seen clearly, then B also will not see clearly, and will find the expression more or less ugly, *just as A did.*

It may be observed that we have not taken into consideration two other cases: that of A having a clear and B an obscure vision; and that of A having an obscure and B a clear vision. Philosophically speaking, these two cases are *impossible.*

Spiritual activity, precisely because it is activity, is not a caprice, but a spiritual necessity; and it cannot solve a definite aesthetic problem, save in one way, which is the right way. Doubtless certain facts may be adduced, which appear to contradict this deduction. Thus works which seem beautiful to artists, are judged to be ugly by the critics; while works with which the artists were displeased and judged imperfect or failures, are held to be beautiful and perfect by the critics. But this does not mean anything, save that one of the two is wrong: either the critics or the artists, or in one case the artist and in another the critic. In fact, the producer of an expression does not always fully realize what has happened in his soul. Haste, vanity, want of reflexion, theoretic prejudices, make people say, and sometimes others almost believe, that works of ours are beautiful, which, if we were truly to turn inwards upon ourselves, we should see ugly, as they really are. Thus poor Don Quixote, when he had mended his helmet as well as he could with cardboard—the helmet that had showed itself to possess but the feeblest force of resistance at the first encounter,—took good care not to test it again with a well-delivered swordthrust, but simply declared and maintained it to be (says the author) *por celada finisima de encaxe.* And in other cases, the same reasons, or opposite but analogous ones, trouble the consciousness of the artist, and cause him to disapprove of what he has successfully produced, or to strive to undo and do again worse, what he has done well, in his artistic spontaneity. An example of this is the *Gerusalemme conquistata.* In the same way, haste, laziness, want of reflexion, theoretic prejudices, personal sympathies, or animosities, and other motives of a similar sort, sometimes cause the critics to proclaim beautiful what is ugly, and ugly what is beautiful. Were they to eliminate such disturbing elements; they would feel the work of art as it really is, and would not leave to posterity, that more diligent and more dispassionate judge, to award the palm, or to do that justice, which they have refused.

It is clear from the preceding theorem, that the judicial activity, which criticizes and recognizes the beautiful, is identical with that which produces it. The only difference lies in the diversity of circumstances, since in the one case it is a question of aesthetic production, in the other of reproduction. The judicial activity is called *taste;* the productive activity is called *genius:* genius and taste are therefore substantially *identical.*

The common remark, that the critic should possess some of the genius of the artist and that the artist should possess taste, reveals a glimpse of this identity; or that there exists an active (productive) taste and a passive (reproductive) taste. But a denial of this is contained in other equally common remarks, as when people speak of taste without genius, or of genius without taste. These last observations are meaningless, unless they be taken as alluding to quantitative differences. In this case, those would be called geniuses without taste who produce works of art, inspired in their culminating parts and neglected and defective in their secondary parts, and those, men of taste without genius, who succeed in obtaining certain isolated or secondary effects, but do not possess the power necessary for a vast artistic synthesis. Analogous explanations can easily be given of other similar propositions. But to posit a substantial difference between genius and taste, between artistic production and reproduction, would render communication and judgment alike inconceivable. How could we judge what remained extraneous to us? How could that which is produced by a given activity be judged by a different activity? The critic will be a small genius, the artist a great genius; the one will have the strength of ten, the other of a hundred; the former, in order to raise himself to the altitude of the latter, will have need of his assistance; but the nature of both must be the same. In order to judge Dante, we must raise ourselves to his level: let it be well understood that empirically we are not Dante, nor Dante we; but in that moment of judgment and contemplation, our spirit is one with that of the poet, and in that moment we and he are one single thing. In this identity alone resides the possibility that our little souls can unite with the great souls, and become great with them, in the universality of the spirit.

Let us remark in passing that what has been said of the aesthetic *judgment* holds good equally for every other activity and for every other judgment; and that scientific, economic, and ethical criticism is effected in a like manner. To limit ourselves to this last, it is only if we place ourselves ideally in the same conditions in which he who took a given resolution found himself, that we can form a judgment as to whether his resolution were moral or immoral. An action would otherwise remain incomprehensible, and therefore impossible to judge. A homicide may be a rascal or a hero: if this be, within limits, indifferent as regards the safety of society, which condemns both to the same punishment, it is not indifferent to him who wishes to distinguish and to judge from the moral point of view, and we cannot dispense with studying again the individual psychology of the homicide, in order to determine the true nature of his deed, not merely in its judicial, but also in its moral aspect. In Ethic, a moral taste or tact is sometimes referred to, which answers to what is generally called moral conscience, that is to say, to the activity itself of good-will.

The explanation above given of aesthetic judgment or reproduction at once affirms and denies the position of the absolutists and relativists, of those, that is to say, who affirm and of those who deny the existence of an absolute taste.

The absolutists, who affirm that they can judge of the beautiful, are right; but the theory on which they found their affirmation is not maintainable. They conceive of the beautiful, that is, of aesthetic value, as of something placed outside the aesthetic activity; as if it were a model or a concept which an artist realizes in his work, and of which the critic avails himself afterwards in order to judge the work itself. Concepts and models alike have no existence in art, for by proclaiming that every art can be judged only in itself, and has its own model in itself, they have attained to the denial of the existence of objective models of beauty, whether they be intellectual concepts, or ideas suspended in the metaphysical sky.

In proclaiming this, the adversaries, the relativists, are perfectly right, and accomplish a progress. However, the initial rationality of their thesis becomes in its turn a false theory. Repeating the old adage that there is no accounting for tastes, they believe that aesthetic expression is of the same nature as the pleasant and the unpleasant, which every one feels in his own way, and as to which there is no disputing. But we know that the pleasant and the unpleasant are utilitarian and practical facts. Thus the relativists deny the peculiarity of the aesthetic fact, again confounding expression with impression, the theoretic with the practical.

The true solution lies in rejecting alike relativism or psychologism, and false absolutism; and in recognizing that the criterion of taste is absolute, but absolute in a different way from that of the intellect, which is developed by reason. The criterion of taste is absolute, with the intuitive absoluteness of the imagination. Thus every act of expressive activity, which is so really, will be recognized as beautiful, and every fact in which expressive activity and passivity are found engaged with one another in an unfinished struggle, will be recognized as ugly.

There lies, between absolutists and relativists, a third class, which may be called that of the relative relativists. These affirm the existence of absolute values in other fields, such as Logic and Ethic, but deny their existence in the field of Aesthetic. To them it appears natural and justifiable to dispute about science and morality; because science rests on the universal, common to all men, and morality on duty, which is also a law of human nature; but how, they say, can one dispute about art, which rests on imagination? Not only, however, is the imaginative activity universal and belongs to human nature, like the logical concept and practical duty; but we must oppose a capital objection to this intermediary thesis. If the absolute nature of the imagination were denied, we should be obliged to deny also that of intellectual or conceptual truth, and, implicitly, of morality. Does not morality presuppose logical distinctions? How could these be known, otherwise than by expressions and words, that is to say, in imaginative form? If the absoluteness of the imagination were removed, spiritual life would tremble to its base. One individual would no longer understand another, nor indeed his own self of a moment before, which, when considered a moment after, is already another individual.

Nevertheless, variety of judgments is an indisputable fact. Men are at variance in their logical, ethical, and economical appreciations; and they are equally, or even more at variance in their aesthetic appreciations. If certain reasons detailed by us, above, such as haste, prejudices, passions, etc., may be held to lessen the importance of this disagreement, they do not thereby annul it. We have been cautious, when speaking of the stimuli of reproduction, for we said that reproduction takes place, *if all the other conditions remain equal.* Do they remain equal? Does the hypothesis correspond to reality?

It would appear not. In order to reproduce several times an impression by employing a suitable physical stimulus, it is necessary that this stimulus be not changed, and that the organism remain in the same psychical conditions as those in which was experienced the impression that it is desired to reproduce. Now it is a fact, that the physical stimulus is continually changing, and in like manner the psychological conditions.

Oil paintings grow dark, frescoes pale, statues lose noses, hands, and legs, architecture becomes totally or partially a ruin, the tradition of the execution of a piece of music is lost, the text of a poem is corrupted by bad copyists or bad printing. These are obvious instances of the changes which daily occur in objects or physical stimuli. As regards psychological conditions, we will not dwell upon the cases of deafness or blindness, that is to say, upon the loss of entire orders of psychical impressions; these cases are secondary and of less importance compared with the fundamental, daily, inevitable, and perpetual changes of the society around us, and of the internal conditions of our individual life. The phonic manifestations, that is, the words and verses of the Dantesque *Commedia*, must produce a very different impression on a citizen engaged in the politics of the third Rome, to that experienced by a well-informed and intimate contemporary of the poet. The Madonna of Cimabue is still in the Church of Santa Maria Novella; but does she speak to the visitor of to-day as she spoke to the Florentines of the thirteenth century? Even though she were not also darkened by time, would not the impression be altogether different? And finally, how can a poem composed in youth make the same impression on the same individual poet when he re-reads it in his old age, with his psychic dispositions altogether changed?

It is true, that certain aestheticians have attempted a distinction between stimuli and stimuli, between *natural and conventional* signs. They would grant to the former a constant effect on all; to the latter, only on a limited circle. In their belief, signs employed in painting are natural, while the words of poetry are conventional. But the difference between the one and the other is only of degree. It has often been affirmed that painting is a language which all understand, while with poetry it is otherwise. Here, for example, Leonardo placed one of the prerogatives of his art, "which hath not need of interpreters of different languages as have letters," and in it man and brute find satisfaction. He relates the anecdote of that portrait of the father of a family, "which the little grandchildren were wont to caress while they were still in swaddling-clothes, and the dogs and cats of the house in like manner." But other anecdotes, such as those of the savages who took the portrait of a soldier for a boat, or considered the portrait of a man on horseback as furnished with only one leg, are apt to shake one's faith in the understanding of painting by sucklings, dogs, and cats. Fortunately, no arduous researches are necessary to convince oneself that pictures, poetry, and every work of art, produce no effects save on souls prepared to receive them. Natural signs do not exist; because they are all conventional in a like manner, or, to speak with greater exactitude, all are *historically conditioned.*

This being so, how are we to succeed in causing the expression to be reproduced by means of the physical object? How obtain the same effect, when the conditions are no longer the same? Would it not, rather, seem necessary to conclude that expressions cannot be reproduced, despite the physical instruments made by man for the purpose, and that what is called reproduction consists in ever new expressions? Such would indeed be the conclusion, if the variety of physical and psychic conditions were intrinsically unsurmountable. But since the insuperability has none of the characteristics of necessity, we must, on the contrary, conclude: that the reproduction always occurs, when we can replace ourselves in the conditions in which the stimulus (physical beauty) was produced.

Not only can we replace ourselves in these conditions, as an abstract possibility, but as a matter of fact we do so continually. Individual life, which is communion with ourselves (with our past), and social life, which is communion with our like, would not otherwise be possible.

As regards the physical object, paleographers and philologists, who *restore* to texts their original physiognomy, *restorers* of pictures and of statues, and similar categories of workers, exert themselves to preserve or to give back to the physical object all its primitive energy. These efforts certainly do not always succeed, or are not completely successful, for never, or hardly ever, is it possible to obtain a restoration complete in its smallest details. But the unsurmountable is only accidentally present, and cannot cause us to fail to recognize the favourable results which are nevertheless obtained.

Historical interpretation likewise labours to reintegrate in us historical conditions which have been altered in the course of history. It revives the dead, completes the fragmentary, and affords us the opportunity of seeing a work of art (a physical object) as its author saw it, at the moment of production.

A condition of this historical labour is tradition, with the help of which it is possible to collect the scattered rays and cause them to converge on one centre. With the help of memory, we surround the physical stimulus with all the facts among which it arose; and thus we make it possible for it to react upon us, as it acted upon him who produced it.

When the tradition is broken, interpretation is arrested; in this case, the products of the past remain *silent* for us. Thus the expressions contained in the Etruscan or Messapian inscriptions are unattainable; thus we still hear discussions among ethnographers as to certain products of the art of savages, whether they be pictures or writings; thus archaeologists and prehistorians are not always able to establish with certainty, whether the figures found on the ceramic of a certain region, and on other instruments employed, be of a religious or of a profane nature. But the arrest of interpretation, as that of restoration, is never a definitely unsurmountable barrier; and the daily discoveries of historical sources and of new methods of better exploiting antiquity, which we may hope to see ever improving, link up broken tradition.

We do not wish to deny that erroneous historical interpretation produces at times what we may term *palimpsests*, new expressions imposed upon the antique, artistic imaginings instead of historical reproductions. The so-called fascination of the past depends in part upon these expressions of ours, which we weave into historical expressions. Thus in hellenic plastic art has been discovered the calm and serene intuition of life of those peoples, who feel, nevertheless, so poignantly, the universality of sorrow; thus has recently been discerned on the faces of the Byzantine saints "the terror of the millennium," a terror which is an equivoke, or an artifical legend invented by modern scholars. But *historical criticism* tends precisely to circumscribe *vain imaginings* and to establish with exactitude the point of view from which we must look.

Thus we live in communication with other men of the present and of the past; and we must not conclude, because sometimes, and indeed often, we find ourselves face to face with the unknown or the badly known, that when we believe we are engaged in a dialogue, we are always speaking a monologue; nor that we are unable even to repeat the monologue which, in the past, we held with ourselves.

Monroe C. Beardsley

Reasons and Judgments

A critic who offers to improve our acquaintance with literary works by
giving interpretations of them takes on the character of a guide. And if he
is a discriminating guide, capable of helping us choose best where to
spend our limited time, he cannot avoid evaluations. Inevitably, we ask
him to tell us, from time to time, how good a poem or a novel is. This tell-
ing-how-good is what I shall mean by "judgment."

Used car salesmen, baseball scouts, and real estate appraisers working at their chosen trades are engaged in activities that can present many
philosophical puzzles. But some philosophers hold that when it comes to
judging in aesthetic contexts—that is, the judging of works of art, including literary works of art—special puzzles turn up that have no parallel in
other spheres of evaluation. They hold that critical evaluations are radically different from other kinds. My present purpose is to see whether this
fear is justified.

There seems to be at least a prima facie case for suspecting that critical judgment has something rather queer about it. Consider what might
be called "the Anomaly of Critical Argument." It is well pointed up by
some remarks of T. S. Eliot in an essay on Ben Jonson:

> To be universally accepted, to be damned by the praise that
> quenches all desire to read the book ... this is the most perfect
> conspiracy of approval. ... No critic has succeeded in making him
> appear pleasurable or even interesting.[1]

For my present purpose it does not matter whether Eliot is right about the
critics and the critics right about Ben Jonson. Let us assume that the situation is as Eliot describes it. We then have a favorable judgment of Ben
Jonson's plays—say that they are very good plays. And we presumably
have various reasons given by the critics to support this judgment. So as
far as the abstract argument goes, it may be sound and rationally compelling. And yet, says Eliot, there is something hollow in this logical achievement: the readers who are put in possession of the argument are, in one

important respect, no better off than before, since they are still unable to extract aesthetic enjoyment from the works themselves.

What is the point of making a literary judgment and arguing for it? My answer to this question—which I shall defend here—is simple and old-fashioned. It is to inform someone how good a literary work is. But philosophers are rightly suspicious of this so-called "informing," if it merely evokes verbal agreement but brings no further satisfaction to the hearer. And so they sometimes conclude that the essential point of judging must not be to give information, but something else: to get someone to like (or dislike) the work, to get someone to pay attention to the work, to promote the work, to get someone to praise or condemn the work, etc. Now I do not doubt in the least that people who utter judgments of literary works often have such ends in view. Certainly that is true of book reviewers, of librarians, of employees of the Virginia Kirkus service. They expect decisions and actions to follow on what they say. But there is a proximate end in judging—namely, to provide information about value—and I do not see how those remoter ends could be attained except by such a means.

I grant that there is something disturbingly anomalous about critical evaluations, and I hope to show how these peculiar features can be explained without treating critical judgments as *sui generis*, and without abandoning the view that critical judgments are supported by reasons in a perfectly straightforward way. But to do this we must undertake a fairly careful analysis of the nature of critical judgments and of the arguments used to support them.

1.

Clear thinking about the difficult problems of literary judgment calls for several crucial distinctions, which are often neglected. One is the distinction I have just suggested between the proximate and the remote ends of judgment or—to reintroduce one of the technical terms I have borrowed from J. L. Austin—between the perlocutionary act of *informing* (which is something that can be done directly by language) and the further consequences of this act (for example, having a book published, increasing its sales, getting it revised, etc.). Another Austinian distinction is between perlocutionary acts and the illocutionary acts on which they are based. The point of a given utterance may be to inform, but the informing is done by one or more illocutionary acts, such as reporting, describing, analyzing, explaining, predicting—or *judging*. To get at the nature of judging and to find out whether it is peculiar, or in what ways it is peculiar, we must study it in itself as an illocutionary act—quite apart from any further ends it may be used to achieve.

As I noted earlier, J. L. Austin, who isolated the concept of illocutionary acts, and William Alston, who has studied them extensively, have shown that what distinguishes a particular sort of illocutionary act is the set of conditions that the speaker represents as holding, or takes responsibility for, in performing the act. To formulate these conditions is to give the linguistic rules that govern the particular kind of act. For example, one rule is that the word "hello" is to be said when meeting someone, but not when about to part from someone (in short, "hello" is used to perform the illocutionary act of greeting).

I take it that the question the critical judge tries to answer is: "How good a literary work is X?" where X is the name of a poem, novel, or whatever. The answer will be that it is a magnificent literary work, a first-rate one, an extremely good one, a very good one, an average one, an inferior one, a miserable one—or another judgment that will fit in somewhere along this spectrum of praise and condemnation. The judgment may not be framed in terms of literary works in general, but in terms of acknowledged species: "*The Mill on the Floss* is a good novel," " 'Blackberry Winter' is a good short story," " 'Dover Beach' is a good poem." To say that "Dover Beach" is a good poem is, of course, not exactly the same as to say that it is a good literary work; but for present purposes I think we are safe in setting aside this difference.

There is a parallel distinction that I also propose to set aside, with due warning. To say that X is a good literary work is to make a judgment of literary goodness (i.e., of goodness as literature), but since there is a legitimate sense in which literary works can be said to form a subclass of works of art, judgments of literary goodness can also be classified as judgments of "artistic goodness. This, then, is the way I shall characterize the judgments to be discussed here, for example, Granville Hicks in the *Saturday Review:*

> I continue to believe that Norman Mailer's *An American Dream* is
> an uncommonly bad novel and Saul Bellow's *Herzog* an
> uncommonly good one.

Our task is to understand such judgments of artistic goodness in the domain of literature. And the fires question concerns the *subject* of such judgments. That is, what kind of thing is it that we are judging?

When one critic praises a novel for the skill in writing that it displays while another laments that the skill has been exercised to so little effect, it is not that they are making contradictory judgments and supporting them by different reasons. They are in fact judging different things: one, a property of the author (for strictly speaking, only living things can have skill); the other, a property of the finished work. When Stanley Edgar Ilyman writes that

> *An American Dream* is a dreadful novel, perhaps the worst I have
> read since beginning this column, since it is infinitely more
> pretentious than the competition,

perhaps he, too, is judging two different kinds of thing in the same sentence. I am not certain of this, because the word "pretentious" can refer to a quality of a literary work, a disparity between promises and fulfillments within the work itself. But there is a suggestion in this judgment that it contains two parts. First, the critic seems to decide that the novel is poor in its own terms. Then he detects in it signs that the author thought he was writing, and claimed to be writing, something very good; it is pretentiousness in this sense that seems to make the critic rate the novel even lower than he did at first. But then there really are two judgments: the first is (or ought to be) directed toward the work, and the second toward the author.

Here are some of the possible subjects of critical judgment:

1. We judge a performance—in terms of how skillfully the writing of the poem has been done.
2. We judge an execution—in terms of how successfully the poet's intention has been carried out.
3. We judge a production—in terms of how adequately a particular reading aloud of the poem realizes its potentialities.
4. We judge a person (that is, the author)—in terms of how good a poet he is.
5. We judge an object (that is, the poem)—in terms of its actual or possible effects.

I am sure that critics have judged all these things (and others) more or less reasonably, depending on the evidence available; but quite often they have mixed them up or slipped from one to another. Now, I do not want, at the moment, to enter into a discussion of the peculiar problems of each of these five types of judgment, and I am even willing, in a burst of unwonted charitableness, to allow that there is some use in all five of them. But I am concerned to insist on two things: (1) that the fifth type, the judgment of the work itself as an object, is a distinct kind of judgment, not to be confused with the others; and (2) that when we say that X is a good poem, it is precisely this type of judgment that we are making: we are not judging the poet, or his performance or execution, or his culture or his psychological states, or anything but the poem itself.

On some level of philosophical sophistication, I confess, eyebrows may justifiably be raised over my use of the term "object." Considering the objects that lie about us most familiarly and serve as examples by which the use of this term is taught, a poem is indeed an odd sort of ob-

ject. But, odd or not, a poem has a public character, a determinable quidd-
ity, that lays it open to interpretation—and, by the same token, to judgment. I will not pause to cite examples of misrepresentations of the
subject of critical judgment by philosophers who have talked as though
the whole business were like awarding blue ribbons in a tournament, or
sentencing a prisoner, or calling a runner out at first, or something else
equally remote from the critic's business. But when I emphasize the term
"object" it is to contrast the judgment of poems with all these distinct—
though no doubt related—activities.

2.

If we are straight about the subject of judgments of artistic goodness, we
are now ready for a closer examination of their predicate. The term "judgment" covers a variety of linguistic activities that seem to deserve somewhat disparate treatment. We judge distances and weights (before we have
measured them); we judge the criminality of actions and the legality of
contractual claims; we judge beauty contests and art competitions. But
what, more specifically and helpfully, are we doing when we judge literary
works in terms of their artistic goodness? I say that we are estimating the
artistic goodness of those works. This formula is not to be accepted without some misgiving. Two aspects of it plainly call for further explanation:
(1) why is the kind of illocutionary act involved in critical judging said to
be that of *estimating* something? (2) what is the *estimatum*, the property
of artistic goodness?

   I do not know exactly how to show that *estimate* is the *mot juste* for
what the critic does in his evaluative role. It seems to me that when I examine the elements of estimating as an illocutionary act, I find them present in the act of literary judging. Consider a typical case of estimating,
say, that of the representative of the moving company who comes to tell
you what it will cost to move your worldly goods. His estimate has at
least the following features:

1. The cost is a matter of degree; what he tells you is *how much* it is.
   Similarly, artistic goodness is a matter of degree, since some literary
   works are said to be better or worse than others.
2. The mover is not in a position to give an exact estimate of the cost. If
   he were able to calculate or to measure the total cost, he would not
   have to estimate it; he could *report* it. Similarly, the critic cannot assign a number to his appraisal of the literary work or rate it on a scale;
   he can only use terms like "extremely good" and "slightly better than
   such-and-such a poem."

3. The mover is not in a position to be certain how much it will cost, because he cannot be sure that he has taken every item into account. Similarly, the critic cannot be certain of his judgment of artistic goodness, though (like the mover) he may be justified in having some confidence in it.
4. Further investigation may provide evidence to correct the mover's estimate. In fact, when the van is loaded, it will be weighed, and the result will be a bill that is both exact and definitive. Similarly, the critic can learn more about the poem and come to understand it better, and thus correct his judgment.
5. The mover's estimate is based on observation and deliberation; he must take into account the facts of the situation (such as the amount and types of furniture, the number of books, etc.). Otherwise he would be merely *guessing.* Similarly, the critic bases his judgment on a study of the actual features of the work he is judging, and weighs their significance for his judgment.
6. Thus, the mover's estimate may be said to be reached by a process of reasoning in that the facts he takes into aaccount serve as data by which his estimate can be defended. And similarly, the critic, in deliberating before judging, transforms his literary facts into reasons.

The fourth point of comparison has perhaps the most obvious weakness. In most ordinary contexts, estimating is quantitative: the estimator aims to approximate a quantity that can, in principle, be measured exactly; and characteristically he formulates his estimate in terms such as "about a hundred yards away" or "roughly two hundred pounds, give or take a little." The literary critic, of course, has no instrument analogous to the mover's scale and adding machine, so there is no question of checking his estimate ultimately by a calculation based on measurement. What he has instead is the possibility that he or someone else can actualize in direct experience the degree of artistic goodness he estimates to be present. Seeing two trees across a field, I make an (inexact) estimate of their distance-difference by judging that one is a good deal farther away than the other. When I walk closer, I can see that such is the case. Similarly, I can judge the artistic goodness of one sonnet or play to be a good deal greater than that of another, and when it is experienced by someone capable of appreciating it fully, this estimate, too, may be confirmed.

It must be granted, then, that there is a use of "estimate"—probably its most frequent use—in which the possibility of measurement is presupposed, and this is not the sense in which the literary critic estimates artistic goodness. But I think there is also a weaker (non-quantitative) sense of "estimate"—or at least I think we can form such a weaker sense—in which we can legitimately and illuminatingly speak of the literary critic as making an estimate.[2]

The sixth point of comparison is the hardest to substantiate: let us take up that task. There are two very different ways in which (philosophers would say) reasons could be relevant to the critic's judgments. Reasons in what I think we can call the "ordinary" sense are reasons that have a bearing on the *truth* of the judgments. And the relevance of such reasons presupposes that the judgments can be true or false. This is indeed my view. But there might be reasons for making a certain judgment that are not reasons for saying it is true, if it should be the case that judgments cannot be true or false. For example, suppose that judging a poem is like saying, "By the authority vested in me by the Commonwealth, I hereby confer upon you the degree of Doctor of Laws." In that case, there could be reasons (even excellent reasons) for awarding the (honorary) degree, but the utterance that constitutes the awarding of the degree is not itself something that can sensibly be called true or false. So our first question is whether in fact critical judgments have a truth-value—i.e., are either true or false.

In his tentative classification of illocutionary acts, J. L. Austin marks out a class of "Verdictives," which includes, among other things, estimating, reckoning, and appraising.[3] We do not properly speak, he says, of verdictives as true or false. We "may estimate rightly or wrongly, for example, that it is half past two," but we do not estimate this truly or false.[4] But, as P. H. Nowell-Smith has argued,[5] although the words "true" and "truly" do not go with "estimate" as idiomatically as "rightly" or "correctly," an estimate surely involves a claim to truth, which may be allowed or disallowed. Suppose I estimate that the room is about twenty feet long. Then the question is whether it is *true* that the room is about twenty feet long. If so, then I have estimated rightly, and my estimate is approximately correct. In the same way, if a poem really is very good, and I say it is, then what I am saying is true. For in estimating the poem's artistic goodness, I am also making a statement about the poem. These are not really two separate illocutionary acts. There is an illocutionary act that can be called "making a statement," as when one deposes certain things at the police station and signs the typescript. But when one judges, estimates, predicts, guesses, reckons, diagnoses, locates, identifies, describes, analyzes, explains, etc. (to take some of Austin's list of verdictives), all these illocutionary acts have something in common, namely, making a claim to truth. And therefore it makes sense to ask for reasons to support that claim.

3.

I now turn to the third element in the judgment of artistic goodness— what I have called the "estimatum" or property to be judged. What is artistic goodness? Unfortunately, a reasonably complete answer to this question, together with an adequate defense, is beyond the scope of this discussion. I have wrestled with it on previous occasions,[6] and can only give a bit of the story here. The concept of goodness is undoubtedly a complex and philosophically puzzling one. For example, if we speak of artistic goodness, we are distinguishing a certain kind of goodness (of which literature-type goodness is a species) from other kinds of goodness (such as the kinds characteristic of governments or razors or houses or drivers). But there seems to be a variety of things that artistic goodness might consist in. To make this point clear, we require another distinction.

Imagine any object—anything you like—that we would all agree to have some sort and some degree of goodness: let us say, this chocolate ice cream cone. Not everyone likes chocolate ice cream, of course, so not everyone can take advantage of its goodness—or, as we might say, *actualize* its goodness. And some people are more fond of chocolate ice cream cones than others are, so if we should give it to X to eat, he will actualize more of its goodness than Y, who would have preferred pistachio. Each consumption of a chocolate ice cream cone may be regarded as an attempt to actualize its goodness. Many of these encounters are only half-successful. Yet if someone does not enjoy the cone, we do not say it is not good, but that he is oblivious to its goodness; and if the cone melts before anyone gets to taste it, we should not say that it never was good, but only what a pity it is that its goodness was wasted. So there is, we might say, actualized goodness and unactualized goodness.

Now I certainly do not want to suggest that literary works are in important respects anything like chocolate ice cream cones, and having introduced my distinction by this simple example, I hasten to apply it where it most matters for present purposes. A poem has some artistic goodness; and since (unlike the ice cream cone) it can be consumed more than once, we can distinguish various experiences of reading it. These encounters will vary in the amounts of that goodness they actualize and (inversely) leave unactualized. Now I ask what it is that the critic estimates when he estimates the artistic goodness of a poem. There are several possibilities:

1. The greatest amount of artistic goodness that has been actualized so far in any one encounter with the poem (let us call this the poem's *aesthetic attainment*).
2. The average amount of artistic goodness that has been actualized so far in encounter with the poem (let us call this the poem's *aesthetic dependability*).
3. The sum (if this makes sense) of all the amounts of goodness that have been or will be actualized in all encounters with the poem (let us call this the poem's *total aesthetic worth*).

4. The average amount of artistic goodness actualized in all encounters with the poem, past, present, and future (let us call this the poem's *mean aesthetic worth*).
5. The greatest amount of artistic goodness that *can* be actualized in an encounter with the poem (let us call this the poem's *aesthetic value*).

If we make a number of distinctions of this sort—and no doubt more could be contrived—we can obtain a clearer idea of what the critic estimates. We see that some of these estimates would normally be far beyond the competence of a critic; and so, if he is sensible, these cannot be what he is trying to make. For example, it would hardly ever be possible for a critic to make a reliable estimate of (3), total aesthetic worth. Even if we waive the nagging question whether it makes any sense to add up goodnesses, the critic would have to have detailed information about past, present, and future encounters with the poem.[7] The same hopelessness pertains to (4), mean aesthetic worth. It might be a little less formidable a task to estimate (2), aesthetic dependability—one could do it from a random sample of personal testimonies. But what critic, in deciding how good a work is, goes through a process of questionnaires and statistical manipulations? He does not think it is his job to count noses or take depositions—evidently, therefore, he is not trying to make this sort of estimate. Aesthetic attainment (1) might be possible to estimate in many cases, if the critic either is acquainted with an unsurpassed reader of the poem or can claim to be one himself. There is, however, a logical difficulty about saying that past aesthetic attainment is what the critic is estimating when he tells us how good the poem is. For suppose he discovers the greatest amount of goodness actualized by any reader so far, and rates the poem as quite good. And then suppose he himself, or another, goes back to the poem next week, with fuller understanding or a less distracted mind, and succeeds in actualizing even greater goodness, so that he then judges the poem to be very good. If in both cases he was estimating aesthetic attainment, then both estimates were correct; therefore, he must say that the poem has become artistically better in the course of that week. Obviously this would be a silly thing to say; it is not the poem that has changed, but its reader. Therefore, a critic's judgment is not an estimate of aesthetic attainment.

By a process of elimination, we are left with (5), aesthetic value, which is the greatest amount of artistic goodness that the poem allows of actualizing in any one encounter with it. This, I am convinced, is what the critic estimates. In making his estimate, he relies, of course, on experiences that he and others have had, but he is not limited to them; for sometimes, by analyzing the poem, he can reasonably infer that its aesthetic value is greater than what has already been actualized. There are many problems here that I do not attempt to deal with now. But at least we can see, I think, why the critic's decision about the poem's aesthetic value is, indeed, an estimate in the sense previously analyzed: that he can only make a somewhat rough judgment, which is subject to correction by future experience but yet is based on reasons.

4.

It is this last term that we must now consider: the reasonableness of the critic's estimates of aesthetic value. This is the problem of justification: what grounds are capable of supporting the critic's judgments? I think it would be best to begin with examples. They will be handy to refer to.

> To my mind, then, *The Cantos* is a poem lacking in significant action, lacking in order, and lacking in authority; and all these failings derive from the theories of language, of knowledge, and of reality upon which the poem is built.[8]

> By this time nearly everyone who is interested must know that John O'Hara's new novel, *From the Terrace*, is a bad book.... The novel is hollow at the center.... O'Hara's failure is that the key situation in Alfred's life, the emotional center around which the rest of the book is built, is simply unbelievable.... Conflicts are prepared, then dropped before their resolution; characters are developed, then disappear just as we are becoming interested in them. (Richard Schickel in *The Progressive*)

There are, of course, a good many philosophical problems about the reasoning of critics; I plan to deal with only one of them here, though I think a fundamental one. To get to that problem, I have to take for granted a few propositions that I have defended elsewhere, and one very important proposition in particular. I hope it will be agreed that a critic who knows how good (artistically) a poem is can sometimes explain (at last partially) the degree of goodness it has. For example, if Hynes is right in his disparagement of *The Cantos*, then in noting their lack of significant action, order, and authority, he is presenting *reasons why* the poem is not good (as a whole). For he is claiming that these deficiencies help to keep it from being excellent.

My assumption, then, is that it is possible for critics to give explanations for the degree of artistic goodness that is to be found in the works they study. Explanations are *reasons why*. But our problem here has to do with reasons in a different sense: reasons that one gives to support a proposition in an argument—in short, justifying reasons rather than explaining reasons. Let us call a reason why something is the case an *explanation*, and a reason for believing that something is the case a *justification*.

The same true statement can, of course, be both in different contexts. Suppose the car's motor will not start. One person knows that the motor will not start and inquires after the explanation: he learns that the battery is dead. Another person is told that the battery is dead, and he *infers* that the motor will not start. For the first person, the statement "The battery is dead" is an explanation of the motor's failure to start; for the second person, it is a justification for believing that the motor will not start.

The problem I now wish to place before you is simply this: can critical judgments be justified? Or, in other words, can reasons be given for accepting them? I must take account of an ingenious and noteworthy argument put forth recently by Michael Scriven—an argument that purports to show the impossibility of critical reasoning, in this sense.[9] Scriven's main line of thought depends upon a fundamental characteristic of successful arguing, which he brings out very cogently. Let us take as our model of argument the schema:

Reason; *therefore,* Conclusion.

That is, the minimal argument consists of two statements that are both asserted to be true, and a claim that there is a logical connection between them, in virtue of which acceptance of the reason carries with it some degree of rational obligation to accept the conclusion. In order to play any role in our acquisition of knowledge, an argument must satisfy what Scriven calls the "independence requirement": that is, it must be possible for us to know that the reason is true, and also to know that it is a reason for the conclusion, *before* knowing that the conclusion is true. For an argument is supposed to help us toward the conclusion by supporting it and soliciting our belief in it; but if we must believe the conclusion before we can decide whether to believe the reason, or whether to believe that the reason *is* a reason, then the argument is of no use to our thinking.

Scriven's view is that most (though not all) critical argument falls into this trap, that is, fails to satisfy the independence requirement. To see why he holds this view, consider a fairly typical example: "The speaker's situation in this poem is too vaguely delineated; *therefore,* the poem is not very good."[10] The word "too" in the first statement is the first thing to note. Its role is clearly essential. The critic does not tell us exactly how vaguely delineated the speaker's situation is in this poem; he only tells us that the delineation has some degree of vagueness, and this degree of vagueness detracts from artistic goodness *in this particular poem.*

Since most of the features in poems that critics cite in support of their judgments are matters of degree, there are countless instances where the word "too" must be tacitly understood, even when it is not supplied. For example, when Hynes says that *The Cantos* are "lacking in order" and "lacking in authority," I suppose he does not mean that these qualities are totally absent, but that they are very little in evidence, and, more relevantly, that they are *insufficiently* in evidence to satisfy (so to speak) the needs of this poem. When Schickel says that in the O'Hara novel "conflicts are prepared, then dropped before their resolution," this is more of an either-or matter, yet disparity between preparation and resolution is a matter of degree, and the main claim is that the degree is too considerable here.

Now it may be difficult for different critics, even if they have equally precise vocabularies, to be sure they are in agreement on just how vague the delineation of situation is, or how much authority there is in *The Cantos*, or how great is the disparity between preparation and resolution in the O'Hara novel. But let us suppose that they do agree on these matters. The next question for them to decide, as critical judges, is whether the degree of vagueness, authority, or disparity is right for this particular work, or whether it is too much or too little. If they were in possession of a manual supplied by some Aesthetic Bureau of Standards, this question could be answered mechanically—in roughly the same way the experts determine that the pollution of the atmosphere or the radioactivity of milk or the bacteria count of the ocean has risen above what they call, euphemistically, the "acceptable" level. Maybe there is an acceptable level of air pollution—considering what we would have to forego if we were to eliminate it entirely. But there is no such thing in literature as an acceptable level of vagueness in delineation or lack of authority or disparity between preparation and resolution. The very same level of vagueness in the speaker's situation that interferes with the artistic goodness of one poem will enhance the artistic goodness of another. So that when the critic tries to decide whether this particular degree of some feature is a merit or a defect in this work, he must see what it does *here*.

But can the critic know how this degree of vagueness affects the goodness of this poem unless he knows how good this poem is? For it seems that to know that the vagueness detracts from goodness, he must be able to explain the privation of goodness as in part due to the vagueness. But the critic is in no position to explain *why* the poem is not very good until after he *knows* that it is not very good. If the decision about merits and defects depends on a prior ability to give explanations, and the ability to give explanations depends on a prior knowledge of how good (or poor) the poem is, then the statements about merits and defects cannot function as the critic's justification of how good (or poor) the poem is. He would have to know how good it is before he knew how good it is. The sample arguments we have been analyzing, then, cannot be genuine arguments. No critic could discover how good a work of literature is by *first* deciding whether the situation is too vague, the work too lacking in authority, the novel's conflicts too little resolved. Such is Michael Scriven's conclusion. As he remarks,

It seems all too clear that the degree of agreement about when unity is needed and present to the needed or desirable degree does not exceed the degree of our initial agreement about the merit of the work of art.[11]

Suppose, for the moment, that Scriven is right in holding that the critic (in nearly all cases, remember) knows how good the poem is without having to do any reasoning to reach this conclusion. How, then, *does* he know how good the poem is? Well, of course, he has read, he has experienced, the poem; in doing so, he has actualized some portion of its artistic goodness. By direct experience he knows at least this much: that the poem permits the actualization of a certin amount of goodness. Now if the critic's judgment were merely a report of the maximal goodness he has himself experienced in the poem, then we could say that he knows his judgment is true by direct experience. After he acquires that knowledge, he can undertake the task of trying to explain the poem's goodness by seeing how its features contribute to it.

But a critic's judgment, we have seen, is not a report; it is an estimate. And estimating takes study, or at least allows for it. Even if a critic reads the poem and has a flair for quick judgments, so that he makes up his mind at once that it is a masterpiece or a failure—nevertheless, when he begins to analyze it in order to explain, if he can, what is so good about it, or so wrong with it, the process of discovering these explanations may well strengthen his original judgment, or may lead him to revise or even abandon it. And in that case, the explanations are functioning as (partial) justifications, even for him. For what he is supposed to do, after all, is not merely to give us an introspective report on how much he has so far gotten out of the poem, but a judicious estimate of what *can* be gotten out of it. Sometimes the critic can do this without reasons, even if his judgment goes beyond his experience. For example, he may enjoy the poem very much when he reads it the first time; but he may realize that he is fatigued and distracted, and so he may judge that it is probably even better than his experience has informed him that it is. But that is more in the nature of a good guess than an estimate. A serious estimate will require a discrimination of parts and relations, and some thought about their multiple interconnections; in short, it will be *reasoned*. And if the critic could not use reasons in making his judgments, I do not see how he could make very good judgments—as he sometimes does.

Scriven's argument goes wrong, I believe, when he says that the critic cannot decide whether a property of the poem contributes to goodness or detracts from goodness unless he already knows how good the poem is. I agree that he cannot give an adequate explanation of goodness until he knows how much goodness is there to be explained. But the process of deciding what is a merit or defect does not presuppose knowledge of the poem's final worth.

Consider again an example already used. How does the critic decide that the following three features of the O'Hara novel are defects? (1) The "key situation in Alfred's life" is unbelievable; (2) there is a sharp disparity between conflicts and resolutions; (3) characters are developed but disappear "just as we are becoming interested in them." He examines these features to see how they cooperate with other features or how they inhibit them; he looks to see whether these features, in this particular setting, as qualified and partly shaped by other factors in the novel, weaken or strengthen certain basic properties of the work: such properties as unity and the intensity of its regional qualities. I take it that the reason why the conflict-resolution disparity and the sudden disappearance of interesting characters are defects is that, taken together with everything else in the novel, they severely damage the coherence and completeness of the novel. And I take it that the reason why the unbelievability of the key situation is a defect is that it prevents the dramatic quality of the novel from rising to a high level of intensity. Thus it is possible to know what defects a novel has before knowing how good or poor it is.

The difference between my view and Scriven's now becomes explicit. In the sentence I quoted from him, he treats unity the same way I would treat such properties as vagueness of situation or conflict-resolution disparity. Concerning these latter properties of a work, it is quite true that whether they are merits or defects depends on the context in which they appear. But such properties as unity and intensity of regional quality are not that sort, I hold; these basic properties always count in one direction; they always contribute to the artistic goodness of the work in the degree to which they are present. Scriven disputes this claim, and argues (I think in a somewhat desultory fashion) that unity is not always a desirable feature of works of art. I will not enter into this question at the moment, having dealt with it before. If it is not regarded as taking unfair advantage of a friendly opponent, I would even be prepared to regard Scriven's argument as a further support of my own position. Scriven shows that *if* all features of literary works depend on their contexts to determine whether they are defects or merits or neutral features, *then* it would follow that critics cannot use reasons to arrive at their judgment. But *if*, as I claim, these judgments are estimates, then some reasons *must* be used by the critics in arriving at them, and *therefore* there must be some basic features of literary works that are always merits or defects— just as I say that unity and intensity of regional quality are always worth having in a literary work, while (conversely) confusion and insipidity are never worth having (assuming that we are concerned only with artistic goodness, not other kinds). But my main purpose here is not so much to defend my notion of basic critical criteria as to lay out, however briefly, my conception of how rational judgments of literary works are possible.

It is worth noting, I think, that even if we accepted Scriven's main line of argument, it would not wholly eliminate justifying reasons from our dealings with literature. For even if the *critic* cannot use justifying reasons, others may. When I use the term "critic" in this context, I mean someone who has read and judged the work (he has at least that much authority, though he is not necessarily a professional). I will use the term "layman," no doubt very arbitrarily, to refer to anyone who has not read the work, but who asks for the critic's judgment of it—perhaps in order to decide whether he should read it. Now even if Scriven is right in holding that the critic does not use reasons to reach his judgment of the work, still, after he has judged it, he can explain why the work has the degree of goodness he has judged it to have. When the layman receives these explanatory propositions from the critic, *his* situation is reversed: he can take the explanations as justifications and use them to reason his way to a judgment—not a conclusive one, of course, but one having some probability.

There are difficulties with this suggestion, I know, but I am inclined to think they can be overcome if we are allowed to make my assumption that certain general features of literary works are one-way criteria of judgment: unity, complexity, and intensity of regional quality. Without that assumption, it is doubtful that we can formulate a statement that will express at once an explanation for the critic and a justification for the layman. If, for example, the critic's explanation of why a poem is poor is that it is "studded with too many too-obtrusive details," this cannot serve as a justification for the layman, for in accepting it as such, he must take for granted the conclusion that it is supposed to help him to reach (namely, that the poem is made poor by these details). Thus the layman is in the same logical predicament as the critic. However, in my view, the critic can formulate his explanation in this way: "The poem is studded with this many details, which are obtrusive to such-and-such a degree, and these details detract (considerably) from the unity of the poem." *This* statement can be accepted by the layman without begging any questions, and though he cannot infer that the poem is necessarily poor, he can put this information together with other information from the critic and make a judgment that is more than a mere guess.

If one were partial to paradoxes, it would be tempting to say (if we accept Scriven's argument) that the critic does not have justifying reasons, but gives them, whereas the layman may have justifying reasons, but cannot give them (though he can pass along some he has already been given). But the temptation to propound paradoxes must always be fought. It is fortunate that we can take the easy way out and prevent the temptation from arising in the first place. For it seems that, despite their important difference in stance, critic and layman are alike in being able to have (justifying) reasons for their judgments, if they care for them.

5.

It is time to return to the quotation from T. S. Eliot that I began with and to the anomaly that I extracted from it. Perhaps we can now see how the layman (in my peculiar use of this term) can indeed have reasons for regarding the plays of Ben Jonson as great without being tempted to read them, and without being equipped to enjoy them if he does. For even if the critic convinces him of their greatness, what he is convincing him of (remember) is an estimate of what can be obtained from them by a highly qualified reader. And the layman—indeed, any one of us in sane moments—is quite prepared to admit the greatness of works whose artistic goodness he is not qualified (by native talent, by training, or by inclination) to actualize.

Nevertheless, it remains true (Eliot points out the rare case) that for the most part the critic's justifying reasons and explanations are of use to the layman. They bring out features of the works that had escaped his notice and enable him to do a better job at actualizing his share of the poem's artistic goodness. This is the element of truth in a view that has sometimes been espoused by philosophers to whom the subtleties and complexities of critical practice have been an anguish: generally speaking, the usefulness of the critic's justifying reasons to those laymen who come to him for advice consists less in what they learn about the *goodness* of the work than in what they learn about its *meaning*. The interesting point of an argument supporting a critical judgment may turn out to be the light it sheds on interpretation.

I think a good deal of obfuscation has been introduced into discussions of critical argument because of a failure to give adequate consideration to the difference between the role of the informing critic and the role of the layman in search of information.

For example, I have said that the critic, acting as judge, *estimates* artistic goodness. Now suppose he presents his best estimate to the layman and makes it convincing. The layman is then justified in expressing his own belief that the poem is a good one. But in doing so, he is performing a somewhat different illocutionary act from that of the critic. The critic was making an estimate; but the layman is not making an estimate, he is only repeating someone else's estimate. Perhaps this subtle difference has been one of the many things contributing to widespread skepticism about the whole concept of *persuasion* in criticism—just as Eliot was being somewhat skeptical, or at least dubious, in wondering whether persuasion about artistic goodness is very meaningful when it is separated from enjoyment.

Another aspect of this same asymmetry is pointed up by the phrase with which I began as a characteristic formula for critical judgment: " 'Fern Hill' is a good poem." Now I think there is a certain suggestion in this formula—not part of what it states, perhaps, but still strongly there—that it is an endorsement of the work. If someone pointed to a car and said, "That is a good car," we would take him to be professing some degree of authority—we would naturally suppose that he knows whereof he speaks, because he has driven it successfully, or at least has driven other cars of the same year and model. If he is only going by hearsay and has never driven that car or any like it, it would be less misleading for him to say something like, "I understand that's a good car" or "That's a good car, I'm told." Similarly, if someone says, " 'Fern Hill' is a good poem," without further qualification of the source of his claim, we take him to suggest that he has both read the poem and actualized some portion of its goodness. To say " 'Fern Hill' is a good poem, but I've never read it" is odd. To say " 'Fern Hill' is a good poem, but I have never enjoyed reading it" is also odd, in a similar way.

I think this element of suggestion in the expression "a good X" has helped to lure people into personal relativism. Philosophers have asked, "Does it make sense to judge something good when you don't like it, or to judge it poor when you do?" Other philosophers have said, "Yes—there is no contradiction." Yet there is the appearance of a contradiction if I say " 'Fern Hill' is a good poem, but I don't like it at all," because when I say it is a good poem, I suggest that I like it. There is something odd here. But it is not really a proof of relativism. For it is perfectly correct to say, "I have excellent reasons to believe (you have convinced me) that 'Fern Hill' is a good poem, though not on the basis of any enjoyment I have myself obtained from it." That is making the same pair of statements, without the suggestion, and there is nothing odd about it. In fact, a layman who reads a history of English literature—and indeed a playgoer who reads the reviews before he sees the performance—will often be in exactly this situation.

There are, then, puzzles about the transferability or viability of critical judgments, but they are not insoluble puzzles, and they do not show that there is no such thing as argument and persuasion in criticism. I cannot think of a better way to crystallize the point of view I am defending here than to take issue with a rather sour remark that Samuel Johnson once made in his *Idler:*

Criticism is a study by which men grow important and formidable at a very small expense. The power of invention has been conferred by nature upon few, and the labor of learning those sciences which may by mere labor be obtained is too great to be willingly endured; but every man can exert such judgment as he has upon the works of others, and he whom nature has made weak and idleness keeps ignorant may yet support his vanity by the name of a critic.

All professions can be debased, and criticism, like a metropolitan police force or college faculty, has its share of phonies and sadists. But if I am right, when one man exerts "such judgment as he has upon the works of others," he subjects himself to some rather exacting standards by which the better judgment can be discriminated from the worse. This is not a realm where anything goes. And if the critic cannot claim to possess the power of invention that would have made him a poet, he may claim to possess something very precious—the ability to lead others to what is good. This is what gives him not merely the name of a critic but the substance.

NOTES

1. *Essays on Elizabethan Drama* (New York: Harvest Books, 1956), p. 65.
2. Cf. F. E. Sparshott, *The Concept of Criticism*, pp. 120–21. Though I do not accept his main view, that what a critic criticizes is always a "performance," and that "criticism" and "performance" are "correlative terms" (p. 42), I am glad to find support in his way of connecting "estimating" with "evaluating."

   Hans Eichner has argued that a critical judgment is a prediction: when A says to B, "X is a good work of art," he means (in the "expert" sense): "If you are seriously interested in the art form to which X belongs, if your experience is wide enough, and if you are prepared to take trouble over X, you will like it" (see "The Meaning of 'Good' in Aesthetic Judgments," *British Journal of Aesthetics* 3 [1963]: 308). I do not understand how a critic could possibly make such predictions about his readers, when he does not know them—unless we take the "predictions" as tautologies ("If you have enough interest, experience, and willingness to take trouble, to make you like X, you will like X").
3. *How to Do Things with Words*, p. 150.
4. Ibid., p. 140; cf. p. 152.
5. P. H. Nowell-Smith, "Acts and Locutions," in W. H. Capitan and D. D. Merrill, eds., *Art, Mind, and Religion* (Pittsburgh: University of Pittsburgh Press, 1967), p. 18. This paper argues persuasively that claims to truth are involved in many more kinds of illocutionary act than was realized, or at least conceded, by Austin. Cf. John R. Searle, "Austin on Locutionary and Illocutionary Acts," *Philosophical Review* 77 (October 1968): 405–24.
6. See "The Aesthetic Point of View," forthcoming in the *Proceedings of the International Philosophy Year* at the State University of New York at Brockport; also in *Metaphilosophy* 1 (January 1970): 39–58.

7. It is true that some of the reasons that critics actually give are logically relevant, not to judgments of aesthetic value but to judgments of total or mean aesthetic worth. For example, that the poem is easily understood (or, on the other hand, is obscure) does not—in my view—have any bearing on its aesthetic value, but it does affect the accessibility or availability of the poem, and hence the number of readers who will be able to enjoy it. (On the concept of total aesthetic worth and related concepts, see my "Aesthetic Welfare," forthcoming in the *Proceedings of the VI International Congress of Aesthetics* [Uppsala, 1968].)

8. Samuel Hynes, "Whitman, Pound, and the Prose Tradition," p. 131.

9. See Scriven, "The Objectivity of Aesthetic Evaluation," *Monist* 50 (1966): 159–87, and *Primary Philosophy* (New York: McGraw-Hill, 1966), chap. 3.

10. Cf. Wittgenstein's musical example, "The bass is too heavy; it moves too much," reported by G. E. Moore, *Philosophical Papers* (New York: Collier, 1962), p. 307; and Harold Osborne, "Reasons and Description in Criticism," *Monist* 50 (1966): 204–12. Excellent examples of critical "too"-statements are provided by Harold Clurman, reviewing *The Prime of Miss Jean Brodie* in *The Nation* (my italics): "The production suffers from *overemphasis.* Michael Langham has directed it with *sledge-hammer insistence* on what the script itself makes *abundantly evident* and readily enjoyable. Zoe Caldwell ... is a brilliant actress. But her portrayal of Jean Brodie is *much too stressed* and studded with *obtrusive detail.* Even the personage's plainness is *overdone* by an unbecoming wig and *unneeded exaggeration* in makeup. Miss Brodie thus becomes freakish. . . . "

11. Scriven, "The Objectivity of Aesthetic Evaluation," p. 179.

Barbara Herrnstein Smith

Contingencies of Value

1. The Exile of Evaluation

It is a curious feature of literary studies in America that one of the most venerable, central, theoretically significant, and pragmatically inescapable set of problems relating to literature has not been a subject of serious inquiry for the past fifty years. I refer here to the fact not merely that the study of literary evaluation has been, as we might say, "neglected," but that the entire problematic of value and evaluation has been evaded and explicitly exiled by the literary academy. It is clear, for example, that there has been no broad and sustained investigation of literary evaluation that could compare to the constant and recently intensified attention devoted to every aspect of literary *interpretation*. The past decades have witnessed an extraordinary proliferation of theories, approaches, movements, and entire disciplines focused on interpretive criticism, among them (to recite a familiar litany) New Criticism, structuralism, psychoanalytic criticism, reader-response criticism, reception aesthetics, speech-act theory, deconstructionism, communications theory, semiotics, and hermeneutics. At the same time, however, aside from a number of scattered and secondary essays by theorists and critics who are usually otherwise occupied,[1] no one in particular has been concerned with questions of literacy value and evaluation, and such questions regularly go begging—and, of course, begged—even among those whose inquiries into other matters are most rigorous, substantial, and sophisticated.

Reasons for the specific disparity of attention are not hard to locate. One is the obvious attachment of problems of interpretation and meaning to the more general preoccupation with language that has dominated the entire century and probably, as well, the fact that disciplines such as linguistics and the philosophy of language are more accessible to literary scholars than the corresponding disciplines, especially economics and sociology, that are more broadly concerned with the nature of value and evaluative behavior. The reasons for the general neglect and exile, how-

463

ever, are more complex, reflecting, among other things, the fact that literary studies in America, from the time of its inception as an institutionalized academic discipline, has been shaped by two conflicting and mutually compromising intellectual traditions and ideologies, namely—or roughly namely—positivistic philological scholarship and humanistic pedagogy. That is, while professors of literature have sought to claim for their activities the rigor, objectivity, cognitive substantiality, and progress associated with science and the empirical disciplines, they have also attempted to remain faithful to the essentially conservative and didactic mission of humanistic studies: to honor and preserve the culture's traditionally esteemed objects—in this case, its canonized texts—and to illuminate and transmit the traditional cultural values presumably embodied in them. One consequence or manifestation of this conflict has been the continuous absorption of "literary theory" in America with institutional debates over the proper methods and objectives of the academic *study* of literature and, with respect to the topic at hand, the drastic confinement of its concern with literary evaluation to debates over the cognitive status of evaluative criticism and its proper place, if any, in the discipline.

A bit of history will be helpful here. In accord with the traditional empiricist doctrine of a fundamental split or discontinuity between fact and value (or description and evaluation, or knowledge and judgment), it was possible to regard the emerging distinction within literary studies between "scholarship" and "criticism" as a reasonable division of labor. Thus, the scholar who devoted himself to locating and assembling the historical and philological facts necessary to edit and annotate the works of, say, Bartholomew Griffin might remark that, although Griffin was no doubt a less fashionable poet than such contemporaries as Spenser and Shakespeare, the serious and responsible scholar must go about his work in a serious and responsible manner, leaving questions of literary merit "to the critics." The gesture that accompanied the remark, however, was likely to signal not professional deference but intellectual condescension; for the presumably evenhanded distribution of the intellectual responsibilities of literary study—the determination of facts to the scholar and value to the critic—depended on an always questionable and increasingly questioned set of assumptions: namely, that literary value was a determinate property of texts and that the critic, by virtue of certain innate and acquired capacities (taste, sensibility, etc., which could be seen as counterparts to the scholar's industry and erudition), was someone specifically equipped to discriminate it.

The magisterial mode of literary evaluation that issued from this set of assumptions (and which, in Anglo-American criticism, characteristically reproduced itself after the image—and in the voice—of Dr. Johnson

Eliot) was practiced most notably by F. R. Leavis in England and, in America, perhaps most egregiously, by Yvor Winters. Its reaches and a taste of its once familiar flavor can be recalled in this passage from Leavis' *Revaluation:*

> There are, of course, discriminations to be made: Tennyson, for
> instance, is a much better poet than any of the pre-Raphaelites. And
> Christina Rossetti deserves to be set apart from them and credited
> with her own thin and limited but very notable distinction....
> There is, too, Emily Brontë, who has hardly yet had full justice as a
> poet. I will record, without offering it as a checked and deliberated
> judgment, the remembered impression that her *Cold in the earth* is
> the finest poem in the nineteenth-century part of *The Oxford Book
> of English Verse.*[2]

Such unabashed "debaucheries of judiciousness" (as Northrop Frye would later characterize them) were, however, increasingly seen as embarrassments to the discipline, and the practice of evaluative criticism became more defensive, at least partly in response to the renewed and updated authority given to axiological skepticism.

In the thirties and forties, a number of prominent philosophers, among them A. J. Ayer and Rudolph Carnap, began to argue that value judgments are not merely distinct from empirically verifiable statements of fact but vacuous pseudostatements, at best suasive and commendatory, at worst simply the emotive expressions of personal sentiment, and in any case neither reflecting nor producing genuine knowledge.[3] For the positivistic literary scholar, such arguments reinforced his impression that the work of his critical colleague was the intellectually insubstantial activity of a dilettante, while the true discipline of literary studies was exhibited in his own labors, in which he had always sought to achieve a rigor and objectivity as free as possible from the contamination of value ascription. In the institutional struggles that ensued, various maneuvers were developed to secure for "criticism" not only a central place in the discipline but also an intellectual status equal in respectability to that of empirical science and what was commonly referred to as "serious scholarship."

One obvious tactic, still favored in many quarters of the literary academy, was to invoke the humanistic mission of literary studies and turn the fact-value split against the scholars' claim of centrality. Thus Winters would maintain that while science was value-neutral—or, as he put it, "amoral"—literary studies had moral responsibilities. The function of historical scholarship and philology was, accordingly, ancillary: specifically, it was "to lay the groundwork for criticism," while the important job was, precisely, to evaluate literature.[4] For Winters, this meant to declare, forthrightly and unequivocally, what was good and bad literature (which was to say, "moral" or "decadent" literature), and he did not hesitate, himself, to rank-order not only poets and poems but also literary genres, verse forms, and entire centuries.

Winters had a genius for unequivocality that was imitated but never matched by his numerous followers. In any case, a more common tactic, exemplified by a number of the New Critics, was to devise some formulation of critical activity that bridged the fact-value split or at least unobtrusively edged the two sides together. Thus, in 1951, W. K. Wimsatt, Jr., in an important essay titled "Explication as Criticism," observed that it was necessary to find "an escape between the two extremes of sheer affectivism and sheer scientific neutralism" and attempted to demonstrate how evaluation could be assimilated into the typical New Critical production of increasingly exquisite explications and fine-grained analyses: "But then, finally, it is possible to conceive and produce instances where explication in the neutral sense is so integrated with special and local value intimations that it rises from neutrality gradually and convincingly to the point of total judgment."[5]

It may be recalled here that Wimsatt's attempt to expose "the affective fallacy" was directed largely at the "psychological theory of value" developed by I. A. Richards in the twenties, which Wimsatt charged with amounting to subjectivism and leading to impressionism and relativism. Richards' theory was, however, in effect an updated rehearsal of the eighteenth-century empiricist-normative account and, like the latter, designed to *rebut* axiological skepticism.[6] An adequate theory of criticism, Richards wrote, must be able to answer such questions as "What gives the experience of reading a certain poem its value?" and "Why is one opinion about works of art not as good as another?";[7] and while the first of these questions no doubt seemed to Wimsatt altogether different from what, for him, would have been the more proper question of what gives *the poem itself* its value, the second of them makes Richards' normative objectives quite clear. Indeed, he consistently put his psycho-neurological account of value in the service of canonical judgments and repeatedly translated it into versions of evaluative absolutism and objectivism. Thus, the remarkable chapter on "Badness in Poetry" in *Principles of Literary Criticism* concludes its excruciating examination of the failure of a sonnet by Ella Wheeler Wilcox to produce a "high level of organization" of "adequate [neural] impulses" with Richards' observation that, although "those who enjoy [the sonnet] certainly seem to enjoy it to a high degree," nevertheless, with good and bad poetry, as with brandy and beer, the "actual universal preference of those who have tried both fairly is the same as superiority in value of one over the other. Keats, by universal qualified opinion, is a more efficient poet than Wilcox, and that is the same as saying his works are more valuable."[8] The invocation of an "actual" universality coupled with such question-begging hedges as "fairly" and "qualified" is, as we shall see, characteristic of traditional empiricist-normative accounts. It was not, one suspects, its alleged relativism that made Richards' theory so unabsorbable by the literary academy but rather the raw jargon and unedifying physiology that attended it.

The boldest move in the mid-century effort to give disciplinary respectability and cognitive substance to criticism was, or course, Frye's call upon it to redefine itself as a project that banished evaluation altogether. In his "Polemical Introduction" to the *Anatomy of Criticism*, Frye insisted that, if criticism was ever to become a "field of genuine learning" (significantly exemplified by "chemistry or philology"), it would have to "snip . . . off and throw . . . away" that part that had "no organic connection with [it],"—namely, evaluation.[9] For Frye, the shifting assessments and rank-orderings made by critics were not only a noncumulative accumulation of subjective judgments but also irrelevant to "real criticism," since he believed, echoing and endorsing Eliot, that "the existing monuments of literature form an ideal order among themselves." "This," Frye commented, "is criticism, and very fundamental criticism. Much of this book attempts to annotate it" (*AC*, p. 18).

In what proved to be a memorable passage, he derided "all the literary chit-chat which makes the reputations of poets boom and crash in an imaginary stock-exchange," and observed:

> This sort of thing cannot be part of any systematic study, for a systematic study can only progress: whatever dithers or vacillates or reacts is merely leisure-class gossip. The history of taste is no more a part of the *structure* of criticism than the Huxley-Wilberforce debate is a part of the structure of biological science. [*AC*, p. 18]

In view of Frye's Platonic conception of literature and positivistic conception of science, it is not surprising that he failed to recognize that his analogy here cuts both ways. For not only could the Huxley-Wilberforce debate be seen as very much a part of the "structure" of biological science (which, like that of any other science, including any science of literature, is by no means independent of its own intellectual, social, and institutional history), but, since the "order" of "the existing monuments of literature" is the distinctly sublunary product of, among other things, evaluative practices, any truly systematic study of literature would sooner or later have to include a study of *those practices*. In other words, the structure of criticism cannot be so readily disengaged from the history of taste because they are mutually implicating and incorporating.

Joining as it did both an appeal to scientific objectivity and a humanistic conception of literature, while at the same time extending the promise of a high calling and bright future to a project pursued in the name of "criticism," Frye's effort to banish evaluation from literary study was remarkably effective—at least to the extent of haunting a generation of literary scholars, critics, and teachers, many of whom are still inclined to apologize for making overt value judgments, as if for some temporary intellectual or moral lapse.[10] It was hardly the last word on the subject, however, and as late as 1968 we find E. D. Hirsch, Jr., attempting to rehabilitate the cognitive status of evaluative criticism in an essay significantly titled "Evaluation as Knowledge." In the essay, Hirsch argues that the value judgment of a literary work, when properly directed to the work itself and not to a "distorted version of it," closely coordinated with a correct interpretation of its objective meaning and rationally justified with reference to specific criteria, *does* constitute a genuine proposition and, therefore, like a "pure description," does "qualify as objective knowledge."[11] Since just about every concept engaged by Hirsch's argument is at issue in contemporary epistemology and critical theory, it is not surprising that it did not settle the question of the intellectual status of evaluative criticism—for Hirsch or anyone else.[12]

The debate over the proper place of evaluation in literary studies remains unresolved and is, I believe, unresolvable in the terms in which it has been formulated. Meanwhile, although evaluative criticism remains intellectually suspect, it certainly continues to be practiced as a magisterial privilege in the classrooms of the literary academy and granted admission to its journals as long as it comes under cover of other presumably more objective types of literary study, such as historical description, textual analysis, or explication. At the same time, however, the fact that literary evaluation is not merely an aspect of formal academic criticism but a complex set of social and cultural activities central to the very nature of literature has been obscured, and an entire domain that is properly the object of theoretical, historical, and empirical exploration has been lost to serious inquiry.

Although I confine my comments here primarily to the American literary academy and to Anglo-American critical theory, the situation—and its intellectual and institutional history—has not been altogether different in continental Europe. The dominance of language- and interpretation-centered theories, movements, and approaches, for example, is clearly international, and versions of the positivist/humanist conflict have shaped the development of literary studies in Europe as well. Certain exceptions are, however, instructive. When, in the twenties and thirties, East European theorists also sought to transform literary studies into a progressive, systematic science, the problematic of value and evaluation was not excluded from the project. For example, the historically variable functions of texts and the interrelations among canonical and noncanonical works and other cultural products and activities were recognized and documented by, among others, Jurij Tynjanov and Mikhail Bakhtin; and

Jan Mukařovský's explorations of the general question of aesthetic value were both original and substantial.[13] Also, studies in the sociology of literature, especially in France and Germany, and the project of reception aesthetics have concerned themselves with aspects of literary evaluation.[14] It should also be noted, however, that the study of value and evaluation remained relatively undeveloped in the later work of formalists and structuralists,[15] while Marxist literary theory has only recently begun to move from minimal revisions of orthodox aesthetic axiology toward a radical reformulation.[16] It may be added that, although the theoretical perspective, conceptual structures, and analytic techniques developed by Jacques Derrida are potentially of great interest here (especially in conjunction with the renewed attention to Nietzsche), their radical axiological implications remain largely unexplored,[17] and, insofar as it has been appropriated by American critical theory, deconstruction has been put almost entirely in the service of antihermeneutics, which is to say that it has been absorbed by our preemptive occupation with interpretive criticism. Recent moves toward opening the question of value and evaluation in the American literary academy have come primarily from those who have sought to subject its canon to dramatic revaluation, notably feminist critics. Although their efforts have been significant to that end, they have not, however, amounted as yet to the articulation of a well-developed non-canonical theory of value and evaluation.

One of the major effects of prohibiting or inhibiting explicit evaluation is to forestall the exhibition and obviate the possible acknowledgment of divergent systems of value and thus to ratify, by default, established evaluative authority. It is worth noting that in none of the debates of the forties and fifties was the traditional academic canon itself questioned, and that where evaluative authority was not ringingly affirmed, asserted, or self-justified, it was simply assumed. Thus Frye himself could speak almost in one breath of the need to "get rid of ... all casual, sentimental, and prejudiced value-judgments" as "the first step in developing a genuine poetics" and of "the masterpieces of literature" which are "the materials of literary criticism" (*AC*, pp. 18, 15). The identity of those masterpieces, it seemed, could be taken for granted or followed more or less automatically from the "direct value-judgement of informed good taste" or "certain literary values ... fully established by critical experience" (*AC*, pp. 27, 20).

In a passage of particular interest, Frye wrote:

> Comparative estimates of value are really inferences, most valid when silent ones, from critical practice. ... The critic will find soon, and constantly, that Milton is a more rewarding and suggestive poet to work with than Blackmore. But the more obvious this becomes, the less time he will want to waste belaboring the point. [*AC*, p. 25]

In addition to the noteworthy correlation of validity with silence (comparable, to some extent, to Wimsatt's discreet "intimations" of value), two other aspects of Frye's remarks here repay some attention. First, in claiming that it is altogether obvious that Milton, rather than Blackmore, is "a more rewarding and suggestive poet [for the critic] to work with," Frye begged the question of *what kind of work* the critic would be doing. For surely if one were concerned with a question such as the relation of canonical and noncanonical texts in the system of literary value in eighteenth-century England, one would find Blackmore just as rewarding and suggestive *to work with* as Milton. Both here and in his repeated insistence that the "material" of criticism must be "the masterpieces of literature" (he refers also to "a feeling we have all had: that the study of mediocre works of art remains a random and peripheral form of critical experience" [*AC*, p. 17]), Frye exhibits a severely limited conception of the potential domain of literary study and of the sort of problems and phenomena with which it could or should deal. In this conceptual and methodological confinement, however (which betrays the conservative force of the ideology of traditional humanism even in the laboratories of the new progressive poetics), he has been joined by just about every other member of the Anglo-American literary academy during the past fifty years.

The second point of interest in Frye's remarks is his significant conjoining of Milton with Blackmore as an illustration of the sort of comparative estimate that is so obvious as not to need belaboring. Blackmore, we recall, was the author of an ambitious epic poem, *The Creation*, notable in literary history primarily as the occasion of some faint praise from Dr. Johnson and otherwise as a topos of literary disvalue; its function—indeed, one might say, its *value*—has been to stand as an instance of bad poetry. This handy conjunction, however (and similar ones, such as Shakespeare and Edgar Guest, John Keats and Joyce Kilmer, T. S. Eliot and Ella Wheeler Wilcox, that occur repeatedly in the debates outlined above), evades the more difficult and consequential questions of judgment posed by genuine evaluative diversity and conflict: questions that are posed, for example, by specific claims of value made for noncanonical works (such as modern texts, especially highly innovative ones, and such culturally exotic works as oral or tribal literature, popular literature, and "ethnic" literature) and also by judgments of literary value made by or on behalf of what might be called noncanonical or culturally exotic audiences (such as all those readers who are not now students, critics, or professors of literature and perhaps never were and never will be within the academy or on its outskirts).

The evasion is dramatized when conflicts of judgment arising from fundamental and perhaps irreconcilable diverity of interest are exhibited in currently charged political contexts. A specific example will illustrate my point here. In 1977 a study of Langston Hughes' poetry was published by Onwuchekwa Jemie, a Nigerian-born, American-educated poet and critic, at that time associate professor of English and Afro-American literature at the University of Minnesota. In one section of his study, Jemie discusses Hughes' poetic cycle, "Madame," in relation to Eliot's "The Love Song of J. Alfred Prufrock" and Ezra Pound's "Hugh Selwyn Mauberly," comparing various formal and thematic aspects of the three works. He observes, for example, that each of them is "consistent in language, tone and attitude with the socio-psychological milieu which it explores: the ghetto dialect and sassy humor [in Hughes' work], the cynical polished talk of literary London [in Pound's], and the bookish ruminations of Prufrock's active mind in inactive body"; he then concludes pointedly: "In short, to fault one poem for not being more like the other, for not dealing with the matter and in the manner of the other, is to err in judgment."[18] Soon after its publication, a reviewer of Jemie's book in the London *Times Literary Supplement* took it very much to task for, among other things, its "painfully irrelevant comparisons," citing the passage quoted above.[19] And, a few weeks later, there appeared in *TLS* an extraordinary letter to the editor from Chinweizu, himself a Nigerian-born, American-educated writer and critic. Responding to the review and particularly to the phrase, "painfully irrelevant comparisons," he shot back:

> Painful to whom? Irrelevant to whom? To idolators of white genius? Who says that Shakespeare, Aristophanes, Dante, Milton, Dostoevsky, Joyce, Pound, Sartre, Eliot, etc. are the last word in literary achievement, unequalled anywhere? ... The point of these comparisons is not to thrust a black face among these local idols of Europe which, to our grave injury, have been bloated into "universality"; rather it is to help heave them out of our way, clear them from our skies by making clear ... that we have, among our own, the equals and betters of these chaps. ... In this day and age, British preferences do not count in the Black World. As Langston Hughes himself put it half a century ago: "If white people are pleased, we are glad. If they are not, it doesn't matter."[20]

This brief case history in the problem of literary evaluation illustrates, among other things, what genuine evaluative conflict sounds like. (It also illustrates that, contrary to Frye's assertion, the history of taste is not "a history where there are no facts" [*AC*, p. 18], though we have barely begun to recognize either how to chronicle its episodes and shape its narrative or its significance not only for "the structure of criticism" but also for the structure of "literature.") I would suggest that it is, also among other things, the very possibility of that sound that is being evaded in Anglo-American literary studies and, furthermore, that when the sound

reaches the intensity that we hear in Chinweizu's letter, the literary academy has no way to acknowledge it except, perhaps, in the language of
counteroutrage.[21]

It is clear that, with respect to the central pragmatic issues as well as
theoretical problems of literary value and evaluation, American critical
theory has simply painted itself out of the picture. Beguiled by the humanist's fantasy of transcendence, endurance, and universality, it has
been unable to acknowledge the most fundamental character of literary
value, which is its mutability and diversity. And, at the same time, mag-
netized by the goals and ideology of a naive scientism, distracted by the
arid concerns of philosophic axiology, obsessed by a misplaced quest for
"objectivity," and confined in its very conception of literary studies by
the narrow intellectual traditions and professional allegiances of the literary academy, it has foreclosed from its own domain the possibility of
investigating the dynamics of that mutability and understanding the nature of that diversity.

The type of investigation I have in mind here would seek neither to
establish normative "criteria," devise presumptively objective evaluative
procedures, nor discover grounds for the "justification" of critical judgments or practices. It would not, in short, be a literary axiology or, in effect, the counterpart for evaluative criticism of what a literary hermeneutics offers to be for interpretive criticism. It would seek, rather, to clarify
the nature of literary—and, more broadly, aesthetic—value in conjunction with a more general rethinking of the concept of value; to explore the
multiple forms and functions of literary evaluation, institutional as well
as individual, in relation to the circumstantial constraints and conditions
to which they are responsive; to chronicle "the history of taste" in relation to a general model of historical evaluative dynamics and specific local conditions; and to describe and account for the various phenomena and
activities that appear to be involved in literary and aesthetic evaluation
in relation to our more general understanding—as it is and as it develops—of human culture and behavior.

The sort of inquiry suggested here (which obviously could not be pursued within the confines of literary study or critical theory as they are
presently conceived and demarcated) might be expected to make its accounts internally consistent, externally connectable, and amenable to
continuous extension and refinement; for it is thus that the theoretical
power and productivity of those accounts would be served and secured.
This is not, however, to imagine a monolithic intellectual project that
would offer to yield an ultimately comprehensive, unified, and objective
account of its subject; for to imagine it thus would, of course, be to repeat,
only on a grander scale, elements of the raw positivism and naive scientism that were, in part, responsible for both the exile of evaluation and the

confinements of modern critical theory. What is desirable, rather, is an inquiry pursued with the recognition that, like any other intellectual enterprise, it would consist, at any given time, of a set of heterogeneous projects; that the conceptual structures and methodological practices adopted in those projects would themselves be historically and otherwise contingent (reflecting, among other things, prevailing or currently interesting conceptual structures and methods in related areas of inquiry); that whatever other value the descriptions and accounts produced by any of those projects might and undoubtedly would have (as indices of twentieth-century thought, for example, to future historians), their specific value as descriptions and accounts would be a function of how well they made intelligible the phenomena within their domain to whoever, at whatever time and from whatever perspective, had an interest in them; and that its pursuit would be shaped by—that is, energized and transformed in response to—those interests, and its descriptions and accounts continuously and variously interpreted and employed in accord with them.[22]

The discussion that follows is designed to suggest a theoretical framework for such an inquiry.[23]

2. The Economics of Literary and Aesthetic Value

All value is radically contingent, being neither an inherent property of objects nor an arbitrary projection of subjects but, rather, the product of the dynamics of an economic system. It is readily granted, of course, that it is in relation to a system of that sort that commodities such as gold, bread, and paperback editions of *Moby-Dick* acquire the value indicated by their market prices. It is traditional, however, both in economic and aesthetic theory as well as in informal discourse, to distinguish sharply between the value of an entity in that sense (that is, its "exchange-value") and some other type of value that may be referred to as its utility (or "use-value") or, especially with respect to so-called "nonutilitarian" objects such as artworks or works of literature, as its "intrinsic value." Thus, it might be said that whereas the fluctuating price of a particular paperback edition of *Moby-Dick* is a function of such variables as supply and demand, production and distribution costs, and the publisher's calculation of corporate profits, these factors do not affect the value of *Moby-Dick* as experienced by an individual reader or its intrinsic value as a work of literature. These distinctions, however, are not as clear-cut as may appear.

Like its price in the marketplace, the value of an entity to an individual subject is *also* the product of the dynamics of an economic system, specifically the personal economy constituted by the subject's needs, interests, and resources—biological, psychological, material, and experiential. Like any other economy, moreover, this too is a continuously fluctuating or shifting system, for our individual needs, interests, and resources are themselves functions of our continuously changing states in relation to an environment that may be relatively stable but is never absolutely fixed. The two systems are, it may be noted, not only analogous but also interactive and interdependent; for part of our environment *is* the market economy, and, conversely, the market economy is comprised, in part, of the diverse personal economies of individual producers, distributors, consumers, and so forth.

The traditional discourse of value—including a number of terms I have used here, such as "subject," "object," "needs," "interests," and, indeed, "value" itself—reflects an arbitrary arresting, segmentation, and hypostasization of the continuous process of our interactions with our environments—or what could also be described as the continuous interplay among multiple configurable systems. It is difficult to devise (and would be, perhaps, impossible to sustain) a truly Heraclitean discourse that did not reflect such conceptual operations, but we may recognize that, insofar as such terms project images of discrete acts, agents, and entities, fixed attributes, unidirectional forces, and simple causal and temporal relationships, they obscure the dynamics of value and reinforce dubious concepts of noncontingency—that is, concepts such as "intrinsic," "objective," "absolute," "universal," and "transcendent." It is necessary, therefore, to emphasize a number of other interactive relationships and forms of interdependence that are fragmented by our language and commonly ignored in critical theory and aesthetic axiology.

First, as I have already suggested, a subject's experience of an entity is always a function of his or her personal economy: that is, the specific "existence" of an object or event, its integrity, coherence, and boundaries, the category of entities to which it "belongs" and its specific "features," "qualities," or "properties" are all the variable products of the subject's engagement with his or her environment under a particular set of conditions. Not only is an entity always experienced under more or less different conditions, but the various experiences do not yield a simple cumulative (corrected, improved, deeper, more thorough, or complete) knowledge of the entity because they are not additive. Rather, each experience of an entity frames it in a different role and constitutes it as a different configuration, with different "properties" foregrounded and repressed. Moreover, the subject's experiences of an entity are not discrete or, strictly speaking, successive, because recollection and anticipation always overlay perception and the units of what we call "experience" themselves vary and overlap.

Second, what we speak of as a subject's "needs," "interests," and "purposes" are not only always changing (and it may be noted here that a subject's "self"—or that on behalf of which s/he may be said to act with "self-interest"—is also variable, being multiply reconstituted in terms of different roles and relationships), but they are also not altogether independent of or prior to the entities that satisfy or implement them; that is, entities also produce the needs and interests they satisfy and evoke the purposes they implement. Moreover, because our purposes are continuously transformed and redirected by the objects we produce in the very process of implementing them, and because of the complex interrelations among human needs, technological production, and cultural practices, there is a continuous process of mutual modification between our desires and our universe.[24]

Of particular significance for the value of "works of art" and "literature" is the interactive relation between the *classification* of an entity and the functions it is expected or desired to perform. In perceiving an object or artifact in terms of some category—*as*, for example, "a clock," "a dictionary," "a doorstop," "a curio"—we implicitly isolate and foreground certain of its possible functions and typically refer its value to the extent to which it performs those functions more or less effectively. But the relation between function and classification also operates in reverse: thus, under conditions that produce the "need" for a door-stopping object or an "interest" in Victorian artifacts, certain properties and possible functions of various objects in the neighborhood will be foregrounded, and both the classification and value of those objects will follow accordingly. As we commonly put it, one will "realize" the value of the dictionary *as* a doorstop or "appreciate" the value of the clock *as* a curio.[25] (The mutually defining relations among classification, function, and value are nicely exhibited in the *OED*'s definition of "curio" as "an object of art, piece of bric-à-brac, etc., valued as a curiosity," which is, of course, something like—and no less accurate than—defining "clock" as "an object valued as a clock.") It may be noted here that human beings have evolved as distinctly opportunistic creatures and that our survival, both as individuals and as a species, continues to be enhanced by our ability and inclination to reclassify objects and to "realize" and "appreciate" novel and alternate functions for them—which is also to "misuse" them and to fail to respect their presumed purposes and conventional generic classifications.

The various forms of interdependence emphasized here have considerable bearing on what may be recognized as the economics of literary and aesthetic value. The traditional—idealist, humanist, genteel—tendency to isolate or protect certain aspects of life and culture, among them works of art and literature, from consideration in economic terms has had the effect of mystifying the nature—or, more accurately, the dynamics—of their value. In view of the arbitrariness of the exclusion, it is not surprising that the languages of aesthetics and economics nevertheless tend to drift toward each other and that their segregation must be constantly patrolled.[26] (Thus, an aesthetician deplores a pun on "appreciation" appearing in an article on art investment and warns of the dangers of confusing "the uniqueness of a painting that gives it scarcity value ... with its unique value as a work of art."][27] To those for whom terms such as "utility," "effectiveness," and "function" suggest gross pragmatic instrumentality, crass material desires, and the satisfaction of animal needs, a concept such as use-value will be seen as irrelevant to or clearly to be distinguished from aesthetic value. There is, however, no good reason to confine the domain of the utilitarian to objects that serve only immediate, specific, and unexalted ends or, for that matter, to assume that the value of artworks has altogether nothing to do with pragmatic instrumentality or animal needs.[28] The recurrent impulse or effort to define aesthetic value by contradistinction to all forms of utility or as the negation of all other nameable sources of interest or forms of value—hedonic, practical, sentimental, ornamental, historical, ideological, and so forth—is, in effect, to define it out of existence; for when all such particular utilities, interests, and sources of value have been subtracted, nothing remains. Or, to put this in other terms: the "essential value" of an artwork consists of everything from which it is usually distinguished.

To be sure, various candidates have been proposed for a pure, nonutilitarian, interest-free, and, in effect, value-free source of aesthetic value, such as the eliciting of "intrinsically rewarding" intellectual, sensory, or perceptual activities, or Kant's "free play of the cognitive faculties." A strict accounting of any of these seemingly gratuitous activities, however, would bring us sooner or later to their biological utility and/or survival value (and indeed to something very much like "animal needs"). For although we may be individually motivated to engage in them "for their own sake" (which is to say, for the sake of the gratifications they provide), our doing so apparently yields a long-term profit in enhanced cognitive development, behavioral flexibility, and thus biological fitness, and our general tendency to do so is in all likelihood the product of evolutionary mechanisms.[29] Moreover, as I have pointed out elsewhere, the occasioning of such activities (or "experiences") is not confined to "works of art" and therefore cannot, without circularity, be said to constitute the defining "aesthetic function" of the objects so labeled.[30] More generally, it may be observed that since there are no functions performed by artworks that may be specified as unique to them and also no way to distinguish the "rewards" provided by the art-related experiences or behavior from those provided by innumerable other kinds of experience and behavior, any distinctions drawn between "aesthetic" and "non- (or "extra-) aesthetic" value are fundamentally problematic.[31]

Suggestions of the radically contingent nature of aesthetic value are commonly countered by evidence of apparent noncontingent value: for example, the endurance of certain classic canonical works (the invocation of Homer being a topos of the critical tradition) and, if not quite Pope's "gen'ral chorus of mankind," then at least the convergent sentiments of people of education and discrimination. Certainly any theory of aesthetic value must be able to account for continuity, stability, and apparent consensus as well as for drift, shift, and diversity. The tendency throughout formal aesthetic axiology has been to explain the constancies and convergences by the inherent qualities of the objects and/or some set of presumed human universals and to explain the variabilities and divergences by the errors, defects, and biases of individual subjects. The classic development of this account is found in Hume's essay, *Of the Standard of Taste*, where the "catholic and universal beauty" is seen to be the result of

> [t]he relation which nature has placed between the form and the sentiment.... We shall be able to ascertain its influence ... from the durable admiration which attends those works that have survived all the caprices of mode and fashion, all the mistakes of ignorance and envy.
>
> The same Homer who pleased at Athens two thousand years ago, is still admired at Paris and London. All the changes of climate, government, religion and language have not been able to obscure his glory....
>
> It appears then, that amidst all the variety and caprice of taste, there are certain general principles of approbation and blame, whose influence a careful eye may trace in all the operations of the mind. Some particular forms or qualities, from the original structure of the internal fabric are calculated to please, and others to displease; and if they fail of their effect in any particular instance, it is from some apparent defect or imperfection in the organ.
>
> Many and frequent are the defects ... which prevent or weaken the influence of those general principles.[32]

The essay continues by enumerating and elaborating these defects, introducing the familiar catalog (already given vivid expression in, among other places, Pope's *Essay on Criticism:* "Of all the causes which conspire to blind / Man's erring judgment and misguide the mind") with an analogy, also a commonplace of the tradition, between "the perfect beauty," as agreed upon by men "in a sound state of the organ," and "the true and real colors" of objects as they appear "in daylight to the eye of a man in health."[33]

The following is a more recent statement of the traditional view:

> False judgments and intuitions of an object can only be corrected if
> there is a correct and permanently valid intuition of an object. . . .
> The relativity of value judgments merely proves that subjective
> judgments are conjoined with the person, that mistaken
> judgments—of which there is no dearth in the history of
> literature—are always the fault of the person.
>
> . . . Just as the universal validity of a mathematical proposition
> does not necessarily imply that everyone can understand it, "but
> merely that everyone who understands it must agree with it," so the
> universal validity of aesthetic value does not necessarily mean that
> evidence of it is felt by everyone. Aesthetic values demand an
> adequate attitude, a trained or reliably functioning organ. Moreover,
> the fact that the history of literature contains, albeit tacitly, a firm
> gradation of valuable works of art is an indication that values
> transcend historicity.
>
> . . . The value-feeling organ must not be encumbered with
> prejudgments, pre-feelings, or arbitrarily formed opinions if it
> wishes to address itself adequately to the object, a process that is by
> no means always easy, . . . for the human being is in part—an
> external but not uninfluential part—a historical creature,
> embedded in a whole cluster of behavior compulsions that stem
> from his environment.[34]

This conflation of, among others, Hume, Kant, Nicolai Hartmann, and
Roman Ingarden is remarkable only in making particularly flagrant the
logical incoherence of the standard account, whether in its empiricist,
idealist, or phenomenological guise.

Given a more sophisticated formulation, Hume's belief that the individual experience of "beauty" can be related to "forms" and "qualities"
that gratify human beings "naturally" by virtue of certain physiological
structures and psychological mechanisms is probably not altogether
without foundation.[35] Taken as a ground for the justification of normative
claims, however, and transformed accordingly into a model of standards-
and-deviations, it obliged him (as it did and does many others) to interpret
as so many instances of individual pathology what are, rather, the variable
products of the interaction between, on the one hand, certain *relatively*
uniform innate structures, mechanisms, and tendencies and, on the
other, innumerable cultural and contextual variables as well as other individual variables—the latter including particulars of personal history,
temperament, age, and so forth. What produces evaluative consensus,
such as it is, is not the healthy functioning of universal organs but the
playing out of the *same* dynamics and variable contingencies that produce evaluative divergences.

Although value is always subject-relative, not all value is equally subject-variable. Within a particular community, the tastes and preferences of subjects—that is, their tendency to find more satisfaction of a particular kind in one rather than another of some array of comparable items and to select among them accordingly—will be conspicuously *divergent* (or indeed idiosyncratic) to the extent that the satisfactions in question are themselves functions of types of needs, interests, and resources that (*a*) vary individually along a wide spectrum, (*b*) are especially resistant, if not altogether intractable, to cultural channeling, and/ or (*c*) are especially responsive to circumstantial context. Conversely, their tastes and preferences will tend to be similar to the extent that the satisfactions in question are functions of types of needs, interests, and resources that (*a*) vary individually within a narrow spectrum, (*b*) are especially tractable to cultural channeling, and (*c*) remain fairly stable under a variety of conditions.

Insofar as satisfactions ("aesthetic" or any other: erotic, for example) with regard to some array of objects are functions of needs, interests, and resources of the first kind, preferences for those objects will appear "subjective," "eccentric," "stubborn," and "capricious." Insofar as they are functions of the second, preferences will seem so obvious, "natural," and "rational" as not to appear to be matters of taste at all. Indeed, it is precisely under the latter conditions that the value of particular objects will appear to be inherent, that distinctions or gradations of value among them will appear to reduce to differences in the properties or qualities of the objects themselves, and that explicit judgments of their value will appear to be objective. In short, here as elsewhere, a co-incidence of contingencies among individual subjects will be interpreted by those subjects as noncontingency.

Because we are dealing here not with two opposed sets of discrete determinants but with the possibility of widely differing specifications for a large number of complexly interacting variables, we may expect to find a continuous exhibition of every degree of divergence and convergence among the subjects in a particular community over the course of its history, depending in each instance on the extent of the disparity and uniformity of each of the relevant contingencies *and* on the strength of various social practices and cultural institutions that control the exhibition of extreme "deviance."[36] It may be noted that the latter—that is, the normative mechanisms within a community that suppress divergence and tend to obscure as well as deny the contingency of value—will always have, as their counterpart, a *counter*mechanism that permits a recognition of that contingency and a more or less genial acknowledgement of the inevitability of divergence: hence the ineradicability, in spite of the efforts of establishment axiology, of what might be called folk-relativism: "Chacun à son goût"; "De gustibus ... "; "One man's meat is another's poison"; and so forth.

The prevailing structure of tastes and preferences (and the consequent illusion of a consensus based on objective value) will always be implicitly threatened or directly challenged by the divergent tastes and preferences of some subjects within the community (for example, those not yet adequately acculturated, such as the young, and others with "uncultivated" tastes, such as provincials and social upstarts) as well as by most subjects outside it or, more significantly, on its *periphery* and who thus have occasion to interact with its members (for example, exotic visitors, immigrants, colonials, and members of various minority or marginalized groups). Consequently, institutions of evaluative authority will be called upon repeatedly to devise arguments and procedures that validate the community's established tastes and preferences, thereby warding off barbarism and the constant apparition of an imminent collapse of standards and also justifying the exercise of their own normative authority. In Hume's words, "It is natural to seek a Standard of Taste; a rule by which the various sentiments of men may be reconciled; at least a decision afforded confirming one sentiment and denying another"—the usefulness of such a rule to the latter end being illustrated in the essay by that memorable vignette of the barbarian in the drawing room who "would assert an equality of genius and elegance between Ogilby and Milton or Bunyan and Addison" and what ensues: "Though there may be found *persons* who give preference to the former authors, *no one* pays attention to such taste; and *we* pronounce without scruple the sentiment of these pretended critics to be absurd and ridiculous."[37] The sequence emphasized here is no less telling than the embarrassment of the argument by the examples.

Both informally, as in the drawing rooms of men of cultivation and discrimination or the classrooms of the literary academy, and formally, as in Hume's essay and throughout the central tradition of Western critical theory, the validation commonly takes the form of privileging absolutely—that is, "standard"-izing—the particular contingencies that govern the preferences of the members of the group and discounting or, as suggested above, pathologizing all other contingencies.[38] Thus it will be assumed or maintained: (*a*) that the particular *functions* they expect and desire the class of objects in question (for example, "works of art" or "literature") to perform are their intrinsic or proper functions, all other expected, desired, or emergent functions being inappropriate, irrelevant, extrinsic, abuses of the true nature of those objects or violations of their authorially intended or generically intrinsic purposes; (*b*) that the particular *conditions* (circumstantial, technological, institutional, and so forth) under which the members of the group typically interact with those objects are suitable, standard, or necessary for their proper appreciation, all other conditions being irregular, unsuitable, substandard, or outlandish; and, perhaps most significantly, (c) that the particular *subjects* who compose the members of the group are of sound mind and body, duly trained and informed, and generally competent, all other subjects being defective, deficient, or deprived—suffering from crudenesses of sensibility, diseases and distortions of perception, weaknesses of character, impoverishment of background-and-education, cultural or historical biases, ideological or personal prejudices, and/or undeveloped, corrupted, or jaded tastes.

With regard to this last point (c), we may recall here the familiar specifications of the "ideal critic" as one who, in addition to possessing various exemplary natural endowments and cultural competencies, has, through exacting feats of self-liberation, freed himself of all forms of particularity and individuality, all special interests (or, as in Kant, all interests whatsoever), and thus of all bias—which is to say, one who is "free" of everything in relation to which any experience or judgment of value occurs. (In these respects, the ideal critic of aesthetic axiology is the exact counterpart of the "ideal reader" of literary hermeneutics.)

We may also note, with regard to the first point (a), that the privileging of a particular set of functions for artworks or works of literature may be (and often is) itself justified on the grounds that the performance of such functions serves some higher individual, social, or transcendent good, such as the psychic health of the reader, the brotherhood of mankind, the glorification of God, the project of human emancipation, or the survival of Western civilization. Any selection from among these alternate and to some extent mutually exclusive higher goods, however, would itself require justification in terms of some yet *higher* good, and there is no absolute stopping point for this theoretically infinite regress of judgments and justifications. This is not to say that certain functions of artworks do not serve higher—or at least more general, comprehensive, or longer-range—goods better than others. It is to say, however, that our selection among higher goods, like our selection among any array of goods, will always be contingent.

3. The Multiple Forms, Functions, and Contexts of Evaluative Behavior

It follows from the conception of value outlined here that evaluations are not discrete acts or episodes punctuating experience but indistinguishable from the very processes of acting and experiencing themselves. In other words, for a responsive creature, to exist is to evaluate. We are always calculating how things "figure" for us—always pricing them, so to speak, in relation to the total economy of our personal universe. Throughout our lives, we perform a continuous succession of rapid-fire cost-benefit analyses, estimating the probable "worthwhileness" of alternate courses of action in relation to our always limited resources of time and energy, assessing, re-assessing, and classifying entities with respect to their probable capacity to satisfy our current needs and desires and to serve our emergent interests and long-range plans and purposes. We tend to become most conscious of our own evaluative behavior when the need to select among an array of alternate "goods" and/or to resolve an internal "contest of sentiments" moves us to specifically verbal or other symbolic forms of cost accounting: thus we draw up our lists of pros and cons, lose sleep, and bore our friends by overtly rehearsing our options, estimating the risks and probable outcomes of various actions, and so forth. Most of these calculations, however, are performed intuitively and inarticulately, and many of them are so recurrent that the habitual arithmetic becomes part of our personality and comprises the very style of our being and behavior, forming what we may call our principles or tastes—and what others may call our biases and prejudices.

I have been speaking up to this point of the evaluations we make for ourselves. As social creatures, however, we also evaluate for one another through various kinds of individual acts and also through various institutional practices. The long-standing preoccupation of aesthetic axiology with the logical form and cognitive substance of verbal "value judgments" and, in particular, with debates over their "validity," "truth-value," and "verifiability," has obscured the operation and significance of institutional and other less overt forms of evaluation. It has also deflected attention from the social contexts, functions, and consequences of all forms of aesthetic and literary evaluation, including their complex productive relation to literary and aesthetic value. Although I am more concerned here with the latter questions and shall return to them below, some comments on *explicit* aesthetic judgments (and on certain familiar axiological perplexities regarding them) are in order.

Evaluations are among the most fundamental forms of social communication and probably among the most primitive benefits of social interaction. (Animals—insects and birds as well as mammals—evaluate *for* one another, that is, signal to other members of their group the "quality" of a food supply or territory by some form of specialized overt behavior.)[39] We not only produce but also solicit and seek out both "expressions of personal sentiment" and "objective judgments of value" because, although neither will (for nothing can) give us "knowledge" of *the* value of an object, both may let us know other things we could find useful. For example, other people's reports of how well certain objects have gratified them, though "mere expressions of subjective likes and dislikes," may nevertheless be useful to us if we ourselves have produced those objects or if—as lovers, say, or parents or potential associates—we have an independently motivated interest in the current states, specific responses, or general structure of tastes and preferences of those people. Also, an assertion that some object (for example, some artwork) is good, great, bad, or middling can, no matter how magisterially delivered or with what attendant claims or convictions of absoluteness, usually be unpacked as a judgment of its *contingent* value: specifically, as the evaluator's observation and/or estimate of how well that object, relative to others of the same implied category, has performed and/or is likely to perform certain particular (though taken-for-granted) functions for some particular (though only implicitly defined) set of subjects under some particular (unspecified but assumed) set or range of conditions. Any evaluation, therefore, is "cognitively substantial" in the sense of being potentially informative about *something.* The actual interest of that information, however, and hence the value of that evaluation to *us* (and "we" are always heterogeneous) will vary, depending on, among other things, the extent to which we have any interest in the object evaluated, believe that we take for granted the same taken-for-granted functions and assume the same assumed conditions, and also think that we (or others whose interests are of interest to us) are among that implicitly defined set of subjects—or, of course, the extent to which we have an interest in the evaluator's sentiments by reason of our independently motivated interest in him or her.

In view of the centrality of the question in post-Kantian aesthetic axiology, it may be noted that if the set of relevant subjects implied by an evaluation is not contextually defined or otherwise indicated, it will usually be appropriately taken to consist of the evaluator himself and all others whom s/he believes are *like* himself or herself in the pertinent respects. Of course, some evaluators believe that *all* other people are—or should be—like themselves in the pertinent respects: hence, apparently, the curious and distracting notion that every aesthetic judgment "claims universal subjective validity."[40] The familiar subjectivist/objectivist controversy is commonly seen to turn on whether, in making an aesthetic judgment, I speak "for myself *alone*" or "for *everyone.*" A consideration of the social functions of such judgments, however, suggests that, if such a formulation is wanted at all, it should be that, in making aesthetic judgments, I tend to speak "for myself *and some others.*"

We may also consider here what is thought to be the suspect propositional status of value judgments as distinguished from and compared to that of so-called factual statements and the consequent demotion of the former to the status of "pseudostatements." There is, of course, no way for us to be certain that someone's reports of his or her personal likes or dislikes are sincere, or that the estimates and observations offered are the estimates and observations actually made. Like all other utterances, value judgments are context-dependent and shaped by the relation of the speaker to his or her audience and by the structure of interests that sustains the verbal transaction between them. (In effect, there is no such thing as an honest opinion.) For this reason, we will always interpret (supplement and discount) evaluations in the light of other knowledge we have of the evaluator (or think we have: there is no absolute end to this regress, though in practice we do the best we can), including our sense—on whatever grounds—of the possibility of flattery or other kinds of deception: the evaluator may be the author's personal friend or professional rival, s/he may not want to hurt the cook's feelings, s/he may want to recommend himself or herself by creating the impression that s/he shares our tastes, and so forth. In all these respects, however, value judgments are no different from any other kind of utterance, and neither their reliability nor their "validity" as "propositions" is any more (or any less) compromised by these possibilities than that of any other type of verbal behavior, from someone's saying (or otherwise implying) that s/he has a headache to his or her solemn report of the measurement of a scientific instrument.

There is a tenacious conviction among those who argue these questions that unless one judgment can be said or shown to be more "valid" than another, then all judgments must be "equal" or "equally valid." Indeed, it is the horror or apparent absurdity of such egalitarianism that commonly gives force to the charge that "relativism" produces social chaos or is a logically untenable position. While the radical contingency of all value certainly does imply that no value judgment can be more valid than another in the sense of being a more accurate statement of *the* value of an object (for the latter concept then becomes vacuous), it does not follow that all value judgments are equal or equally valid. On the contrary, what does follow is that the concept of "validity" is *inappropriate* with regard to evaluations and that there is no nontrivial parameter with respect to which they *could* be "equal." This is not to say that no evaluations can be better or worse than others. What must be emphasized, however, is that the value—the "goodness" or "badness"—of an evaluation, like that of anything else (including any other type of utterance), is *itself* contingent, and thus a matter not of its abstract "truth-value" but of how well it performs various desired/able functions for the various people who may at any time be concretely involved with it. In the case of an aesthetic evaluation, these people will always include the evaluator, who will have his or her own particular interest in the various effects of the judgments s/he produces, and may also include anyone from the artist to a potential publisher or patron, various current or future audiences of the work, and perhaps someone who just likes to know what's going on and what other people think is going on. Each of them will have his or her own interest in the evaluation, and it will be better or worse for each of them in relation to a different set of desired/able functions. What all this suggests is that the obsessive debates over the cognitive substance, logical status, and "truth-value" of aesthetic judgments are not only unresolvable in the terms given but, strictly speaking, pointless.

As was indicated above, the value of an explicit verbal evaluation— that is, its utility to those who produce and receive it—will, like that of any other type of utterance, always be a function of specific features of the various transactions of which it may be a part, including the relevant interests of the speaker and any of those who, at any time, become members of his or her de facto audience. It follows that the value of a value judgment may also be quite minimal or negative. For example, depending on specific (and readily imaginable) contextual features, an aesthetic judgment may be excruciatingly *uninteresting* to the listener or elicited from the speaker at considerable expense to himself or herself. Also, aesthetic judgments, like any other use of language, may be intimidating, coercive, and otherwise socially and politically oppressive. If they ??? propositional status (and "justifying" them—that is, giving a show of justice to their claims of objectivity or universal validity—will not eliminate the oppression) but, once again, because of the nature of the transactions of which they are a part, particularly the social or political relationship between the evaluator and his or her audience (professor and student, for example, or censor and citizen) and the structure of power that governs that relationship.[41] We may return now from the discussion of individual overt value judgments to the more general consideration of evaluative behavior, normative institutions, and the social mechanisms by which literary and aesthetic value are produced.

4. The Cultural Re-Production of Value

We do not move about in a raw universe. Not only are the objects we encounter always to some extent pre-interpreted and preclassified for us by our particular cultures and languages, but also pre-evaluated, bearing the marks and signs of their prior valuings and evaluations by our fellow creatures. Indeed, preclassification is itself a form of pre-evaluation, for the labels or category names under which we encounter objects not only, as was suggested earlier, foreground certain of their possible functions but also operate as signs—in effect, as culturally certified endorsements—of their more or less effective performance of those functions.

Like all other objects, works of art and literature bear the marks of their own evaluational history, signs of value that acquire their force by virtue of various social and cultural practices and, in this case, certain highly specialized and elaborated institutions. The labels "art" and "literature" are, of course, commonly signs of membership in distinctly honorific categories. The particular functions that may be endorsed by these labels, however, are, unlike those of "doorstops" and "clocks," neither narrowly confined nor readily specifiable but, on the contrary, exceptionally heterogeneous, mutable, and elusive. To the extent—always limited—that the relation between these labels and a particular set of expected and desired functions is stabilized within a community, it is largely through the normative activities of various institutions: most significantly, the literary and aesthetic academy which, among other things, develops pedagogic and other acculturative mechanisms directed at maintaining at least (and, commonly, at most) a *sub*population of the community whose members "appreciate the value" of works of art and literature "as such." That is, by providing them with "necessary backgrounds," teaching them "appropriate skills," "cultivating their interests," and, generally, "developing their tastes," the academy produces generation after generation of subjects for whom the objects and texts thus labeled do indeed perform the functions thus privileged, thereby insuring the continuity of mutually ???.

It will be instructive at this point to consider the very beginning of a work's valuational history, namely, its initial evaluation by the artist (here, the author); for it is not only a prefiguration of all the subsequent acts of evaluation of which the work will become the subject but also a model or paradigm of all evaluative activity generally. I refer here not merely to that ultimate gesture of authorial judgment that must exhibit itself negatively—that is, in the author's either letting the work stand or ripping it up—but to the thousand individual acts of approval and rejection, preference and assessment, trial and revision that constitute the entire process of literary composition. The work we receive is not so much the achieved consummation of that process as its enforced abandonment: "abandonment" not because the author's techniques are inadequate to his or her goals but because the goals themselves are inevitably multiple, mixed, mutually competing, and thus mutually constraining, and also because they are inevitably unstable, changing their nature and relative potency and priority during the very course of composition. The completed work is thus always, in a sense, a temporary truce among contending forces, achieved at the point of exhaustion, that is, the literal depletion of the author's current resources or, given the most fundamental principle of the economics of existence, at the point when the author simply has something else—more worthwhile—to do: when, in other words, the time and energy s/he would have to give to further tinkering, testing, and adjustment are no longer compensated for by an adequately rewarding sense of continuing interest in the process or increased satisfaction in the product.

It is for comparable reasons that we, as readers of the work, will later let our own experience of it stand: not because we have fully "appreciated" the work, not because we have exhausted all its possible sources of interest and hence of value, but because we, too, ultimately have something else—more worthwhile—to do. The reader's experience of the work is pre-figured—that is, both calculated and pre-enacted—by the author in other ways as well: for, in selecting this word, adjusting that turn of phrase, preferring this rhyme to that, the author is all the while testing the local and global effectiveness of each decision by impersonating in advance his or her various presumptive audiences, who thereby themselves participate in shaping the work they will later read. Every literary work—and, more generally, artwork—is thus the product of a complex evaluative feedback loop that embraces not only the ever-shifting economy of the artist's own interests and resources as they evolve during and in reaction to the process of composition, but also all the shifting economies of his or her assumed and imagined audiences, including those who do not yet exist but whose emergent interests, variable conditions of encounter, and rival sources of gratification the artist will attempt to predict—or will intuitively surmise—and to which, among other things, his or her own sense of the fittingness of each decision will be responsive.[43]

But this also describes all the other diverse forms of evaluation by which the work will be subsequently marked and its value reproduced and transmitted: that is, the innumerable implicit acts of evaluation performed by those who, as may happen, publish the work, purchase, preserve, display, quote, cite, translate, perform, allude to, and imitate it; the more explicit but casual judgments made, debated, and negotiated in informal contexts by readers and by all those others in whose personal economies the work, in some way, "figures"; and the highly specialized institutionalized forms of evaluation exhibited in the more or less professional activities of scholars, teachers, and academic or journalistic critics—not only their full-dress reviews and explicit rank-orderings, evaluations, and revaluations, but also such activities as the awarding of literary prizes, the commissioning and publishing of articles about certain works, the compiling of anthologies, the writing of introductions, the construction of department curricula, and the drawing up of class reading lists. All these forms of evaluation, whether overt or covert, verbal or inarticulate, and whether performed by the common reader, professional reviewer, big-time bookseller, or small-town librarian, have functions and effects that are significant in the production and maintenance or destruction of literary value, both reflecting and contributing to the various economies in relation to which a work acquires value. And each of the evaluative acts mentioned, like those of the author, represents a set of individual economic decisions, an ajudication among competing claims for limited resources of time, space, energy, attention—or, of course, money—and also, insofar as the evaluation in a socially responsive act or part of a social transaction, a set of surmises, assumptions, or predictions regarding the personal economies of other people.

Although, as I have emphasized, the evaluation of texts is not confined to the formal critical judgments issued within the rooms of the literary academy or upon the pages of its associated publications, the activities of the academy certainly figure significantly in the production of literary value. For example, the repeated inclusion of a particular work in literary anthologies not only promotes the value of that work but goes some distance toward creating its value, as does also its repeated appearance on reading lists or its frequent citation or quotation by professors, scholars, and academic critics. For all these acts, at the least, have the effect of drawing the work into the orbit of attention of a population of potential readers; and, by making it more accessible to the interests of those readers (while, as indicated above, at the same time shaping and supplying the very interests in relation to which they will experience the work), they make it more likely both that the work will be experienced at all and also that it will be experienced as valuable.

The converse side to this process is well known. Those who are in positions to edit anthologies and prepare reading lists are obviously those who occupy positions of some cultural power; and their acts of evaluation—represented in what they exclude as well as in what they include—constitute not merely recommendations of value but, for the reasons just mentioned, also determinants of value. Moreover, since they will usually exclude not only what they take to be inferior literature but also what they take to be nonliterary, subliterary, or paraliterary, their selections not only imply certain "criteria" of literary value, which may in fact be made explicit, but, more significantly, they produce and maintain certain definitions of "literature" and, thereby, certain assumptions about the desired and expected functions of the texts so classified and about the interests of their appropriate audiences, all of which are usually not explicit and, for that reason, less likely to be questioned, challenged, or even noticed. Thus the privileging power of evaluative authority may be very great, even when it is manifested inarticulately.[44] The academic activities described here, however, are only a small part of the complex process of literary canonization.

When we consider the cultural re-production of value on a larger time scale, the model of evaluative dynamics outlined above suggests that the "survival" or "endurance" of a text—and, it may be, its achievement of high canonical status not only as a "work of literature" but as a "classic"—is the product neither of the objectively (in the Marxist sense) conspiratorial force of establishment institutions nor of the continuous appreciation of the timeless virtues of a fixed object by succeeding generations of isolated readers, but, rather, of a series of continuous interactions among a variably constituted object, emergent conditions, and mechanisms of cultural selection and transmission. These interactions are, in certain respects, analogous to those by virtue of which biological species evolve and survive and also analogous to those through which artistic choices evolve and are found fit or fitting by the individual artist. The operation of these cultural-historical dynamics may be briefly indicated here in quite general terms.

At a given time and under the contemporary conditions of available materials, technology, and techniques, a particular object—let us say a verbal artifact or text—may perform certain desired/able functions quite well for some set of subjects. It will do so by virtue of certain of its "properties" as they have been specifically constituted—framed, foregrounded, and configured—by those subjects under those conditions and in accord with their particular needs, interests, and resources—and also perhaps largely as pre-figured by the artist who, as described earlier, in the very process of producing the work and continuously evaluating its fitness and adjusting it accordingly, will have multiply and variably constituted it. Two points implied by this description need emphasis here. One is that the value of a work—that is, its effectiveness in performing ??? of subjects—is not independent of authorial design, labor, and skill. The second, however, is that what may be spoken of as the "properties" of the work—its "structure," "features," "qualities," and, of course, its "meanings"—are not fixed, given, or inherent in the work "itself" but are at every point the variable products of some subject's interaction with it. (It is thus never "the *same* Homer.") To the extent that any aspect of a work is recurrently constituted in similar ways by various subjects at various times, it will be because the subjects who do the constituting, *including the author*, are themselves similar, not only in being human creatures and in occupying a particular universe that may be, for them, in many respects recurrent or relatively continuous and stable, but also in inheriting from one another, through mechanisms of cultural transmission, certain ways of interacting with that universe, including certain ways of interacting with texts and "works of literature."

An object or artifact that performs certain desired/able functions particularly well at a given time for some community of subjects, being perhaps not only "fit" but exemplary—that is, "the best of its kind"—under those conditions, will have an immediate survival advantage; for, relative to (or in competition with) other comparable objects or artifacts available at that time, it will not only be better protected from physical deterioration but will also be more frequently used or widely exhibited and, if it is a text or verbal artifact, more frequently read or recited, copied or reprinted, translated, imitated, cited, and commented upon—in short, culturally re-produced—and thus will be more readily available to perform those or other functions for other subjects at a subsequent time.

Two possible trajectories ensue:

1. If, on the one hand, under the changing and emergent conditions of that subsequent time, the functions for which the text was earlier valued are no longer desired/able or if, in competition with comparable works (including, now, those newly produced with newly available materials and techniques), it no longer performs those original functions particularly well, it will, accordingly, be less well maintained and less frequently cited and recited so that its visibility as well as interest will fade, and it will survive, if at all, simply as a physical relic. It may, of course, be subsequently valued specifically *as* a relic (for its archeological or "historical" interest), in which case it *will* be performing desired/able functions and pursue the trajectory described below. It may also be subsequently "rediscovered" as an "unjustly neglected masterpiece," either when the functions it had originally performed are again desired/able or, what is more likely, when different of its properties and possible functions become foregrounded by a new set of subjects with emergent interests and purposes.

2. If, on the other hand, under changing conditions and in competition with newly produced and other re-produced works, it continues to perform *some* desired/able functions particularly well, even if not the same ones for which it was initially valued (and, accordingly, by virtue of *other* newly foregrounded or differently framed or configured properties—including, once again, emergent "meanings"), it will continue to be cited and recited, continue to be visible and available to succeeding generations of subjects, and thus continue to be culturally re-produced. A work that has in this way survived for some time can always move into a trajectory of extinction through the sudden emergence or gradual conjunction of unfavorable conditions of the kind described above under (1). There are, however, a number of reasons why, once it has achieved canonical status, it will be more secured from that risk.

First, when the value of a work is seen as unquestionable, those of its features that would, in a noncanonical work, be found alienating—for example, technically crude, philosophically naive, or narrowly topical— will be glozed over or backgrounded. In particular, features that conflict intolerably with the interests and ideologies of subsequent subjects (and, in the West, with those generally benign "humanistic" values for which canonical works are commonly celebrated)—for example, incidents or sentiments of brutality, bigotry, and racial, sexual, or national chauvinism—will be repressed or rationalized, and there will be a tendency among humanistic scholars and academic critics to "save the text" by transferring the locus of its interest to more formal or structural features and/or allegorizing its potentially alienating ideology to some more general ("universal") level where it becomes more tolerable and also more readily interpretable in terms of contemporary ideologies. Thus we make texts timeless by suppressing their temporality. (It may be added that to those scholars and critics for whom those features are not only palatable but for whom the value of the canonical works consists precisely in their "embodying" and "preserving" such "traditional values," the transfer of the locus of value to formal properties will be seen as a descent into formalism and "aestheticism," and the tendency to allegorize it too generally or to interpret it too readily in terms of "modern values" will be seen not as saving the text but as betraying it.)

Second, in addition to whatever various and perhaps continuously differing functions a work performs for succeeding generations of individual subjects, it will also begin to perform certain characteristic cultural functions by virtue of the very fact that it *has* endured—that is, the functions of a canonical work as such—and will be valued and preserved accordingly: as a witness to lost innocence, former glory, and/or apparently persistent communal interests and "values" and thus a banner of communal identity; as a reservoir of images, archtypes, and topoi—characters and episodes, passages and verbal tags—repeatedly invoked and recurrently applied to new situations and circumstances; and as a stylistic and generic exemplar that will energize the production of subsequent works and texts (upon which the latter will be modeled and by which, as a normative "touchstone," they will be measured). In these ways, the canonical work begins increasingly not merely to survive within but to shape and create the culture in which its value is produced and transmitted and, for that very reason, to perpetuate the conditions of its own flourishing. Nothing endures like endurance.

To the extent that we develop within and are formed by a culture that is itself constituted in part *by* canonical texts, it is not surprising that those texts seem, as Hans-Georg Gadamer puts it, to "speak" to us "directly" and even "specially":

> The classical is what is preserved precisely because it signifies and interprets itself; [that is,] that which speaks in such a way that it is not a statement about what is past, as mere testimony to something that needs to be interpreted, but says something to the present as if it were said specially to us. ... This is just what the word "classical" means, that the duration of the power of a work to speak directly is fundamentally unlimited.[45]

It is hardly, however, as Gadamer implies here, because such texts are uniquely self-mediated or unmediated and hence not needful of interpretation but, rather, because they have already been so thoroughly mediated—evaluated as well as interpreted—for us by the very culture and cultural institutions through which they have been preserved and by which we ourselves have been formed.

What is commonly referred to as "the test of time" (Gadamer, for example, characterizes "the classical" as "a notable mode of 'being historical,' that historical process of preservation that through the constant proving of itself sets before us something that is true")[46] is not, as the figure implies, an impersonal and impartial mechanism; for the cultural institutions through which it operates (schools, libraries, theaters, museums, publishing and printing houses, editorial boards, prize-awarding commissions, state censors, etc.) are, of course, all managed by persons (who, by definition, are those with cultural power and commonly other forms of power as well), and, since the texts that are selected and preserved by "time" will always tend to be those which "fit" (and, indeed, have often been *designed* to fit) their characteristic needs, interests, resources, and purposes, that testing mechanism has its own built-in partialities accumulated in and thus *intensified by* time. For example, the characteristic resources of the culturally dominant members of a community include access to specific training and the opportunity and occasion to develop not only competence in a larger number of cultural codes but also a large number of diverse (or "cosmopolitan") interests. The works that are differentially re-produced, therefore, will often be those that gratify the exercise of such competencies and engage interests of that kind: specifically, works that are structurally complex and, in the technical sense, information-rich—and which, by virtue of those very qualities, are especially amenable to multiple reconfiguration, more likely to enter into relation with the emergent interests of various subjects, and thus more readily adaptable to emergent conditions.[47] Also, as is often remarked, since those with cultural power tend to be members of socially, economically, and politically established classes (or to serve them and identify their own interests with theirs), the texts that survive will tend to be those that appear to reflect and reinforce establishment ideologies. However much canonical works may be seen to "question" secular vanities such as wealth, social position, and political power, "remind" their readers of more elevated values and virtues, and oblige them to "confront" such hard truths and harsh realities as their own mortality and the hidden griefs of obscure people, they would not be found to please long and well if they were seen to undercut establishment interests *radically* or to subvert the ideologies that support them *effectively*. (Construing them to the latter ends, of course, is one of the characteristic ways in which those with antiestablishment interests participate in the cultural re-production of canonical texts and thus in their endurance as well.)

It is clear that the needs, interests, and purposes of culturally and otherwise dominant members of a community do not exclusively or totally determine which works survive. The antiquity and longevity of domestic proverbs, popular tales, children's verbal games, and the entire phenomenon of what we call "folklore," which occurs through the same or corresponding mechanisms of cultural selection and re-production as those described above specifically for "texts," demonstrate that the "endurance" of a verbal artifact (if not its achievement of *academic* canonical status as a "work of literature"—many folkloric works do, however, perform all the functions described above as characteristic of canonical works *as such*) may be more or less independent of institutions controlled by those with political power. Moreover, the interests and purposes of the latter must always operate in interaction with non- or antiestablishment interests and purposes as well as with various other contingencies and "accidents of time" over which they have limited, if any, control, from the burning of libraries to political and social revolutions, religious iconoclasms, and shifts of dominance among entire languages and cultures.

As the preceding discussion suggests, the value of a literary work is continuously produced and re-produced by the very acts of implicit and explicit evaluation that are frequently invoked as "reflecting" its value and therefore as being evidence of it. In other words, what are commonly taken to be the *signs* of literary value are, in effect, also its *springs*. The endurance of a classic canonical author such as Homer, then, owes not to the alleged transcultural or universal value of his works but, on the contrary, to the continuity of their circulation in a particular culture. Repeatedly cited and recited, translated, taught and imitated, and thoroughly enmeshed in the network of intertextuality that continuously *constitutes* the high culture of the orthodoxly educated population of the West (and the Western-educated population of the rest of the world), that highly variable entity we refer to as "Homer" recurrently enters our experience in relation to a large number and variety of our interests and thus can perform a large number of various functions for us and obviously has performed them for many of us over a good bit of the history of our culture. It is well to recall, however, that there are many people in the world who are not—or are not yet, or choose not to be—among the orthodoxly educated population of the West: people who do not encounter Western classics at all or who encounter them under cultural and institutional conditions very different from those of American and European college professors and their students. The fact that Homer, Dante, and Shakespeare do not figure significantly in the personal economies of these peo-

ple, do not perform individual or social functions that gratify their interests, *do not have value for them,* might properly be taken as qualifying
the claims of transcendent universal value made for such works. As we
know, however, it is routinely taken instead as evidence or confirmation
of the cultural deficiency—or, more piously, "deprivation"—of such people. The fact that other verbal artifacts (not necessarily "works of literature" or even "texts") and other objects and events (not necessarily
"works of art" or even artifacts) have performed and do perform for them
the various functions that Homer, Dante, and Shakespeare perform for us
and, moreover, that the possibility of performing the totality of such functions is always distributed over the totality of texts, artifacts, objects, and
events—a possibility continuously realized and thus a value continuously "appreciated"—commonly cannot be grasped or acknowledged by
the custodians of the Western canon.

NOTES

1. The most recent of these include E. D. Hirsch, Jr., *The Aims of Interpreta-
    tion* (Chicago, 1976), esp. the essays "Evaluation as Knowledge" (1968) and
    "Privileged Criteria in Evaluation" (1969); Murray Krieger, "Literary Analy-
    sis and Evaluation—and the Ambidextrous Critic," in *Criticism: Specula-
    tive and Analytic Essays,* ed. L. S. Dembo (Madison, Wis., 1968); a number
    of brief essays by Anglo-American as well as continental European theorists
    in *Problems of Literary Evaluation,* ed. Joseph Strelka (University Park, Pa.
    and London, 1969); and the chapters on value and evaluation in John Ellis,
    The Theory of Literary Criticism (Berkeley and Los Angeles, 1974), John
    Reichert, *Making Sense of Literature* (Chicago, 1977), and Jeffrey Sammons,
    Literary Sociology and Practical Criticism (Bloomington, Ind. and London,
    1977). All of them either participate directly in the self-justifying academic
    debates outlined below or are haunted by them into equivocation.
2. F. R. Leavis, *Revaluation: Tradition and Development in English Poetry*
    (London, 1936; New York, 1963), pp. 5–6.
3. See esp. A. J. Ayer, *Language, Truth, and Logic* (London, 1936).
4. Yvor Winters, *The Function of Criticism* (Denver, 1957), p. 17.
5. W. K. Wimsatt, Jr., *The Verbal Icon* (Louisville, Ky., 1954), p. 250.
6. See the discussion of David Hume below, pp. 15–18.
7. I. A. Richards, *Principles of Literary Criticism* (1924; London, 1960), pp. 5–
    6. "The two pillars upon which a theory of criticism must rest," Richards
    declared, "are an account of value and an account of communication" (p. 25).
    It was, of course, the latter that subsequently became the overriding concern
    of critical theory.
8. Ibid., p. 206.
9. Northrop Frye, *Anatomy of Criticism: Four Essays* (Princeton, N.J., 1957),
    pp. 18, 19; all further references to this work, abbreviated *AC,* will be in-
    cluded in the text.

10. It should be recalled that, like many others (e.g., Hirsch [see n. 12 below]), Frye continued to maintain that *interpretive* criticism could lay claim to objectivity. See his remarks in a paper delivered in 1967: "The fundamental critical act . . . is the act of recognition, seeing what is there, as distinguished from merely seeing in a Narcissus mirror of our own experience and social and moral prejudice. . . . When a critic interprets, he is talking about his poet; when he evaluates, he is talking about himself" ("Value Judgements," in *Criticism: Speculative and Analytic Essays*, p. 39).

11. Hirsch, *The Aims of Interpretation*, p. 108. See also n. 40 below, for Hirsch's neo-Kantian formulation.

12. In a recent unpublished essay, "Literary Value: The Short History of a Modern Confusion" (1980), Hirsch argues that, although literary *meaning* is determinate, literary value is not. With respect to the latter, however, he concludes that "there are some stable principles"—namely, ethical ones—"that escape the chaos of purely personal relativity" (p. 22). As will be seen in the analysis below, "personal relativity" neither produces chaos nor is in itself chaotic. The escape route of ethical principles and other appeals to higher goods are discussed below (p. 19).

13. See Jurij Tynjanov, "On Literary Evolution" (Moscow, 1927), trans. Ladislav Matejka and Krystyna Pomorska, in *Readings in Russian Poetics*, ed. Matejka and Pomorska (Cambridge, Mass., 1971); Mikhail Bakhtin, *Rabelais and His World* (Moscow, 1965), trans. Helene Iswolsky (Cambridge, Mass., 1968); and Jan Mukařovský, *Aesthetic Norm, Function, and Value as Social Facts* (Prague, 1934), trans. Mark E. Suino (Ann Arbor, Mich., 1970).

14. For surveys and discussions, see Sammons, *Literary Sociology and Practical Criticism*, and Rien T. Segers, *The Evaluation of Literary Texts: An Experimental Investigation into the Rationalization of Value Judgments with Reference to Semiotics and Esthetics of Reception* (Lisse, 1978). For a recent study of considerable interest, see Jacques Leenhardt and Pierre Józsa, *Lire la lecture: Essai du sociologie de la lecture* (Paris, 1982).

15. It is not mentioned as such, e.g., in Jonathan Culler's *Structuralist Poetics: Structuralism, Linguistics, and the Study of Literature* (Ithaca, N.Y., 1975).

16. See, e.g., the thoroughly equivocal discussions of "objective value" in Stefan Morawski, *Inquiries into Fundamentals of Aesthetics* (Cambridge, Mass. and London, 1974), and the revalorization of the standard Eng. Lit. canon in Althusserian terms in Terry Eagleton, *Criticism and Ideology: A Study in Marxist Literary Theory* (London, 1976), pp. 162–87. For other discussions of this point, see Hans Robert Jauss, "The Idealist Embarrassment: Observations on Marxist Aesthetics," *New Literary History* 7 (Autumn 1975): 191–208; Raymond Williams, *Marxism and Literature* (Oxford, 1977), esp. pp. 45–54 and 151–57; Tony Bennett, *Formalism and Marxism* (London, 1979), esp. pp. 172–75; and Peter Widdowson, " 'Literary Value' and the Reconstruction of Criticism," *Literature and History* 6 (1980): 138–50. See also n. 33 below.

17. See, however, Arkady Plotnitsky, "Constraints of the Unbound: Transformation, Value, and Literary Interpretation" (Ph.D. diss., University of Pennsylvania, 1982), for an extensive and sophisticated effort along such lines.

18. Onwuchekwa Jemie, *Langston Hughes: An Introduction to the Poetry* (New York, 1976), p. 184.

19. C. W. B. Bigsby, "Hand in Hand with the Blues," *Times Literary Supplement,* 17 June 1977, p. 734.

20. Chinweizu, letter to the editor, *Times Literary Supplement,* 15 July 1977, p. 871.

21. Thus Sammons, in his embattled book, writes of "the elements ... in the canon of great literature" to which we should be attentive so that, faced with charges of elitism, "we will not have to stand mute before claims that inarticulateness, ignorance, occult mumbling, and loutishness are just as good as fine literature" (*Literary Sociology and Practical Criticism*, p. 134).

22. See Gonzalo Munévar, *Radical Knowledge: A Philosophical Inquiry into the Nature and Limits of Science* (Indianapolis, 1981), for an elaboration of a "performance model" of scientific activity along the lines implied here.

23. For a companion piece to the present essay, see my "Fixed Marks and Variable Constancies: A Parable of Literary Value," *Poetics Today* 1 (Autumn 1979): 7–31.

24. Some aspects of this process are discussed by Pierre Bourdieu in "La Métamorphose des goûts," *Questions de sociologie* (Paris, 1980), pp. 161–72. The more general interrelations among human "needs and wants," cultural practices, and economic production have been examined by Marshall Sahlins in *Culture and Practical Reason* (Chicago, 1976), Mary Douglas in *The World of Goods* (New York, 1979), and Jean Baudrillard in *For a Critique of the Political Economy of the Sign* (Paris, 1972), trans. Charles Levin (St. Louis, 1981). Although Baudrillard's critical analysis of the concept of "use-value"—and, with it, of "sign value"—is of considerable interest for a semiotics of the marketplace, his effort to develop, "as a basis for the practical overthrow of political economy" (p. 122), a theory of a value "beyond value" (created out of what he calls "symbolic exchange") is less successful, partly because of its utopian anthropology and partly because the value in question does not escape economic accounting.

25. For an excellent analysis of the relation between classification and value, see Michael Thompson, *Rubbish Theory: The Creation and Destruction of Value* (Oxford, 1979), esp. pp. 13–56.

26. The magnetism or recurrent mutually metaphoric relation between economic and aesthetic—especially literary—discourse is documented and discussed by Marc Shell in *The Economy of Literature* (Baltimore, 1978) and Kurt Heinzelman in *The Economics of the Imagination* (Amherst, Mass., 1980).

27. Andrew Harrison, *Making and Thinking* (Indianapolis, 1978), p. 100.

28. See George J. Stigler and Gary S. Becker, "De gustibus non est disputandum," *American Economics Review* 67 (March 1977): 76–90, for an ingenious and influential attempt (at the opposite extreme, perhaps, of Baudrillard's [see n. 24 above]) to demonstrate that differences and changes of behavior (including aesthetic behavior) that appear to be matters of "taste" and, as such, beyond explanation in economic terms can be accounted for (*a*)

as functions of subtle forms of "price" and "income" and (*b*) on the usual (utilitarian) assumption that we always behave, all things considered, so as to maximize utility. As Stigler and Becker acknowledge, recent experimental studies of "choice behavior" in human (and other) subjects suggest that this latter assumption itself requires modification.

29. See Robert Fagen, *Animal Play Behavior* (Oxford, 1981), pp. 248–358, for an extensive analysis of "intrinsically rewarding" physical activities and an account of the evolutionary mechanisms that apparently produce and sustain them.

30. See the related discussion of "cognitive play" in my *On the Margins of Discourse: The Relation of Literature to Language* (Chicago, 1978), pp. 116–24.

31. Monroe Beardsley's "instrumentalist" (that is, utilitarian) theory of aesthetic value (*Aesthetics: Problems in the Philosophy of Criticism* [New York, 1958], pp. 524–76) and Mukařovský's otherwise quite subtle exploration of these questions (see n. 13, above) do not altogether escape the confinements and circularities of formalist conceptions of, respectively, "aesthetic experience" and "aesthetic function."

32. David Hume, "*Of the Standard of Taste*" *and Other Essays*, ed. John W. Lenz (Indianapolis, 1965), pp. 8–10.

33. Ibid., p. 10. At the conclusion of the essay, Hume almost—but not quite— —reinstalls the very *de gustibus* arguments that the standard of taste was presumably designed to answer: "But where there is such a diversity in the internal frame or external situation as is entirely blameless on both sides, ... a certain degree of diversity of judgment is unavoidable and we seek in vain a standard by which we can reconcile the contrary sentiments" (pp. 19–20). Of course, the qualification ("as is entirely blameless on both sides") that keeps this from being a total turnabout also introduces a new normative consideration (how to determine whether or not—or to what extent—something "in the internal frame or external situation" is *blamable*) and thus moves again toward the type of potentially infinite regress into which all axiologies typically tumble.

34. Walter Hinderer, "Literary Value Judgments and Value Cognition," trans. Leila Vannewitz, in *Problems of Literary Evaluation*, pp. 58–59.

35. The discipline of "empirical aesthetics" has been developed out of precisely such a belief. For a recent survey and discussion of its findings, see Hans and Shulamith Kreitler, *Psychology of the Arts* (Durham, N.C., 1972). See also n. 47 below.

36. See Morse Peckham, *Explanation and Power: The Control of Human Behavior* (New York, 1979), for an account of deviance (or what he calls "the delta effect") as the product of the relation between cultural practices and the randomness of behavior and, more generally, for a highly original discussion of the processes and institutions of cultural channeling.

37. Hume, "*Of the Standard of Taste*," pp. 5, 7.

38. Communities are of all sizes and so are drawing rooms: the provincials, colonials, and marginalized groups mentioned above (including the young), insofar as they constitute social communities, may also be expected to have

prevailing structures of tastes and preferences and to control them in the same ways as do more obviously "establishment" groups. Folk-relativism is neither confined to the folk nor always exhibited by them.

39. To the extent that such forms of behavior are under the control of innate mechanisms that respond directly to—or, in effect, "register"—the conditions in question, they are not, strictly speaking, verbal or symbolic. For this reason, such evaluations may be "objective" in a way that, for better or worse, no human value judgment can be.

40. Kant's tortured attempt, which occupies most of *The Critique of Judgment*, to ground such a claim on the possibility of a cognition of pure aesthetic value (that is, "beauty") produced by nothing but the free operation of universal cognitive faculties has been recently revived and supplemented by Hirsch's attempt to ground it on the possibility of "correct interpretation," specifically the "re-cognition" of that "universally valid cognition of a work . . . constituted by the kind of subjective stance adopted in its creation" (*The Aims of Interpretation*, pp. 105–6). For a recent and very thorough examination of *The Critique of Judgment*, see Paul Guyer, *Kant and the Claims of Taste* (Cambridge, Mass. and London, 1979); for a thoroughly irreverent examination of it, see Jacques Derrida, "Economimesis," trans. Richard Klein, *Diacritics* 2 (Summer 1981): 3–25.

41. I discuss these and related aspects of verbal transactions in *On the Margins of Discourse*, pp. 15–24 and 82–106, and in "Narrative Versions, Narrative Theories," *Critical Inquiry* 7 (Autumn 1980): 225–26 and 231–36.

42. Pierre Macherey and Etienne Balibar analyze some aspects of this process in "Literature as an Ideological Form: Some Marxist Propositions," trans. James Kavanagh, *Praxis* 5 (1981): 43–58.

43. See Howard Becker, *Art Worlds* (Berkeley, Los Angeles, and London, 1982), pp. 198–209, for a description of some of the specific constraints that shape both the process and its termination and, more generally, for a useful account of the ways in which artworks are produced by "social networks."

44. For a well-documented illustration of the point, see Nina Baym, "Melodramas of Beset Manhood: How Theories of American Fiction Exclude Women Authors," *American Quarterly* 33 (Summer 1981): 125–39. In addition to anthologies, Baym mentions historical studies, psychological and sociological theories of literary production, and particular methods of literary interpretation.

45. Hans-Georg Gadamer, *Truth and Method*, trans. Sheed and Ward, Ltd. (New York, 1982), pp. 257–58.

46. Ibid., p. 255.

47. Structural complexity and information-richness are, of course, subject-relative as "qualities" and also experientially subject-variable: that is, we apparently differ individually in our tolerance for complexity in various sensory/perceptual modes and in our competence in processing information in different codes, so that what is interestingly complex and engagingly information-rich to one subject may be intolerably chaotic to another. See Gerda Smets, *Aesthetic Judgment and Arousal* (Louvain, 1973), and Sven Sand-

ström, *A Common Taste in Art: An Experimental Attempt* (Lund, 1977), for two recent studies relevant to the point. Its relation to the general problem of aesthetic and literary value, itself a very complex matter, cannot be pursued here but is discussed briefly in *On the Margins of Discourse*, pp. 116–24.

Appendix A
Supplementary Readings

One: Theory

Terry Eagleton, "Conclusion: Political Criticism"
John Crowe Ransom, "Criticism, Inc."
Murray Krieger, "The Vanity of Theory and Its Value"
Susan Sontag, "Against Interpretation"
Richard Rorty, "Nineteenth-Century Idealism and Twentieth-Century Textualism"

Two: Literature

John M. Ellis, "The Definition of Literature"
Paul Valéry, "Poetry and Abstract Thought"
Jean-Paul Sartre, "What Is Writing?"
Jan Mukařovský, "Standard Language and Poetic Language"
Martin Heidegger, "The Origin of the Work of Art"

Three: Author

E. D. Hirsch, Jr., "In Defense of the Author"
Ervin Panovsky, "The Concept of Artistic Volition"
Georges Poulet, "Criticism and the Experience of Interiority"
Leon Edel, "Literature and Biography"
Roland Barthes, "Authors and Writers"

Four: Tradition

Hayden White, "The Problem of Change in Literary History"
Thomas S. Kuhn, "Postscript—1969"
Hans Robert Jauss, "Literary History as a Challenge to Literary Theory"
E. H. Gombrich, "The Analysis of Vision in the Arts"
Jorge Luis Borges, "Pierre Menard, Author of the Quixote"

Five: Conventions

Jonathan Culler, "Literary Competence"
Alastair Fowler, "The Life and Death of Literary Forms"
Harry Levin, "Notes on Convention"
Dan Ben-Amos, "Analytical Categories and Ethnic Genres"
Mary Louise Pratt, "Literary Cooperation and Implicature"

Six: Style

Meyer Shapiro, "Style"
Stephen Ullman, "Stylistics and Semantics"
Amado Alonso, "The Stylistic Interpretation of Literary Texts"
Michael Riffaterre, "Criteria for Style Analysis"
Cesare Segre, "The Stylistic Synthesis"

Seven: Narrative

Seymour Chatman, "Story Existents: Character"
E. M. Forster, "Plot"
Gerard Genette, "Time and Narrative in *A la recherche du temps perdu*"
Gerald Prince, "Introduction to the Study of the Narratee"
Erving Goffman, "The Frame Analysis of Talk"

Eight: Interpretation

R. S. Crane, "Toward a More Adequate Criticism of Poetic Structure"
Arthur C. Danto, "The Appreciation and Interpretation of Works of Art"
Hans-Georg Gadamer, "Language as the Medium of Hermeneutical Experience"
Edward Said, "Opponents, Audiences, Constituencies, and Community"
Steven Knapp and Walter Michaels, "Against Theory"

Nine: Reception

Geoffrey Hartman, "The Work of Reading"
Lev Semonovich Vygotski, "Art as Catharsis"
I. A. Richards, "Multiple Definition"
Erich Auerbach, "The Emergence of the Literary Public"
Richard Ohmann, "The Social Definition of Literature"

Ten: Evaluation

Elder Olson, "On Value Judgments in the Arts"
Eliseo Vivas, "The Esthetic Judgment"
Georg Lukács, "Healthy and Sick Art"
Jury Lotman, "On 'Bad' and 'Good' Poetry"
Walter Benjamin, "The Work of Art in the Age of Mechanical
      Reproduction"

Appendix B
Chronology

1909:   Benedetto Croce, "Taste and the Reproduction of Art."

1919:   T. S. Eliot, "Tradition and the Individual Talent."

1920:   Ervin Panovsky, "The Concept of Artistic Volition."

1923:   Boris Tomashevsky, "Literature and Biography."

1925:   Lev Semonovich Vygotski, "Art as Catharsis."

1927:   E. M. Forster, "The Plot."

1928:   Jurij Tynjanov and Roman Jakobson, "Problems in the Study of Literature and Language."

1929:   Mixail Baxtin, "Discourse Typology in Prose."

            Jurij Tynjanov, "On Literary Evolution."

1932:   Jan Mukařovský, "Standard Language and Poetic Language."

1933:   I. A. Richards, "Multiple Definition."

1935:   Martin Heidegger, "The Origin of the Work of Art."

1936:   Walter Benjamin, "The Work of Art in the Age of Mechanical Reproduction."

            Eliseo Vivas, "The Esthetic Judgment."

1938:   John Crowe Ransom, "Criticism, Inc."

1939:   Jorge Luis Borges, "Pierre Menard, Author of the Quixote."

            Paul Valéry, "Poetry and Abstract Thought."

1941:   Kenneth Burke, "[Symbolic Action]."

1942:   Amado Alonso, "The Stylistic Interpretation of Literary Texts."

            René Wellek, "The Mode of Existence of the Literary Work."

1943:   Yvor Winters, "Preliminary Problems."

1946:   W. K. Wimsatt, Jr. and Monroe C. Beardsley, "The Intentional Fallacy."

1947:   Cleanth Brooks, "The Heresy of Paraphrase."

1948:   Jean-Paul Sartre, "What Is Writing?"

         Leo Spitzer, "Linguistics and Literary History."

1950:   Harry Levin, "Noted on Convention."

1951:   Jorge Luis Borges, "Kafka and His Precursors."

         Northrop Frye, "The Archetypes of Literature."

1952:   Georg Lukács, "Healthy and Sick Art"

1953:   M. H. Abrams, "Orientation of Critical Theories."

         R. S. Crane, "Toward a More Adequate Criticism of Poetic Structure."

         Meyer Shapiro, "Style."

1958:   Erich Auerbach, "The Emergence of the Literary Public in Western Europe."

1959:   Michael Riffaterre, "Criteria for Style Analysis."

1960:   Roland Barthes, "Authors and Writers."

         Hans-Georg Gadamer, "Language as the Medium of Hermeneutical Experience."

         E. H. Gombrich, "The Analysis of Vision in the Arts."

1961:   Wayne C. Booth, "Distance and Point-of-View: An Essay in Classification."

1963:   Michel Foucault, "What Is an Author?"

1964:   Susan Sontag, "Against Interpretation."

1966:   Jacques Derrida, "Structure, Sign, and Play in the Human Sciences."

1967:   Leon Edel, "Literature and Biography."

         E. D. Hirsch, Jr., "In Defense of the Author."

         Hans Robert Jauss, "Literary History as a Challenge to Literary Theory"

1969:   Dan Ben-Amos, "Analytical Categories and Ethnic Genres."

          A. J. Greimas, "Elements of a Narrative Grammar" [rev. 1977].

          Thomas S. Kuhn, "Postscript—1969."

1970:   Monroe C. Beardsley, "Reasons and Judgments."

          Gerard Genette, "Time and Narrative in *A la recherche du temps perdu.*"

          Georges Poulet, "Criticism and the Experience of Interiority."

          Tzvetan Todorov, "Literary Genres."

1972:   Wolfgang Iser, "The Reading Process: A Phenomenological Approach."

1973:   Gerald Prince, "Introduction to the Study of the Narratee."

          Cesare Segre, "The Stylistic Synthesis."

1974:   John M. Ellis, "The Definition of Literature."

          Hans-Robert Jauss, "Literary History as a Challenge to Literary Theory."

          Elder Olson, "On Value Judgments in the Arts."

1975:   Harold Bloom, "The Dialectics of Poetic Tradition."

          Jonathan Culler, "Literary Competence."

          Nelson Goodman, "The Status of Style."

          Walter J. Ong, S. J., "The Writer's Audience Is Always a Fiction."

          Hayden White, "The Problem of Change in Literary History."

1976:   Murray Krieger, "The Vanity of Theory and Its Value."

          Jury Lotman, "On 'Bad' and 'Good' Poetry."

1978:   Seymour Chatman, "Story-Existents: Character."

1979:   Umberto Eco, "Introduction (sec. 0.1, "How to Produce Texts by Reading Them"; sec. 0.2, "The Model Reader")."

          Stanley Fish, "Demonstration vs. Persuasion: Two Models of Critical Activity."

1980:   Geoffrey Hartman, "The Work of Reading."

1981:   Mary Louise Pratt, "Literary Cooperation and Implicature."

Paul Ricoeur, "What Is a Text? Explanation and Understanding."

Richard Rorty, "Nineteenth-Century Idealism and Twentieth-Century Textualism."

1982:   Steven Knapp and Walter Benn Michaels, "Against Theory."

Julia Kristeva, "Psychoanalysis and the Polis."

Edward Said, "Opponents, Audiences, Constituencies, and Community."

1983:   Arthur C. Danto, "The Appreciation and Interpretation of Works of Art."

Terry Eagleton, "Conclusion: Political Criticism."

Barbara Herrnstein Smith, "Contingencies of Value."

Appendix C
Sources

Abrams, M. H. "Orientation of Critical Theories." In *The Mirror and the Lamp: Romantic Theory and the Critical Tradition*. New York: Oxford Univ. Press, 1953. Pp. 3–29.

Amado Alonso. "The Stylistic Interpretation of Literary Texts," *Modern Language Notes*, 57, No. 7 (Nov. 1942), 489–96.

Erich Auerbach. "The Emergence of the Literary Public in Western Europe." In *Literary Language and Its Public in Late Latin Antiquity and in the Middle Ages*. 1958; rpt. London: Routeledge and Kegan Paul, 1965. Pp. 237–52.

Roland Barthes. "Authors and Writers" [1960]. In *Critical Essays*. Tr. Richard Howard. Evanston: Northwestern Univ. Press, 1972. Pp. [141]–50.

Monroe C. Beardsley. "Reasons and Judgments." In *The Possibility of Criticism*. Detroit: Wayne State Univ. Press, 1970. Pp. 62–88, 89–111.

Dan Ben-Amos. "Analytical Categories and Ethnic Genres." *Genre*, 2, No. 3 (Sept. 1969), 275–301.

Mixail Baxtin. "Discourse Typology in Prose" [1929]. Tr. Richard Balthazar and I. R. Titunik. In *Readings in Russian Poetics: Formalist and Structuralist Views*. Ed. Ladislav Matejka and Krystyna Pomorska. Ann Arbor: Michigan Slavic Publications, 1978. Pp. 176–96.

Walter Benjamin. "The Work of Art in the Age of Mechanical Reproduction" [1936]. In *Illuminations*. New York: Schocken, 1969. Pp. 217–52.

Harold Bloom. "The Dialectics of Poetic Tradition. In *A Map of Misreading*. New York: Oxford Univ. Press, 1975. Pp. 27–40."

Wayne C. Booth. "Distance and Point-of-View: An Essay in Classification." *Essays in Criticism*, 11 (1961), 60–79.

Jorge Luis Borges. "Pierre Menard, Author of the Quixote" [1939], "Kafka and His Precursors" [1951]. In *Borges: A Reader*. Ed. Emir Rodriguez and Alastair Reid. New York: Dutton, 1981. Pp. 96–103, 242–43.

Cleanth Brooks. "The Heresy of Paraphrase." In *The Well Wrought Urn: Studies in the Structure of Poetry*. New York: Harcourt, Brace and World, 1947. Pp. 192–214.

Kenneth Burke. "[Symbolic Action] [1941]." In *The Philosophy of Literary Form: Studies in Symbolic Action.* 2nd edn. Baton Rouge: Louisiana State Univ. Press, 1967. Pp. 1–25.

Seymour Chatman. "Story-Existents: Character." In *Story and Discourse: Narrative Structure in Fiction and Film.* Ithaca: Cornell Univ. Press, 1978. Pp. 107–38.

R. S. Crane. "Toward a More Adequate Criticism of Poetic Structure." In *The Languages of Criticism and the Structure of Poetry.* Toronto: Univ. of Toronto Press, 1953. Pp. 140–94.

Benedetto Croce. "Taste and the Reproduction of Art." In *Aesthetic as Science of Expression and General Linguistic.* Tr. Douglas Ainslie. London: Macmillan, 1909. Pp. 194–210.

Jonathan Culler. "Literary Competence." In *Structuralist Poetics: Structuralism, Linguistics and the Study of Literature.* Ithaca: Cornell Univ. Press, 1975. Pp. 113–30.

Arthur C. Danto. "The Appreciation and Interpretation of Works of Art." In *Relativism in the Arts.* Ed. Betty Jean Craige. Athens: Univ. of Georgia Press, 1983. Pp. [21]–44.

Jacques Derrida. "Structure, Sign, and Play in the Human Sciences" [1966]. In *The Structuralist Controversy: The Languages of Criticism and the Sciences of Man.* Baltimore: Johns Hopkins Univ. Press, 1970. Pp. 134–56.

Terry Eagleton. "Conclusion: Political Criticism." In *Literary Theory: An Introduction.* Oxford: Basil Blackwell, 1983. Pp. 194–217.

Umberto Eco. "Introduction (sec. 0.1, "How to Produce Texts by Reading Them"; sec. 0.2, "The Model Reader")." In *The Role of the Reader: Explorations in the Semiotics of Texts.* Bloomington: Indiana Univ. Press, 1979. Pp. 3–11.

Leon Edel. "Literature and Biography." In *Relations of Literary Study.* Ed. James Thorpe. New York: Modern language Assn. of America, 1967. Pp. 57–72.

T. S. Eliot. "Tradition and the Individual Talent" [1919]. In *The Sacred Wood.* London: Faber, 1920. Pp. 47–59.

John M. Ellis. "The Definition of Literature." In *The Theory of Literature: A Logical Analysis.* Berkeley: Univ. of California Press, 1974. Pp. 24–53.

Stanley Fish. "Demonstration vs. Persuasion: Two Models of Critical Activity" [1979]. In *Is There a Text in This Class: The Authority of Interpretive Communities.* Cambridge, MA: Harvard Univ. Press, 1980. Pp. 322–28.

E. M. Forster. "The Plot." In *Aspects of the Novel.* 1927; rpt. New York: Harvest, 1964. Pp. 83–103.

Michel Foucault. "What Is an Author?" [1963]. In *Language, Counter-Memory, Practice: Selected Essays and Interviews.* Ed. Donald Bouchard. Ithaca: Cornell Univ. Press, 1977. Pp. 113–38.

Alastair Fowler. "The Life and Death of Literary Forms." *New Literary History,* 2, No. 2 (Winter 1971), 199–216.

Northrop Frye. "The Archetypes of Literature." In *Kenyon Review,* 13 (1951), 92–110.

Hans-Georg Gadamer. "Language as the Medium of Hermeneutical Experience" [1960]. In *Truth and Method.* Trans. William Glen-Doepel. New York: Crossroad, 1982. Pp. 345–66.

Gerard Genette. "Time and Narrative in *A la recherche du temps perdu*" [1970]. Trans. Paul de Man. In *Aspects of Narrative.* Ed. J. Hillis Miller. New York: Columbia Univ. Press, 1970. Pp. 93–118.

Erving Goffman. "The Frame Analysis of Talk." In *Frame Analysis: An Essay in the Organization of Experience.* Cambridge, MA: Harvard Univ. Press, 1974. Pp. 496–559.

E. H. Gombrich. "The Analysis of Vision in the Arts," X–XI [1960]. In *Art and Illusion: A Study in the Psychology of Pictorial Representation.* 3rd edn. London: Phaidon, 1968. Pp. 265–75.

Nelson Goodman. "The Status of Style." *Critical Inquiry,* 1 (June 1975), 799–811.

A. J. Greimas. "Elements of a Narrative Grammar." *Diacritics,* 7 (March 1977), pp. 23–40.

Geoffrey Hartman. "The Work of Reading." In *Criticism in the Wilderness: The Study of Literature Today.* New Haven: Yale Univ. Press, 1980. Pp. 161–88.

E. D. Hirsch, Jr. "In Defense of the Author." In *Validity in Interpretation.* New Haven: Yale Univ. Press, 1967. Pp. 1–23.

Martin Heidegger. "The Origin of the Work of Art" [1935]. In *Poetry, Language, Thought.* Ed. Alfred Hofstadter. New York: Harper and Row, 1971. Pp. 15–39.

Wolfgang Iser. "The Reading Process: A Phenomenological Approach." *New Literary History,* 3 (1972), 279–99.

Hans Robert Jauss. "Literary History as a Challenge to Literary Theory [1967]." Tr. Elizabeth Benzinger. *New Literary History,* 2, No. 1 (Autumn 1970), [7]–37.

Steven Knapp and Walter Benn Michaels. "Against Theory." *Critical Inquiry,* 9 (Summer 1982), 723–42.

Julia Kristeva. "Psychoanalysis and the Polis." Tr. Margaret Waller. *Critical Inquiry,* 9, No. 1 (Sept. 1982), 77–92.

Murray Krieger. "The Vanity of Theory and Its Value." In *Theory of Criticism: A Tradition and Its System.* Baltimore: Johns Hopkins Univ. Press, 1976. Pp. 3–8.

Thomas S. Kuhn. "Postscript—1969." In *The Structure of Scientific Revolutions*. 2nd edn. International Encyclopedia of Unified Science, 2, No. 2. Chicago: Univ. of Chicago Press, 1970. Pp. 174–210.

Harry Levin. "Notes on Convention." In *Perspectives of Criticism*. Ed. Harry Levin. Cambridge, MA: Harvard Univ. Press, 1950. Pp. [55]–83.

Jury Lotman. "On 'Bad' and 'Good' Poetry." In *Analysis of the Poetic Text*. Ann Arbor: Ardis, 1976. Pp. 127–31.

Georg Lukács. "Healthy or Sick Art?" [1952]. In *Writer and Critic and Other Essays*. Ed. and tr. Arthur D. Kahn. New York: Grosset and Dunlap, 1970. Pp. 103–09.

Jan Mukařovský. "Standard Language and Poetic Language" [1932]. In *A Prague School Reader on Esthetics, Literary Structure, and Style*. Ed. Paul Garvin. Washington: Georgetown Univ. Press, 1964. Pp. 17–30.

Richard Ohmann. "The Social Definition of Literature." In *What Is Literature?* Ed. Paul Hernadi. Bloomington: Indiana Univ. Press, 1978. Pp. 89–101.

Elder Olson. "On Value Judgments in the Arts." *Critical Inquiry*, 1 (Sept. 1974), 71–90.

Walter J. Ong, S. J. "The Writer's Audience Is Always a Fiction." *PMLA*, 90 (Jan. 1975), 9–21.

Ervin Panovsky. "The Concept of Artistic Volition" [1920], *Critical Inquiry*, 8 (Autumn 1981), 17–23.

Georges Poulet. "Criticism and the Experience of Interiority." In *The Structuralist Controversy: The Languages of Criticism and the Sciences of Man*. Baltimore: Johns Hopkins Univ. Press, 1970. Pp. 56–72.

Mary Louise Pratt. "Literary Cooperation and Implicature." In *Essays in Modern Stylistics*. Ed. Donald C. Freeman. London/New York: Methuen, 1981. Pp. [377]–412.

Gerald Prince. "Introduction to the Study of the Narratee" [1973]. In *Reader-Response Criticism: From Formalism to Post-Structuralism*. Ed. Jane P. Tompkins. Baltimore: Johns Hopkins Univ. Press, 1980. Pp. 7–25.

John Crowe Ransom. "Criticism, Inc." [1938]. In *The World's Body*. 1938; rpt. Baton Rouge: Louisiana State Univ. Press, 1968. Pp. 327–50.

I. A. Richards. "Multiple Definition [1933]." In *Proceedings of the Aristotelian Society*, 34 (1933–34), 31–50.

Michael Riffaterre. "Criteria for Style Analysis." *Word*, 15, No. 1 (April 1959), 154–74.

Paul Ricoeur. "What Is a Text? Explanation and Understanding." In *Hermeneutics and the Human Sciences: Essays on Language, Action and Interpretation.* Ed., tr. John B. Thompson. Cambridge (UK): Cambridge Univ. Press; Paris: Editions de la Maison des Sciences de l'Homme, 1981. Pp. 145–64.

Richard Rorty. "Nineteenth-Century Idealism and Twentieth-Century Textualism." *The Monist,* 64 (April 1981), 155–74.

Edward Said. "Opponents, Audiences, Constituencies, and Community." *Critical Inquiry,* 9, No. 1 (Sept. 1982), 1–26.

Jean-Paul Sartre. "What Is Writing?" In *What Is Literature?* 1948; rpt. London: Methuen, 1950. Pp. 1–25.

Cesare Segre. "The Stylistic Synthesis." In *Semiotics and Literary Criticism.* The Hague: Mouton, 1973. Pp. 18–25.

Meyer Shapiro. "Style." In *Anthropology Today.* Ed. A. L. Kroeber. Chicago: Univ. of Chicago Press, 1953. Pp. 287–312.

Barbara Herrnstein Smith. "Contingencies of Value." *Critical Inquiry,* 10, No. 1 (Sept. 1983), 1–35.

Leo Spitzer. "Linguistics and Literary History." In *Linguistics and Literary History: Essays in Stylistics.* Princeton: Princeton Univ. Press, 1948. Pp. 1–39.

Susan Sontag. "Against Interpretation" [1964]. In *Against Interpretation.* New York: Farrar, Straus and Giroux, 1965. Pp. 3–14.

Tzvetan Todorov. "Literary Genres" [1970]. In *The Fantastic: A Structural Approach to a Literary Genre.* Ithaca: Cornell Univ. Press, 1975. Pp. [3]–23.

Boris Tomashevsky. "Literature and Biography" [1923]. In *Russian Poetics: Formalist and Structuralist Views.* Ed. Ladislav Matejka and Krystyna Pomorska. Cambridge, MA: MIT Press, 1971. Pp. 47–55.

Jurij Tynjanov. "On Literary Evolution" [1929]. In *Russian Poetics: Formalist and Structuralist Views.* Ed. Ladislav Matejka and Krystyna Pomorska. Cambridge, MA: MIT Press, 1971. Pp. 66–78.

Jurij Tynjanov and Roman Jakobson. "Problems in the Study of Literature and Language" [1928]. In *Russian Poetics: Formalist and Structuralist Views.* Ed. Ladislav Matejka and Krystyna Pomorska. Cambridge, MA: MIT Press, 1971. Pp. 79–81.

Stephen Ullmann. "Stylistics and Semantics." In *Meaning and Style: Collected Papers.* Oxford: Basil Blackwell, 1973. Pp. 40–63.

Paul Valéry. "Poetry and Abstract Thought [1939]." In *The Art of Poetry.* Tr. Denise Folliot. The Collected Works of Paul Valery, 7. Ed. Jackson Matthews. London: Routeledge and Kegan Paul, 1958. Pp. 52–81.

Eliseo Vivas. "The Esthetic Judgment." *The Journal of Philosophy,* 33, No. 3 (30 Jan. 1936), 57–69.

Lev Semonovich Vygotski. "Art as Catharsis" [1925]. In *The Psychology of Art.* Cambridge, MA: MIT Press, 1971. Pp. 192–215.

René Wellek. "The Mode of Existence of the Literary Work." *Southern Review,* 7 (Spring 1942), 735–54.

Hayden White. "The Problem of Change in Literary History," *New Literary History,* 7, No. 1 (Autumn 1975), [97]–111.

Ludwig Wittgenstein. *Philosophical Investigations.* Sec. 156–67 and 197–203 [1953]. 3rd edn. Oxford: Blackwell, 1967. Pp. 61–68, 80–82.

W. K. Wimsatt, Jr. and Monroe C. Beardsley." "The Intentional Fallacy" [1946]. In *The Verbal Icon: Studies in the Meaning of Poetry.* Lexington, KY: Univ. of Kentucky Press, 1954. Pp. 3–18.

Yvor Winters. "Preliminary Problems." In *The Anatomy of Nonsense.* Norfolk, Conn.: New Directions, 1943. Pp. 9–22.

Index of Names